Democratic institutions are never done;
they are like living tissue, always a-making.
It is a strenuous thing, this of living the
life of a free people . . .

WOODROW WILSON

Second Edition

IN QUEST

OF

FREEDOM

American Political Thought
and Practice

ALPHEUS THOMAS MASON

McCormick Professor of Jurisprudence Emeritus
Princeton University

RICHARD H. LEACH

Professor of Political Science
Duke University

PRENTICE-HALL, INC.   Englewood Cliffs, New Jersey

Library of Congress Cataloging in Publication Data

MASON, ALPHEUS THOMAS
　　In quest of freedom.

　　Includes bibliographical references.
　　1. United States–Politics and government.
2. Political science–History–United States.
I. Leach, Richard H., joint author. II. Title.
JK31.M35 1973　　　320.9'73　　　72-3774
ISBN　0-13-453712-2

10　9　8　7　6　5　4　3　2　1

Printed in the United States of America

Prentice-Hall International, Inc., London
Prentice-Hall of Australia, Pty. Ltd., Sydney
Prentice-Hall of Canada, Ltd., Toronto
Prentice-Hall of India Private Limited, New Delhi
Prentice-Hall of Japan, Inc., Tokyo

To CHRISTINE
and
BETTY, again

CONTENTS

PREFACE

American politics esteems aggressive, self-reliant individuals whose tireless energy and unfaltering faith supply the primary impetus to progress. Political doctrine evolved slowly in the United States and, quite naturally, took an empirical or pragmatic form; throughout, philosophy has been subservient to, and the tool of, statesmanship. The doers themselves have done most of our political thinking. This book, therefore, highlights the actual participants in the affairs of state, the men of "light and leading," though it does not neglect those not in positions of power. Drawn largely from primary sources and presented in historical context, it confronts the reader with live issues, exhibiting our best minds in action—opposing, discussing, deliberating, compromising, and deciding.

American statesmen have been disinclined to probe the mysteries of authority and obedience. Neither abstract political speculation nor the "grand design" has appealed to them. Jefferson, though known as a thinker, is valued for his works rather than for his political philosophy. His writings, like those of other major figures featured in this volume—James Otis, John Adams, John Taylor, J. C. Calhoun, Thorstein Veblen, Woodrow Wilson, Franklin D. Roosevelt—were responses to the challenges presented by specific issues and problems; they were not occasioned by the urge to speculate in the abstract. The American pioneer was a man of action who cleared the forest, conquered the foe, and established institutions of government. Succeeding generations followed that example; they molded and adapted political institutions as conditions, not the dictates of theory, demanded. Although they continued on the unending quest for freedom, their thought emerged in response to events rather than arising from speculation. The contemplative men—Thoreau, Bellamy, Bourne—who indulged in what Justice Holmes once called the "isolated joy of the thinker"—were seldom influential in their own times.

This is not to say that there have not been great conflicts over public policy. There have, and in their resolution a variety of points of view have been sincerely and reasonably advanced. Indeed, nonconformity, dissent, and resistance to tedious procedures and cumbersome methods form an important part of the American political tradition. Lincoln caught the central theme of American political conflict when he asked, "Must a government of necessity be too strong for the liberties of its people, or too weak to maintain its own existence?" Despite more than 180 years of debate, compromise, and decision, it is still relevant to try to find answers to that and to the following questions: What is the nature and scope of equality? What is the appropriate relation between the state and the people? Which majority should rule—local or national? How should various branches of the government be related to each other under conditions of unprecedented international tension? Which should be given priority—governmental power or human rights?

Each generation has made its own peculiar contribution to the stream of American thought on these basic issues, resulting in an accumulated storehouse of material continuously drawn upon in today's debate. As the story is told in the pages that follow, the reader will find the stark judgments of history acting on past events. Whatever wisdom or merit our actions had at certain crucial junctures—1776, 1789, 1861, 1933, 1954—the things then said and done fall short of final solutions. Underscored are the endless adventures of politics and the unrelenting demands of democratic citizenship. Underscored too is the openendedness of the American political debate.

A much quoted passage in de Tocqueville's *Democracy in America* makes a remarkable prediction of how two great nations, America and Russia, would in time be locked in a power struggle. "The principal instrument of the former," he wrote, "is freedom, of the latter servitude." Less known is another prophecy, published as the introductory poem to the 1775 volume of the London periodical, *The Gentleman's Magazine*, in which the writer portrays the role America would play in the unending quest of freedom. After expressing sorrow at the

> Friends, brothers, parents in the blood
> Of brothers, friends, and sons inbrued!

the poem ends with a glowing forecast:

> At length, when all these contests cease,
> And Britain weary'd rests in peace,
> Our sons, beneath yon Western skies
> Shall see one vast republic rise;
> Another Athens, Sparta, Rome
> Shall there unbounded sway assume;
> Thither her ball shall Empire roll,
> And Europe's pamper'd states controul,
> Though Xerxes rul'd and lash'd the sea,
> The Greeks of old thus would be free . . .

This book tries to portray how that prophecy has been fulfilled.

By now, the authors have lost count of the students, colleagues, and friends who have helped shape their thoughts and put them into readable prose. The dedication, however, reveals their major debt. Hopefully, others will know how much their contributions are appreciated.

A. T. M.
R. H. L.

CHAPTER ONE

TAPROOTS
OF FREEDOM

The origins of American political ideas and institutions are both remote and near at hand. Many of our political precepts were first developed in ancient Greece and Rome and are found in such "elementary books of public right"[1] as Plato's *Republic*, Aristotle's *Politics*, and Cicero's *De Republica*. Other ideas have come down from the great thinkers of the Middle Ages—from St. Augustine and St. Thomas Aquinas, from Marsiglio of Padua and Nicholas of Cusa. More important than any of these is our English heritage. Because this continent was settled almost entirely by immigrants from England, much of American political thought comes as a direct inheritance from the mother country. It is significant not only that this nation was founded by Englishmen, but also that seventeenth-century English culture served as the filter through which the congenial ideas of the past reached our forefathers. Viewed in this light, the contributions of the remote past, though not unimportant, are secondary and of value chiefly as they appear in English theory and practice at the time of the settlement on this continent.

---

[1] The oft-quoted remark of Thomas Jefferson, *The Writings of Thomas Jefferson*, Memorial ed. (Washington, D.C.: Thomas Jefferson Memorial Association, 1903), XVI, 118.

1

What, then, were the political conceptions prevailing in England in the turbulent years after 1600? What political ideas did the émigrés take with them to the New World?

First of all, seventeenth-century Englishmen had long been accustomed to at least an indirect role in government. From Anglo-Saxon and Angevin times, "strong and weak kings alike had followed the practice of calling the leading people of the country together, seeking information and advice from them, turning over much of the public business to them, and, in many matters at least, deferring tò their wishes and opinions."[2] Gradually, this practice became institutionalized in Parliament, which by the end of Elizabeth I's long reign in 1603 was on the threshold of exerting final and complete supremacy over the crown.

For years before that time, Parliament had functioned only intermittently and with little or no effect on royal despotism. Its place in the English constitutional system had nevertheless been recognized, even by the most arbitrary monarchs, and its power expounded by such writers as Glanvill, Bracton, and Fortescue. It was, moreover, widely accepted by the people. At that time, Parliament was representative only of the upper classes in English society, but already those classes demanded representation as a right, and the continued expansion of the House of Commons, even under the Tudors, gave promise that the principle would be further extended.

Representation was not regarded as a sterile right. A definite concept of parliamentary power had grown up along with it, so that by 1603 the laws of the realm in general, and tax laws in particular, were enacted with Parliament's advice, consent, and authority. Although consent of the governed in English politics had yet to be stated as a theory, it was slowly coming into practice.

England in the seventeenth century entertained a well-developed notion of guaranteed personal rights, or, to put it differently, of limited government. As early as 1100, Henry I granted a charter of liberties to his subjects, and, in 1215, John I affixed his mark to the Great Charter, signifying his assent to the principle (though hardly the practice) that certain rights were beyond even his reach. Although the Magna Carta was an instrument of its times and dealt mainly with feudal rights and privileges, and chiefly with those of the barons, it served as the symbol and ark of English liberty during the first decades of the seventeenth century, and supporters of Parliament relied on it in their claims against the king.

Furthermore, a strong sense of local autonomy had long prevailed in England. At the level of the town and the shire, the people since Saxon days had been accustomed to self-government. By 1600 the habit was so ingrained that its extension seemed entirely logical.

Finally, a robust body of common law, existing since the seventeenth century, had come to stand between the people of England, on the one

---

[2] Frederick A. Ogg, *English Government and Politics*, 2nd ed. (New York: Macmillan, 1936), p. 12.

hand, and the exercise of arbitrary power on the other. Distinctively English, the common law had begun with the customs of the people. With the passage of time it jelled into a substantial corpus juris. Rising above all other claimants and equated with perfect reason, the common law emerged supreme and decisive in 1607, when Sir Edward Coke, chief justice of the Court of Common Pleas, applied it to the king himself. More than anything else, the common law persuaded the English people to revere rule of law rather than that of men. Devotion to this maxim finally expressed itself in the theory that revolutionary action was justified against those who abused it.

All these factors and developments combined to create, in seventeenth-century England, a strong sense of *constitutionalism*. Haltingly and tentatively, Englishmen had come to believe that certain fundamental rights of the individual necessitated limited government. They were particularly insistent that certain forms and procedures be acknowledged and followed by all who wielded political authority.[3]

As long as government did not deviate too greatly from this evolving pattern (generally throughout the fifteenth and sixteenth centuries it did not), most Englishmen were content. Few concerted attempts were made to rationalize the course of this slow evolutionary process: no theorists came forth with a clear and cohesive articulation of what constitutionalism meant. It was nevertheless widely felt. Although implicit, constitutionalism by the time of American colonization was a vital political force that only the most reckless would have challenged.

Challenge came, however, in the years after 1603 from the royal family that succeeded Elizabeth. The Stuarts were not in sympathy with the idea of restraints on royal power; in opposition to it, they put forth a reaffirmation of the outdated divine right theory of absolute monarchy. In particular, James I and Charles I challenged what the rising merchant-capitalists considered their economic "rights" and what were widely regarded as basic religious "rights." Unlike the Tudors, both rulers often opposed the economic interests of the powerful merchants and capitalists and disregarded the religious beliefs and practices of their subjects. The result was a long series of struggles beginning as early as 1628, when an angry Parliament forced the Petition of Right on the reluctant Charles I. Sixty years elapsed before Parliament at last emerged the victor.

During those years a veritable flood of political literature engulfed England and overflowed into the colonies. Abstract questions of political power and natural rights were burning topics of the day. In a sort of last-gasp effort to bolster absolutism, its proponents encountered a torrent of rebuttal and refutation from partisans of the parliamentary cause. For the first time democratic ideas and devices were discussed and promoted, and the implications of constitutionalism were explored. Although England herself utilized only a few of the ideas thus released, these ideas

---

[3] See Francis D. Wormuth, *The Origins of Modern Constitutionalism* (New York: Harper & Brothers, 1939), especially Chap. 1.

flourished later on in the more fertile American soil. Indeed, colonization began during this period of civil war and revolution, many of the first colonists themselves being active partisans in the struggle.

PROPERTY AND POLITICS:
THE PUTNEY DEBATES

The first, and in many ways the most significant, expositions of political thought during the civil war period were the product not of political philosophers but of discontented soldiers in the parliamentary army. By 1647 Charles I had been captured, and the revolution seemed to have accomplished its objectives, at least as far as Parliament was concerned. The army, however, dissatisfied with the fruits of victory, became restless as the religiously oriented Parliament continued to neglect it. Many of the common soldiers felt that all the benefits to be derived from the king's defeat were being diverted to the upper classes, of which Parliament was largely representative. Their conviction was strengthened when Parliament threatened to demobilize the army without appropriating funds to pay the troops and without providing some sort of guarantee of the political rights of the English people. Under the leadership of a militant radical group know as the Levellers,[4] the demands of the rank and file were framed in "An Agreement of the Free People of England,"[5] published in 1649. By this compact, if acted upon by Parliament, they hoped to secure, among other things, manhood suffrage.

The ideas at the heart of the "Agreement" were the concept of natural rights ("native rights," to use its terminology), consent of the governed, the right of all to free worship, and equality before and under the law. It declared that the functions of government could only be performed by a Parliament representative "of this nation" and acting for the safety and well-being of all the English people. Viewing Parliament's power as delegated by the people, it envisaged a broad suffrage, measured "according to the number of the inhabitants" of England. Finally, the "Agreement" proposed the adoption of biennial Parliaments and a written constitution. In short, the "Agreement" was by far the most democratic political document that had yet appeared in England.

In the end, however, the proposal never reached Parliament. The officers, having already sent to Parliament their own scheme for moderate reform, known as the "Declaration of the Army," were unwilling to prejudice the chance of its acceptance by presentation of another, more radical, proposition. But the "Agreement" did not die at the officers' hands. They agreed to discuss it with representatives from the ranks, and from the extended debate between the two sides, held at Putney in the

---

[4] See Henry N. Brailsford, *The Levellers and the English Revolution*, Christopher Hill, ed. (Stanford, Calif.: Stanford University Press, 1961).
[5] The "Agreement" can be found in *Introduction to Contemporary Civilization in the West*, 2nd ed. (New York: Columbia University Press, 1954), I, 871–73.

fall of 1647, emerged a remarkable picture of the political climate of the time.

The debates, surprisingly enough, showed much agreement between the officers and the rank and file, indicating the extent to which the idea of constitutionalism pervaded the nation. Both sides believed government rested on compact—one of many liberal ideas that had been discussed somewhat earlier by Richard Hooker.[6] All the parties recognized the existence of a higher, or natural, law—the law of nature. In varying degrees, all recognized the institution of property as basic in politics. They disagreed, however, about the relationship of the three concepts: compact, higher law, and property.

As spokesmen for the officers, Oliver Cromwell and his son-in-law, Commissary General Henry Ireton, stressed the irrevocable nature of a compact and expressed their belief that all rights, especially property, were based upon it. To them submission of the "Declaration of the Army" constituted a compact, precluding the later "Agreement," despite its reputed advantages, or even its justness. Said Ireton:

> The great foundation of justice between man and man . . . [is] that we should keep covenant with another. Covenants freely made, freely entered into, must be kept one with another. Take away that, I do not know what ground there is of any thing you can call any man's right.[7]

The common soldiers saw it quite differently. To them compact, though basic to the constitution of government, was neither irrevocable nor final. They elevated justice over compact, rather than compact over justice. As Mr. Wildman (evidently a civilian representative of the soldiers) put it:

> A principle much spreading . . . is this: that when persons once be engaged, though the Engagement appears to be unjust, yet the person must set down and suffer under it; and that therefore, in case a Parliament, as a true Parliament, does anything unjustly, if we be engaged to submit to the laws that they shall make, if they make an unjust law, though they make an unrighteous law, yet we must swear obedience. I confess to me this principle is very dangerous . . . it is contrary to the laws of nature and nations. . . .

There was dispute, too, over the role of natural law and its relation to the compact on which society was based. The soldiers invoked "higher law" as the final arbiter of right, against which all acts were to be tested. The officers, on the other hand, though not denying the force of natural law, considered it too uncertain a guide and potentially dangerous to property. Compacts, Ireton thought, secured property, and without them the propertied would be at the mercy of the propertyless. "By the law of nature," he observed, "you have no more right to this land or anything

---

[6] See E. T. Davies, *The Political Ideas of Richard Hooker* (London: Society for Promoting Christian Knowledge, 1946) and John Shirley, *Richard Hooker and Contemporary Political Ideas* (London: Church Historical Society, 1949).
[7] These and the following quotations are from C. H. Firth, ed., *The Clarke Papers* (Westminster: Camden Society, 1891), I, 226–367.

else than I have. . . . For matter of goods, that which does fence me from [the right] which another man may claim by the law of nature of taking my goods, that which makes it mine really and civilly is the law."

A second major difference arose over representation. The "Agreement" demanded that members of Parliament be elected by "the people of England." Said Mr. Pettus for the soldiers: "we judge that all inhabitants that have not lost their birth-right should have an equal voice in Elections." Colonel Rainboro[8] declared that

> every man born in England cannot, ought not, neither by the law of God or the law of nature, . . . be exempted from the choice of those who are to make laws, for him to live under, and for him, for aught I know, to lose his life under.

Rainboro could find nothing in the law of God or of nature saying that "a Lord should choose 20 Burgesses, and a Gentleman but two or a poor man should choose none." Rich and poor alike had reason, and God intended that it be recognized and used in the processes of government, not denied by an arbitrary property qualification. As Mr. Wildman put it:

> I conceive that the undeniable maxim of government is that all government is in the free consent of the people. If so, then upon that account there is no person that is under a just government or hath justly his own, unless he by his own free consent be put under that government . . . there are no laws that . . . any man is bound to . . . that are not made by those whom he doth consent to. And therefore I should humbly move that if the question be stated which would soonest bring things to an issue it might rather be this: whether any person can justly be bound by law who doth not give his consent that such persons shall make laws for him.

In opposition General Ireton insisted that because protection of property was the primary purpose of government, only those having a proprietary interest in the kingdom should have the right to vote. To him, and to his fellow officers, and indeed to the bulk of the English upper classes, political power was tied to property, and their union was mutually exclusive. In response to the claim that birthright alone gave an equal right to a voice in elections, Ireton declared unequivocally that "no person has a right to an interest or a share in disposing or determining the affairs of the Kingdom . . . that has not a permanent fixed interest in this Kingdom."

Spokesmen for the soldiers were not oblivious to the importance of property. They agreed that men "put themselves into forms of government that they may preserve property. . . ." But they argued that natural law, and Divine law beyond it, offered sufficient protection for property, and that protection of persons as well as estate was an end of government. The officers, in turn, did not deny God's law, but believed that it determined only generals, not particulars such as property: it was clearly not enough by itself. Civil law protected property, and those who made it must perforce have been propertied.

---

[8] The spelling of his name is uncertain; it may be Rainsborough or Rainborrow.

The officers, in short, were fearful. Give all the right to vote without reference to property, Ireton observed, and "why may not those men vote against all property? . . . Show me what you will stop at, wherein you will fence any man in a property by this rule. . . . Property is of human constitution. . . ." Fearing invasion of the rights of property, Ireton raised the specter of anarchy. He pleaded with the soldiers "to suffer for quietness's sake rather than make a great disturbance."

The soldiers, on the other hand, stressed personality. Because the foundation of all law, including the law of property, "lies in the people," no one is excluded under the law of God and of nature "from the choice of those who are to make laws for him to live under." Men agreed to come into civil society "that they who were chosen might preserve property." Accordingly, to give every man a choice "is not to destroy it." Anticipating twentieth-century American values, Rainboro observed:

> Really I think that the poorest he that is in England has a life to live as the richest he; and therefore truly, Sir, I think it's clear, that every man that is to live under a Government ought first by his own consent to put himself under that Government; and I do think that the poorest man in England is not at all bound in a strict sense to that Government that he has not had a voice to put himself under. . . .

For what, Rainboro asked, had the soldiers fought, if not to assure a government whose "chief end is to preserve persons as well as estates. . . ?"

Rainboro and his followers thought they, not the officers, were taking the long view—the conservative approach. Security for established institutions lay on the side of reform rather than in stubborn resistance to change. "Truly, Sir," Rainboro remarked, "I do very much care whether [there be] a King, or no King, Lords or no Lords, property or no property; and I think if we do not all take care, we shall all have none of these very shortly. . . . I do think that the main cause why Almighty God gave men reason . . . was that they should make use of that reason, and that they should improve it for that end and purpose that God gave it."

Although neither side at Putney succeeded in convincing the other, these historic debates set the stage for interminable controversy concerning issues and values as hotly contested now as they were in 1647— dissent and civil disobedience, persons versus property, "one man, one vote."[9]

---

[9] For twentieth-century discussions of certain seventeenth-century issues at Putney, see Abe Fortas, *Concerning Dissent and Civil Disobedience* (New York: New American Library, 1968) and Harold Zinn, *Disobedience and Democracy: Nine Fallacies On Law and Order* (New York: Vintage Books, 1968). See also Hugo Adam Bedeau, ed., *Civil Disobedience: Theory and Practice* (New York: Pegasus, 1969); N. F. Cantor, *The Age of Protest: Dissent and Rebellion in the Twentieth Century* (New York: Hawthorne, 1969); S. E. Morrison, E. Merk, and F. Freidel, *Dissent in Three American Wars* (Cambridge, Mass.: Harvard University Press, 1969); and A. T. Mason, "To Be More Safe: America's Continuing Dilemma," *Virginia Quarterly Review*, XLV (Autumn, 1969) 545–62.

PROPERTY AND POLITICS: JOHN LOCKE

The immediate significance of the Putney debates was to supply a sort of proving ground for the ideas John Locke (1632–1704) utilized forty years later in writing his celebrated treatise on civil government. As restated by Locke,[10] the arguments of Rainboro and Ireton helped reinforce the thinking of countless colonial leaders.

Locke's approach, like that of the debaters at Putney, was realistic. By the time he wrote his *Second Treatise of Civil Government* in 1690, England's experiment in republicanism had failed, the monarchy had been restored, and the second series of struggles between king and Parliament had been concluded. In these struggles neither Charles II nor James II had been able to turn back the forces of constitutionalism. James II was finally compelled to abdicate. The "Convention Parliament" had named William of Orange his successor and had laid down the conditions under which he might assume the throne. Parliamentary supremacy had been secured; the Glorious Revolution was an accomplished fact.

Well born and well educated, Locke was suited by temperament and experience to explain and justify this *fait accompli*.[11] Although not original, he was perhaps the best synthesizer of his time. His experience had given him a good understanding of seventeenth-century British politics. So convincing were Locke's conclusions that he not only supplied a tract of his times, but also passed on to later generations one of the most impressive political utterances ever written.

The *Second Treatise* explained the origin of two great institutions in the modern world—property and government. Locke derived property from a condition of primitive communism, in which the things of the world were held in common. But whenever man mixed his own labor with natural things, he transmuted them into personal property:

> . . . every man has a "property" in his own "person." This nobody has any right to but himself. . . . Whatsoever, then, he removes out of the state that Nature hath provided and left it in, he hath mixed his labour with it, and joined to it something that is his own, and thereby makes it his property. . . . For this "labour" being the unquestionable property of the labourer, no man but he can have a right to what that is once joined to. . . .[12]

---

[10] See Sterling P. Lamprecht, *The Moral and Political Philosophy of John Locke* (New York: Columbia University Press, 1918) and Maurice W. Cranston, *John Locke, A Biography* (New York: Macmillan, 1957).

[11] Peter Laslett has demonstrated that the conventional view of Locke as the apologist of the Glorious Revolution is in error. He has contended that "the whole work was written before 1683." See the Laslett edition of Locke's *Two Treatises of Civil Government* (Cambridge: Cambridge University Press, 1960), pp. 45–66. Locke has also been reinterpreted, with an emphasis on the theological character of his political thought, in John Dunn, *The Political Thought of John Locke* (New York: Cambridge University Press, 1969) and in M. Seligler, *The Liberal Politics of John Locke* (London: Allen & Unwin, 1968).

[12] This and the following quotations are from John Locke, *Second Treatise of Civil Government*, Everyman's Library (London: J. M. Dent, 1924; rpt. 1943), Chap. 5.

To the things with which man mixed his own labor, Locke added the labor performed for him by servants and beasts. Thus, the individual in the natural state owned "the grass [his] horse has bit, the turfs [his] servant has cut, and the ore [he has dug] in any place where [he has] a right to them in common with others. . . ." These things became his property "without the assignation or consent of anybody."

But man had property only in those things he could use without spoiling: he might not hold against the claims of society any property —though it were the work of his own hands—if it might spoil before being used. With the invention of money, however, it came to pass that men could rightfully possess more than they could use. Men could then enlarge their possessions unequally.

> It is plain that the consent of men have agreed to a disproportionate and unequal possession of the earth—I mean out of the bounds of society and compact; for in governments the laws regulate it; they having, by consent, found out and agreed in a way how a man may, rightfully and without injury, possess more land than he himself can make use of by receiving gold and silver, which may continue long in a man's possession, without decaying for the overplus, and agreeing those metals should have a value.

This development gave rise to the condition that so disturbed General Ireton at Putney. In a moneyed society men could be political equals but economic unequals. In the state of nature, without compact or government, natural law protected private property. But now natural law did not suffice. Locke believed that men found it necessary to institute government to protect property and presumably to guarantee each man his holdings. Ireton had been fearful that once men without property were accorded political rights, the propertyless would use their power to invade and destroy property. It was this juxtaposition of economic inequality with political equality that gave rise to the "inconvenience" that Locke believed men experienced in the state of nature and for which civil society was the remedy.

It is important to note that Locke used the term property to cover more than material goods. It covered life and liberty as well. The "inconveniences" of the state of nature induced men to seek out other men and join together in the common task of preserving "their lives, liberties and estates." Protection of property in this broader sense constituted for Locke the end of government.

THE ORIGIN OF POLITICAL SOCIETY

Locke's concept of the state of nature is basic not only to his explanation of the origin of property, but also to his theory of government. His explorations were hypothetical. He did not pretend that man (except possibly the American Indian) had ever lived in this state. Rather, he tried to explain how man might be reasonably supposed to have begun political existence. Thus, the state of nature served as a philosophical device to demonstrate how society might be safeguarded against a two-fold danger: absolutism and anarchy.

State of Nature

Locke saw man's primeval condition—indeed, human nature itself—in two aspects. From one point of view, human life was characterized by "peace, good will, mutual assistance and preservation." The state of nature Locke described as a condition of "perfect equality"—"all being kings," "every one ha[ving] executive power of the law of nature." It was governed not by fear, but by reason and the law of nature—a higher rule, one more easily understood than the "fancies and intricate contrivances of mere men." The law of nature tells men that they ought not to interfere with other men's lives and possessions. Because the law of nature was "that measure God has set to the actions of men for their mutual security," society was a natural condition, not an artificial creation. Its essence lay in man's God-given sense of moral obligation.

But Locke also saw the state of nature as full of danger and continual fears, marred by the corruption of vicious and degenerate men. Had it not been for this viciousness there would have been no need for men to leave this "great and natural community." That man found it necessary to abandon his natural condition seemed a misfortune, for he had enjoyed in a state of nature the two basic rights every free society seeks to attain: freedom and equality. But note how Locke defined these terms. "Perfect freedom" meant the right of men "to order their actions and dispose of their possessions as they think fit, within the bounds of the law of nature, without asking leave or depending upon the will of any other man." Freedom was thus the right to act within the law.

"Perfect equality" was also precisely defined. It existed in the sense that in a state of nature "there is no superiority or jurisdiction of one over another." Each man was equally an executive, equally a king; each man was authorized to interpret and enforce natural law—even in cases wherein his own interests were involved. This situation naturally gave rise to "inconveniences"—the absence of known positive law, the want of a common authority to interpret it, the lack of a common power to enforce it.

The state of nature was thus "full of fears and continual dangers," not because men lacked law and "government," but because they did not consider natural law binding upon them. So, not unreasonably, men were induced to join with others for the preservation of their lives, liberties, and estates.

Social Compact

The social compact or contract was the device Locke's harassed men used for making the transition from the great and natural community to civil society. An instrument of reason, the social contract created the political community. The parties to it were individuals. It was an agreement of all with all. Every man must join the compact, or he would not be bound. To gain the ends men desired—security for their lives, liberties, and estates— they must pay a high price, reckoned in terms of two precious human values: freedom and equality. The essence of the compact was the common surrender to the community of certain rights individuals enjoyed in the state of nature. Thereafter the individual was no longer free to do "whatever he thinks fit for the preservation of himself and the rest of mankind." He now consented "to be regulated by laws made by the society, so far as the preservation of himself and the rest of that society shall require." And note this addendum—"which laws of society in many things confine the liberty he had by the law of nature."

In coming into the political community, the individual also surrendered "perfect equality." The individual "wholly gives up" the power to punish. In short man was no longer his own executive, no longer a "king." He was subject to government.

Political Community—Civil Society—The State

In this transition to civil society through the social compact, one authority was substituted for the multiplicity of executives existing in the state of nature. "The essence of union," Locke observed, "consists in having one will." Civil society demanded the ability to speak through a single authority, and this surrender of executive power to the community was irrevocable. "The power that every man gave the society when he entered into it can never revert to the individual again, but will always remain in the community. Without this, there could be no community, no commonwealth."

How could civil society achieve oneness? How could one will be achieved? Locke's answer was unequivocal. In joining the political community men tacitly consented "to be bound by the vote of the majority. Once civil society was "established, the majority has the declaring and keeping of that will." The majority bound the minority. Locke passed over one of the toughest questions of political theory—why *should* the majority rule? Nor did he deal with the possibility that the majority might sometimes be wrong. Side-stepping the moral aspect, he gave a utilitarian justification for majority rule. The alternative to majority rule was unanimity—"the consent of every individual." But to obtain unanimous consent in the face of an unavoidable variety of options and conflicts of interest was "next to impossible." Add to this the "infirmities of health" and the claims of "avocations," and it was evident that insistence on unanimity would doom political society at the outset. Besides considerations of expediency, force justified majority rule.

> For that which acts any community, being only the consent of the individuals of it, and it being one body, must move one way, it is necessary the body should move that way whither the greater force carries it, which is the consent

of the majority, or else it is impossible it should act or continue one body, one community, which the consent of every individual that united into it agreed that it should; and so every one is bound by that consent to be concluded by the majority.

Government

By majority vote the political community established government, in which Locke, like Hooker before him, affirmed "the supreme authority of the legislative power."[13] In Locke's system the legislature "is not only the supreme power of the commonwealth, but sacred and unalterable in the hands where the community have once placed it." But its supremacy was limited: (1) the legislature must not rule "by arbitrary, extemporary decrees, but . . . only by promulgated standing law"; (2) the law ought to be designed for no other end than the good of the people; (3) property was not secure if the legislature might take it arbitrarily without the individual's consent; (4) the legislature might not delegate its lawmaking power, legislative power being delegated by the people, not inherent in the legislature. In addition to these specific limitations on the legislature, Locke added two others: separation of powers and right of revolution. The most conspicuous feature of Locke's constitutionalism is the number and variety of limits on power.

In effect, however, these limitations were only paper guarantees. Government's obligation to rule under promulgated standing law provided no legally enforceable bar against either the legislature or the executive. On the altar of *prerogative*, the executive might defy law, including promulgated standing law. Prerogative, by definition, was power in the executive to act without a rule, power to act for "the public good" according to discretion—without the prescription of a law, and sometimes even against it. Nor was separation of powers designed to weaken the legislature. Although Locke mentioned it as a barrier against abuse of power, this maxim was of importance to him chiefly as the mark of a "well-ordered" commonwealth.

Likewise, the right of revolution was less a restriction on, than an inducement to, just and equitable government. It was a kind of reserve force, a weapon of last resort, a gun behind the door. Knowledge of its existence would influence rulers and ruled alike. It would put the fear of God in the rulers' hearts and make them less inclined to abuse power. Subjects were presumed to be reasonable too: they would not fly to drastic remedies at the first grievance. Locke held no brief for a government subject to continual and direct pressure from the masses. The right of revolution was a recipe for its avoidance, assuring security in place of insecurity—"the best fence against Rebellion," "the probablest means to hinder it."

---

[13] J. R. Pole, *Political Representation in England and the Origins of the American Republic* (London: Macmillan, 1966), p. 503.

Locke's faith in reason was well-nigh unbounded. He thought in terms of what reasonable men would do. Just as they would leave the state of nature only by their consent, so they would create a government limited in power. They would surrender only as much of their natural freedom as would enable the government to carry out their will and act for their good. The rest they would retain. "The great end of men's entering into society being the enjoyment of their properties in peace and safety," they would not create a government they could not control. Its power they would limit "to the public good of the society," and to it they would never give the right "to destroy, enslave, or designedly to impoverish the subjects." Nor would they entrust government to one man.

> Absolute monarchs are but men; and if government is to be the remedy of those evils which necessarily follow from men's being judges in their own cases, and the state of nature is therefore not to be endured, I desire to know what kind of government that is, and how much better it is than the state of nature, where one man commanding a multitude has the liberty to be judge in his own case, and may do to all his subjects whatever he pleases without the least ability to any one to question or control those who execute his pleasure.

Reasonable men would put their faith in a legislature deriving its power from "a positive voluntary grant" by the people and endowed by them with "only a fiduciary power to act for certain ends."

Locke attempted to fuse liberty and authority, but he provided no means, short of revolution, by which aggrieved individuals or minorities could safeguard their rights against the arbitrary acts of a government enjoying majority support.

> For if [tyranny] reach no farther than some private men's cases, though they have a right to defend themselves, and to recover by force, what by unlawful force is taken from them; yet the right to do so, will not easily engage them in a contest, wherein they are sure to perish. . . .

Thus, he left unresolved the dilemma that would arise if the people's chosen representatives should violate their trust under the social compact and the "promulgated established laws." Who, then, must judge the transgressor? In the absence of a "judicature on earth to decide," Locke answered, "God in heaven is judge"—presumably a Lockean euphemism for prayer—or force.

Locke's constitutionalism boils down essentially to political checks— those imposed at elections plus the hope that rulers and ruled alike would be guided by considerations of justice and common sense. Whether in a state of nature or in civil society, "keeping of faith belongs to men as men." It has been suggested that Locke was unreasonable "only in his faith in reason."[14]

---

[14] See N. C. Phillips, "Political Philosophy and Political Fact: The Evidence of John Locke," in *Liberty and Learning: Essays in Honor of Sir James Hight* (Christchurch: Whitcombe and Thombs, 1950), p. 208. See also Louis Arenilla, "The Notion of Civil Disobedience According to Locke," *Diogenes*, No. 35 (Fall, 1961), 109–35.

In evolving his theory Locke drew from the arguments on both sides at Putney. In a sense, he bridged the gap between them. Like the spokesmen for the common soldiers—particularly Rainboro—he set natural law above civil law. But, like Ireton, he regarded property as society's chief concern, and thus conceived of natural law as operating primarily for its protection. If acceptance of the right of revolution as a check on tyranny—a proposal made by the rank and file at Putney—makes him seem liberal, his assumption that it would be applied only when property rights were violated makes him seem conservative. Perhaps this duality explains Locke's appeal in America.

Moreover, many factors in American society made his individualistic norms meaningful: the frontier was literally a state of nature, and the Mayflower Compact a concrete example of his hypothetical social contract. In the debates preceding the Revolution, Locke's ideas supplied theoretical ammunition for the colonists. Perhaps no other single person had more influence on the colonial mind. During the revolutionary period Locke was referred to as "the ingenious," "the incomparable Mr. Locke." Jefferson incorporated into the Declaration of Independence sentences virtually word for word from the *Second Treatise*. Most of the Founding Fathers were familiar with Locke's arguments and reasoning, the *Second Treatise* having long been a standard text in colonial colleges. In him, and in the arguments of the protagonists at Putney before him, they could find all the theory they needed to oppose despotism and arbitrary rule. Consent of the governed, majority rule, the idea of natural rights independent of and limiting government, and the right to revolt —all were adopted with enthusiasm by our revolutionary forebears and continue to influence American political thinking.[15]

Neither the idea of a constitution limiting and superintending the operations of the supreme legislative authority nor the system of judicial review—a unique feature of American constitutionalism—formed a part of Locke's system. For Americans his political thought was wanting on the institutional side.

PROPERTY AND POLITICS: JAMES HARRINGTON

As important as Locke is to an understanding of American politics, he must share the honors with others, such as Algernon Sidney—whose *Discourses Concerning Government* (1704) reemphasized the idea that power lay originally with the people and must be exercised by their consent

---

[15] Pole, *Political Representation*, p. 17. Pole did not find that Locke had exerted "any effective influence on the political thought of the colonists until Thomas Jefferson. . . . Yet Locke epitomized certain doctrines, without which the American revolutionaries would have found it difficult to explain their activities either to the opinion of mankind or even to themselves." For a perceptive discussion of the authoritarian element in Locke, see Jason Aronson, "Shaftesbury on Locke," *American Political Science Review*, LIII (1959), 1101–4.

through representation—and particularly with James Harrington (1611–1677) and Charles de Montesquieu (1689–1755).

Harrington's influence was both theoretical and practical.[16] Closely attached to both Charles I and Charles II, Harrington had great hopes that England would adopt republicanism under Oliver Cromwell. To that end he created a fictitious commonwealth and designed for it what he conceived to be a model government. The result was his *Oceana*, published in 1656. Unlike the utopias of Plato and Sir Thomas More, *Oceana* was meant not for the skies nor for some spot on earth that did not exist, but for England. The hero of the story is Cromwell, who calls in experts to help him frame a constitution. Cromwell is named Protector, and the new order succeeds famously. At the height of its glory, the Protector retires to private life, leaving England the happiest land in the world. The first part, entitled "The Preliminaries, showing the Principles of Government," yielded enduring theoretical concepts that have been woven into the American political fabric. *Oceana* was also the source of certain practical devices peculiarly suited to American politics.

A lifelong observer of political institutions and a close student of history, Harrington, like Ireton before him, held that those possessed of "the permanent interest of the land" had the right to rule: he discovered that property in fact did govern in England. Thus, he concluded that political power was a concomitant of property and that government, to be stable and effective, must truly reflect the property balance in the country.[17] To Harrington property meant primarily land, except in the cities, "where revenue is in trade." Where one man was the sole landlord of a territory, he should rule absolutely; where a few owned the land, such government as had existed earlier in England would be proper—mixed monarchy, he called it; and where land ownership was widespread, the government should be a commonwealth, or republic. To neglect the property balance and maintain the wrong type of government by force was sheer tyranny.

> Holding the government not according to the balance, it is not natural, but violent: and therefore if it be at the devotion of a prince, it is *tyranny;* if at the devotion of the few, *oligarchy;* or if in the power of the people, *anarchy.*[18]

Concerned about the recent turmoil resulting from the civil wars, Harrington sought to provide a formula for the permanent achievement of good government. Because property was then widely held in England,

---

[16] See Charles Blitzer, *An Immortal Commonwealth: The Political Thought of James Harrington* (New Haven, Conn.: Yale University Press, 1960).

[17] Harrington took specific issue with his absolutist contemporary Thomas Hobbes, who tried to demonstrate that society and morals, as well as the state, rest on physical force. Harrington was almost modern in his defiant challenge of the author of *Leviathan* (1651), saying that an army is "a beast that has a big belly and must be fed."

[18] Quoted in Theodore W. Dwight, "Harrington and His Influence upon American Political Institutions and Political Thought," *Political Science Quarterly,* II (March, 1887), 37.

it followed from his reasoning that only the commonwealth form was possible and right. As a plea for the adoption of republican principles, *Oceana* became a tract of the times.

Closely associated with Harrington's idea of property balance was his assertion that the true commonwealth must be an empire of laws, not of men: ". . . if the liberty of a man consists in the empire of his reason, the absence whereof would betray him to the bondage of his passions, then the liberty of a commonwealth consists in the empire of her laws, the absence whereof would betray her to the lust of tyrants."[19] The authority of a commonwealth, in other words, could not safely be lodged in men but must be placed in laws. In no other way could reason and virtue be dominant over passion and vice.

Harrington realized that it would be difficult to achieve and maintain an empire of laws. Its basis must be a balance of property; the organs of government constructed on that basis must themselves be balanced, so that the common interest rather than one particular interest or group of interests would be ascendant. That balance could be secured, however, and the common interest promoted, by entrusting government to three separate sets of hands. What should be enacted as law would be discovered during the course of debate among "the wiser, or at least less foolish" part of the people—the intellectual aristocrats—who would then propose laws embodying their discoveries to the whole people for their concurrence. The people, guided by right reason, would follow the counsel of this natural senate, and from it they would "discover things that they never thought on; or [be] cleared in divers truths which had formerly perplexed them." They would come to rely on it as their "stay and comfort" and would be led to see that the interest of each lay in the interest of all. One other element was necessary to perfect the balance: a magistracy, answerable to the people, to carry out the laws. The combination of the senate proposing, the people resolving, and the magistracy executing would provide a balanced and stable government—an empire of laws.

Although he had faith in the principle of balance as the mainspring of commonwealth, Harrington nevertheless believed it needed to be safeguarded. Particularly, the property balance needed to be maintained, and to assure that it would be, he conceived the idea of "an equal Agrarian . . . a perpetual law establishing and preserving the balance of dominion by such a distribution that no one man or number of men . . . [could] come to overpower the whole people by their possession in lands." By its operation Harrington sought to prevent destruction, through a subsequent shift in the ownership of land, of the basis for republicanism.

Harrington was not content with one institution "for safeguarding the State." He foreshadowed Madison, in *Federalist* Number 51, in the belief

---

[19] These and the following quotations in this section are from James Harrington, *The Oceana and Other Works*, ed. J. Toland (London: Becket, Cadell and Evans, 1771), *passim.*

that "auxiliary precautions" were necessary. He advocated equal rotation in office, so that all the people might serve in their turn as magistrates; "equal rotation is equal vicissitude in government," he wrote, and it alone made sure that the "life or natural motion of a commonwealth" would be sustained. Believing a written constitution, popularly ratified, to be basic, he placed great reliance on the elective principle with short terms of office and the secret ballot. These, he declared, "increased the freedom of [the people's] judgment." He suggested also the separation of powers and guaranteed religious freedom. In this practical work of constructing a free government, Harrington contributed even more than Locke. In the establishment of free government, *Oceana* served as a guidebook.

> Again and again one is tempted to substitute the name America for Oceana and spell his new England with a capital N. The written constitution, the unlimited extension of the elective principle, and the separation of the three functions of government lie at the root of American political theory. . . .[20]

Harrington's mark is evident in the founding of the proprietary colonies of Carolina, New Jersey, and Pennsylvania. In Carolina the organization of the colony was based on landholding, indicating acceptance of his belief that "empire follows property." In New Jersey and Pennsylvania his republican views were mirrored in the deliberations of William Penn. "Penn's early plans closely resemble Harrington's model. Thus, the republican stream irrigated the green country town of Penn's Quaker commonwealth and flowed out into the American continent."[21]

"The din of the great English rebellion," Theodore Dwight observed, "and the rejoicings at its close had scarcely ceased to ring in men's ears, when our greater and more successful rebellion was inaugurated by men who had studied the writings of these great English radicals and had fully imbibed their spirit. Our statesmen knew the thoughts of Harrington . . . as we know those of Washington, Adams, Hamilton, and Jefferson."[22] Indeed, Harrington was so widely read that his influence carried on into the postrevolutionary period and was evident in the framing of state constitutions—especially those of Virginia, Pennsylvania, New York, the Carolinas, and Massachusetts—and in the debate on the Articles of Confederation. In his "Thoughts on Government Applicable to the Present State of the American Colonies" of 1776, John Adams asked for "an 'empire of laws,' which could only be achieved by a division of the legislature into two houses, by the separation of the three functions of government, and by rotation" in office.[23] Adams insisted on the elective principle and suggested indirect election for the upper house. The

---

[20] H. F. Russell-Smith, *Harrington and His Oceana. A Study of a 17th Century Utopia and Its Influence in America* (Cambridge: Cambridge University Press, 1914), p. 152.
[21] Pole, *Political Representation*, p. 13.
[22] Dwight, "Harrington and His Influence," p. 3.
[23] Dwight, "Harrington and His Influence," p. 192.

prescriptions of *Oceana* are most clearly reflected in Adams's "Defense of the Constitutions of the United States," parts of which were known to the delegates to the Constitutional Convention in 1787—an indication of the popularity and influence exerted by Harrington.

POLITICS AND LIBERTY:
CHARLES DE MONTESQUIEU

While the names of Locke and Harrington are associated with a proliferation of ideas, Charles Louis de Secondat, Baron de Montesquieu,[24] is remembered primarily for one contribution, the doctrine of separation of powers. Locke and Harrington had touched upon that idea, but "it is Montesquieu, and Montesquieu alone, who developed a genuine doctrine of separate powers."[25] Oddly enough, in Montesquieu's great work, *The Spirit of the Laws*, published in Paris in 1748, it was only one aspect of a systematic study of politics and society. It fitted the colonial experience so neatly that separation of powers soon became regarded as a political axiom. James Madison, while noting that ". . . the preservation of liberty requires that the three great departments of power should be separate and distinct," cited "the oracle who is always consulted . . . on this subject . . . the celebrated Montesquieu."[26] Jefferson called *The Spirit of the Laws* "the most precious gift the present age has received." Hamilton cited Book XI as "a luminous abridgement of the principal arguments in favor of the Union." Many years later Oliver Wendell Holmes, Jr., writing an introduction to a new edition, spoke of Montesquieu as a "great and many-sided genius," "a precursor . . . in so many ways," whose book "has done as much to remodel the world as any product of the eighteenth century. . . ."[27] In any case Montesquieu's solution to the problem of how best to protect individual liberty has become a basic tenet of American constitutionalism.

Certainly its creator did not intend it that way. He wrote as one of France's leading literary figures and addressed himself to the situation existing in France. Louis XV's despotism was becoming more and more oppressive, and the first tremors of resistance and revolt were already being felt. Montesquieu, a serious student of history, and particularly

---

[24] See Robert Shackleton, *Montesquieu: A Critical Biography* (London: Oxford University Press, 1961) and Henry J. Merry, *Montesquieu's System of Natural Government* (Indiana: Purdue University Studies, 1969).

[25] Franz Neuman in his introduction to *Montesquieu's The Spirit of the Laws* (New York: Hafner, 1949), p. ix. J.R. Pole has written that separation of powers came from "the dark lessons inculcated by British history in the eighteenth century" and from state constitutions and their operation, as well as from Montesquieu. Pole, *Political Representation*, pp. 510–11.

[26] *The Federalist*, Modern Library ed. (New York: Random House, 1937), p. 313.

[27] Max Lerner, ed., *The Mind and Faith of Justice Holmes* (Boston: Little, Brown, 1943), p. 382.

informed on English political institutions, sought to present what changes he concluded to be necessary.

Not a revolutionary, nor even a democrat, the aristocratic Montesquieu was attracted to monarchy as the best form of government. Yet the meaning of liberty was of intense concern. Although little else in the thirty-one books of *The Spirit of the Laws* intrigued colonial imaginations, his formula in Book XI for assuring personal liberty certainly did.

To Montesquieu liberty was not unrestrained freedom. Rather, it was the right "of doing whatever the laws permit."[28] It was freedom under law, not freedom from law. Moreover, it was peculiarly the product of governments so constituted that power became a check on power. Montesquieu's study convinced him that, of all governments, England's guaranteed the most liberty. In England power was divided and checked, belonging neither to King nor Commons nor Lords, but to all three. Although Montesquieu did not understand the practical nature of English government, he nevertheless reflected what was still accepted as theory. To him English government alone was so constituted that no man need be afraid of another. For it recognized that

> when the legislative and executive powers are united in the same person, or in the same body of magistrates, there can be no liberty; because apprehensions may arise, lest the same monarch or senate should enact tyrannical laws, to execute them in a tyrannical manner. Again, there is no liberty if the judicial power be not separated from the legislative and executive. Were it joined with the legislative, the life and liberty of the subject would be exposed to arbitrary control, for the judge would be then the legislator. Were it joined to the executive power, the judge might behave with violence and oppression. There would be an end of everything, were the same man or the same body, whether of the nobles or of the people, to exercise those three powers, that of enacting laws, that of executing the public resolutions, and of trying the causes of individuals.

In England each power was placed at least partially in different hands, each endowed with rights of restraint and control over the others. "Here then," Montesquieu concluded, "is the fundamental constitution of . . . government." "The legislative body being composed of two parts, they check one another by the mutual privilege of rejecting. They are both restrained by the executive power, as the executive is by the legislative." Montesquieu dismissed the judiciary as "next to nothing," and so did not assign it the important checking role it has been given in the United States. His theory was broad enough, however, to include the courts when they began to exercise judicial review, for judicial review logically forms part of the essence of the separation of powers doctrine.

Locke, Harrington, and Montesquieu are conspicuous among the authorities confidently relied on, especially during the revolutionary and

---

[28] *The Spirit of the Laws.* The quotations are from pp. 619, 465, and 472 of F. W. Coker, *Readings in Political Philosophy* (New York: Macmillan, 1914), pp. 439–74.

formative periods of American history. It is highly probable, however, that Americans were influenced more by experience than by great names. "Is it not the glory of the people of America," Madison asks in *Federalist* Number 14, "that, while they have paid a decent regard to the opinions of former times and other nations, they have not suffered a blind veneration for antiquity, for custom, or for names, to overrule the suggestions of their own good sense, the knowledge of their own situations, and the lessons of their own experience?"

CHAPTER TWO

STRUGGLE FOR FREEDOM
IN THE
BIBLE COMMONWEALTH

Although the colonists brought with them from England a great many political precepts, the development of a distinctively American political thought began almost as soon as the first settlers arrived in the New World. One hundred sixty-nine years elapsed between the settlement at Jamestown and July 4, 1776. By then the Second Continental Congress could proclaim a number of ideas as *American* political verities.

The thirteen colonies shared unequally in the development of those ideas. From New York to the South, the pattern of colonial life was very much like what the colonists had left behind. Thus, the settlers of the Northern Neck of Virginia quickly developed "an ambitious landed society,"[1] reminiscent of England's. New York began its English existence in 1664 under laws drafted by one of orthodoxy's strongest supporters, the duke of York, later James II. Articulation of distinctly American political philosophy could hardly have been expected from such quarters. Nor was ideological independence, with a few isolated but significant exceptions, readily forthcoming.

---

[1] Title of Vol. I, Chap. 1 of Douglas S. Freeman, *George Washington* (New York: Scribner's, 1948).

Unconsciously at first and then deliberately, the Puritans and particularly the Puritan clergy in New England led the movement. Driven out by persecution at home, the Puritans sought freedom in America. They would have been surprised, perhaps shocked, had they realized that their theocratic state structure contained not only fertile soil for the growth of freedom but also some sturdy seedlings. As John Quincy Adams noted in 1836:

> The popular movement of the American revolution had been preceded by a foreseeing and directing mind. . . . [Not by one mind] but by a pervading mind, which . . . may be traced back to the first Puritan settlers of Plymouth and of Massachusetts Bay.[2]

The Puritans came to America to establish a religious system. In the words of one of them:

> Necessity may presse some, novelties draw on others; hopes of gaine in time to come may prevaile with a third sort; but that the most and most sincere and godly part have the advancement of the Gospel for their scope I am confident.[3]

Puritanism meant unquestioning acceptance of God's sovereignty. The Bible, containing His law, had to be accepted as interpreted by the clergy. Creation of a perfect Christian community required that the state, a lesser sphere, be one with the church. Church and state alike were of divine order; both were in the service of God. To disobey or resist either was to subvert His sovereignty.

"Let no man . . . deceive himself, since he cannot resist God," John Calvin declared in his *Institutes*. "No policy can be successfully established unless piety be its first care."

But to Calvinists, morality reinforced by religion was not enough. To secure property and public order, the state must punish idolatry, heresy, slander, blasphemy, and nonconformity. Presumably clear and explicit, truth was contained in the written word of God; the primary duty of the rulers was to guard and preserve it. In Calvin's theocracy nonmembers could not hold civil office. Equality formed no part of the Puritan creed: enjoyment of civil rights was limited to "saints," foreordained to salvation. Calvin was averse to both disorder and anarchy, and he considered

---

[2] John Quincy Adams, *An Eulogy on the Life and Character of James Madison*, September 27, 1836 (Boston: American Stationers' Company, 1836), p. 6. The Pilgrims, who settled at Plymouth, were somewhat more liberal, more democratic, than their Puritan brethren of Massachusetts Bay, with whom they were finally united under a new charter in 1692. "The democratic spirit prevailing at Plymouth is indicated by the fact that in the early years legislation was shared by all freemen. . . . Not to accept election when first chosen to office was a serious, punishable offense." Fred Krinsky, *The Politics of Religion in America* (Beverly Hills, Calif.: Glencoe Press, 1969), p. 18.

[3] Quoted in A. T. Mason, *Free Government in the Making* (New York: Oxford University Press, 1965), p. 51.

democracy synonymous with chaos. It meant an elevation of the rabble above the devout, a perversion of Christian values, a brazen insult to reason.

Nor did Calvin's American followers believe differently. John Winthrop (1588–1649), first governor of Massachusetts Bay Colony and a powerful Puritan leader, dubbed democracy "the meanest and worst of all forms of Government . . . of least continuance and fullest of troubles."[4] "God Almightie in his most holy and wise providence," Winthrop averred, "hath soe disposed of the Condicion of mankind, as in all times some must be rich, some poor, some highe and eminent in power and dignities; others meane and in subieccion." Instead of equality God had ordained inequality, no man being "made more honorable than another or more wealthy, etc. out of any particular or singular respect to himself but for the glory of his creator and the Common Good of the Creature, man."[5] Inequality arose out of the degree of one's godliness, and none were more godly than the Puritans. They believed themselves to be God's chosen people, being sure that to them alone had been given the keys to the heavenly kingdom. They alone, as His select on earth, were entitled to rights as citizens.

They believed God has chosen for them their way of government, whose leadership lay chiefly with the ministers of His Gospel. The purpose of life on earth being to carry out His plan, who but they could interpret His everlasting law as revealed in the Bible? To their authority and to that of the civil magistrates, who shared with the clergy responsibility for maintaining the purity of God's kingdom on earth, citizens were to "quietly and cheerfully submit"; true liberty consisted in "upholding the honor and power of [their] authority. . . ."[6] "[F]or when the people have chosen men to be their rulers, and to make their laws, and bound themselves by oath to submit thereto," Winthrop observed in his journal, "now to combine together (a lesser part of them) in a public petition to have any order repealed, which is not repugnant to the law of God, savors of resisting an ordinance of God."[7]

The Puritans could no more have been expected to advocate a separation of church and state than any of their European contemporaries. If they "separated" from the Anglican church, it was over doctrinal and procedural questions, not because they desired to tear church and state

---

[4] From Winthrop's "Replye on the Negative Vote," quoted in James Truslow Adams, *The Epic of America* (Boston: Little, Brown, 1931), p. 53.

[5] John Winthrop, "A Modell of Christian Charity," a sermon delivered aboard the *Arabella*, 1630, *Winthrop Papers* (Boston: Massachusetts Historical Society, 1931), II, 282.

[6] John Winthrop, "Speech to the General Court," July 3, 1645, *Old South Leaflets*, III, No. 66, 10.

[7] John Winthrop, *Journal*, May 22, 1639, quoted in Perry Miller and Thomas H. Johnson, *The Puritans* (New York: American Book, 1938), p. 203. For a full discussion of Winthrop's influence, see George Lee Haskins, *Law and Authority in Early Massachusetts* (New York: Macmillan, 1960) and Edmund S. Morgan, *The Puritan Dilemma. The Story of John Winthrop* (Boston: Little, Brown, 1958).

asunder. With most people of the age, they believed that church and state were properly one and that the highest purpose of the state was to serve the interests of the church. To them, as to John Cotton (1584–1652), long minister of Boston's First Church and the Bay Colony's leading theologian, it was suitable for the church to prescribe rules for individuals and "Yea, [for] the commonwealth too, so farre as both of them are subordinate to spiritual ends. . . ."[8]

So believing, they set out to demonstrate their belief. Theocracy, they believed with John Cotton, was the "best forme of government in the commonwealth, as well as in the church." In the Puritans' well-ordered state, voters were hand picked "for their devotion to the Puritan church."[9] Those who ran for civil office had both to be within the fold and to have the support of the clergy if they hoped for election. The election sermon was long regarded as a duty of the minister, on whom the people were to rely for guidance at the polls. The duty of magistrates, on the other hand—as outlined in *A Platform of Church Discipline*, accepted by the General Court of Massachusetts in 1649—was "to take care of matters of religion" and at the same time to include within their purview "matters of godliness; yea, of all godliness."[10] Moreover, the coercive power of magistrates was to be exerted to prevent schisms within the church as well as within society.

Nor was toleration a part of the Puritan philosophy. Nathaniel Ward (1578–1652), minister at Ipswich (Aggawam), Massachusetts, from 1634 to 1636, and author of the Body of Liberties (1641), the first code of law in Massachusetts, expressed the general feeling in his *Simple Cobbler of Aggawam*: "God doth no where in his word tolerate Christian States, to give Tolerations to . . . adversaries of his Truth, if they have power in their hands to suppress them." With most of his contemporaries, he could hold: "That State is wise, that will improve all paines and patience rather to compose, than tolerate differences in Religion."[11] To him the state was the agent of the church, and its primary duty was to ensure the state against attacks by false religionists; no arguments based on natural rights, popular sovereignty, or natural law could persuade Ward otherwise. His devout authoritarianism did permit enjoyment of God-given liberties, but the precise limits of such liberties he left quite vague. Hatred of allegedly false opinions—and in this he was in the company of most of the first wave of Puritans—would seem to preclude all civil and religious views not in accord with his own.

---

[8] From a letter of John Cotton to Lord Say and Seal, 1636, quoted in Miller and Johnson, *The Puritans*, pp. 209–10. The rest of the passage seems to suggest the possibility of a separation of church and state in civil affairs: "God's institutions may be close and compact, and coordinate one to another, and yet not confounded."

[9] Thomas J. Wertenbaker, *The Puritan Oligarchy* (New York: Scribner's, 1947), p. 76.

[10] "A Platform of Church Discipline," reprinted in Cotton Mather, *Magnalia Christi Americana* (Hartford, Conn.: Silus Andrus, 1855), II, 211–36.

[11] Nathaniel Ward, *The Simple Cobbler of Aggawam* (London, 1647); reprinted in part in Miller and Johnson, *The Puritans*, pp. 226–36.

THE COVENANT: THEORY
OF THE PURITAN STATE

Puritan New England was politically so unlike America today that it is difficult to understand fully. Representing in some respects a retrogression from the slowly evolving constitutional pattern of seventeenth-century England, the bleak Zion of Puritanism had more in common with latter-day totalitarianism than with free government. Despite its forbidding appearance, that rigid and uncompromising theocracy contained at least three elements intimating recognizable concepts of free government: Puritan reliance on compact, or covenant, fervent attachment to the right of local self-government, and firm belief in limited government.

The concept of covenant was a basic religious tenet. It had come to be relied upon heavily at the beginning of the Puritan revolution in England, at which time a number of early separatists, chief among them Robert Browne, began to assert, as a part of their argument against the Anglican church, that the proper basis of the church was not an organization, a hierarchy, or a dogma, but a compact made between individual believers joining together to worship God. Gradually this view became common in English Puritanism, and the English settlers brought it with them to the New World. Here the idea was joined with another, slowly developing in England for a century or more—the principle of consent. The combination of covenant (or compact) and consent was destined to become a vital force in colonial, as well as later, political thinking.

"Its free for any man to offer to joyn with another who is fit for fellowship, or to refuse," Thomas Hooker (1586–1647), one of the founders of Connecticut, wrote in his major work, *Survey of the Summe of Church Discipline*, published in 1648. "Its as feee [sic] for another to reject or receive such who offer, and therefore they that do joyn, it is by their own free consent and mutuall ingagement on both sides . . . it is not every relation, but such an ingagement, which issues from free consent, that makes the covenant." Hooker's thought on the covenant as the basis of social organization is so closely akin to Locke's that it has been suggested that the author of the *Summe of Church-Discipline* might have written Chapters 7 and 8 of the *Second Treatise*.[12] Even Governor Winthrop, no divine and no democrat, declared that "the Lord hath given us leave to drawe our own Articles" and spoke of "the worke wee have in hand" being by "mutuall consent."[13] He was referring, of course, to ecclesiastical affairs, but because each congregation formed by the covenant, not only a church, but also (in the colonies) a society and body politic,[14] the covenant was quite as significant in politics as in religion. The famous

---

[12] Clinton Rossiter, *Seedtime of the Republic* (New York: Harcourt, Brace, Jovanovich 1953), p. 172.
[13] Winthrop "A Modell of Christian Charity," pp. 293–94.
[14] The Southold (Long Island) church, established in 1640, served, according to a commemorative tablet, as "meeting house, church, fort, court, and prison."

Mayflower Compact of the Pilgrims has long been properly regarded as a foundation stone in the building of free government in America. For it not only bound the signatories together in the worship of God, but also "constituted an original contract for the establishment of a new community" and a new government.[15]

With only a few exceptions, however, the Puritans did not carry the contract-consent principle to its full implications. Commonly accepted was Winthrop's conviction that the compact had little or no meaning once the body politic was formed. Nevertheless, the founders of Connecticut, Providence, and New Haven followed the example of the passengers on the Mayflower when they broke away to form separate colonies, and the compact soon became widely regarded as the legitimate basis of both church and state. A full half-century before Locke wrote his *Second Treatise*, the idea of the compact was familiar to colonial Puritans. Locke's exegesis thus provided a cogent rationalization of an old political practice.

LOCAL SELF-GOVERNMENT: PURITAN PRACTICE

The idea of compact as the foundation of church and state, combined with several other forces, firmly established local autonomy within Puritan political practice and, thus, in American political thought. In the first place the Puritans, as Englishmen, had been used to a certain amount of autonomy. Second, Puritan colonization took place during hectic years in English politics, and the little groups of settlers that managed to survive in the New World were long virtually ignored by king and Parliament. Charles I had granted the "Governor and Company of the Massachusetts Bay in New England" the usual charter, which entrusted the government of the emigrants very largely to the members of the company itself. Because of the pressure of events in England, very little subsequent supervision was accorded the affairs of the Puritan Commonwealth. Moreover, the very remoteness of New England furthered the chances for self-government. The difficulties of trans-Atlantic travel and communication alone minimized effective English supervision, and the distances between New England towns, magnified by the Indian menace and lack of good roads, worked against centralized control.

Also, Puritan theology emphasized independent congregational control of ecclesiastical matters. The congregation, when constituted as the town meeting, quite naturally handled local civic affairs as well as church matters. Thus, the town meeting "could at one moment be considering the matter of the common fence around a grain field and the next, if it so chose, convert itself into the congregation without leaving the meeting

---

[15] J. Mark Jacobson, *The Development of American Political Thought* (New York: Appleton-Century-Crofts, 1932), p. 61.

room, and proceed to discipline wayward brothers or sisters, or elect a deacon, or receive a person to communion."[16] The Puritan freemen quickly became as jealous of their political independence as of their religious freedom. There is much to be said for the assertion frequently made that the congregational form of worship in New England provided the seedbed for free government. Certainly nowhere else in western Europe or in the American colonies was so much political independence possible.

The availability of free land and the joy with which men and women, long starved for land, made it their own served also to inspire an exaggerated sense of local concern and a desire for self-government. "It was this 'land in the woods' as a possibility for almost every inhabitant of America that was to prove one of the most powerful of the forces which worked toward a democracy of feeling and outlook. . . ."[17]

Finally, the Puritans were insistent upon limitations of power. John Cotton argued "that all power that is on earth be limited, Church-power or other. . . . It is counted a matter of danger to the State to limit Prerogatives; but it is a further danger, not to have them limited." Everyone, magistrates and people alike, was subject to checks set by fundamental law and basic right. "It is wholesome and safe to be dealt withall as God deales with the vast Sea; *Hitherto shalt thou come, but there shalt thou stay thy proud waves.* . . . So let there be due bounds set." In no other way could the corruptness in man's nature be restrained and his soul saved.[18]

DISSENT FROM PURITAN THEOCRACY

Perhaps even more important than the sprigs of democratic theory and practice that took root in the arid authoritarian soil of Puritan New England was the vigorous and ultimately victorious body of clerical dissent stimulated by the Bible Commonwealth. Puritanism itself was the result of dissent (beginning with John Wyclif, if not before), and in the Bay Colony it reached its perfection. Puritan authority being "right" and God ordained, no dissent was permitted. Indeed, to pull away from what was solemnly presented as God's final word was regarded as sin punishable by banishment or death. Despite repeated attempts to stamp it out, the spirit of dissent was not to be stifled. Instances of it had plagued the Puritan colonies from the first year of their existence. In the end the protesters—Roger Williams, Thomas Hooker, John Wise, and Jonathan Mayhew—carried the day.

---

[16] Wertenbaker, *The Puritan Oligarchy*, p. 69.
[17] J. T. Adams, *The Epic of America*, p. 38.
[18] John Cotton, "Limitation of Government" (1646), quoted in Miller and Johnson, *The Puritans*, pp. 212–14.

Roger Williams

The most prominent of the early dissenters, "by all odds the most exciting character in the story of colonial liberty,"[19] was Roger Williams (c. 1603–1684). Williams was born in London and educated at Charterhouse and Cambridge. Although he was a protégé of Sir Edward Coke, his intensely religious nature led him to take Anglican orders instead of following his mentor into the law. Williams soon drifted into Puritanism, emigrating in 1631 to Massachusetts, where his differences with other colonial church leaders quickly led to difficulties.

Williams began his pulpit career as an Anglican; later he turned to separatism, and ended as a Seeker. Never certain that he had reached absolute truth, he was constantly striving for fuller understanding of God and man. Because such a liberal religious attitude fitted awkwardly into the Bay Colony authoritarianism, he was removed from his Salem pastorate. Religious unorthodoxy was but a single facet of his betrayal. He opposed the required oath of fidelity and denied the power of magistrates to enforce purely religious commandments. He denounced the grants of land to the colonists as "unjust usurpations upon others' possessions"—those of the Indians, from whom the land had been wrested without any semblance of legality. Tried in October 1635 for preaching "Newe and dangerous opinions, against the authoritie of magistrates," he was ordered out of the colony by the General Court. After some delay he complied with the order and fled south in the spring of 1636. Settling on land purchased from the Narragansett Indians, he founded the town of Providence. Before long it was joined by sister towns and became the colony of Rhode Island. There Williams worked and preached for the rest of his life, putting into practice his advanced religious and political ideas. A theologian rather than a statesman, he became celebrated as *the* prophet of religious freedom and as the founder of America's first democratic government.[20]

Much of Williams's philosophy was due to his own uncertainty about religious fundamentals. Not sure himself what was right and convinced that no one had yet founded the "true Church of God," he objected to enforced conformity with official dogma. With startling modernity he denied the power of civil magistrates in ecclesiastical affairs; he saw no reason for the connection of church and state; and he was against the doctrine of persecution for cause of conscience.[21] Although Christ had

[19] Rossiter, *Seedtime of the Republic*, p. 192.
[20] See Perry Miller, *Roger Williams: His Contributions to the American Tradition* (New York: Atheneum, 1962), pp. 28–29. See also Mario Calamandrei, "Neglected Aspects of Roger Williams' Thought," *Church History*, XXI (1952), 239–58.
[21] Williams engaged in an extended controversy with John Cotton over these points. The essence of Williams's theory is stated in his work of 1644, *The Bloody Tenent of Persecution for Cause of Conscience Discussed* (1644) (Providence: Narragansett Club Publications, 1870), III, 3–425, *passim*, from which these quotations are taken.

provided "spiritual *antidotes* and *preservatives* against the spiritual *sickness, sores, weaknesses, dangers* of his *Church* and people . . . he [had] never appointed the *civill Sword* for either *antidote* or *remedy*, as an *addition* to those *Spiritualls*. . . ." Instead, Christ had put spiritual weapons into the hands of church officers to equip them to guard the soul, and had left for civil officers the care of "bodies and goods."

In attempting to combine two distinct functions, orthodox ministers were victims of "ignorance and blind zeal," forgetting that ". . . *Gods people* were and ought to be *Non-conformitants*, not daring either to be *restrained* from the *true*, or *constrained* to *false* Worship. . . ." There was no justification whatever for using civil power to enforce religious beliefs or to persecute for conscience's sake. "*Stocks, whips, prisons, swords, gibbets, stakes, &c*" directly contradicted the spirit and practice of the Prince of Peace. Even more tragic, they were futile: instead of uniting all men in Christ, they only succeeded in destroying civil peace and subverting the welfare of the commonwealth. The precise intention of Scripture could not be ascertained with the icy certainty claimed by the Massachusetts clergy. Williams thus wanted church and state separated to protect the church from corruption by the power of the state.

Although Williams was primarily a man of God, not a politician, circumstances forced him into a political role. In it he proved to be the most advanced political thinker of his time. For him government was merely the creature of the sovereign people, subject to their control. The social contract had a continuing significance. It implied that the people, having consented to the creation of a government, might parcel out its functions, control its actions, and change its form whenever they so desired. Williams manifested an intense concern, also, for natural law and natural rights. Religious liberty was of course the chief natural right, but he also insisted —and the institutions of Rhode Island reflected that insistence—on recognition of the rights guaranteed in the Magna Carta. Under his leadership Providence and its sister towns enjoyed remarkably liberal government. Popular elections, the referendum, the right of recall, religious liberty, and numerous personal freedoms were its hallmarks. This unique combination of theory and practice bred in Rhode Island a spirit of rampant agrarian democracy, which remained alive long after Rhode Island entered the Union.

Thomas Hooker

A contemporary of Roger Williams, perhaps less well known as a dissenter today, was Thomas Hooker. A native of Leicestershire, England, and a graduate of Emmanuel College, Cambridge, he became an eminent nonconformist preacher. His particular brand of nonconformity, however, soon rendered him *persona non grata* to Archbishop Laud, and he was forced to flee to Holland. From there, in 1633, he emigrated to Massachusetts. For three years he was pastor at Newtown (Cambridge), but in

1636 he led his land-hungry congregation westward to the banks of the
Connecticut River. On the site of a Dutch trading post, he established
the city of Hartford and the colony of Connecticut. Although historians
disagree about Hooker's significance, it is quite clear "that he represents
the forces of liberty inherent in Puritanism more dramatically than any
other colonial of the seventeenth century. . . ."[22] His role was harder
than Williams's. Williams broke with the reigning oligarchy and pursued
his independent way; Hooker remained steadfastly orthodox. Within the
limits of his faith, he had to plant and nurture "in New England soil the
seeds of democracy hidden away in the brittle pod of Puritanism."[23] One
working from the inside, the other challenging from without, Hooker and
Williams together laid the groundwork for democratic theory upon which
later generations built with notable success.

Hooker believed in the ecclesiastical equality of all men and in the
resultant necessity for their free consent to a compact forming both
church and state. The concept of popular sovereignty inherent in the
covenant had vitality for Hooker (as for Williams) even after the people
had entered into it. As a listener remembered the main point in one of
Hooker's sermons, he thought not only that "the choice of public magistrates [belonged] unto the people, by God's own allowance," but also
that, having once elected "officers and magistrates, it is in their power,
also, to set the bounds and limitations of [that] power. . . ."[24]

Hooker's faith in "the privilege of election, which belongs to the people," his conviction that magistrates were to seek the advice and defer to
the judgment of the people on all "matters of greater consequence, which
concern the common good," his willingness to let the people restrict the
exercise of magistrates' power, set him, like Williams, apart from all his
contemporaries. So, too, did his insistence that magistrates act according
to established law. Anticipating Harrington, Hooker remarked:

> And we know in other Countries, had not the law overruled the lusts of
> men and the crooked ends of judges many times, both places and people had
> been . . . past all relief, in many cases of difficulty. You will know what the
> Heathen man said by the candle light of common sense: The law is not sub-
> ject to passion, nor to be taken aside with self-seeking ends, and therefore
> ought to have chief rule over rulers themselves.[25]

Should the law not prevail over the whim of the magistrates, the people
had the reserved right "to proceed against any officer 'that goes aside.' "[26]

---

[22] Clinton Rossiter, "Thomas Hooker," *New England Quarterly*, XXV (December, 1952),
460.
[23] Rossiter, "Thomas Hooker," p. 488.
[24] Thomas Hooker's Sermon to the General Court, May 31, 1638, *Connecticut Historical
Society Collections*, I, 20.
[25] Thomas Hooker's Letter to Governor Winthrop, Autumn, 1638, reprinted in *Connecticut Collections*, pp. 11–12.
[26] Merle Curti, *The Growth of American Thought* (New York: Harper & Brothers,
1943), p. 118.

Like Roger Williams, Hooker was mainly a religious thinker. His *Survey of the Summe of Church Discipline* is primarily a statement of congregational church policy. It makes clear, however, Hooker's belief that, within the church, the congregation was sovereign and that church officers owed more allegiance to the people than the people owed submission to them. The celebrated Fundamental Orders of Connecticut, the written foundation of the colony, adopted in 1639, reflected Hooker's belief. They embodied a well-developed concept of popular sovereignty; they made use of the covenant principle; and they created a truly representative government. They provided that the freemen in the colony, without limitation, religious or otherwise, should elect once a year a governor and a board of magistrates, as well as designate deputies to the General Court. To this court was entrusted all legislative power. The people's sovereignty was further protected by the existence of the right in the General Court to call erring magistrates to account, by the fact that its sessions were independent of the governor and magistrates, by the power of the veto vested in the governor, and by the power of the General Court to amend or abolish the Fundamental Orders themselves. If in other ways the Fundamental Orders were less liberal, they nevertheless served to move Connecticut away from the rigid theocracy of its parent colony toward the democratic practices of today.[27] Because of Hooker's "mighty preaching," Professor Alexander Johnston designated Hartford "the birthplace of American democracy."[28]

Williams and Hooker were exceptions to the political rule. Although they anticipated the future, New England as a whole remained staunchly Puritan. Yet their ideas, like the contents of Pandora's box—once loosed, elaborated upon, and spread abroad—began to take hold. By the beginning of the eighteenth century, the theocratic mold had cracked and was beginning to break apart completely.[29] In its place a secular society, increasingly democratic in tone, emerged and gradually became rationalized into general acceptance.

John Wise

In the philosophy of John Wise (1652–1725) one can see how far, by the beginning of the eighteenth century, the movement had progressed. Wise

---

[27] See Mary J. A. Jones, *Congregational Commonwealth, Connecticut 1636–1662* (Middletown, Conn.: Wesleyan University Press, 1968). But see also Richard L. Bushman, *From Puritan to Yankee. Character and the Social Order in Connecticut 1690–1765* (Cambridge, Mass.: Harvard University Press, 1967), who has argued that by 1690, "the Puritan rulers of Connecticut valued order above all other social ventures" (p. 3) and that they "conceived their function to be the containment of the wicked passions" of the populace (p. 4). All of Chap. 1, "Law and Authority," provides an interesting commentary on the erosion of Hooker's values in latter-day Connecticut.

[28] Alexander Johnston, *Connecticut* (Boston: Houghton Mifflin, 1893), p. 73.

[29] See Wertenbaker, *The Puritan Oligarchy*, Chaps. 5–8, for an excellent discussion of the forces responsible for the dissolution of the Puritan oligarchy.

was minister at Ipswich, Massachusetts, from 1680 until his death. Educated at Harvard College, he remained at the forefront of democratic activity in the colonies the rest of his life. Although he attracted notice as early as 1687, when he led the people of Ipswich in resistance to the taxes levied without consent by Governor Andros and his council through the General Court, it was not until 1710 that Wise brought out his first book, *Churches Quarrel Espoused*. From it, and from his later *Vindication of the Government of the New England Churches* (first published in 1717), both of which were characteristically addressed to ecclesiastical problems, can be gleaned the first virtually complete theory of democratic politics in America. Much further than either Williams or Hooker, Wise developed a theory of politics based on natural rights.

Wise considered man as originally "in a state of natural being, as a free-born subject under the crown of heaven . . . owing homage to none but God himself," and guided in his actions by natural law, "the dictates of right reason."[30] Reason led man quickly to see that when some men went contrary to the law of nature and abused it, the safety of others was imperiled and government became a necessity. Reason also taught man that any particular government must suit "the temper and inclination" of the people and thus could only be properly established by "human free-compacts," not by "divine institution." "Nothing can be God's ordinance," Wise wrote in *Vindication of Government*, "but what he has particularly declared to be such; there is no particular form of civil government described in God's word, neither does Nature prompt it." Governments were not formed by God; they were formed by men.

These assumptions led Wise to examine the forces directing men in their choice of governments. He saw men "cloathed" by God with three "immunities," each guiding them inevitably toward democracy: the first, "that he is most properly the subject of the law of nature . . . [and lives] agreeably with [it]"; the second, "an original liberty instampt upon his rational nature"; the third, that "every man must be acknowledged equal to every man, since all subjection and all command are equally banished on both sides. . . ." So immunized, each man could judge for himself the course most conducive to his happiness and welfare, and reason dictated that men so conditioned would inevitably choose democracy, the "form of government, which the light of nature does highly value, and often directs to, as most agreeable to the just and natural prerogatives of human beings."

Wise relied on the compact theory for the establishment of free government. He thought three covenants were necessary to protect the people and to assure observance of "the formal reason of government . . . the will of [the] community: one among the people, to form the society"; another, "to set up some particular species of government" over that society; and the third, to bind those on whom authority was conferred to

---

[30] John Wise, *A Vindication of the Government of New England Churches* (Boston: John Boyles, 1772), Chap. 2. The quotations in these paragraphs are from pp. 22–44.

guard "the common peace, and welfare. And the subjects on the other hand, to yield them faithful obedience."

Such reasoning led men to prefer democracy. Only that form of government, in states or in churches, permitted the people to exercise their sovereignty and kept them free from the "arbitrary measures of particular men." Only democracy embodied the principle that the happiness of the people was the end of the state. Only democracy could be "rationally imagined" by free and equal men. Like Hooker, Wise visualized no restrictions on the suffrage, at least among freemen. Like Williams he emphasized natural rights, holding: "The end of all good government is to . . . promote . . . the good of every man in all his rights, his life, liberty, estate, honour, &c. without injury or abuse done to any."

Wise's books, at the outset, had only religious influence, their purpose being solely to present a defense of congregational church government against centralized Presbyterianism. But the political applications of his thinking did not lose their validity, and when the need for a well-conceived body of democratic doctrine arose in the days just before the Revolution, Wise's works were reprinted and widely read. Much more than either Williams or Hooker, from whom Wise must have received inspiration and guidance, he affected future events. His clear exposition of theory is probably more significant in the evolution of modern American political thought than any other in the colonies up to that time.

Jonathan Mayhew

As the years passed, the ideas espoused by Williams, Hooker, and Wise became more characteristic of New England than the earlier Puritan conceptions. By the mid-1700s only one further major tenet was needed to make their theory a rounded whole, ready to be acted on in 1776. More than anyone else, the Reverend Jonathan Mayhew (1720–1766), minister of West Church in Boston, filled that need. Mayhew was a theologian so liberal in politics that only two other clergymen attended his ordination in 1747.[31] He took a stand unhesitatingly on public issues—his sermon in 1750 on the anniversary of the execution of Charles I being perhaps the most influential of a great many attempts to guide the public mind in the darkening days before the Revolution. In his *Discourse Concerning Unlimited Submission and Non-Resistance to Higher Powers,* Mayhew added the finishing touch to prerevolutionary theory by clearly stating the right of resistance to arbitrary authority. Unlimited submission seemed to him "a monstrous, unaccountable doctrine," nowhere countenanced by the Scriptures. In its stead he substituted the principle of lawful resistance.

---

[31] Miller and Johnson, *The Puritans,* p. 277. For a biography of Mayhew, see Charles W. Akers, *Called Unto Liberty: A Life of Jonathan Mayhew, 1720–1766* (Cambridge, Mass.: Harvard University Press, 1964).

We may very safely assert these two things in general, without undermining government: One is, That no civil rulers are to be obeyed when they enjoin things that are inconsistent with the commands of God . . . disobedience to them is a duty, not a crime. . . . Another thing that may be asserted with equal truth and safety is, That no government is to be submitted to, at the *expence* of that which is the *sole end* of all government,—the common good and safety of society. . . . If . . . in any case, the common safety and utility would not be promoted by submission to government, but the contrary, there is no ground or motive for obedience and submission, but, for the contrary.[32]

Government was a trust, "committed by the people, to those who are vested with it . . . All besides is mere lawless force and usurpation; neither God nor nature, having given any man a right of dominion over any society, independently of that society's approbation, and consent to be governed by him. . . ." Mayhew did not, however, argue for resistance at every turn. As children must as a rule obey their parents, but may resist them in extreme cases, so the people of a state as a rule owed submission to those they had set over them—but not in all cases. If those in authority abused their trust *"to such a degree*, that neither the law of reason, nor of religion, requires . . . obedience or submission," the people were absolved of the duty and might take back the authority and vest it in others. Rulers, declared Mayhew, had "no authority from God to do mischief."

To say that subjects in general are not proper judges when their governors oppress them, and play the tyrant; and when they defend their rights, administer justice impartially and promote the public welfare, is as great *treason* as ever man uttered; . . . 'tis treason, not against one *single* man, but the State—against the whole body politic;—'tis treason against mankind, 'tis treason against common sense;—'tis against God. And this impious principle lays the foundation for justifying all the tyranny and oppression that ever any prince was guilty of. The people know for what end they set up and maintain their governors; and they are the proper judges when they execute their *trust* as they ought to do it.

Mayhew did not fear that adherence to such precepts would overturn civil society. He knew that men would endure a great deal of tyranny and oppression before acting against their rulers. Mayhew's reasoning, joined with Locke's similar exposition, provided the underlying premises of the Declaration of Independence.

So far had beliefs changed from those of their Puritan ancestors that Mayhew's sermon might have been repeated by a large number of third- and fourth-generation New England clergy. From an earlier advocacy of subjection to absolute governmental power, the clergy's position had

---

[32] The quotations here are from Jonathan Mayhew, "A Discourse Concerning Unlimited Submission," in John W. Thornton, ed., *The Pulpit of the American Revolution*, 2nd ed. (Boston: D. Lothrop, 1876), pp. 53–104, *passim.*

slowly shifted to the fiduciary nature of government and advocacy of the people's right of resistance. But its position of leadership had not diminished, and its influence remained great in politics, as in other fields. In an age when leadership from the pulpit was expected and the sanction of the clergy was considered necessary for any successful enterprise, no other way of making so fundamental a shift acceptable to the people would have been possible.

Indeed, the New England clergy provided "unbroken lines of transmission" from the seventeenth-century philosophy of John Locke to the American Revolution. Long before 1763, ideas proclaimed every Sunday and in special election sermons made familiar to church-going New Englanders not only the doctrines of natural rights, social contract, and the right of resistance, but also the fundamental principle of American constitutional law, that government, like its citizens, is bound by law and that when it transcends these limits, it cannot claim validity.

Seven years before the beginning of tax troubles with England, many colonists had heard ringing words from the pulpit concerning the inestimable value of their chartered privileges and their rights as Englishmen, of law and constitution as contrasted with tyranny and arbitrary government, and of the danger of becoming slaves and losing all their freedom, civil and religious. They had heard rebellion itself justified in defense of their chartered rights and liberties, a fact "never sufficiently realized by historians."

The assertion that "the constitutional Convention and the written constitution were the children of the pulpit" may be extreme, but there is ample justification for the conclusion that one line in the search for the origin of fundamental constitutional doctrines and the reasons for America's devotion to them "runs back to the New England ministers who, for a hundred years and more, accepted and taught a religious people with unquestioning faith, giving them the sanction of divine law."[33]

---

[33] Alice M. Baldwin, *The New England Clergy and the American Revolution* (Durham, N.C.: Duke University Press, 1928), pp. 13, 19, 79, 88, 98, 134, 172.

CHAPTER THREE

FORGING INDEPENDENCE

The distinctively American pattern of political thought developed slowly, almost imperceptibly. It might never have flowered, despite growing acceptance of the liberating doctrines of Colonel Rainboro and John Locke, and their endorsement by leading colonial clergymen, had not the congenial relations existing before 1760 between the colonies and Great Britain been drastically altered. Although the philosophy of revolution had already made its way into colonial thinking, there had nowhere been occasion or desire to translate that theory into action. But after 1763 Anglo-American relations were subjected to a series of rude and increasingly severe shocks, and in the space of little more than twelve years, the colonists had formulated and acted upon a full-grown philosophy of revolution and independence.

At least until the early 1760s, colonial Americans generally regarded themselves as Britons, loyal subjects of the king and citizens of the empire. That circumstances could force them away from the mother country toward independence few recognized and most would have denied. The remoteness of the colonies from England had permitted them to adjust their politics to the realities of frontier life, unhindered in the main by irrelevant English precedents and customs. It did not occur to most of the colonists that their ways had become sufficiently different from those in England to warrant theoretical exploration. The colonists were simply too busy to worry about the full implications of their evolving way of life. Occupied in opening up a new country and building their fortunes, they asked only to be allowed to follow their pursuits. As late as 1776, the average American colonist would hardly have impressed anyone as a potential supporter of radical political doctrines.[1]

THE PAMPHLET WAR: 1763-1776

The Seven Years' War (1756-1763)—the French and Indian War on this side of the Atlantic—and especially the repeated attempts by king and Parliament to convince the colonies to share its costs changed the colonial situation irrevocably. During the war the gap between the colonists and their British brethren became evident, and by 1776 it seemed entirely wise and right to the colonists "to dissolve the political bonds" that connected them with England and "to assume among the Powers of the earth, the separate and equal station to which the Laws of Nature and of Nature's God" entitled them. "Decent respect to the opinions of mankind" moved them to state the peculiar ends to which they were about to dedicate themselves. Specific reasons for the break were listed in the Declaration of Independence and need no elaboration here. Suffice it to say that the end of the French and Indian War marked a dividing line in Anglo-American relations after which nothing was ever again the same. From then until July 4, 1776, it became increasingly obvious that Americans were no longer Englishmen and that they would have to readjust their governmental arrangements.

Actions on the part of king and Parliament that would formerly have gone unchallenged were now queried and resisted. Bitter agitation developed against Parliament's authority to tax the colonies and concerning the broader issue of the power of king and Parliament. As a result the years between the Treaty of Paris and the Declaration of Independence were marked by uninterrupted discussion of the political relationship between the mother country and the colonies. Just as the years of civil war in England set off a literary avalanche, so did the postwar years in America drench the colonists with a flood of pamphlets, books, broadsides, and speeches presenting the pros and cons of contemporary political developments. As the period drew to a close, an ever clearer theory of American, as distinct from colonial, politics became evident. Separate principles that had been heretofore only incidentally and even casually

---

[1] See Richard L. Merritt, *Symbols of American Community 1735-1775* (New Haven, Conn.: Yale University Press, 1966) for an analysis of popular attitudes in colonial America.

stated were brought into sharp alignment and effectively synthesized.[2] With the Stamp Act colonial thinking began to merge into a single channel flowing toward independence. Unlike the earlier period, when only a few men, chiefly Puritans, concerned themselves with political theory, the decade just before the Revolution was crowded with contenders. If it is true, as John Adams believed, that the Revolution was, in effect, over before it began, having been accomplished "in the minds and hearts of the people," much credit must be given to the host of pamphleteers and letterwriters who, between 1763 and 1776, labored so diligently to bring it about. This was, indeed, the "seedtime of the Republic."

Benjamin Franklin: The Case for Representation

In general the arguments of the pamphleteers went through three phases, each successively broader and bolder until, after the Revolution and independence had occurred, they were comprehensive enough to appeal to all mankind. In the early days of the controversy, it was common to argue that the answer to Anglo-American troubles could be found in colonial representation in Parliament. Benjamin Franklin (1706–1790), already an elder statesman, made this approach. As early as 1754, when his ill-fated Albany Plan (which Franklin had drafted as a means of uniting the colonies for military purposes) was still under discussion, Franklin diagnosed the root of the colonial difficulty. Referring to the British counterproposal of parliamentary taxation—a suggested substitute for his own idea of taxation by a central legislative council in the colonies—he wrote Governor William Shirley: "Excluding the people of the colonies from all share in the choice of the grand council will give extreme dissatisfaction; as well as taxing them by act of Parliament, where they have no representation."[3]

Recognizing that the distance of the colonies from England and the incompetence of many governors and counselors combined to produce a poor understanding of colonial attitudes, Franklin argued that colonial representation in Parliament would overcome these difficulties. If Great

---

[2] See, in particular, Carl Becker, *The Eve of the Revolution* (New Haven, Conn.: Yale University Press, 1918) and John C. Miller, *Origins of the American Revolution* (Boston: Little, Brown, 1943) for detailed discussions of the years between 1760 and 1776. See also Bernard Bailyn, *Pamphlets of the American Revolution, 1750–1776* (Cambridge, Mass.: Harvard University Press, 1965). Bailyn's *The Theological Origins of the American Revolution* (Cambridge, Mass.: Harvard University Press, 1967) is an enlarged version of the introduction to *Pamphlets*.

[3] Benjamin Franklin to Governor William Shirley, December 18, 1754, reprinted in Jared Sparks, ed., *The Works of Benjamin Franklin* (Boston: Townsend, MacCoun, 1882), pp. 57–63. For a description of Franklin's political theory, see Paul W. Connor, *Poor Richard's Politicks: Benjamin Franklin and His New Order* (New York: Oxford University Press, 1965) and Alfred O. Aldridge, *Benjamin Franklin: Philosopher and Man* (Philadelphia: Lippincott, 1965).

Britain would open Parliament to colonial representation and repeal all restraints on colonial trade and manufactures, the result would be a union acceptable to the colonies, "agreeable to the nature of [the] English constitution, and to English liberty," and advantageous in the extreme to England itself.

"I look upon the colonies," Franklin wrote Shirley, "as so many countries gained to Great Britain," affording her a great variety of produce and materials for more manufactures, increasing her shipping, enlarging her empire and commerce, and increasing "her strength, her wealth, and the numbers of her people" far beyond what she otherwise might have expected. In short, "the best interest of the whole" would be served by "*uniting the colonies* more intimately with Great Britain, by allowing them *representatives in Parliament.* . . ."

The passage of thirteen years produced a revision of Franklin's thinking. His years of service as an agent in London for Pennsylvania and other colonies gave him deep insight into British imperial relations and clear comprehension of the basic points of dispute. Franklin's shift in outlook marked the progression from arguments characteristic of the first stage of the controversy to those of the second. Although still desirous of a "consolidating union," based on equal representation of all parts of the empire in Parliament, he now recognized that in neither the law, nor the institutions, nor the disposition of England was such a union any longer possible. Passage of the Stamp Act in 1764 and the fierce reaction it produced had complicated the whole colonial problem. By 1767 the belief was widespread in America that Parliament's sovereignty over the colonies and its right to tax were limited, perhaps nonexistent.

Why not accept the colonial assertion, Franklin suggested in 1767.[4] To abandon the claim of parliamentary sovereignty over the internal affairs of the colonies would avoid "great mischief"—the alienation "of the affections of the people of America" toward England—as well as the probable destruction of the empire. In any case Franklin persevered, introducing a theme eventually introduced into the Declaration of Independence: the allegiance of the colonies was properly to the king and to him alone. Thus, even though, through force of habit and because it had been deemed necessary "for the common good of the empire," the power to regulate its general commerce had been placed in Parliament, it did not follow that Parliament also possessed the right to impose internal taxes on the colonies. Because the king alone was sovereign over them, Parliament possessed only limited authority over the colonies.

Franklin, like so many of the colonists, accepted initially the distinction between external and internal taxation. On reexamination of his ideas on trade and commerce, however, he discarded the main tenets of mercantilism. In "The Causes of the American Discontents," written in 1768, he observed:

---

[4] F. L. Mott and C. E. Jorgenson, *Benjamin Franklin, Representative Selections* (New York: American Book, 1936), p. 325.

There cannot be a stronger natural right than that of a man's making the best profit he can of the natural produce of his lands, provided he does not thereby hurt the State in general. Iron is to be found everywhere in America and beaver are the natural produce of that country: hats and nails and steel are wanted there as well as here. It is of no importance to the common welfare of the empire, whether a subject of the king gets his living making hats on this, or on that side of the water.[5]

It was even more important for England than for America to change her approach to the conflict. For, as Franklin predicted as early as 1751, the Americans "will, in another Century, be more than the People of *England,* and the greatest Number of *Englishmen* will be on this Side of the Water."[6] In time America would be of much greater political significance than the "tiny island." To "surrender" nonexistent rights would cost her but little, Franklin declared in 1767. Moreover, it would save for England and for the empire

an immense territory, favored by Nature with all advantages of climate, soil, great navigable rivers, lakes, &c., [that] must become a great country, populous and mighty; and will in a less time than is generally conceived, be able to shake off any shackles that may be imposed upon her, and perhaps place them on the imposers.[7]

Because he loved England and wished to preserve "that fine and noble China Vase, the British Empire,"[8] Franklin urged a policy of "kind usage and tenderness" for colonial privileges. The seeds of liberty had already been sown in America and were not to be uprooted. He hoped that king and Parliament would heed his warning.

"Kind usage and tenderness" for American privileges was not to be embodied in the policies of the ministers of George III, and as proof after proof piled up, reliance on them was slowly abandoned. Franklin thus straddled, as it were, the first two stages in the development of the colonial argument—the case for representation and the broader appeal for colonial rights under the British constitution. As the years went by and he became less hopeful of the simple solution of representation, others assumed active leadership in the raging controversy.

James Otis: The Case
for Higher Law

The most prominent group among those who formulated the colonial argument were the lawyers, and heading the list was the fiery Bostonian

---

[5] Sparks, *Works of Franklin,* IV, 251.
[6] Verner Winslow Crane, *Benjamin Franklin: Englishman and American* (Baltimore: Williams & Wilkins, 1936), p. 63.
[7] Mott and Jorgenson, *Benjamin Franklin,* p. 329.
[8] Letter to Lord Howe, Philadelphia, July 30, 1776, reprinted in Mott and Jorgenson, *Benjamin Franklin,* p. 386.

James Otis (1725–1783). Otis was among the most vociferous New Englanders in opposition to British colonial measures. As head of the Massachusetts Committee of Correspondence, he vigorously denounced the
Stamp Act and spearheaded formation of the Stamp Act Congress. In
1769 he was attacked for his utterances against the Townshend Acts
by an irate commissioner of customs and so severely beaten as to end his
public career. But he was, in fact, hardly more anxious to defy the
British government than was Franklin or other colonial leaders. Although
arguing strenuously against the Stamp Act, he nonetheless declared, "Let
the parliament lay what burthens they please on us, we must, it is our
duty to submit and patiently bear them, till they will be pleased to relieve
us." Otis hoped to settle the difficulties with Great Britain within the
framework of the empire, and his suggestions for their solution did not
at first include independence.

Otis is chiefly remembered for his *Rights of the British Colonies
Asserted and Proved*, published in 1764.[9] Prefacing the colonial case with
systematic theory, Otis steered a course between Locke and Harrington.
Accepting property as basic, Otis argued that even if "the security of
property is one end of government," it was absurd to "assert that *one*
end of government is the foundation of government." The difficulty he
saw in the theories of Locke and Harrington was that they made government seem "an *arbitrary* thing, depending merely on *compact* or *human
will* for its existence," whereas in reality government had its "everlasting
foundation in the *unchangeable will* of God, the author of nature, whose
laws never vary" and was "most evidently founded *on the necessities of*
[*human*] *nature*." It followed that the end of government was "the *good*
of mankind" and that its great duties were

> above all things to provide for the security, the quiet, and happy enjoyment
> of life, liberty, and property. There is no one act which a government can
> have a *right* to make, that does not tend to the advancement of the security,
> tranquility, and prosperity of the people.

To Otis power so founded and oriented must be "*originally and ultimately* in the people," given in trust and conditioned by the necessity of
continual concern for their good. Its form might be left to the determination of each society. Whichever form was chosen, however, the administrators were equally subject to popular control. Should they "deviate
from truth, justice and equity, they verge towards tyranny, and are to
be opposed; and if they prove incorrigible, they will be *deposed* by the
people, if the people are not rendered too abject."

Applying these general principles, which had by 1764 attained relatively wide currency in the colonies, Otis turned his attention to the
status of the colonies. The colonists were merely "men, the common

---

[9] James Otis, *The Rights of the British Colonies Asserted and Proved* (Boston: Edes and
Gill, 1764).

children of the same Creator with their brethren of Great Britain."
Although they resided in a *"territory disjoined* or remote from the
mother country . . . [they were] entitled to as *ample* rights, liberties,
and privileges as the subjects of the mother country. . . . If [these were]
taken from them without their consent," they, like their fellow citizens
at home, would be "so far enslaved." On the other hand, the colonists
were subject to the supreme lawful authority of Parliament, but no more
so than their brethren in Great Britain. Thus, they were quite as justified
as their English cousins in expecting Parliament to stay within the bounds
set by God and nature. In its actions Parliament, neither at home nor
across the Atlantic, could rightfully "make itself arbitrary," dispense
justice by other than *"known settled rules,* and by duly *authorized independent judges . . . take from any man any part of his property,* without his consent in *person, or by representation . . .* [or] *transfer the
power of making laws to any other hands."*

With such principles of law and justice embodied in the British constitution, how was it, Otis asked, "that all the . . . colonies, who are
without one representative in the house of Commons, should be taxed
by the British parliament?" Taxes so imposed were "absolutely irreconcilable with the rights of the Colonists, as British subjects, and as men."
Taxation without representation would lead inevitably to slavery and
the destruction of all civil rights, for "if a man is not his own *assessor*
in person, or by deputy, his liberty is done, or lays entirely at the mercy
of others."

Following Locke, Otis reasoned that Parliament was uncontrollable
except by the people themselves. Coupled with this was the proposition
that certain rights, guaranteed by God, nature, and the British constitution, were beyond the reach of parliamentary power. Going beyond
Locke, he suggested, in the famous Writs of Assistance Case of 1761, a
specific way of keeping Parliament within bounds. The colonial court
had been confronted with the question whether a British customs officer
could lawfully secure a general warrant permitting searches for stolen
goods. Although it was denied that Parliament had authorized any such
warrants, Otis queried Parliament's power to authorize general warrants
in the first place. The language he used anticipated American thought
of later years:

> An Act against the Constitution is void: an Act against natural Equity is
> void: and if an Act of Parliament should be made, in the very Words of this
> Petition, it would be void. The Executive Courts must pass such Acts into
> disuse.[10]

Otis repeated this argument in *The Rights of the British Colonies
Asserted and Proved,* insisting that constitutional and natural law set

---

[10] Josiah Quincy, Jr., *Reports of Cases Argued and Adjudged in the Superior Court of
Judicature of the Province of Massachusetts Bay Between 1761 and 1772* (Boston: Little,
Brown, 1865), p. 474.

more than paper restrictions on parliamentary power; they were judicially enforceable guarantees.

> Parliaments are in all cases to declare what is for the good of the whole; but it is not the declaration of Parliament that makes it so: There must be in every instance, a higher authority, viz. GOD. Should an act of parliament be against any of His natural laws . . . their declaration would be contrary to eternal truth, equity and justice, and consequently void: and so it would be adjudged by the parliament itself, when convinced of their mistake. . . . When such mistake is evident and palpable . . . the judges of the executive courts have declared the act of a whole parliament void.

The "grandeur of the British constitution," as Otis envisaged it, consisted in a system in which the parts operated as "a perpetual check and balance" to each other. If the supreme executive errs, it is informed by the supreme legislative in Parliament; if the supreme legislative errs, it is informed by the supreme executive in the king's courts of law. "This is government! This is a constitution!" he exclaimed.

Many years later John Adams saw the birth of "the child Independence" in Otis's repudiation of parliamentary sovereignty.[11] Otis also conceived at this time his unique contribution to the American theory and practice of free government—that seemingly undemocratic device for obliging government to control itself: judicial review.

John Dickinson:
Precursor of Federalism

John Dickinson (1732–1808), a noted Philadelphia lawyer and a spokesman for the prosperous colonial Whigs—roused to action by the Townshend Acts—began in November 1767 a series of articles in the *Pennsylvania Chronicle*, entitled "Letters from a Farmer in Pennsylvania."[12] He criticized parliamentary taxation of the colonies, but drew a careful line between Parliament's legal authority to regulate colonial trade, which he cheerfully admitted as necessary for the welfare of the empire, and its right to levy internal taxes, which he denied. Until passage of the Stamp Act, Parliament had legislated only to regulate trade for the benefit of the whole empire. Thereafter Parliament began imposing duties on America for the purpose of raising revenue—quite a different thing, "a most dangerous innovation," and prejudicial in the extreme to the cherished freedom of Englishmen. Under the British constitution such taxes could be laid only by consent of the people or of their representatives. Besides, taxes for revenue violated the tacit assumption under-

---

[11] William Tudor, *The Life of James Otis* (Boston: Wells and Lilly, 1823), p. 61.
[12] John Dickinson, *Letters from a Farmer in Pennsylvania* (New York: The Outlook Co., 1903); see especially letters II and III, pp. 13–35. The *Letters* have been reprinted with an introduction and notes by Forrest McDonald, A Spectrum Book (Englewood Cliffs, N.J.: Prentice-Hall, 1962).

lying the settlement of the colonies, that Great Britain should manufacture for the colonies while they supplied her with raw materials. Under that profitable arrangement America had become "a country of planters, farmers, and fishermen," confident that (except for the quite proper impositions Parliament laid on trade) their importations from England would not be molested in any way. Now, however, Parliament sought to levy taxes on those importations.

"Rouse yourselves," Dickinson urged his fellow colonists, "and behold the ruin hanging over your heads. If [you] *once* admit that Great Britain may lay duties upon her exportations to us, *for the purpose of levying money on us only*, she then will have nothing to do, but to lay those duties on the articles which she prohibits us to manufacture—and the tragedy of American liberty is finished."

While Dickinson urged his compatriots to stir themselves, he cautioned against radical action. "The cause of liberty is a cause of too much dignity to be sullied by turbulence and tumult." Resistance by force he particularly feared, not only because of the disrupting effects of war itself, but also because "if once we are separated from our mother country, what new form of government shall we accept, or where shall we find another Britain, to supply our loss?" Like most colonists in the years before 1776, Dickinson deemed the prospect of independence too fearful to contemplate. Of course, there were evils. "Every government, at some time or other," Dickinson calmly observed, "falls into wrong measures." In the face of these, however, he urged patience: the people should resort to constitutional modes of remedy and exert the right of petition. Even if the mother country showed "an inveterate resolution" to annihilate the liberties of the governed, the colonies could not act with too much caution. Revolution would be the worst conceivable calamity. It might start a chain reaction. "People do not reform with moderation." Beginning merely as a protest against certain acts of Parliament, colonial agitation ran the risk, Dickinson thought, of developing into widespread democratic upheaval. "The stream of revolution, once started, could not be confined within narrow banks, but [would] spread abroad upon the land,"[13] bringing with it a variety of social changes, all tending toward a "levelling democracy."[14]

Dickinson preferred the safe way, a road dictated by necessity—one that did not require the colonies either to leave the fold or to become abject slaves of Parliament. In effect he advocated federalism: Parliament would legislate for external matters, the colonial assemblies would regulate internal matters—both acting directly on individuals, both sovereign and supreme in their fields, yet operating within the same unit, the British Empire. If only Britain would recognize the necessity of adopting such policy! If only the colonies would act moderately and with patience!

---

[13] J. Franklin Jameson, *The American Revolution Considered as a Social Movement* (New York: Peter Smith, 1950), p. 9.
[14] Jameson, *The American Revolution*, p. 18.

Franklin, Otis, and Dickinson confined themselves primarily to considerations of the colonies' position within the British Empire. Their appeal was to the British constitution and to the "undoubted rights of Englishmen." With other ministers in power and another king on the throne, their ideas might well have provided the basis for adjustment and reconciliation along the lines eventually followed by those parts of the empire remaining after the defection of the colonies in 1776. For a while, indeed, it seemed that adjustment on some such basis was possible. After the Stamp Act fiasco and the string of events culminating in the Boston Massacre, colonial tempers subsided, and for one reason or another most of the colonial leaders refrained from taking the ultimate step. In Britain, too, concern waned, until "American affairs were barely mentioned in Parliament, and a few paragraphs in the *Annual Register* were thought sufficient to chronicle for English readers events of interest across the Atlantic."[15] On both sides the time seemed ripe for the resumption of harmony. Unfortunately, English leaders lacked the foresight to see the possibilities and, after the brief respite, continued on their blundering course. In the colonies themselves, despite the tranquil appearance of things, forces were at work that would have made any attempt at adjustment difficult. In any case, the opportunity slipped away, and in 1774 the imposition of the tea tax raised the old questions in considerably exacerbated form.

Building on Natural Rights:
Wilson, Hamilton, and Adams

When the colonial arguments resumed, they were urged more forcefully. In this third and last phase they were based on the broadest possible conception of natural rights, appeal to which finally succeeded in carrying the day.

James Wilson (1742–1798), a protégé of John Dickinson, at first questioned the absolute legislative authority of Parliament and tried to draw a line defining parliamentary power over the colonies. But he finally discovered that "such a line does not exist." Because the colonies had no share in the British Parliament, they were not, under fundamental maxims of justice and the British constitution, "bound by the acts of the British Parliament."

> All men are, by nature, equal and free: no one has a right to any authority over another without his consent: all lawful government is founded on the consent of those who are subject to it: such consent was given with a view to ensure and to increase the happiness of the governed, above what they could enjoy in an independent and unconnected state of nature. The consequence is, that the happiness of the society is the first law of every government.[16]

---

[15] Becker, *Eve of Revolution*, pp. 150–51.

[16] "Considerations on the Nature and Extent of the Legislative Authority of the British Parliament," August 17, 1774, reprinted in James DeWitt Andrews, ed., *The Works of James Wilson* (Chicago: Callaghan and Company, 1896), II, 501–43.

Distinguishing between allegiance to the king and obedience to Parliament, Wilson contended that the former was founded on *protection*, the latter on *representation*. For want of representation, "the superiority of Great Britain over the colonies ought . . . to be rejected." Thus, the only tie to the mother country in effect was that of "the heart," binding "fellow subjects under the allegiance of the same prince."

By 1774, however, others—among them the youthful insurgent Alexander Hamilton (1755–1804)—foresaw the need of destroying even this link. Only so could natural rights be vindicated and independence achieved. Revolution would put political power where it belonged—in the hands of legislatures and governors of the colonies' own choosing. In his first significant paper, "A Full Vindication,"[17] Hamilton, still a student at King's College (now Columbia University), moved directly to the assertion that there was "no recourse" but forcible resistance. Hamilton defined freedom simply as government by laws to which consent had been given, either in person or through representatives. The alternative, to be "governed by the will of another," was slavery. Reason did not admit of the latter. Instead, it dictated that "all men have one common original: they participate in one common nature, and consequently have one common right." Both the spirit of the English constitution and the specific words of the colonial charters prohibited "the idea of legislation, or taxation, when the subject is not represented." Hamilton thus broadened the base of the colonial argument to the limit: the pretensions of Parliament were "contradictory to the law of nature, subversive of the British constitution, and destructive of the faith of the most solemn compacts." Remonstrance and petition having failed, there was but one course to follow—resistance *vi et armis*, i.e., revolution, and the declaration of colonial independence.

John Adams (1735–1826) joined Hamilton in 1775, entering into a series of debates in the *Boston Gazette*, under the pen name of Novanglus,[18] with the brilliant Tory lawyer Daniel Leonard (1740–1829), who signed himself Massachusettensis. Originally a moderate, his Novanglus Letters reveal how far the moderates had moved in the few years since Dickinson's "Letters from a Pennsylvania Farmer." In his debate with Leonard, Adams developed perhaps the most complete presentation so far of the liberal colonial position. "Our rhetorical magician," he wrote, can offer only one proposition in his "long string of pretended absurdities"—"that it is absolutely necessary there . . . be a supreme power,

---

[17] Alexander Hamilton, "A Full Vindication of the Measures of the Congress from the Calumnies of Their Enemies," December 15, 1774 (New York: James Rivington, 1774), reprinted in John C. Hamilton, ed., *The Works of Alexander Hamilton* (New York: Charles S. Francis, 1851), II, 1–36.

[18] John Adams, *Novanglus and Massachusettensis* (Boston: Hews and Goss, 1819). The quotations in these paragraphs are from pp. 94–102. For a fuller view of Adams's role, see Page Smith, *John Adams* (Garden City, N.Y.: Doubleday, 1962), I (1735–1784). See also Paul R. Conkin, *Puritans and Pragmatists* (New York: Dodd, Mead, 1968), Chap. 4, "John Adams."

coextensive with all the dominions." With that proposition Adams sharply disagreed. He thought there was "nothing in the law of nations, which is only the law of right reason, applied to the conduct of nations, that requires that the emigrants from a state should continue, or be made part of the state. The practice of nations has been different."

Adams was no more troubled by parliamentary regulation of colonial trade than Dickinson. That right had been granted by "the voluntary act of the colonies, their free cheerful consent." What bothered Adams was Leonard's assertion of parliamentary control in *all cases*. In return for renunciation of that claim and for recognition, instead, of the principle that the provincial legislatures were the only supreme authorities in the colonies, Adams was quite willing to allow parliamentary jurisdiction over the high seas. The colonial charters, after all, authorized no colonial control over them. Indeed, "here is a line fairly drawn between the rights of Britain and the rights of the colonies, viz. the banks of the ocean, or low water mark. . . ." On the one side, British power was quite proper and constitutional; on the other, the colonial legislatures were supreme, even to the extent that they might alter "provincial constitutions" without parliamentary consent. Adams thought that "America will never allow that Parliament has any authority to alter their constitution at all. She is wholly penetrated with a sense of the necessity of resisting it, at all hazards."

Adams assured Massachusettensis that such a division of authority was not destructive of the empire. It was, instead, the only way to preserve it, for without recognition of the supremacy of the American legislatures over internal affairs, Britain would lose her colonies. In any case, their tie with Great Britain was through the king, by virtue of the colonial charters. "It ought to be remembered," Adams wrote, "that there was a revolution here, as well as in England, and that we made an original, express contract with King William as well as the people of England." By that contract "we are a part of the British dominions, that is of the king of Great Britain, and it is our interest and duty to continue so. It is equally our interest and duty to continue subject to the authority of parliament, in the regulation of our trade, *as long as she shall leave us to govern our internal policy, and to give and grant our own money, and no longer.*"[19] As for British liberties, Adams declared them to be

> but certain rights of nature, reserved to the citizen, by the English constitution, which rights cleaved to our ancestors, when they crossed the Atlantic, and would have inhered in them, if instead of coming to New England, they had gone to Outaheite or Patagonia, even although they had taken no patent or charter from the king at all.

In short, these rights attached to men as men, not as British subjects. Any attempt to reduce those liberties in America, Adams warned, would be resisted.

---

[19] Adams, *Novanglus*, p. 94.

Even at that late date Adams did not *want* independence. He wished only to go back to the status quo that existed before 1763. Then the colonists actually enjoyed "more liberty than the British constitution allows." "If we enjoy the British constitution in greater purity and perfection than they do in England . . . whose fault is this? Not ours." For 150 years the colonies had been allowed to tax themselves and govern their internal affairs as they thought best, while Parliament had governed trade. Adams hoped this arrangement might continue. But "it is honestly confessed," he warned, "rather than become subject to the absolute authority of parliament, in all cases of taxation and internal polity, they will be driven to throw off that of regulating trade."

THE BUGLE CALL FOR
INDEPENDENCE: THOMAS PAINE

By 1775 four main ideas had been advanced in the colonies' argument with Great Britain: (1) the right of representation (though important populous communities in England, such as Sheffield, Birmingham, and Leeds, were still unrepresented); (2) denial of the supremacy of Parliament (an antiquated theory after the revolution of 1688 and the Act of Settlement); (3) assertion of the king's relation to the colonies (either outmoded or not realized until the Commonwealth of Nations agreement in 1931); and (4) a theory of higher law (though advocated in England by the eminent Lord Coke and in America by James Otis, it was not sanctioned in the mother country).

If their proponents pushed ever harder toward revolution and independence, they did so only against considerable opposition. Especially formidable opponents were Samuel Seabury (1729–1796), the eminent Anglican clergyman, and Daniel Leonard, the Boston lawyer, who epitomized the Tory position, exposing the false logic in the arguments and emphasizing the evils that rebellion would unleash.[20] They, and others, were persuasive enough to delay the final rupture. Lingering doubts and hopes for reconciliation still exerted a powerful hold. Sorely needed were the gifts of an agitator and propagandist to fuse the arguments and translate them into a rousing bugle call for independence. Into this breach came the agitator Thomas Paine (1737–1809). A fairly recent newcomer from England, Paine brought the weapon of propaganda to bear on political targets and was not deterred by the cautionary dialectics beclouding the constitutional arguments. "Volumes have been written on the subject of the struggle between England and America," Paine pointed out. "Men of all ranks have embarked in the controversy, from different motives, and

---

[20] See Samuel Seabury, "A View of the Controversy Between Great Britain and Her Colonies," (New York: James Rivington, 1774) and Daniel Leonard (Massachusettensis), "Letters Addressed to the Inhabitants of the Province of Massachusetts Bay" (Boston: Hews and Goss, 1819).

with various designs: but all have been ineffectual, and the period of debate is closed. Arms, as the last resource, must decide the contest."[21]

In his *Common Sense*, published in January 1776, Paine abandoned all arguments save those based on natural rights. The "RIGHTS OF MANKIND" and the "FREE AND INDEPENDENT STATES OF AMERICA" were inviolably linked. "A government of our own is our natural right"; revolution was necessary to secure it.

Paine's basic assumption was that society and government were separable, the one permanent, the other transitory—society, a natural blessing, government, "the badge of lost innocence," the result of man's wickedness. John Dickinson's fear of the future if the colonies cut themselves off from Great Britain Paine rejected as sheer nonsense. The only concern the colonists need have was that their form of government be the one most likely to assure security "with the least expense and greatest benefit" and that it be in accord with the "principle in nature." "The so much boasted constitution of England" was emphatically the wrong government for America.

A master at satire, Paine pictured the English government as tyrannical because of its hereditary aspects; absurd because, while it provided the Commons power to check the king by withholding supplies, it gave the king power to check the Commons by use of the veto; ridiculous because it embodied the monarchical principle. Recognizing in America, as elsewhere, that it was the "pride of kings which throws mankind into confusion," Paine systematically destroyed the case for loyalty to the king and unequivocally demanded revolution. "The sun never shined on a cause of greater worth," he wrote. " 'Tis . . . the affair . . . of a continent—of at least one-eighth part of the habitable globe. 'Tis not the concern of a day, a year, or an age; posterity are virtually involved in the contest, and will be more or less affected, even to the end of time, by the proceedings now. Now is the seed time of continental union, faith, and honor." There was not a single advantage in adhering to the empire. Not even the concept of England as the mother country softened Paine's determination to be free. "Europe, and not England, is the parent country of America," he declared. "This new world hath been the asylum for the persecuted lovers of civil and religious liberty from *every part* of Europe." Colonial commerce, as well as colonial government, would be improved by separation. For England to presume to rule America was for the tail to wag the dog. Paine therefore concluded that "everything that is right or natural pleads for separation."

Paine's greatest service to the American cause was not as a thinker but as a catalyst:

The marvelous power which this untitled and impecunious penman wielded over the minds of men and over the course of events, during the

---

[21] Philip S. Foner, ed., *The Complete Writings of Thomas Paine* (New York: Citadel Press, 1945), I, 17.

entire period of our Revolution, was essentially the power of a great journalist. . . . All that he wrote was suggested by an occasion, and was meant for one. By some process of his own he knew just what the people thought, feared, wished, loved, and hated: he knew it better than they knew it themselves.[22]

By standing squarely against further delay and by championing immediate and unconditional independence, *Common Sense* brought the colonies to the brink of revolution and pushed them firmly—and irrevocably—over the edge.

REVOLUTION ACCOMPLISHED

The colonial mind, fearful of the consequences, arrived at separation and independence reluctantly, only after considering various alternatives. It also moved toward revolution conservatively; indeed, among all the revolutionaries the world has ever seen, the Americans of 1776 were perhaps the most reluctant. "The American leaders, including those of the Constitutional Convention—legislators, soldiers, merchants, lawyers—were a sober lot, given neither to grandiloquence nor fanaticism. There was not a Rousseau or a Robespierre among them. . . . As a matter of fact, it may be doubted whether the leaders of the American Revolution were revolutionists at all, in the conventional sense."[23] By and large, the essential concern of the colonists dealt with the relationship that should exist between themselves and the British government, not with fundamental changes in either the social or the political order. They accepted preservation of property, respect for individual rights, and maintenance of British law as axiomatic. Talk and thought of democracy were almost wholly negative.

The revolutionaries of 1776 were cautious, sober men. They were revolutionaries by chance rather than choice. The colonists did not relish a break with the mother country, and a substantial number, including John Dickinson, never agreed with that decision. The First Continental Congress, an extralegal body, was called September 5, 1774, not to declare independence but "to consult on the present state of the colonies . . . and to deliberate and determine upon wise and proper measures . . . for the recovery and establishment of their just rights and liberties . . . and the restoration of union and harmony between Great Britain and the colonies, most ardently desired by all good men."[24]

---

[22] Moses Coit Tyler, *The Literary History of the American Revolution* (New York: G. P. Putnam's Sons, 1897), I, 17. See Cecelia M. Kenyon, "Where Paine Went Wrong," *American Political Science Review*, XLV, No. 4 (December, 1951), 1086–99.

[23] Saul K. Padover, "Well-off, Middle-Aged Rebels," *Saturday Review*, August 19, 1967, p. 30.

[24] Massachusetts's instructions to her delegates, quoted in Edmund C. Burnell, *The Continental Congress* (New York: Macmillan, 1941), p. 35.

Nor did the Second Continental Congress of the following year mean to dissolve the tie. As late as August 25, 1775, Jefferson, though outraged by the power the British Parliament had "assumed," confessed that "I am sincerely one of those [who still wish for union] . . . and would rather be in dependence on Great Britain, properly limited, than on any other Nation on earth."[25]

SELF-EVIDENT TRUTHS ENSHRINED

Britain did nothing to counteract the mounting fervor for independence. Heeding Paine's clamor, several colonies declared their independence of Britain and, in the spring and early summer of 1776, formed governments of their own. Pressure mounted for a unanimous declaration of independence. On June 7 Richard Henry Lee of Virginia introduced in the Second Continental Congress the motion that "these United Colonies are, and of right ought to be, free and independent States. . . ." A committee consisting of John Adams, Benjamin Franklin, Thomas Jefferson, Robert R. Livingston, and Roger Sherman was appointed to prepare a declaration to that effect, and during the next month, worked on Jefferson's first draft. At last, on July 4, 1776, the Congress formally adopted the document.

Perhaps no one was better equipped than Jefferson (1743–1826) to crystallize American ideas and beliefs and to present them to the world. His whole career had been spent in the public service. Although a serious and fertile political thinker, Jefferson did not look upon the Declaration of Independence as the proper vehicle for "originality of principle or sentiment." Rather, he sought to set down "an expression of the American mind." What he attempted, and what he actually did, was "not to find out new principles, or new arguments, never before thought of, not merely to say things which had never been said before; but to place before mankind the common sense of the subject, [in] terms so plain and firm as to command their assent, and to justify ourselves in the independent stand we [were] impelled to take."[26] The great strength of the Declaration was that it said what everyone in America was thinking.

In view of the antecedents leading to the Declaration, a disproportionate amount of space is given to the king's wrongdoings. No mention is made of Parliament. Besides specific grievances against a particular king, there was a fundamental presupposition against all kings. Denouncing his bad motives no less than his bad acts, Jefferson declared that the king had manifested a deliberate and persistent purpose to establish absolute tyranny over the colonies. In the spirit of Locke, Jefferson pointed

---

[25] *The Writings of Thomas Jefferson*, IV, 30.
[26] Thomas Jefferson to Henry Lee, May 8, 1825, quoted in Julian P. Boyd, *The Declaration of Independence* (Princeton, N.J.: Princeton University Press, 1945), p. 2.

out that the colonies had suffered and petitioned against continued injustice—all to no avail.

The Declaration is significant for what it omits. Besides omission of the
word Parliament, no reference is made to what had been much stressed,
the rights of British subjects. Being committed now to independence, the
authors of the document had to consider the more exalted level of the
rights of man. On this elevated plane both Parliament and the rights of
British subjects could be ignored as irrelevant. Because the king had
broken his contract by repeated acts of usurpation, the colonists, as a free
people, renounced the allegiance they had formerly professed.

Several ambiguities appear in the document. In his first draft Jefferson
used the title: "A Declaration by The Representatives of the *United
States of America* in General Congress Assembled." In his opening line
Jefferson wrote: "When in the course of human events it becomes necessary for *one people* to dissolve the political bonds which have connected
them with another. . . ." On July 19, 1776, Congress voted that the
Declaration be embossed on parchment with the title: "The Unanimous
Declaration of The *Thirteen* United States of America." Was the Declaration an act of the people of the thirteen colonies or an act of the people
of America? In later years this question became a matter of crucial
importance.

Certain writers have made much of Jefferson's substitution of the
phrase "pursuit of happiness" for the narrower term "property," as in the
Virginia Bill of Rights of June 12, 1776. "Samuel Adams and other followers of Locke had been content," V. L. Parrington observed in his *Main
Currents in American Thought,* "with the classical enumeration of life,
liberty, and property; but in Jefferson's hands the English doctrine was
given a revolutionary shift." Parrington interpreted Jefferson's change as
marking "a complete break with the Whiggish doctrine of property rights
that Locke had bequeathed to the English middle class, and the substitution of a broader sociological conception. . . ."[27] Dr. Julian P. Boyd set
the matter in truer perspective:

> Jefferson's inclusion of the "pursuit of happiness" as an indefeasible right
> does not warrant the assumption that this was a new philosophy of govern-
> ment, distinctively American . . . Jefferson only indicated in the Declara-
> tion certain unalienable rights and *among* these were life, liberty, and the
> pursuit of happiness. . . . That he differed with Locke in the choice of this
> phrase is infinitely less important than that he and the people for whom he
> spoke grounded their Declaration upon Locke's great justification of revolu-

---

[27] V. L. Parrington, *Main Currents in American Thought* (New York: Harcourt, Brace,
1930), I, 344. George Mason, author of the Virginia Declaration of Rights, which preceded the Declaration of Independence, listed man's "inherent natural rights" as
"Enjoyment of Life and Liberty, with the means of acquiring and possessing Property,
and pursuing and obtaining Happiness and Safety." For a more realistic discussion, see
John H. Schaar, ". . . And the Pursuit of Happiness," *Virginia Quarterly Review,*
Winter, 1970, pp. 1–26.

tion. For revolution, in both the Jeffersonian and the Lockian sense, is merely the ultimate means of pursuing happiness. . . .[28]

In a similar vein Merrill Jensen wrote:

> The central issue in seventeenth-century New England was not social equality, manhood suffrage, women's rights or sympathy for the Levellers. . . . The central issue was the source of authority for the establishment of government. The English view was that no government could exist in a colony without a grant of power from the crown. The opposite view, held by certain English dissenters in New England, was that a group of people could create a valid government for themselves by means of a covenant, compact or constitution. The authors of the Mayflower Compact and the Fundamental Orders of Connecticut operated on this assumption, although they did not carry it to the logical conclusion and call it democracy as did the people in Rhode Island. It is the basic assumption of the Declaration of Independence, a portion of which reads much like the words of Roger Williams written 132 years earlier.[29]

The political essence of the Declaration is the philosophy of natural rights that had been developing in England and the colonies for over a century: the belief that man's original equality is an endowment of God, and that by right of birth all men are equal, not in condition or ability but in basic rights; the "self-evident truth" that men possess these rights because they are human beings, regardless of race, color, or creed; the conviction that whenever a government becomes destructive of its proper ends—the protection of those rights—the people may alter or abolish it and institute a new one more in keeping with their safety and happiness.

Although these ideas were familiar, the action endorsed was novel. In America, for the first time, a political society formally declared its purpose, enumerated some of man's natural rights, and affirmed the right of revolution. Jefferson's words are historic and of continuing significance. They summed up the progress of centuries toward free government and built a platform on which future development was to take place.

While the Declaration states certain self-evident truths, it does not prove them, nor could they have been proved. Some of the verities were being falsified even as they were pronounced. Among man's God-given rights were life, liberty, and equality. Yet the newspapers of the day carried copies of the Declaration along with advertisements of slaves and indentured servants, giving brandmarks on the necks of human beings as identification. The principle that just governments derive their powers from the consent of the governed had yet to be realized. For many years important offices carried property qualifications, as did the exercise of the

---

[28] Boyd, *The Declaration*, pp. 3–4.
[29] Merrill Jensen, "Democracy and the American Revolution," *Huntington Library Quarterly*, XX, No. 4 (August, 1957), 325. His comprehensive book *The Founding of a Nation: A History of the American Revolution, 1763–1776* (New York: Oxford University Press, 1968) covers the entire prerevolutionary struggle.

right of suffrage. In 1776 the number consenting to government was but a small part of the adult population. Besides qualifications of property there were also those of religion for voting and office holding. The word "people" had a relatively narrow connotation: slaves were not people; men without property were not people. Those whose voices counted in public affairs were freeholders, taxpayers, and Christians—particularly Protestants.[30]

This is not to detract from the noble instrument, not to endorse George Santayana's scathing characterization of it as "a piece of literature, a salad of illusions,"[31] but rather to underscore its basic ideals. Its principles, though never unanimously accepted and sometimes frontally attacked— as by loyalists during the Revolution and by John C. Calhoun and George Fitzhugh during the struggle to wipe out Negro slavery—have nevertheless motivated every latter-day liberal impulse. The Declaration of Independence, cast in terms of all mankind, set up, as Lincoln said, a "standard maxim for free society, which should be familiar to all, and revered by all; constantly looked to, constantly labored for, and even though never perfectly attained, constantly approximated. . . ." Its authors meant it to be "a stumbling block to all those who in after time might seek to turn a free people back into the hateful paths of despotism."[32]

---

[30] Charles E. Merriam, *A History of American Political Theories* (New York: Macmillan, 1928), pp. 87–88.

[31] George Santayana, *The Middle Span*, quoted in Edward Dumbauld, *The Declaration of Independence and What It Means Today* (Norman, Okla.: University of Oklahoma Press, 1950), p. 55.

[32] Speech in Springfield, Illinois, June 26, 1857, John G. Nicolay and John Hay, eds., *Complete Works of Abraham Lincoln* (New York: Francis D. Tandy, 1905), II, 331. See Harry V. Jaffa, *Equality and Liberty. Theory and Practice in American Politics* (New York: Oxford University Press, 1965) for an examination of how the Declaration of Independence has been interpreted by later generations of Americans. See also R. R. Palmer, "The American Revolution's Influence Then & Now," *University*, Winter, 1967–1968, 3–7 and Richard B. Morris, *The American Revolution Reconsidered* (New York: Harper & Row, 1967).

CHAPTER FOUR

REVOLUTIONARY IDEAS
ON THE
ANVIL OF EXPERIENCE

Eloquent proclamation of independence in the Declaration of Independence was one thing; positive action to secure it was quite another. More than once during the decade after the Revolution, the new Republic teetered. The most optimistic patriots were filled with foreboding and despair, for "the same spirit of liberty which made the colonists resist George III and choose independence, was an almost fatal handicap in the fight for independence. And it would have been fatal but for George Washington and French assistance."[1] The Revolution did not create a nation; it only set the colonies free. "In the period of the . . . Revolution we . . . discover a number of enthusiasms: for the safety and prosperity of Virginia or New York, for the cause of justice; for the rights of Englishmen. What is missing is anything that might be called widespread enthusiasm for the birth of a new nation: the United States of America."[2] Most important, the Revolution failed to established a structure of effective national government. Indeed, it operated in the opposite direction.

---

[1] Samuel E. Morison, *The Oxford History of the American People* (New York: Oxford University Press, 1965), p. 226.
[2] Daniel Boorstin, *The Genius of American Politics* (Chicago: University of Chicago Press, 1953), p. 73.

In the prerevolutionary discussions the difficulties that would arise for want of a common power had been clearly anticipated. Because separation from Britain would make the states independent of one another— that is, place them in a "state of nature"—Daniel Leonard, Samuel Seabury, and John Dickinson shied away from independence. When it became *fait accompli*, Dickinson, remaining consistent, demanded that the Articles of Confederation establish a sovereign central government. After adopting Richard Henry Lee's resolution for independence, the Second Continental Congress appointed a committee to draw up a constitution for the "United Colonies." That committee, under Dickinson's leadership, promptly produced a draft with great possibilities for centralization. In his version few limitations were placed on the powers of Congress, and no guarantee of the sovereignty of states was inserted. In the convention of 1787, James Wilson recalled that Dickinson had intended to establish a national government, and one may speculate that had he been successful, America might have been spared the "critical period," 1783–1787. Dickinson's draft was rejected. Adopted in its place was a document—the Articles of Confederation—that declared unequivocally that "each State retains its sovereignty, freedom and independence."

WEAKNESS AT THE CENTER: CONGRESS AND THE ARTICLES OF CONFEDERATION

After lengthy debate in the Continental Congress and further delay in making necessary changes, the Articles of Confederation became the new nation's first charter of government. Submitted to the states for ratification in July 1777, they were accepted by every state save Maryland, which withheld endorsement until March 1781.

The Articles had no congeniality of principle with the Declaration of Independence. The Declaration stressed the rights of man, proclaimed popular sovereignty, and asserted the right of revolution. The Articles constituted a victory for the political units called states. The two documents were consistent with their own principles; together they formed neither a consistent whole nor an enduring framework of government. Needing unanimous approval, they became effective too late to meet the governmental needs of the United States. In the interval the Continental Congress continued to operate as a de facto national government. Although it did a creditable job in some ways, especially in concluding the war and in handling foreign affairs, Congress was, to say the least, diffident in its exercise of power. Into this power vacuum stepped the state governments. The infant Republic was thus, at the outset, divided between a weak central authority and strong de jure state governments claiming sovereignty. The latter very quickly became the paramount force in American politics.

As early as 1780 Alexander Hamilton became convinced that to counter state power, Congress "should have considered themselves invested with full power *to preserve the republic from harm*. . . . Undefined powers are discretionary powers, limited only by the object for which they were given; in the present case, the independence and freedom of America." Diffidence in the face of urgent need for bold action was not the basic problem. Congress simply lacked powers "competent to the public exigencies." This could be remedied in one of two ways: by "resuming and exercising" the powers necessary for the safety of the nation or by "calling immediately a convention of all the States, with full authority to conclude finally upon a General Confederation, stating to them, beforehand, explicitly, the evils arising from a want of power in Congress. . . ." "The sooner the better," Hamilton wrote. "Our disorders are too violent to admit of a common or lingering remedy."[3]

Nor was the situation improved when the Articles were finally ratified. Having freed themselves from the tyrannical rule of Great Britain, the authors of the Articles went to extremes in the other direction.

Rather than creating a union, the Articles of Confederation merely bound the states together in "a league of friendship." Under them the states retained control over their delegates to Congress, even to the extent of paying their salaries, and it was only through the agency of the states that individual citizens could be affected by national power. Moreover, the powers granted the central government were few in number and their exercise extremely difficult. Even fundamental powers such as taxation and the control of commerce were denied the national government. An executive arm and a national judiciary were wanting. Carrying out or enforcing national laws had to be done through the states.

The source of trouble was not merely lack of power; it was also a matter of practical politics. Congress at work was ludicrous, forced to wander from place to place—Princeton, Annapolis, Trenton in 1783, and finally New York in 1785—and constantly plagued by lack of a quorum. The few successful acts it was able to pass, such as the Northwest Ordinance of 1787, the most significant act in the period of the Confederation, were overshadowed by failure in almost every other area. In short, both the Articles and the Congress they created were weak reeds on which to build the future.

WEAKNESS IN THE PARTS: STATE GOVERNMENTS

The states, with which the major responsibility lay, were themselves far from perfect instruments of government. Constantly quarrelling with each other, they, too, were strapped for power. Greatly influenced by revolutionary principles and prejudices, the new constitutions embodied phrases from the Declaration of Independence, and some were prefaced by the Declaration itself. Evidence of revolutionary doctrine is manifest in what

---

[3] Hamilton to James Duane, September 3, 1780, Hamilton, *Works of Hamilton*, I, 150–57.

was included as well as in what was omitted. Distrust of government, particularly the executive, had been deeply ingrained in the American character by prerevolutionary experience. Therefore, all monarchical and aristocratic features had to be eliminated. In every state the legislature enjoyed almost unlimited power. Except for protection afforded individual freedom by bills of rights, few obstacles were placed in the way of legislative dominance. In six states (New York, New Jersey, Virginia, South Carolina, North Carolina, and New Hampshire) nothing prevented the legislature from amending the state constitution by an ordinary enactment. In five states (Virginia, North Carolina, South Carolina, New Jersey, and New York) the legislature appointed nearly all the officers of the state. No state allowed its governor a final veto upon legislation, and in only three (South Carolina, Massachusetts, and New York) did he have even a partial veto. The judiciary was likewise subordinated. In Connecticut, Rhode Island, and Massachusetts the judges were selected by the legislature, and in every state except South Carolina the lawmakers fixed judicial salaries. Several constitutions permitted the legislature to eliminate existing courts, change their composition, and limit their functions. All such features constitute clear evidence that those who drafted the first constitutions were more concerned with limiting the powers of the states than with making them viable instruments of government.

It became evident not only that the states were, like the national government under the Articles of Confederation, handicapped by poorly constructed and imperfectly balanced constitutional systems, but also that governmental action, both before and after the Articles had become effective, often contributed more to confusion and disorder than to union and strength. Responsible though the states were for meeting congressional requisitions of money and troops, they consistently failed to do so, even in the midst of the war. The "partial compliance with the Requisitions of Congress in some of the States, and . . . [the] failure of punctuality in others," Washington observed, ". . . served . . . to accumulate the expenses of the War, and to frustrate the best concerted Plans. . . ." This would have led, he said, to "the dissolution of any Army less patient, less virtuous, and less persevering, than that which I have had the honor to command."[4]

Moreover, the currency situation was chaotic. The states issued their own money, often without adequate backing, and with so much unbacked currency in circulation and so little commercial activity, its value depreciated. Class conflict between debtors, who thoroughly enjoyed and supported the situation, and creditors, whose suffering steadily increased, gradually became acute. Cheap money parties flourished in all thirteen states and were victorious at the polls in seven. The immediate result was a series of statutes suspending actions on debts, authorizing payment in kind and even in land, and threatening to render creditors and property

---

[4] George Washington to Governor Livingston, June 12, 1783, Mary A. Benjamin, ed., *The Collector* (New York: Bowker, 1947), LX, No. 2, 30.

owners insecure or insolvent.[5] Where rag money parties were not victorious, they were strong enough to engender fear. In Massachusetts conflict
flared into open rebellion. With no effective constitutional safeguards to
protect them, the propertied classes began to distrust the revolutionary
emphasis on liberty: it seemed to lead, as Hamilton observed, to contempt
and disregard of all authority. By 1786 gloom was widespread and the
outlook for the United States cloudy. There was "no supreme power to
interpose, and discord and animosity" were everywhere.[6] Revolutionary
political theory had served to inspire the first act of the great American
drama; it did not provide a formula for carrying the nation into the
second act.

THE REMEDY ADVANCED: HAMILTON

The thinking that led to the formulation of a counter-balancing, comple-
mentary, and better-rounded theory began as soon as the implications of
political life under the Articles became obvious.

Alexander Hamilton, in the forefront of those seeking solutions, traced
all evils to "a want of power in Congress": lack of power to "interfere
with the internal policy of the States," inability to control "the entire
formation and disposal of our military forces," the denial to Congress of
power of the purse—these were the chief causes of trouble. The greatest
danger confronting America was want of power in the central government
to unite the states and direct their common forces toward "the interest
and happiness of the whole."[7]

"A little time hence, some of the States will be powerful empires,"
Hamilton warned, "and we are so remote from other nations, that we
shall have all the leisure and opportunity we can wish, to cut each other's
throats." The remedy was simple: replace the existing Confederation with
"a solid coercive union", and give Congress complete sovereignty over the
whole country, "except as to that part of internal police which relates to
the rights of property and life among individuals, and to raising money
by internal taxes."[8] "In a government framed for durable liberty, no less
regard must be paid to giving the magistrate a proper degree of authority,
to make and execute the laws with vigor, than to guard against encroachments upon the rights of the community. As too much power leads to
despotism, too little leads to anarchy, and both eventually to the ruin of
the people." The central government was growing weaker as the states

---

[5] See E. S. Corwin, "Progress of Constitutional Theory Between the Declaration of
Independence and the Meeting of the Philadelphia Convention," *American Historical
Review*, XXX (April, 1925), 511–13, 519.
[6] Seabury, "A View of the Controversy," p. 127.
[7] Hamilton to James Duane, Hamilton, *Works of Hamilton*. Hamilton communicated
these ideas to General John Sullivan of New Hampshire in November 1779. See Mason,
Free Government, p. 137.
[8] Letter to James Duane, Hamilton, *Works of Hamilton*.

sapped its prerogatives; if the *"speedy* and *violent end"* of the nation were to be prevented, union under one government with sufficient power to act must soon be accomplished.[9]

Just as dangerous, Hamilton felt, to the welfare of the United States as the lack of centralized power was the concentration of power in Congress. "Congress is, properly, a deliberative corps; and it forgets itself when it attempts to play the executive. It is impossible that a body, numerous as it is, constantly fluctuating, can ever act with sufficient decision, or with system." Hamilton called for the creation of executive departments administered by individuals who, operating under the direction of Congress, would supply the "method and energy" in administration heretofore lacking.[10]

Also necessary was a solution of the nation's financial problems. Although Hamilton believed a foreign loan was the first necessity, he thought that to provide Congress with steady and regular income and the nation with a single stable currency was equally important. Providing Congress with income might be accomplished by empowering it to raise revenue from the sale of lands, taxes, and duties on trade; providing for a currency, by establishing a bank "on the joint credit of the public and of individuals." Moneyed men, Hamilton reasoned, must be made to feel an immediate and selfish interest in the nation's survival. To bring them into a national bank and guarantee them all or part of the profits from its operations would be the surest way to create such an interest.[11]

Experience and common sense also demonstrated that trade, to be prosperous, needed governmental encouragement and restraints. The states were not, however, the proper repositories of such power. They might have been, Hamilton declared, had they had "distinct interests" and had they been unconnected with each other. But exactly the contrary was true. They were "parts of a whole, with a common interest in trade. . . . ; there ought to be a "common direction in that as in all other matters." Regulation of trade would also provide a convenient source of revenue for the central government.[12] Finally, Hamilton considered it necessary to form some kind of permanent military force independent of the states. He had seen at first hand the terrible results of an army of fluctuating size, concluding that "all our military misfortunes, three-fourths of our

---

[9] Alexander Hamilton, "The Continentalist," July 12, 1781 to July 4, 1782, reprinted in Henry Cabot Lodge, ed., *The Works of Alexander Hamilton* (New York: Putnam's, 1904), pp. 243–87.

[10] Letter to James Duane, Hamilton, *Works of Hamilton.*

[11] Letter to James Duane, Hamilton, *Works of Hamilton.*

[12] Hamilton "The Continentalist." Hamilton might have been familiar with the comment of Joseph Galloway (c. 1731–1803) to the First Continental Congress in 1774:

Is it not necessary that the trade of the empire should be regulated by some power or other? Can the empire hold together without it? No. Who shall regulate it? Shall the Legislature[s of each colony]? It can't be pretended. Our legislative powers extend no further than the limits of our governments. Where shall it then be placed? There is a necessity that an American Legislature should be set up. . . .

Quoted in Mason, *Free Government*, p. 134.

civil embarrassments" were due to this "pregnant source of evil." He therefore advocated complete surrender to the national government of the power of raising, officering, paying, supplying, and directing the army. "Congress would then have a solid basis of authority and consequence: for, to me, it is an axiom, that in our constitution, an army is essential to the American Union."[13]

Although Hamilton was convinced of the utility of his remedies, he realized that they were not viewed enthusiastically by many of his compatriots, fearful lest the rights they had so recently wrested from one strong government be surrendered to another. When state politicians capitalized on that concern, Hamilton countered with the argument that it was "difficult to assign any good reason why Congress should be more liable to abuse the powers with which they are entrusted than the State Assemblies." Indeed, Hamilton thought it very likely "that Congress will be in general better composed for abilities, as well as for integrity, than any assembly in the continent."[14]

Hamilton challenged Americans to contemplate the consequences of failure to take the steps he advocated: "want of revenue and of power," "immediate risk to our independence, . . . the dangers of all the . . . evils of a precarious Union," the sacrifice of "the landed interest and the laboring poor" to the trading interest in the community, and "the deficiency of a wholesome concert and provident superintendence to advance the general prosperity. . . ." With such dreadful prospects in store, Hamilton hoped that "the seductions of some immediate advantage or exemption" would not lure the states to sacrifice the future to the present.[15]

Hamilton's chief objectives were a stronger union and a more energetic national government. He stressed the necessity of power, order, and security for the preservation of liberty. Hamilton resigned from Washington's staff in 1781, after Yorktown, and began to prepare systematically for a revitalized central authority.

George Washington shared Hamilton's forebodings. He agreed "that arbitrary power is most easily established, on the ruins of Liberty abused to licentiousness." By the summer of 1783, Washington's profound concern prompted him to send a circular letter to several state governors, in which he set forth the things "essential to the well being, I may even venture to say, to the existence of the United States as an independent Power." First and foremost he placed "an indissoluble Union of the States under one Federal Head." "It is indispensable to the happiness of the individual States," he wrote, "that there should be lodged some where a Supreme Power, to regulate and govern the general concerns of the confederated Republic. . . ." It was only in "our united Character as an Empire" that other countries acknowledged American power. Without

---

[13] Letter of James Duane, Hamilton, *Works of Hamilton.*
[14] Hamilton, "The Continentalist."
[15] Hamilton, "The Continentalist."

"an entire conformity to the spirit of Union," Washington concluded, "we shall be left nearly in a State of Nature." Union alone could avoid the perils of "a natural and necessary progression from the extreme of Anarchy, to the extreme of Tyranny."[16] Union alone could protect the rights of mankind for which the Revolution itself had been fought.

THE REMEDY FURTHER ADVANCED: JEFFERSON, MADISON, ADAMS

Hamilton's and Washington's approaches reflected a concern with national problems. Others were motivated by the evils within the states.

Thomas Jefferson shared Hamilton's sense of urgency. As early as 1783, he told Edmund Randolph that unless the bond of the confederacy were strengthened, "the States will go to war with each other in defiance of Congress."[17] But Jefferson was concerned particularly with affairs in his own state.

In his wonderfully perceptive *Notes on Virginia* Jefferson expressed his distrust of unqualified democracy and of majority rule. The two houses of the Virginia legislature were too much alike. The very purpose of having a two house legislature was "to introduce the influence of different interests or different principles." Virginia did not receive from the separation "those benefits which a proper complication of principles is capable of producing. . . ." Worse, all power in the state gravitated toward the legislature. "The concentrating [of power] in the same hands is precisely the definition of despotic government. It will be no alleviation that these powers will be exercised by a plurality of hands, and not by a single one. One hundred and seventy-three despots would surely be as oppressive as one. . . . An *elective despotism* was not the government we fought for, but one which should be founded on free principles . . . in which the powers of government should be so divided and balanced among several bodies of magistracy, as that no one could transcend their legal limits, without being effectually checked and restrained by the others." Jefferson argued that the three great departments of government—executive, legislative, and judicial—should not only be separate and distinct, but also kept apart by ample and effectual barriers erected between them. From his experience as governor of Virginia, he knew first hand the danger of leaving the executive and the judiciary subject to the will of the legislature. The only way to guard against "corruption and tyranny" was to prevent it by incorporating the principles of separation of powers and of checks and balances so strongly favored a few years later by the Philadelphia Convention.

Moreover, the Virginia Constitution of 1776 was merely an ordinance of the legislature, of "no higher authority than the other ordinances of

---

[16] Letter to Governor Livingston, Benjamin, *The Collector.*
[17] Quoted in Mason, *Free Government*, p. 138.

the same session." Jefferson therefore advanced the need for a written constitution stemming directly from the people.

His sharpest criticism of the Virginia Constitution, however, was the possibility of dictatorship under it. The legislature could fix its own quorum, could, in fact, "create a *dictator*, invested with every power legislative, executive, and judiciary, civil and military, of life and of death, over our persons and over our properties." "Every lineament" of republican government, express or implied, opposed the idea of dictatorship, he exclaimed. Must those who had fought "from a pure love of liberty, and a sense of injured rights, who determined to make every sacrifice, and to meet every danger, for the re-establishment of those rights on a firm basis now surrender those same rights 'into a single hand'?" "The very thought alone was treason against the people. . . ." Lest such an eventuality materialize, Jefferson begged his fellow Virginians to be sensible of the dangers and to

> apply, at a proper season, the proper remedy, which is a convention to fix the constitution, to amend its defects, to bind up the several branches of government by certain laws, which when they transgress, their acts shall become nullities; to render unnecessary an appeal to the people, or in other words a rebellion, on every infraction of their rights, on the peril that their acquiescence shall be constructed into an intention to surrender those rights.

Jefferson was not active in the movement that led to the convention of 1787. In 1784 he went to France as American minister and stayed until 1790. In a sense, however, he remained on the battle line through his close friend James Madison. For Madison's use he selected and shipped to America innumerable volumes of ancient and modern history, contributing to Madison's already considerable knowledge of the theory and practice of government. His mastery is reflected in his *Vices of the Political System of the United States,* finished just before the Constitutional Convention opened in late May 1787. This essay probes deeply into the nature of free government.

James Madison and the Control of Factions

Madison was at one with Hamilton in identifying want of power in Congress as a cardinal weakness of the Articles of Confederation. "A sanction is essential to the idea of law," Madison wrote, "as coercion is to that of Government. The federal system being destitute of both, wants the great vital principle of a Political Constitution." The cure was as simple to Madison as it had been to Hamilton: give the national government power to secure the obedience of individual citizens to its laws.

Unlike Hamilton, however, Madison believed that a republican government could be successfully adapted to an extensive territory. Convinced that public affairs were too often decided "by the superior force of an interested and overbearing majority" rather than by "the rules of justice and rights of the minor party," he wrote to James Monroe:

There is no maxim, in my opinion, which is more liable to be misapplied, and which therefore needs more elucidation, than the current one, that the interest of the majority is the political standard of right and wrong. Taking the word "interest" as synonymous with "ultimate happiness," in which sense it is qualified with every necessary moral ingredient, the proposition is no doubt true. But taking it in the popular sense, as referring to the immediate augmentation of property and wealth, nothing can be more false. In the latter sense, it would be the interest of the majority, in every community, to despoil and enslave the minority of individuals, and in a Federal community, to make a similar sacrifice of the minority of the component states. In fact, it is only reestablishing, under another name and a more specious form, force as a measure of right.[18]

Madison measured the principle of majority rule by the realities of human nature and found it inadequate. He saw not only that representatives of the people were motivated by ambition and personal interest rather than by concern for the public good, but also that the people themselves were divided into "different interests and factions,"[19] each of which selfishly sought control of the affairs of state to promote its own interests. Creditors and debtors, rich and poor, farmers, merchants, and manufacturers, religious sects and political parties, regions, and the owners of different kinds of property—all sought preference for themselves. If any one faction obtained majority support, nothing in the state constitutions prevented it "from unjust violation of the rights and interests" of all the other interests.

What then was the remedy? Unlike Locke, Madison refused to consider unqualified majority rule as an irremediable inconvenience. "The great desideratum in Government," Madison observed, "is such a modification of the sovereignty as will render it sufficiently neutral between the different interests and factions, to controul one part of the society from invading the rights of another, and at the same time sufficiently controuled itself, from setting up an interest adverse to that of the whole Society." The vast expanse of the country was a partial guarantee that such a desideratum would be observed in the United States, for it worked automatically to give those "who may feel a common sentiment . . . less opportunity of communication and concert." Also needed was the choice of representatives by "a process of elections as will most certainly extract from the mass of the society the purest and noblest characters which it contains."

---

[18] James Madison to James Monroe, October 5, 1788, printed in *Letters and Other Writings of James Madison* (Philadelphia: J. B. Lippincott, 1865), I, 250–51.
[19] Madison derived his idea of "factions" from the Scottish philosopher David Hume's *Idea of a Perfect Commonwealth*, published in 1752. See Douglass Adair, "That Politics May Be Reduced to a Science: David Hume, James Madison, and the Tenth *Federalist*," *Huntington Library Quarterly*, XX (August, 1957) 343–60.

Still more important was the need for external correctives for the "injustice" of state laws, namely, a federal convention and a new constitution.

John Adams and the Idea of Balance

It remained for John Adams to make the final contribution to the "science of government," American style, in his detailed two-volume *Defence of the Constitutions of Government of the United States of America,* published in 1787–1788. Adams's work has been described as a "treasure in insight."[20] The first volume was published just as the Philadelphia Convention was beginning. Of its influence Dr. Rush remarked: "Mr. Adams's book has diffused such excellent principles among us that there is little doubt of our adopting a vigorous and compounded Federal legislature."[21]

Adams, like Madison, drew heavily from history and concluded "that the people's rights and liberties, and the democratical mixture in a constitution, can never be preserved without a strong executive, or, in other words, without separating the executive from the legislative power." Separation of powers and checks and balances were the sine qua non of free government.

The idea of *balance* was as central to Adams's constitutionalism as to Madison's. "If the executive power, or any considerable part of it, is left in the hands . . . of an . . . assembly, it will corrupt the legislature as necessarily as rust corrupts iron . . . and when the legislature is corrupted, the people are undone." Legislative and executive powers were fundamentally different, and thus properly to be exercised by different agencies. The executive should be maintained separately and endowed with a veto. Balance and separation of power would prevent government from being subjected to "everlasting fluctuations, revolutions, and horrors" by the people, on the one hand, and from being converted into "the instrument of a few grandees," on the other.

Although Adams added little to the doctrine of separation of powers, he clarified the people's role in free government. He denied the assertion that the people "never think of usurping over other men's rights, but mind which way to preserve their own."[22] Such belief could lead, Adams contended, to the destruction of free government. Experience showed that oppression was natural in all societies, and no man, no group, no class was immune to its drives. Individuals consistently tried to invade the rights of others, parties oppressed parties, and majorities almost universally persecuted minorities. Private interests, of individuals or of groups,

---

[20] Clinton Rossiter, "The Legacy of John Adams," *Yale Review,* XLVI (Summer, 1957), 533.

[21] Benjamin Rush to Richard Price, June 2, 1787, printed in Lyman H. Butterfield, ed., *Letters of Benjamin Rush* (Princeton, N.J.: Princeton University Press, 1951), I, 418.

[22] Marchamont Nedham, *The Excellency of a Free State* (London: Millar, Codell, Kearsly and H. Parker, 1767), p. 2.

were naturally preferred to the interest of the nation as a whole. "Some provision must be made in the constitution, in favor of justice, to compel all to respect the common right, the public good, the universal law, in preference to all private and partial considerations."[23] The problem of government was twofold: to safeguard society from the overriding ambitions of aristocracy, the existence of which was as inevitable as it was beneficial, and to prevent the majority from usurping the rights of the minority. Nature's seamy side was a common affliction. "My opinion is, and always has been, that absolute power intoxicates alike despots, monarchs, aristocrats, and democrats, and Jacobins, and *sans culottes*."[24]

But far from repudiating democracy, Adams extolled its virtues: "Democracy must be respected; democracy must be honored; democracy must be cherished; democracy must be an essential, an integral part of the sovereignty, and have a control over the whole government, or moral liberty cannot exist. . . ."[25] Democracy, however, like aristocracy, must be subjected to restraint.

Adams had a profound understanding of the relationship of property to political power. Better than anyone else at the time he caught the meaning of Harrington's *Oceana* and applied its reasoning to the American situation. He found it inevitable that there would be rich and poor— perhaps in the ratio of eight or nine poor persons to every wealthy one. Obviously, measures were necessary to prevent invasion of the rights of the one by the action of the eight or nine—measures more reliable than faith that the poor would "never think of usurping over other men's rights." "Property is surely a right of mankind as real as liberty," Adams countered, and the rich surely had as sacred a right to their property as the poor had to their liberty. Sounding a Madisonian note, he wrote:

> Perhaps, at first, prejudice, habit, shame, or fear, principle or religion, would restrain the poor from attacking the rich, and the idle from usurping on the industrious; but the time would not be long before courage and enterprise would come, and pretexts be invented by degrees, to countenance the majority in dividing all the property among them, or at least, in sharing it equally with its present possessors. . . . What would be the consequence of this? The idle, the vicious, the intemperate, would rush into the utmost extravagance of debauchery, sell and spend all their share, and then demand a new division of those who purchased from them. The moment the idea is admitted into society, that property is not as sacred as the laws of God, and that there is not a force of law and public justice to protect it, anarchy and tyranny commence. . . .[26]

All men were afflicted with unruly passions—"self-interest, private avidity, ambition, and avarice." Neither "benevolence and generous affec-

---

[23] Charles F. Adams, ed., *The Works of John Adams* (Boston: Little, Brown, 1851), VI, 6–7.
[24] Rossiter, "Legacy of Adams," p. 542.
[25] Rossiter, "Legacy of Adams," p. 543.
[26] Adams, *The Works of John Adams,* VI, 8–9.

tions" nor self-denial was enough to restrain them. Therefore, "rational and prudent precautions" had to be taken to assure that property—and other rights—would not be made the victim of man's natural selfishness.

Adams recognized that, for republican government to remain stable, restraints on the minority and majority alike must be applied. Control "the selfish avidity of the governor, by the senate and house; of the senate, by the governor and house; and of the house, by the governor and senate."[27] In particular, give the minority a negative on the majority, by giving the rich separate representation in a senate. Let the people be represented in a house of representatives. Create an "executive power, vested with a negative," equal to both houses, "to hold the balance even between them, and decide when they cannot agree." Put the final defense of liberty in independent courts of law. Keep the executive and judicial power out of the legislature's control, for in any representative assembly, "the honest men are generally nearly equally divided in sentiment, and, therefore, the vicious and unprincipled . . . always follow the most profligate leader, him who bribes the highest, and sets all decency and shame at defiance."

THE REMEDY: A CONSTITUTIONAL CONVENTION

By 1787 Hamilton, Washington, Jefferson, Madison, and Adams had set the stage for reexamination of the basis of government in the United States. It was one thing, however, to identify the causes of the crisis; it was something else to channel American thought and action to alleviate it. The Confederation was not unpopular; it was "just the sort of loose arrangement most favorable to democratic self-rule. . . . It was for achieving exactly this object . . . that the Confederation's strongest supporters —such leaders as Samuel Adams, Patrick Henry, Thomas Burke, and Richard Henry Lee—pushed the colonies into the Revolution in the first place."[28] To turn them—and a majority of the American people—from such an arrangement and back in the direction of stronger and more centralized government was a formidable task. Even after the issues were crystallized, the movement still lacked a sense of urgency. Needed was an incident or a man to do, in 1787, what Tom Paine had done so effectively with his *Common Sense* in 1776.

Shays's Rebellion: Catalytic Agent

Such an incident came quite fortuitously in the summer and fall of 1786 in the guise of Shays's Rebellion in Massachusetts. This militant popular uprising constituted an armed attack on lawyers and courts, an intimi-

---

[27] Adams, *Works of John Adams*, 57–58.
[28] Stanley Elkins and Eric McKitrick, "The Founding Fathers: Young Men of the Revolution," *Political Science Quarterly* LXXVI (June, 1961), 192.

dation of the legislature, and a threat to property. Shays's appeal for repudiation of debts provided the very object lesson in democratic idiocy needed by friends of public power, and they fully exploited their opportunity.

The principal sower of the seeds of fear was General Henry Knox of Massachusetts. From him Washington received almost daily bulletins. On October 23, 1786, the general painted a dreadful picture: "The theoretic government of Massachusetts has given way, and its laws are trampled under foot. . . . Their creed is that the property of the United States has been protected from the confiscation of Britain by the joint exertions of all, and therefore ought to be the common property of all. This dreadful situation has alarmed every man of principle and property in New England. . . . Our government must be braced, changed, or altered to secure our lives and property."[29]

News of Shays's Rebellion alarmed many American leaders. "When Massachusetts appealed to the Confederation for help, Congress was unable to do a thing. That was the final argument to sway many Americans in favor of a stronger federal government."[30]

Hysteria, particularly among men of property, was so widespread that some feared chaos might lead to monarchy or military dictatorship. Conservative dissatisfaction with the Articles of Confederation was strongest in Massachusetts, leading to an "inchoate but threatening body of opinion . . . that all republican government was impracticable and that even monarchy might be preferable."[31] Indeed, both George Washington and Prince Henry of Brandenberg were nominated to assume an American crown.[32] Fortunately, neither was receptive. Even so, the possibility that liberty might be destroyed from the Right, combined with the impact of popular uprisings, contributed incalculably to the efforts of those determined to safeguard free institutions.

The Revolution Continued

The major force pushing the nation toward correction, however, was the fact that the revolution of 1776 was incomplete. The Declaration of Independence itself indicates both negative and positive aspects of revolution: the right of the people "to alter or abolish" a tyrannical government, and the right "to institute a new government, laying its foundations on such principles as to them seem more likely to effect their safety and happiness." Only the former was accomplished in 1776. Although the war was

---

[29] Quoted in Mason, *Free Government*, p. 185.
[30] Morison, *History of American People*, p. 304.
[31] Robert A. East, "The Massachusetts Conservatives in the Critical Period," in R. B. Morris, ed., *The Era of the American Revolution* (New York: Columbia University Press, 1939), p. 376.
[32] Louise Dunbar, "A Study of 'Monarchical' Tendencies in the United States from 1776 to 1801," *University of Illinois Studies in the Social Sciences*, X (March 1922), 7–164. See also Charles A. Beard, *The Republic* (New York: Viking, 1945), p. 25.

over, the revolution of 1776 was still to be completed. Then began what Samuel E. Morison called "the Creative Period in Politics, 1785–1788."[33] By then, as Hamilton noted in *Federalist* Number 9:

> The science of politics . . . like most other sciences had received great improvement. The efficacy of various principles is now well understood, which were either not known at all or imperfectly known to the ancients. The regular distribution of power into distinct departments; the introduction of legislative balances and checks; the institution of courts composed of judges holding their offices during good behavior; the representation of the people in the legislature by deputies of their own election; these are either wholly new discoveries, or have made their principal progress toward perfection in modern times.[34]

New knowledge, combined with experience, facilitated the next step in the endless quest for free government.

In 1776 political checks imposed at the ballot box and remedy by resort to revolution were considered the only safeguards against arbitrary government. This was the essence of Locke. The author of the *Second Treatise*, like the framers of the state constitutions, included certain institutional checks, but these were hardly more than paper limitations. For the delegates about to meet in Philadelphia to frame the new federal constitution, Locke's formulas were not enough. Among the most important innovations of the Confederation period was the use initiated within the states of an auxiliary check obliging government to control itself. Professor Corwin put it this way:

> The abuses resulting from the hitherto undifferentiated character of "legislative power" was met by the idea that it was something intrinsically distinct from judicial power and that therefore it was exceeded when it interfered with the dispensation of justice through the ordinary courts. Then building upon this result, the finality of judicial determinations was represented as extending to the interpretation of the standing law, a proposition which when brought into association with the notion of a higher law, yielded the initial form of the doctrine of judicial review.

Thus, the two primary objectives of those who favored the calling of a Constitutional Convention were fused into one. "The problem of providing adequate safeguards for private rights and adequate powers for a national government was one and the same problem, inasmuch as a strengthened national government could be made a make-weight against the swollen prerogatives of the state legislatures."[35] The desideratum yet

---

[33] Morison, *History of American People*, title of Chap. 20. See also Gordon S. Wood, *The Creation of the American Republic* (Chapel Hill, N.C.: University of North Carolina Press, 1969).

[34] *Federalist* Number 9.

[35] Corwin, "Progress of Constitutional Theory," p. 536.

to be found for republican government was "some disinterested and dispassionate umpire in disputes between different passions and interests in the State."[36]

No period in American history has been more productive of theoretical and institutional development than the eleven years between 1776 and 1787. Within scarcely more than a decade, America was changed from a subordinate part of an empire to an independent republic, from colonies to states, from a loosely knit Confederacy to a federated union. *Revolution* alone would seem adequate to describe this remarkable transformation. Yet, as Edmund Burke understood so well, that word in the American context must be construed to mean something very different from what occurred as a result of the French Revolution. The Americans, unlike the French, did not begin by "despising everything that belonged to them."[37] Even the revolution that marked the break with England was limited. In the chaos and travail that followed independence, the basic precepts formulated in 1776 were not abandoned. Rather, they were reexamined and reoriented in the light of reason and experience.

Reorientation was accomplished in the face of opposition. Defenders of the Articles of Confederation, most of whom became Anti-Federalists after 1787, reiterated the arguments that had earlier proved successful in defeating John Dickinson's original draft of the Articles. By 1787 there was general agreement, even among Anti-Federalists, that action was necessary. The time had come to tighten the bonds of union—to complete the revolution of 1776.[38]

---

[36] Merrill Jensen, *The New Nation* (New York: Knopf, 1950), p. 427.

[37] Edmund Burke, *Reflections on the French Revolution* (New York: Merrill), p. 18.

[38] See B. F. Wright, *Consensus and Continuity, 1776–1789* (Boston: Boston University Press, 1958).

CHAPTER FIVE

TIGHTENING
THE BONDS OF UNION

The initial step toward the establishment of a new government was taken early in September 1786, when Virginia invited the other states to join in conference at Annapolis to discuss trade and commerce between the several states. The meeting was poorly attended and, measured solely in terms of its stated objectives, was a dismal failure. The twelve commissioners, representing five states, convened on September 11 and broke up September 14. The session, though short, lasted long enough for the delegates to discover that a remedy even for the evils affecting commerce and trade must be found in some broader constitutional framework. This required the cooperation of all states and considerable enlargement of the commissioners' authority. At Annapolis only New Jersey's delegates were empowered to discuss "other important matters."

The result was the adoption of Alexander Hamilton's resolution declaring that small attendance alone precluded the commissioners' proceeding "to the business of their mission." But their sense of urgency moved them to declare the "earnest and unanimous wish that speedy measures may be taken to effect a general meeting of the states in a future convention for the same and such other purposes as the situation of public affairs may be found to require." The resolution went on to record the further reflection that "the power of regulating trade is of such comprehensive extent, and will enter so far into the general system of the Federal Government, that to give it efficacy, and to obviate questions and doubts concerning its precise nature and limits, may require a correspondent adjustment of the federal system." The resolutions ended with the proposal that all the states appoint commissioners "to meet at Philadelphia on the second Monday in May next, to take into consideration the situation of the United States, to devise such further provisions as shall appear to them necessary to render the Constitution of the Federal Government *adequate to the exigencies of the Union."*

The report of the Annapolis Commissioners came before the Congress in October with the expectation that Congress would recommend the action suggested. The matter was opposed, however, on technical grounds, and it was not until the situation worsened—not only between but also within the states—that Congress finally, on February 21, 1787, adopted the Annapolis resolutions. The states, with the exception of Rhode Island, began immediately to choose delegates to represent them in the forthcoming convention. Eight of the Annapolis Commissioners, including Alexander Hamilton, James Madison, Edmund Randolph, and John Dickinson, were again selected. Virginia provided the project buoyant expectancy by choosing George Washington as one of her delegates.[1] He was the Convention's unanimous choice as presiding officer.

THE DEMIGODS GATHER

On April 8, 1787, a few weeks before the Convention delegates assembled in Philadelphia, James Madison, anticipating that "some leading proposition would be expected from Virginia," wrote Washington and Governor Edmund Randolph concerning the central issue—federalism. To Randolph he said:

> I hold it for a fundamental point, that an individual independence of the States is utterly irreconcilable with the idea of an aggregate sovereignty. I think, at the same time, that a consolidation of the States into one simple republic is not less attainable than it would be inexpedient. Let it be tried then whether any middle ground can be taken which will at once support a due supremacy of the national authority, and leave in force the local authorities so far as they can be subordinately useful.[2]

The members of the Convention constituted a varied and distinguished group, ranging in age from twenty-six to eighty-one. Twenty-nine were

---

[1] See Arthur N. Holcombe, "The Role of Washington in the Framing of the Constitution," *Huntington Library Quarterly,* XIX (August, 1950), 317–34.
[2] Quoted in Mason, *The States Rights Debate: Anti-federalism and the Constitution* (New York: Oxford University Press, 1972), p. 61.

university graduates. The twenty-six nongraduates included two of the most distinguished of them all—Washington and Franklin. For the most part the members of the Convention were not the same men who had accepted Jefferson's draft of the Declaration; only eight of the fifty-nine had signed that document. They were, in a sense, a new generation in American political life.

Certain eminent leaders of the Revolution were conspicuously absent: Jefferson was at his diplomatic post in France; Patrick Henry "smelt a rat" and declined to serve as a delegate from Virginia; Samuel Adams and Richard Henry Lee avoided any move that might sanction the aversion they shared so strongly—consolidated government. Deprived of such men, the Convention's most persuasive delegates were nationalists. Had anti-federalist leadership been stronger, the result might have been quite different.

The framers shared many of the same prejudices and preferences. The theory that society tends to divide into classes along economic lines was accepted without argument. Property was freely equated with liberty and happiness. Suffrage was accepted as one of the fundamental articles of republican government, yet all agreed that the evils which the Convention had been called to mitigate were caused by excesses of democracy. Few, however, supported the opposite extreme of providing no role for the people at all. The venerable Franklin, then eighty-one and acknowledged to be the "first civilized American," expressed his distaste for "everything that tended to debase the common people." "The virtue and public spirit of our common people" during the Revolution, he recalled, contributed "principally to the favorable issue of it."[3] Although most delegates accepted Franklin's outlook, they were disturbed by the almost certain prospect that the masses would in time become politically dominant. Even at the end, the ability of the people to govern themselves was doubted.

A twofold objective prompted the Convention's efforts: to provide more adequate power and energy in the central government, and to secure private rights against the evil of faction—especially the superior force of an interested and overbearing majority. What the Convention could accomplish was, of course, problematical. A turning point in the nation's affairs was apparent, but certain states were unwilling to authorize their delegates to do more than "revise" the Articles of Confederation. Not a single legislature of the twelve states sending delegates authorized them to make the basic changes that Hamilton, Madison, and Adams had long been advocating. Yet the very first resolution put before the Convention, presented on May 29, proposed drastic change. Discussion during the next two weeks convinced a majority of the delegates that mere amendment would not render the Articles of Confederation "adequate to the exigencies of the Union," that the only hope of the infant nation lay in proceed-

---

[3] Quoted in Mason, *Free Government*, pp. 190–91.

ing "upon lines of somewhat radical reform."[4] In defiance of instructions, the delegates began the arduous task of reconstructing the constitutional foundations of American politics. Looking back, the accomplishment seems remarkable, almost miraculous.

Because of their willingness to violate specific instructions, the framers of the Constitution have been accused of harboring ulterior motives.[5] More particularly, they have been credited with the desire to secure economic protection and preferment for themselves and their class. Charles A. Beard's systematic effort to sustain such charges is not persuasive. It seems, rather, that the majority of the delegates resolved to ignore their instructions and strike out boldly on the basis of new knowledge and of experience.[6] Their "theoretical prepossessions" were those of men of affairs—men of commerce and the court room, of the legislative chamber and the battlefield—to whom the practical limitations of the Articles and the injustices flowing from the state governments had become increasingly irksome. Their collective experience had taught them that human nature in its frailty needed "the power of a good political constitution to control" it.[7] So believing, they could hardly have been expected to do less than attempt to replace the Articles of Confederation with a new constitution. That the new charter of government protected their own financial condition appears only coincidental.

Partial refutation of the charge of self-interest is contained in the roster of the Convention's leading delegates. Besides Washington, Franklin, Hamilton, Dickinson, Madison, George Wythe, and James Wilson, it included William Paterson of New Jersey, Gouverneur Morris of Pennsylvania, Rufus King, then of Massachusetts, George Mason of Virginia, and C. C. Pinckney of South Carolina. Although men of this stature were not in the majority, all were, nevertheless, men of integrity and character; however much their various positions seem now to reflect self-interest, it is more probable that their presence in Philadelphia represented sincere convictions, arrived at after careful study and thought. Jefferson described the delegates as "an assembly of demi-gods." Although this is an exaggeration, it cannot be doubted that the men who drafted the Constitution were eminently qualified by knowledge and experience to construct a viable system of government.

---

[4] Max Farrand, *The Framing of the Constitution of the United States* (New Haven, Conn:. Yale University Press, 1913), p. 74.
[5] See J. Allen Smith, *The Spirit of the American Government* (New York: Macmillan, 1912); Charles A. Beard, *An Economic Interpretation of the Constitution* (New York: Macmillan, 1929); and Parrington, *Main Currents*. For refutations of this thesis, see Robert E. Brown, *Charles Beard and the Constitution* (Princeton, N.J.: Princeton University Press, 1956) and Forrest McDonald, *We the People: The Economic Origins of the Constitution* (Chicago: Chicago University Press, 1958).
[6] Corwin, "Progress of Constitutional Theory," p. 511.
[7] Richard Hofstadter, *The American Political Tradition and the Men Who Made It* (New York: Knopf, 1948), p. 3.

RANDOLPH'S FEDERALIST PLAN

The Convention was finally organized on May 25.[8] To assure frank and honest discussion, the delegates agreed to proceed behind closed doors. The delegates met continually until September 17, at which time the finished Constitution was referred to the states and the Convention adjourned sine die. Debate centered from the beginning on two major proposals, based on different theoretical assumptions. One proposal, since known as the Virginia Plan, was basically Madison's, though introduced on May 29 by Edmund Randolph (1753–1813), a prominent Virginia statesman and governor of that state. The plan was predicated on the theory of national sovereignty. After pointing out the defects of the Articles of Confederation, Randolph continued:

> Let us not be afraid to view with a steady eye the perils with which we are surrounded. Look at the public countenance from New Hampshire to Georgia. Are we not on the eve of War, which is only prevented by the hope from this Convention?
>
> Our chief danger arises from the democratic parts of our constitutions. It is a maxim which I hold incontrovertible that the powers of government exercised by the people swallows up the other branches. None of the constitutions have provided sufficient checks against the democracy.[9]

Randolph proposed a bicameral national legislature empowered "to legislate in all cases to which the separate States are incompetent, or in which the harmony of the United States may be interrupted by the exercise of individual legislation," and to veto any state law it deemed contrary to the national constitution. By implication, the national legislature itself would decide the cases "to which the separate States are incompetent," and that power, plus its veto of state legislation, would have demolished the idea of state sovereignty. The Virginia Plan also called

---

[8] Two historical accounts of the Convention are Farrand, *Framing of the Constitution* and Carl Van Doren, *The Great Rehearsal* (New York: Viking, 1948). See also William W. Crosskey, *Politics and the Constitution in the History of the United States* (Chicago: University of Chicago Press, 1953). For a day-by-day account of the Convention, see Catherine D. Bowen, *Miracle at Philadelphia* (Boston: Little, Brown, 1966). See also David G. Smith, *The Convention and the Constitution. The Political Ideas of the Founding Fathers* (New York: St. Martin's 1965); Paul Eidelberg, *The Philosophy of the American Constitution* (New York: Free Press, 1968); and John P. Roche, "The Founding Fathers: A Reform Caucus in Action," *American Political Science Review*, LIX (1961), 799–816.

[9] Unless otherwise noted the quotations from the Convention debates are from Vols. I and II of Max Farrand, ed., *The Records of the Federal Convention of 1787* (New Haven, Conn.: Yale University Press, 1911).

for a national executive and a national judiciary to strengthen execution and enforcement of national laws. Under its terms national officials would bring the central government directly to bear on individuals. No longer could the states, through failure to heed the laws of Congress or through the authority of their courts, shield individuals from the coercive power of the national government. Although the states would still function, they would do so more as minions and less as lords.

The Virginia Plan also embodied the theory of separated and balanced powers in the national government. Madison having been its guiding spirit, it could hardly have been otherwise. The legislature would be divided against itself—one house elected by the people, the other, indirectly by the state legislatures—each presumably reflecting counterbalancing interests. Each house would have an equal right to initiate legislation. The proposed national executive would be endowed with "general authority to execute the National laws." It would be chosen by the legislature and be ineligible a second time. Judicial power would be vested in a national judiciary of one or more supreme tribunals. Judges would hold office during good behavior and thus be out of reach of both the legislature and the executive. Lest the legislature become tyrannical, the opportunity to review its every act would be granted to a Council of Revision, consisting of the executive and "a convenient number of the National Judiciary." Having resolved itself into the Committee of the Whole, the Convention proceeded to discuss the plan point by point.

PATERSON AND STATE SOVEREIGNTY

Representatives of the smaller states quickly became dissatisfied with the way things were going. William Paterson (1745–1806), attorney general of New Jersey before he became a delegate to the convention, came forward on June 16 with a substitute plan. Anticipating only such enlargement of the Articles of Confederation as would render them "adequate to the exigencies of Government, and the preservation of the Union," his proposal would have perpetuated state sovereignty. Throughout, Paterson sought to protect the states as dominant centers of government. Although additional legislative powers were to be vested in the national Congress, all punishment for contravening acts of Congress was first to be "adjudged by the Common Law Judiciarys" of the several states. The proposal not only declared that none of the legislative powers vested in the United States in Congress should be exercised without the consent of a specified number of states, but also provided that the national executive should be removable by Congress on the application of a majority of the state governors.

Oddly enough, Paterson's sixth resolution contained a statement of what was later regarded as the keystone of national supremacy—Article VI, section 2 of the adopted Constitution. Paterson's version read:

Resolved that all Acts of the United States in Congress, made by virtue and in pursuance of the powers hereby and by the articles of confederation vested in them, and all treaties made and ratified under the authority of the United States shall be the supreme law of the respective States so far forth as those Acts or Treaties shall relate to the said States or their Citizens, and that the Judiciary of the several States shall be bound thereby in their decisions, any thing in the respective laws of the Individual States to the contrary notwithstanding. . . .

Presumably a substitute for the overall national veto of state acts proposed in the Randolph Plan, this otherwise strongly nationalistic statement was weakened by the assertion that the supremacy of congressional acts applied only "so far as those Acts . . . shall relate to the said States or their Citizens." While permitting state judges to observe such acts, the resolution also permitted them to decide how far those very acts related to the states and to their citizens. Opportunity for operation of the States' rights principle was still open, despite the strong language and contrary tone of this resolution.

The New Jersey Plan, as Paterson's proposal came to be called, like the Virginia Plan, embodied the theory of separation of powers, but with much less elaboration. A legislature of enlarged power would be provided and a plural executive chosen by Congress, endowed with "general authority to execute the federal acts." A federal judiciary would consist of "a supreme Tribunal . . . appointed by the Executive. . . ." Paterson's explanation of his plan made it obvious that he thought of separation of powers much more as a device to limit the power of the national government vis-à-vis the states than as a method of dividing powers and functions within the federal government itself. He met Randolph's assertion that a two-branch legislature was necessary "for the purpose of a check" with emphatic denial. "The reason of the precaution is not applicable to this case," he explained. "Within a particular State, when party heat prevails, such a check may be necessary. In a body such as Congress, it is less necessary, and besides, the delegations of the different States are checks on each other." The people at large did not complain of Congress, Paterson asserted. The important thing was to keep power diffused so that "the lesser states" would not be sacrificed to the larger or to the national government.

HAMILTON'S BRITISH MODEL

On June 18 Alexander Hamilton submitted a third plan of government. Coming from such a highly respected source, it might have been expected to receive serious and immediate attention. That it failed to do so is significant. For Hamilton, neither the Virginia nor the New Jersey Plan gave promise of a truly efficacious government. Neither took account sufficiently of the obvious fact that "the passions . . . of avarice, ambition, interest, which govern most individuals, and all public bodies, [fell] into the current of the States, and [did] not flow in the stream of the General Government." With so much natural advantage, the states would always constitute "an overmatch for the general government." Only a plan that would create so complete a sovereignty in the national government "as will turn all the strong principles and passions above mentioned on its side" would succeed in overcoming that great advantage. Neither of the other two plans met this difficulty; neither, therefore, would do. Instead, a system must be adopted that would permit the general power to "swallow up the State powers, [lest] it . . . be swallowed up by them." On this ground the British model recommended itself.

The essence of Hamilton's plan was a strong executive to maintain justice between the classes, along with a representative assembly "to give the entire mass of people an effective control over government." Unlike many other delegates, including Madison, Hamilton surprisingly favored the extension of the franchise to all white males.

Lest it "shock the public opinion," Hamilton did not actually propose abolition of the states and their incorporation into a unitary government, as in Great Britain. In so large a country subordinate authorities were necessary, but only as "corporations for local purposes." "For any of the great purposes of commerce, revenue, or agriculture," the states were altogether inadequate. The British model attracted Hamilton because it met the most important criteria—stability and permanency. In support of this view, Hamilton said:

> I believe the British government forms the best method the world ever produced, and such has been its progress in the minds of the many that this truth gradually gains ground. This government has for its object *public strength* and *individual security*. It is said with us to be unattainable. If it was once formed it would maintain itself. All communities divide themselves into the few and the many. The first are rich and well born, the other the mass of the people. The voice of the people has been said to be the voice of God; and however generally this maxim has been quoted and believed, it is not true in fact. The people are turbulent and changing; they seldom judge or determine right. Give therefore to the first class a distinct permanent share in the government. They will check the unsteadiness of the second, and as they cannot receive any advantage by a change, they therefore will ever maintain good government. Can a democratic assembly, who annually revolve in the mass of the people, be supposed steadily to pursue the public good? Nothing but a permanent body can check the imprudence of democracy. Their turbulent and uncontrouling disposition requires checks. . . .

Strong government was essential to protect property from "the amazing violence and turbulence of the democratic spirit." No temporary senate would suffice. Let its members, like those of the House of Lords in England, be chosen for life or at least during good behavior. As for popular election of the executive—that was a manifest absurdity, for only "men of little character" would be chosen by the people for such a post. Instead, let the executive be for life, if the "best citizens" were secured to fill it. With these protections Hamilton thought the British example of a lower house elected by the people might safely be followed in America. The Senate and the executive constituted as he proposed would serve to prevent "every pernicious innovation" from materializing. Here, as in England, property would be secure, and government would be rendered stable.

Hamilton's plan received a cool reception, and shortly after its presentation, he returned to New York, where he remained for the duration of the Convention, thus depriving that body of his undeniable talents.

THEORETICAL CONSIDERATIONS

Hamilton's suggestions brought the submission of raw material, as it were, to a close.[10] The delegates then entered into three months of debate and resolution, compromise and concession. Out of it emerged the seven articles that form the Constitution of 1787, a document noted for its practicality and brevity. Indeed, so concise was the Constitution that it hardly seems an expression of theory at all. Unlike the Massachusetts Constitution of 1776, which carefully spelled out separation of powers, the framers of the national constitution made that theory implicit only in the arrangement of Articles I, II, and III. So it is with other theories that might logically have been expected to be lodged in the Constitution. On its surface the Constitution seems to stand apart from the stream of theoretical development in English and American politics of the century and a half preceding it. On closer examination, however, the discussion in the Convention was one long exercise in the application of that very development to an immediately practical situation. The Convention debates thus provide the theoretical underpinnings for provisions relating to the position of the states in the Union, the nature of each of the three branches of the government, and the questions of representation and suffrage. The expressions of contemporary philosophy in Madison's *Notes* form a précis of the theory of free government as it was understood by the Founding Fathers. Credit for that record goes not to the Convention secretary, William Jackson, who did little more than record ayes and noes on specific questions, but to James Madison. His *Notes*[11] have served almost to recreate the drama of the scene. Because he kept such a detailed record of what was said at the Convention, quite as much as for the fact that he was primarily responsible for the drafting of the Virginia Plan, he has been accorded the title Father of the Constitution.

---

[10] Charles C. Pinckney (1757–1824) of South Carolina also submitted a plan to the Convention, but its exact provisions are not known.

[11] James Madison, *Journal of the Federal Convention* (Chicago: Albert, Scott, 1894).

NATURE OF THE UNION:
THE CONNECTICUT COMPROMISE

The Virginia Plan, stressing national power, necessitated an examination of the nature of the union. From the beginning most of the delegates were wary of an entirely centralized government; exactly what degree of decentralization was proper they were not so sure. To William Paterson and to Luther Martin of Maryland confederation meant, in Paterson's words, "sovereignty in the members . . . [and] sovereignty supposes equality." Because the Declaration of Independence implied the equality of the several states, the Convention could not alter this implication by raising over them a general government with power to govern individuals within them, as suggested in the Virginia Plan.

In the end the Convention decided that neither confederation and state sovereignty nor complete consolidation squared with the requirements of free government. Madison, who throughout the debate indicated his fear of majority factions, caught the feeling that probably animated a majority of the delegates. He opposed the confederate form because it had established a poor record for the protection of minority rights. In "digesting a plan which in its operation would decide forever the fate of Republican Government we ought not only to provide every guard to liberty that its preservation could require," but also to "be equally careful to supply the defects which our own experience has particularly pointed out." Outstanding among those defects—the evil that perhaps more than anything else had produced the Convention—was interference with "the security of private rights, and the steady dispensation of Justice" by the legislatures of the states and the inability of the Confederation Congress to halt it.

"What has been the source of those laws complained of among ourselves?" Madison inquired. "Has it not been the real or supposed interest of the major number? Debtors have defrauded their creditors. The landed interest has borne hard on the mercantile interest. The Holders of one species of property have thrown a disproportion of taxes on the holders of another species." In the internal administration of the states, "violations of Contracts had become familiar in the form of depreciated paper made a legal tender, of property substituted for money, of Instalment laws, and of the occlusions of the Courts of Justice. . . ." "Was it to be supposed that republican liberty could long exist under the abuses of it practiced in [some of] the States?" Madison asked. The answer was clear. Admitting the division of all civilized societies, republican as well as others, "into different Sects, Factions, and interests," and recognizing that whenever "a majority are united by a common interest or passion, the rights of the minority are in danger," the people might still be assured of their protection by enlarging the unit of government, thereby dividing "the community into so great a number of interests and parties, that in the first place a majority will not be likely at the same moment to have a common interest separate from that of the whole or of the minority;

and in the second place, that in case they should have such an interest, they may not be apt to unite in the pursuit of it." A republican government, Madison concluded, should be framed "on such a scale and in such a form as will control all the evils which have been experienced." In short, it should be framed within a union, capable of strong national government.

James Wilson (1742–1798) and Rufus King (1755–1827) conceived of the Union in another way. Wilson did not favor a national government that "would swallow up the State governments. . . ." Instead, he realized that they were "absolutely necessary for certain purposes which the former could not reach" and thus were to be preserved "on friendly terms." After all, claims to state sovereignty were mere "metaphysical distinctions." Just as men in Locke's state of nature, having been equally "kings," had given up their liberty and equality on entering civil society, so the states must yield their sovereignty on entering the Union. "Federal liberty is to States, what civil liberty, is to private individuals. And States are not more unwilling to purchase it, by the necessary concession of their political sovereignty, than the savage is to purchase civil liberty by the surrender of the personal sovereignty which he enjoys in a State of Nature." "If New Jersey will not part with her sovereignty," Wilson warned, "it is vain to talk of Government."

Wilson's words implied absolute surrender of state sovereignty. The lawyer Rufus King,[12] who had helped draft the famous Ordinance of 1787, was not so positive. He argued that the states were not sovereign to the extent often claimed. There were a number of the peculiar features of sovereignty never possessed by the states—the power to make war and peace, for example, and the power to make alliances and treaties. "Considering them as political Beings, they were dumb, for they could not speak to any foreign Sovereign whatever. They were deaf, for they could not hear any propositions from such Sovereign. They had not even the organs or faculties of defence or offence, for they could not of themselves raise troops, or equip vessels for war." Yet, in other ways, particularly in regard to internal affairs, the states had a considerable portion of sovereignty. Out of respect for internal affairs, King suggested, the Union should embrace the idea of confederation; out of need for a sovereign power to deal with war and foreign affairs, the Union should also embrace the idea of consolidation.

The views of Wilson and King were more balanced than those of Hamilton, on the one hand, or of Paterson and Martin, on the other, and thus more representative of the feeling of a majority of delegates. They were also a good deal more ambiguous. Because the Convention was willing to embrace neither the theory of consolidated union nor that of weak confederation, they were forced into ambiguity. That ambiguity was not resolved in the finished Constitution. The delegates arrived at no clear

---

[12] For King's part in the Convention, see Robert Ernst, *Rufus King, American Federalist* (Chapel Hill, N.C.: University of North Carolina Press, 1968), Chaps. 5–7.

definition of exactly what they were creating. To have attempted to do so might have wrecked the Convention. In fact, more than once the argument over the nature of the Union and over the closely related issue of proportional versus equal representation in Congress nearly broke up the Convention. The proponents of confederation were small-state men, who shared with Paterson the fear that in a union the small states would be swallowed up. "Give the large States an influence in proportion to their magnitude," Paterson observed, "and what will be the consequence? Their ambition will be proportionally increased, and the small States will have everything to fear." Their only defense lay in absolute equality.

Madison tried to allay such fears. Would the small states, he asked, really be endangered by entering into a union, as proposed in the Virginia Plan? Would the large states use their power to destroy the other states? Were Massachusetts, Pennsylvania, and Virginia in fact united by some common interest that set them against the remaining states and imperiled their existence? He doubted it. In point of location, commodities produced, "manners, Religion and other circumstances, which sometimes beget affection between different communities, they were not more assimilated than the other states." Nor was mere size a guarantee of a single-mindedness among the large states. "The journals of Congress did not present any peculiar association of these States in the votes recorded." If there were in reality nothing to be feared from the combined power of the big three, there was even less to be feared from them singly. The best assurance that the interests of the small states would be safeguarded, Madison concluded, was to create a general government with "sufficient energy and permanency" to operate on all the states. Each would then be secure from the others.

So tenaciously did the two sides cling to their arguments that at one point in the proceedings it looked as if the Convention would be deadlocked. On June 28 Madison himself suggested the hard "either or" alternatives: "The two extremes before us are a perfect separation and a perfect incorporation of the 13 States." The Convention was enabled to continue its work only by the famous Connecticut Compromise, the contribution of Dr. William Samuel Johnson, delegate from Connecticut. The cause of the impasse, as Dr. Johnson saw it, was that no one had recognized the twofold character of the states. They could be regarded as "districts of people" and as "political societies." In the first capacity, the small states had nothing to fear from the proposed plan of union; in the second, however, "they must be armed with some power of self-defense."

> As in some respects the States are to be considered in their political capacity, and in others as districts of individual citizens, the two ideas embraced on different sides, instead of being opposed to each other, ought to be combined; that in *one* branch [of the national legislature] the *people* ought to be represented; in the *other*, the States.

Oliver Ellsworth (1745–1807), an eminent Connecticut lawyer destined to become third Chief Justice of the United States, adopted Johnson's idea and proposed that both these principles be accepted. Let recognition be given to the states, to satisfy the proponents of state sovereignty, and to the people, according to their numbers, to satisfy the proponents of union. The legislature would then be partly national and partly federal. Proportional representation in the first branch, in conformity with the national principle, "would secure the large States against the small," while "an equality of voices" in the second branch would "secure the small states against the large." Ellsworth hoped "that on this middle ground a compromise would take place," and, after a little more debate, it did.

A crucial battle had apparently been won, though the impression remained that a basic Federalist principle had been sacrificed. Jonathan Dayton of New Jersey dubbed the Connecticut Compromise "an amphibious monster." The Senate having been made "a palladium of residuary sovereignty," he foresaw that "seeds of rivalry" would be planted. Nationalists insisted that no government could be solid or lasting unless representation were based on the people. Gunning Bedford of Delaware observed that there was "no middle way between a perfect consolidation and a mere confederacy of States"; yet he, like the majority, accepted the compromise, being willing to put off correction of the defects "10, 15, or 20 years."

The Connecticut Compromise has occupied an important place in the development of American political thought, as much for what it did not do as for what it did. It not only made possible the continuation and triumphant conclusion of the Convention by providing a precedent for resolution of other conflicts, but also began what has since become traditional in American politics—an inclination toward compromise. It did not, however, resolve the issue that underlay the debate—that of the nature of the Union. It failed to meet James Wilson's valid point: "Can we forget for whom we are forming a government? Is it for men, or for the imaginary beings called States? . . . It is all a mere illusion of names. We talk of States, till we forget what they are composed of." The immediate effect of the Connecticut Compromise was to break a deadlock; the long-run consequence was to bolster a states' rights psychology, leading directly to the Kentucky and Virginia Resolutions of 1798, the Hartford Convention of 1812, the Nullification Act of 1832, and finally to secession and the Civil War. It was only after the war's conclusion that the ambiguity created by the Connecticut Compromise was resolved. But not entirely so: the seeds of controversy planted in that historic compromise of 1787 are still bearing fruit today.[13]

THE LEGISLATURE

The delegates agreed almost without comment that the national legislature ought to consist of two houses. Influenced by Montesquieu and more

---

[13] See Mason, *The States Rights Debate* and Eidelberg, *Philosophy of the Constitution.*

recently by Adams's *Defence of the Constitutions*, the delegates quickly accepted a division of legislative power as an essential of free government. It was less easy to agree on the proper basis for the selection of the legislature. In some quarters "the people" were very much distrusted. Thus, Roger Sherman (1721–1793) of Connecticut, prominent in both colonial and state politics, argued that the people "want information and are constantly liable to be misled." They should "have as little to do as may be" with the government. Elbridge Gerry (1744–1814), one of Massachusetts's leading statesmen, agreed wholeheartedly. He was "still republican but had been taught by experience the danger of the levilling spirit." To Gerry republican government meant government by "men of honor and character," not government by the people. "The evils we experience," he remarked, "flow from the excess of democracy. The people do not want virtue; but are the dupes of pretended patriots." In practical terms, therefore, both Sherman and Gerry advocated a minimal role for the people and suggested indirect election of both houses of the Congress by state legislatures.

On the other side, George Mason (1725–1792), author of the Virginia Declaration of Rights, argued that republican government meant government by men who knew and sympathized with every part of the community, men taken from the people in different parts of the Republic. Nor did the current reaction against democratic excesses in the state legislatures alter Mason's conviction. Although there had formerly been too much democracy, the Convention should not "incautiously run into the opposite extreme." "Notwithstanding the oppressions and injustice experienced among us from democracy," Mason cautioned, "the genius of the people is in favor of it, and the genius of the people must be consulted." James Wilson endorsed these sentiments. For him republicanism entailed "as broad a basis as possible [for] the federal pyramid." It required a government which enjoyed "the confidence of the people." Wilson thought the people should be permitted to choose their own representatives. Besides, the state legislatures were already strong enough without making them the electors of the national legislature.

James Madison likewise considered popular election of at least one of the two houses of Congress "as essential to every plan of free government," and he opposed pushing the people too far into the background, lest the "necessary sympathy between them and their rulers and officers [be] too little felt." Madison was convinced that the new government would be much more stable and durable "if it should rest on the solid foundation of the people themselves than if it should stand merely on the pillars of the Legislatures."

The prevailing view appeared to be that democracy needed restraint, not elimination, and that the democratic principle was not applicable to both houses of Congress. If free government required that at least one branch of the legislature be drawn directly from the people, it was equally important that the other branch represent the states. James Wilson insisted that every part of the national government "ought to flow immediately from the legitimate source of all authority . . . the people at large," divided into "proper districts" for the purpose of choosing members of the Senate. But a majority of the delegates preferred election of the upper house by the states, thus assuring that the "Citizens of the States would be represented both *individually* and *collectively*."[14] Election of the Senate by the state legislatures was favored "as a method of representing the states as states in the national government. . . . Both from former habit and present reasons . . . a federated republic [was preferred] to a consolidated nation."[15]

Madison provided the clearest exposition of why the upper house should be removed from control of the people themselves. It would balance the "impetuous counsels" apt to emanate from the lower house, whose members (unlike the enlightened members of the Senate) were apt to err "from fickleness and passion." More important, the Senate would serve as the guardian of minorities. Madison again referred to the different classes and interests into which society was divided and the ever-present danger that "the major interest might under sudden impulses be tempted to commit injustice on the minority." Reminding the delegates that the population was not even then "one homogeneous mass," Madison warned:

> In framing a system which we wish to last for ages, we should not lose sight of the changes which ages will produce. An increase in population will of necessity increase the proportion of those who will labour under all the hardships of life, and secretly sigh for a more equal distribution of its blessings. These may in time outnumber those who are placed above the feelings of indigence. According to the equal laws of suffrage, the power will slide into the hands of the former.

Madison thought that the creation of a body in the government "sufficiently respectable for its wisdom and virtue" to throw its weight on the side of minorities would be both proper and effective. In short, the Senate would "supply the defects which our own experience has particularly pointed out." Much the same views were expressed by Gouverneur Morris (1752–1816), who helped draft New York's first state constitution before he moved to Philadelphia about 1780. The object of the second house was "to check the precipitation, changeableness, and excesses of the first branch." Like Madison and Hamilton, Morris had watched state legislatures in action, and he dreaded the possibility that similar excesses might occur in the national legislature. They would not if "the popular interest," represented in the lower house, were checked by "the aristocratic interest," represented in the upper. Like Adams and Franklin, Morris recognized the danger from the rich. Properly constituted, "a select and sagacious body of men" would also serve as a check on them. "A firm government alone can protect our liberties. . . . We should remember

---

[14] The words of William Pierce, June 6, 1787, Farrand, *Records*, I, 137.
[15] Van Doren, *Great Rehearsal*, p. 70.

that the people never act from reason alone. The rich will take advantage of their passions and make these the instruments for oppressing them. . . . The only security against encroachments will be a [Senate] instituted to watch against them on all sides."

The other question to settle was the extent of power that would be given to the national legislature. Should these powers be left indefinite or specifically enumerated? Alert to possible inroads on the states, Hugh Williamson of North Carolina objected that to leave them indefinite might be to "restrain the States from regulating their internal" affairs. Indefinite power in the central authority would, Elbridge Gerry objected, "enslave the States." Hamilton, Madison, and Wilson stood firm, the last explaining that it was impossible to draw a line dividing state and national powers. "When we come near the line," he explained, "it cannot be found. . . . A discretion must be left on one side or the other. . . . Will it not be most safely lodged on the side of the National Government? . . . What danger is there that the whole will unnecessarily sacrifice a part? But reverse the case, and leave the whole at the mercy of each part, and will not the general interest be continually sacrificed to local interests?" A "middle ground" was apparently found.[16] Proposed for ratification was a national government of powers that were enumerated but still "indefinite" under the "necessary and proper" clause. Like the Connecticut Compromise, this decision has also had a far-reaching effect.

THE EXECUTIVE BRANCH

American experience before 1787 offered no example of a republican executive, and "the British model . . . was inapplicable to the situation of this country; the extent of which was so great, and the manners so republican. . . ."[17] Nor was the example of the state or colonial governors particularly helpful. The greater diversity of opinion regarding the executive can be seen by comparing Articles I and II of the finished Constitution. The detailed nature of the former was possible because the framers were in basic agreement about the legislature; the brevity and restraint of the latter reflects diverse opinions and lack of experience with an appropriate executive.

The Virginia Plan called for a separately constituted executive, but it did not specify whether it should be single or plural. The New Jersey Plan spoke of "Executives." The delegates shied away from a single executive, not so much because they disliked the idea as because it was inevitably associated with British monarchy. Like Edmund Randolph, the delegates recognized that "the fixt genius of the people of America required a different form of Government." On the other hand, their experience with a plural executive under the Articles of Confederation

---

[16] See Robert H. Birkby, "Politics of Accommodation: The Origin of the Supremacy Clause," *Western Political Quarterly*, XIX (March, 1966), 123–35.

[17] The words of James Wilson, June 1, 1787, Farrand, *Records*, I, 66.

had been disillusioning. In the end they adopted the single executive (despite its unhappy associations) not only because it would produce the most energy, vigor, and dispatch, but also because it would "feel the greatest responsibility and administer the public affairs best."[18] Roger Sherman's suggestion that "the Executive magistracy [was] nothing more than an institution for carrying the will of the Legislature into effect" and should therefore consist of whatever number that body should from time to time decide was fortunately rejected.

Both the Virginia and New Jersey Plans proposed election of the executive by the national legislature. To their authors, as to most of the delegates to the Convention, Gouverneur Morris being perhaps the outstanding exception, this seemed to be the only logical method of election consistent with republicanism. Morris argued that the president "ought to be elected by the people at large, by the freeholders of the Country." This seemed the only logical method consistent with republicanism. The Convention agreed with George Mason—that "a Government which is to last ought at least to be practicable." This would not be the case "if the . . . election should be left to the people at large . . . It would be as unnatural to refer the choice of a proper character for Chief Magistrate to the people, as it would, to refer a trial of colours to a blind man. The extent of the Country renders it impossible that the people can have the requisite capacity to judge of the respective pretensions of the candidates."

Objections were also raised to election by the legislature. Morris thought a president so elected would become "the mere creature of the Legislature." James Wilson contended that "a particular objection . . . against . . . election by the Legislature was that the Executive in that case would be too dependent to stand the mediator between the intrigues and sinister views of the Representatives and the general interests and liberties of the people." Invoking the principle of the separation of powers, Madison asked how independence in the executive could be assured if the president were dependent on Congress for his appointment? "A dependence of the Executive on the Legislature, would render it the Executor as well as the maker of laws; and . . . according to the observations of Montesquieu, tyrannical laws may be made [to] be executed in a tyrannical manner. . . . It [is] absolutely necessary to a well constituted Republic that the two . . . should be kept distinct and independent of each other."

These arguments carried the day, but rejection of both popular choice and legislative election left the Convention without a solution. A number of alternatives were presented, but none were acceptable, either on practical or theoretical grounds. Finally, it was agreed that election by electors squared with republicanism and did not present the difficulties of the other modes. James Wilson had suggested something like the Electoral College early in the summer, and finally, near the end of the session, the Convention adopted the idea without enthusiasm. Perhaps nothing

---

[18] The words of John Rutledge, June 1, 1787, Farrand, *Records*, I, 65.

revealed so clearly the Founding Fathers' distrust of democracy as the Electoral College. Indeed, the reluctant adoption of the College reveals the dilemma the Convention continually faced. As realists they distrusted the people both collectively and as individuals, but they did not feel that the people either could or should be ignored. The Electoral College took cognizance of both horns of the dilemma, and as unsatisfactory as it had first appeared, it was therefore acceptable.

The dilemma arose again in the discussion of executive functions. It was agreed, as Gouverneur Morris described it, that "one great object of the Executive is to control the Legislature. The Legislature will continually seek to aggrandize and perpetuate themselves; and will seize those critical moments produced by war, invasion or convulsion for that purpose. It is necessary then that the Executive Magistrate should be the guardian of the people, even of the lower classes, against Legislative tyranny. . . ." While Morris contended that the people must be admitted into republican government, he believed, as well, that they must be protected against themselves. Madison expressed the same thought:

> Experience had proved a tendency in our governments to throw all power into the Legislative vortex. The Executives of the States are in general little more than Cyphers; the legislatures omnipotent. If no effectual check be devised for restraining the instability and encroachments of the latter, a revolution of some kind or other would be inevitable. The preservation of Republican Government therefore required some expedient for the purpose, but required evidently at the same time that in devising it, the genuine principles of that form should be kept in view.

One such expedient was the executive veto. Despite George Mason's objection that a veto would "give up all the rights of the people to a single Magistrate," and Franklin's fear that such a device would enable the executive officer to extort money from the legislature, the Convention adopted it. Acceptance of the veto, like the use of so many other checks and balances, reflects the Founding Fathers' concern that popular power needed restraint.

The framers were less sure of the other functions the executive should perform; in the end they left the definition of "executive power" to the president himself, thereby providing a far more powerful executive than might have been expected.

Both plans before the Convention proposed that the executive be ineligible for a second time, primarily because both conceived that he would be chosen by the legislature and thus would inevitably court legislative favor throughout his first term. After considerable debate, and after the Electoral College scheme was agreed upon, that idea was abandoned. What effect, Gouverneur Morris asked, would limiting the eligibility of the executive have?

> 1. It will destroy the great incitement to merit public esteem by taking away the hope of being rewarded with a reappointment. . . . The love of

fame is the great spring to noble and illustrious actions. Shut the Civil road to glory and he may be compelled to seek it by the sword. 2. It will tempt him to make the most of the short space of time allotted him, to accumulate wealth and provide for his friends. 3. It will produce violations of the very Constitution it is meant to secure. In moments of pressing danger the tried abilities and established character of a favorite magistrate will prevail over respect for the forms of the Constitution.

Morris's views prevailed; the final draft of the Constitution contained no mention of reeligibility.

Nor did either plan originally visualize a four-year term. Instead, both contemplated long terms—perhaps seven years. On the Convention floor some sentiment was expressed in favor of service "during good behavior." Morris, outspoken in favor of popular election of the president, seconded a motion "to strike out seven years, and insert 'during good behavior.' " "This [is] the way to get a good Government," he exclaimed. He was "indifferent how the Executive should be chosen, provided he held his place by this tenure." Madison thought a long term would be a better guarantee of executive independence than a short one. The four-year term was settled upon as a compromise, for it seemed long enough to pull the executive a little away from the people, but not long enough to let him forget them.

THE JUDICIARY

Virtually every member of the Convention considered an independent national judiciary essential to free government. The details—namely, the mode of its appointment, the tenure of its judges, and its jurisdiction— were settled with remarkable speed. There was less agreement upon judicial organization. No one opposed the creation of the Supreme Court, but states' rights sympathizers argued that the national government should use state tribunals as its courts of first instance, and that from them an appeal to the Supreme Court would be sufficient to protect the national interest and secure the uniformity necessary in a federal system. Federalists, on the other hand, reasoned that such a scheme would provide no adequate protection from local prejudice in the first—and often only— trial and that it would lead to an overwhelming number of appeals to the Supreme Court. They urged, therefore, the establishment of national inferior courts. The Convention, unable to decide which line of thinking to accept, finally left the establishment of inferior courts to Congress.

Convention discussion did not focus directly on judicial review, for it was assumed by virtually everyone that courts might properly pass judgment on the constitutionality of legislative acts. Debate arose, however, in connection with the proposed Council of Revision. Better than any other source except *Federalist* Numbers 78–82, this debate illuminates contemporary opinion of the judiciary's role in a free society. All arguments stressed the value of judicial review as a check on popular power.

James Wilson, to be one of the first justices appointed to the Supreme Court, declared that

> the Judiciary ought to have an opportunity of remonstrating against projected encroachments on the people . . . Laws may be unjust, may be unwise, may be dangerous, may be destructive; and yet not be so unconstitutional as to justify the Judges in refusing to give them effect. Let them have a share in the Revisionary power, and they will have an opportunity of taking notice of these characters [sic] of a law, and of counteracting, by the weight of their opinions the improper views of the Legislature.

Madison thought the council would be "useful to the Community at large as an additional check against a pursuit of those unwise and unjust measures which constituted so great a portion of our calamities" during the Confederation. George Mason described its greatest advantage as restraint against the passage of "unjust and pernicious laws." "It would have the effect not only of hindering the final passage of such laws; but would discourage demagogues from attempting to get them passed. . . ."

But should judges, it was asked, be associated with the enterprise? Could they be presumed to possess any peculiar knowledge of public policy? To Elbridge Gerry such a council not only would combine the three branches of government, but also would make "Statesmen of the Judges." It would make judges—who, he thought, would represent the people better than the executive—"the guardians of the Rights of the people." Luther Martin (1748–1826)

> considered the association of the Judges with the Executive as a dangerous innovation; as well as one which could not produce the particular advantage expected from it. A knowledge of mankind, and of Legislative affairs cannot be presumed to belong in a higher degree to the Judges than to the Legislature . . . As to the Constitutionality of laws, that point will come before the Judges in their proper official character. In this character they have a negative on the laws. Join them with the Executive in the Revision and they will have a double negative. It is necessary that the Supreme Judiciary should have the confidence of the people. This will soon be lost, if they are employed in the task of remonstrating against popular measures of the Legislature.

The thought was also expressed that judges were of all men the least fit for the function assigned to them in the plan for the Council of Revision: "Judges ought never to give their opinion on a law until it comes before them."[19]

The final decision of the Convention was to omit the revisionary function altogether, both as institutionalized in a council and as formulated in Madison's proposal that all acts before they become laws should be submitted to the Supreme Court as well as to the president for approval. Despite this omission the framers expressed themselves almost unani-

---

[19] The words of John Rutledge, July 21, 1787, Farrand, *Records*, II, 80.

mously in favor of a strong and positive role for the judiciary. Only a handful disapproved of the doctrine that judges as expositors of the Constitution should have authority to declare a law void. The vast majority agreed with Gouverneur Morris that the courts should decline to give the weight of the law to "a direct violation of the Constitution." Such a control over the legislature might have its inconveniences, Morris admitted, but it was nevertheless necessary. "The most virtuous citizens," he reasoned, "will often as members of a legislative body concur in measures which afterwards in their private capacity they will be ashamed of." Republican government must of necessity offer some protection against this tendency, and the courts should rightfully be empowered to give it. So much support for judicial review is further evidence that the framers lacked faith in the people: they distrusted unrestrained popular government and unqualified majority rule.

THE BASIS OF REPRESENTATION

Perhaps the knottiest problems arose in trying to determine the proper basis for popular representation in the House of Representatives and qualifications for suffrage and office holding. It was one thing to agree on a tripartite government and to cast a role for the people in one of those parts; it was quite another to decide who was to fill it. Some, James Wilson among them, felt that "with respect to this object, as well as to other *personal* rights, numbers were surely the natural and precise measure of Representation." Charles Pinckney agreed with Wilson on the more limited ground that the number of inhabitants was "the only just and practicable rule." Several others, Gouverneur Morris outstanding among them, thought that numbers—along with another measure such as property—were the proper standard. As Morris put it, "Property ought to be taken into the estimate as well as the number of inhabitants. [If] Life and Liberty were generally said to be of more value than property, [an] accurate view of the matter would nevertheless prove that property was the main object of Society. [As such] certainly it ought to be one measure of the influence due to those who were to be affected by the Government."

Most men considered property the principal value of society, the great object of government—"the only just measure of representation." The majority, echoing General Ireton at Putney over a century before, believed that men without property were not to be trusted with political power. As Madison told the delegates:

> Viewing the subject on its merits alone, the freeholders of the country would be the safest depositories of Republican liberty. In future times a great majority of the people will not only be without landed, but [without] any other sort of property. These will either combine under the influence of their common situation, in which case, the rights of property and the public liberty [will not be secure]; or which is more probable, they will become

the tools of opulence and ambition, in which case there will be equal danger on another side.

There was another reason that property should be the rule for representation: sectionalism demanded it. If numbers were made the rule, it was feared that "the Atlantic states will be subjected to the Western." Said Gouverneur Morris: "Numbers would [not] be a just rule at any time. . . . Among other objections it must be apparent they would not be able to furnish men equally enlightened, to share in the administration of our common interests. The busy haunts of men, not the remote wilderness, [are] the proper school of political talents. If the Western people get the power into their hands they will ruin the Atlantic interests. The Back members are always most averse to the best measures."

Just as the Founding Fathers felt strongly about property as the basis for representation, they regarded it also as the proper basis for the suffrage and for political office. Restricting the vote and office holding to property holders was a "necessary defence against the dangerous influence of those multitudes without property and without principle, with which our Country like all others, will in time abound."[20] Property and principle, property and wisdom, were generally equated.

Surprisingly, however, these conservative views did not prevail. The Convention finally entrusted the election of the House simply to "the People of the several States."[21] Despite its almost unanimous conviction, the Convention could not, Mason argued, raise a property barrier in the Constitution, because eight or nine states had already "extended the right of suffrage beyond the freeholders. What will the people there say, if they should be disfranchised?" Besides, Mason went on, most people felt "too strongly the remains of ancient prejudices." Because the proponents of property had won out in England, and a freehold was a qualification there, "it is imagined to be the only proper one" for America. In truth, however, as Colonel Rainboro had pointed out at Putney, every man "having evidence of attachment to and permanent common interest with the Society ought to share in all its rights and privileges." Property was not the only evidence of a permanent attachment. "Ought the merchant, the monied man, the parent of a number of children whose fortunes are to be pursued in [this country], to be viewed as suspicious characters, and unworthy to be trusted with the common rights of their fellow Citizens?"

Practical arguments also led the framers to omit a constitutional prescription for office holding. In spite of their strong bent toward property as a requirement for participation in public affairs, the delegates rejected it as an idea they feared and mistrusted. They created a system of government that would lessen the dangers of popular participation, or at least alleviate them. Checks and balances, federalism, an indirectly chosen

---

[20] The words of John Dickinson, August 7, 1787, Farrand, *Records*, II, 202.
[21] Article I, section 2 of the Constitution.

Senate to exercise a restraining hand, a strong executive equally remote from the people, and an independent judiciary to guard the Constitution and to keep the several parts of the Republic in balance—these would operate to keep popular passion and ignorance in check. With such a system the framers believed the country would be safe, even in the people's hands.

The matter of representation fell afoul of a question that plagued the Convention until near the end. Delegates from Southern states argued that regardless of whether property or numbers were the rule for representation, slaves should be included along with the white people in the final count. Northern delegates rejected this idea. Did that mean, asked William Paterson, that if property were accepted as the basis for representation, a man in Virginia would have "a number of votes in proportion to the number of his slaves?" Or, if numbers were chosen, would Southerners demand that Negroes be represented in the general government when they were not represented as such in the states "to which they belong"? To Gouverneur Morris claims for Negro representation set up a distinction between Northern and Southern states. He could not see why only Negroes should win specific mention among the many kinds of property. Southern delegates countered with the argument that for the very reason that slaves were property—and an especially valuable kind of property at that—"an equal representation ought to be allowed for them in a Government which was instituted principally for the protection of property, and was itself supported by property."[22]

No logical solution presented itself; Southern delegates remained adamant in the belief that slave representation be allowed. In the end it was agreed that three-fifths of the slaves should be entitled to representation. As George Mason said, slaves, valuable though they were, were not equal to freemen and therefore should not be equally represented; but "the Southern States [had] this peculiar species of property, over and above the other species of property common to all the States," and this was entitled to some representation. The three-fifths figure was chosen as a compromise, and as with other compromises that went into the Constitution, it could not be explained so much in terms of logic and theory as on grounds of practical necessity.

THE NEW CONSTITUTION IS SIGNED

By August 6 a printed first draft of the Constitution was made available to the delegates; a revised second printing was ready by September 12. On September 17, 1787, 109 days after the delegates had convened, the convention completed its task. Two days later the delegates released the document to the public; they did so with misgivings. "It is too probable," Washington solemnly told the delegates, "that no plan we propose will

---

[22] The words of Pierce Butler, July 11, 1787, Farrand, *Records*, I, 580–81.

be adopted. Perhaps another dreadful conflict is to be sustained. If, *to please the people*, we offer what we ourselves disapprove, how can we afterward defend our work? Let us raise a standard to which the wise and the honest can repair; the event is in the hands of God. . . ."[23]

Although Washington and others were doubtful, the document framed by the Convention has served to round out the American political creed.

Far from representing seizure of power by a few American aristocrats, as charged by Beard, the Constitution was in fact the logical conclusion of the revolutionary effort, creating a government consistent with the dominant middle-class values and ideas of the nation.[24] It was itself revolutionary,[25] not only in the sense that it went into effect on ratification by nine states instead of by all (as required by the Articles of Confederation for amendment), but also in the more fundamental sense that it derived its authority from the people and rested on their consent. In *Federalist* Number 43, Madison invoked "the absolute necessity of the case; the great principle of self-preservation; the transcendent law of nature and of nature's God, which declares that the safety and happiness of society are the objects at which all political institutions aim, and to which all such institutions must be sacrificed." Reverting to Jefferson's positive concept of "revolution," Madison held that it was available as an original power in the people, to be used not only against acts of oppression but also in securing their safety and happiness. By adopting the Constitution they would perform the ultimate act of sovereignty.

The Declaration of Independence and the Articles of Confederation emphasized individual rights and popular power, weak government and legislative supremacy. The Constitution recognized the defects in such an imbalance and corrected them, without overturning the basic principles that underlay them. Thus, it provided processes through which the people might exercise political authority, safeguarded from the violence of popular passion. At the same time it brought strength and order to government and introduced a balance of power between the various organs and units of government.

If not wholly satisfactory to anyone, it was an acceptable representation of the best efforts of its framers, reflecting the belief that perhaps no better constitution could ever be produced. The tasks ahead were still formidable. Conventions in nine states had to ratify the Constitution before it would become effective. As the delegates left Independence Hall, the words of Morris and Hamilton rang in their ears. Upon the adoption of the Constitution, Morris had said, rested the answer to "the great question . . . shall there be a national Government or not? . . . this must take place or a general anarchy will be the alternative." Admitting that "no man's ideas were more remote from the plan [adopted] than

---

[23] Mason, *Free Government*, p. 192.
[24] For a detailed examination of this thesis, see Robert E. Brown, *Reinterpretation of the Formation of the American Constitution* (Boston: Boston University Press, 1963).
[25] See Madison's *Federalist* Number 40.

his own," Hamilton felt that it was impossible "to deliberate between anarchy and convulsion, on one side, and the chance of good arising from the plan, on the other."

Friends of the Constitution were soberly reflective and hopeful. Franklin dramatized the moment: as the last members of the convention filed past him to sign the Constitution, he observed to those around him that he had wondered throughout the Convention whether the sun painted on the wall back of the president's chair was a rising or a setting sun. As he saw delegate after delegate affix his signature, Franklin had, at last, "the happiness to know that it [was] a rising . . . sun."

CHAPTER SIX

THE CONSTITUTION CRITICIZED, EXPLAINED, AND ENDORSED

The framers of the Constitution were uncertain of the soundness of their proposal; they were even more so of its ratification. Without either blessings or encouragement, Congress, to which a draft had been submitted on September 20, merely passed the Constitution on to the states "in conformity to the resolves of the Convention."[1]

The first reactions in the states were favorable: Delaware, Pennsylvania, and New Jersey ratified within ten days of each other in December; Georgia and Connecticut followed in January. By June 21, 1788, conventions in Massachusetts, Maryland, South Carolina, and New Hampshire had brought the number of ratifying states to the required nine. The Constitution could then, in accordance with the words of Article VII, be put into operation "between the States so ratifying the same." Virginia ratified five days later, and New York within the next month. The expiring Congress thereupon notified the states of ratification and arranged for the election of a new Congress and a president. March 4, 1789 was appointed as the day for the new government to begin functioning. On

---

[1] For various resolutions leading to the Convention and the Constitution, see *Federalist* Number 40.

April 30 President Washington was inaugurated, only a little over nineteen months after the Constitutional Convention had adjourned.

So rapid an acceptance by the people did not mean that the framers' forebodings were groundless. The Constitution went into effect with far from unanimous approval and with bitter opposition. It is probable that only a minority favored its adoption. The rest either were indifferent or were actively opposed to ratification. In the Massachusetts, New Hampshire, Virginia, and New York conventions, the conflict was bitter and the final votes close—Massachusetts, 187 to 168; New Hampshire, 57 to 47; Virginia, 89 to 79; and New York, 30 to 27. North Carolina's convention was so hostile that it voted in July 1788, 184 to 83, to postpone ratification until a long string of amendments was adopted. It did not enter the Union until November 21, 1789. Rhode Island resisted even longer. It was May 29, 1790, before sufficient support could be mustered to secure its endorsement. In those six states, and in some of the others as well, approval came only after a stubborn fight, in the process of which another pamphlet war was waged.[2] The antifederalists, as opponents of ratification were quickly tagged, fought against it strenuously.

CRITICISM FROM PARIS

Jefferson's reaction from Paris was that there were "very good articles in it, and very bad. I do not know which preponderate."[3] He had not expected such sweeping changes and the establishment of so strong a national government, suspecting that the "convention ha[d] been too much impressed by the insurrection of Massachusetts; and in the spur of the moment they are setting up a kite to keep the hen yard in order." Rather than react so sharply, the Convention, Jefferson thought, might have accepted such popular outbursts as inevitable, and he gloried in a rebellion "so honorably conducted." "God forbid," he went on, "we should ever be twenty years without such a rebellion. . . . The tree of liberty must be refreshed from time to time with the blood of patriots and tyrants. It is its natural manure."

Jefferson was displeased not only by the Convention's overreaction but also by its procedures. He was critical of the Convention's secrecy: "I am

---

[2] On the closeness of the ratification fight, see the map on p. 118 of Richard B. Morris, ed., *Encyclopedia of American History* (New York: Harper & Row, 1961). For a general work on the opposing sides, see John D. Lewis, ed., *Anti-Federalists versus Federalists: Selected Documents* (San Francisco: Chandler, 1967). See also Cecelia M. Kenyon, *The Anti-Federalists* (Indianapolis: Bobbs-Merrill, 1966); Jackson T. Main, *The Antifederalists, Critics of the Constitution, 1781–1788* (Chapel Hill, N.C.: Universty of North Carolina Press, 1961); and Morton Borden, ed., *The Antifederalist Papers* (East Lansing, Mich.: Michigan State University Press, 1965).

[3] Jefferson's criticisms are found in a number of letters to various correspondents in *The Writings of Thomas Jefferson*, VI, 8–11, 227, 259, 371–73, 380, 386–89, 394, and VII, 36–37, 322.

sorry they began their deliberations by so abominable a precedent as that of tying up the tongues of their members."

His objections also included matters of substance. "As to the Constitution," he wrote Edward Carrington, "There is a great mass of good in it . . . but there is also to me, a bitter pill or two." Jefferson spelled out his feeling to Madison:

> I like much the general idea of framing a government, which should go on of itself, peaceably, without needing continual recurrence to the State legislatures. I like the organization of the government into legislative, judiciary and executive. I like the power given the legislature to levy taxes, and for that reason solely, I approve of the greater house being chosen by the people directly. For though I think a house so chosen . . . will be very illy qualified to legislate for the Union, for foreign nations etc., yet this evil does not weigh against the good of preserving inviolate the fundamental principle that the people are not to be taxed but by representatives immediately chosen by themselves.
>
> I am captivated by the compromise of the opposite claims of the great and little States, of the latter to equal and the former to proportional influence. I am much pleased, too, with the substitution of the method of voting by person, instead of that of voting by States; and I like the negative given to the Executive, conjointly with a third of either House. . . . There are other good things of less moment.
>
> I will now tell you what I do not like. First, the omission of a bill of rights, providing clearly and without aid of sophism, for freedom of religion, freedom of the press, protection against standing armies, restriction of monopolies, the eternal and unremitting force of the habeas corpus laws, and trials by jury in all matters of fact triable by the laws of the land, and not by the laws of nations. . . . Let me add, that a bill of rights is what the people are entitled to against every government on earth, general or particular; and what no just government should refuse or rest on inference.

Jefferson also made clear his dislike of the failure to provide for rotation in office, particularly in the presidency. Coming across the Atlantic just as the battle for ratification was intensifying, these opinions supplied the antifederalists with potent ammunition in the battle against ratification. In so using Jefferson's comments, they aligned him on the wrong side, for he was finally persuaded that "the great mass and groundwork [of the Constitution] was good" and that its adoption was to be "prayed for." By March 1789 reflection had even led him to conclude that "the Constitution . . . is unquestionably the wisest ever yet presented to men. . . ."

Throughout the debates Jefferson was apparently less concerned with what the delegates had accomplished than with how they had done it. Apart from the secrecy of its procedures, the Convention was for him a happy demonstration of the effectiveness of reason in statecraft. Here was gratifying proof of how varying interests and divergent opinions could be brought into constructive accord by "assembling the wise men of the State, instead of assembling armies." "We can surely boast of having set the world a beautiful example of a government reformed by reason alone without bloodshed."

Even though Jefferson finally supported the Constitution, his "influence on opinion" was, as Dumas Malone said, "probably against the Constitution, since his earliest comments were the least favorable and the fight in America was practically over before anybody there was informed of his final acceptance of the new frame of government."[4] Jefferson's criticism of the Constitution embarrassed Madison, particularly in the Virginia ratifying convention. Invoking this high authority, Patrick Henry rose in the convention to point out how "this illustrious citizen advises you to reject this government till it be amended. . . . At a great distance from us, he remembers and studies our happiness . . . he thinks . . . of bills of rights—thinks of those little despised things called *maxims*. Let us follow the sage advice of this common friend of our happiness."[5]

CRITICISM AT HOME:
THE ANTI-FEDERALIST CASE

Yates and Lansing

Besides the incalculable advantage of Jefferson's apparent support, the antifederalists were greatly assisted by the argument of four delegates to the Constitutional Convention. In New York, Robert Yates (1738–1801), a state supreme court judge, and John Lansing (1754–1829), mayor of Albany—neither of whom had played a prominent role in the Convention—were among the new Constitution's bitterest foes. Indeed, they left Philadelphia in mid-July and returned home to oppose the Convention's work. Both were extremely suspicious of the trend toward centralization so clearly manifest in the Convention. Writing in the *New York Journal* of June 13, 1788, under the name "Sydney," Yates gave a lurid account of the doings in Philadelphia:

> We can scarcely entertain a doubt but that a plan has long since been framed to subvert the confederation; that that plan has been matured with the most persevering industry and unremitted attention, and that the objects expressed in the preamble to the constitution, that is "to promote the general welfare and secure the blessings of liberty to ourselves and our posterity," were merely the ostensible, and not the real reasons of its framers. [The Convention's] . . . journals have not been published even to this day, but will no doubt continue buried in the dark womb of suspicious secrecy. . . .[6]

---

[4] Quoted in Dumas Malone, *Jefferson and the Rights of Man* (Boston: Little, Brown, 1951), p. 170.
[5] Jonathan Elliot, *The Debates in the Several State Conventions on the Adoption of the Federal Constitution* (Philadelphia: Lippincott, 1901), III, 152–53. The correspondence between Jefferson and Madison on the Bill of Rights, including their shifting positions, is reprinted in Mason, *The States Rights Debate*, pp. 170–89.
[6] P. L. Ford, ed., *Essays on the Constitution of the United States . . . 1787–1788* (Brooklyn: Historical Printing Club, 1892), p. 298.

Back in New York, Yates and Lansing disregarded the Convention's pledge of secrecy and warned Governor Clinton, and through him the people of New York, that "a consolidation of the United States into one government" was an imminent possibility.[7] They contended that the powers under which the Convention had acted did not contemplate abandonment of the principle of state sovereignty and that it was utterly impracticable, on the grounds of distance and expense, to think of establishing a general government "pervading every part of the United States, and extending essential benefits to all." The argument that such a government, "however guarded by declarations of rights, or cautionary provisions, must unavoidably, in a short time, be productive of the destruction of the civil liberty of such citizens who could be effectually coerced by it" seemed valid to others besides Yates and Lansing. Throughout the New York campaign antifederalists pressed this point with telling effect.

In his *Letters of Brutus* Yates took judicial review for granted and pointed out its dangers. As he saw it, the judges, under the Constitution, would be beyond reproof—a "situation altogether unprecedented in a free country." Given the "general and indefinite" nature of the Constitution, they would be in a position "to supply what is wanting [in the wording of the Constitution] by their own decisions. . . ." "The reason and spirit of the constitution" would thus be wholly their determination. The worst effect would be the subversion of individual states.

> Every adjudication of the supreme court, on any question that may arise upon the nature and extent of the general government, will affect the limits of the state jurisdiction. In proportion as the former enlarge the exercise of their powers, will that of the latter be restricted.

"If . . . the legislature pass any laws, inconsistent with the sense the judges put upon the constitution, they will declare it void; and therefore in this respect their power is superior to that of the legislature. . . . In short, they are independent of the people, of the legislature, and of every power under heaven. Men placed in this situation will generally soon feel themselves independent of heaven itself."

Elbridge Gerry

Arguments similar to those of Lansing and Yates were marshalled by Elbridge Gerry in Massachusetts. Gerry refused to sign the Constitution, predicting civil war in the United States between the party "devoted to Democracy, the worst . . . of all political evils," and the equally power-

---

[7] Robert Yates and John Lansing, To the Governor of New York, Containing Their Reasons For Not Subscribing to the Federal Constitution, *Senate Documents*, XV, 60th Cong., 2nd sess., 1908–1909, p. 190. See also Yates's *Letters of Brutus*, 1788, published originally in the *New York Journal and Weekly Register* and reprinted in full in E. S. Corwin, *Court over Constitution* (Princeton, N.J.: Princeton University Press, 1938), pp. 231–62. For excerpts, see A. T. Mason, *The States Rights Debate*, pp. 107–13.

ful party at the other extreme.[8] Fearing disaster, he "could not . . . by signing the Constitution pledge himself to abide by it at all events." Having refused to sign the Constitution, Gerry entered the lists against "this many headed monster, of such motley mixture, that its enemies cannot trace a feature of Democratic or Republican extract; nor have its friends the courage to denominate a Monarchy, an Aristocracy, or an Oligarchy. . . ." Instead, it was given "the happy epithet of a *Federal Republic*." The strange form of the Constitution did not bother Gerry so much as the secrecy of its birth, the "rapidity of its growth, and the fatal consequences of suffering it to live to the age of maturity."

Nor were these the only things that troubled him. The Constitution left the limits of judicial power undefined; it did not provide for annual elections; it lacked a bill of rights. "The rights of individuals ought to be the primary object of all government, and cannot be too securely guarded by the most explicit declarations in their favor." Without frequent elections, Gerry feared, growth of corruption in government would occur. Without rotation in office the Union might be the victim of perpetual office holders. He did not like the ambiguity left in the relationship between the executive and legislative branches of the national government. Furthermore, a single legislative body, governing a territory as large as the United States, was "an insuperable objection. . . ."

Gerry assumed that the majority felt as he did. The events of the preceding decade had induced him to favor an indissoluble union, but attachment to the ideal of state sovereignty made acceptable only a union that permitted the states to retain their "separate sovereignties and independence." He opposed the Constitution because it would force the states to become "tributaries to a consolidated fabric of aristocratic tyranny," located in a remote and alien federal city that by the words of the Constitution itself was to be governed independently of the states. Finally, he was sure that the Constitution would lay the foundation for a "Government of *force* and *fraud*," that the people would be bled for taxes at every pore, and that the people's liberties would "soon be terminated."[9]

George Mason

Opposition also came from the venerable George Mason. Prominent throughout the Convention, he had made a wide reputation for breadth of vision, wise judgment, cogent arguments, and devotion to republican government. His early approval of the purposes of the Convention had, however, changed to foreboding; it became increasingly evident to him that a "total alteration" of the confederate form was in prospect. He not only objected to individual items in the draft Constitution, but also abhorred "the precipitate and intemperate, not to say indecent, manner in which the business was conducted during the last weeks of the Conven-

[8] Elbridge Gerry, September 17, 1787, quoted in Farrand, *Records*, II, 647.
[9] Gerry, in Farrand, *Records*, II, 647.

tion, after the patrons of this new plan had a decided majority in their favor."[10]

Although he remained in Philadelphia until the close of the Convention and continued to participate in debate, Mason refused to sign the document and made public his reasons.[11] The absence of a bill of rights worried him, for he feared that because the Constitution was specifically paramount to state laws and constitutions, "declarations of rights, in the separate states" would not be secure after its adoption. He objected also to the fact that "in the House of Representatives there is not the substance, but the shadow only of representation." The Senate, with its power of altering money bills, its influence over the president, and its long and continuous tenure, would effectively "destroy any balance in the government, and enable [it] to accomplish what usurpation [it] pleases, upon the rights and liberties of the people." Mason also criticized the proposed federal court system, fearing it would absorb those of the states. Nor did Mason like the absence of a presidential council to give "proper information and advice." Without such a council the president might become a tool of the Senate or be directed by "minions and favorites" in the government. These features of the new government would render it "a moderate aristocracy" from the beginning, and whether "in its operation [it would] produce a monarchy, or a corrupt oppressive aristocracy" remained to be seen. Moreover, Mason thought it wrong that the federal government was restrained from prohibiting the slave trade for twenty years and that a specific provision had been made against the use of ex post facto laws, which necessity and the public safety might at times require.

Finally, Mason objected to the Constitution's requirement of only a majority of Congress for the passage of legislation affecting commerce and navigation. Therein lay the ruin of the South, "for such rigid and premature regulations may be made, as will enable the merchants of the northern and eastern states not only to demand an exorbitant freight, but to monopolize the purchase of the commodities, at their own price . . . to the great injury of the landed interest, and the impoverishment of the people [of the South]." He also voiced a common fear of Southern planter interests, that the "necessary and proper clause"[12] would permit Congress to extend its power over so wide a field that the state legislatures would have "no security for the powers now presumed to remain to them; or the people for their rights."

---

[10] Quoted in Mason, *Free Government*, p. 243.

[11] Mason's objections were published in the *Philadelphia Packet*, October 4, 1789, and are reprinted in P. L. Ford, *Pamphlets on the Constitution . . . 1787–1788* (Brooklyn: Historical Printing Club, 1888), pp. 327–32 under the title "Objections." For a welcome addition to the literature on Mason, see Robert A. Rutland, ed., *The Papers of George Mason*, (Chapel Hill, N.C.: University of North Carolina Press, 1970).

[12] Article I, section 8, paragraph 18: "The Congress shall have power to make all laws which shall be necessary and proper for carrying into execution the foregoing powers, and all other powers vested by this Constitution in the government of the United States, or in any department thereof."

Richard Henry Lee

Mason's objections were made after serious thought and with patriotic motives. Neither partisan nor quibbling, they were accorded considerable weight, especially in Virginia, where the struggle for ratification was crucial. Also weighty in Virginia were the arguments of Richard Henry Lee (1732–1794), an eminent Virginia statesman, who when the Constitution was made public, vigorously opposed it in the Congress and, in the fall and winter of 1787–1788, published a series of *Letters from the Federal Farmer to the Republican,* aimed at the "deliberate and thinking men, who must establish and secure governments on free principles."[13]

In the first place, Lee thought proponents of the Constitution were much too eager to have it ratified, too anxious to shut the door against examination of its details.

> I see the danger . . . arise principally from the conduct and views of two very unprincipled parties in the United States—two fires, between which the honest and substantial people have long found themselves situated. One party is composed of little insurgents, men in debt, who want no law, and who want a share of the property of others . . . levellers, Shayites. . . . The other party is composed of a few, but more dangerous men [who] avariciously grasp at all power and property . . . [who] dislike . . . free and equal government. . . . Between these two parties is the weight of the community, the men of middling property, men not in debt on the one hand, and men, on the other, content with republican governments, and not aiming at immense fortunes, offices, and powers.

The first party in 1787 had brought forth the Constitutional Convention; there the second party had attempted to establish in great haste "a politer kind of government" than the Articles of Confederation. Lee argued that the Constitution should not be accepted save after close scrutiny and full approval of a majority of the people.

Lee admitted the need for a stronger government, but he questioned whether the Constitution met that need, not being "calculated equally to preserve the rights of all orders of men in the community." As it stood, the Constitution left too little power in the hands of the people and permitted too much to be exercised by the "artful and ever active aristocracy." A bill of rights would "give security to the just rights of human nature; and better secure from injury the discordant interests of the different parts of this union." He anticipated that the Constitution would change the United States from thirteen republics into "one consolidated government." With remarkable foresight, he observed: "Whether such a change can ever be effected in any manner; whether it can be effected without convulsions and civil wars; whether such a change will not totally destroy the liberties of this country—time only can determine."

---

[13] Lee's Letters are reproduced in Ford, *Pamphlets,* pp. 277–325.

LUTHER MARTIN,
PATRICK HENRY, AND SAMUEL ADAMS

"It is, in its very *introduction*," Luther Martin complained of the new Constitution, "declared to be a compact between the people of the United States, as individuals; and it is to be ratified by the *people* at large, in their capacity *as individuals*." All this "would be quite right and proper, if there were *no State Governments*, if *all the people* of this continent were in a *state of nature*, and we were forming one *national government* for *them as individuals*."[14] For Martin even the equality of state representation in the Senate could not disguise "their favorite object—destruction of the State governments and the introduction of Monarchy." It was, he said, "only consenting, after they had struggled to put *both their feet on our necks*, to take *one of them off*, provided we would consent to let them *keep the other on*, when they knew . . . that by being permitted to keep on that one foot, they should *afterwards be able to place the other foot on whenever they pleased*."

Patrick Henry (1736–1799), one of Virginia's most prominent lawyers, explained why members of the Convention proposed alteration, not revision, of the Articles:

> I am sure they [members of the Convention] were fully impressed with the necessity of forming a great consolidated government, instead of a confederation. That this is a consolidated system is demonstrably clear, and the danger of such a government is, to my mind, very striking. I have the highest veneration for those gentlemen, but, sir, give me leave to demand, What right had they to say, *We, the People?* My political curiosity, exclusive of my anxious solicitude for the public welfare, leads me to ask, Who authorized them to speak the language of *We, the People*, instead of *We, the States?* . . . If the states be not the agents of this compact, it must be one great, consolidated, national government of the people of all the states.[15]

Samuel Adams (1722–1803) sounded the same note in Massachusetts:

> I am not able to conceive why the Wisdom of the Convention led them to give Preference to the former [national government] before the latter [sovereign states]. If the several states in the Union are to become one entire Nation, under one Legislature, the powers of which shall extend to every Subject of Legislation, and its laws be Supreme and control the whole, the Idea of Sovereignty in those States must be lost. . . . I confess, as I enter the Building I stumble at the Threshold. I meet with a National Government, instead of a Federal Union.[16]

---

[14] Luther Martin, "Genuine Information," delivered to the legislature of the state of Maryland, November 29, 1787, reprinted in Farrand, *Records*, III, 193. Martin's emphasis.

[15] Elliot, *The Debates*, III, 22.

[16] H. A. Cushing, ed., *The Writings of Samuel Adams* (New York: Putnam's, 1908), IV, 324.

"Whether the Constitution be good or bad," George Mason observed, going to the heart of the matter, "it is a national government, and no longer a Confederation."[17]

Despite differences of detail, the anti-federalist arguments were all of one piece. They stressed the need for a bill of rights, expressed fear of the Constitution's implications for state sovereignty, and pointed to flaws in procedural and mechanical details. They were all predicated on the assumption that, somehow, the Constitution was constructed on principles different from those that had motivated the Declaration of Independence and the Articles of Confederation, that its basic premises were incompatible with those of the earlier documents.

John Quincy Adams recognized early that antifederalist criticism was not wholly lacking in merit, that "omission of a clear and explicit Declaration of Rights was a great defect in the Constitution as presented by the Convention to the people."[18]

> These rights are not . . . fundamental because they find mention in the written instrument; they find mention there because they are fundamental. . . . The written constitution is, in short, but a nucleus or core of a much wider region of private rights, which, though not reduced to black and white, are as fully entitled to the protection of government as if defined in the minutest detail.[19]

Few would deny today that the Constitution is stronger for the addition of the first eight amendments.

The antifederalists' criticism served to point up what has been repeatedly demonstrated since 1787: that the creed embodied in the Declaration of Independence and the idea of state sovereignty have enduring vitality.

THE CONSTITUTION EXPLAINED

For ratification of the Constitution, the primary debt is owed to the federalists, a group of men, led by Hamilton, who saw the need for a stronger central government if the United States were to survive. This nucleus, which later developed into the Federalist Party, carried the day for ratification in the state conventions and provided the new nation with an enduring thread of political thought. Prominent Federalists were James Wilson, Theodore Sedgwick (1746–1813),[20] James Madison, and Alexander Hamilton. The Federalist argument for ratification was based on the belief that

---

[17] Elliot, *The Debates*, III, 29.

[18] J. Q. Adams, *The Jubilee of the Constitution* (New York: Samuel Colman, 1839), p. 45.

[19] Edward S. Corwin, "The Basic Doctrine of American Constitutional Law," *Michigan Law Review*, XII (February, 1914), 1–2.

[20] See Richard E. Welch, Jr., *Theodore Sedgwick, Federalist* (Wesleyan, Conn.: Wesleyan University Press, 1965).

in its principles . . . [the Constitution] is purely democratical; varying indeed, in its form, in order to admit all the advantages, and to exclude all the disadvantages which are incidental of the known and established constitutions of government. But when we take an extensive and accurate view of the streams of power that appear through this great and comprehensive plan, when we contemplate the variety of their directions, the force and dignity of their currents . . . we shall be able to trace them all to one great and noble source, THE PEOPLE.[21]

As a consequence state sovereignty was an impossibility. "Upon what principle," Wilson asked, "is it contended that the sovereign power resides in the state governments?" The *people* were sovereign, the states merely pretenders—perhaps usurpers. The Declaration of Independence had confirmed the inherent and inalienable right of the people to form governments of their choosing. The Constitutional Convention fulfilled America's commitment to free government.

The most painstaking exposition of the new Constitution, and one of the most profound political treatises ever written, is *The Federalist*.[22] A series of eighty-five lengthy papers by James Madison, Alexander Hamilton, and John Jay—written under the name Publius[23] and totaling

[21] Words of James Wilson, quoted in Mason, *Free Government*, pp. 245–46.
[22] There are several good editions. The Edward G. Bourne edition (Washington, D.C.: M. Walter Dunne, 1901) has been used here. See Gottfried Dietze, *The Federalist. A Classic on Federalism and Free Government* (Baltimore: Johns Hopkins, 1960) for a perceptive analysis of the essays. There is a considerable literature on *The Federalist*. See, among others, A. T. Mason, "The Federalist: A Split Personality," *American Historical Review*, LVII (1952), 625; Benjamin F. Wright, "The Federalist on the Nature of Man," *Ethics*, XLIX, No. 2, Part II (January, 1949); Martin Diamond, "Democracy and *The Federalist*: A Reconstruction of the Framers' Intent," *American Political Science Review*, LIII (March, 1959), 52–68; James P. Scanlan, "*The Federalist* and Human Nature," *Review of Politics*, XXI (October, 1959), 657–77; and Maynard Smith, "Reason, Passion and Political Freedom in *The Federalist*," *Journal of Politics*, XXII (August, 1960), 525–44.
[23] For a considerable time the authors of *The Federalist* were not known. It was the fashion of the time to write under a nom de plume, and none of the authors divulged his identity. During the writing Hamilton and Madison took special pains to guard their secret, sometimes going so far as to speculate about the possible authorship of the essays. See Henry Cabot Lodge, ed., *The Works of Alexander Hamilton* (New York: Putnam's, 1903), IX, pp. 427, 431. Just before he died in 1804, Hamilton claimed to have written sixty-three, while Madison, in 1818, approved an edition by Jacob Gideon in which he claimed he had written twenty-nine. For a long time, dispute was rife among historians over the authorship of some of the papers. Thanks to recent scholarship, the dispute seems settled, and the distribution seems set as follows: Jay, five (Numbers 2–5, 64); Hamilton; fifty-one (Numbers 1, 6–9, 11–13, 15–17, 21–36, 59–61, 65–85); Hamilton and Madison together, three (Numbers 18–20); and Madison, the remaining twenty-six. See E. G. Bourne, "The Authorship of *The Federalist*," *American Historical Review*, II (April, 1897), 443–60; Douglass Adair, "The Authorship of the Disputed *Federalist* Papers," *William and Mary Quarterly*, 3rd series, I (April and July, 1944), 97–122, 235–64. Using mathematical analysis and a computer, Professors Frederick Mosteller of Harvard and David L. Wallace of the University of Chicago found that the disputed essays—Numbers 49–58, 62, and 63—belong to Madison rather than to Hamilton, *New York Times*, September 10, 1962, pp. 1, 24.

some 175,000 words—it appeared in the New York press between October 27, 1787, and August 15, 1788. The primary purpose was to present the case for ratification in New York. A seasoned diplomat, Jay (1745–1829) was a key participant because of his extensive knowledge of and experience in foreign affairs. Madison was indispensable not only because he was "the best informed man of any point in debate,"[24] but also because of his unrivaled grasp of the Convention's proceedings. The idea of preparing the papers sprang from the fertile mind of Hamilton.

They appeared in book form in the spring of 1788, and though they came too late to be of real significance in New York, they immediately impressed contemporary readers, as they did Oliver Wendell Holmes many years later, as "a truly original and wonderful production."[25] Each essay was carefully, if hurriedly, written. Elevated in tone, the pettiness and partisan spirit that sometimes marked antifederalist objections was much less in evidence.

The Federalist was prepared as a propaganda tract rather than as a treatise on political theory. As an exercise in special pleading, it reflects certain of the shortcomings of such efforts. "It is repetitious," Edward Mead Earle observed. "It is not always frank; Hamilton, . . . preferred a national to a federal government, and he was contemptuous of popular opinion; but he loyally and vigorously supported, much in the relation of lawyer to client, the Constitution for which he felt comparatively little enthusiasm."[26]

The Federalist embodies four main arguments: (1) the necessity of prompt and effective action because of acknowledged defects in the Articles of Confederation; (2) the urgency of a unitary system, acting directly on individuals and possessed of coercive power to avoid imperium in imperio; (3) the peculiar adaptability of the republican form of government to a great extent of territory and widely divergent interests; and (4) the necessity of providing more effectually for the securing of private rights—especially of property and contract—harassed and violated in the several states by "interested and over-bearing majorities."

The authors divided the labor of writing *The Federalist* along the lines of their special aptitudes and interests. Since 1780 Hamilton had been citing want of power in Congress as the crucial defeat in the existing system. It was natural, therefore, that he should seek to demonstrate how the Constitution provided the remedy. Madison, though not ignoring the

---

[24] "Notes of Major William Pierce on the Federal Convention of 1787," *American Historical Review*, III (January, 1898), 331.

[25] Oliver Wendell Holmes, "Speech on John Marshall," February 4, 1901, reproduced in Max Lerner, ed., *The Mind and Faith of Justice Holmes* (Boston: Little, Brown, 1946), p. 384. ,

[26] Edward Mead Earle, Introduction to *The Federalist*, Modern Library ed. (New York: Random House, 1937), p. xi. Professor W. W. Crosskey has declared that *The Federalist* contains "much of sophistry; much that is merely distractive; and some things, particularly in the parts that Madison wrote, which come perilously near falsehood." *Politics and the Constitution*, I, 8–9.

need for greater energy in the central government, had been denouncing legislative encroachments on vested rights as among the most grievous wrongs. He therefore devoted the bulk of his attention to demonstrating how the Constitution corrected that evil.

Jay's contribution was important chiefly because it upheld the necessity of forming at once a strong and united nation. Without such unity the United States could not long remain safe from foreign danger and influence. His papers also contain a specific argument in defense of that provision of Article II, section 2 of the Constitution providing for the approval of treaties by the Senate. Although Jay's work cannot be dismissed as insignificant, it is the papers of Hamilton and Madison that give *The Federalist* enduring value.

The Federalist: Hamilton

Profoundly concerned about the lack of power in the national government, Hamilton set out to demonstrate how the Constitution remedied this defect. His Number 15 is particularly revealing. Opponents of the Constitution, Hamilton charged, were willing to admit "that the government of the United States is destitute of energy," but they were "against conferring upon it those powers which are requisite to supply that energy. They seem still to aim at things repugnant and irreconcilable, at an augmentation of federal authority, without a diminution of State authority; at sovereignty in the Union, and complete independence in the members." The Constitution strengthened the power of the national government by extending its authority beyond the states in their "CORPORATE OR COLLECTIVE CAPACITIES" to the people themselves. Hamilton understood that even an increase in power would be ineffectual if a sanction were not provided. The Confederation government could exert a sanction neither on the sovereign states nor on the people. It scarcely deserved the name of government: no prudent man would commit his happiness to it. The Constitution offered a government in power as well as in name. Its laws could be enforced directly upon individuals; no longer could they be regarded by the states as "mere recommendations which [they might] observe or disregard at their option."

In particular, Hamilton pointed out how the national government provided for in the Constitution would permit "the natural strength and resources of the country [to be] directed to a common interest," rather than dissipated as they had been under the Articles of Confederation; how it would enable adequate revenue to be collected; and how it would provide for effective national defense. He denied in Number 23 that the additional powers granted the national government were "too extensive for the OBJECTS" confided to the federal administration, "or, in other words, for the management of our NATIONAL INTERESTS." In fact, it seemed to him that "the extent of the country, is the strongest argument in favor of an energetic government; for any other can certainly never preserve the Union of so large an empire." Indeed, for Hamilton, the Constitution was chiefly significant as a grant of power. The core of it was in enumeration of the congressional authority (Article I, section 8, paragraphs 1 to 18 inclusive) and in the supremacy clause (Article VI, section 2).

The Federalist: Madison

Madison, on the other hand, had been consistently concerned with the danger to property rights, which were suffering from "injustice of the laws of the States." For him an important object of the Constitution was to limit state legislative power: Article I, section 10 was therefore among its most important provisions. His outstanding *Federalist* papers, Numbers 10 and 51, were dedicated to demonstrating how the Constitution alleviated the subversive effects of state laws on the vested rights of property and contract. He reiterated, in Number 10, the point he had argued before and during the Convention, that society was everywhere tainted by "a factious spirit," which united some citizens in a common cause and set them against "the rights of other citizens, or the permanent and aggregate interests of the community." Minority factions did not worry Madison. They might, he admitted, "clog the administration" or "convulse the society," but he concluded (too easily perhaps) that the republican principle would enable "the majority to defeat its sinister views by regular vote." Majority factions, such as those of the debtor class that had seized legislative reins in a number of states, gave Madison deep concern. These were capable of sacrificing to their own interests "both the public good and the rights of other citizens." Legislation emanating from such factional control of state legislatures had cast discredit on the fundamental principle of republican government—namely, that majority rule is the safest guardian both of public good and of private rights. Madison likened unrestricted majority rule to a state of nature: "In a society under the forms of which the stronger faction can readily unite and oppress the weaker, anarchy may as truly be said to reign as in a state of nature, where the weaker individual is not secured against the violence of the stronger. . . ." How to control majority factions, and thus protect the rights of individuals and minorities, was the chief problem to be met.

Two cures for factions suggested themselves: remove the cause, or control the effects. The former was not practicable, for the factious spirit was "sown in the nature of man"; factions were so integral a part of human nature as to be irremovable. The effect of factions might still be controlled, however. Neither a democratic, nor an authoritarian, nor an egalitarian remedy was acceptable: the first was inimical to property rights; the second would destroy liberty; and the third was neither feasible nor practical. The Constitution created yet another alternative, one admirably designed to control factions: republican government. Of all the forms of government, it alone met the first desideratum of good government—"To secure the public good and private rights against the danger of . . . faction, and at the same time to preserve the spirit and the form of popular government." Both because it confided the actual powers of government to "a small number of citizens elected by the rest" and because of the size of both the citizenry and the country in the United States, a "Compound Republic," a well-constructed union, seemed the best answer to the unavoidable problem of factions.

There was no point on which Madison was so categorical as on his rejection of the shortcut remedy for factions: destruction of liberty. "Liberty is to faction what air is to fire," he wrote in Number 10. Yet liberty must be preserved.

> As long as the reason of man continues fallible, and he is at liberty to exercise it, different opinions will be formed. As long as the connection subsists between his reason and his self-love, his opinions and his passions will have a reciprocal influence on each other; and the former will be objects to which the latter attach themselves. The diversity in the faculties of men, from which the rights of property originate, is not less an insuperable obstacle to a uniformity of interests. The protection of these faculties is the first object of government.

The great variety of factions and the tendency of one to neutralize the corrupting effects of the other had suggested the underlying principle of the Constitution. Under it "the interior structure of government" had been so contrived that "its several constituent parts may by their mutual relations, be the means of keeping each other in their proper place." The Constitution guaranteed that public opinion would be refined and enlarged by forcing it through "the medium of a chosen body of citizens, whose wisdom may best discern the true interest of their country, and whose patriotism and love of justice will be least likely to sacrifice it to temporary or partial considerations." The states would serve as additional elements in the refining process, and the vast expanse of the United States, encompassing every variety of economic, geographic, social, religious, and sectional interest, would further serve to control the effects of faction. "Extend the sphere, and you take in a greater variety of parties and interests; you make it less probable that a majority of the whole will have a common motive to invade the rights of other citizens." The flame of faction might be kindled in a particular state, but it could never spread "a general conflagration" through the rest of the nation.

The control of factions enjoying majority support was the Constitution's main objective. "In framing a government which is to be administered by men over men, the great difficulty lies in this: you must first enable the government to control the governed; and in the next place oblige it to control itself. A dependence on the people is, no doubt, the primary control of the government; but experience has taught mankind the necessity of auxiliary precautions." Within the framework of republican government, the Constitution embodied a number of precautions— a two-house legislature, each elected on a different basis and with somewhat different principles of action; the executive veto; a federal government in which "the power surrendered by the people is first divided between two distinct governments, and then the portion allotted to each subdivided among distinct and separate departments"; and judicial review—the power of the Supreme Court, in cases properly before it, to construe legislative acts and determine whether they square with the provisions of the Constitution.

In short, the Constitution, as Madison explained it, was built on the theory that "you may cover whole skins of parchment with limitations but power alone can limit power."[27] History as well as American experience reinforced the "policy of supplying, by opposite and rival interests, the defect of better motives. . . ."

THE FEDERALIST: SPLIT PERSONALITY

Madison's reference in Number 10 to "the superior force of an interested and overbearing majority" indicates an unwillingness to accept unqualified majority rule. Throughout the essays Hamilton and Madison repeatedly demonstrated their distrust of a government subject to the continual, direct pressure of the people. In Number 71 Hamilton explained:

> The republican principle demands that the deliberate sense of the community should govern the conduct of those to whom they intrust the management of their affairs; but it does not require an unqualified complaisance to every sudden breeze of passion or to every transient impulse which the people may receive from the arts of men, who flatter their prejudices to betray their interests.

Hamilton's enthusiastic endorsement of "a vigorous Executive,"[28] of judicial review,[29] of the Electoral College as a device for electing the president,[30] and of the veto,[31] and Madison's approval of the Constitution's provision for a difficult amending process[32] and for the indirect election and relatively long tenure of office for senators[33]—all must be interpreted as proof that the Constitution was not oriented toward unqualified popular government.

Although *The Federalist* speaks with one voice in enunciating basic principles, it reveals a divergence between its authors on others—a divergence so marked that Douglass Adair described *The Federalist* as having a

---

[27] John Randolph (1773–1833), long a representative of Virginia in Congress, quoted in W. C. Bruce, *John Randolph of Roanoke* (New York: Putnam's, 1922), II, 211.
[28] *Federalist* Number 71.
[29] *Federalist* Number 78.
[30] *Federalist* Number 68.
[31] *Federalist* Number 73.
[32] *Federalist* Number 49 and 50.
[33] *Federalist* Number 62.

"split personality."[34] Hamilton, for instance, saw the new government as constituting a "consolidated system," a "Union under one government," a "perfect subordination [of the states] to the general authority of the Union."[35] Madison was much less inclined to speak in terms of consolidation. In his celebrated Number 39, he contended that

> the proposed Constitution . . . is, in strictness, neither a national or a federal Constitution, but a composition of both. In its foundation it is federal, not national; in the sources from which the ordinary powers of the government are drawn, it is partly federal and partly national; in the operation of these powers, it is national, not federal; in the extent of them, again, it is federal, not national; . . . in the authoritative mode of introducing amendments, it is neither wholly federal nor wholly national; [and] in ratifying the Constitution [in which case each State] is considered as a sovereign body, independent of all others, and only to be bound by its own voluntary act. . . . the . . . Constitution will, if established, be a *federal* and not a *national* constitution.

To Madison the Constitution represented "an improvement on the theory of free government,"[36] for under it "the power surrendered by the people is first divided between two distinct governments, and then the portion allotted to each subdivided among the distinct and separate departments. Hence a double security arises to the rights of the people. The different governments will control each other, at the same time that each will be controlled by itself."[37] To Hamilton, on the other hand, the states interfered with the establishment in government of a will independent of society and were to be suffered only because of popular attachment to them. Hamilton brushed aside Madison's refinements as a distinction "more subtle than accurate . . . in the main, arbitrary . . . supported neither by principle nor precedent."[38] It was precisely the ambiguity latent in Madison's concept of the nature of the Union that led to so much anguish during the tragic years 1861–1865. Madison's theory that the Constitution was "founded on the assent and ratification of the people of America, not as individuals composing one entire nation, but as composing the distinct and independent States to which they respectively belong" is the more noteworthy in light of its novelty. In 1787 "People of the States" and "People of America" were not, as *Federalist* Number 39 implies, antagonistic concepts. The polar ideas familiar to the men of that day—"Government" and "People"—were inherited from

---

[34] Professor John D. Lewis denies that *The Federalist* is afflicted with a "split personality," an aspect discernible to contemporary observers and scholars alike. See his *Anti-Federalists versus Federalists*, p. 49n.
[35] *Federalist* Number 9. Hamilton was careful to add, however, that "it would still be, in fact and in theory, an association of states, or a confederacy. The proposed Constitution, far from implying an abolition of the State Governments . . . leaves in their possession certain exclusive and very important portions of sovereign power."
[36] Hunt, *Writings of Madison*, VI, 92.
[37] *Federalist* Number 51.
[38] *Federalist* Number 9.

Locke. Government was universally regarded as the creation of people; people meant an aggregation of individuals endowed with the natural right to determine their form of government. A constitution represented a fresh manifestation of the inexhaustible, inalienable right of people to govern themselves. Madison's refinement of these basic ideas provided valuable ammunition in the hands of those who, in later years, made an abortive attempt to destroy the Union.[39]

Madison and Hamilton also disagreed about the nature and scope of the powers granted to the new government. Madison held "that the great principles of the Constitution proposed by the Convention may be considered less as absolutely new than as an expansion of the principles which are found in the Articles of Confederation."[40] In Number 45 he declared: "If the new Constitution be examined with accuracy and candor, it will be found that the change which it proposes consists much less in the addition of NEW POWERS to the Union, than in the invigoration of its ORIGINAL POWERS." After all, he explained, "the powers delegated by the proposed Constitution to the federal government are few and defined."

Hamilton, arguing as if Madison were his opponent rather than his colleague, spoke in Number 23 of "an entire change in the first principles of the system." What is more, he devoted no fewer than six essays[41] to the inadequacies of government under the Articles of Confederation. This suggests his belief that a fresh start was necessary. Nor did Hamilton agree with Madison's assertion that the new government possessed only a few defined powers. For Hamilton the objects of the national government were general and the powers granted it for achieving them were undefined, even undefinable. It would be, he declared, both "unwise and dangerous to deny the federal government an unconfined authority, as to all those objects which are intrusted to its management. . . . A government, the constitution of which renders it unfit to be trusted with all the powers which a free people *ought to delegate to any government*, would be an unsafe and improper depository of the NATIONAL INTERESTS." "Not to confer . . . a degree of power commensurate to the end, would be to violate the most obvious rules of prudence and propriety, and improvidently to trust the great interests of the nation to hands which are disabled from managing them with vigor and success."[42]

The powers granted the national government were not only different in degree, as Madison suggested, but also different in kind. Hamilton conceived Article I, section 8, read in conjunction with Article VI, section 2, to mean a great deal more than mere "invigoration of original powers." To him the combination resulted in a grant of enough power to

---

[39] See, E. S. Corwin, *The Doctrine of Judicial Review* (Princeton, N.J.: Princeton University Press, 1914), pp. 81–108, 198, and his "National Power and State Interposition, 1787–1861," *Michigan Law Review*, X (May, 1912), 535–51.
[40] *Federalist* Number 40.
[41] *Federalist* Numbers 15, 16, 17, 21, 22, and 23.
[42] *Federalist* Number 23.

satisfy the greatest "extent and variety of national exigencies" it was possible to foresee.[43] The Constitution, in other words, granted *means* in the same broad spirit that it set forth *ends*.

Hamilton and Madison also disagreed about the proper directions for the exercise of national power. In Number 45 Madison registered his belief that it should be applied chiefly in the field of foreign affairs and in times of emergency and war. Hamilton, on the other hand, regarded the national government as properly constituting the dominant force in both domestic and foreign affairs.

Other differences divided the authors. Hamilton was as sensitive to the evil of "factions" as his collaborator. But whereas Madison saw them as multifarious, and "the various and unequal distribution of property" as only the "most common and durable source" thereof, Hamilton saw the social cleavage more exclusively grounded in economics. For him every community was divided "into a few and the many," rich and poor, debtors and creditors. Hamilton's case, as he stated it in Number 9, was a firm union and a national government with "coercive" powers acting directly on individuals: these together would repress domestic factions and insurrections. So different from Madison's ideas were these that John Quincy Adams described Hamilton's Number 9 and Madison's Number 10 as "rival dissertations upon Faction and its remedy."[44]

Adams might have made the contrast even sharper by adding Madison's Number 51 and Hamilton's Numbers 70, 71, 76, and 78, in which the New Yorker elaborated his remedy for factions, stressing the need of "a vigorous Executive," "the advantage of permanency in a wise system of administration," of duration in office of "considerable extent," of "independence" in government, and of judicial review as the final guarantor of "the majesty of national authority."

An authoritarian note is evident throughout Hamilton's discussion of executive and judicial power. In Number 71 he advanced the sentiment that though the people commonly intend the public good, they do not always reason rightly about the means of promoting it. The exalted role carved out for the executive and judiciary, especially the latter, suggests Hamilton's faith in a superior intelligence beholding all the passions of men without experiencing any of them. Hamilton was naturally less outspoken in *The Federalist* than he had been at the convention, but he made no less clear his conviction that an independent will in government, immune from fluctuating gusts of popular passion, is an essential safeguard against "domestic insurrection and factions." The effect, he wrote in Number 71, is not to enthrone authoritarianism nor to flout popular government, but rather to safeguard "the people" when their "interests . . . are at variance with their inclinations," giving them "time and opportunity for more cool and sedate reflection." Moreover, "the sole and undivided responsibility of one man will naturally beget a livelier

---

[43] *Federalist* Number 23.
[44] J. Q. Adams, *An Eulogy on Madison*, p. 32.

sense of duty and a more exact regard to reputation. . . . This supposition of universal venality in human nature is little less an error in political reasoning, than the supposition of universal rectitude" (Number 76).

One discovers in Madison's essays no such confidence.[45] In Number 51 he held that government must be obliged "to control itself" through a "policy of supplying, by opposite and rival interests, the defects of better motives." In Number 48 he observed: "It will not be denied, that power is of an encroaching nature, and that it ought to be effectually restrained from passing the limits assigned to it." Even when Madison spoke of energy and stability as essential to security and good government, he was wont to temper his stand with caution. In the achievement of his principal objective—"energy in government" combined "with the inviolable attention due to liberty and the republican form"—there is no suggestion that he shared Hamilton's faith that "responsibility" and office holding "during good behavior" would develop "impartiality" and the "requisite integrity" in government (Numbers 76 and 78). "On comparing . . . these valuable ingredients [energy and stability] with the vital principles of liberty," Madison commented in Number 37, "we must perceive at once the difficulty of mingling them together in their due proportions."

Madison's approach was consistently pluralistic. For him the states need not be obliterated; they were well adapted to a broad expanse of territory and helpful in serving the ends of a "well-constructed union"— liberty and justice. "If they were abolished, the general government," he wrote in Number 14, "would be compelled by the principle of self-preservation, to reinstate them in their proper jurisdiction." Hamilton, on the other hand, believed that the great size of the country, torn by warring factions, necessitated a consolidated system with "unconfined," "coercive power" poised at one center. If the states continued, as under the Articles of Confederation, as members of a "partial" union, "frequent and violent contests with each other" would be inevitable (Number 6).

---

[45] In *Federalist* Number 55, Madison seemed to qualify his earlier misgivings on human nature, but the context makes clear the contrast with Hamilton. "As there is a degree of depravity in mankind which requires a certain degree of circumspection and distrust, so there are other qualities in human nature which justify a certain portion of esteem and confidence. Republican government presupposes the existence of these qualities in a higher degree than any other form. Were the pictures which have been drawn by the politically jealous of some among us faithful likeness of the human character, the inference would be, that there is not sufficient virtue among men for self-government; and nothing less than the chains of despotism can restrain them from destroying and devouring one another." In the Virginia Constitutional Convention of 1829–1830, Madison again cautioned that government means power and that the necessity of placing power in human hands means that it is apt to be abused. The danger of abuse is greatest when men act in a body, and because conscience alone is not a sufficient check, safeguards for minority rights must be found in the structure of government. Thus, Madison conceded that the slavery interest would have to be incorporated into the government in order to guard against the oppressive taxation that might result from the government's falling into the hands of nonslaveowners. *Proceedings and Debates of the Virginia Constitutional Convention of 1829–1830* (Richmond: Samuel Shepherd, 1830), p. 538.

In contrast, Madison envisaged, in Number 51, a counterpoised system. Just as in a society—composed of sects, interests, classes, and parties—ambition checks ambition, vice checks vice, and interest sets itself against interest, so within the government a structure provided an institutional expression of social diversity, of action and counteraction.

Hamilton's and Madison's divergence is further reflected in their views of the authority from which the Constitution emanates. For Hamilton the crucial infirmity of the system it was to replace was congenital—"it never had ratification by the PEOPLE." To avoid the "gross heresy"—that a *"party* to a *compact* has a right to revoke that *compact"*—"the fabric of American empire ought to rest on the solid basis of THE CONSENT OF THE PEOPLE" (Number 22). The Constitution corrected "the great and radical vice . . . *Legislation* for *States* . . . as contradistinguished from the individuals of which they consist." "If we are unwilling," Hamilton commented, going to the heart of his nationalist creed, "to be placed in this perilous situation; if we still adhere to the design of a national government, or, which is the same thing, of a superintending power, under the direction of a common council, we must resolve to incorporate into our plan those ingredients which may be considered as forming the characteristic difference between a league and a government; we must extend the authority of the Union to the persons of the citizens,—the only proper objects of government" (Number 15).

One cannot always be certain in identifying the stand of either Hamilton or Madison. Their interpretations became less categorical when either author entered the province of the other. Thus, Madison's nationalism in Number 14 is qualified in Numbers 39 and 40. The diminutive scope of the power he accorded Congress in Numbers 40 and 45 he lost sight of in Number 44: "No axiom is more clearly established in law, or in reason, than that wherever the end is required, the means are authorized; wherever a general power to do a thing is given, every particular power necessary for doing it is included." In later years Hamilton made this "axiom" his own.

Similarly, Hamilton's bold nationalist stand in Numbers 9, 15, and 22, his inference that the Constitution, as a logical necessity, eliminated every vestige of the old relationship of states as members of a "League," is toned down, even neutralized, elsewhere. "An entire consolidation," he remarked in Number 32, "of the States into one complete national sovereignty would imply an entire subordination of the parts; and whatever powers might remain in them, would be altogether dependent on the general will. But as the plan of the convention aims only at a partial union or consolidation, the State governments would clearly retain all the rights of sovereignty which they before had, and which were not by that act, *exclusively* delegated to the United States." In case of conflict even in the crucial matter of taxation, Hamilton suggested the desirability of "reciprocal forbearances" (Number 32). Anticipating the provisions of the Tenth Amendment, he declared "that the States will retain all *pre-existing* authorities which may not be exclusively delegated to the federal head"

(Number 82). To quiet the fears of those antagonistic to greatly enlarged central authority, Hamilton used language that seemed to sanction the "gross heresy" he so roundly condemned in Number 22, that "a party to a compact has a right to revoke that compact." In Number 17 he suggested that the division of powers between the central and state governments was such that the states would have "so decided an empire over their respective citizens as to render them at all times a complete counterpoise, and, not infrequently, dangerous rivals to the power of the Union." In Number 26 he referred to the state legislatures as "suspicious and jealous guardians of the rights of the citizens against encroachments from the federal government" and suggested that they "will be ready enough, if any thing improper appears, to sound the alarm to the people, and not only to be the VOICE, but, if necessary, the ARM of their discontent." Ambiguities such as these on the part of both Hamilton and Madison indicate that the renowned *Federalist* may suffer from schizophrenia, a malady worse than that identified by Adair.

THE FEDERALIST: EXEGESIS OF FREE GOVERNMENT

That Hamilton and Madison cooperated effectively in this joint enterprise is a matter of history. One reason they could do so is that the particular division of labor served to prevent any head-on clash or at least to obscure basic antagonisms. Another is that there were between them certain important areas of agreement. Both men entertained a pessimistic view of human nature. Government is necessary, they agreed, because men are not angels. "What is government itself," Madison commented, "but the greatest of all reflections on human nature?" "Why has government been instituted at all?" Hamilton asked. Because, he answered, "the passions of men will not conform to the dictates of reason and justice, without constraint." This distrustful refrain runs indistinguishably throughout the various numbers of *The Federalist*.

Regardless of authorship, the essays stressed the "caprice and wickedness of man," the "depravity of human nature," "the folly and wickedness of Mankind." In Madison's essays, no less than in Hamilton's, one notes the conviction that "men are ambitious, vindictive, and rapacious," that "momentary passions and immediate interest," rather than "considerations of policy, utility, or justice," are dominant drives in politics. The authors of *The Federalist*—like Montesquieu, the oracle to whom both Hamilton and Madison paid great deference—were convinced that "virtue itself has need of limits."

Nor did the collaborators look forward, eventually (as did Karl Marx in 1848) to some earthly paradise emerging either from a changed economic and social environment or from a spiritual regeneration. "Have we not already seen enough," Hamilton observed with disdain, "of the fallacy and extravagance of those idle theories which have amused us with promises of an exemption from the imperfections, weaknesses, and evils incident to society in every shape? Is it not time to awake from the deceitful dream of a golden age, and to adopt as a practical maxim for the direction of our political conduct that we, as well as the other inhabitants of the globe, are yet remote from the happy empire of perfect wisdom and perfect virtue?" (Number 6). Human nature being what it is, man must employ his feeble contrivance of reason in building institutional fences around unconquerable human avarice and greed.

Hamilton and Madison also agreed that the Articles of Confederation were inadequate to cope with the wide variety of controversies that grow out of the "caprice and wickedness of man" (Number 57). In Number 16 Hamilton called the Articles "an odious engine of government," so "radically vicious and unsound, as to admit not of amendment but by entire change in its leading feature." Madison's language was somewhat less drastic and his stand less unequivocal, but in Number 37 he agreed that the Articles were based on "principles which are fallacious; that we must consequently change this first foundation, and with it the superstructure resting on it."

Finally, Hamilton and Madison agreed that in a free society, "inequality of property" was inevitable. For them it was axiomatic that "inequality would exist as long as liberty existed," and the primary task of government was to protect "liberty"—i.e., "the different and unequal faculties of acquiring property," from which "the different degrees and kinds of property immediately" result.[46] Growing out of these inevitable inequalities, society, as envisaged by both men, was torn by strife and struggle, the major manifestation of discord being identified as "factions."

THE CONSTITUTION DUBIOUSLY ENDORSED

Despite the vigor of their defense the authors of *The Federalist* were not completely persuaded of the merits of the instrument they espoused. In Number 37 Madison freely indulged in his apologies: "A faultless plan was not to be expected," he reminded his readers; the "errors [in the Constitution] may be chargeable on the fallibility to which the convention, as a body of men, were liable. . . ." The Convention operated under so many difficulties that it was hardly likely that "the final act" would be entirely acceptable.

Hamilton's feelings were equally mixed. In the opening number of *The Federalist*, he confessed misgivings toward the project he was launching: "The consciousness of good intentions disdains ambiguity," he said. "My arguments will be open to all, and may be judged of by all. . . .

---

[46] Madison, in *Federalist* Number 10. "It was certainly true," Hamilton remarked on the floor of the Constitutional Convention, June 26, 1787, "that nothing like an equality of property existed: that an inequality would exist as long as liberty existed, and that it would unavoidably result from that very liberty itself. This inequality of property constituted the great and fundamental distinction in Society." Farrand, *Records*, I, 424.

My motives must remain in the depository of my own breast." Then, as on September 17 when he signed the Constitution, the choice between anarchy and convulsion and the chance of good government under the Constitution was an easy one. He knew that even this chance would be lost unless a strong national authority could be immediately established. "A good administration will conciliate the confidence and affection of the people, and perhaps enable the government to acquire more consistency than the proposed constitution seems to promise for so great a country. It may then triumph altogether over the State governments, and reduce them to an entire subordination, dividing the larger States into smaller districts."[47]

In the opening and concluding numbers Hamilton sounded a tolerant note: "We are not always sure," he observed in the first essay, "that those who advocate the truth are influenced by purer principles than their antagonists. We, upon many occasions, see wise and good men on the wrong as well as on the right side of questions of the first magnitude to society." The closing essay ends on the same note:

> I never expect to see a perfect work from imperfect man. The result of the deliberations of all collective bodies must necessarily be a compound, as well of the errors and prejudices, as of the good sense and wisdom, of the individuals of whom they are composed. The compacts which are to embrace thirteen distinct States in a common bond of amity and union, must as necessarily be a compromise of as many dissimilar interests and inclinations. How can perfection spring from such materials?

The Constitution was "the best which our political situation, habits and opinions will admit, and superior to any the revolution has produced." Better to adopt it, misgivings notwithstanding, "than to prolong the precarious state of our national affairs, and to expose the Union to the jeopardy of successive experiments, in the chimerical pursuit of a perfect plan."[48]

Neither the equivocation of the authors regarding the Constitution's virtues nor the ambiguity of their interpretation of it appears to have lessened the impact of their effort. For those unable to detect in Hamilton's and Madison's words the seeds of future strife, *The Federalist's* split personality might have made their defense more rather than less effective. In any event, this debater's handbook quickly rose from the lowly status of propaganda to the elevated station of an authoritative treatise. It has long been accepted as a political classic. Jefferson read it "with care, pleasure and improvement," describing it as "the best commentary on the principles of government ever written."[49] Washington wrote Hamil-

---

[47] Lodge, *Works of Hamilton*, I, 423. Compare these sentiments with those expressed in *Federalist* Numbers 26, 28, 32, 81, and 82.
[48] *Federalist* Number 85.
[49] Letter to James Madison, November 18, 1788, *Writings of Thomas Jefferson*, VII, 183.

ton that "perusal of the political papers under the signature of Publius has afforded me great satisfaction. I shall consider them as claiming a most distinguished place in my library."[50] Chief Justice Marshall later elevated *The Federalist* to semiofficial status, citing it repeatedly as authority in judicial opinions. Jurists ever since have followed his example. By 1825, Jefferson could refer to it as "an authority to which appeal is habitually made by all, and rarely declined or denied by any, as evidence of the general opinion of those who framed and of those who accepted the Constitution of the United States as its genuine meaning."[51]

The ratification of the Constitution, to which *The Federalist* was primarily directed, avoided what might have been an awkward detour in America's quest for freedom. With the exception of such fundamental concepts as justice and equality, which hark back to Greece and Rome, the theory on which the Constitution is based was the product of the post-Renaissance revolutionary movements in Europe and America. Sanctity of private rights, separation of powers, the idea of compact, a written constitution and its exaltation as the supreme law of the land, coupled with limitations imposed on the exercise of governmental power at all levels—all this had evolved in close association with revolutions of the seventeenth and eighteenth centuries. The Constitution's underlying theory was basically revolutionary. Furthermore, the provision making the Constitution effective on ratification by *nine* States, given through *conventions* called for the purpose, clearly indicates, as Professor Corwin said, that the Constitution was "in the legal sense, an act of revolution."[52] Finally, the federal system, basic to the entire Constitution though not without American antecedents, marked a sharp break with precedent and practice.

By the time the Convention had completed its work and its product had been ratified, certain characteristics of the American political fabric were clear. In each stage of its development, the same strands are discernible. On the one hand, there were economic power, interests, property, and minority rights; on the other, popular power, numbers, persons, and majority rule. The entire revolutionary period in England and America can be described in terms of a conflict between these forces; the expression of these various elements in the developing American system can be generally ascribed to partisans of one side or the other.

By 1787 the concept of *free government* had been formulated and institutionalized. A way had been found to weld into one consistent work the seemingly irreconcilable elements of liberty and restraint. No one could be certain that this "proximate" solution would be a happy one; nor have the intervening years been without struggle, conflict, and war.

---

[50] Quoted in Jared Sparks, ed., *The Writings of George Washington* (New York: Harper & Brothers, 1847–1848), IX, 149.
[51] Quoted in Mason, *Free Government*, p. 252.
[52] Edward S. Corwin, *The Constitution and What It Means Today*, 9th ed. (Princeton, N.J.: Princeton University Press, 1947), p. 152.

These, indeed were inevitable: "A free society is a society always in agitation."[53]

---

[53] Words of Montesquieu, quoted in Julian P. Boyd, "A People Divided," *North Carolina Historical Review*, XLVII (April, 1970), 162.

CHAPTER SEVEN

STRESS
ON NATIONAL POWER:
HAMILTON AND MARSHALL

"The Constitution," as John Quincy Adams truly said, "had been extorted from the grinding necessity of a reluctant nation."[1] Establishment of the new government was hardly less demanding. It was one thing to blueprint the machinery of rulership; it was something else altogether to supply the motive power of governing, to strike out on a bold new course, to break away from the bias and prejudice of old ways and institutions.

A constitution is a lifeless thing, a paper contrivance, at most a license to begin governing. However meritorious the document of 1787 as it came from the hands of the framers, the new political system might be good or bad depending on the men empowered to launch it. With energetic leaders of insight, daring, and imagination, the experiment might succeed. In the hands of weak men, blind to what the nation might become, the Constitution, prepared with so much care and accepted with reservation, might fail. "Governments, like clocks," William Penn observed, "go from the motion men give them."

George Washington was the Electoral College's obvious choice for president. As chief executive his immediate goals were to settle the points

---

[1] J. Q. Adams, *Jubilee of the Constitution*, p. 55.

that remained at issue with Great Britain and to put the nation on a firm and stable financial basis. To that end he appointed Jefferson Secretary of State and Hamilton Secretary of the Treasury. Although Washington's leadership and prestige were valuable—indeed, probably indispensable— he soon discovered, as have all his successors, that practical considerations required him to leave the administration and even much of the formulation of policy to his chief subordinate officers. Fulfillment of the framers' hopes thus rested primarily on the shoulders of Hamilton and Jefferson.

ALEXANDER HAMILTON: NATIONALIST LEADER

Hamilton[2] quickly became the dominant figure in the administration, so much so that Jefferson, unable to reconcile his views with those of Hamilton, left the cabinet in 1793. From then until his resignation, Hamilton was chiefly responsible for demonstrating the power available in the Constitution.

Born a British subject in the French West Indies, Hamilton was an illegitimate son of poverty-stricken parents. His origins are so obscure that researchers have had difficulty in establishing the date of his birth.[3] We know that at fifteen he came to this country to study and that in less than a year, he was prepared for college. During his freshman year violent outbreaks precipitated the revolutionary struggle, and, determined to be a part of it, he first became a pamphleteer, writing *Full Vindication* (1774) and *The Farmer Refuted* (1775). When the war broke out, he quit college and pamphleteering and joined a volunteer body known as Hearts of Oak.

His rise in the military was extraordinary. In March 1776, a few days before Washington drove Sir William Howe from Boston, Hamilton, then twenty-one, was appointed to a captaincy. A year later he became aide-de-camp to Washington with the rank of lieutenant colonel. Then began a close relationship that lasted throughout their lives, a relationship that might well have shaped the course of American history. Experience as Washington's military secretary gave Hamilton an insight into America's needs and problems unequalled by that of any of his contemporaries, save perhaps Washington himself. Throughout the critical period Hamilton

---

[2] Besides the books mentioned in footnotes, reference should be made to John C. Miller, *Alexander Hamilton: Portrait in Paradox* (New York: Harper & Row, 1959); Jacob E. Cooke, ed., *Alexander Hamilton: A Profile* (New York: Hill & Wang, 1967); and Gerald Stourzh, *Alexander Hamilton and the Idea of Republican Government* (Stanford, Calif.: Stanford University Press, 1970).

[3] Citing the record of the Probate Court of Christiansted, St. Croix, February 22, 1768, which was convened at the death of Hamilton's mother to divide her possessions, Broadus Mitchell has concluded that the date of Hamilton's birth is 1755, not 1757. Broadus Mitchell, *Heritage from Hamilton, 1755–1788* (New York: Columbia University Press, 1957), p. 4.

was conspicuous among those in the vanguard of affairs, trying to produce the event.[4] Although his contributions at Annapolis, in Philadelphia, and as an author of *The Federalist* loom large, Hamilton played his greatest role in Washington's administration. Conceiving of the presidency in the royal pattern, there being no precedent for a democratic executive, Washington did not expect to exert his leadership openly. That function he delegated to Hamilton. In appointing the thirty-two-year-old New Yorker to the treasury post, the president provided him an unparalleled vantage point from which to drive toward his goal—"a Great Republic, tranquil and prosperous at home and respectable abroad."[5]

The first years of the United States, especially those comprising George Washington's administrations, were crucial for the future of America. The United States was then neither a nation nor a geographical unit. It was, rather, a philosophical image of what might be. The enemies of the Constitution, though temporarily discouraged, were numerous and powerful. The drift of opinion, despite ratification of the Constitution, was predominantly agrarian and inclined to favor state power. Purposeful, bold, and immediate action was needed; "additional buttresses to the Constitution"[6] were required. Realizing that he had to move against economic agrarianism and political localism, Hamilton set out to construct for his nationalist policy a fortress of precedent so solid that only revolution could dislodge it.

ESTABLISHING PUBLIC CREDIT

In the early years no man did more than Hamilton to launch the new government.[7] He took office on September 11, 1789. Ten days later the House of Representatives called on him to submit a plan for adequate support of public credit. The secretary was eager to respond. By January 14, 1790, he had prepared his first report, a brilliant tour de force, abounding in facts, figures, and argument. Hamilton strongly recommended the assumption by the national government of all state and federal debts. Believing this to be "the price of liberty" and "a powerful cement to our Union," he urged the national government to take responsibility for payment in full (including interest in arrears) of all creditors

---

[4] Hamilton's political strategy was derived from the first Philippic of Demosthenes' orations: "As a general marches at the head of his troops, so ought wise politicians, if I dare use the expression, to march at the head of affairs; insomuch that they ought not to wait the *event*, to know what measures to take; but the measures which they have taken ought to produce the *event*."

[5] Quoted in Mason, *Free Government*, p. 329.

[6] Quoted in F. C. Prescott, *Alexander Hamilton and Thomas Jefferson* (New York: American Book, 1934), p. xxxi.

[7] See Clinton Rossiter, *Alexander Hamilton and the Constitution* (New York: Harcourt, Brace & World, 1964). See also Leonard D. White, *The Federalists: A Study in Administrative History* (New York: Macmillan, 1964).

of the United States and of the several states. These policies he thought essential to placing public credit on a sound footing.[8]

Assumption of the debts was also necessary to "consolidate popular support behind the federal government . . . and win the confidence of business interests . . . by creating a sorely needed credit medium." Hamilton's objective was to induce the wealthy to look to the national government rather than to the states and to rely on national power rather than on state power for the security of their capital and repayment of their loans. "It cannot but merit particular attention," he wrote, "that among ourselves, the most enlightened friends of good government are those whose expectations are the highest," i.e., the public creditors. "The advantage [to them], from the increased value of that part of their property which constitutes the public debt, needs no explanation." To justify and preserve their confidence, as well as "to promote the increasing respectability of the American name; to answer the calls of justice; to restore landed property to its due value; to furnish new resources, both to agriculture and commerce; to cement more closely the union of the States; to add to their security against foreign attack; to establish public order on the basis of an upright and liberal policy"—these were "the great and invaluable ends to be secured by a proper and adequate provision, at the present period, for the support of public credit."[9]

Yet he had no intention of

> acceding to the position, in the latitude in which it is sometimes laid down, that "public debts are public benefits"—a position inviting to prodigality and liable to dangerous abuse. . . . [Instead, he wished] to see it incorporated as a fundamental maxim in the system of public credit of the United States, that the creation of debt should always be accompanied with the means of extinguishment.[10]

To assure the attainment of these ends, Hamilton recommended the immediate creation of a sinking fund and the establishment of a national bank. In a letter of 1780 to Robert Morris, then in charge of congressional finances, he had made a detailed and cogent plea for a national bank. This, he had said, would also serve to enlist the support of the moneyed interests. They would relish the project and make it their own.

Congress accepted his recommendations. By the Funding Act of 1790, it provided for an issue of bonds to replace the state bonds and the old Continental and Confederation bonds still outstanding, and by the Act of February 8, 1791, it established the United States Bank. The latter action clashed with the laissez faire theory of Adam Smith that was making such headway in America; it was also queried on constitutional grounds. Leading the opposition in the House was Hamilton's erstwhile

---

[8] See D. F. Swanson, *The Origins of Hamilton's Fiscal Policies* (Gainesville, Fla.: University of Florida Press, 1963).

[9] Lodge, *Works of Hamilton*, II, 227, 231–32.

[10] Lodge, *Works of Hamilton*, II, 283.

Federalist collaborator, James Madison. The Constitution, Madison argued, conferred on the national government only limited power, and that, he said, was the Convention's intention. But the House turned thumbs down on Madison's arguments by a vote of two to one. Hamilton and his friends exulted, but not for long, for Madison's opposition raised doubts in the mind of President Washington himself. For advice the President turned to Attorney General Edmund Randolph and Secretary of State Thomas Jefferson. Both considered the bank unconstitutional.

Creation of a joint-stock bank, Jefferson contended, did not come within the orbit of congressional power, either by express grant of the Constitution (in Article I, section 8) or by implication. To take any action not clearly authorized by the Constitution would render meaningless the concept of delegated power and open to Congress the whole field of state and local power. Washington was greatly disturbed by the existence of these diametrically opposed views. In his perplexity the President turned to Secretary of War Henry Knox. "Constitutional," General Knox responded. This assurance, and Hamilton's persuasive *Opinion on the Constitutionality of the Bank of the United States* of February 23, 1791, led the president to sign the bill into law.

Broadening the Base of National Power

Working at his usual breakneck speed, Hamilton produced an opinion destined to become a classic in all later discussions of national power. Next to *The Federalist*, his argument on the constitutionality of the bank is perhaps the most important single contribution to American political thought in the first years of the Union. In it Hamilton made the first substantial statement of the doctrine of implied powers, which he had earlier suggested. It was wrong, he thought, to interpret the grant of power to Congress narrowly. The Constitution surely granted Congress all the powers not specifically prohibited and those needed to carry out the powers expressly granted by Article I, section 8. To Hamilton it appeared axiomatic

> that this *general principle* is *inherent* in the very *definition* of government, and *essential* to every step of the progress to be made by that of the United States, namely: That every power vested in a government is in its nature *sovereign*, and includes, by *force* of the *term*, a right to employ all the *means* requisite and fairly applicable to the attainment of the *ends* of such power, and which are not precluded by restrictions and exceptions specified in the Constitution, or not immoral, or not contrary to the *essential ends* of political society.

The notion that division of sovereign powers between the national government and the states rendered this general proposition inapplicable did not impress the Secretary. Federalism did not restrain the authority of either government from achieving its proper objects. The power to erect

corporations was unquestionably such an object, and consequently incident to the power "of the United States, in *relation* to the *objects*
intrusted to [its] management. . . ." Nor did the Tenth Amendment
invalidate the axiom. To be sure, it provided that "all powers not delegated to the United States by the Constitution, nor prohibited by it to
the States, are reserved to the States, or to the people." But that was
merely a truism: the only limit federalism imposed was that the national
government could establish corporations only in the certain fields of
legislation to which it was permitted entrance. "Fair reasoning and construction . . . [based on] the general principles and general ends of
government" amply demonstrated that Congress possessed three kinds of
power: expressly delegated, implied, and resulting powers. It seemed to
Hamilton that authority to create a corporation was properly an implied
power. A corporation was a natural means for carrying into execution
several specific objects of the national government, at least those of collecting taxes and regulating trade with foreign countries. Although the
power to establish a corporation was not granted in words, it could certainly be implied as a logical way of achieving those ends. Because it was
the province of the national government to regulate those objects, it was
equally within its province to employ any means related "to its regulation
to the best and greatest advantage"—in this case, the incorporation of a
bank.

The power contended for was not a new or independent power. It
did not destroy the constitutional relationship between national and state
power. It was merely an implied power, incident to specified powers and
objects of national concern, a plenary and sovereign power like any specifically delegated power.

"It is no valid objection . . . to say that its[exercise] is calculated to
extend the power of the General Government" into the sphere of state
power.

> The same thing has been said . . . with regard to every exercise of power
> by *implication* or *construction*. . . . The truth is . . . difficulties on this
> point are inherent in the nature of the Federal Constitution; they result
> inevitably from a division of the legislative power. The consequence of this
> division is, that there will be cases clearly within the power of the National
> Government; others, clearly without its powers; and a third class, which will
> leave room for controversy and difference of opinion, and concerning which
> a reasonable latitude of judgment must be allowed.

Jefferson informed the President that the Constitution limited the
extensive use of implied powers by permitting only the enactment of
laws *necessary* for carrying into execution a specifically granted power. To
his mind, "necessary" was restrictive and was to be read as if qualified by
the words "absolutely" or "indispensably." In emphatically rejecting such
reasoning, Hamilton laid the basis for future broad interpretations of the
Constitution's so-called elastic clause. Both grammatically and in common usage, he pointed out, "necessary" often meant no more than "*need-*

ful, requisite, incidental, useful, or *conducive to.*" "It is a common mode
of expression to say, that it is *necessary* for a government . . . to do this
or that thing, when nothing more is intended or understood, than that
the interests of the government . . . require, or will be promoted by,
the doing of this or that thing. The imagination can be at no loss for
exemplifications of the use of the word in this sense. And it is the true
one in which it is to be understood as used in the Constitution." To argue
as Jefferson did was to misinterpret the intent of the Convention, which
was "by that clause, to give a liberal latitude to the exercise of the
specified powers."

Jefferson's interpretation would prevent the use of national power in
many desirable and advantageous situations and thus operate to the
detriment of the public good. Hamilton reminded Congress that many
of the subjects over which the Constitution granted it power were basic
to the "general administration of the affairs" of the nation. Liberal construction must be the rule.

> The means by which national exigencies are to be provided for, national
> inconveniences obviated, national prosperity promoted, are of such infinite
> variety, extent, and complexity, that there must of necessity be great latitude
> of discretion in the selection and application of those means.

Of course, Hamilton reasoned, no government had a right to do merely
what it pleased. Neither, however, was it denied power to enact laws
necessary and proper for accomplishing its purposes. The test of constitutionality was not the degree to which a measure was necessary, but
"the *relation* between the measure and the *end*; between the *nature* of
the *means* employed towards the execution of a power, and the object of
that power. . . . If the *end* be clearly comprehended within any of the
specified powers, and if the measure have an obvious relation to that *end,*
and is not forbidden by any particular provision of the Constitution, it
may safely be deemed to come within the compass of the national
authority."[11]

Even before his arguments for the bank were accepted by Congress,
Hamilton came forward with another proposal. Embodied in his *Report
on the Establishment of a Mint,* and sent to Congress on January 28, 1791,
were his recommendations for the minting of silver dollars and the setting
of a fifteen-to-one monetary standard. So quickly did Congress enact the
secretary's proposal that he was hailed as all powerful before Congress,
failing in nothing he attempted to do. These plaudits seemed none too
extravagant, especially when he succeeded presently in getting Congress
to authorize government encouragement of industry. To accomplish that
objective, Hamilton submitted to Congress the third of his trilogy of
reports, the *Report on the Subject of Manufactures.*[12]

---

[11] Lodge, *Works of Hamilton,* III, 445–58.
[12] Lodge, *Works of Hamilton,* IV, 70–198.

Shoring up the Economic Foundations

The secretary had long been convinced that manufacturing provided an essential key to national power and greatness. As early as 1774, he suggested: "If, by the necessity of the thing, manufactures should once be established, and take root among us, they will pave the way still more to the future grandeur and glory of America."[13] Nothing in the intervening years changed his view. He did not deny the importance of agriculture, but he did query any exclusive predilection in favor of it.

In his report, based on a questionnaire distributed internationally, Hamilton urged government aid for the establishment of manufacturing on two closely related grounds, military security and national economic development. The premise from which he argued was a simple one: that America's future greatness lay in domestic manufacturing. Continued preoccupation with agriculture could result in a small and inconsequential nation, but support of manufactures would produce "a positive augmentation of the produce and revenue of the society" and would be responsible for a more efficient division of labor, the more extensive use of machinery, an increase in employment opportunities, the attraction of emigrants, the creation of a "greater scope for the diversity of talents, and dispositions, which discriminate men from each other," the expansion of the fields of enterprise, and the creation of "a more certain and steady demand for the surplus produce of the soil." All these would redound to the future wealth, independence, and security of America. Their realization depended, however, on the establishment of manufacturing on a firm basis. To that end Hamilton recommended a panoply of government assistance and protection—government aid to inventors, the imposition of tariffs, the granting of bounties, and use of the funded debt as a source of capital for the expansion of the nation's infant industries. Hamilton did not conceive of himself as a protectionist, but his various recommendations have become identified with the concept of protectionism.

In support of national power to encourage industry, Hamilton elaborated his concept of implied powers. The specific delegation of power to Congress to raise money (Article I, section 8) was made in effect "plenary and indefinite" by the phrase which followed it: "To pay the debts and provide for the common defense and general welfare of the United States." The term "general welfare" was added because the Constitution's framers meant it to convey something more than what was included in the first two purposes for which Congress might raise money; "otherwise, numerous exigencies incident to the affairs of a nation would have been left without a provision." This comprehensive phrase was used because they realized that the power of the national government to appropriate its revenues should not be confined to any limits narrower than the gen-

---

[13] Lodge, *Works of Hamilton*, I, 19.

eral welfare of the nation and because they intended it to cover "a vast variety of particulars, which are susceptible neither of specification or definition." Only Congress could decide, in each case, what objects properly concerned the general welfare. It could constitutionally appropriate money to accomplish the broad objects set out in the Constitution. Certainly, he concluded, "the general interests of learning, of agriculture, of manufactures . . . of commerce" were objects for which Congress might spend without violating constitutional limitations.[14] Hamilton's *Report* did not move Congress to immediate action, but his reasoning was ultimately accepted.

HAMILTON'S CONSTITUTION ASSAYED

Hamilton's program began the transformation of America from a parochial, agrarian community into the predominantly industrial nation it is today.

> With his report on manufactures Hamilton hoped to place into position the third, and most enduring, buttress of the nation. With a sound financial structure, with a national bank to make it viable, with a prosperous hum of machinery rising from every city and town in the land, he felt that the future might be faced with a degree of confidence hitherto unknown.[15]

The foundation of Hamilton's nationalist structure was threefold: political, legal, and economic. Even in the days of the sailing vessel and vast distances, he realized that America's might must be built on unconquerable economic power. Military strength had to be laid on foundations of industrialism. As a means to preserve order at home and protect this country politically, economically, and militarily against foreign danger, he favored capitalism as a centralizing force. Economic independence required balance between agriculture, manufacture, and commerce, and it was the business of government to achieve this balance. Hamilton believed in a planned economy.

To portray Hamilton as an advocate of the twentieth-century welfare state is unwarranted. Remarks in the *Report on Manufactures* and elsewhere indicate his lack of sympathy with social planning in the modern sense. Indeed, he was always less concerned with humanitarian objectives than with refuting the idea that production, prices, and profits were the automatic results of the operation of natural economic laws. He promoted the counterproposal that political action is always necessary to regulate a nation's economic life to the best advantage of its people. What is more, he demonstrated that the Constitution endowed the national government with sufficient power to meet this objective. So forcefully did he argue

---

[14] Lodge, *Works of Hamilton*, IV, 151–52.
[15] Nathan Schachner, *Alexander Hamilton* (New York: Appleton-Century-Crofts, 1946), p. 277.

that his theories, formulated during the stress of the first years under the Constitution, have served as the basis for all later government activity in connection with the national economy, including a vast social welfare program.

Hamilton's career suggests a man who both knew what he wanted and could devise strategies best calculated to achieve it. A staunch nationalist, he was bold, calculating, coldly logical, and realistic. Human kindness and warm emotions were not his attributes. Despite his achievements, though great and basic, one notes traces of intellectual arrogance, cynical contempt for the masses, impatience with those intellectually less well endowed, and unbounded ambition. His absorbing concern for a national system of credit, finance, and industry shows little or no concern for the social consequences of his policies. Conspicuously absent from Hamilton's program for building the great American empire is any provision for education. He could perhaps never have said (with Jefferson) that the individual is capable of a development that cannot even be imagined.

HAMILTON'S CONSTITUTION OPPOSED

Hamilton's contribution seems all the greater when the forces aroused against his policies are recalled. These policies provoked fear and distrust and, finally, concerted opposition. Jefferson had been suspicious of Hamilton from the beginning of their association. By 1792, after Hamilton had laid his several reports before Congress and had succeeded in getting a large part of his program adopted, Jefferson was convinced, as he wrote Washington, that the Hamiltonian party in Congress—"a corrupt squadron," he called it—was intent on destroying the states and replacing them with a consolidated system, thus paving the way for a monarchy. In reply Washington conceded that "there might be desires," but he could not believe that "there were designs." Unwilling to accept either Washington's distinction or his seeming acquiescence in Hamilton's policies, Jefferson became even less trusting. As Hamilton's program of national power unfolded, Jefferson and his followers became hostile to it. Jefferson, now thinking of Hamilton as a scheming monarchist, began to record in a secret notebook conversations and observations that seemed to confirm his suspicions. Long afterward, when the passions of the time had died away, he published his notes under the title *Anas*. He still believed that the contest had been "between the advocates of republican, and those of kingly government."

For his part, Hamilton denounced Jefferson and his growing group of followers, which included James Madison, as "pretended republicans," "mere speculatists," and "philosophic politicians," accusing them of being inspired by French revolutionists. The feeling engendered in this contest between two opposed philosophies of government can be seen from Hamilton's remarks to Colonel Edward Carrington, written late in the spring of 1792. His political creed, he told Carrington, included two essential points—"first, the necessity of Union to the respectability and happiness of this country, and second, the necessity of an efficient general government to maintain the Union." With these views Hamilton had understood Madison to be in agreement. Had he thought otherwise, he would not have accepted the Treasury post. Imagine his surprise in discovering Madison joined with Jefferson in opposition on fundamental questions of policy; worse, Madison, either "from a spirit of rivalship, or some other cause, had become personally unfriendly" to him. "Mr. Madison, cooperating with Mr. Jefferson [was] at the head of a faction decidedly hostile to me and my administration"—a faction motivated by views "subversive of the principles of good government and dangerous to the Union, peace, and happiness of the country."[16]

Since the first session of Congress, Hamilton reported to Carrington, Madison and Jefferson had been found among those "who are disposed to narrow the federal authority," leaving as much as possible to the states. What a strange turn of events! Not long before, Madison feared national authority would be subverted by the more powerful states. Now "his measures . . . [were based] on an opposite supposition."[17]

Hamilton believed the Jeffersonian party in error in both domestic policy and foreign affairs. It leaned excessively toward the French and treated the British too coldly to suit his tastes. Jefferson's experiences as ambassador to France, Hamilton reasoned, had permitted him to see government "only on the side of its abuses," and, consequently, he had been attracted by the revolutionary arguments. Such an attraction, however, deviated from "the true path" for the United States, which was a neutral and pacific policy toward all countries.

If Jefferson had begun to jot down Hamilton's idiosyncrasies, Hamilton had at least given considerable thought to Jefferson's peculiarities. The difficulty might well have been, Hamilton confided to Carrington, that Jefferson had come into the cabinet "with a too partial idea of his own powers; and with the expectation of a greater share in the direction of our councils than he has in reality enjoyed. I am not sure that he had not peculiarly marked out for himself the department of the finances." Moreover, he aimed "with ardent desire at the Presidential chair," and this ambition clouded his thinking with considerations of popularity. In any case, Hamilton feared, Jefferson and his party were now attempting to subvert his own position and would stop at nothing to accomplish that objective.

Hamilton's letter to Carrington is significant not only for its evidence of personal friction in the development of American political thought,

---

[16] Alexander Hamilton to Colonel Edward Carrington, May 26, 1792, Lodge, *Works of Hamilton*, IX, 513–35, *passim*.
[17] See Richard Hofstadter, *The Idea of a Party System* (Berkeley, Calif.: University of California Press, 1969); William Nesbit Chambers, *Political Parties in a New Nation: The American Experience, 1776–1809* (New York: Oxford University Press, 1963). See also Lisle A. Rose, *Prologue to Democracy: The Federalists in the South, 1789–1800* (Lexington, Ky.: University of Kentucky Press, 1968).

but also for its concise statement of the Hamiltonian platform of national power: the Union, an efficient and strong national government, state governments "circumscribed within bounds, consistent with the preservation of the national government," "a liberal construction of the powers of the national government" to protect it from the depredations of the large and powerful states, "equality of political rights, exclusive of all hereditary distinction." "I am affectionately attached to the republican theory. . . . [and] I have strong hopes for the success of that theory," Hamilton declared. But "I ought also to add that . . . I consider its success as yet a problem. It is yet to be determined by experience whether it is consistent with that stability and order in government which are essential to public strength and private security and happiness."

The chief ground for Hamilton's doubt was the prevalence of the "spirit of faction and anarchy." If Jefferson, Madison, and the lesser Republicans persisted in their efforts to stir that spirit into action, the Union and all it stood for, Hamilton thought, would be in serious straits. They had forgotten, Hamilton feared, "an old, but a very just, though a coarse saying, that it is much easier to raise the devil than to lay him." What Hamilton described to Carrington was the birth of the American political party system, which Hamilton saw in the black and white terms of personal rivalry.

The Jeffersonians continued their drive and soon could boast a sizable following, especially on the frontier and in the less heavily populated areas of the mountains. It was precisely there that the Hamiltonian program faced its first severe test. To help the national government amass the resources needed to assume the burden of state debts, Hamilton proposed an excise tax on the domestic manufacture of liquor. Congress responded in 1791 by laying a heavy excise tax on whisky, the most important cash product of the back country farmers of western Pennsylvania, Virginia, and North Carolina. The tax at once aroused the farmers' ire. Strong in their preference for the Jeffersonian principle of weak government, they offered opposition to its collection. Denunciatory resolutions were adopted by representatives of the western farmers at a meeting in Brownsville, Pennsylvania, in 1791, and again in Pittsburgh in 1792. Meanwhile, the farmers paid no taxes, and the lives of the government revenue collectors were threatened. Neither a modification in the law nor a warning proclamation from President Washington was effective in quelling the rebellion. Instead, explosive revolutionary slogans began to be shouted in the back country, and in 1794, after a final attempt at conciliation, Washington ordered a militia force of some fifteen thousand men into the region. Without firing a shot, the militia carried the day. Indeed, no resistance was offered. A score or more prisoners were taken and sent to Philadelphia to be tried for treason; some were later convicted but eventually pardoned. The affair ended in a complete victory for the national government and for Hamilton's revenue program. It set the back country, however, onto an anti-federalist tack that was to have significant effects in later years.

In Hamilton's eyes the outbreak was not only a disruption of the fiscal program vital to the success of the national government, but also an example of the Jacobin radicalism he had long been accusing Jefferson and his followers of fostering. To him it was nothing less than an overt challenge to the power, integrity, and dignity of the new government. He probably welcomed the affair, however, for putting it down successfully might add immeasurably to national power and prestige. In a series of papers addressed "To the People of the United States," and written under the pseudonym Tully,[18] Hamilton gave vent to his feelings. Although the size of the "rebellion" made Hamilton's elaborate broadside seem ridiculous, his arguments for law and order were so impressive that they have become an integral part of American constitutionalism.

No republic could lose its liberty "from any other cause than that of anarchy, to which a contempt of the laws is the high-road." Governments were generally of two kinds: of force and of law. The latter could only be preserved and the former avoided if laws were respected and obeyed. Government meant control; it necessitated power, both to keep certain individuals from doing injury to others or to the public good, and to lead them in cooperation toward a common end. Free governments rested only on "a sacred respect for the constitutional law." To rely on force would lead them away from freedom into slavery, for if force became "the ordinary instrument of government," liberty was at an end. Subversion of these tenets was treason, treason "against society, against liberty, against every thing that ought to be clear to a free, enlightened, and prudent people." Thus, the resistance offered in the west to "a solemn constitutional act" was nothing less than "a criminal infraction of the social compact, an inversion of the fundamental principles of republican government, and a daring attack upon [popular] sovereignty"; as such, it must be withstood and defeated. The President must not only use force, if necessary, to carry out his constitutional obligation, but also offer resistance to any "seditious combinations" against the law, wherever they arose, if "the hydra Anarchy" were to be avoided. To keep intact the "goodly fabric" that the framers of the Constitution had established, the majority must govern, the nation must rule, the general will must prevail over that of a faction. There was no other alternative to chaos.

Hamilton stated the issue posed by the Whisky Rebellion with dramatic simplicity: "Shall the majority govern or be governed? Shall the nation rule or be ruled? Shall the general will prevail or the will of a faction? Shall there be a government or no government?" In reply to his own questions, Hamilton suggested that any man who does not agree that force ought to be used to compel insurgents to obey the laws is not a good citizen.

> Such a man, however he may prate and babble republicanism, is not a republican; he attempts to set up the *will* of a part against the *will* of the

---

[18] Lodge, *Works of Hamilton*, VI, 410–26.

whole, the *will* of a *faction* against the *will* of the *nation*, the pleasure of a *few* against *your* pleasure, the violence of a lawless combination against the sacred authority of laws pronounced under your indisputable commission. . . .

Hamilton saw another issue at stake: the preeminence of national power. When Governor Mifflin of Pennsylvania communicated to President Washington his own willingness to cooperate in restoring law and order, his suggestion was flatly rejected. The answer was drafted by Hamilton, and signed by Washington and Randolph:

> It is a matter of some regret, that the course which has been suggested by you, as proper to be pursued, seems to have contemplated Pennsylvania in a light too separate and unconnected. The propriety of that course, in most, if not in all respects would be susceptible of little question if there were no federal government, federal laws, federal judiciary, or federal officers. . . .

More was at stake than restoration of peace, law, and order:

> The people of the United States have established a government for the management of their general interests; they have instituted executive organs for administering that government; and their representatives have established the rules by which these organs are to act. When their authority and that of their government is attacked, by lawless combinations of the citizens of part of a State, they could never be expected to approve that the care of vindicating their authority, of enforcing their laws, should be transferred from the officers of their own government to those of a State.

There seems no justification for the claim that Hamilton used these events in an attempt to subvert the Constitution and change the form of government. Rather, it is reasonable to believe that his intention was to strengthen the part of the system that he considered most beneficial to society. "His only client," Broadus Mitchell wrote, "was the whole country. In a crisis of confusion at home and abroad, he sought stability and system in which a young nation could mature."[19] In Jefferson's eyes, however, he was bent on destroying the very principles that the Virginian considered most important: the agrarian society and sturdy individualism.

Hamilton's essay on the Whisky Rebellion was for all practical purposes his valedictory. Having seen most of his program embodied into law, but hard pressed financially (his annual salary was $3,500), he resigned as Secretary of the Treasury on January 31, 1795. Increasingly opposed by the popular current, even within his own party, Hamilton began to lose his influence. He continued, however, to advise Washington, assisting him in preparing the Farewell Address.

During the short span of his official career, Hamilton put flesh on the skeleton of national power, bolstering every step with his well-rounded creed. His arguments did not seem to prevail; indeed, the Republican Party's victory at the polls in 1800 and its continuance in power for the next generation seemed to belie them.

---

[19] Broadus Mitchell, *Alexander Hamilton* (New York: Macmillan, 1957–1962), I, xii.

HAMILTON'S CONSTITUTION
REINFORCED: JOHN MARSHALL

John Adams's last act as president was the appointment of John Marshall as chief justice of the United States. Marshall not only shared Hamilton's views, but also had actively supported him. As chief justice, Marshall anchored the Hamiltonian precepts in the solid rock of judicial precedent —a more substantial victory, in the long run, than Jefferson's triumph at the polls.[20]

Jefferson considered Marshall's appointment a federalist conspiracy to perpetuate control even after political defeat. The federalists, he wrote, "have retired into the Judiciary as a stronghold . . . and from that battery all the works of Republicanism are to be beaten down and destroyed."[21] Jefferson made it sound exceedingly simple for the Supreme Court to nullify his program. This, however, was not so. When Marshall took over, the Supreme Court had little or no prestige. In *Federalist* Number 78, Hamilton described it "the least dangerous" branch of the government. Despite the Convention's almost unanimous support of judicial review, it had not yet been established in practice. The Supreme Court had, indeed, achieved so little distinction that John Jay had earlier declined Adams's offer to become chief justice again. The first chief justice, Jay resigned to accept the governorship of New York. In 1800 he was convinced that the Court labored under so many handicaps that it would neither "obtain the energy, weight, and dignity essential to its affording due support to the national government nor acquire the public confidence and respect that, as the last resort of the justice of the nation, it should possess."[22]

By the time Marshall went on the Court (February 4, 1801), the Constitution seemed to Hamilton to have become a "frail and worthless fabric."[23] Rescue could come none too soon.

In the nick of time, John Marshall took on this herculean task. The nationalist zeal of Marshall and Hamilton was indistinguishable. They

---

[20] See Samuel J. Konefsky, *John Marshall and Alexander Hamilton: Architects of the Constitution* (New York: Macmillan, 1963). With Marshall in mind, John Quincy Adams rated the office of Chief Justice higher than the presidency, "because the power of constructing the law is almost equivalent to the power of enacting it. The office of Chief Justice of the Supreme Court is held for life, that of the President of the United States only for four, or at most for eight, years. The office of Chief Justice requires a mind of energy sufficient to influence generally the minds of a majority of his associates—to accommodate his judgment to theirs, or theirs to his own—and a judgment capable of abiding the test of time and of giving satisfaction to the public." Charles F. Adams, ed., *Memoirs of John Quincy Adams* (Philadelphia: Lippincott, 1874–1877), IX, 250–51.
[21] Quoted in Edward S. Corwin, *John Marshall and the Constitution* (New Haven, Conn.: Yale University Press, 1919), p. 23.
[22] Corwin, *Marshall and the Constitution*, pp. 23–24.
[23] Quoted in Prescott, *Hamilton and Jefferson*, p. 172.

were also one in their distrust of democracy, and in the priority they accorded property. Commenting in January of 1787 on Shays' Rebellion and similar democratic outbursts, the future chief justice had come to fear "that those have truth on their side who say that man is incapable of governing himself."[24] A year later, pressing for ratification of the Constitution, Marshall argued that the choice was between free government and the despotism of unchecked popular rule. The supporters of the Constitution, he declared, considered the former "as the best means of protecting liberty." One of the "favorite maxims" of free government was "a strict observance of justice and public faith, and a steady adherence to virtue. . . . Would to Heaven that these principles had been observed" under the Articles of Confederation![25]

On the Court, Marshall's distrust of popular rule hardened into basic constitutional tenets. In 1809 he wrote: "I consider the interference of the [state] legislature in the management of our private affairs . . . as . . . dangerous and unwise." For Chief Justice Marshall, Article 1, section 10, was thus the only safeguard in the original Constitution for the rights of property and contract against state action. In *Fletcher* v. *Peck* (1810) and in the Dartmouth College Case (1819), he found constitutional and even higher legal bases for carrying out his belief in vested rights. He hoped that through education the people might in time be better able to exercise the responsibilities of self-government. By 1827, however, he wondered whether there were grounds for optimism, for "as our country fills up how shall we escape the evils which have followed a dense population?"[26]

To Marshall the subordinate position of the judiciary in the national government—and its consequent inability to assert the principles in which he believed—must have appeared as a challenge. In any event he moved with the precision and force of a military strategist to change the situation. As his first step he established in judicial decisions what Hamilton had asserted so forcibly in theory—the right of the Supreme Court to give final interpretation of the Constitution, in regard not only to acts of Congress but also to the acts of state legislatures and state court decisions involving the Constitution. The first goal was accomplished in 1803, within two years after assuming office, in *Marbury* v. *Madison*,[27] and the second in 1819, in *McCulloch* v. *Maryland*.[28]

The Power of the Courts Asserted

Marbury v. *Madison* arose as a result of Adams's last-minute appointments to the federal bench. He named William Marbury a justice of the peace for the District of Columbia. Marbury's commission had been

---

[24] Quoted in A. J. Beveridge, *The Life of John Marshall* (Boston: Houghton, Mifflin, 1919), I, 302.
[25] J. Elliot, *The Debates*, III, 222–23.
[26] Quoted in Beveridge, *Life of Marshall*, IV, 472.
[27] 1 Cranch 137 (1803).
[28] 4 Wheaton 316 (1819).

signed but not delivered when Adams left office. Among Jefferson's first acts as president was to order James Madison, whom he had appointed secretary of state, not to surrender it. Under the terms of the Judiciary Act of 1789, Marbury brought an original suit in the Supreme Court, asking for the delivery of his commission. The suit presented a perfect case for assertion of judicial review, and the chief justice quickly seized the opportunity. That Marbury had a right to his commission Marshall willingly admitted. That the laws of his country afforded him a remedy and that a writ of mandamus, as provided in the Judiciary Act of 1789, was the proper remedy he also admitted. But that the Supreme Court was the proper tribunal for granting a mandamus in such a case he denied; in so doing, he declared unconstitutional section 13 of the Judiciary Act, which authorized the Supreme Court to issue writs of mandamus in such cases. Under his decision Congress could not add to the category of cases enumerated in the Constitution in which the Supreme Court might exercise original jurisdiction.

To give weight to the opinion, Marshall spelled out the underlying theory of judicial review more fully than Hamilton had done in *Federalist* Number 78. Although *Marbury* v. *Madison* has remained central to the system of American constitutional law and stands as Marshall's most distinctive contribution, the credit is not all his. Probably no one saw the potentiality of judicial review, or recognized its legitimacy more unqualifiedly, than Robert Yates in his 1788 *Letters of Brutus* (1788).[29] Hamilton explored the same ground in *Federalist* Number 78:

> The interpretation of the laws is the proper and peculiar province of the courts. A constitution is, in fact, and must be regarded by the judges, as a fundamental law. It therefore belongs to them to ascertain its meaning, as well as the meaning of any particular act. . . . If there should happen to be an irreconcilable variance between the two, that which has the superior obligation and validity ought, of course, to be preferred. . . .

Marbury v. *Madison* is significant as an exercise in judicial creativity and for its theoretical foundations, which go back to the Declaration of Independence. The Court's duty in regard to matters of constitutionality arose out of the fact that the Constitution had been created by the people —a "very great exertion," not to be "frequently repeated." The principles on which the people had acted were deemed fundamental and "designed to be permanent." In the Constitution the powers of Congress were defined and limited; "and that those limits may not be mistaken, or forgotten, the Constitution is written." That being the case, Marshall inquired: "To what purpose are powers limited, and to what purpose is that limitation committed to writing, if these limits may, at any time, be passed by those intended to be restrained?" The answer seemed obvious. The Constitution was designed to control legislative acts repugnant to it. If this were not so, then "written Constitutions are absurd attempts, on

---

[29] See Chapter 6, pp. 99–100, *supra*.

the part of the people, to limit a power in its own nature illimitable." It followed that courts could not give effect to unconstitutional laws. To argue otherwise would be "an absurdity too gross to be insisted on."

> It is emphatically the province and duty of the judicial department to say what the law is. Those who apply the rule to particular cases, must of necessity expound and interpret that rule. If two laws conflict with each other, the courts must decide on the operation of each.

It was "of the very essence of judicial duty" that they do so; the principle of separation of powers reinforces this responsibility. As Marshall put it years later in *McCulloch* v. *Maryland*: "On the Supreme Court of the United States has the Constitution of our country devolved [the] important duty [of deciding questions of constitutionality]. This tribunal *alone* can make such decisions." In all cases in which legislative acts contravened the Constitution, the Supreme Court must uphold the Constitution. It has no other choice.

Chief Justice Marshall, like Hamilton in *Federalist* Number 78, was at special pains to square the Court's limiting and protective function with that other requisite of free government, the notion that legitimate power is derived from the people and must ultimately reflect their will. Judicial review assumes that the power of the people is superior to both legislatures and courts and that when the will of the legislature declared in statutes differs from that of the people declared in the Constitution, the judges will be governed by the latter. It is thus the "will of the people" that the courts discover and declare. As Marshall described it, the judicial process is quite simple: the Constitution is placed beside the law in question to determine whether they agree with each other.

Thus, *Marbury* v. *Madison* is notable not only because it established judicial review but also because Marshall, in asserting this power, set forth the notion that the judicial process is essentially an exercise in mechanics. Supreme Court justices do not make constitutional law; they merely discover the Constitution's meaning. To Marshall judicial power, as contradistinguished from the power of the laws, had no existence. Courts were mere instruments of the law and could will nothing. Under this theory constitutional interpretation consists in finding ultimate meanings that are clear only to judges. To others, whether Congress or the executive, constitutional meaning is necessarily obscure. The only final and authoritative mouthpiece of the Constitution is the Supreme Court. In theory judicial review has the special virtue of never violating the original instrument. To legitimize judicial review, Marshall combined mechanics and theology.

Marshall's decision represented an important political coup. Both his decision and his opinion were thinly veiled lessons to Jeffersonian Republicans, who, feeling that the federalists were attempting to entrench their repudiated philosophy in the federal courts, were seeking to curb the powers of the judiciary. The sole point at issue in *Marbury* v. *Madison* was whether the Supreme Court had jurisdiction in the case, but the Chief Justice could not resist *obiter dicta* (nonbinding, incidental judicial opinions) to demonstrate to Jefferson and his party (and to the public at large) that it was they, not the federalists, who in fact sought to subvert the Constitution. That Marshall managed to strike at Jefferson while not only preserving the Court but also enhancing greatly its power is a testimony to his statesmanship.

Strength of the National Government Fortified

Sixteen years later, in the great case of *McCulloch* v. *Maryland*, Chief Justice Marshall advanced the cause of national legislative power. By 1819, when the *McCulloch* case came before the Court, belief in State's rights and a minimal national government had almost triumphed over the precepts Hamilton had sought to establish. Marshall, like a great many others, was growing increasingly concerned about the dangers that would confront the nation should the doctrine of national supremacy be rejected. The *McCulloch* case gave him a long-awaited opportunity to move in the opposite direction.

McCulloch v. *Maryland* is probably Marshall's greatest opinion; certainly it has since been recognized as the classic statement of the nationalist point of view and has probably been cited more than any other judicial expression before or since.[30] In it are reflected the conclusions of the better part of a lifetime devoted to the advancement of nationalism. The *McCulloch* opinion also revealed Marshall's "qualities as a judicial stylist: his 'tiger instinct for the jugular vein,'; his rigorous pursuit of logical consequences; his power of stating a case . . . his scorn of [qualifications]; the pith and balance of his phrasing . . . the developing momentum of his argument; above all, his audacious use of the *obiter dictum*."[31] He leaned heavily on Hamilton's 1791 opinion on the constitutionality of the bank,[32] as well as on the arguments of counsel in the case, particularly those of Daniel Webster. But, as always, he reinforced, refined, and illuminated these with his own masterful constitutional theory.

The facts of the case are simple. The charter establishing the national bank was proposed by Hamilton in 1791, and it expired in 1811. In 1816 Congress granted it another charter. From the beginning the second Bank of the United States was unpopular in several sections of the country because it sought to control the unregulated issuance of currency by state banks. Charges were made that it was too powerful and that it operated

---

[30] Francis H. Heller, *Introduction to American Constitutional Law* (New York: Harper, 1952), p. 98.

[31] Corwin, *Marshall and the Constitution*, p. 130.

[32] Hamilton also anticipated Marshall's reasoning in *Federalist* Number 23—"the means ought to be proportioned to the end"—as well as in his argument in favor of the constitutionality of the national bank.

too much in the interests of the commercial classes. A number of state legislatures passed either resolutions or legislative enactments against it. Maryland passed an act in 1818 levying a tax on the notes of all banks or branches of banks in the state not chartered by the state legislature. It was aimed directly at the Bank of the United States, and when McCulloch, cashier of the Baltimore branch, issued bank notes on which no tax had been paid, the battle was on. Appealed to the Supreme Court, this case gave Marshall his superb opportunity.

Counsel for Maryland—among them Luther Martin, the ardent states' rights advocate of the Constitutional Convention—put forth the proposition that the Constitution did not emanate from the people; it was "the act of sovereign independent states," and as a result, the powers of the national government "must be exercised in subordination to the states, who alone possess supreme dominion." This was the same proposition that Hamilton had combatted in the early days of Washington's administration. It was popular in 1819, nurtured as it had been by the Republican Party of Jefferson and Madison. Marshall knew that his opinion on this point alone would "essentially influence the great operations of the government" from that time on. He determined, therefore, to quash the proposition completely.

Although the Constitutional Convention was composed of delegates elected by the state legislatures, Marshall began, its product was approved by the *people* of the United States, in convention. "It is true, they assembled in their several states—and where else should they have assembled?" Nor did that fact make their adoption of the Constitution a state act. It remained an act of the people. Thus, the Constitution, Marshall concluded, derived its authority from the people. Their act was final and "of complete obligation . . . and [binding on] the state sovereignties." "The government of the Union, then (whatever may be the influence of this fact on the case), is, emphatically, and truly, a government of the people. In form and in substance it emanates from them. Its powers are granted by them, and are to be exercised directly on them, and for their benefit."

Counsel for Maryland raised the question of the nature of the Constitution not so much as a general inquiry but as an inquiry into the nature and scope of national power. Marshall moved next to meet this argument. It was true, he admitted, that the national government was one of limited, enumerated powers; that principle was now "universally admitted." It was nevertheless "the universal consent of mankind" that "the government of the Union, though limited in its powers, is supreme within its sphere of action." It was the government of all; and the whole, in the areas over which it had power, must necessarily bind its several parts. Reason and common sense demonstrated the truth of this assertion, and the framers of the Constitution had specifically spelled it out in Article VI, section 2. For Marshall this should be enough to convince even the most skeptical.

Coming to the specific exercise of national power in the case before him, Marshall reasoned that although power to establish a bank or create a corporation was not among the enumerated powers in the Constitution, there was "no phrase in the instrument which, like the Articles of Confederation, exclude[s] incidental or implied powers; and which requires that everything granted should be expressly and minutely described." Whether particular powers not enumerated, but not prohibited, lay properly with the national government or with the states was left, even in the Tenth Amendment, to "a fair construction of the whole instrument."

> A constitution, to contain an accurate detail of all the subdivisions of which its great powers will admit, and of all the means by which they may be carried into execution, would partake of [the] prolixity of a legal code, and could scarcely be embraced by the human mind. It would probably never be understood by the public. Its nature, therefore, requires that only its great outlines should be marked, its important objects designated, and the minor ingredients which compose those objects be deduced from the nature of the objects themselves. . . . In considering this question, then, we must never forget that it is a constitution we are expounding.

In other words, although it was appropriate and right that ends were listed and powers enumerated in the Constitution, it would be in vain to expect mention of the various and manifold means appropriate to those ends.

It was equally unreasonable, Marshall went on, to expect that the framers of the Constitution, having listed such important ends of the national government as laying and collecting taxes, borrowing money, and regulating commerce, intended to "clog and embarrass [their] execution by withholding the most appropriate means." The framers could not have intended to withhold from Congress a choice of means or even to limit the choice of means by requiring a demonstration of its necessity and propriety. To be sure, the Constitution gave Congress the power to make all laws *necessary* and *proper* for carrying into execution the other enumerated powers. But those words could not rightfully be given a restrictive meaning—despite Jefferson's claim in reaction to Hamilton's bank proposal and the claim of counsel for Maryland—lest the additional grant of power be construed as excluding "the choice of means, and [leaving] to Congress, in each case, that [means] only which is most direct and simple." Instead, Marshall maintained, it must be recognized that *necessary* and *proper*, used in the Constitution as anywhere else, conveyed, as Hamilton had insisted, more than a single idea. They were not confined to "a fixed character"; nor did they always import the same degree of urgency. Like all words they were used in various senses; thus, in their construction, "the subject, the context, the intention of the person using them, are all to be taken into view."

> We admit, as all must admit, that the powers of the government are limited, and that its limits are not to be transcended. But we think the sound construction of the constitution must allow to the national legislature that discretion, with respect to the means by which the powers it confers are to be carried into execution, which will enable that body to perform the high

duties assigned to it, in the manner most beneficial to the people. Let the end be legitimate, let it be within the scope of the constitution, and all means which are appropriate, which are plainly adapted to that end, which are not prohibited, but consist with the letter and spirit of the constitution, are constitutional.

The question at issue was the power to create a corporation, a bank. Was it a legitimate exercise of national power? Or was it, as counsel for Maryland contended, in contradiction to the Constitution? Both the states and the national government could create corporations, Marshall answered, as one of the prerogatives of sovereignty, each in its own sphere. It had merely to be demonstrated, in the case of the national government, that the creation of a corporation was reasonably related to one of its legitimate ends. That could easily be established. Nothing in the Constitution, in the arguments of counsel, or in the circumstances of the case suggested that any particular reason could be advanced for excluding the use of a bank, if required for fiscal operations. Indeed, the bank was "a convenient, a useful, and essential instrument in the prosecution of its fiscal operations." It was enough for the Court to say that both the act establishing the Bank of the United States and the establishment of a branch in Maryland were constitutional and proper.

It remained, then, for Marshall to deal with Maryland's tax on what was thus a legitimate branch of the national government. On this question, as throughout the case, Marshall's reasoning was broad, directed not only toward settling the issue raised in the case but also toward setting a precedent. He could easily have declared the Maryland statute discriminatory or void, for it was obviously aimed directly at a national agency and thus patently unconstitutional both by the terms of Article VI, section 2, and by the general construction of the Constitution. Such a decision would have been in accord with what he had already written and would have given firm support to the concept of national power that he was so anxious to advance. Marshall, however, went much further. To achieve his object, he formulated the principle that the states had no power "to tax the means employed by the government of the Union, for the execution of its powers." Those means operated for the benefit of all and were selected by the representatives of all; no one state had the power or right to interfere with or attempt to nullify their operation; nor was the permission or authorization of any state necessary. Moreover, the power to tax, as Webster had said in arguing the case, involved the power to destroy. "The power to destroy may defeat and render useless the power to create," Marshall declared. There is "a plain repugnance," he argued, "in conferring on one government a power to control the constitutional measures of another, which other, with respect to those very measures, is declared to be supreme over that which exerts the control." This seemed to him an undeniable proposition. Confidence in state government could not be relied upon to prevent its exercising power designed to destroy the national government. Only the absolute denial of that power to the states would be an adequate safeguard. In the last analysis, it was a question of supremacy, and it was clear to Marshall that "if the right of the states to tax the means employed by the general government be conceded, the declaration that the Constitution, and the laws made in pursuance thereof, shall be the supreme law of the land, is an empty and unmeaning declaration." This Marshall would not allow, and he made use of his decision to prevent it from happening.

Marshall had other opportunities before his death in 1835 to support the Hamiltonian principles of national power and strong government and to develop them even further. The current of the times ran counter to his efforts, however, and they did not receive widespread contemporary approval. It was not until our own time that Marshall's precepts, in the main extensions of the Hamilton philosophy, triumphed in American politics and jurisprudence. For many years they have been virtually uncontested.[33]

HAMILTON AND MARSHALL: NATION BUILDERS

For the development of national power as a main tenet of American political thought, credit lies chiefly with Hamilton and Marshall. The first phase of the American Revolution had been predicated upon the assumption that men had a right and a responsibility to decide for themselves when their government was intolerable. This was the relatively easy, negative aspect. The positive, and far harder, one required demonstration of the practical meaning of that right by erecting a new governmental fabric to replace one that had proved inadequate. Hamilton served the United States in both phases of the Revolution, but it was during the second—when the war-inspired unity had broken down and interest was pitted against interest—that he stamped American history indelibly with a mark characteristically his own.

It remained for John Marshall to translate Hamilton's ideas into principles of constitutional law. Their efforts were so intertwined that appraisal of their separate contributions is difficult. Marshall has been lauded as a nation maker, a state builder, and has been conceded credit equal to, if not greater than, that given Hamilton in laying the solid foundations of a supreme and powerful national government. Justice Holmes, speaking on the one hundredth anniversary of Marshall's appointment as chief justice, was impressed more by Hamilton than by the chief justice. A part of Marshall's greatness, Holmes wrote in 1901, consisted in his "being *there*"—on the Supreme Court, and in the center chair—at the right time in the nation's history. He doubted "whether, after Hamilton and the Constitution itself, Marshall's work proved more than a

---

[33] See Robert K. Faulkner, *The Jurisprudence of John Marshall* (Princeton, N.J.: Princeton University Press, 1968).

strong intellect, a good style, personal ascendancy in his court, courage, justice, and the convictions of his party."[34] In Holmes's view Marshall lacked originality; he did not go beyond Hamilton; his opinions opened up no wider vistas.

Hamilton's contributions were both theoretical and practical. As secretary of the treasury, he not only supplied the theory of national power on which Marshall later built so enduringly, but also acted to give that theory concrete meaning. John Marshall secured and extended Hamilton's work even though the latter's archenemy, Thomas Jefferson, was in power. Working against the political tide, Chief Justice Marshall established judicial precedents for national power during a period when centrifugal forces were gaining momentum. Professor Corwin stressed Marshall's accomplishments and the effectiveness of his method:

> It was no ordinary skill and courage which, assisted by great office, gave enduring definition to the purposes of the Constitution at the very time when the whole trend of public opinion was setting in most strongly against them. . . . Not one of the cases which elicited his great opinions but might easily have been decided on comparatively narrow grounds in precisely the same way in which he decided it on broad, general principles, but with the probable result that it would never again have been heard of outside the law courts. . . .[35]

At the end of his Anniversary Speech, Holmes gave Marshall high praise:

> When I consider his might, his justice, and his wisdom, I do fully believe that if American law were to be represented by a single figure, sceptic and worshipper alike would agree without dispute that the figure could be one alone, and that one John Marshall. . . . Time has been on Marshall's side; the theory for which Hamilton argued, and he decided, and Webster spoke, and Grant fought, and Lincoln died, is now our cornerstone.[36]

Hamilton and Marshall formulated "for a people whose thought was permeated with legalism the principles on which the integrity and ordered growth of their nation have depended."[37] So much cannot be said for any other pair of statesmen in American history—unless Hamilton's (or Marshall's) name be joined with that of his great antagonist, Thomas Jefferson.

---

[34] Oliver Wendell Holmes, *Collected Legal Papers* (New York: Harcourt, Brace, 1921), p. 269.
[35] Corwin, *Marshall and the Constitution*, pp. 22–23.
[36] Holmes, *Legal Papers*, p. 270.
[37] Corwin, *Marshall and the Constitution*, p. 230.

CHAPTER EIGHT

STRESS ON FUNDAMENTAL RIGHTS: MADISON, JEFFERSON, AND TAYLOR

Power builders make an indispensable contribution to a nation's greatness. So do those who question power. The latter determine whether we use power or power uses us. Hamilton's and Marshall's primary concern was the establishment of national power. But they tended to underestimate an equally important aspect of free government—limitations. A delegate to the Pennsylvania ratifying convention put the point succinctly:

> So loosely, so inaccurately are the powers which are enumerated in this constitution defined, that it will be impossible, without . . . [a bill of rights], to ascertain the limits of authority, and to declare when government has degenerated into oppression.[1]

Without a bill of rights fixing the limits of national power over the rights of individuals, the anti-federalists had insisted, the Constitution was incomplete. In convention after convention, the want of a bill of rights weighed heavily in the discussions. Although in the end the Constitution was ratified by eleven states, a number did so with "recommen-

---

[1] Quoted in Mason, *Free Government*, p. 309.

datory" amendments. The need to satisfy the demand for a bill of rights was finally acknowledged by federalists and anti-federalists alike.

The problem was twofold: how to get the amendments incorporated into the Constitution and what to include among the rights so protected. Ratification in New York had only been achieved at the price of a circular letter to other states, calling for another Convention to provide the amendments demanded. James Madison took the lead in defusing such a dangerous suggestion, dangerous because, as Washington perceived, it would "set everything afloat again."[2] Why not use the new instrument of government itself to provide its own corrective? It was Madison's sincere opinion

> that the Constitution ought to be revised, and that the first Congress meeting under it ought to prepare and recommend to the States for ratification, the most satisfactory provision for all essential rights, particularly the rights of Conscience in the fullest latitude, the freedom of press, trials by jury, security against general warrants, etc.[3]

Having been elected a representative to Congress from Virginia, Madison, prodded by Jefferson, took the lead both in proposing the amendments (on June 8, 1789)[4] and in piloting them through Congress. From the list submitted came the first eight amendments to the Constitution, including guarantees of freedom of speech, press, religion, petition, and assembly; a variety of procedural safeguards—those against unreasonable search, seizure, and warrants of arrest; a blanket provision that no person be deprived of life, liberty, or property without due process of law; and specific protections for persons accused of crime. Lest certain "natural rights" be omitted, Madison included the so-called "forgotten ninth amendment," stating that the enumeration, in the Constitution, of certain rights was not to deny or disparage the existence of other rights belonging to the people of a free society.

Specific safeguards against government encroachment on individual rights were not enough. To quiet anti-federalist fears that an overbearing central government would destroy the states, Madison reluctantly included a further amendment—the tenth: "The powers not delegated to the United States by this Constitution, nor prohibited by it to the States, are reserved to the States respectively, or to the people thereof." He successfully resisted heavy pressure to insert "expressly" before the word "delegated," thus once again defeating men of states' rights persuasion in their attempt to circumscribe national power. Omission of "expressly" made the Tenth Amendment redundant, merely another way of expressing the substance of Article VI, section 2, of the Constitution—the so-called Supremacy Clause. Even so, the door was left ajar, opening the way to an unending struggle for states' rights.

---

[2] Mason, *Free Government*, p. 313.
[3] Mason, *Free Government*, p. 314.
[4] *Annals U.S. Congress*, 1st Cong. (1789), I, 440–60.

The campaign for a bill of rights began as a seemingly partisan maneuver to defeat ratification of the Constitution. It ended with the desired goals being generally accepted by all. The fundamental rights of people in a free society were given no greater moral sanction by their being incorporated into the supreme law of the land; but by that act, rights formerly natural became civil. Individuals could thereafter look to courts for their protection and fulfillment, and courts—thanks to the antifederalist drive—could look to the Constitution, particularly to the Bill of Rights, for standards. Incorporation of the Bill of Rights into the Constitution made the courts the special guardians of those rights, "an impenetrable bulwark against every assumption of power in the legislature or executive. . . ." The dilemma John Locke had posed, that is, who shall decide in case of conflict between the government and the people, had been doubly answered—by providing *judges* to ascertain when the peoples' representatives had broken the social compact and by arming them with *standards* to guide them in arriving at their decision. By these means the system of free government was immeasurably strengthened and popular support more widely secured.

THE JEFFERSON REVOLUTION

To many the actions taken by the Washington and Adams administrations under Federalist leadership seemed to threaten the accomplishment of national purpose. The Federalists not only seemed to favor the needs of the great merchants and landowners of New England and the Middle Atlantic states in their attempt to encourage industry and establish a well-ordered sociey, but also were pro-British in foreign affairs. These attitudes increasingly separated them from the majority of the electorate. As a result of their effective public relations effort and their superior political organization, the Jeffersonians swamped the Federalists in the election of 1800. After Jefferson's election, which he called a revolution, Hamilton despaired for his party, for the Constitution, and for the country. All his efforts seemed to have been in vain.

No such dramatic lamentations marred Jefferson's prospects in taking office, on March 4, 1801, as the third President of the United States. "The revolution of 1800 was," he said two days later, "as real a revolution in the principles of our government as that of 1776 was in its form."

In a letter to John Dickinson, Jefferson made a more specific indictment of the course on which the Federalists had led the nation and expressed his determination to effect a "perfect consolidation":

> The storm through which we have passed has been tremendous indeed. The tough sides of our Argosie have been thoroughly tried. Her strength has stood the waves into which she was steered with a view to sink her. We shall put her on her republican tack, and she will now show by the beauty of her motion the skill of her builders. . . I hope to see shortly a perfect consolidation, to effect which nothing shall be spared on my part, short of the abandonment of

the principles of our revolution. A just and solid republican government maintained here will be a standing monument and example for the aim and imitation of the people of other countries; and I join with you in the hope and belief that they will see from our example, that a free government is of all others the most energetic; that the enquiry which has been excited among the mass of mankind by our revolution and its consequences, will ameliorate the condition of man over a great portion of the globe. What a satisfaction have we in the contemplation of the benevolent effects of our efforts, compared with those of the leaders on the other side, who have discountenanced all advances in science as dangerous innovations, have endeavored to render philosophy and republicanism terms of reproach, to persuade us that man cannot be governed but by the rod, etc. I shall have the happiness of living and dying in the contrary hope.[5]

As head of the triumphant Democratic-Republican party, Jefferson portrayed the nation in his inaugural address as in "the full tide of successful experiment," and rated the national government as "the world's best hope." "I know," his message continued, "that some honest men have feared that a republican government cannot be strong; that this government is not strong enough . . . I believe this, on the contrary, the strongest government on earth." Obviously, the ingredients of national strength Jefferson considered essential bore little or no resemblance to those stressed by Hamilton and Marshall,[6] and no one was more acutely conscious of these divergencies than the protagonists themselves. The safest reliance of every government was on men's interests, Hamilton believed. Jefferson, on the other hand, upheld government's responsiveness to the people. For him the people were the safest and most honest, though not necessarily the wisest, depository of the public interest. Responsibility, exercised by the people, was a powerful engine in a free government. He deemed the inconveniences attending too much liberty less worrisome than those attending too little liberty and opposed consolidation—Federalist style—convinced that only by the distribution of power could good government be effected. The true guardians of liberty in this country were the state governments. For Jefferson these were among the elements on which he relied for achieving "a perfect consolidation."

The "revolution" of 1800 represented the completion of another cycle in the characteristic pattern of American politics. The Declaration of Independence and the period that followed it—indeed, the Revolutionary War itself—were devoted to loosening bonds and minimizing control. During the years 1783–1787 difficulties verging on chaos sparked a movement toward a more energetic government. The period before the Constitutional Convention and immediately following it, years of Federalist

---

[5] Thomas Jefferson to John Dickinson, March 6, 1801, Paul Leicester Ford, ed., *The Works of Thomas Jefferson* (New York: G. P. Putnam's Sons, 1905), IX, 201–2.
[6] See Julian P. Boyd, "Jefferson's 'Empire of Liberty,'" *Virginia Quarterly Review* XXIV (Autumn, 1948), 538–54. See also Gilbert Chinard, *Thomas Jefferson*, 2nd ed. (Ann Arbor, Mich.: University of Michigan, 1966), especially Book IV.

supremacy, represented a swing of the pendulum toward order, security, and power. The Constitution institutionalized that trend. By 1800 the movement launched by the Washington and Adams administrations had spent itself, and the same forces that had swung the political pendulum in 1776 toward emphasis on natural rights swayed it in that direction again. Just as Jefferson's words in 1776 had given voice to the rights side of the American dichotomy, so their author led the movement stressing rights as the proper basis of governmental policy. Seemingly antagonistic, the philosophies of Hamilton and Jefferson have been fused in the mainstream of American political thought, furnishing both the essence and the enduring strength of free government.

Jefferson's election did not, however, terminate vigorous government action, nor even the broad construction of the Constitution. On occasion Jefferson carried liberal construction to its limits. Whereas Hamilton and Marshall looked upon the Constitution as primarily a grant of power, Jefferson was inclined to stress its guarantees of freedom. Thus, the triumph of the Democratic-Republican party under Jefferson's leadership meant the resumption of that always popular and appealing theme of American politics, the rights of free men. On this foundation Jefferson built his own "Empire of Liberty."

THE CONSTITUTION AS A COMPACT OF STATES

The difference between Jefferson and the Federalists is revealed most clearly in their varying conceptions of federalism. Hamilton and Marshall were inclined to favor national power at the expense of the states. This balance, they believed, had been struck by the Constitution itself. Jefferson, on the other hand, saw the Constitution in terms of preservation "to the states [of] the powers not yielded by them to the Union, and to the legislature of the Union [of] its . . . share in the division of powers." He opposed "transferring all the powers of the States to the general government."[7] On the contrary, he favored "preservation to the States of those rights unquestionably remaining with them."[8] The Federalist program threatened "to sink the State governments, consolidate them into one, and to monarchize that." Jefferson preferred to keep government localized, believing that the United States was even then "too large to have all its affairs directed by a single government." Administrative difficulties and a diminution of the people's ability to control their public servants would follow any increase of national power at the cost of the states. "What an augmentation of the field for jobbing, speculating, plundering, office-building and office hunting would be produced by an

---

[7] To Elbridge Gerry, January 26, 1779, Ford, *Works of Jefferson*, IX, 18.
[8] To Gideon Granger, August 13, 1800, Ford, *Works of Jefferson*, IX, 138–39.

assumption of all the State powers into the hands of the general govern-ment," Jefferson wrote Gideon Granger. "The true theory of our Con-stitution is surely the wisest and best, that the States are independent as to everything within themselves, and united as to everything respecting foreign nations."[9]

Jefferson's conception of federalism is perhaps most distinctly visible in the Kentucky Resolutions of 1798. (Madison wrote a similar resolution for the Virginia legislature, also in 1798.) Drafted by Jefferson and passed by the Kentucky legislature in reaction to the Alien and Sedition Acts, the resolutions viewed the Constitution as a compact of sovereign states. Because the Constitution did not unequivocally preclude "state sover-eignty," such an assertion could easily be made. Jefferson believed that

> to this compact [the Constitution] each State acceded as a State, and is an integral party, its co-States forming, as to itself, the other party; that the gov-ernment created by this compact was not made the exclusive or final judge of the extent of the powers delegated to itself; . . . but that as in all other cases of compact among parties having no common Judge, each party has an equal right to judge for itself, as well of infractions as of the mode and mea-sure of redress.[10]

Jefferson invited other states to concur in declaring the Alien and Sedi-tion Acts void and of no force.

That Jefferson placed no absolute value on union is clearly reflected in his letter of August 23, 1799, to Madison:

> Express in affectionate and conciliatory language our warm attachment to union with our sister-states, and to the instrument and principles by which we are united; that we are willing to sacrifice to this every thing except those rights of self government the securing of which was the object of that com-pact; that not at all disposed to make every measure of error or wrong a cause of scission, we are willing to view with indulgence, to wait with patience till those passions & delusions shall have passed over which the federal govern-ment have artfully & successfully excited to cover its own abuses & to conceal its designs; fully confident that the good sense of the American people and their attachment to those very rights which we are now vindicating will, before it shall be too late, rally with us round the true principles of our fed-eral compact. But determined, were we to be disappointed in this, to sever ourselves from that union we so much value, rather than give up the rights of self government which we have reserved, & in which alone we see liberty, safety & happiness.[11]

---

[9] Ford, *Works of Jefferson*, IX, 140.

[10] Ford, *Works of Jefferson*, VIII 458–59.

[11] Quoted in Adrienne Koch and Harry Ammon, "The Virginia and Kentucky Resolu-tions: An Episode in Jefferson's and Madison's Defense of Civil Liberties," *William and Mary Quarterly*, V (April, 1948), 166. A further Kentucky Resolution, adopted in 1799, provided a formal process for nullification of objectionable acts.

THE NATIONAL GOVERNMENT:
POLICEMAN OF THE UNION

Jefferson's conviction that the Constitution was in truth a compact and that state sovereignty lay at its base led him to ideas entirely opposed to the Federalist conception of the national government's proper influence. Hamilton and Marshall did not seek to confine national activities within restricted limits. Jefferson, on the other hand, repeatedly spoke out for a small and inactive central authority, for a "simple and economical mode of government."[12] No friend of energetic government by his own admission, he favored "a government rigorously frugal and simple, applying all the possible savings of the public revenue to the discharge of the national debt; and not for a multiplication of officers and salaries merely to make partisans, and for increasing, by every device, the public debt, on the principle of its being a public blessing." Government must have authority enough to prevent men from injuring one another, to eliminate artificial barriers to equality of opportunity, and to spread the advantages of education among all the people. These and other matters internal he confided to the states; the national government's chief responsibility was foreign affairs. But he wanted no national army in peacetime, favoring reliance on the militia until actual invasion, and thought only of "such a naval force . . . as may protect our coasts and harbors" and not of a navy "which, by its own expenses and the external wars in which it will implicate us, will grind us with public burdens, and sink us under them."[13] Nor did he favor a large diplomatic establishment, believing that commerce should be free and that the United States should engage in no treaties or political connections with other countries. "Let the general government be reduced to foreign concerns only," Jefferson declared, "and let our affairs be disentangled from those of all other nations, except as to commerce, which the merchants will manage the better, the more they are left free to manage for themselves, and our general government may be reduced to a very simple organization, and a very inexpensive one; a few plain duties to be performed by a few servants."[14]

Jefferson's conviction that the national government need perform only "a few plain duties" stemmed from his conception of the United States as primarily agricultural. Unlike Hamilton and, to some degree, Marshall, who looked ahead to a time when the United States would be a great industrial empire, Jefferson thought of agriculture as America's economic mainstay.

> He sprang from a society deep-rooted in an agrarian economy, and he wished to preserve that society. Born on the Virginia frontier, he had never

---

[12] Ford, *Works of Jefferson*, IX, 140.
[13] To Elbridge Gerry, Ford, *Works of Jefferson*, IX, 18.
[14] To Gideon Granger, Ford, *Works of Jefferson*, IX, 140.

seen a hamlet so large as twenty houses before his eighteenth year; his neighbors and associates were capable and vigorous frontier democrats, who managed the affairs of local government with the same homespun skill that went to their farming.[15]

The states and local governments were thus "the most competent administrations for our domestic concerns," and he saw no reason to give the national government any more power than was necessary for preserving "peace at home and safety abroad."[16]

THE FOCUS OF FREE GOVERNMENT: FREE INDIVIDUALS

Equally important in explaining Jefferson's preference for simple and economical government is the fact that his chief attention was directed toward freedom rather than control. To him the sum of good government was that it should leave men free "to regulate their own pursuits of industry and improvement." His concern was directed more to the portion of their lives that men possessed free from governmental restraint than to the smaller portion regulated by government. He thought that government should not step far beyond the role of policeman. "Still one thing more," Jefferson observed in his First Inaugural Address, "a wise and frugal government, which shall restrain men from injuring one another . . . and shall not take from the mouth of labor the bread it has earned. This is the sum of good government, and this is necessary to close the circle of our felicities."[17]

Whereas Hamilton doubted the wisdom of too much liberty and thus devoted his public career to strengthening the role of government in the nation's life, Jefferson sought to minimize that role and to elevate the individual, who was born with God-given unalienable rights. To violate these rights or to ignore man's infinite capacity for development was to sever the very roots of national strength. Jefferson believed that the worth of the state is commensurate with the worth of the individuals composing it. He made freedom the proper concern of government, central to everything else—freedom of religion, freedom of speech, freedom of the press, "the progress of science in all its branches,"[18] the equal right of all men to the use of their faculties and to the acquisitions of their industry, freedom of persons under the protection of *habeas corpus*, and trial by jury. To assure the perpetuation of these freedoms was an adequate role for the national

---

[15] Parrington, *Main Currents*, I, 345.

[16] First Inaugural Address, Ford, *Works of Jefferson*, IX, 198.

[17] Ford, *Works of Jefferson*, IX, p. 197. Jefferson's concern for weak government was not wholly shared by his fellow Virginians. See Wiley E. Hodges, "Pro-Governmentalism in Virginia, 1787–1836: A Pragmatic Liberal Pattern in the Political Heritage," *The Journal of Politics*, XXV (May, 1963), 333–60.

[18] To Elbridge Gerry, Ford, *Works of Jefferson*, IX, 18.

government, and the degree to which it secured them was the index of its success.

Most important was the invigoration of man and society, the quickening and informing of public policy and action by exposing them to all the divergent and shifting currents of doctrine. "Reason and free inquiry are the only effectual agents against error," he proclaimed in *Notes on Virginia*. "It is error alone which needs the support of government. Truth can stand by itself." He reiterated an unwavering belief in "freedom of religion, and against all manoeuvres to bring about legal ascendancy of one sect over another; [in] freedom of the press, and against all violations of the Constitution to silence by force and not by reason the complaints or criticisms, just or unjust, of our citizens against the conduct of their agents."[19] Bitter experience under the Alien and Sedition Acts validated this belief. In his First Inaugural Address he reechoed it with the challenge: "If there be any among us who would wish to dissolve this Union or change its republican form, let them stand undisturbed as monuments of the safety with which error of opinion may be tolerated when reason is left free to combat it."[20]

Jefferson believed that republican government, seen as the instrument of the people themselves, was of all forms of government most likely to preserve and extend men's freedom. In his First Inaugural Address, he spoke of majority rule as a "sacred principle," and called for "absolute acquiescence" in its decisions. But the majority will "to be rightful must be reasonable," for "the minority possess their equal rights, which equal law must protect. . . ."[21] So great was his confidence "in the natural integrity and discretion of the people, and in the safety and extent to which they might trust themselves with a control over their government,"[22] that the fear of the people often expressed by Hamilton never troubled him.

Not even Jefferson's confidence in the people was unqualified. Since his earliest days in public office, his attention and interest had been directed toward education. The fundamental prerequisite of a free society was an enlightened citizenry. "If a nation expects to be ignorant and free, in a state of civilization, it expects what never was and never will be."[23] "To give information to the people" was the most certain and the most legitimate function of government. In his *Notes on Virginia*, Jefferson wrote:

> History, by apprising [the people] of the past, will enable them to judge of the future; it will avail them of the experience of other nations and other times; it will qualify them as judges of the actions and designs of men; it will

[19] Ford, *Works of Jefferson*, IX, 180.
[20] First Inaugural Address, Ford, *Works of Jefferson*, IX, 195.
[21] Ford, *Works of Jefferson*, IX, 195.
[22] To John Melish, January 13, 1813, Ford, *Works of Jefferson*, XI, 279.
[23] Saul K. Padover, ed., *The Complete Jefferson*, (New York: Duell, Sloan & Pearce, 1943), p. 149.

enable them to know ambition under every disguise it may assume; and knowing it, to defeat its views. In every government on earth is some trace of human weakness, some germ of corruption and degeneracy, which cunning will discover, and wickedness insensibly open, cultivate and improve. Every government degenerates when trusted to the rulers of the people alone. The people themselves, therefore, are its only safe depositories. And to render even them safe their minds must be improved to a certain degree.[24]

Acting on this belief, Jefferson had prepared a bill for the Virginia legislature providing for a system of public education in free ward schools, in which reading, writing, and common arithmetic would be taught; for those who distinguished themselves, it would provide "a higher degree of education at a distant school"; and finally, for the most promising students, it would provide education at a university, "where all the useful sciences should be taught."[25] The bill was not adopted, but the University of Virginia, a later product of Jefferson's interest in education, furthered his idea. The University of Virginia has been characterized as "the lengthened shadow of one man." Chartered in 1819 and opened for instruction in 1825, with Jefferson as its first rector and with both Madison and Monroe on its first Board of Visitors, it was designed to offer instruction in ancient and modern languages, mathematics, natural philosophy (physics and astronomy), natural history (chemistry and botany), moral philosophy (ethics and metaphysics), anatomy and medicine, law, and engineering. Courses in "this institution," Jefferson said, "will be based on the illimitable freedom of the human mind. For here we are not afraid to follow truth wherever it may lead, nor to tolerate any error, so long as reason is left free to combat it."[26]

Also helpful in alleviating the risks of majority rule, Jefferson believed, was a "natural aristocracy among men," based on virtue and talent. "It would have been inconsistent in creation to have formed man for the social state, and not to have provided virtue and wisdom enough to manage the concerns of the society," he declared.[27] The American system of government provided effectually for election of those who possessed such virtue and wisdom—those "natural *aristoi*"—in numbers sufficient to secure good government. Given the proper moral and physical conditions, the citizens of the United States were qualified to select "the able and good for the direction of their government." The only auxiliary precautions needed were "a jealous care of the right of election by the people, a mild and safe corrective of abuses which are lopped by the sword of revolution where peaceable remedies are unprovided,"[28] and "a recur-

---

[24] *Notes on Virginia*, Ford, *Works of Jefferson*, IV, 64.
[25] To John Adams, October 28, 1813, Ford, *Works of Jefferson*, XI, 346.
[26] Quoted in Gordon E. Baker, "Thomas Jefferson on Academic Freedom," *American Association of University Professors Bulletin*, XXXIX (Autumn, 1953), 378.
[27] To John Adams, October 28, 1813, in *Notes on Virginia*, Ford, *Works of Jefferson*, IX, 343.
[28] First Inaugural Address, Ford, *Works of Jefferson*, IX, 198.

rence of elections at such short periods as will enable [the people] to displace an unfaithful servant, before the mischief he meditates may be irremediable."[29] Jefferson abhorred Hamilton's artificial aristocracy of family and fortune, denouncing it for its constant attempts to occupy all the places of power and profit in society.

Republican government meant, above all, the "ingredient of the direct action of the citizens," "the control of the people over the organs of their government."[30] To illustrate his point, he quoted these lines:

> "What constitutes a State?
> Not high-raised battlements, or labor'd mound,
>   Thick wall, or moated gate;
> Not cities proud, with spires and turrets crown'd;
>   No: men, high-minded men;
>   Men, who their duties know;
> But know their rights; and, knowing, dare maintain.
>   These constitute a State."[31]

Republicanism so defined did not exist at either the local or national level. "In the General Government," he observed, "the House of Representatives is mainly republican; the Senate scarcely so at all, as not elected by the people directly, and so long secured even against those who do elect them; the Executive more republican than the Senate, from its shorter term, its election by the people, *in practice* (for they vote for A only on an assurance that he will vote for B), and because, *in practice, also,* a principle of rotation seems to be in a course of establishment; the judiciary independent of the nation, their coercion by impeachment being found nugatory." All this indicated that there was "less of republicanism [in the United States] than ought to have been expected. . . ." The people had "less regular control over their agents, than their rights and their interest require," a fault ascribed to the influence of European "speculators" on government, who, frightened by the masses of their own cities, had come to fear the people and thus to advocate circumscription of their part in government.[32] The proper balance could yet be struck by asserting the right of popular election and by exercise of the right of revolution. The possibilities of the first should be exhausted before the dangers of the second were let loose, but he did not think the people should hesitate to use revolution if they found it necessary.

GOVERNMENT: A POPULAR INSTRUMENT

Obviously, Jefferson did not regard constitutions with sanctimonious reverence. He did not deem them like the ark of the convenant—too

---

[29] To John Adams, *Notes on Virginia*, Ford, *Works of Jefferson*, XI, 349.
[30] To John Taylor, May 28, 1816, Ford, *Works of Jefferson*, XI, 529, 532.
[31] Ford, *Works of Jefferson*, XI, 531.
[32] Ford, *Works of Jefferson*, XI, 531–32.

sacred to be touched. He did not speak of the Constitution, as Marshall did, as a "very great exertion," not frequently to be repeated. "Laws and institutions must go hand in hand with the progress of the human mind."

> As that becomes more developed, more enlightened, as new discoveries are made, new truths disclosed, and manners and opinions change with the change of circumstances, institutions must advance also, and keep pace with the times. We might as well require a man to wear still the coat which fitted him when a boy, as civilized society to remain ever under the regimen of their barbarous ancestors.[33]

Jefferson dismissed stability and order, which seemed so desirable and necessary to Hamilton and Marshall, as a handicap to national development. Believing that each generation was capable of taking care of itself, of ordering its own affairs, he advocated the right of each new generation to choose the form of government it believed most conducive to its own happiness. The Constitution should provide an opportunity for such a choice at regular intervals. "This corporeal globe, and everything upon it, belong to its present corporeal inhabitants, during their generation. They alone have a right to direct what is the concern of themselves alone, and to declare the law of that direction; and this declaration can only be made by their majority."[34]

Jefferson's concept of government by the laws of the living reduced the role of the federal courts. Their function was to protect men's rights against legislative and executive encroachment. Neither judicial precedent nor contemporary constitutional interpretation was binding on the coordinate branches of government. Marshall explicitly upheld, against any claim by Congress, the President, or the states, the Court's right to determine the Constitution's meaning. Jefferson refused to confide such exclusive and final authority anywhere save in a majority of the people. "Absolute acquiescence in the decisions of the majority" was the "vital principle" of republican government, and he did not believe this principle could be ignored, particularly by a body so remote from the people as the courts. Courts had a function, an important one, but he could find nothing in the Constitution or in the theory of republican government that gave the Supreme Court an exclusive judgment of the constitutionality of legislation. Each branch should pass on the validity of acts pertaining to matters within its jurisdiction. It was possible, Jefferson admitted, "that contradictory decisions may arise in such case, and produce inconvenience. . . . Yet the prudence of the public functionaries, and authority of public opinion, will generally produce accommodation."[35]

The view that legislative interpretation was final had merit because of its safety—"there being in the body of the nation a control over [the

---

[33] To Samuel Kercheval, July 12, 1816, Ford, *Works of Jefferson*, XII, 12.
[34] Ford, *Works of Jefferson*, XII, 13–14.
[35] To W. H. Torrance, June 11, 1815, Ford, *Works of Jefferson*, XI, 474.

legislature], which, if expressed by rejection on the subsequent exercise of their elective franchise, enlists public opinion against their exposition, and encourages a judge or executive on a future occasion to adhere to their former opinion."[36] Although he preferred a legislative to a judicial interpretation, Jefferson was not inclined to credit the legislature with any great responsibility for advancing the nation's republicanism. Republicanism was not furthered by the Constitution but by the spirit of the people, which would oblige even a despot to govern in a republican manner. "In government, as well as in every other business of life," Jefferson concluded, "it is by division and subdivision of duties alone, that all matters, great and small can be managed to perfection. And the whole is cemented by giving to every citizen, personally, a part in the administration of the public affairs."[37]

CONSISTENCY THROUGH INCONSISTENCY

Jefferson's primary interest lay in "responsive government."[38] Everything else was of secondary importance. Through the years, as conditions changed, Jefferson's thinking changed too. He brought new policies and new concepts to the support of his main object or altered old ones. It never troubled him that the ground on which he was arguing had become soft. He merely shifted his position. "Apparently inconsistent, changing his program with the changing times, he seemed to his enemies devoid of principle, a shallow demagogue who incited the mob in order to dupe the people."[39] Yet Jefferson, contradictory and many sided as he was, never swerved from his central belief, that the most important work of society was to preserve the rights God had given equally to all men. Nothing was unchangeable but the inherent and inalienable rights of man.

Devotion to these "eternal verities" was perhaps the only stable and consistent element of his philosophy. In 1787, for example, he even seemed to favor judicial review, voicing regret that the judiciary had not been associated with the president in exercising the veto and even suggesting that the Supreme Court might have been given a similar or separate veto power. In the abstract, it seemed to him that such a power vested in the Court provided an additional safeguard for individual rights. In the spring of 1787, when Madison wrote him, proposing that the federal government be given a negative on state legislatures in all cases whatsoever, Jefferson answered that this was a new idea to him.

> Would not an appeal from the state judicatures to a federal court in all cases where the act of confederation controlled the question be as effectual

---

[36] Ford, *Works of Jefferson*, XI, 475.
[37] To Samuel Kercheval, Ford, *Works of Jefferson*, XII, 9.
[38] Parrington, *Main Currents*, I, 351.
[39] Parrington, *Main Currents*, I, 343.

a remedy and exactly commensurate with the defect? It will be said that this court may encroach on the jurisdiction of the state courts. It may. But there will be a power, to wit, Congress, to watch and restrain them. But place the same authority in Congress itself, and there will be no power above them to perform the same office. They will restrain within due bounds a jurisdiction exercised by others much more vigorously than if exercised by themselves.[40]

In these early endorsements, however, Jefferson never imagined that he would be confronted with such a formidable adversary as John Marshall. With the chief justice specifically in mind, he wrote years later:

> It is not enough that honest men are appointed judges. All know the influence of interest on the mind of man, and how unconsciously his judgment is warped by that influence. To this bias add that of the esprit de corps, of their peculiar maxim and creed, that "it is the office of a good judge to enlarge his jurisdiction," and the absence of responsibility, and how can we expect impartial decision between the General government, of which they are themselves so eminent a part, and an individual state from which they have nothing to hope or fear? We have seen too that, contrary to all correct example, they are in the habit of going out of the question before them, to throw an anchor ahead and grapple further hold for future advance of power.[41]

Having endured as president the painful experience of trying to pilot the impeachment proceedings of Supreme Court Justice Samuel Chase through Congress, Jefferson concluded that "impeachment is a farce which will not be tried again."[42] In 1823, many years after retirement, he wrote:

> At the establishment of our constitutions, the judiciary bodies were supposed to be the most helpless and harmless members of the government. Experience, however, soon showed in what way they were to become the most dangerous; that the insufficiency of the means provided for their removal gave them a freehold and irresponsibility in office.[43]

Jefferson's apparent about-face was due to changed circumstances. As an explanation Dumas Malone suggests that "a deeper consistency" might have been involved; "continued advocacy of a balanced government" and opposition to such "tyrannies as seemed most menacing at a particular time."[44]

It was not judicial *review*, in any case, but judicial *supremacy* that aroused Jefferson's ire. He was adamant in his belief that each branch of the federal government is coordinate with the others and that each should interpret the Constitution in its own way; in cases of conflict, an appeal

---

[40] To James Madison, March 15, 1789, Ford, *Works of Jefferson*, V, 461.

[41] Ford, *Works of Jefferson*, I, 122 (autobiography).

[42] To William Giles, April 20, 1807, Ford, *Works of Jefferson*, X, 387.

[43] A. A. Lipscomb, ed., *The Writings of Thomas Jefferson*, Library ed. (Washington, D.C., 1903), XV, 487.

[44] Malone, *Jefferson*, p. 163.

to the people as the final judge afforded the proper method of determining which interpretation should prevail.

Other "inconsistencies," some more glaring, may be noted. Jefferson's espousal of free inquiry and expression, his faith in reason, are unrivaled in American history. But he was not invariably freedom's champion. When difficulties arose in finding a professor of law for the University of Virginia unaffected with subversive Federalist principles, he proposed a "previous prescription" of texts as well as close examination of the professor's beliefs.

> In most public seminaries, text-books are prescribed to each of the several schools, as the *norma docendi* in that school; and this is generally done by authority of the trustees. I should not propose this generally in our University, because, I believe none of us are so much at the heights of science in the several branches as to undertake this; and therefore that it will be better left to the professors, until occasion of interference shall be given. But there is one branch in which we are the best judges, in which heresies may be taught, of so interesting a character to our own state, and to the United States, as to make it a duty in us to lay down the principles which shall be taught. It is that of Government. Mr. Gilmer being withdrawn, we know not who his successor may be. He may be a Richmond lawyer, or one of that school of quondam federalism, now consolidation. It is our duty to guard against the dissemination of such principles among our youth, and the diffusion of that poison, by a previous prescription of the texts to be followed in their discourses.[45]

Once again Jefferson's departure from his own principles can be partially explained, though not justified, by changed conditions. Jefferson noted that many young Virginians were going north to college, and he feared that they would imbibe dangerous political doctrines. To him, letting the Federalists educate the youth of the South seemed bad strategy. He anticipated that if Virginia did not spend more on education, she would be too weak to oppose the "overwhelming mass of light and science by which she will be surrounded." New York was making "gigantic efforts" in education, and Massachusetts had long been the most influential of all states because of her lead in education. He hoped that the University of Virginia would relieve the dependence of the South on northern universities and would possibly attract some northern youth as well, thus creating friendships that would help cement the Union. As sectional conflicts deepened, he looked to the university as a source of solidarity, as "a nursery of Republican patriots as well as genuine scholars." Northern "seminaries were no longer proper for Southern or Western students."

> Harvard will still prime it over us, with her twenty professors. How many of our youths she now has, learning the lessons of anti-Missourianism, I know

---

[45] Baker, "Jefferson on Academic Freedom."

not; but a gentleman lately from Princeton, told me that he saw there the list of students at that place and that more than half were Virginians. These will return home, no doubt, deeply impressed with the sacred principles of our holy alliance of Restrictionists.[46]

Before censuring Jefferson too severely, one should bear in mind the elevated plane on which he stood and the fact that present-day professional standards of academic freedom have been achieved only after years of hard struggle. In his espousal of academic inquiry, Jefferson was far ahead of his time. Even now the academic profession is unable to present a united front in freedom's defense.

One other example of his inconsistency may be cited. Opposed to "energetic government," Jefferson upbraided the Federalists for their attempts to expand the national government. Yet, as president, Jefferson himself stretched national power further than either of his Federalist predecessors, further even than Hamilton and Marshall had ventured. Extreme examples are his embargo program, the Louisiana Purchase, and his recommendation of a national university. Jefferson tried to explain these actions, noting:

> A strict observance of the written laws is doubtless *one* of the high duties of a good citizen, but it is not *the highest*. The laws of necessity, of selfpreservation, of saving our country when in danger, are of higher obligation. To lose our country by a scrupulous adherence to written law would be to lose the law itself, with life, liberty and property and all those who are enjoying them with us; thus absurdly sacrificing the end to the means. . . . It is incumbent on those only who accept of great charges, to risk themselves on great occasions, when the safety of the nation, or some of its very high interests are at stake.[47]

In his own mind Jefferson's motives remained the same—preservation and expansion of human liberty in the United States. Because both the embargo and the Louisiana Purchase were necessary to achieve that purpose, the constitutional barrier did not deter him.

> The dominant principle of his [Jefferson's] creed was that all powers belonged to the people, and that governments, constitutions, laws, precedent,

---

[46] Quoted in Baker, "Jefferson on Academic Freedom," p. 384.
[47] It is quite clear that this explanation did not fully satisfy Jefferson himself: "I had rather ask an enlargement of power from the nation, where it is found necessary, than to assume it by a construction which would make our powers boundless. Our peculiar security is in the possession of a written Constitution. Let us not make it a blank paper by construction. I say the same as to the opinion of those who consider the grant of the treaty-making power as boundless. If it is, then we have no Constitution. . . . If, however, our friends shall think differently, certainly I shall acquiesce with satisfaction, confiding that the good sense of our country will correct the evil of construction when it shall produce ill effects." Ford, *Works of Jefferson*, IV, 498–505; VIII, 234, 241–45.

and all other artificial clogs and "protections" are entitled to respect and obedience only as they fulfilled their limited function of aiding—not curtailing—the greatest freedom of the individual.[48]

APOSTLE OF HUMAN RIGHTS

Less than a month before he died, at the age of 83, Jefferson reiterated the essence of his faith. The mayor of Washington, D.C., invited him, as one of the surviving signers of the Declaration of Independence, to participate in the fiftieth anniversary celebration of the signing of that document. Jefferson could not go because of poor health, but in his reply to the mayor, he spoke of the choice America had made, a choice he believed would

> be, (to some parts sooner, to others later, but finally to all) the signal of arousing men to burst the chains [which bind them] and to assume the blessings and security of self government. That form which we have substituted restores the free right to the unbounded exercise of reason and freedom of opinion. All eyes are opened, or opening, to the rights of man. The general spread of the light of science has already laid open to every view the palpable truth, that the mass of mankind has not been born with saddles on their backs, nor a favored few booted and spurred, ready to ride them legitimately, by the grace of God. These are grounds of hope for others. For [our]selves let the annual return of this day, forever refresh our recollections of these rights, and an undiminished devotion to them.[49]

Jefferson has attracted enthusiastic partisans and equally vehement detractors. So wide were his interests and so facile his mind that his contributions embraced every aspect of American life. He played a significant role not only in the development of American politics, but also in the growth of American science, architecture, education, philosophy, and agriculture. No name in American political history has shone more brightly in terms of "hostility against every form of tyranny over the mind of man." This unvarying stress on the individual supplies the key to an understanding of what he meant by "strong government." Embodying the Enlightenment thinking of his generation, Jefferson's affinity for the heavenly city of the eighteenth-century philosophers sharply distinguishes his political ideas from those of Hamilton or Marshall. Not denying the importance of a strong militia, a sound economy, and a rich supply of resources to national well-being, Jefferson ultimately rested nationhood upon a cluster of ideals in the possession of the citizens. For the author of the Declaration of Independence, these were the rights of man. A spa-

---

[48] Anthony M. Lewis, "Jefferson's *Summary View* as a Chart of Political Union," *William and Mary Quarterly*, V (January, 1948), 34.
[49] To R. C. Weightman, June 16, 1826, *The Writings of Thomas Jefferson*, Memorial ed., XVI, 182.

cious conception of nationality is basic to Jefferson's political philosophy, as well as to his political behavior: "His was a constructive achievement," Julian Boyd observed, "grounded upon an enlarged view of man in relation to his potentialities and to the society in which he moves . . . His wholehearted and undeviating acceptance of the idea and meaning of nationhood were characterized by a faith, a vision, and an elevation of purpose that made him all but unique among the Founding Fathers."

The government of the United States was strong not only in the ideal sense, but also in the very practical sense that it enjoyed the uncoerced and willing support of the people. Its strength lay in the fact that the formal structure was buttressed by principles that alone could assure the rights of man. Republicanism, with its ear sensitively attuned to the wishes of the people, was of all forms of government the only one that could provide a political structure capable of maintaining harmony between political practice and the spirit of freedom. Because "a just and solid republican government" found its strength in national consensus, it was "of all others the most energetic."

Emphasizing the spiritual rather than the tangible ingredients of nationhood, Jefferson paid relatively little attention to constitutional form and structure. "Methods of arranging and distributing political power," Boyd wrote, "were not among Jefferson's absolutes . . . Understanding history, he perceived that laws and constitutions merely codify and do not create the elements of nationhood. The monumental achievements of American constitutionalism . . . were the written expressions of a people already unified in ideals, as Jefferson clearly perceived." Perhaps better than any of his contemporaries he sensed the fact that the people, too, believed in their national destiny. "The salient fact that we have too long overlooked," Boyd concluded, "is that the cardinal principle of Jefferson's life was his uncompromising devotion to the union because of its identity with human rights."[50]

To the end of his days, Jefferson regarded government as an enemy of freedom rather than as a handmaiden. He had a peculiar distaste for governing. "An honest man can feel no pleasure in the exercise of power over his fellow citizens," he said. "Power is not alluring to pure minds." "There never has been a moment in my life in which I should not have gladly relinquished office for the enjoyment of my family, my farm, my friends and my books."[51] As an old man he posed for himself the question: "Is my Country the Better for my Having Lived at All?" His reply listed four accomplishments—none concerned with governing, all directed toward further freeing or emancipating men: the Declaration of Independence and the Virginia statutes proclaiming religious freedom, the abolishment of primogeniture and entail, and the prohibition of the importation of slaves. On his tombstone at Monticello, the epitaph Jefferson wrote for himself proclaims:

---

[50] Boyd, *The Declaration*, pp. 543–46, *passim*.
[51] Ford, *Works of Jefferson*, XI, 279.

Here was buried Thomas Jefferson, author of the Declaration of American Independence, of the Statute of Virginia for religious freedom, and father of the University of Virginia.

The man who had been elected president of the United States for two terms and served his state as a party leader and governor omitted all mention of these distinctions, thereby suggesting his conviction that "the greatest service which can be rendered any country is to add a useful plant to its culture." Woodrow Wilson may have hit upon the key to Jefferson's significance: it did not consist "in any one of his achievements, but in his attitude toward mankind."[52]

JEFFERSONIAN IDEAS SYSTEMATIZED: JOHN TAYLOR

Jefferson's contribution to American political thought was one of orientation, emphasis, and direction. Nowhere did he crystallize his own philosophy or develop it systematically. Only now, during the process of assembling his voluminous works in a multivolume edition, is it becoming possible to get an overall view. He opposed Federalist doctrines all his life, but his attacks were piecemeal and sometimes impromptu. It remained for others to elaborate the Jeffersonian position.

That task was undertaken by John Taylor (1753–1824) of Caroline County, Virginia. A lawyer, Taylor had served in the Revolutionary War, rising to the rank of lieutenant colonel. He was long a member of the Virginia House of Delegates (1779–1781, 1783–1785, 1796–1800) and of the United States Senate (1792–1794, 1803, 1822–1824). Although he maintained a large degree of political independence, he generally walked in the same paths as Jefferson. His pamphlet of 1794 entitled *Definition of Parties; or the Political Effects of the Paper System Considered* prepared the way for later Republican attacks on Hamilton's fiscal policies. He introduced the Virginia Resolutions of 1798 to the Virginia House of Delegates, and went so far on that occasion as to propose dissolution of the Union and formation of a southern confederacy.

Taylor is remembered chiefly for his *An Inquiry into the Principles and Policy of the Government of the United States* (1814), which Charles A. Beard praised as the "single immortal work in political science since . . . *The Federalist,*" for his *Construction Construed and Constitutions Vindicated* (1820), *Tyranny Unmasked* (1822), and *New Views of*

---

[52] Quoted in Mason, *Free Government.* In a recent biography of Jefferson, Thomas Fleming, *The Man From Monticello. An Intimate Life of Thomas Jefferson* (New York: William Morrow, 1969) the author has concluded: "Jefferson's last and best legacy is his life. . . . No real understanding of the man . . . can be achieved merely by studying his ideas. It is his life that tells us . . . the many meanings of a reasoned commitment to freedom. . . ." (pp. 385–86).

the Constitution of the United States (1823). In all these works Taylor attacked Hamilton's financial programs and the aristocracy he was convinced would result from their operation. Even more vehement in his defense of agrarianism than Jefferson, Taylor denounced Federalist policies as creating a new aristocracy of wealth, an "aristocracy of paper and patronage," inimical to an agricultural society. He agreed that a few would often possess "the mass of the renown, virtue, talents and wealth of a nation" and that in such cases they not only might but "probably ought to" form an aristocracy. But if such an aristocracy were not present, it ought not to be created by legal enactment. As he saw it, that was precisely the effect, if not the intention, of Hamilton's policies. Just as the priesthood and the nobility had once oppressed the majority of the people, so the banking system, central to Hamilton's program, was oppressing the common people of America.

Such policies as the funding system, the Bank of the United States, and the protective tariff not only put existing generations under the tutelage of the past, but also redounded to the benefit of the new paper-money aristocracy rather than to the benefit of the farmer. The result was that the people daily grew less free, and their rights were steadily being diminished. Good government had of necessity to follow what Taylor described as "the elemental political axiom," that its power be exercised for the good of the whole nation. The Federalists had reversed the maxim. The sharpest barbs of Taylor's pen were reserved for an attack on the protective tariff. The bulk of *Tyranny Unmasked* was devoted to arguments against it. It was "a tax upon the rich and the poor of the whole community," on all consumers "for the exclusive benefit of the rich of one occupation. This is aristocracy in its worst character."[53] To justify passing laws favorable to a few and injurious to the best interests of the many, the Federalists had deliberately misconstrued the Constitution. It was not the fault of the document itself. It would stand vindicated when the Federalists' "artful conversion of good words, into knavish dogmas" was brought to a stop.[54]

In *Construction Construed and Constitutions Vindicated*, Taylor lashed out at John Marshall's doctrine of implied powers. The people had granted legislative power only to their representatives. Under the Lockean principle this power could not be delegated. Yet Congress had created a bank with the power to regulate the national currency. "Now I ask, if [this power] is not both a formal and substantial legislative power? What is legislative power? Something able to dispense good or harm to a community. Cannot bank directors do this? Somebody has said that money *governs* the world. Have those who govern money no governing powers?" They undoubtedly did. They composed a perfect aristocracy, "exercising an absolute power over the national currency," an aristocracy that operated in complete disregard for republican principles. It could only be

---

[53] Quoted in Mason, *Free Government*, p. 373.
[54] Mason, *Free Government*, p. 63.

controlled by removing its cause—the misinterpretation of the Constitution that supported it.[55]

Taylor not only conceived of the Bank of the United States as violating republican principles, but also was convinced that, like the entire Federalist program, it ran directly counter to the Republican tenet of weak government. Taylor asked his readers to "turn your eyes toward a government accoutred in the complete panoply of fleets, armies, banks, funding systems, pensions, bounties, corporations, exclusive privileges . . . in short, possessing an absolute power to distribute property, according to the pleasure, the pride, the interest, the ambition, and the avarice of its administrators; and consider whether such a government is the servant or the master of the nation?"[56] Carrying his dislike of energetic government beyond Jefferson's, Taylor held that *any* power in the national government to distribute, or even affect, property per se rendered the government bad. "Freedom of property," he believed, "will beget civil liberty, as freedom of conscience has begotten religious. The success of one experiment proves the other to be practicable . . . Had the freedom of religion been established in England at the Reformation, a mass of civil war, national inquietude and oppression would have been avoided. A greater mass of these evils was foreseen by the framers of the Union, and attempted to be avoided, by restricting the powers given to Congress, and by retaining to the states those powers united with the local interests, habits and opinions of each state; in fact, by securing the freedom of property."[57]

By the time Taylor wrote these words, it was too late to unseat such doctrines or divest the national government of its already considerable power. Taylor's arguments were nevertheless those of a large number of American people, and they particularly appealed to Southerners when the slavery issue arose in the 1850s. Combined with the idea of nullification, which Jefferson and Madison fostered in 1798–1799, Taylor's well-constructed theory of extreme localism played a significant role in American politics, despite its poor timing. In his last book, *New Views of the Constitution*, he carried the States' rights doctrine to the very brink of secession.

Although Taylor adopted Madison's distinction between national and federal government, he rejected the idea that the Constitution had, as Madison suggested, embodied both concepts. In a federal system, Taylor insisted, the Constitution itself was supreme. This supremacy bound all the instruments of government, including the Supreme Court, and it constituted "an admonition to all departments, both state and federal, that they were bound to obey the restrictions it imposes." It could not be, as Marshall contended, that the Supreme Court had the final right to interpret the Constitution. Instead, this right of construction, which

---

[55] Mason, *Free Government*, pp. 319–20.
[56] Mason, *Free Government*, p. 12.
[57] Mason, *Free Government*, pp. 16–18.

"must be attached to the right of alteration, or the latter right would be destroyed," belonged to the states "because they made [the Constitution], and not [to] a consolidated people, because such a people did not make it; the right of construction is attached to the altering power, and not given to its own agents under the fictions assumed to sustain a national government, namely, that a consolidated people existed. . . ."[58]

> In the creation of the federal government, the states exercised the highest act of sovereignty, and they may, if they please, repeat the proof of their sovereignty, by its annihilation. But the union possesses no innate sovereignty, like the states; it was not self-constituted, it is conventional, and of course subordinate to the sovereignties by which it was formed. . . . I have no idea of a sovereignty constituted upon better ground than that of each state, nor of one which can be pretended to on worse, than that claimed for the federal government. . . .

Small wonder that Taylor has been called a "prophet of secession"!

Such a conception of sovereignty quite naturally led Taylor, as it had Jefferson, to the conclusion that the national government was confined to the exercise of its delegated powers only. It led him also to the strained conclusion that whereas the people were actually supreme within the several states, they were not a party to the federal union. There, supremacy was to be found in three-fourths of the states. Because of the two different supremacies, Taylor thought neither the states nor the United States were subject to the laws or judgments of the other. "Reason, compact, and a common interest, and not a supreme power, [were] the only resources for settling" the collisions such a division of power inevitably produced.[59]

Taylor's argument served to add vigor to the popular states' rights philosophy and to discredit Federalist principles, thus paving the way for Jacksonian Democracy. Throughout his writing runs a strong note of pessimism, "occasionally almost an elegiac note, as if he were lamenting a world mortally wounded by change."[60] Faith even in his own party faltered as he saw Jefferson, and later Madison and Monroe, accept some of the principal planks of the hated Federalist platform. Jefferson retreated from some of his theoretical positions, and Madison and Monroe, "lacking either the will or the capacity to work out a program in terms of their own . . . philosophy, were forced to beat a faltering but unmistakable retreat from the original Jeffersonian positions."[61] Madison gave his approval to the Second Bank of the United States in 1816 and even endorsed the tariff. The Jeffersonian party, by deviating from the true principles of free government, had become "tinctured with the folly of

---

[58] Quoted in Mason, *Free Government*, p. 400.
[59] John Taylor, *New Views of the Constitution of the United States* (Washington, D.C.: Printed for the author, 1823), p. 379.
[60] Arthur M. Schlesinger, Jr., *The Age of Jackson* (Boston: Little, Brown, 1946), p. 25.
[61] Schlesinger, *Age of Jackson*, p. 18.

certain sympathies, towards strong parties, popularity, and noise."[62] The people had been deserted by their own champions. Of course, no desertion had actually taken place. The merit of Hamilton's program had simply proved itself, and Democratic-Republican leaders had moved perforce to adopt parts of it. By the time Taylor wrote his last book in 1823, the United States was clearly moving in the direction of an integrated industrial economy; so there was little left for him to do but bemoan America's departure from the simple agricultural way of life and demand a return to the earlier status quo. With Taylor, Jeffersonian agrarianism and belief in states' rights became a dissenting minority movement, bucking the Hamiltonian tide until defeated on the battlefield in 1865.

THE JEFFERSONIAN HERITAGE

Jefferson's victory in 1800 afforded an opportunity to redress the nationalist dominance achieved under the administrations of Washington and Adams. The Jeffersonians stressed state sovereignty in opposition to the concept of a consolidated union; they were more concerned with the role of the people in government and with the supremacy of the majority, more inclined to elevate individual rights to a dominant position among constitutional principles. Any appraisal of the Jeffersonian influence must take these facts into account. Certainly the emphasis on state sovereignty, especially as developed by John Taylor and the southern theorists who followed him, has been a disruptive influence in American politics. In fairness to Jefferson, it should be pointed out, as Charles A. Beard took pains to do in *The Republic*, that Jefferson was disinclined toward secession and never proposed it openly. Indeed, "in practice and in his addresses to the country, Jefferson stood by the Constitution and voiced a conviction that constitutional principles should guide the nation."[63] In his First Inaugural Address, Jefferson described "the preservation of the General Government in its whole constitutional vigor, as the sheet anchor of our peace at home and our safety abroad." Yet Jefferson cannot escape responsibility for advancing the cause of secession. It was his partisans, or some of them, who made the states' rights doctrine the potent force in American politics that it became after 1850.

Jefferson's reiteration of faith in the individual, his belief in a government resting on the consent of the governed first stated in the Declaration of Independence, were a healthy counterbalance. Federalist leaders, except perhaps John Marshall, were aristocrats by orientation if not by birth, and as a result their policies and programs often overlooked considerations of popular interest and support. By 1800 the nation needed reaf-

---

[62] John Taylor to James Monroe, January 31, 1811, in "Letters of John Taylor," *The John P. Branch Historical Papers of Randolph-Macon College (1901–1918)*, II, 317.
[63] Charles A. Beard, *The Republic* (New York: Viking, 1946), p. 62.

firmation of faith in the people, of faith in "the common reason of society," as well as reassertion of men's fundamental rights. Jefferson's firm conviction stimulated a broad-gauged movement in the 1820s and 1830s to expand the base of political power, bringing about still another "revolution," one in which the tenets of his creed were reaffirmed and extended.

CHAPTER NINE

THE BASE
OF FREEDOM EXPANDED

After the Louisiana Purchase and the War of 1812, American public attention began to turn westward, stimulating an effort destined to exert the influence on American life Frederick Jackson Turner later described as central to an understanding of American history. Industrialism expanded rapidly, and the means of transportation improved, facilitating settlement of the West. Gradually Madison's prediction at the Philadelphia Convention was fulfilled: "An increase of population will of necessity increase the proportion of those who will labour under all the hardships of life, and secretly sigh for a more equal distribution of its blessings. These may in time outnumber those who are placed above the feelings of indigence. According to the equal laws of suffrage, the power will slide into the hands of the former."

The 1820s witnessed this process in action, and it was the states that undertook to adjust to it. Their goal was to approach in fact what Jefferson had proclaimed in the Declaration of Independence.

DEFECTS OF THE
EARLY STATE CONSTITUTIONS

Even before the Declaration of Independence, a number of states had adopted constitutions. Rhode Island and Connecticut simply reenacted their liberal colonial charters. The other eleven states drafted new constitutions. All the original state constitutions had been framed and adopted, as New York convention delegate P. R. Livingston recalled in 1821, "in an hour of extreme peril, amidst the noise of musketry and the thunder of cannon. We all knew that deliberations, under such circumstances, were in some measure erroneous."[1] Reform was warranted on many grounds. Jefferson's criticism of the Virginia Constitution of 1776 applied with equal force to the constitutions of other states.[2]

In most cases the new constitutions had been framed by revolutionary provincial congresses, the Massachusetts Constitution of 1780 being the first to be popularly ratified. Each of the original constitutions proclaimed the supremacy of law and reflected the current belief in natural rights. Some were prefaced with the Declaration of Independence. All paid lip service to Montesquieu's principle of separation of powers, though none made full use of the corollary doctrine of checks and balances. All created independent judiciaries, in most cases appointed by the governor or the legislature for life or for good behavior. All reflected the contemporary distrust of executive power and consequently assigned to legislatures the chief powers of government. In most cases the executive branch was subordinated to the legislature; in some states even the governor was chosen by the legislature. Aside from those imposed by bills of rights, the legislatures were subject to few limitations.

Although professing belief in popular sovereignty, the early state constitutions were not democratic documents. Every one limited the right of suffrage and confined the concept of the "people" to persons meeting either property or taxpaying qualifications. There was little in any of the first constitutions supporting the principle of equality asserted in the Declaration of Independence; the elevated proposition that "governments are instituted among men, deriving their just powers from the consent of the governed" fell far short of realization. "Every man, having property in, a common interest with, and an attachment to the community ought to have the right to the suffrage," the Maryland Constitution of 1776 declared. The Virginia Constitution incorporated almost the same words. None of the other constitutions deviated from this general pattern. All demonstrated that "the Revolution brought no marked change in the suffrage laws . . . The position of the propertied classes remained almost as secure after, as it had before, independence."[3] In addition to property qualifications on the suffrage, several states imposed religious requirements.

[1] P. R. Livingston, in *Proceedings and Debates of the Convention of 1821, Assembled for the Purpose of Amending the Constitution of the State of New York* (Albany, 1821).
[2] See Oscar Handlin, *The Popular Sources of Political Authority. Documents on the Massachusetts Constitution of 1780* (Cambridge, Mass.: Belknap Press of Harvard University Press, 1966).
[3] Edward M. Sait, *American Parties and Elections*, rev. ed. (New York: Appleton-Century-Crofts, 1939), p. 24.

Religious tests and property qualifications were required also for office holding; "those other than trinitarian Protestants frequently found themselves disqualified."[4] In the first Constitution of South Carolina, for example, office holders were required to take an oath. Atheists and deists were denied both suffrage and office holding by the provision that "all persons and religious societies who acknowledge that there is one God, and a future state of rewards and punishments, and that God is to be publicly worshipped, shall be freely tolerated." Property qualifications for office holding were imposed in most states, the amount usually higher than that set for voting, and the more elevated the office, the larger the amount.

The undemocratic nature of the early constitutions was also manifest in the fact that the legislatures, although dominant, were not truly representative of the people. The older tidewater areas were everywhere given more than their share of representation, while the new back country sections were poorly represented.

Continuance into the nineteenth century of aristocratic features in the early state constitutions might have been due, as Charles A. Beard believed, to "apathy and lack of understanding of the significance of politics."[5] A vast majority of Americans had long been accustomed to restricted suffrage and property qualifications for office holding. In an agricultural society oriented toward land values, it seemed proper that political power should attach itself to land ownership. The fact that voters constituted only 3.6 percent of the population[6] did not strike most Americans as incongruous. In any case, there had been little pressure for the removal of such restrictions.

THE GROWING DEMAND FOR REFORM

A number of factors contributed to the demand for wider political participation. In the War of 1812 many Americans fighting for their country did not have the privilege of voting. As the western territories were settled and came as states into the Union, they carried with them an egalitarianism absent in the more settled seaboard areas. Pioneer conditions and the availability of land to all (in 1820, the minimum price of public land was $2 per acre; by 1830, it had been reduced to $1.25, and sales were authorized in smaller units) made arbitrary distinctions restricting suffrage and office holding seem unreasonable. Kentucky entered the Union in 1792 with a constitution that allowed all free white males of full age to vote for members of the lower house. By amendment in 1799 popular election was extended to the election of the senate and the gov-

---

[4] Jeanette P. and Roy F. Nichols, *The Growth of American Democracy* (New York: Appleton-Century-Crofts, 1939), p. 82.
[5] Charles A. Beard, *An Economic Interpretation of the Constitution of the United States* (New York: Macmillan, 1947), p. 284.
[6] Richard Hofstadter, *The American Political Tradition and the Men Who Made It* (New York: Knopf, 1948), p. 50.

ernor. The Tennessee Constitution of 1796 provided for direct election of both houses of the state legislature and of the governor. These states pioneered; other western states followed as they joined the Union.

Pressure for the eradication of political privilege also arose out of the development Madison had foreseen: by the 1820s a propertyless class had developed in the industrializing East, a group—largely native American—that insisted on equal political rights. It has been suggested that "the trend toward popular activity in politics was heightened by the panic of 1819, which set class against class for the first time since the Jeffersonian era." Thousands of debtors found themselves pushed to the wall by their creditors and in defense turned to politics. "For the first time many Americans thought of politics as having an intimate relation to their welfare."[7] Reexamination of the restrictions that kept them disfranchised was demanded, and the states were forced to respond.

Yet the leading political figures of the day, faced with demands for corrections, were hesitant to make changes. Most of them not only were opposed to change as such, but also were particularly distrustful of the idea that public policy determination should become the subject of mass participation. The established leaders agreed with Chancellor James Kent (1763–1847), first chief judge of the New York Supreme Court and then presiding judge of the State Court of Chancery (hence his title of Chancellor), that any attempt to remodel the state constitutions in the direction of greater popular control was a "bold and hazardous experiment." To liberalize the New York Constitution, Kent declared, would suggest that "we were disposed to arraign the goodness of Providence."[8] Pressure from farmers and workers was not to be repulsed, however, and the desperate struggle of experienced political leaders to preserve the privileged position of the propertied in state and local politics ultimately proved unsuccessful.

Their case was handicapped from the start by victories already achieved not only in the West but also in several of the older states. Quietly and almost unobtrusively, Pennsylvania dropped property qualifications for suffrage in 1776; New Hampshire, property qualifications in 1784 and tax qualifications in 1792; Georgia, property qualifications in 1789 and tax qualifications in 1798; and Delaware, property qualifications in 1792. By 1821 property qualifications had been abandoned by seven of the original thirteen states and the requirement of tax payment by three. Universal manhood suffrage had already acquired a firm foothold in American politics. By the time the issues raised by the panic of 1819 forced the propertied to consider the safety of their own political positions, it was already too late for a successful defense. Against democratic convictions they could only offer, as someone has remarked, "historical learning and dialectical skill." The march of democracy could be delayed but not stopped.

Between 1820 and 1830 contests were waged in the leading states of

---

[7] Hofstadter, *American Political Tradition*, pp. 50–51.
[8] Livingston, in *Proceedings and Debates*, p. 219.

Massachusetts, New York, and Virginia.[9] Assembled in the conventions of these states were some of the nation's most prominent citizens, men whose public services dated from the revolutionary period. Delegates to the Massachusetts Convention of 1820 included John Adams, then eighty-five, who emerged from retirement to attend; Joseph Story (1779–1845), an Associate Justice of the Supreme Court and father of the reborn Harvard Law School; and Daniel Webster (1782–1852), longtime member of the United States Senate. Chancellor Kent headed the list of notables in New York. All were ardent defenders of the status quo. In opposition were men less distinguished but no less determined to achieve constitutional revision than others were to maintain the status quo. Thus, while Chancellor Kent and his counterparts in Massachusetts and Virginia staunchly defended the principles embodied in the constitutions of the revolutionary period, obscure delegates argued that failure to liberalize them would mean a continuing violation of those fundamental rights for which American patriots had spent their blood and treasure.

PROPERTY AND THE SUFFRAGE

The Conservative Case in the North: Kent, Story, and Webster

The debates centered primarily on proposals to remove the property restrictions on suffrage. In their attempt to win voting privileges, non-freeholders argued from the familiar premise of natural rights, only to meet resistance at the hands of conservative leaders, who asserted that extension of suffrage would forge for the masses a political weapon enabling them to encroach upon the rights of property. In New York Chancellor Kent[10] condemned universal suffrage:

> The tendency of universal suffrage is to jeopardize the rights of property and the principles of liberty. There is a constant tendency in human society, and the history of every age proves it; there is a tendency in the poor to covet and to share the plunder of the rich; in the debtor to relax or avoid the obligation of contracts; in the majority to tyrannize over the minority, and trample down their rights; in the indolent and the profligate, to cast the whole burdens of society upon the industrious and the virtuous; and *there is a tendency in ambitious and wicked men, to inflame these combustible materials.* It requires a vigilant government, and a firm administration of justice, to counteract that tendency. Thou shalt not covet; thou shalt not steal; are divine injunctions induced by this miserable depravity of our nature.[10]

---

[9] See Merrill D. Peterson, ed., *Democracy, Liberty, and Property: the State Constitutional Conventions of the 1820's* (Indianapolis: Liberal Arts Press, 1965). See also Gilman Ostrander, *The Rights of Man in America, 1606–1861* (Columbia, Mo.: University of Missouri Press, 1960) and Chilton Williamson, *American Suffrage from Property to Democracy, 1760–1860* (Princeton, N.J.: Princeton University Press, 1960).

[10] This and the following Kent remarks are from *Proceedings and Debates*, pp. 164, 221.

The force of that mighty engine, universal suffrage, was capable of sweeping everything before it.

> Our governments are becoming downright democracies. . . . The principle of universal suffrage, which is now running a triumphant career from Maine to Louisiana, is an awful power, which, like gunpowder, or the steam engine, or the press itself, may be rendered mighty in mischief as well as in blessings. We have to fear inflammatory appeals to the worst passions of the worst men in society; and we have greatly to dread the disciplined force of fierce and vindictive majorities, headed by leaders flattering their weaknesses and passions, and turning their vengeance upon the heads and fortunes of minorities, under the forms of law. It requires all our wisdom and all our patriotism to surround our institutions with a rampart against the corruption and violence of party spirit. We must ingraft something like quarantine laws into our constitution to prevent the introduction and rage of this great moral pestilence.

The convention finally gave the vote, despite Kent's vehement protest, to men who paid taxes or who had served in the militia or performed labor on the public highways.

> The notion that every man who works a day on the road, or serves an idle hour in the militia, is entitled as of right to an equal participation in the whole power of the government, is most unreasonable, and has no foundation in justice. We had better at once discard . . . such a nominal test of merit. If such persons have an equal share in one branch of the legislature, it is surely as much as they can in justice or policy demand. Society is an association for the protection of property as well as of life, and the individual who contributes only one cent to the common stock, ought not to have the same power and influence in directing the property concerns of the partnership, as he who contributes his thousands. He will not have the same inducements to care, and diligence, and fidelity.

Anticipating the laissez faire dogma current two generations later, Kent explained:

> The sense of property is graciously bestowed on mankind for the purpose of rousing them from sloth, and stimulating them to action; and so long as the right of acquisition is exercised in conformity to the social relations and the moral obligations which spring from them, it ought to be sacredly protected. The natural and active sense of property pervades the foundations of social improvement. It leads to the cultivation of the earth, the institution of government, the establishment of justice, the acquisition of the comforts of life, the growth of the useful arts, the spirit of commerce, the productions of taste, the erections of charity and the display of the benevolent affections.[11]

The votes of men without property—and, consequently, destitute of character—would be easily commanded by their masters, to the extreme

---

[11] Quoted in John Horton, *James Kent: A Study in Conservatism* (New York: Appleton-Century-Crofts, 1939), p. 275.

peril of established agrarian power. To avoid this danger, the men of property must perpetuate this qualification.

> Who can undertake to calculate with any precision, how many millions of people, this great state [New York] will contain in the course of this and the next century, and who can estimate the future extent and magnitude of our commercial ports? The disproportion between the men of property, and the men of no property, will be in every society in a ratio to its commerce, wealth, and population. We are no longer to remain plain and simple republics of farmers. . . .[12]

Manufacturing and commerce were destined to become paramount; New York City, with its "unwieldy population, and with the burdensome pauperism, of an European metropolis," would rule the state. Property must be guarded against this "wild and savage licentiousness."

Kent believed that the fate of the Republic hung in the balance; privilege was being threatened.

> Universal suffrage once granted, is granted forever, and never can be recalled. There is no retrograde step in the rear of democracy.

Story said much the same thing in the Massachusetts Convention. It must always be a question of the highest moment, he thought, "how the property-holding part of the Community may be sustained against the inroads of poverty and vice."[13] Like Kent, Story insisted that the state senate, as a bulwark for property, remain undisturbed. He regarded property as the source of every comfort and advantage; every man from the poorest to the wealthiest should be equally interested in its security and preservation. For property brought many blessings, not only to those who possessed it but also to the general community. Story was willing to allow representation of the people in the lower house, but he insisted that property continue to have special protection in the upper. He was sure that all would agree that this was in everyone's interest:

> Property is continually changing like the waves of the sea. . . The richest man among us may be brought down to the humblest level; and the child with scarcely clothes to cover his nakedness, may rise to the highest office. . . .

Story and his supporters, however, fought a losing battle. Looking back, he was convinced that justice had miscarried:

> There was a pretty strong body of Radicals, who seemed well disposed to get rid of all the great and fundamental barriers of the Constitution."[14]

---

[12] *Proceedings and Debates*, p. 221.
[13] *Journal of Debates and Proceedings in the Convention of Delegates Chosen to Review the Constitution of Massachusetts* (Boston, 1853), pp. 285–86.
[14] W. W. Story, *Life and Letters of Joseph Story* (Boston: Little, Brown, 1851), I, 395.

To Daniel Webster the argument that property constituted the proper basis of representation in the Massachusetts senate derived both from the principle of separation of powers and from the even more basic principle that "in the absence of military force, political power naturally and necessarily goes into the hands which hold the property." Political power naturally gravitated toward property. "In my judgment," Webster declared, "a republican form of government rests, not more on political constitutions, than on those laws which regulate the descent and transmission of property." In the United States property ownership was widespread. Our governments had been founded on recognition of man's pervading interest in its preservation. As Harrington had demonstrated in *Oceana*, it had been founded legitimately. This state of things had been brought about not by constitutional magic nor by "the mere manner of organizing the government," but by laws regulating "the descent and transmission of property":

> The true principle of a free and popular government would seem to be, so to construct it as to give to all, or at least to a very great majority, an interest in its preservation; to found it, as other things are, founded on man's interest. The stability of government requires that those who desire its continuance should be more powerful than those who desire its dissolution. . . . In this country, we have actual existing systems of government, in the protection of which it would seem a great majority, both in numbers and in other means of power and influence, must see their interest.[15]

A great revolution over property would have to take place before our government could be moved from its republican base.

> If the nature of our institutions be to found government on property, and that it should look to those who hold property for its protection, it is entirely just that property should have its due weight and consideration in political arrangements. Life and personal liberty are, no doubt, to be protected by law; but property is also to be protected by law, and is the fund out of which the means for protecting life and liberty are usually furnished. We have no experience that teaches us that any other rights are safe, where property is not safe. Confiscation and plunder are generally in revolutionary commotions, not far before banishment, imprisonment and death.

If these were correct political maxims, then, Webster believed, property ought to have "its due weight and consideration, in political arrangements." In Massachusetts property paid five-sixths of the public taxes, and it supported the schools. These were reasons enough for it to retain its special place in the structure of the legislature that it had occupied for forty years. "As to the *right* of apportioning Senators upon this principle," Webster remarked, "I do not understand how there can be a question about it."

---

[15] *Journal of Debates*, pp. 311–12. The remaining quotations are from page 317.

All government is a modification of general principles and general truths, with a view to practical utility. Personal liberty, for instance, is a clear right, and is to be provided for; but it is not a clearer right than the right of property, though it may be more important. It is therefore entitled to protection. But property is also to be protected; and when it is remembered, how great a portion of the people of this State possess property, I cannot understand how its protection or its influence is hostile to their rights and privileges.

The Conservative
Case in the South

At the Virginia Convention of 1829–1830, in which all realized that change was only a matter of time, apologists for the status quo sounded a note of desperation. Included in the conservative ranks were men who had distinguished themselves in the nation's service: John Marshall, former President James Monroe, John Randolph of Roanoke (1773–1833), who had represented Virginia almost thirty years in Congress, and Abel P. Upshur (1790–1844), then a state judge and later Secretary of the Navy and of State in John Tyler's cabinet. The most vociferous opponents of change were Judge Upshur and John Randolph. Delegates from the western part of the state spoke at length of the necessity for majority rule. Such talk bored Judge Upshur, especially because it was paraded as a self-evident truth or else "assumed as a postulate." No one, he said, had ever demonstrated its validity—certainly no one in the convention. The majority rule principle, therefore, demanded careful examination.

"There are two kinds of majority," Upshur explained. "There is a majority in *interest*, as well as a majority in *number*."[16] Only the former was a right under natural law; the latter was an innovation introduced by man after he reached the social state.

What if the principle of majority rule were accepted in Virginia, Upshur asked. What then would be the basis of representation? "*All* are counted, in making up the majority, and each one of the majority ought of consequence to possess a share in its rights." Thus, women should be admitted to the polls, and minors as well. "If you go on population alone, as the basis of representation, you will be obliged to go the length of giving the elective franchise to every human being over twenty-one years," and perhaps even to those under twenty-one years. Where was the limit? There was none. If the principle of majority rule were adhered to, there could be no qualifications at all. "If you establish any disqualification whatever, there is no *natural necessity*, nor even a *moral certainty*, that a majority in any given community, will not come within the exception." It was manifestly ridiculous to conceive of suffrage without restriction. "There is no one among us so wild and visionary, as to desire universal suffrage," Upshur exclaimed. "In truth . . . *there are no original princi-*

---

[16] All the quotations in this section are from *Proceedings and Debates of the Virginia State Convention of 1829–1830* (Richmond: Ritchie and Cook, 1830), pp. 66–79, *passim.*

ples of government at all . . . The principles of Government, are those principles only, which the people who form the Government, choose to *adopt and apply to themselves.* Principles do not *precede*, but spring out of Government." The delegates should therefore ignore abstract principles plucked out of the air and realistically consider the requirements of "our interests and necessities."

Upshur admitted, as a general proposition, that the majority should rule. If an identity of interests existed among the constituent members of the body politic, no other rule would be equitable and just. "But our interests are not identical, and the difference between us arises from property alone. We therefore contend that property ought to be considered, in fixing the basis of representation." In the last analysis, society is made up of only two elements: persons and property. There are personal rights and personal obligations in society. But "society cannot exist without property . . . And of these two, it may be fairly asserted that property is not only of *equal* but even of *more* importance." Every society that has withdrawn protection from property has soon succumbed to disorder and violence. Without property society and government would become impossible. Man in society has two basic obligations: to bear arms and to pay taxes. The requirement to bear arms and thus protect society reciprocates the protection society affords individual rights. Similarly, the requirement to pay taxes reciprocates the protection government affords property. Such is the agreement between government and the taxpayer. It was in support of this very principle that the American Revolution was fought. What must be the nature of this protection? Slaves being so important an element in the Virginia economy, there must be ironclad guarantees that taxation of the slaveholders would never be oppressive. Man is governed by interest, and the western majority brought into being by an extension of the franchise would be quick to shift the tax burden for internal improvements to the eastern slavocracy. Furthermore, how could this majority, even assuming they would honor their word and act under restraint, guarantee that their posterity would do the same? Society, indeed, could not exist without property; "it constitutes the full half of its being. Take away all protection from property, and our next business is to cut each other's throats. All experience proves this. The safety of men depends on the safety of property . . . And shall it not then be protected?" "It appears to me," Upshur concluded, "that I need only announce the proposition, to secure the assent of every gentleman present."

Upshur was a good reporter: the "gentlemen" in the Virginia Convention were unanimously in favor of protecting property by basing suffrage upon it. Fearing change, John Randolph joined in opposition to all innovation. The best service the Convention could render, he said, was to dissolve itself and leave Virginia with the old constitution intact.

Distrust of man and of democracy was basic to Randolph's conservatism. "I must be permitted to say, that there exists, in the nature of man . . . a disposition to escape from our own proper duties, to undertake the duties of somebody or anybody else."[17] Man could not be trusted with the liberties of another, and above all, Randolph loved *his* liberty. Governments, like all human institutions, were repositories of power and quite capable of abuse. Paper limitations could not prevent abuses of power; only power could check power. "With all the fanatical and preposterous theories about the rights of man (the *theories*, and not the rights themselves, I speak of), there is nothing but power that can restrain power . . . I have no faith in parchment, sir, I have no faith in the abracadabra of the constitution." The principle of equality, moreover, was demonstrably false. "Sir, my only objection is, that these principles, pushed to their extreme consequences—that all men are born free and equal—I can never assent to for the best of all reasons, because it is not true. . . ."[18] Democracy was the evil to be avoided.

> But all this, I suppose, is in obedience to the all-prevailing principle that *vox populi vox dei*; aye, Sir, the all-prevailing principle that Numbers and Numbers alone, are to regulate all things in political society, in the very teeth of those abstract natural rights of man which constitute the only shadow of claim to exercise this monstrous tyranny.[19]

"Mr. Chairman," Randolph shouted, "I am a practical man. I go for solid security, and I never will, knowingly, take any other." Property should determine the franchise.

> Will you go into joint stock with those *"vagabonds"* and that *"rabble"* . . . who never mean to have a freehold? the profligate, the homeless . . . who . . . hang very loosely on society, but stick very closely to her skirts, and who are determined to pick up their vile and infamous bread, by every dispicable means? I call on the young non-freeholders, the sons of freeholders . . . to wait, and not to unite themselves with those who, in the nature of things, can have no permanent interest in the Commonwealth."

Nature herself ordained the first principle of politics, that power and property go together. The corrupt nature of the poor prevented ownership of property. The taxes of the wealthy should not be used to support them. Were he but a younger man, Randolph threatened, he would move from Virginia rather than live "under King Numbers. I would not be his steward—nor make him my task-master. I would obey the principle of self-preservation—a principle we find in the brute creation, in flying from this mischief." "Sir, I see no wisdom in making this provision for future changes . . . Almost any thing is better than this perpetual uncertainty. . . . Sir, how often must I repeat, that *change* is not *reform*." The "monstrous claims" of "King Numbers" were not worth discussion.

---

[17] Quoted in Russell Kirk, *The Conservative Mind* (Chicago: Henry Regnery, 1953), p. 138.
[18] Kirk, *Conservative Mind*, pp. 139, 141.
[19] *Proceedings of Virginia Convention*. The Randolph quotations here are from pp. 313–21, 445, 790.

It is the first time in my life, that I ever heard of a government, which was to divorce property from power. . . . The moment you have separated the two, that very moment property will go in search of power, and power in search of property . . . the two sexes do not more certainly, nor by a more unerring law, gravitate to each other, than power and property.

Although professing sympathy for the poor, Randolph could not see why "that ragged fellow staggering from the whiskey shop, and . . . that slattern who has gone there to reclaim him" should be granted political power. Why encourage their belief "that all things must be done for them by the government, and that they are to do nothing for themselves? . . ." Why endanger the security of property by exposing it to invasion by the ragged, the idle, the vicious, the ignorant?

> "Stick to what you have got; stick to your Constitution; stick to your Right of Suffrage. Don't give up your freehold representation. We have seen enough of the opposite system and too much."

THE CASE FOR REFORM

Less eminent delegates in all three states were quick to refute the conservatives. David Buel, Jr. of the New York Convention pointed out that the argument of the conservatives was based on an invalid comparison between Europe and America. In Europe great landed estates were possessed by a few; the masses were poor "and without that attachment to the government which is found among the owners of the soil, . . . the poor envy and hate the rich, and mobs and insurrections sometimes render property insecure. Did I believe that our population would degenerate into such a state, I should hesitate in extending the right of suffrage but I confess I have no fears."

Things were different in the United States. Laws for regulating descents, and for converting entailed estates into fee simple, had gradually increased the number of landholders. American territory had been rapidly divided and subdivided. Dissemination of information was creating equality of opportunity and accentuating widespread distribution of property. In such a society a combination of the mercantile and manufacturing interests would be the only one powerful enough to weaken the landholders, but their natural relationship was that of rivalry. Another possibility was a union of the poor against the rich, but Buel thought it unlikely that those without property could ever combine so successfully as to have a majority in both houses of a legislature unfriendly to landholders. Pointing to the day of diverse property ownership, Buel dismissed as groundless the conservative fear that the unpropertied would rise up against the propertied.

> The supposition that, at some future day, when the poor shall become numerous, they may imitate the radicals of England, or the Jacobins of France; that

they may rise, in the majesty of their strength, and usurp the property of the landholders, is so unlikely to be realized that we may dismiss all fear arising from that source.[20]

Partisans of the people were obviously unimpressed with the "class struggle" ideas fostered by the good American conservatives. Property was sacrosanct in the minds of the poor as well as of the rich. "Every member of this convention," remarked P. R. Livingston at the New York Convention, "is a friend of property and to the landed interest."[21] Most men in America desired property, and it was not logical to assume that they would seek to destroy what they themselves hoped to obtain. A democrat of considerable wealth,[22] Livingston expressed complete faith in the people: "In a republican government, it will not be denied that all the power of the legislature is vested in, and emanates from, the people." It appeared to him "a solecism to say the people would assent to measures which would be injurious to their own good—that it should be in the power of a minority to rule a majority."[23]

Livingston was supported by another delegate, John Cramer, who thought it inconsistent to believe that men who could be trusted to handle muskets and bayonets "in your defense in war" could not be trusted at the ballot box. It was not the miser, "the monied Shylock," the speculator, who spilled his blood to defend his country. Rather, "it is the poor and hardy soldier . . . the veteran to whom you allow the privilege to fight, but not to vote. If there is value in the right of suffrage, or reliance to be placed upon our fellow citizens in time of war, where, I ask, is the justice of withholding that right in times of peace and safety?" "And why are these men to be excluded?" Cramer persisted. "Not because they are not virtuous, not because they are not meritorious; but . . . because they are poor and dependent, and can have no will of their own, and will vote as the man who feeds them and clothes them may direct . . . I know of no men in this country who are not dependent. The rich man is as much dependent upon the poor man for his labor, as the poor man is upon the rich for his wages."[24] Although acknowledging the role of wealth in society, Livingston reminded the Convention that of itself wealth was powerless "without the hand of labour." Rather than controlling labor, money was itself controlled by labor.

> When the farmer cradles his wheat and harvests his hay, he does not find the labourer on his knees before him at the close of the day, solicitous for further employment; but it is the farmer who takes off his hat, pays him his wages, and requests his return on the morrow.[25]

---

[20] Buel's remarks are in *Proceedings and Debates*, p. 243.
[21] *Proceedings and Debates*, p. 224.
[22] Dixon R. Fox, *The Decline of Aristocracy in the Politics of New York* (New York: Columbia University Press, 1919), p. 240.
[23] *Proceedings and Debates*, pp. 50, 59.
[24] *Proceedings and Debates*, p. 239.
[25] *Proceedings and Debates*, p. 225.

Striking the same telling note in the Massachusetts Convention, Holder Slocum asked who were the ones excluded from voting. "The laboring parts of society," he answered, the same class of men who "achieved our independence." Deprived of voting rights, these men could only watch "the rich putting in their votes 'like Patience on *the* monument, smiling at Grief.' If a man was a Newton or a Locke, if he is poor, he may stand by and see his liberties voted away."[26]

In Virginia, delegate Philip Doddridge used a frontier analogy to good effect:

> One Indian, we are told, enters society with two bows and arrows; another with one, and a third with none, while another brings nothing but his age, his infirmities and his wants. From these facts, it is attempted to draw the conclusion, that he who brings the most property to protect, is entitled to the most influence in Government, instead of the obvious one, that he should be subjected to the greatest share of the expenses of its protection. It has certainly been left to the men of Virginia of the present day to make this discovery in the science of Government. . . .
>
> We have often heard that wealth gives power, or that wealth itself, is power. By this axiom I suppose, is meant nothing more than the natural and moral influence which wealth gives to the possessor, by increasing his means of doing good or evil. Whenever power is directly conferred on wealth by Government, the additional power thus conferred, is a corrupt one. It is a *privilege* conferred contrary to the Bill of Rights, because not conferred *for merit or public services.* . . . It is an immoral distinction that is conferred, because it makes no discrimination between the possessors of estates honestly acquired, and those of ill-gotten stores.
>
> Do I misrepresent or exaggerate when I say your doctrine makes me a slave? . . . We [in the West] are a majority of individual units in the State, and your equals in intelligence and virtue, moral and political. Yet you say we must obey you. You declare that the rule of the minority has never oppressed us, nor visited us with practical evil; but of this we are the best judges. We have felt your weight and have suffered under misrule.[27]

Doddridge cautioned conservatives to

> look at the census of 1790, . . . [there you will] discover . . . that a race is rising up with astonishing rapidity, sufficiently strong and powerful to burst asunder any chain by which you may attempt to bind them, with as much ease as the thread parts in a candle blaze. . . .[28]

In Virginia, as in New York and Massachusetts, the obscure delegates harked back to the fundamentals of 1776. A memorial from "a numerous and respectable body of citizens, the non-freeholders of the city of Richmond," gave a full catalog of arguments for liberalizing suffrage.[29]

---

[26] *Journal of Debates,* p. 252.
[27] *Proceedings of Virginia Convention,* pp. 83–84, 88.
[28] *Proceedings of Virginia Convention,* pp. 86–87.
[29] *Proceedings of Virginia Convention,* pp. 25–30, *passim.*

Debarred by lack of property from the right of suffrage, the memorialists contended that their hold on every other right was thereby rendered insecure. Freedom and the security of rights could be guaranteed only by participation in the formation of a society's political institutions and in the control of those who administered them. To deny the members of any class participation was to pass them by as though they were "aliens or slaves, . . . destitute of interest, or unworthy of a voice, in measures involving their future political destiny." Virginians had been taught, the memorialists went on, that all men were "by nature equally free and independent, and have certain rights," and that "a majority of the community hath an indubitable, unalienable, and indefeasible right to reform, alter or abolish the Government" in order to protect those rights. Exclusion of those without a freehold from suffrage did violence to these precepts. Many of the memorialists possessed land; "many, though not proprietors, [were] yet cultivators of the soil: others [were] engaged in avocations of a different nature, often as useful, pre-supposing no less integrity, requiring as much intelligence, and as fixed a residence, as agricultural pursuits." "Virtue, intelligence, are not among the products of the soil," nor was the possession of property "to be confounded with the sacred flame of patriotism." Moreover, if no "invidious distinctions" as to property were drawn between citizens of the state in time of danger and war, why should they be drawn in time of peace? Nonfreeholders were no more inclined to abuse the right of suffrage than their fellow men of whatever class.

> If we are sincerely republican [the memorial continued], we must give our confidence to the principles we profess. We have been taught by our fathers, that all power is vested in, and derived from the people; not the freeholders: that the majority of the community, in whom abides the physical force, have also the political right of creating and remoulding at will, their civil institutions. Nor can this right be anywhere more safely deposited. The generality of mankind, doubtless, desire to become owners of property: left free to reap the fruit of their labours, they will seek to acquire it honestly. It can never be their interest to overburthen, or render precarious, what they themselves desire to enjoy in peace. But should they ever prove as base as the argument supposes, force alone; arms, not votes, could effect their designs; and when that shall be attempted, what virtue is there in Constitutional restrictions, in mere wax and paper, to withstand it? To deny to the great body of the people all share in the Government; on suspicion that they may deprive others of their property, to rob them in advance of their rights; to look to a privileged order as the fountain and depository of all power; is to depart from the fundamental maxims, to destroy the chief beauty, the characteristic feature, indeed, of Republican Government.[30]

These were the principles on which the "infant Republic" had been founded. These verities had received "the deliberate sanction of the most enlightened friends of liberty, throughout the world." "*Sovereignty of the*

---

[30] *Proceedings of Virginia Convention,* p. 28.

people, the *equality of men,* and the *right of the majority,"* delegate John R. Cooke asserted, were the principles that had enabled Virginia to abolish privilege and substitute "an elective magistracy, deriving their power *from* the people, and responsible *to* the people." These principles had never been revoked. The present Convention, Cooke argued, had it within its power to remove the inconsistency that had grown up between "theoretical principles" and "practical regulations" and to demonstrate that it was not necessary (as Randolph and Upshur argued) "to restrain . . . this many-headed and hungry monster, *the many,* by some artificial regulation in *the Constitution.* . . ." Man, as the Virginia Bill of Rights correctly implied, was not by nature either a wolf or a tiger. He was endowed with "the *social feeling;* the feeling of attachment to those around him," with a conscience, and the love or fear of God, all of which combined to give him a love of property as "the great engrossing passion" of his life. "The *very* desire for property implies the power to possess it *securely.*" Men, freeholders and nonfreeholders alike, respected property if for no other reason than that all had the desire to possess it; thus, no distinctions were necessary in granting suffrage. The Convention must return Virginia to the "great and sacred truths." All classes were "sagacious enough to know and follow their *real* interest," and in following it to live in accord with the principles of free government.[31]

REFORM CARRIES THE DAY

The movement away from privileged orders and the dominance of the landed aristocracy had become too strong to be successfully resisted. Experience on the frontier had raised man's opinion of his own capabilities; the demand for equal rights no longer seemed dangerous. Thus, Webster's and Story's desperate defense of the old order was unsuccessful in Massachusetts. Even before New York the Bay State turned its back on the idea that property must have representation in the senate. "Our government is one of the people," a Massachusetts delegate asserted, "not a government of property."[32] Property was not competent to sustain a free government. Rather, free government rested upon the intelligence of the people. Such arguments, expressing the dominant spirit of the times, presaged Jacksonian Democracy.

Although a majority of the New York Convention could not be persuaded to remove property qualifications for voting, these steps were accomplished four years later in the Empire State. By then the people of New York had rejected the argument that the turf "is of all things the most sacred, and that for its security, you must have thirty-two grave turf senators from the soil, in that *Sanctum Sanctorum,* the senate chamber, and then all your rights will be safe. No matter whether they possess

---

[31] *Proceedings of Virginia Convention,* pp. 53–61.
[32] Thomas Lincoln, *Journal of Debates,* p. 265.

intelligence, if they are selected by your rich landowners, all is well."[33] The fact that all state constitutions formed or amended in the preceding thirty years had "discarded this odious, this aristocratical, this worse than useless, feature, from their political charts" helped to convince New York that it, too, might properly follow suit, without suffering the dire consequences Kent predicted.

In Virginia conservative resistance continued another twenty years. John Randolph's fear of "King Numbers" and Judge Upshur's fear that an extension of suffrage would lead directly to an invasion of property rights prevailed. For defenders of the status quo the fate of republican government was at stake. Chief Justice Marshall, then seventy-four, indicated his views to Justice Story, his colleague on the bench, before the Convention opened:

> We shall have a good deal of division and a good deal of heat, I fear, in our convention. The freehold principle will, I believe, be lost. It will, however, be supported with zeal. If that zeal should be successful I should not regret it. If we find that a decided majority is against retaining it I should prefer making a compromise by which a substantial property qualification may be preserved in exchange for it.
> I fear the excessive . . . democratic spirit, coincident to victory after a hard fought battle continued to the last extremity may lead to universal suffrage or something very near it.[34]

So persuaded, Virginians did not see fit to remove the property qualification from suffrage until 1850.[35]

Nor were they any more successful in changing judicial organization, even though the judiciary, under the Constitution of 1776, had become (according to Marshall's biographer) "the very negation of democracy," a "rigid and self-perpetuating" oligarchy. It had even assumed the right of nominating the governor's new appointments to the bench. Its members were virtually irremovable, so much so that one member of the convention charged that the inability of the legislature to remove a judge resulted in the perpetuation of "a privileged corps in a free community."

The judiciary article in the new constitution, drafted by the chief justice himself, embodied almost no change. Indeed, in some respects, it was even more conservative than the one it replaced. The convention took away from the legislature all control over the appointment of state judges —confiding the power solely in the governor—and even voted to sustain "the old Federalist idea that judges should continue to hold their positions and receive their salaries, even though their offices were abolished."[36]

---

[33] John Cramer, *Proceedings and Debates*, p. 238.
[34] Beveridge, *Life of Marshall*, p. 470.
[35] Virginians shared Chancellor Kent's fears that once universal suffrage was granted it could not be rescinded. See above, p. 176.
[36] Beveridge, *Life of Marshall*, p. 496.

There was an important distinction between abolishing a court and removing a judge, Marshall argued. Although courts could be abolished or altered by legislative enactment, judges were "permanent in their office." Proper doctrine required that judges be untouchable; how else preserve their independence? How else keep them from being "dependent altogether upon the breath of the Legislature"? How else keep them as bulwarks of property against the tyranny of majorities? A majority at the convention accepted his arguments and carried their spirit into the constitution.

POPULAR POWER ADVANCED

In the decade following 1820 three important states, Massachusetts, New York, and Virginia, broadened the foundation of popular power. Once they had done so, the movement's success throughout the nation was assured. Twenty years later manhood suffrage became a reality. The liberalism that finally triumphed in securing manhood suffrage stimulated other innovations. Women began to demand equal rights; free public schools became common; the class system began to disintegrate, even in the tidewater areas. Conservatives continued to block these efforts, however, and, as their success in the Virginia Convention shows, their creed did not lose its vitality. In economic terms the conflict represented a struggle between those who believed class war inevitable in an industrial society unless high constitutional fences were erected to protect the few against the many, and those who were confident that politics in America would follow a course altogether different from that of Europe. In a country like America, the Kent-Randolph notion of social stratification (which ironically anticipated Karl Marx) was altogether inapplicable. There would be no class struggle here, where all respected property and hoped to attain it.

After the liberal triumph in the state constitutional conventions, the conservatives, loyal followers of Harrington in thinking that political power and property were inextricably linked, found themselves in an awkward position. If their belief that economic antagonism inevitably divided society along economic lines were accepted at face value, it would be logical for the liberals to use their newly won political power to attack property. Faced with this dangerous possibility, the diehards did a quick about-face. Discarding their old claims, they accepted the opposing liberal thesis that America differed from Europe, that the doctrines of class war did not apply in the United States, and that all elements of American society possessed a common interest in maintaining the institution of private property. Relaxation of the conservative position after 1830 did not, however, end conflict and struggle. Other vexing issues loomed, and after 1870 the battle was renewed with increased vigor and animosity. By then the liberal movement, increasingly reflected in legislation, seemed well-nigh irresistible; a fight to the finish seemed inevitable.

One cannot read these historic debates without sensing the great and continuing paradox that permeates American political thought and action. Warring against each other in all these conventions were the moral ideals of freedom, the basic axioms Jefferson wrote into the Declaration of Independence, and the impassioned insistence that "inevitable" economic equality must be protected by specific constitutional safeguards. To many, as to Daniel Webster, who saw the threat most clearly, it was obvious that narrowly concentrated economic power would put a heavy strain on free government. "A great equality of condition," he said, "is the true basis, most certainly, of popular government." With uncanny prescience he anticipated the crucial issue ahead:

> The freest government, if it could exist, would not be long acceptable, if the tendency of the laws were to create a rapid accumulation of property in few hands, and to render the great mass of the population dependent and pennyless. In such a case, the popular power must break in upon the rights of property, or else the influence of property must limit and control the exercise of popular power.[37]

Webster forecast the dynamics of American politics after 1870. Popular power did begin to "break in"—that is, to regulate property rights—and the influence of property did find effective ways of controlling—or evading—popular power. Webster not only foreshadowed conservative and liberal strategy but also divined the issue that remains crucial in our own time.

---

[37] *Journal of Debates*, p. 312.

CHAPTER TEN

JACKSONIAN DEMOCRACY: THE COMMON MAN TRIUMPHANT

The political upsurge of the 1820s, which expanded the role of the masses, escalated in the 1830s. By then the "common man" had developed a deep interest in, and an equally deep conviction of, the importance of change. "With the crowding into Washington of farmers, planters, and lawyers elected to Congress from the new states of the West and South . . . attacks on the Republicanism which had absorbed Federalism became irrepressible."[1] Andrew Jackson (1767–1845), soldier, lawyer, Tennessee political figure, and national hero after the Battle of New Orleans, became the leader of the mounting protest. Jackson identified himself so fully with popular grievances that historians have fallen into the habit of referring to this many-faceted movement as Jacksonian Democracy.[2]

Although the Age of Jackson has long been a favorite topic for scholarly and semipopular research, Jackson himself remains an enigma.

---

[1] Charles A. and Mary R. Beard, *A Basic History of the United States* (New York: The New Home Library, 1944), p. 249.
[2] See Margaret L. Coit, *Andrew Jackson* (Boston: Houghton Mifflin, 1965); Marquis James, *Andrew Jackson, Portrait of a President* (New York: Grosset & Dunlap, 1967); and Marvin Meyers, *The Jacksonian Persuasion. Politics and Belief* (Stanford, Calif.: Stanford University Press, 1966).

Charles M. Wiltse's observation, made in 1948, is still true: "Those who have succeeded in giving Jackson either a consistent policy or an intelligible political philosophy have been able to do so . . . only on the basis of incomplete analysis or misinterpretation of essential facts."[3] Like Jefferson, Jackson left his philosophy uncodified; but in his case no one else undertook the task for him. Because Jackson was primarily a man of action, Jacksonianism is difficult to evaluate.[4] Any attempt to formulate a unified creed runs the risk of giving undue coherence to a complex and variegated movement.

Jackson first moved into national prominence in the election of 1824. By then the Federalist—Democratic-Republican dichotomy had disappeared. For a while an "era of good feeling" existed. Hamilton's and Marshall's ideas of national power, serving the great commercial and financial interests through the United States Bank, the protective tariff, bounties, and internal improvements, were widely endorsed.

By the mid-twenties dissidents in the Democratic-Republican party had begun to call themselves simply "Democrats." Yet they were neither sufficiently numerous nor sufficiently well organized to win the 1824 election. Nevertheless, Jackson and John Quincy Adams—the son of President John Adams and secretary of state under James Monroe—emerged as strong figures. Because neither received a majority of votes, the election was thrown into the House of Representatives, and after a prolonged and hotly contested struggle, Adams emerged the victor. The circumstances of Adams' victory,[5] the support of John C. Calhoun in the South and Martin Van Buren in New York, and a steady increase both in Democratic party strength and in Jackson's own popularity combined to carry him into the White House in 1828 with four times the number of votes he had received in 1824. The Jackson tide ran full in 1832, the year "Old Hickory" was reelected. It did not begin to ebb until well into the presidency of Martin Van Buren, Jackson's handpicked successor.

So long a hold on the presidency, and indeed upon the national government,[6] provided ample time for considerable development in American political thought. Jackson shared the ideas of the West and South and of the working classes of the eastern seaboard rather than those of the business and financial "Establishment." His constituents were the frontier

---

[3] Charles M. Wiltse, *John C. Calhoun, Nullifier, 1829–1839* (Indianapolis: Bobbs-Merrill, 1949), p. 429. James L. Bugg, in his *Jacksonian Democracy: Myth or Reality?* (New York: Holt, Rinehart & Winston, 1965), has suggested five schools of Jackson historiography. See also Alfred A. Cave, *Jacksonian Democracy and the Historians* (Gainesville, Fla.: University of Florida Press, 1964) and Charles Sellers, Jr., "Andrew Jackson versus the Historians," *The Mississippi Valley Historical Review*, XLIV (March, 1958), 615–34.

[4] Schlesinger, *Age of Jackson*, p. 517.

[5] Henry Clay, who ran fourth in the election for president in 1824, was appointed Secretary of State by Adams, thereby raising the still-repeated charge that Adams and Clay had made a deal for votes in the House of Representatives.

[6] Jackson himself appointed five Supreme Court justices, including Roger B. Taney, Marshall's successor as chief justice; Van Buren in four years (1837–1841) appointed two others.

beneficiaries of the government's land policy, which enhanced individual ownership, and the rising eastern industrial working class, members of which looked forward confidently to independence in their own shop or factory. Tools of production were still relatively simple, inexpensive, and easily obtained. It is little wonder that the visiting Frenchman Alexis de Tocqueville was impressed. "Nothing struck me more forcibly," he wrote in the early 1830s, "than the general equality of condition [in the United States]. . . . There is not one country in the world where man more confidently reaches toward the future, where he feels with so much pride that his intelligence makes him master of the universe, that he can fashion it to his liking."[7]

Both material and spiritual resources impressed de Tocqueville. The familiar tag "rugged individualism" is used appropriately, without risk of ridicule, to describe the economic condition and the political state of mind that flourished during these years. Jackson, understanding the implications of these developments, led an aggressive middle-class movement dedicated to the "common man" and to a political and an economic democracy. Cheaper printing opened new avenues of information, and the emergence of the platform speaker personalized and popularized issues. By these devices Jackson presented himself, over Congress, as the one representative of all the people. To accomplish his objectives, he relied heavily on executive power, on extensive use of patronage and the presidential veto, and on a bold challenge to the Supreme Court. "Jackson's Presidency was, in truth, no mere revival of the office—it was a remaking of it."[8]

Between the election of 1828 and Jackson's inauguration, the country might well have wondered what kind of man and administration it had summoned to power. "His experience neither in state nor in national politics," Arthur Schlesinger, Jr., observed, "afforded clear indication of what could be expected from him."[9] Elected without a platform, he was vaguely expected to be "different from what the people imagined Adams had been."[10] It was believed that Jackson was committed to change and that he could be trusted to act for all the people, not for just a class, a section, or a special interest.

Jackson's orientation toward the people and his confidence in the average man's capacity for politics come out strongly in his first annual message to Congress.[11] Politics was a "very simple thing." "The duties of all public officers are . . . so plain and simple," runs an oft-quoted line, "that men of intelligence may readily qualify themselves for their performance." To open public offices to a greater number of the people,

---

[7] de Tocqueville, *Democracy in America*, I, 1.
[8] Edward S. Corwin, *The President: Office and Powers*. 2nd ed. (New York: New York University Press, 1941), p. 21.
[9] Schlesinger, *Age of Jackson*, p. 37.
[10] Hofstadter, *American Political Tradition*, p. 54.
[11] James D. Richardson, ed., *Messages and Papers of the Presidents* (Washington, D.C.: Bureau of National Literature and Art, 1909), II, 442–52, *passim*.

Jackson proposed rotation in office. Offices long held came to be considered by their occupants "as a species of property," and the public interest was likely to be neglected. The government's efficiency and "official industry and integrity" would be better secured by limiting all public appointments to four years. Limited tenure would give "healthful action to the system" by continually emphasizing the principle that government was "an instrument erected solely for the service of the people." The notion of a vested interest in government jobs by a few office holders would thus be prevented.

Even more essential for the proper representation of the people was the necessity of altering the method of presidential election. Jackson's own experience in 1824 taught him that "to the people belongs the right of electing their chief magistrate; it was never designed that their choice should . . . be defeated, either by the intervention of electoral colleges or by . . . the House of Representatives. Experience proves that in proportion as agents to execute the will of the people are multiplied there is danger of their wishes being frustrated. . . . So far . . . as the people can with convenience speak, it is safer for them to express their own will." In all cases Jackson believed that policy required "that as few impediments as possible should exist to the free operation of the public will." If the majority were to govern, then a system that produced minority presidents must be altered.

Jackson's first annual message demonstrated both the Jeffersonian basis of his political thinking and deviations from it. Speaking of the difficulty of regulating governmental conduct to the advantage of the three "cardinal interests" of American economic life—agriculture, commerce, and manufacturing—he voiced regret that "the complicated restrictions which now embarrass the intercourse of nations could not by common consent be abolished, and commerce allowed to flow in those channels to which individual enterprise, always its surest guide, might direct it." Unfortunately, however, the United States was forced by the actions of other nations to enact commercial legislation preventing injury to its own trade. It was also necessary—and here Jackson pulled away somewhat from his Jeffersonian mooring—to use governmental power "to harmonize the conflicting interests of our agriculture, our commerce, and our manufactures." Whereas the Jeffersonians urged weak government as a first principle, Jackson seemed to favor a strong government, active in behalf of the people, instead of the landed and moneyed aristocracy that flourished in the absence of such a harmonizing agent. But he immediately retreated from so positive an assertion, remarking that to legislate frequently in behalf of any branch of industry or commerce "should never be attempted but with the utmost caution" and without "patriotic determination to promote the great interests of the whole." Nor was national power to be used to promote one section over another. Nevertheless, Jackson, in words full of implications for latter-day liberalism, invited Congress' "particular attention" to agriculture and recommended the application of "the fostering care of Government." Indeed, Jacksonian Democracy bridged a vital gap in the Jeffersonian creed. Jeffersonians insisted on weak government, but their insistence left unanswered the crucial question, What would prevent the control of powerful economic interests from spreading over the entire nation with no active government to prevent it? The "whole moral of the Jacksonian experience," on the other hand, was "that only a strong people's government could break up the power of concentrated wealth."[12] Andrew Jackson set the pattern for all subsequent "strong presidents."

JACKSON AND THE CONSTITUTION

Jackson's attitude toward the scope of national power under the Constitution also indicates divergence from Jefferson. In his first address to Congress, he advocated distribution of surplus revenue to the several states. "Should this measure be found unwarranted by the Constitution, it would be expedient to propose to the States an amendment authorizing it." Although recognizing that "this was intended to be a government of limited and specific, and not general, powers," and that it was the duty of the people of the United States "to preserve for it the character intended by its framers," he felt that if "experience points out the necessity for an enlargement of these [national] powers," it was quite proper to seek such an expansion.

Although Jackson disagreed with Jefferson about the use of governmental power, he placed himself alongside his predecessor in two other respects: state sovereignty and state power and the limited role of the Supreme Court. In cases of doubt about the use of national power, Jackson recommended "an appeal to the source of power," the several states. If change must be made, "let us apply for it to those for whose benefit it is to be exercized, and not undermine the whole system by a resort to overstrained constructions."

Jackson agreed with Jefferson that "the great mass of legislation relating to our internal affairs was intended to be left where the Federal Convention found it—in the State governments." Nothing was clearer to Jackson "than that we are chiefly indebted for the success of the Constitution under which we are now acting to the watchful and auxiliary operation of the State authorities. This is not the reflection of a day, but belongs to the most deeply rooted convictions of my mind. I cannot, therefore, too strongly or too earnestly . . . warn you against all encroachments upon the legitimate sphere of State sovereignty. Sustained by its healthful and invigorating influence the federal system can never fall."

Jackson also shared Jefferson's sharp feeling of rivalry with the Supreme Court. His alleged reaction to Marshall's decision in *Worcester* v. *Georgia*

---

[12] Schlesinger, *Age of Jackson*, p. 517.

is one illustration; his tart statement in vetoing the bank bill is another.[13] Proponents of the bank had argued that its constitutionality, having been specifically upheld in the famous case of *McCulloch* v. *Maryland*, should be regarded as settled. Not so, retorted Jackson. In language reminiscent of Jefferson's, he declared:

> If the opinion of the Supreme Court covered the whole ground of this act, it ought not to control the coordinate authorities of this Government. The Congress, the Executive, and the Court must each for itself be guided by its own opinion of the Constitution. Each public officer who takes an oath to support the Constitution swears that he will support it as he understands it, and not as it is understood by others. It is as much the duty of the House of Representatives, of the Senate, and of the President to decide upon the constitutionality of any bill or resolution which may be presented to them for passage or approval as it is of the supreme judges when it may be brought before them for judicial decision.

Jackson would give a court decision no more weight "over Congress than the opinion of Congress has over the judges. . . ." And the President was, of course, independent of both. A Supreme Court opinion was entitled only to "such influence as the force of [its] reasoning may deserve." Like Jefferson, Jackson would rely on separation of powers to destroy the peculiar role of the judiciary that Marshall asserted in *Marbury* v. *Madison*. "It is the exclusive province of Congress and the President," Jackson argued, "to determine whether this or that particular power, privilege, or exemption is 'necessary and proper' " and therefore constitutional. From their decision there was no appeal to the courts of justice. For a number of years after John Marshall's death in 1835, these Jeffersonian and Jacksonian sentiments were reflected in Supreme Court opinions. It is ironical that a strong Jacksonian, Roger B. Taney, should have led the Court in precisely the opposite direction in the ill-fated *Dred Scott* case of 1857.

ECONOMIC DEMOCRACY ADVANCED

During Jackson's administrations, federalism and judicial power did not loom so large as questions of economic democracy. Thus, although Jackson was attached to the principle of state sovereignty, he had not much opportunity to act upon it. And if he distrusted judicial power in the abstract, his confidence in the Supreme Court increased in direct proportion to the number of his appointments to it. Much closer to the political currents of the time was Jackson's deep conviction that a strong stand must be taken "against all new grants of monopolies and exclusive privi-

---

[13] 6 Peters 515 (1832). Jackson is supposed to have said, in learning of that decision: "John Marshall has made his decision, now let him enforce it." The bank veto is in Richardson, *Messages of Presidents*, pp. 576–91.

leges, against any prostitution of our Government to the advancement of the few at the expense of the many. . . ."

His targets were the Kents and Upshurs in politics, who, as representatives of property, saw the problem of government primarily in terms of "how the property-holding part of the community may be sustained against inroads of poverty and vice." They believed that property was the basic feature of society and that, to promote the general welfare, government must give protection and aid to any trade or industry needing support. John Marshall strengthened their case considerably in 1819 by his opinion in *Dartmouth College* v. *Woodward*,[14] wherein he held that any direct state interference with corporate rights of property and contract guaranteed by the terms of Article I, section 10, of the Constitution must have been authorized in the charter. Individual rights of property and contract fixed the contours within which the states could exercise their power over corporations. Free from legislative interference were the charters not only of charitable and educational institutions, such as Dartmouth College, but also those of profit-seeking monopolies. The consequences of this broad interpretation were far reaching.

In the 1820s corporations were springing up everywhere "in response to the necessity for larger and more constant business units and because of the convenience and profit of such organizations. Marshall's opinion was a tremendous stimulant to this natural economic tendency. It reassured investors in corporate securities and gave confidence and steadiness to the business world. . . . [It] made corporate franchises infinitely more valuable and strengthened the motives for procuring them, even by corruption."[15] Corporate rights, entrenched behind impregnable charters, threatened to become untouchable, remote from public control. That is why Jackson was so profoundly concerned lest the foundation of popular government itself be undermined by corporations enjoying exclusive privileges under charters granted by government and construed by John Marshall as inviolable.

The dynamism of the Jacksonian movement resulted in large part from the reaction of the ordinary man to the manner in which state legislatures handled the incorporation of new companies springing up in every section of the country. Except for laws with partial coverage in New York and Connecticut, the states did not have general incorporation statutes. Banks, railroads, manufacturing enterprises, and other profit-making businesses wishing to incorporate had to apply to the state legislature for a special act of incorporation. The way was thus left open to favoritism and corruption. Many corporations not only were conceived in sin but also were often given the privileges of a monopoly in their field. It is no wonder that in many states, the bargaining and trading away of chartered privi-

---

[14] 4 Wheaton 518 (1819). For an illuminating essay on the contemporary circumstances of the case, see Richard W. Marin, "Will to Resist: The Dartmouth College Case," *Dartmouth Alumni Magazine*, April, 1969.
[15] Beveridge, *Life of Marshall*, pp. 276, 278.

leges seemed to be the only business of the legislature, nor that the planter, the farmer, the mechanic, and the laborer were vehement in their denunciation of monopolies. "We cannot pass the bounds of the city without paying tribute to monopoly," it was said; "our bread, our meat, our vegetables, our fuel, all, all pay tribute to monopolists." William Leggett of the *New York Post* declared that "not a road can be opened, not a bridge can be built, not a canal can be dug, but a charter of exclusive privilege must be granted for the purpose."[16] To a people with a tenacious hold upon their freedom and nurtured on Jeffersonian doctrine, it began to appear that a new tyranny was gaining strength. As the people's spokesman, and convinced of the danger, Jackson was anxious to attack head-on and subdue the tyranny.

The passage of a bill to renew the charter of the Second Bank of the United States gave him the opportunity he sought. Although the charter did not expire until 1836, Jackson's opponents in Congress—particularly the friends of Henry Clay, anxious to push him into the presidency in 1832—sent a bill to the White House in July 1832 for a new charter. Jackson promptly returned it to Congress with his veto. His veto message, largely prepared by Taney, then attorney general, embodied a forthright statement of his belief that privilege is as wrong, as undemocratic, in economics as in politics.

Jackson opposed the national bank on a number of specific grounds: it was neither a necessary nor a proper governmental device, and it might be "so organized as . . . to infringe on . . . the reserved rights of the States." The bill for its recharter had been passed without executive advice or consent. He opposed it in particular, however, because it favored only a few of the nation's "opulent citizens." Like all monopolies and exclusive privileges, it existed "at the expense of the public which ought to [but did not] receive a fair equivalent."

It is to be regretted that the rich and powerful too often bend the acts of government to their selfish purposes. Distinctions in society will always exist under every just government. Equality of talents, of education, or of wealth cannot be produced by human institutions. In the full enjoyment of the gifts of Heaven and the fruits of superior industry, economy, and virtue, every man is equally entitled to protection by law; but when the laws undertake to add to these natural and just advantages artificial distinctions, to grant titles, gratuities, and exclusive privileges, to make the rich richer and the potent more powerful, the humble members of society—the farmers, mechanics, and laborers—who have neither the time nor means of securing like favors to themselves, have a right to complain of the injustice of their government. . . . Many of our rich men have not been content with equal protection and equal benefits, but have besought us to make them richer by act of Congress. By attempting to gratify their desires we have in the results of our legislation . . . [created] a fearful commotion which threatens to shake the foundations of our Union. . . .

---

[16] Quoted in Hofstadter, *American Political Tradition*, p. 57.

These views were heard with alarm by "the rich" and with enthusiasm by "the humble members of society," and gave evidence that Webster's prediction in the Massachusetts Convention was no idle conjecture.

Jackson's veto message set the stage for another battle between the philosophy of government declaring that property should control the state and the philosophy denying that property had a superior claim to governmental privileges and benefits.[17] For the time being, the latter was victorious: Jackson was easily returned to office in 1832 and Van Buren chosen to carry on in 1836. For the next three decades, other issues crowded out the struggle over the role of property in government. After the Civil War the problem returned with renewed intensity. When it did, the Jacksonian position was a vital link in the argument against privilege.

JACKSON AND GOVERNMENTAL POWER

In October 1836 Jackson, looking forward to retirement, wrote Taney, whom he had switched to Secretary of the Treasury in 1833, that he would like to make a farewell address. What should go into it? "Your farewell address," Taney replied, "should be exclusively devoted to those great and enduring principles upon which our institutions are founded, and without which the blessings of freedom cannot be preserved."[18] Taney accepted Jackson's commission to draft the address, but worked in close collaboration with the President. Delivered on March 4, 1837, it provided a comprehensive statement of the Jacksonian creed.[19] Throughout, Jackson emphasized his faith in the common people. "Never for a moment believe," he cautioned, "that the great body of the citizens of [the United States] can deliberately intend to do wrong. They may, under the influence of temporary excitement or misguided opinions, commit mistakes; they may be misled for a time by the suggestions of self-interest; but in a community so enlightened and patriotic as the people of the United States argument will soon make them sensible of their errors, and when convinced they will be ready to repair them." To "march to the highest point of national prosperity," they needed to be true to themselves and to their own "good sense and practical judgment."

Again Jackson warned against permitting a combination of interests to undermine free institutions. Corporations and wealthy individuals would ever seek to win "designing politicians" to their cause and "to engross all power in the hands of the few and to govern by corruption or force. . . ." He cited the bank as one example of the devices that "the moneyed power" might use to achieve that object and as another "profuse expenditure" for such purposes as internal improvement. He congratu-

---

[17] Schlesinger, *Age of Jackson*, p. 92.
[18] Quoted in Mason, *Free Government*, p. 444.
[19] The farewell address is reproduced in Richardson, *Messages of Presidents*, III, 292–308.

lated the people on their victory over the bank and added that "no nation
but the freemen of the United States could have come out victorious from
such a contest; yet, if you had not conquered, the Government would
have passed from the hands of the many to the hands of the few, and thus
organized money power from its secret conclave would have dictated the
choice of your highest officers and compelled you to make peace or war,
as best suited their own wishes. The forms of your Government might for
a time have remained, but its living spirit would have departed from it."

Speaking as a true follower of Jeffersonian Republicanism, Jackson
urged perpetual caution against the tendency of the national government
"to overstep the boundaries marked out for it by the Constitution." "Its
legitimate authority," he declared, "is abundantly sufficient for all the
purposes for which it was created, and its powers being expressly enumerated, there can be no justification for claiming anything beyond them."
If "the principle of constructive powers" or the argument of temporary
necessity were ever successful in justifying the assumption "of a power not
given by the Constitution, the General Government [would] before long
absorb all the powers of legislation" into "a single consolidated government." The Constitution fixed an appropriate sphere of activity for the
national government and one for the states. "Each state has the unques-
tionable right to regulate its own internal concerns according to its own
pleasure . . . while it does not interfere with the rights of the people of
other States or the rights of the Union"; the successful operation of the
whole depended on the strict observance of both.

If these words pointed backward, they nevertheless represented a large
segment of Democratic party support, and Jackson was bound to say
them. But he demonstrated that his thinking had advanced from the
restricted Jeffersonian concept of national power. Thus, he accented the
fact that "coercive powers confided [to] the general government" were
necessary to enable the federal government to enforce its supremacy upon
the states, and he insisted that its supremacy be maintained. It was chiefly
the federal government's abuse of the taxing power that he feared, and
this he charged to the use of influence and not to the existence of the
power itself. Although he could see the states' side, he accepted the necessity of union and of maintaining a strong and active national government
over it. In the last analysis, his strongest allegiance was to the latter.
George Washington himself had opposed sectionalism, Jackson recalled.
Nor could those aiding the formation of regional parties be unmindful
of the blessings the Constitution had conferred: the nation's common
prosperity, the proud claim to citizenship in a great country, freedom from
the burden of the heavy taxes for armament that small nations had to
bear. Although admitting that state pride was legitimate, that national
laws might work injustice on the states, and that a state might, in extreme
circumstances, resort to force of arms in defense of its rights, Jackson
offered no adequate definition of such rights and thus left open the question of the precise conditions under which revolt was justifiable. The
affections of a loyal people, he suggested, are always a surer guarantee of

of national security than coercive measures imposed by the federal government.[20]

As early as 1837, Jackson foresaw that "mutual suspicions and reproaches" between the states might "in time create mutual hostility, and [that] artful and designing men [might] be found who [were] ready to foment these fatal divisions and to inflame the natural jealousies of different sections of the country." Extremists in both the North and the South were making systematic efforts "to sow the seeds of discord between different parts of the United States and to place party divisions directly upon geographical distinctions; to excite the *South* against the *North* and the *North* against the *South*. . . ." There was nothing to be gained by such efforts, Jackson declared, except the opportunity to see "controversies which are now debated and settled in the halls of legislation . . . tried on fields of battle and determined by the sword." Almost fifty years' experience under the Constitution and the Union it had created had proved that free government was "no longer a doubtful experiment." The Constitution had successfully "preserved unimpaired the liberties of the people [and] secured the rights of property. . . ." Moreover, it had made it possible for the United States to flourish "beyond any former example in the history of nations." "It is no longer a question whether this great country can remain happily united and flourish. . . ." "Experience, the unerring test of all human undertakings, has shown the wisdom and foresight of those who founded it, and has proved that in the Union of these States there is a sure foundation for the brightest hopes of freedom and for the happiness of the people. At every hazard and by every sacrifice this Union must be preserved."

POPULAR SOVEREIGNTY
AND THE POLICE POWER

Jackson did not live to see the Union torn asunder, but he did see his ideas set in the bedrock of constitutional law. In the summer of 1835, John Marshall died, and Jackson rewarded his faithful aide Roger B. Taney (1777–1864) with an appointment as chief justice of the Supreme Court.[21] He now had named a majority of the Court. Taney, a Baltimore lawyer and earlier a Federalist leader in Maryland, was the most distinguished of all Jackson's appointments. He had amply demonstrated his loyalty to Jacksonian concepts of free government, and with a Democratic majority on the Court to support him, there was speculation that the Federalist doctrines Marshall had so carefully nurtured would be cast

---

[20] J. L. Blau, *Social Theories of Jacksonian Democracy* (New York: Hafner, 1947), pp. 4–8.

[21] Jackson had appointed Taney as an associate justice of the Court a year earlier, but the Senate refused confirmation, largely because of Taney's role as secretary of the treasury, at which time he withdrew federal funds from the Bank of the United States.

aside and replaced by a new set of principles. In fact, nothing of the sort happened. As interpreted by the Taney Court, Jacksonianism shifted emphasis, not substance. For the most part, the Taney Court followed well-marked judicial paths, deviating only slightly from Marshall's nationalism and introducing the stress Jackson himself paid states' rights.

Taney had at least one thing in common with his distinguished predecessor. Like Marshall he moved against the dominant political trend. Confronted with the abolitionist movement and national action designed to destroy slavery, Taney interposed constitutional roadblocks and finally brought down on his head a storm of protest. The Court became the focus of fierce controversy, with the Chief Justice featured as the villain in the plot.

Both Marshall and Taney were leaders in support of administrations in which they had been cabinet officers. Each had to meet strong opposition. Despite these seemingly untoward circumstances and criticism of unparalleled bitterness, Marshall and Taney shaped our constitutional development in their own image. Yet these eminent Chief Justices entertained views of the Constitution, of the Union, and of national power not easily reconciled. Marshall's contributions to nationalistic theory and action, increasingly vindicated by history, clearly overshadow those of Taney. Yet Taney's "enduring contributions to a workable adjustment of the theoretical distribution of authority between the two governments for a single people place Taney second only to Marshall in the constitutional history of our country."[22] (This appraisal predates the chief justiceship of Earl Warren [1953–1969].)

"Taney's mind," Thomas Reed Powell wrote

> seems to me markedly neater than that of Marshall, and his arguments are less open to refutation. Marshall was more intricate, more philosophical, cleverer at turning sharp corners, and his elocution is more sonorous than Taney's, gifts which doubtless are literary virtues but not necessarily judicial ones. Marshall was a nation builder, which Taney was not. As a creative statesman Marshall built superstructures on the foundation laid by the Fathers, but Taney in my view kept closer to that foundation than did Marshall, with always the tragic exception of his *Dred Scott* enormity as to the absence of national power to forbid slavery in the territories.[23]

The Taney Court was inclined, as the Marshall Court was not, to permit exercise of state police power at the expense of private rights. Indeed, Taney's first major opinion, in *Charles River Bridge* v. *Warren Bridge*,[24] veered "from the rigidity of the *Dartmouth College* ruling in the direction of narrowing the immunities of corporations and enlarging the scope

---

[22] Felix Frankfurter, "Taney and the Commerce Clause," *Harvard Law Review*, XLIX (1936), 1286, 1302.
[23] Thomas Reed Powell, *Vagaries and Varieties in Constitutional Interpretation* (New York: Columbia University Press, 1956), p. 150.
[24] 11 Peters 420 (1837).

of social legislation."[25] It reflected the spirit of hostility toward monopoly and exclusive privileges embodied in Jackson's Farewell Address, and the propriety of free enterprise and genuine laissez faire at the state level.

In 1785 Harvard College received from the Massachusetts legislature a charter authorizing construction of a toll bridge over the Charles River. The corporation set up by the charter flourished as population and business in the Boston area expanded. In 1828 the legislature authorized a second bridge, the Warren, which in time was to be operated free of toll. The Charles River Bridge Company immediately sought to enjoin construction of the Warren Bridge on the ground that it would impair the obligation of the contract implicit in the charter granted to the Charles River Bridge Company. The Supreme Judicial Court of Massachusetts dismissed the bill, and a writ of error to the United States Supreme Court was obtained. The case was argued in 1831, but no decision had been reached. It was argued again in 1837, during Taney's first term on the bench. By then the Warren Bridge had been finished and turned over to the state to be operated as a free bridge. Daniel Webster, counsel for the Charles River Bridge Company, argued on the basis of Marshall's reasoning in the *Dartmouth College* case that an implied contract in the charter dictated that no second bridge would ever be authorized or built. Involved was a clear conflict between vested rights, on one side, and public power, on the other.

No rights, Chief Justice Taney ruled, were to be construed as granted except those conferred specifically by the charter itself. It would be "a singular spectacle" if the Supreme Court should enlarge the privileges of American corporations by implication at the same time the courts in England, from which "our system of jurisprudence" was borrowed, were "restraining, within the strictest limits, the spirit of monopoly . . . and confining corporations to the privileges plainly given to them in their charter. . . ." Indeed, both English precedent and previous constructions by the Supreme Court itself emphasized the principle that "in grants by the public nothing passes by implication." "The object and end of all government is to promote the happiness and prosperity of the community by which it is established; and it never can be assumed that the government intended to diminish its power of accomplishing the end for which it was created." Only the "plain words" of a specific contract in the charter, naturally and properly construed, should be relied on as the basis for taking rights away from the public and giving them to a corporation. Especially was this true in a country like the United States, "free, active, and enterprising," "continually advancing in numbers and wealth," daily finding fresh need for new channels of communication, "both for travel and trade, and . . . the comfort, convenience, and prosperity of the people." Here, especially, one should not presume that a state had surrendered "its power of improvement and public accommodation" to a private corporation, for "the whole community [had] an interest in preserving [it]

---

[25] Schlesinger, *Age of Jackson*, p. 324.

. . . undiminished." Government would lose much of its value "if, by implications and presumptions, it was disarmed of the powers necessary to accomplish the ends of its creation, and the functions it was designed to perform transferred to the hands of privileged corporations." The community was interested in promoting its comfort and convenience and in advancing public prosperity "by providing safe, convenient, and cheap ways for the transportation of produce and purposes of travel." Implied contracts could not be allowed to thwart that interest by decreeing that a single corporation had exclusive privileges on a particular line of travel.

The rights of private property must, of course, be "sacredly guarded." No more than Marshall was Taney willing to sacrifice private rights on the altar of public power. But "we must not forget that the community also has rights, and that the happiness and well-being of every citizen depends on their faithful preservation." The important thing was to keep the channels of enterprise free and opportunities to enter them untrammeled.

LAISSEZ FAIRE UPHELD

One does not find in Taney's opinion any trace of the spirit of leveling, no suggestion that government itself undertake, by positive action, promotion of the public good. There is, however, blunt repudiation of the Federalist notion that absolute protection of private property is the surest way to promote the welfare of all. What Jackson and Taney asked of government was evenhanded justice in economic matters. Both desired elimination of economic privilege. Far from assailing property or business enterprise, they were concerned primarily with protecting it against privilege-seeking corporations. By insisting that industry, commerce, and finance be liberated from government-created monopoly privilege, the Jacksonians were apostles of laissez-faire equalled in spirit only by Jefferson himself.

The Jacksonian concept of laissez faire was perhaps best spelled out by Jackson's successor, President Martin Van Buren (1782–1862). Except for Taney he was Jackson's most influential adviser, both before and after his election as vice-president in 1832. Early in Van Buren's administration the inflationary effects of Jackson's veto of the Bank bill and his subsequent deposit of government funds in state banks combined to produce a panic and depression of serious proportions. Van Buren was immediately faced with the necessity of combating both. Business interests complained loudly and presented demands for government action to meet the financial crisis. Van Buren called a special session of Congress for September 4, 1837, but instead of recommending government assistance "to relieve embarrassments arising from losses by revulsions in commerce and credit," he moved in precisely the opposite direction.[26] Being firmly con-

---

[26] Van Buren's Special Session Message is in Richardson, *Messages of Presidents*, III, 324–46.

vinced of the rightness of the Jefferson-Jackson tradition, he seldom deviated from it; when he did, it was only to lend emphasis to a particular point. His main suggestion to Congress was abandonment of the system of depositing government funds in banks, state or national, and creation, instead, of an independent United States treasury to receive and disburse all government monies. Having made his recommendation, he concluded with a sharp exposition on the role of government in economic affairs. A minimum of government interference in national economic life was his guiding principle. Even those who looked to the government for specific aid in crisis situations lost sight of the true ends of government and of the proper use of its power. The national government had been established "to give security to us all in our lawful and honorable pursuits under the lasting safeguard of republican institutions. It was not intended to confer special favors on individuals or on any classes of them, to create systems of agriculture, manufactures, or trade, or to engage in them either separately or in connection with individual citizens or organized associations." If governmental power were exerted in behalf of one class, "equivalent favors" would of necessity have to be extended to every other class, and "the attempt to bestow . . . favors with an equal hand, or even to select those who should most deserve them, would never be successful."

The heart of his own belief, and of Jackson's as well, was that

> all communities are apt to look to government for too much. Even in our own country, where its powers and duties are so strictly limited, we are prone to do so, especially at periods of sudden embarrassment and distress. But this ought not to be. The framers of our excellent Constitution and the people who approved it with calm and sagacious deliberation acted at the time on a sounder principle. They wisely judged that the less government interferes with private pursuits the better for the general prosperity. It is not its legitimate object to make men rich or to repair by direct grants of money or legislation in favor of particular pursuits, losses not incurred in the public service. This would be substantially to use the property of some for the benefit of others. . . . its real duty— . . . the performance of which makes a good government the most precious of human blessings—is to enact and enforce a system of general laws commensurate with, but not exceeding, the objects of its establishment, and to leave every citizen and every interest to reap under its benign protection the rewards of virtue, industry, and prudence.

Van Buren, to a greater extent even than Jackson, insisted on strict construction of the Constitution, using every occasion to declare that the federal government made its greatest contribution "to the security and happiness of the people when limited to the exercise of its conceded powers." Because emergency did not create power, measures to relieve "mercantile embarrassments," no matter how necessary they seemed, violated the rule that government should not interfere with the ordinary pursuits of citizens; such measures were not "within the Constitutional province of the General Government," nor would their adoption "promote the real and permanent welfare of those they might be designed to aid."

Van Buren and the Jacksonians conceived of government neither as the shield of property nor as the friend of the propertyless. Its role was that of a neutral, enacting laws to favor no person or class above any other and relying on the operation of natural economic laws, as exemplified in "the ordinary pursuits of citizens," for the welfare and prosperity of the country. John L. O'Sullivan (1813–1895), founder of the *United States Magazine and Democratic Review,* stated the essence of the Jacksonian creed: "Confidence in the virtue, intelligence, and full capacity for self-government, of the great mass of our people, our industrious, honest, manly, intelligent millions of freemen." It opposed any restraint on "free action," and its basic principle stressed response to the will of the majority.[27]

JACKSONIANISM SUMMARIZED

O'Sullivan, like all Jacksonians, underscored majority rule, but, like them, he also expressed "strong sympathy for minorities . . . [whose] rights have a high moral claim on the right and justice of majorities. . . ." Minority rights were certainly entitled to protection—indeed, "highly pernicious error has often possessed the minds of nearly a whole nation," while only a few "possessed the truth, which the next generation may perhaps recognize and practice." That this was sometimes the case did not mean that popular opinion could never be trusted, that it must always be checked by minority interests and subjected to the " 'more enlightened wisdom' of the 'better classes' . . ." Perhaps better than any of his contemporaries, O'Sullivan summarized Jacksonianism as its exponents understood it.

1. A majority was more likely, as a general rule, at least, to understand and follow its own greatest good than was the minority.
2. A minority was "much more likely to abuse power for the promotion of its own selfish interests, at the expense of the majority of numbers, the substantial and producing mass of the nation, than the latter is to oppress unjustly the former. . . ."
3. There was no natural and original superiority of a minority class above the great mass of a community in intelligence and in competence for the duties of government. The "general diffusion of education" and the existence of a free press gave all equal "access to every species of knowledge important to the great interests of the community." The operation of "a perfectly free democratic system which [abolished] all artificial distinctions, and, [prevented] the accumulation of any social obstacles to advancement, . . . [permitted] the free development of every germ of talent, wherever it . . . [chanced] to exist, whether on the proud mountain summit, in the humble valley, or by the wayside of common life."

---

[27] O'Sullivan's essay is in the introduction to *The United States Magazine and Democratic Review,* October, 1837.

4. Neither majorities nor minorities might use the power of government to further their selfish ends. In societies in which government was "understood as a central consolidated power, managing and directing the various general interests of society," the possibilities of a tyrannical majority or minority in power was ever present, and the peace and safety of the community was always in jeopardy. No government could safely be trusted "with the power of legislation upon the general interest of society so as to operate directly or indirectly on the industry and property of the community." Legislation was responsible for nine-tenths of all the evil mankind had suffered since the beginning of time. If it would be used to deal with "the general business and interests of the people," the people would forever after be unable to restrict it. "It [would] be perpetually tampering with private interests, and sending forth seeds of corruption which will result in the demoralization of the society."

5. "The best government is that which governs least," which is confined to the administration of justice, the protection of the "natural equal rights of the citizens," and to the preservation of law and order. "The voluntary principle, the principle of freedom," is the true rule for democratic governments to follow. "The natural laws which will establish themselves and find their own level are the best laws. . . . This is the fundamental principle of the philosophy of democracy, to furnish a system of administration of justice, and then leave all the business and interests of society to themselves, to free competition and association; in a word, to the voluntary principle." Adherence to this principle alone "affords a satisfactory and perfect solution to the great problem, otherwise unsolved, of the relative rights of majorities and minorities."

6. In a truly democratic society, as in nature itself, "precipitate radical changes" were not productive of good. Neither, however, was slavish veneration of "the wisdom of our fathers." Democracy and experimentation were handmaidens; reform was necessary for improvement. If carried on under "the banner of the democratic principle," ventures into the untried and unknown were not dangerous; "it is only necessary to be cautious not to go too fast."

The Age of Jackson changed the direction of American political thought and action. On the one hand, the political capacities of the common man were recognized and given expression—a significant departure from Federalist thought and practice. On the other hand, economic democracy and laissez faire were prescribed and enforced. Although recognizing the sacredness of property rights, the Jacksonians warned that the community also has rights. Both aspects of the Jacksonian revolution are important, although the former for a long time received the greater emphasis. Whereas the stress of Jeffersonianism had been on weak government, Jacksonianism embraced the idea of government acting in behalf of the whole people, to protect them from selfish or privileged minority groups.

Jacksonian Democracy displayed unbounded faith in the future of America. "The Jacksonian movement of revolt . . . was one of aspiration." It was inspired by a desire to open the door of opportunity to all, to give everyone "the chance to grow into something bigger and finer. . . ."[28] Individual self-realization would be fostered not so much by the positive acts of government as by the erasing of privileges, both economic and political, that government itself had been instrumental in creating. Jackson's veto of the bank bill and the clamorous war he waged against financial privilege are conspicuous examples of a far-flung policy.

The nation seemed, during the Age of Jackson, to be closer than at any time before or since to the ideals of the Declaration of Independence.[29] Political democracy was not fully achieved, it is true—not even in the elementary sense of universal manhood suffrage. The blight of slavery had yet to be abolished. But the country had taken long strides in the direction of more responsive and more responsible government. Although de Tocqueville foresaw a "manufacturing aristocracy . . . growing up under our eyes, . . . the harshest which ever existed in the world," the corporation had not yet become dominant. Economic democracy still appeared a viable goal. Indeed, economic equality was very nearly a fact. Any white man might, by his own effort, rise toward a summit of achievement. There was no thought of transferring wealth by government action from the few to the many. With natural resources almost limitless, free men could be trusted to desire what was right and to obtain it.

In the 1830s few realized that another revolution, industrial in character, was already forging new chains to fetter human freedom. Just over the horizon loomed another crisis for free government, precipitated by the rise of the new aristocracy foreseen by de Tocqueville. This struggle drastically altered the climate of American economic and political life. Vanished forever were the conditions that made the Age of Jackson a period of extraordinary progress toward freedom and equality.

---

[28] James Truslow Adams, *The Epic of Democracy* (Boston: Little, Brown, 1931), pp. 173–74.

[29] But see Lee Benson, *The Concept of Jacksonian Democracy. New York as a Test Case* (Princeton, N.J.: Princeton University Press, 1961), who argues that in New York, at least, this conclusion was not borne out.

CHAPTER ELEVEN

THE COMMON MAN
CHALLENGED

The Age of Jackson symbolized triumph for the common man, whether on the farm or in the growing ranks of labor.[1] Owning his land, shop, and tools of production, the working man belonged to the so-called middle class. With vast natural resources and acres of unoccupied land, pre–Civil War America was remarkably homogeneous, and (barring slavery) unstratified by extremes of wealth and poverty. Then the vision of a truly egalitarian society seemed realizable. Democracy and the existing economic pattern, marked by equality, were interchangeable. Economic and political advancement came to nearly everyone who sought it. Only the short-lived panic of 1837 marred the scene.

Yet at the very time the middle class was riding the crest of the wave politically and economically, an opposition movement of considerable strength developed in the social and intellectual spheres. That movement described prewar America as "a cold, unfeeling civilization, bred by commercial interests and isolation, a negative moderation, an excess of pru-

---

[1] See Walter Hugins, *Jacksonian Democracy and the Working Class. A Study of the New York Workingman's Movement 1829–1837* (Stanford, Calif.: Stanford University Press, 1967).

dence, compromise, provincial good taste. It cast a censorious eye on human nature, on all the free flights of the picturesque, the goodly growths of fancy. It offered employment to no one but the decorous and the complacent. It was timid, imitative, tame; worse, it was mean and cruel. It taught the mind of the young to aim at low objects. . . ."[2]

Sensitive members of society, "the imaginative, the impressionable, the perceptive . . . were thoroughly disaffected."[3] Gross materialism—America's overweening concern with business and the acquisition of money—repelled them. For them America's strength was rooted in "ethical and moral standards and precepts," in "democratic faith in man." That faith, rather than profit and the dollar, was "the chief armament of [American] democracy."[4]

Little in the Age of Jackson pleased these romantic individualists, for whom Jacksonian democracy was marked by an incessant drive for gain, vulgarity, the "spoils" of politics, and glorification of the untutored man. God Himself, Henry Thoreau believed, did "not sympathize with the popular movements" of the day.[5] Emerson regarded the election of Andrew Jackson as proof "that government in America was becoming a 'job'—he could think of no more contemptuous word."[6] In 1834 Emerson solemnly declared that "a most unfit person in the Presidency has been doing the worst things; and the worse he grew, the more popular."[7]

By the 1830s and 1840s dissidents had begun to express their displeasure, some under the sponsorship of religious groups, others under secular auspices. Among the most famous of these experiments was Brook Farm, near Boston, which flourished between 1841 and 1847, its avowed purpose being the substitution of brotherly cooperation for selfish competition. To make the point, some turned to literature or combined personal involvement with literary expression. The literary attack was led by Ralph Waldo Emerson, Henry David Thoreau, and Walt Whitman. Included also were Orestes Brownson (1803–1876), editor, novelist, and harsh critic of the capitalist system; Bronson Alcott (1799–1888), schoolmaster and educational reformer; William Henry Channing (1810–1884), clergyman and socialist editor; and Margaret Fuller (1810–1850), writer, conversationalist, and editor. Their combined effort stimulated "the first American Renaissance." Although the slavery crisis in the 1850s and the Civil War diverted the nation's attention, its humanitarian theme has remained significant in American thought.

---

[2] Van Wyck Brooks, *The Flowering of New England 1815–1865*, rev. ed. (New York: Dutton, 1941), p. 181.
[3] Brooks, *Flowering of New England*, p. 180.
[4] David E. Lilienthal, "Our Faith is Mightier Than Our Atom Bomb," *The New York Times Magazine*, March 6, 1949, p. 11.
[5] *The Writings of Henry David Thoreau* (Boston: Houghton Mifflin, 1906), VII, 315.
[6] Perry Miller, "Emersonian Genius and the American Democracy," *New England Quarterly*, XXVI (March, 1953), 29.
[7] Ralph Waldo Emerson to Thomas Carlyle, May 14, 1834, quoted in Miller, "Emersonian Genius."

EMERSON: THE IDEALIST

Ralph Waldo Emerson (1802–1882), poet, essayist, and critic, was born of a long line of Boston ministers. He attended Harvard College, graduating in 1821, and for a while taught in his brother's private school for young ladies. In 1825 he entered Harvard Divinity School and prepared himself for the Unitarian pulpit. Quickly discovering that the church was too confining, he resigned from the ministry to devote his life to creative thinking and writing. Before long his fame as a philosopher had spread far beyond Concord.

Emerson's works are filled with protests against the rampant materialism of his day, its ostentation, its overbearing rich and greedy poor, its lack of thought, its failure to appreciate the finer things of life—beauty, friendship, and love. Men spent their money on trifles and neglected their own personalities: they lost their souls in vainly seeking after "fine garments, handsome apartments, access to public houses and places of amusement."[8] Mercenary impulses accounted for "the selfish and even cruel aspect which belongs to our great mechanical works, to mills, railways, and machinery."[9] It was not so much that the commercial spirit was bad in itself, but rather that it received undue emphasis. "This invasion of Nature by Trade with its Money, its Credit, its Steam, its Railroad," Emerson wrote in his *Journal*, "threatens to upset the balance of man and establish a new universal Monarchy more tyrannical than Babylon or Rome."[10]

Against burgeoning materialism he set the natural world of the spirit. He would willingly trade "this place of brick and stone, these servants, this kitchen, these stables, horses and equipage, this bankstock and file of mortgages . . . all for a little conversation, high, clear and spiritual." "Thought, virtue, beauty were the ends" of life, not the acquisition of goods.[11] "Man was born to be rich," but not in property so much as in "the use of his faculties . . . the union of thought with nature."[12] Emerson therefore urged men to seek harmony with nature, "to try the magic of sincerity, to apply the test of spiritual values to the material forces and mechanical philosophies of the times."[13]

Emerson could not look upon "the Jacksonian rabble with anything but loathing."[14] To accord equal significance to saints and sinners, philosophers and fools, assured a bare level of mediocrity. "Away with this

[8] Edward W. Emerson and Waldo Emerson Forbes, eds., *The Journals of Ralph Waldo Emerson* (Boston: Houghton Mifflin, 1909–1914), V, 285.
[9] Ralph Waldo Emerson, "Essay on Art," *The Complete Essays and Writings of Ralph Waldo Emerson*, Modern Library ed. (New York: Random House, 1940), p. 315.
[10] Emerson and Forbes, *Journals*, V, 285.
[11] Emerson, "Essay on Nature," *Essays and Writings*, p. 418.
[12] Emerson, "Essay on Conduct of Life," *Essays and Writings*, p. 70.
[13] Parrington, *Main Currents*, II, 386.
[14] Miller, "Emersonian Genius," p. 34.

hurrah of the masses," Emerson implored, "and let us have the considerate vote of single men spoken on their honor and their conscience. In old Egypt it was established law that the vote of a prophet be reckoned equal to a hundred hands. I think it was much underestimated."[15] Emerson's "representative man" was he who was able to give voice to what was "just trembling on the lips of all thinking men."[16] Such a man was Daniel Webster, whom Emerson described in his Phi Beta Kappa Poem of 1834:

> A form which Nature cast in the heroic mould.
> Of them who rescued liberty of old;
> He, when the rising storm of party roared,
> Brought his great forehead to the council board,
> There, while hot heads perplexed with fears the state,
> Calm as the morn the manly patriot sate;
> Seemed, when at last his clarion accents broke,
> As if the conscience of the country spoke.

Although Emerson found the America of his day wanting in leaders of Webster's stature, he was nevertheless optimistic that she would produce representative men. Such men were primarily the products of the middle class, and because he considered the representative man *primus inter pares*, reflecting accurately and unselfishly the currents of his own time, Emerson's emphasis was not so undemocratic as it may appear. His greatness lay not in surpassing but in representing his constituency.[17] Such a conviction enabled Emerson to stand as "the first philosopher of the American spirit."[18]

Emerson had sublime faith in the full-grown, well-rounded individual, in "the sufficiency of the private man."[19] He deplored a society whose members "suffered amputation from the trunk, and strut about so many walking monsters—a good finger, a neck, a stomach, an elbow, but never a man."[20] Man by his nature possessed the ability to live according to divine reason; when he learned to exercise that ability, he became a whole individual, a vibrant expression of the Oversoul. Only the institutions of society prevented most men from realizing their full potentialities. The need was to liberate them, to help them free their minds "from false and ignoble loyalties that [they] might serve the true."[21] Once man realized the divinity of his own nature and achieved through the exercise of reason a morality that placed him in a new relationship to his fellows and to the world, his shackles would be removed and he would no longer need any

---

[15] Quoted in Mason, *Free Government*, p. 475.
[16] Emerson and Forbes, *Journal*, II, 282.
[17] Miller, "Emersonian Genius," p. 42.
[18] See John O. McCormick, "Emerson's Theory of Human Greatness," *New England Quarterly* XXVI (September, 1953), 291–314 for an interesting summary discussion of the development of Emerson's belief in genius.
[19] Emerson, "New England Reformers," *Essays and Writings*, p. 451.
[20] Quoted in Mason, *Free Government*, p. 458.
[21] Parrington, *Main Currents*, II, 391.

instruments of force, any government, or indeed, any social institutions. The power of love alone would suffice.

Man's first duty was to develop the fullness of his spiritual nature and power. By his own effort man must fulfill his animal needs. Not even the genius—the representative man—was justified in living on the labor of others. Work was more than a means of sustaining life. It was a process by which man came closer to nature and, thus, found himself. Work was the natural product of man as fruit was of a tree. Just as a weed might be called a plant whose virtues had not yet been discovered, so a man without work was a being whose possibilities remained unexplored. "Was it not the chief disgrace in the world," Van Wyck Brooks wrote in a paraphrase of Emerson, "not to yield that particular fruit which each man was created to bear? . . ."[22]

Emerson and Private Property

Emerson did not share the almost universal devotion of his time to the institution of private property. Work that led solely to its accumulation also led men to "measure their esteem of each other by what each has, and not by what each is." Too great a reliance on property represented a want of reliance on self. In the pursuit of property, men had looked so long "away from themselves and at things that they [had] come to esteem the religious, learned and civil institutions" of society merely as "guards of property."[23] Inordinate concern with property distorted all values. ". . . doubts have arisen," Emerson remarked in his essay on "Politics," "whether too much weight had not been allowed in the laws to property, and such a structure given to our usages as allowed the rich to encroach on the poor, and to keep them poor. . . . [T]here is an instinctive sense, however obscure and yet inarticulate, that the whole constitution of property, on its present tenures, is injurious, and its influences on persons deteriorating and degrading. . . ."[24] "Cultivated" men were coming to be ashamed of their property and to realize that property-mindedness perverted the acts of government. There was a growing feeling, Emerson believed, that government had no special duty toward property and especially that it should not seek to interfere with property. Rather, property should be left to shift for itself, to be regulated by its own natural laws. Then it would flow, as it should, "from the idle and imbecile to the industrious, brave and persevering." "The only safe rule is found in the self-adjusting meter of demand and supply." "Do not legislate . . . give no bounties . . . open the doors of opportunity to talent and virtue; and they will do themselves justice, and property will not be in bad hands."[25]

Such sentiments have enabled latter-day laissez faire theorists to claim

[22] Brooks, *Flowering of New England*, p. 206.
[23] Emerson, "Self-Reliance," *Essays and Writings*, p. 168.
[24] Emerson, "Politics," *Essays and Writings*, p. 425.
[25] Emerson, "Essays on Wealth," *Essays and Writings*, p. 705.

Emerson as their own. But he would not have approved any economic order that narrowed individual opportunity. For him the individual must be free to pursue self-realization unencumbered by either political or economic restriction. "Hands off!" Emerson exclaimed, "let there be no control and no interferences in . . . the affairs of this kingdom of me."[26] The ideal situation was to enjoy freedom so completely that each man might follow his own economic star, checked only by the operation of supply and demand. Artifice and legislation served only to produce "reactions, gluts and bankruptcies."[27]

Emerson and Politics

To Emerson politics was largely immaterial and irrelevant. Government could do little or nothing to change the fundamental laws of economic and social development. Legislation was in any case a pitiful contrivance, unable to bring into being the life men were meant to lead on earth. Beauty would not "come at the call of a legislature";[28] it was futile to expect politics to produce integrity of intellect. Some day, with the emergence of a higher level of civilization, politics would disappear altogether. Men would realize its triviality when compared to emancipation of the individual and development of his divine soul. "Politics is an afterwork, a poor patching. We are always a little late. The evil is done, the law is passed, and we begin the uphill agitation for repeal of that of which we ought to have prevented the enacting. We shall one day learn to supersede politics by education."[29]

In the meantime Emerson found little to applaud in the contemporary political scene. States were inevitably corrupt because "the governments . . . of the world are . . . governments of the rich."[30] The Republic was in poor hands. Political parties lashed themselves into a fury over local and momentary measures to the detriment of the nation. Neither party satisfied him. The Democrats had the best cause; the Whigs, the best men; yet neither recognized that "the highest end of government is the culture of men." Nor was it probable that they ever would. Experience had led him to the conclusion that the solution to America's ills would not be achieved through their efforts. Instead, Emerson was convinced that "the tendencies of the times favor[ed] the idea of self government" and that a movement was under way toward greater reliance on "the influence of private character" in national affairs. "The power of love, as the basis of a State, [had] never been tried." Emerson recommended the experiment:

> When the state-house is the hearth
> Then the perfect state is come,
> The republican at home.

[26] Emerson, "New England Reformers," *Essays and Writings*, p. 451.
[27] Emerson, "Essay on Wealth," *Essays and Writings*, p. 705.
[28] Emerson, "Essay on Art," *Essays and Writings*, p. 314.
[29] Emerson, "Essay on Culture," *Essays and Writings*, p. 722.
[30] Emerson, "Essay on Nature," *Essays and Writings*, p. 418.

The society of Emerson's day bristled with reformist crusades. "In the history of the world," he noted in 1841, "the doctrine of Reform had never such scope as at the present hour, . . . not a kingdom, town, statute, rite, calling, man, or woman, but is threatened by the new spirit."[31] Emerson listed the motley array of dissenters caustically as: "Madmen, and women, men with beards, dunkers, muggletonians, Come-outers, Groaners, Agrarians, Seventh-Day Baptists, Quakers, Abolitionists, Unitarians, and Philosophers."[32] Amid the crowds of uplifters, he ranged himself on the side of weak government, not so much because he was interested (like Jefferson) in men's rights and freedoms as because he wrote as a transcendentalist[33] concerned with men's souls. Salvation, Emerson believed, was a purely individual matter; collective action obscured the real goal. Thus, he was as skeptical of the effectiveness of reform and reformers as of political parties. "Nature . . . does not like our benevolence or our learning much better than she likes our frauds and wars. When we come out of the caucus, or the bank, or the Abolition-convention, or the Temperance-meeting, or the Transcendental-club into the fields and woods, she says to us, 'So hot? my little Sir.' "[34]

"We are all a little worried here with numberless projects of social reform," Emerson wrote his English friend Thomas Carlyle in the fall of 1840. "Not a reading man but has a draft of a new community in his waistcoat pocket." Emerson was mildly interested in the Brook Farm experiment and other causes then occupying the "come-outers," but he remained aloof from them. He distrusted their unbounded enthusiasm and even more the danger to the individual implicit in their collectivist approach. The reform objectives seemed temporary rather than enduring, superficial rather than basic. What in his day passed for root-and-branch imperatives—abolition of war, gambling, intemperance, and slavery— were only "medicating the symptoms" of a basic malady, the stunted, dwarfed individual. Reliance on concert, on association, to cure that malady was futile. If action were to be effective, the approach had to be through each man, through every "secret soul."

Yet reformers eagerly sought Emerson's help. All such solicitations were resisted in deference to the one course he deemed fundamental: "I think *that* the soul of reform; the conviction that not sensuality, not slavery, not war, not imprisonment, not even government are needed,—but in lieu of them all, reliance on the sentiment of man which will work best the more it is trusted."[35] Love, education, and persuasion by example were sure means of reform, the only ones he endorsed and advocated.

Despite his skepticism toward reform projects and his distrustful atti-

---

[31] Emerson, "Man the Reformer," *The Complete Works of Ralph Waldo Emerson,* Concord ed., I, 228.
[32] Charles A. Beard, *Rise of American Civilization* (New York: Macmillan, 1927), I, 728.
[33] Transcendentalism was a literary movement in New England from about 1830 to 1860; it posited a mystical belief in God, in nature, and in individual man.
[34] Quoted in Mason, *Free Government,* pp. 475–76.
[35] Quoted in Mason, *Free Government,* p. 476.

tude toward collective action, Emerson was not afraid of change. "All life is an experiment," he noted in his *Journal* in 1842. "The more experiments you make the better. What if they are a little coarse, and you may get your coat soiled or torn? What if you do fail and get fairly rolled in the dirt once or twice? Up again, you shall never be so afraid of a tumble."[36] "We are to revise the whole of our social structure," he told the Boston Mechanics in 1841, "the State, the school, religion, marriage, trade, science, and explore their foundations in our own nature; we are . . . to clear ourselves of every usage which has not its roots in our own mind. What is man born for but to be a Reformer, a Re-maker, of what man has made; a renouncer of lies; a restorer of truth and good? . . . If there are inconveniences and what is called ruin in the way, [it is] because we have enervated and maimed ourselves. . . ."[37] Yet Emerson was content to be a catalyst, not an activist: "I approve every wild action of experimenters . . . and my only apology for not doing their work is preoccupation of mind. I have work of my own which I know I can do with some success."

Emerson nevertheless became an abolitionist. At first, he had been inclined to accept slavery as a decree of nature, an insurmountable barrier between different degrees of intellect in the different races. Later, he endorsed the abolitionist purpose but denounced their methods as philanthropic—more concerned with bringing reform abroad than at home. "I have not yet conquered my own house. . . . Shall I raise the siege of this hencoop," he asked disdainfully, and "march baffled away to a pretended siege of Babylon?" In time, however, he berated the "old indecent nonsense about the nature of the negro," saying: "It now appears that the negro race is, more than any other, susceptible of rapid civilization." As sectional struggles grew more bitter, slavery became increasingly an economic and political issue. When the proslavery element fought for the annexation of Texas, Emerson urged New England to resist "tooth and nail." He attended several antiannexation meetings, and at one of them delivered an address on "Politics." But while friends like Henry David Thoreau, William Lloyd Garrison, and Wendell Phillipps threw themselves wholeheartedly into the struggle, Emerson remained more or less detached. There were more compelling causes: "I have quite other slaves to free than those negroes, to wit, imprisoned spirits, imprisoned thoughts, far back in the brain of man,—far retired in the heaven of invention, and which, important to the republic of Man, have no watchman, no lover, or defender but I."[38]

Emerson and the American Utopia

The utopia Emerson envisaged, the America he admired, was the ideal—what this country might be. In the effort to achieve it, one should not

---

[36] Emerson and Forbes, *Journals*, VI, 302.
[37] Emerson, "Man the Reformer," *Works*, I, 248.
[38] Mason, *Free Government*, p. 476.

have experiment and reform as ends. "The power which is at once spring and regulator" in all efforts of reform is "the conviction that there is an infinite worthiness in man. . . ."[39] Every institution must be infused with an ideal that bordered on anarchy—perhaps utopia." "The less government we have the better—the fewer laws and the less confided power. The antidote to this abuse of formal government is the influence of private character, the growth of the individual. . . . To educate the wise man the State exists, and with the appearance of the wise man the State expires. The appearance of character makes the State unnecessary. The wise man is the State."[40]

The current trend toward conformity, toward the submersion of the individual, profoundly disturbed Emerson. Society was "everywhere . . . in conspiracy against the manhood of every one of its members. Society is a joint-stock company, in which the members agree, for the better securing of his bread to each shareholder, to surrender the liberty and culture of the eater. The virtue in most respects is conformity. Self-reliance is [society's] aversion. It loves not realities and creators, but names and customs."

> Who so would be a man must be a nonconformist. He who would gather immortal palms must not be hindered by the name of goodness, but must explore if it be goodness. Nothing is at last sacred but the integrity of your own mind. Absolve you to yourself, and you shall have the suffrage of the world. . . . A man is to carry himself in the presence of all opposition as if every thing were titular and ephemeral but he. I am ashamed to think how easily we capitulate to badges and names, to large societies and dead institutions. . . . I hope in these days we have heard the last of conformity and consistency.[41]

Not surprisingly, Emerson viewed the Constitution as a mere mechanical contrivance for holding men to their legal and moral obligations. Neither the auxiliary devices so dear to Madison and Adams nor Hamilton's concept of coercive, overall sovereignty appealed to Emerson. His concern was less for the political union of the many than for the integrity of spirit of each. His essay "New England Reformers" underscores his approach:

> Men will live and communicate, and plough, and reap, and govern, as by added ethereal power, when once they are united. . . . This union must be inward, and not one of covenants, and is to be reached by a reverse of the methods they use. The union is only perfect when all the uniters are isolated. . . . Each man, if he attempts to join himself to others, is on all sides cramped and diminished of his proportion; and the stricter the union the smaller and more pitiful he is. But leave him alone, to recognize in every hour and place the secret soul; he will go up and down doing the works of a true member,

---

[39] Emerson, "Man the Reformer," *Works*, I, 248–49.
[40] Emerson, "Politics," *Works*, III, 215–16.
[41] Emerson, "Self-Reliance," *Works*, II, 49.

and, to the astonishment of all, the work will be done in concert, though no man spoke. Government will be adamantine without any governor. The union must be ideal in actual individualism.[42]

Although utopian, the ideas of Emerson have been influential and abiding. His ideas, sometimes his words, appear in Oliver Wendell Holmes' writings. Holmes' skeptical attitude toward reform and reformers, experiment and change, were borrowed from Emerson. "I used to say," Holmes wrote, "that Emerson's great gift was that of imparting a ferment."[43] Louis D. Brandeis concurred. While a student at the Harvard Law School, he copied in notebooks passages from Emerson's essays, his favorite being "Self-Reliance." "I have read a few sentences of his," Brandeis wrote in 1876, "which are alone enough to make the man immortal."[44] Perhaps no American philosopher has had a greater impact on succeeding generations than Ralph Waldo Emerson. Emerson spoke "for magnanimity and the power of thought; . . . [he] spoke to the active forces waiting in his hearers, eager for the word that would set them free."[45] Liberation was his byword, confidence in the individual, his faith. To this day his message "remains a priceless possession of his countrymen."[46]

THOREAU: WALDEN ICONOCLAST

Among those whom Emerson influenced was his fellow townsman and friend—the essayist, poet, naturalist, surveyor, mystic, and social critic Henry David Thoreau (1817–1862). The son of a lead pencil manufacturer, Thoreau, like Emerson, graduated from Harvard College and taught briefly in a private school. Like Emerson, too, he became a transcendentalist. But whereas Emerson emerged as the great figure of his day, Thoreau achieved slight recognition during his lifetime, and little more for many years after his death. Only since the 1920s (particularly since 1950) has his significance been fully realized.[47] Thoreau's failure to win earlier recognition was due in part to his eccentric manner of life. He gave the impression of indifference toward his fellow man; he seemed cold and impassive[48] and did nothing to alter that opinion. Worse, he deliberately set himself apart from others and pursued an independent course. James Russell Lowell once accused him of withdrawing from his own cen-

---

[42] Emerson, "New England Reformers," *Essays and Writings*, pp. 457–58.

[43] Oliver W. Holmes to John C. H. Wu, quoted in Lerner, ed., *The Mind and Faith of Justice Holmes* (Boston: Little, Brown, 1943), p. 424.

[44] Louis Brandeis to Otto Wehle, November 12, 1876, quoted in A. T. Mason, *Brandeis: A Free Man's Life* (New York: Viking, 1946), p. 38.

[45] Brooks, *Flowering of New England*, pp. 535–36.

[46] Bliss Perry, *The American Spirit in Literature* (New Haven, Conn.: Yale University Press, 1921), p. 130.

[47] See Walter Harding, *The Days of Henry Thoreau* (New York: Knopf, 1965).

[48] Perry, *American Spirit*, p. 132.

tury.[49] The pattern of his life was without counterpart among his contemporaries; indeed, Thoreau seems more like a man of our time.

While the attention of America was turning more and more to enterprise and activity, exploration and exploitation, money and profit, Thoreau moved in the opposite direction, seeming to court material poverty. Although he had learned his father's trade, he made no pretense of following it or any other calling, preferring to work only enough to sustain life. His employment served "to keep [him] at the top of [his] condition and ready for whatever may turn up in heaven or on earth."[50] The less work a man did, the better for him and for his country. Life should be reduced to bare essentials, in order that one might devote himself to the study of nature and of one's self. "I came into this world," he wrote, "not chiefly to make this a good place to live in, but to live in it, be it good or bad."[51] To stay at home and mind one's own business was the best road to follow; wealth could only achieve superfluities. "Money is not required to buy one necessary for the soul." Acting on his belief, he devoted his time to thought and the study of nature. Even more than Emerson, with whom he lived as a young man, Thoreau represented the spirit of transcendentalism. The spiritual perfection of the soul was his chief concern.

Thoreau's Individualism

Like Emerson, Thoreau was an intense believer in individualism. But whereas Emerson was content to live in the community, at least physically, and abide its abuse in return for its comforts, pleasures, and contacts, Thoreau carried his belief to actual withdrawal from society. Emerson supplied the formula; Thoreau applied and proved it. For over two years (1845–1847) he lived at Walden Pond, in the woods near Concord; in communion with the birds, beasts, and flowers, he practiced and recorded the individualism he loved. He abandoned society not because he disliked people or communion with his fellows, but because he sought closer union with them, which could only be acquired by a deeper understanding of the natural world in which all men existed, but in which few lived.

Walden, the account of Thoreau's sojourn in the woods, is the best record of his philosophical thought. Published in 1854, it is at once a naturalist's journal and an essay of social criticism. The story of his two-year retreat on a patch of Emerson's land begins: "When I wrote the following pages . . . I lived alone, in the woods, a mile from any neighbor,

---

[49] Joseph W. Krutch, *Henry David Thoreau* (New York: William Sloane Associates, 1948), p. 252.
[50] Quoted in Perry, *American Spirit*, p. 133. Thoreau was not wholly accurate. Far from a hermit, he "was an inveterate traveler whose friends were legion. He was not an idler, but a surveyor . . . a lecturer . . . an inventive manufacturer . . . and a writer whose output exceeded two million words." John J. McAleer, reviewing Harding, *The Days of Henry Thoreau, America*, January 1, 1966, p. 23.
[51] Quoted in Mason, *Brandeis*, p. 460.

in a house which I had built myself, on the shore of Walden Pond, in Concord . . . and earned my living by the labor of my hands only." As a result of his rendezvous with nature, he became convinced "both by faith and experience, that to maintain one's self on this earth is not a hardship but a pastime, if we will live simply and wisely. . . . It is not necessary that a man should earn his living by the sweat of his brow, unless he sweats easier than I do."[52]

Behind Thoreau's physical retreat lay his conviction that a philosopher must do more than have subtle thoughts, write erudite essays, give learned lectures, urge government action, and back organized reform.

"I went to the woods because I wished to live deliberately, to front only the essential facts of life, and see if I could not learn what it had to teach, and not, when I came to die, discover that I had not lived. . . . I wanted to live deep and suck out all the marrow of life, . . . to put to rout all that was not life, . . . to drive life into a corner, and reduce it to its lowest terms. . . ."[53] A true philosopher must test his philosophy by living it and trying to discover by experience the essential truths. In going to Walden, he was not running away from society's problems; rather, he was working, in his own way, toward their solution.

Walden's thesis, if it can be said to have any, is that men had become too much concerned with comfort, with property, and with the nonessentials of civilization; as a result, they did not live. Revolted, like Emerson, by a society in which "things are in the saddle and ride mankind," Thoreau advocated return to the simple life, flight from too much government and too much trade. In *Walden* Thoreau elaborated the text: "The only wealth is life."[54]

Thoreau on Politics

Neither in *Walden* nor in his earlier book, *A Week on the Concord and Merrimack Rivers*, published in 1849, did Thoreau concern himself primarily with politics, although both, particularly *Walden*, give insight into his concept of the state and government. Had the Mexican War not come along, and later, the bitter struggle over slavery, Thoreau might never have devoted more attention to politics. These events impelled him to take a more positive stand on political questions, with the result that he finally emerged as a reluctant crusader.[55] His position in the political spectrum is one of the most radical of any major American figure.

Thoreau's arrest in 1846 for refusing to pay the Massachusetts poll tax, then levied on all able-bodied males, turned his interest to politics. He objected on grounds of principle, quietly declaring "war with the state,

---

[52] Henry David Thoreau, *Walden, or, Life in the Woods* (Boston: Houghton Mifflin, 1919), pp. 3, 100–101.
[53] Thoreau, *Walden*, pp. 3, 178.
[54] Parrington, *Main Currents*, II, 407.
[55] "The Reluctant Crusader" is the title of a chapter in Joseph Wood Krutch, *Henry David Thoreau* (New York: Sloane, 1948).

after his fashion, by refusing to let his dollar buy 'a man or a musket to shoot one with. . . .' "[56] Whereas others let their fines be paid for them, Thoreau allowed himself to be jailed. After one night behind bars, friends paid his tax and he was released. A delightful yarn has it that Emerson, visiting Thoreau in jail, asked: "Henry, why are you there?" "Waldo," Thoreau shot back, "why are you not here?"

His confinement made a profound impression, out of which grew Civil Disobedience. This classic essay attracted little or no attention at the time but has subsequently been read around the world. "It was Gandhi's source-book in his Indian campaign for Civil Resistance"; it was a significant influence on Martin Luther King, Jr. It "has been read and pondered by thousands who hope to find some way to resist seemingly irresistible force."[57] From *Civil Disobedience* passive resisters of whatever hue have drawn sustenance.

"I heartily accept the motto, 'That government is best which governs least,'" Thoreau wrote, "and I should like to see it acted up to more rapidly and systematically."[58] In fact, he went on, the best government was no government at all, for all government was only an expedient, "a sort of wooden gun to the people themselves." The American people expected a government over them, and so they had one. Yet, Thoreau argued, *it* did not keep the nation free, *it* did not settle the West, *it* did not educate; these things were accomplished by the American people, who probably "would have done somewhat more, if the government had not sometimes got in its way."

> Trade and commerce, if they were not made of india-rubber, would never manage to bounce over the obstacles which legislators are continually putting in their way; and, if one were to judge these men wholly by the effects of their actions and not partly by their intentions, they would deserve to be classed and punished with those mischievous persons who put obstructions on the railroads.

Thoreau did not call for the immediate abolition of government. Rather than join "those who call themselves no-government men," he deliberately disassociated himself from them and asked "not at once [for] no government, but *at once* [for] a better government." A government that governed "not at all" would only be attained when men were prepared for it. In the meantime tyrannical government must be resisted, not all authority flouted. A government having "the sanction and consent of the governed" he supported. Thoreau, then, was more a rebel in the tradition of his forebears than a philosophical anarchist, as is usually sup-

---

[56] Henry Seidel Canby, *Thoreau* (Boston: Houghton Mifflin, 1939), p. 232.

[57] Canby, *Thoreau*, p. 235. Thoreau's most recent biographer, Walter Harding, has found that the essay did not get its title, "Civil Disobedience," until 1866, four years after Thoreau's death.

[58] Henry David Thoreau, *Civil Disobedience, The Writings of Henry David Thoreau* (Boston: Houghton Mifflin, 1906), VI, 356–87.

posed.[59] Power in the hands of the people—and, thus, rule by a majority —was accepted, "not because they are most likely to be in the right, nor because this seems fairest to the minority; but because they are physically the strongest." He objected, in general, to submersion of the individual in the state and, in particular, to government sanction of slavery. Must citizens, he asked, resign their consciences to legislators? If they must, "why has every man a conscience, then? I think we should be men first, and subjects afterward." Respect in a society should be not so much for the law as for the right; the obligations of citizens should therefore not be so much to obey the law as "to do at any time what [they] think right." No right-thinking man could condone slavery.

One who finds it difficult to accept the implications of this conclusion, Thoreau believed, should consider the results of forcing obedience to law rather than to conscience. Men came to serve the state "not as men mainly, but as machines, with their bodies." They forswore the free exercise of their judgment and of their moral sense and "put themselves on a level with wood and earth and stones. . . . They [came to] have the same sort of worth only as horses and dogs. Yet such as these . . . are commonly esteemed good citizens." Only a few, the "heroes, patriots, martyrs, reformers in the great sense, and *men*," served the state with their consciences and repudiated slavery. In most cases these few were necessarily compelled to resist the state and so were treated as enemies. Certainly that was the situation in mid-nineteenth-century America. A *man*, Thoreau declared, could not "without disgrace be associated" with such a government, for it violated his conscience by being "a *slave's* government also."

What, then, could a man do? He could withdraw his support, "both in person and property," and, if necessary, go to jail in protest. For "under a government which imprisons any unjustly, the true place for a just man is also a prison, . . . the only house in a slave State in which a free man can abide with honor." "If any think that their influence would be lost there," he is very much mistaken, Thoreau declared. "If the alternative[s are] to keep all just men in prison" or to give up its errant ways, the state would not long hesitate which to choose. In fact, it had no alternative, for though it had superior physical strength and could carry men off to jail, it could not confine men's "meditations . . . and *they* were really all that was dangerous."

"I could not help being struck with the foolishness of that [jail], which treated me as if I were mere flesh and blood and bones. . . ." By ignoring spiritual strength, by arming itself only with superior physical power, not with superior wit and honesty, the state demonstrated its stupidity. It did not know how to preserve itself save by force, and in the long run, to what avail was force against righteousness? "I was not born to be forced.

I will breathe after my own fashion. Let us see who is the strongest. What force has a multitude? They only can force me who obey a higher law than I. . . . If a plant cannot live according to its nature, it dies; and so a man." And so a state.

Thoreau recognized that "most men think differently from myself" and that statesmen and legislators were the least likely to agree with him. They saw government only from the inside. He saw it from the outside. They were thus unlikely to suggest basic changes and improvements, such as removing the constitutional sanctioning of slavery. That could be accomplished only by sufficient protest from just men, from men not governed by "policy and expediency," who knew that justice could be achieved in America only if the state gave up "war and slavery."

The Right of Revolution Reasserted

What Thoreau envisaged as the answer to tyranny and slavery was a revolution, by passive resistance rather than by force of arms. "A peaceable revolution" could be accomplished by nonpayment of taxes, by refusal to cooperate with the government, and if necessary, by submission to arrest and imprisonment. "Thoreau . . . was not . . . thinking of mass rebellion where motives are mixed and the objective is always power. He was concerned with the individual whose power can only be his integrity."[60] Revolution would be in order, however, only when a government becomes tyrannical beyond endurance. "All machines have their friction," he wrote; "and possibly this does enough good to counterbalance the evil. At any rate, it is a great evil to make a stir about it. But when the friction comes to have its machine, and oppression and robbery are organized, I say, let us not have such a machine any longer." In the battle against tyranny, office holders should resign their positions. "When the subject has refused allegiance, and the officer has resigned his office, then the revolution is accomplished," and the end of slavery in sight.

Government's primary role was the development of the individual. Progress had been made, but much still remained to be done. "Is a democracy, such as we know it," he asked, "the last improvement possible in government? Is it not possible to take a step further towards recognizing and organizing the rights of man?"

> There will never be a really full and enlightened State until the State comes to recognize the individual as a higher and independent power, from which all its own power and authority are derived, and treats him accordingly. I please myself with imagining a State at last which can afford to be just to all men, and to treat the individual with respect . . . which even would not think it inconsistent with its own repose if a few were to live aloof from it, not meddling with it, nor embraced by it, who fulfilled all the duties of neighbors and fellow-men."

---

[60] Canby, *Thoreau*, p. 236.

Until such a state emerged, Thoreau was ready to resist the unjust demands of brute force. Although he did not expect success, he thought resistance would be effective in changing the minds of the men who exercised such force. It was "not futile quietly to declare war upon [the] state."[61]

Civil Disobedience was Thoreau's only systematic discussion of politics. But the idea of resistance is also contained in his *Slavery in Massachusetts,* published in *The Liberator* in 1854, and in his "Plea for Captain John Brown," delivered in 1859. He insisted that the only government a moral man could recognize was one "that establishes justice in the land, never that which establishes injustice," that which represents "the noblest faculties of the mind, and the *whole* heart. . . ." His "Plea" was, in fact, "another essay on the occasional necessity of civil disobedience."

In his *Journal* during Brown's trial, Thoreau went beyond the advocacy of passive resistance: "I do not wish to kill or to be killed but I can foresee circumstances in which both these things would be unavoidable. In extremes I could even be killed."[62] For a rugged individualist, willing to forgo society and absolve himself of any responsibility "to [the] multifarious uncivil chaos named civil government"[63] such a statement amounts almost to an about-face. It "involves (as 'Civil Disobedience' does not) some assumption of 'social responsibility.' "[64] This aspect of Thoreau's thought modifies his tendency toward anarchy, suggesting that had he lived beyond 1862, he might have emerged as a complete citizen.

Thoreau's contribution to American thought must be understood in terms of the transcendentalist movement. Perhaps more than Emerson, (certainly more consistently than he) Thoreau stressed the theme of self-reliance. That idea became a rule of conduct, not an abstraction. Thoreau tried to follow his spirit wherever it led him, and it often led in directions counter to law and to the forces of organized society. In the abstract he stood for the abolition of government, of slavery, of tariffs—indeed, of all restraint. Even the golden rule he considered "by no means a golden rule, but the best of current silver. An honest man would have but little occasion for it. It is golden not to have any rule at all in such a case."[65] Vernon Parrington considered Thoreau "the completest embodiment of the laissez-faire reaction against a regimented social order. . . ."[66] Others

---

[61] Canby, *Thoreau*, p. 238. Thoreau was not the only proponent of civil disobedience of his time. See Edward H. Madden, *Civil Disobedience and Moral Law in Nineteenth-Century American Philosophy* (Seattle, Wash.: University of Washington, 1968). See also Paul F. Power, "On Civil Disobedience in Recent American Democratic Thought," *American Political Science Review*, LXIV (March, 1970), 35–47.

[62] The first quotation is from Henry Seidel Canby, ed., *The Works of Thoreau* (Boston: Houghton Mifflin, 1946), pp. 826, 840. The *Journal* was quoted in Krutch, *Thoreau*, p. 236.

[63] Quoted in Perry, *American Spirit*, p. 133.

[64] Krutch, *Thoreau*, p. 236.

[65] Henry David Thoreau, *A Week on the Concord and Merrimack Rivers* (Boston: J. Munroe, 1849), p. 92.

[66] Parrington, *Main Currents*, II, 413.

have called him the conscience of America. Certainly no other American thinker has ever embraced the doctrine of individualism so concretely.

Although Thoreau lived in Emerson's household for two years, Emerson never seemed to grasp either the subtlety of Thoreau's effort or the significance of his life. In a memorial essay Emerson deplored his friend's lack of ambition, believing that, with his energy and practical ability, his achievements in the world of affairs might have been far greater. "Wanting this," Emerson complained, "instead of engineering for all America, he was the captain of a huckleberry party."[67] Recent appraisals are more perceptive. It is now acknowledged that to an even greater extent than the master himself, Thoreau took to heart and lived by the Emersonian dictum: "The antidote to the abuse of formal government is the growth of the individual." It took eight years to sell the two thousand copies of the first (1854) edition of *Walden*. (Probably that many copies are now sold every week.) An obscure citizen of Concord has become an American of influence. As he phrased it: "Any man more right than his neighbors constitutes a majority of one already"—a bold nineteenth-century aphorism that has turned out to be prophecy.[68]

WHITMAN: BROOKLYN OPTIMIST

Although Walt Whitman had much in common with Emerson and Thoreau, he was very unlike them. Born in New York, largely self-educated, a skillful newspaperman and later a government clerk, Walt Whitman was a man of the people. Unlike the Brahmin Emerson or the eccentric Thoreau, he lived and moved among ordinary, workaday people, befriending and tolerating them and being, in turn, befriended and tolerated by them. His conclusions were derived "from observing and wandering among men." "I am Walt Whitman, liberal and lusty as nature," this sensual man of the people proudly announced.[69] He loved "to ride up and down Broadway all day on an omnibus, sitting beside the driver, listening to the roar of the carts, and sometimes gesticulating and declaiming Homer at the top of his voice." He wrote about love and sex "as if the beasts spoke."[70] He adored men as individuals and in groups; he sought crowds and activity, not solitude and nature. A democrat by conviction, and immersed from childhood in a family that leaned toward the Quakers, Whitman seems in sharp contrast with the Puritan intellectual aristocrats Emerson and Thoreau.

After meeting Whitman on one of his rare trips to New York, Thoreau

[67] Quoted in Mason, *Free Government*, p. 478.
[68] Brooks Atkinson, "Topics: Thoreau's Message After 150 Years," *New York Times*, July 15, 1967, p. 24. See also Joseph Wood Krutch, "Who Was Henry Thoreau?" *Saturday Review*, August 19, 1967, pp. 18–19, 46.
[69] Walt Whitman, "To a Common Prostitute," *Leaves of Grass* (New York: The Heritage Press, 1943), p. 347.
[70] From a letter of Thoreau's, quoted in Canby, *Thoreau*, pp. 414–15.

reported: "Whitman is apparently the greatest democrat the world has ever seen. Kings and aristocracy go by the board at once, as they have long deserved to . . . [but] I am still somewhat in a quandary about him . . . I did not get far in conversation with him . . . and among the few things which I chanced to say, I remember that one was . . . that I did not think much of America or of politics, and so on, which may have been somewhat of a damper to him." Whitman's sensuality bothered Thoreau just as Thoreau's "disdain for men" irked Whitman. Nevertheless, Thoreau believed Whitman had done him "more good than any reading for a long time"[71] and considered the poet "a great fellow."[72] Whitman, in turn, often acknowledged his debt to Thoreau, but he was also puzzled. "Thoreau's great fault was disdain—disdain for men (for Tom, Dick and Harry); inability to appreciate the average life. . . . We had a hot discussion about it—it was a bitter difference." Yet Whitman thought of Thoreau as "a man you would have to like, an interesting man, simple, conclusive."[73]

Whitman also acknowledged Emerson's influence: "I was simmering, simmering. Emerson brought me to a boil."[74] Emerson wrote Whitman a congratulatory note upon publication of the latter's *Leaves of Grass*—one of the few Whitman received—greeting the poet "at the beginning of a great career" and describing it as "the most extraordinary piece of wisdom that America has yet contributed."

Well might the three have admired each other, for they all moved in the same philosophical direction. They reinforced one another's hatred of servitude—legal, economic, or intellectual. Each berated the materialism of commerce and industry; each proclaimed the pursuit of wisdom and belief in the worth and sovereignty of the individual, each drew on the same intellectual resources. All were mystics. Whitman in "Song of Myself" sounds like many a passage from the works of his Boston contemporaries:

> There is that in me—I do not know what it is—but
> I know it is in me.
> . . . .
> It is not chaos or death—it is form, union, plan—
> it is eternal life—it is Happiness.

All were transcendentalists—Thoreau and Emerson by virtue of their Boston Unitarian heritage, Whitman probably because of his Quaker background, with its emphasis on "the inner light." All were individualists—Thoreau and Whitman more by action, Emerson by conviction. Whitman's first poem in *Leaves of Grass*, appropriately enough, is "One's-

---

[71] Thoreau, *Writings*, VI, 296.
[72] Quoted in Canby, *Thoreau*, p. 296.
[73] Canby, *Thoreau*, p. 417.
[74] Quoted in Henry Seidel Canby, *Walt Whitman, An American* (Boston: Houghton Mifflin, 1943), p. 120.

Self I Sing." Many of his writings reflect his belief that in the individual, not in science or material wealth, lay the wellspring of a free, vibrant, democratic America.

> It is not the earth, it is not
>   America who is so great,
> It is I who am great or to be great,
>   it is You up there, or any one,
> It is to walk rapidly through
>   civilization, governments, theories,
> Through poems, pageants, shows,
>   to form individuals
> Underneath all, individuals, I swear
>   nothing is good to me now that
>   ignores individuals.[75]

Whitman made a peculiar contribution. Whereas Thoreau and Emerson emphasized the *single individual*, Whitman glorified people en masse. "Other states indicate themselves in their deputies, . . . but the genius of the United States is not best or most in its executives or legislatures, nor in its ambassadors or authors or colleges or churches or parlors, nor even in its newspapers or inventors—but always most in the common people."[76] Successful democratic government, and indeed the good life itself, depended on each "being one of the mass." Only from the mass, "and from its proper regulation and potency, comes . . . the chance of Individualism."[77] "The great master . . . sees the hiatus in singular eminence. To the perfect shape comes common ground. To be under the general law is great for that is to correspond with it. The master knows that he is unspeakably great and that all are unspeakably great. . . ."[78] In solidarity, in union, men have strength. Not the few but the many are the hope of the future.

This was the central idea in much of Whitman's work, particularly in *Democratic Vistas*, published in 1871. During the Civil War Whitman, serving as a volunteer nurse, developed an even more profound respect for "the majesty and reality of the American people *en masse*."[79] He envisaged America as it might become when "carried far beyond politics."[80] His faith in "people" was deep, yet he recognized stumbling blocks, impeding progress toward the ultimate goal. Besides "the battle . . . between Democracy's convictions [and] aspirations and the People's crudeness, vice, [and] caprices," he sensed an "appalling" danger in universal suffrage. He deplored the lack of distinctively American "forms of

---

[75] Whitman, "By Blue Ontario's Shores," *Leaves*, p. 318.
[76] Whitman, Preface to the 1855 edition of *Leaves of Grass*, reprinted in the Heritage Press ed., p. xxiii.
[77] Walt Whitman, *Democratic Vistas* (Washington, D.C., 1871), pp. 68, 72–74, 79.
[78] Whitman, Preface, p. xxxiii.
[79] Whitman, *Autobiography*, quoted in Parrington, *Main Currents*, III, 77.
[80] Quoted in Mason, *Free Government*, p. 479.

arts, poems, schools, theology," and especially the "want . . . of a class . . . of native Authors, Literatures . . . fit to cope with our occasions, lands, permeating the whole mass of American mentality, taste, belief, breathing into it a new breath of life. . . ." Whitman could not hide his disillusionment. Grant was in the White House, the Gilded Age just over the horizon.

> It is useless to deny it: democracy grows rankly up the thickest, noxious, deadliest plants and fruits of all—brings worse and worse invaders—needs newer, larger, stronger, keener compensations and compellers.
>
> Never was there, perhaps, more hollowness at heart, than at present, and here in the United States . . . we live in an atmosphere of hypocrisy throughout. . . . The depravity of the business classes of our country is not less than has been supposed, but infinitely greater. The official services of America, National, State and municipal, in all their branches and departments, except the Judiciary, are saturated in corruption, bribery, falsehood, mal-administration; and the judiciary is tainted.[81]

There had been "progress," but at too great a cost. "Our New World democracy, however great a success in uplifting the masses out of their sloughs, in materialistic development products, and in a certain highly-deceptive superficial popular intellectuality, is so far an almost complete failure in its social aspects, and in really grand religious, moral, literary and esthetic results." "It is as if we were somehow being endowed with a vast and more and more appointed body, and then left with little or no soul."[82]

Whitman's faith in democracy faltered but did not succumb to despair. He still had confidence in the people—in "their measureless wealth of latent power and capacity, their vast, artistic contrasts of lights and shades . . . their entire reliability in emergencies." American democracy, indeed, had prospects "beyond the proudest claims and wildest hopes" of its enthusiasts.

Whitman: Prophet of America's Future

To Whitman the boast of the present and the future was the conviction that

> the ulterior object of political and all other government, (having, of course, provided for the police, the safety of life, property, and for the basic statute and common law, and their administration . . .) . . . [was] not merely to rule, to repress disorder, etc., but . . . to train communities through all their grades, beginning with individuals and ending there again, to rule themselves.[83]

---

[81] Whitman, *Vistas*, p. 512.
[82] Whitman, *Vistas*, pp. 467–68.
[83] Whitman, *Vistas*, pp. 467–68.

More important than anything else, and "steadily pressing ahead, and strengthening itself," was "the idea of that Something a man is . . . standing apart from all else, divine in his own right . . . sole and untouchable by any canons of authority, or any rule derived from precedent, state-safety, the acts of legislatures, or even from what is called religion, modesty, or art." All other duties, rights, and relations were unimportant beside it. "The radiation of this truth" was "the key of the most significant doings of our immediately preceding three centuries, and has been the political genesis and life of America."[84]

In his glorification of the individual, Whitman never forgot the community. Democracy was to be justified not so much because people were sensible and good or in terms of popular rights as because "good or bad, rights or no rights, the Democratic formula is the only safe and preservative one for coming times. We endow the masses with the suffrage for their own sake, no doubt; then, perhaps still more . . . for community's sake." Union was as compelling a concept as individualism; its preservation, the only guarantee of personal freedom. His poems, especially "Song of the Exposition,"[85] reflect this conviction:

> And thou America,
> Thy offspring towering e'er so high, yet higher Thee
>   above all towering,
> With Victory on thy left, and at thy right hand Law;
> Thou Union holding all, fusing, absorbing, tolerating all,
> Thee, ever thee, I sing.

More than any other nineteenth-century writer, Whitman developed the theme of American nationalism and preached the creed of unity. To him there were no parts, one favored above another, but only the whole. During his early years he had traveled through much of the United States; the essential oneness of the country impressed him deeply.

Whitman's horizons were not bound by the United States. As a poet, the universe was his domain, and as an American, he was intensely concerned that the oneness of all humanity be recognized and protected. "The idea . . . of the Western world one and inseparable"[86] fascinated him. The question, Is this done in reference to universal needs?[87] reflected his most important criteria. Long before the concept of one world became commonplace, Whitman insisted "upon the solidarity of America with all countries of the globe. Particularly in his yearning and thoughtful old age, [he] perceived that humanity has but one heart and that it should have but one will."[88] An isolated United States, shut off from the rest of the world, ran counter to everything Whitman preached.

---

[84] Whitman, *Vistas*, pp. 467–68.
[85] Whitman, *Leaves*, p. 186.
[86] Whitman, "From Paumanok Starting I Fly Like A Bird," *Leaves*, p. 259.
[87] See Whitman, Preface, p. xli.
[88] Perry, *American Spirit*, p. 204.

He valued and encouraged "reformers and revolutionists." They stirred the air; they counterbalanced "inertness and fossilism." "*Vive,* the attack —the perennial assault! *Vive,* the unpopular cause; . . . a Nation like ours . . . is not served by the best men only, but sometimes more by those that provoke it—by the combats they arouse. . . . national rage, fury, discussion, etc." Like Webster in the Massachusetts Convention, he recognized that free government, to be successful, required a wide distribution of property. "The true gravitation-hold of Liberalism in the United States," he wrote, "will be a more universal ownership of property, general homesteads, general comfort—a vast, intertwining reticulation of wealth, . . . a great and varied Nationality, occupying millions of square miles, firmest held and knit by the principles of the safety and endurance of the aggregate of its middling property owners."[89]

Whitman envisioned what America might become. The possibilities of the "Athletic Democracy" were numberless. He hailed the industrial revolution, the rising tide of immigration, the steady filling out of the continent, as significant advances. "The future of the States I harbinge glad and sublime."[90] Like Thoreau and Emerson he cautioned against excessive "refinement and delicatesse," against too great absorption in amassing great fortunes. From the steady pursuit of business, so characteristic of the time, some relief was demanded. "Singleness and normal simplicity, and separation, amid this more and more complex, more and more artificialized, state of society—how pensively we yearn for them."[91]

"Walt Whitman's democracy," Kenneth Rexroth wrote, "is utterly different":

> It is a community of men related by organic satisfactions, in work, love, play, the family, comradeship; a social order whose essence is the liberation and universalization of selfhood. *Leaves of Grass* is not a great work of art just because it has a great program, but [because] it offer[s] point-by-point alternatives to the predatory society. . . . Unlike almost all other ideal societies, Whitman's utopia, which he calls "These States," is not a projection of the outlines of all idealized past into the future, but an attempt to extrapolate the future into the American present. His is a realized eschatology.[92]

No Walden for Whitman. The feverishness of society did not bother him; he regarded it as but a preparatory stage for a calmer and less material future, and looked forward to the fulfillment of its destiny.

> Here first the duties of today, the lessons of the concrete,
> Wealth, order, travel, shelter, products, plenty;
> As of the building of some varied, vast, perpetual edifice,

[89] Whitman, *Vistas,* p. 479.
[90] Whitman, "From Paumanok Starting I Fly Like a Bird," *Leaves,* p. 22.
[91] Whitman, *Vistas,* p. 481.
[92] Kenneth Rexroth, "Classics Revisited XXXV, Walt Whitman," *Saturday Review,* September 3, 1966, p. 43.

> Whence to arise inevitable in time, the towering
>   roofs, the lamps,
> The solid-planted spires tall shooting to the stars.[93]

Whitman's influence is hard to evaluate. In 1918 Bliss Perry ventured the opinion that "to the vast majority of American men and women [Whitman was] still an outsider."[94] The style of his writing worked against popular acceptance.[95] In 1947, however, Van Wyck Brooks concluded that Whitman seemed "the personification and the voice of a happy young country."[96] Thoreau's and Emerson's appeal was intellectual; they acted, in a sense, as the Puritan conscience of nineteenth-century America, reminding the busy country of the value of higher things. Whitman spoke of the same values, but aloud, in trumpet notes.[97] All three sought to turn America's attention back to the individual—Thoreau and Emerson by austere essays, Whitman by forceful, striking, sometimes shocking, poetry and prose.

In 1969, when the last two of five volumes of Whitman's letters were published, the editor, Professor Edwin H. Miller, concluded: "Whitman speaks louder to today's Americans than he did to his contemporaries, for he is both the spokesman of democratic idealism and the voice of dissent from the Establishment." He saw "the taint and the corruption . . . [of] bourgeois life in the United States" and did not hesitate to indict such a way of life. At the same time, he demonstrated "sturdy faith in the common man and his belief in that man's ultimate ability to triumph."[98]

ENDURING VALUE OF TRANSCENDENTALISM

For Henry Seidel Canby, Thoreau and Whitman represent "the two poles of American idealism in literature."[99] He might have included Emerson, for they complemented each other, representing an intellectual and moral attack on materialism and the "organization man" of their day and ours.[100]

Upon certain things this remarkable trio agreed. In an age marked by the drive for material progress, they preferred the pursuit of wisdom, individual creative power, and spiritual sovereignty. They hated any kind of

---

[93] Whitman, *Leaves*, p. 460.
[94] Perry, *American Spirit*, p. 197.
[95] Kenneth Rexroth observed that "whenever [Whitman] found it convenient he spoke of himself as a Quaker and used Quaker language. Much of his strange lingo is not the stilted rhetoric of the self-taught, but simply Quaker talk." Rexroth, "Walt Whitman."
[96] Van Wyck Brooks, *The Times of Melville and Whitman* (New York: Dutton, 1947), p. 191.
[97] Thoreau spoke of *Leaves of Grass* as Whitman's "trumpet-note ringing through the American camp."
[98] Quoted in an interview with Alden Whitman, *New York Times*, June 18, 1969, p. 30.
[99] Canby, *Whitman*, p. 189.
[100] Canby, *Whitman*, p. 189.

servitude—legal, economic, moral, intellectual—and distrusted the dominant motifs in American life: commerce and industrialism. There were also striking differences: Emerson wanted to reform society; Thoreau, seeking a better understanding of society, sought to isolate himself from it; Whitman tried to immerse himself in it.

Ever-present conformism—an abomination to Emerson, Thoreau, and Whitman—undermined their three prerequisites of individualism—*privacy, voluntary association,* and *economic independence.* In 1927, when Justice Brandeis confronted the wiretapping issue, he echoed Thoreau, proclaiming "the right to be let alone—the *most comprehensive* of rights and the right most valued by *civilized* man."[101]

Voluntary association, long thought of as a feasible and desirable means of correcting social and economic ills, has been increasingly replaced by government, exalting the coercive sovereignty so hateful to the transcendentalists. Economic interdependence—not the independence valued by Emerson, Whitman, and Thoreau—has become the hallmark of American life. Each proclaimed the ideal of the masterless man. Today we are largely a nation of hired men, working for one bureaucracy or another—government, business, professional. We need to be reminded that (in the words of a discerning British observer) "the well-springs of American strength are not just iron mines and oil fields, natural gas and fertile soil . . . the best and most effective Americans have always remembered that even more than riches, righteousness exalteth a nation."[102] If Americans remember, it is due in some measure to Emerson, Thoreau, and Whitman. In a final and arresting caveat, Emerson wrote: "Nothing can give you peace but yourself. Nothing can bring you peace but the triumph of principles."[103]

---

[101] Italics added.
[102] D. W. Brogan, "A Plea to America Not to Undersell Herself," *The New York Times Magazine,* November 14, 1948, quoted in Mason, *Free Government,* p. 474.
[103] Emerson, "Self-Reliance," *Essays and Writings,* p. 90.

CHAPTER TWELVE

SLAVERY
AND THE
NATURE OF THE UNION

The mid-nineteenth century was a period of ferment and reform. Everywhere a cause was being pushed, an abuse examined, a new idea advocated. Temperance, land reform, abolition of child labor, flogging in the navy, women's rights, pauperism, amelioration of conditions in prisons and insane asylums, better schools, emancipation of slaves—all had their supporters. Even Thoreau was led to "sign on" to society by "the Pulse of Reform."[1]

Undoubtedly the strongest, the best organized, and the most urgent crusade, in its call for a practice to equal the ideals of its theory, was the movement to end slavery. Slavery, a grim fact in early Greece, had been inherited from even earlier cultures. In the ancient world, as in America, natural differences were cited to justify it. "Those men therefore who are as much inferior to others as the body is to the soul," Aristotle wrote in his *Politics*, "are slaves by nature . . . the proper use of them is their bodies, in which their excellence consists. . . ."

From the time of its introduction in Virginia in 1619, slave labor was primarily justified by its economic advantage. Slaves were themselves a

---

[1] See Chap. 4, "The Pulse of Reform," Allan Nevins, *Ordeal of the Union* (New York: Scribner's, 1947).

form of capital, the value of which rose as the plantation system became more profitable. As Negroes learned mechanical trades, they could easily be exchanged for all kinds of goods or be sold for cash. Finally, slaves made possible the creation of an aristocracy, freed from the necessity of labor, faithfully cared for from the cradle to the grave, able to devote itself to varied civic and social pursuits. As the years went by, slaveholders asserted more boldly the justifications for, and eventually the righteousness of, the system. By 1830 wider use of the cotton gin and the opening up of land in the Southwest (combined with the textile boom in England and New England, with the resultant sharp increase in cotton prices) made the institution seem all the more imperative. "Within a single generation thought and prejudice below the Mason and Dixon line adjusted themselves to economic fact. The Lower South by the time Jackson became president regarded slavery as permanent. . . ."[2] Throughout the South, previous intentions to abandon the institution were replaced with avowals to perpetuate it.

APOLOGISTS FOR SLAVERY

Apologists for slavery became sectional heroes. The most prominent defender and strongest proponent was John C. Calhoun (1782–1850). A South Carolinian and Yale graduate of 1804, aptly described as "The Marx of the Master Class," Calhoun was an uncommonly lucid political thinker. Twice vice-president of the United States, a cabinet member under two presidents, and longtime member of Congress, Calhoun had at first been a nationalist, but (perhaps for opportunistic reasons) became an early exponent of sectionalism. His most earnest efforts, however, were devoted to the defense of slavery as "essential to the peace, safety, and prosperity of the United States." In 1828, denouncing the Tariff of Abominations, he declared the South to be the serf of northern capitalism and predicted the inevitable overthrow of the plantation system and of slavery unless a remedy were soon found. From then until his death, he devoted himself to devising such a remedy and to perfecting a theory of justification.

The Doctrine of Concurrent Majority

For Calhoun, as for Madison, society was not made up of a homogeneous mass but rather of "different and conflicting interests."[3] Examples of diverse interest groups were the North, the South, planters, capitalists,

---

[2] Nevins, *Ordeal of the Union*, p. 137.
[3] August Spain, *The Political Theory of Calhoun* (New York: Bookman Associates, 1951, rpt. Octagon, 1968), p. 129. The standard biography of Calhoun is Charles M. Wiltse, *John C. Calhoun*, 3 vols. (Indianapolis: Bobbs-Merrill, 1944–1951).

laborers, merchants, and farmers. If one or a small alliance were able to control a majority in the government, it would probably be moved by its interests, so distinct from those of the groups in the minority, to abuse its power and slant governmental action in its own direction.[4]

The framers of the Constitution, applying Montesquieu's doctrine, used one branch of the national government to check another, thus preventing any one man or clique from gaining enough power to exceed the limits of the Constitution. Likewise, in distributing the powers of government, they gave only some to the federal branch, the rest being reserved for the states. Thus, only certain powers could be used by an interested majority in the national government to exploit minority interest groups in the states. Madison, in particular, hoped that the natural structure of society would remain truly pluralistic, that a single majority might never become unified enough to enable it consistently to shape the laws in its own interest. This combination of natural pluralism and a contrived separation of powers and checks and balances would, Madison thought, be sufficient to protect the interests of minorities.

Calhoun recognized the beneficial effects of this system, but felt that it failed to protect the interests of the South. As he saw it, the sectional split between North and South divided the nation into two large interests. The Northern majority had grown so large and cohesive that it could—and did—overcome the constitutional checks, in complete disregard of the South. To prevent exploitation of either the government should give both "either a concurrent voice in making and executing the laws or a veto on their execution."[5] This doctrine of "concurrent majorities" Calhoun opposed to the standard rule of a numerical majority, which he thought inevitably became a cloak for the rule of the most powerful. The Northern majority not only was converting legitimate federal authority to its own interest, but also was enabling the national government to seize power from the states. Moreover, the Supreme Court's doctrine of implied powers emboldened national authorities to ignore state protests and transform the federal system.

Calhoun implemented his doctrine of concurrent majorities with that of nullification. An aggrieved Southerner, zealous to protect the basis of the South's economy, Calhoun argued that under the Constitution the states retained virtually full and absolute possession of sovereignty, despite delegation of a part to the national government. Properly interpreted, the Constitution left the states free to nullify enactments they deemed inimical to their interests, and thus enabled them to preserve their peculiar institution—slavery.

Inherited from the Kentucky Resolutions of 1798, this idea was expanded so as to justify the right of a state to secede from the Union. If a state felt its interests were thwarted by remaining in it, a state constitutional convention could merely withdraw the ratification of the ear-

---

[4] Schlesinger, *Age of Jackson*, p. 402.
[5] Hofstadter, *American Political Tradition*, p. 86.

lier convention that had brought the state into the Union.[6] Calhoun's doctrine was further implemented by his suggestion that the United States have two presidents, one from the North and one from the South, each with a veto over legislation.[7] Thus, the Southern minority interest would no longer be at the mercy of the more numerous Northern group, armed with the weapon of majority rule.

Calhoun's doctrine, though designed to preserve the institution of slavery, embodies broader implications, firmly rooted in American belief: the concept that society is a collection of "factions," the recognition that the majority can exploit the minority, and the conviction that power is the only effective limit on power. "No government," wrote Calhoun in 1828, "based on the naked principle that the majority ought to govern, however true the maxim in its proper sense, and under proper restrictions, can preserve its liberty even for a single generation."[8] Restraints on the majority were necessary for the preservation of both liberty and government—and of the slavery system.

In his *Disquisition on Government,* published posthumously,[9] Calhoun broadened his defense of slavery. Building on the assumption that inequality is a necessary consequence of liberty and an indispensable requirement of progress, he argued: "It is a great and dangerous error to suppose that all people are equally entitled to liberty."

> It is a reward to be earned . . . —a reward reserved for the intelligent, the patriotic, the virtuous and deserving;—and not a boon to be bestowed on a people too ignorant, degraded and vicious, to be capable either of appreciating or of enjoying it. Nor is it any disparagement to liberty, that such is, and ought to be the case.

Progress depended on the exertions of individuals to better their condition; if inequality of condition were removed, the incentive of those in the rear "to press forward into [the] files" of the front ranks would also be removed, and the march of civilization would come to a halt. Those who accepted the Declaration of Independence at face value and condemned slavery as contrary to its principles were absolutely wrong. The Declaration assumed something that is contrary to "universal observation" and "destitute of all sound reason," in whatever light it might be regarded. Rejecting the very foundation of the doctrine of natural rights, Calhoun insisted on the fact and propriety of "inequality of condition." Government could do no less than recognize it in all its aspects, slavery included, and indeed provide means for upholding it. The concept of the concurrent majority served this purpose.

Calhoun's defense of the South's peculiar institution was not confined

---

[6] Hofstadter, *American Political Tradition,* pp. 204–5.
[7] Spain, *Theory of Calhoun,* p. 135.
[8] John C. Calhoun, *The South Carolina Exposition and Protest,* reproduced in Richard K. Cralle, ed., *The Works of John C. Calhoun* (New York: Appleton, 1851–1857), VI, 33.
[9] Cralle, *Works of Calhoun,* I, 1–107.

to theoretical disquisitions. Very often he spoke out as directly in behalf of slavery as abolitionists did against it. "Calhoun was the first Southern statesman of primary eminence to say openly . . . what almost all the white South had come to feel": that slavery was not an evil but "a positive good."[10] All civilized societies in history had been founded on slavery; it was "the most safe and stable basis for free institutions in the world." Moreover, it provided the only relationship that enabled blacks and whites to live together. Slavery was beneficial to the Negroes themselves, for in no other system were laborers so carefully cared for and protected: it prevented conflict between labor and capital and so made society less turbulent and property more secure.

> The Southern States are an aggregate . . . of communities, not individuals. "Every plantation is a little community, with the master at its head, who concentrates in himself the united interests of capital and labor, of which he is the common representative." These small communities in the aggregate make the State, in all whose action, labor and capital is "equally represented and perfectly harmonized." In the Union as a whole, the South, accordingly becomes the balance of the system. . . .[11]

FITZHUGH AND HARPER

Slavery had even more passionate defenders than Calhoun. George Fitzhugh (1806–1881), a Southern planter and pamphleteer, regarded abolition as "a surrender to Socialism and Communism . . . to no private property, no church, no law, to free love, free lands, free women and free children." His *Cannibals All! Or, Slaves Without Masters,* published four years before the Civil War,[12] featured pious respect for all forms of property and argued that slavery in the South provided a better labor system than the "White Slave Trade" in the North. The latter was "far more cruel than the Black Slave Trade, because it exacts more of its slaves, and neither protects nor governs them." Free laborers were "overburdened with the cares of family and household, which make [their] freedom an empty and delusive mockery." Once the labors of the day were over, Negro slaves were "free in mind as well as body; for the master provides food, raiment, house, fuel, and everything else necessary to the physical well-being of himself and family." Northern capitalists could not accuse Southern slaveholders of depravity. Their own system was "little better than moral Cannibalism." They prided themselves on living respectably, but the respectable way of living in the North was to make "other people work for you, and [to pay] them nothing for so doing—and [to have] no concern about them after their work is done." How much better the slave

---

[10] Hofstadter, *American Political Tradition,* p. 78.

[11] Hofstadter, *American Political Tradition,* p. 82. For a fuller discussion of Calhoun's political philosophy, see Ralph Lerner, "Calhoun's New Science of Politics," *American Political Science Review,* LVII (December, 1963), 913–32.

[12] *Cannibals All! Or, Slaves Without Masters* (Richmond, Va.: A. Morris, 1857). The quotations here are from pp. 25–361.

system, wherein "the master works nearly as hard for the Negro, as he for the master."

Slavery was a natural and necessary way of life as well as a preferable system of labor. It was sanctioned by "higher law, and is, and ever must be, coeval and coextensive with human nature." Wives were the natural slaves of their husbands, children of their fathers, sailors of their masters, and soldiers of their governments. These were only "a few of its ten thousand modifications." Only when society itself had been dissolved and disintegrated would the sovereignty of the individual be established and the property of man in man be destroyed.

Encouraged by such arguments, Fitzhugh, like Calhoun, disavowed the Declaration of Independence and rejected its concept of consent of the governed. The new states in 1776 were nothing but "self-elected despotisms"; like all governments, they originated in force and were continued by force. "The very term government implies that it is carried on against the consent of the governed." The South recognized, as the northern states did not, that to seek to govern by consent would assume the equality of all men, women, children, and free Negroes—a manifest absurdity. Instead, the South held that "the governing class should be numerous enough to understand, and so situated as to represent fairly, all interests." Such a system provided safe, conservative government. A system of primogeniture and entail would be even better. According to Fitzhugh, "The social institutions of the Jews, as established by Moses and Joshua, most nearly fulfill[ed] the idea of perfect government."

In his defense of slavery, Fitzhugh repudiated the Anglo-American political tradition and adopted a position closely resembling modern totalitarianism. In abandoning the philosophy of natural rights, he developed in its place a rationale for a completely alien system in which liberty and equality were mere cant; no one was free, no one was equal.

Standing beside Fitzhugh was William Harper (1790–1840), a judge of the South Carolina Court of Chancery. In his "Memoir on Slavery," drafted in 1837,[13] he, too, declared that slavery marked progress, not retrogression. "Without it, there can be no accumulation of property, no providence for the future, no . . . comfort or elegancies. . . ." Slaves were wealth, both as property and as creators of capital, and as such, were extremely valuable to a society. Indeed, "property—the accumulation of capital, as it is commonly called—is the first element of civilization," and in the South slaves were the most important type of property. The products of slave labor "furnish more than two-thirds of the materials of our foreign commerce . . . and among the slaveholding States is to be found the great market for all the productions of . . . industry, of whatever kind." The prosperity of both the North and South, as well as "the civilization of their cities," was in large part due to the operation of the slavery system.

---

[13] Reproduced in E. N. Elliott, ed., *Cotton is King, and Pro-Slavery Arguments* (Augusta, Ga., 1860), pp. 552–71.

Slaves were born "in sin and ignorance"; by "temperament and capacity" they were suited to their status of "subjection" and were "not less happy in it than any corresponding class to be found in the world." It was entirely natural that some men should exploit others—just as natural "as that other animals should prey upon each other." So normal to human society was slavery, Harper exclaimed, that "no scheme of emancipation could be carried into effect without the most intolerable mischiefs and calamities to both master and slave, or without probably throwing a large and fertile portion of the earth's surface out of the pale of civilization. . . ."

To Harper, as to Fitzhugh, the theory of natural rights embodied in the Declaration was little more than "a sentimental phrase . . . either palpably false" or without precise meaning. Men were not born free and equal; it was much nearer the truth to say that "no man was ever born free, and that no two men were ever born equal." "Wealth and poverty, fame or obscurity, strength or weakness, knowledge or ignorance, ease or labor, power or subjection," were examples of the unequal condition of man everywhere. Inequality was an inherent characteristic of all societies. It "would exist [even] under the freest and most popular form of government that man could devise, for it was the natural proclivity of man to domineer or to be subservient."

> So when the greatest progress in civil liberty has been made, the enlightened lover of liberty will know that there must remain much inequality, much injustice, much *slavery*, which no human wisdom or virtue will ever be able wholly to prevent or redress.

There were no inalienable rights to life or liberty. Civilized and cultivated men must determine the relations between themselves and "the savage and ignorant." The order "of nature and of God dictated that the being of superior faculties and knowledge, and therefore of superior power, should control and dispose of those who are inferior." In such an order, talk of inalienable rights was nonsense.

SLAVERY ATTACKED

Such arguments were largely confined to the South, where they were widely accepted. Even there, however, support of slavery was not universal, and elsewhere opposition rose steadily. Some realized that slavery did not produce returns proportionate to the effort and capital expended on it. Too much was left to managers and overseers. Accounting was crude and little understood. The plantation system, by favoring investment of surplus capital in more land and more slaves, indefinitely delayed industrialization. Some argued that under slavery, the South would remain in a sort of economic peonage, increasingly dependent on Northern and imported manufactures, increasingly specialized in agriculture, and practically bound to a ruinous single-crop economy. In 1857 H. R. Helper amassed figures and statistics to prove the point.[14]

> The causes which have impeded the progress and prosperity of the South, which have dwindled our commerce, and other similar pursuits, into the most contemptible insignificance; sunk a large majority of the people in galling poverty and ignorance; rendered a small minority conceited and tyrannical, and driven the rest away from their homes; entailed upon us a humiliating dependence on the Free States; disgraced us in the recesses of our own Souls, and brought us under reproach in the eyes of all civilized and enlightened nations—may be traced to one common cause . . . slavery.

Slavery was also criticized on other grounds. It was condemned by "religious thinkers like John Woolman, . . . humanitarians like Benjamin Franklin, and . . . egalitarians like Thomas Paine."[15] James Madison, George Mason, Patrick Henry, and Thomas Jefferson, whose minds were rooted in concepts of natural law, regarded slavery not only as unable to adjust itself to the new conditions of American life but also as sharply in conflict with the Declaration of Independence. Among the charges Jefferson leveled against the King in the original draft of the Declaration was that he had evinced determination "to keep a market place where men should be bought and sold" and that he had "at length prostituted his negative for suppressing any legislative attempt to prohibit and restrain this execrable commerce." "What a stupendous, what an incomprehensive machine is man!" Jefferson exclaimed later on, "who can endure toil, famine, stripes, imprisonment, and death itself, in vindication of his own liberty, and, the next moment be deaf to all those motives whose power supported him through his trial, and inflict on his fellow man a bondage, one hour of which is fraught with more misery than ages of that which he rose in rebellion to oppose. . . . I tremble for my country when I reflect God is just."[16] Washington, a more temperate critic, declared, "I never mean . . . to possess another slave by purchase, it being my *first wishes* to see some plan adopted by which slavery in this country, may be abolished by law."[17] Washington, Jefferson, and Jackson all ultimately freed their slaves, a common practice throughout the country at the time of the Revolution. Emancipation and colonization societies flourished and generated considerable drive in favor of abolition and resettlement.

Antislavery sentiment manifested itself in more concrete ways. In 1778 Virginia prohibited further importation of slaves, and by 1790 most of the other states had followed suit. The Massachusetts Constitution of 1780 declared that "all men are born free and equal." Under this provision

---

[14] Hinton R. Helper, *The Impending Crisis in the South: How to Meet It*, quoted in Mason, *Free Government*, p. 503.
[15] Nevins, *Ordeal of Union*, p. 137.
[16] Quoted in Mason, *Free Government*, p. 503.
[17] Mason, *Free Government*, p. 503.

a slave named Quock Walker won a suit (in 1781) for freedom brought against his master, thus ending slavery in the Bay State. New Jersey provided for eventually abolishing slavery by the Bloomfield Act of 1804. The Congress of the United States, at the expiration of the 1808 constitutional limitation, passed a law prohibiting further importation of slaves. The Missouri Compromise of 1820 prohibited slavery forever in the region north of the parallel 36°30′ (the southern boundary of Missouri). But as Southerners began to use their power in Congress to block further restrictive legislation, progress ground to a halt. Hostility to the system and all it stood for grew rapidly.

The annexation of Texas and the Mexican War intensified opposition. The Fugitive Slave Law enlisted the forces of the federal government in searching out, seizing, and returning escaped slaves. The Kansas-Nebraska Act, repealing the Missouri Compromise, opened Western territory to slavery. Finally, the Dred Scott Case of 1857, declaring that the Negro slave had no rights under law, focused the nation's attention on basic issues of freedom and rights.

THE ABOLITION CRUSADE

Abolitionism, at first merely a reform movement, took on the characteristics of a crusade. Some abolitionists denounced slavery as both ethically and morally contemptible, and described it as a relic of barbarism. Others found it repugnant to the principles of Christianity. Still others declared slavery to be inconsistent with republican government.

Harriet Beecher Stowe (1811–1896) wrote from her personal experience in Kentucky and Ohio. Her *Uncle Tom's Cabin; or, Life Among the Lowly* (published serially in 1851–1852 and in book form in 1852) may have done more than any other single action to arouse the North and anger the South. Wendell Phillips (1811–1884), a Boston aristocrat, lecturer, and reformer, combined exhortation with action and made anti-slavery his chief concern. Elijah P. Lovejoy (1802–1837), a gradual emancipator at first, became the crusade's first martyr. Advocating immediate abolition, he died at the hands of a mob in Alton, Illinois. Other leading abolitionists were Charles G. Finney (1792–1875), president of Oberlin College; Theodore D. Weld (1803–1895), who trained "activists" for the American Anti-Slavery Society in the early days of the crusade; Arthur (1786–1865) and Lewis (1788–1873) Tappan, philanthropists and humanitarians and early organizers of the American Anti-Slavery Society; and James G. Birney (1792–1857), presidential candidate of the Liberty Party in 1840 and 1844.

William Lloyd Garrison: Liberator

The most notorious, and in many ways the most irritating, abolitionist was William Lloyd Garrison (1805–1879). To a large extent, the South's defensive stand was in part at least a reaction against Garrison's fiery exhortations. The self-chosen leader of the militants, Garrison was "an exemplar of the most granitic type of New England Puritanism, a man of intense convictions, of high moral elevation, of arid, colorless, and narrow mind, and of fanatical readiness to submit to any sacrifice."[18] His instrument of reform was his own paper, *The Liberator*, which he first brought out in Boston on January 1, 1831. In that issue he announced: "I will be harsh as truth, and as uncompromising as justice. On this subject [abolition] I do not wish to think, or speak, or write any moderation. I am in earnest—I will not equivocate—I will not excuse—I will not retreat a single inch—and I will be heard." Rejecting halfway measures, he demanded "the instant and wholesale extirpation of slavery, root and branch."[19] Supporters of slavery, those who criticized it mildly, and those who suggested gradual emancipation fell equally under his indictment. He was utterly intolerant of temporary expedients or partial solutions. "Has not the experience of two centuries," he asked, "shown that gradualism in theory is perpetuity in practice? Is there an instance, in the history of the world, where slaves have been educated for freedom by their taskmasters?" Ignoring the stonings and assaults of Boston mobs, he held firmly to his objective, his only interest—immediate emancipation—even after several southern states had put a price on his head.

Garrison's hope, as expressed in the Declaration of Sentiments[20] of the American Anti-Slavery Society, which he helped establish in 1832, was to unite all abolitionists in a single front dedicated to the equality of all men—the right of all to life, liberty, and the pursuit of happiness. He contrasted those principles with the fact that "at least one-sixth part of our countrymen . . . [were] recognized by law, and treated by their fellow-beings, as marketable commodities, as goods . . . [were] plundered . . . of the fruits of their toil . . . enjoy[ed] no constitutional nor legal protection from . . . outrages upon their persons . . . [were] ruthlessly torn asunder . . . at the caprice or pleasure of irresponsible tyrants." Recognizing no excuses or mitigating circumstances, he demanded instant repentance and emancipation of "the oppressed."

No man has a right to enslave or imbrute his brother. . . .
The right to liberty is inalienable. . . . Every man has a right to his own body—to the products of his own labor—to the protection of law—and to the common advantages of society.
It is piracy to buy or steal a native African, and subject him to servitude.
The slaves ought instantly to be set free, and brought under the protection of law. . . .
All those laws which are now in force, admitting the right of slavery, are . . . before God, utterly null and void; being an audacious usurpation of the

---

[18] Nevins, *Ordeal of the Union*, p. 144.
[19] Beard and Beard, *A Basic History*, p. 261.
[20] The Declaration of Sentiments is reproduced in *Selections from the Writings and Speeches of William Lloyd Garrison* (Boston: R. F. Wollcut, 1852), pp. 66–70.

Divine prerogative, a daring infringement on the law of nature, a base over-throw of the very foundations of the social compact . . . and a presumptious transgression of all the holy commandments . . . they ought instantly to be abrogated.

No compensation should be given to the planters emancipating their slaves.

By 1844 Garrison had become convinced that the Constitution itself was but a prop for slavery and therefore should be repudiated. His advocacy of separation of the free states from the slave gave at least lip service to destruction of the Union. Very few were willing to move, as James Russell Lowell remarked in 1848, so directly "over the edge of a precipice."[21] More radical than any of his contemporaries, Garrison effectively used the columns of *The Liberator* (it had an unbroken run of 35 years) to stimulate untold numbers of Americans to think—and eventually to act.

Another approach was taken by Garrison's friend William Ellery Channing (1780–1842). The "Apostle of Unitarianism" and well-known champion of social and humanitarian causes, Channing was a proper and independently wealthy Bostonian and a graduate of Harvard. He did not like controversy for its own sake, as Garrison did, and never formally aligned himself with the abolitionists. Yet his work in behalf of the anti-slavery cause was constant and effective. Moreover, the eminence of his position gave his words great weight, and there is little doubt that his calm and rational approach reached a large audience. Bringing to the movement a humanitarian philosophy, Channing found slavery at war with American ideals. The idea of having property in men contradicted the doctrine of natural rights and the theory of equality to which America was committed. "This deep assurance, that we cannot be rightfully made another's property," he wrote in his pamphlet *Slavery*, published in 1841,[22] "does not rest on the hue of our skins, or the place of our birth, or our strength, or wealth. . . . The consciousness of indestructible rights is a part of our moral being. The consciousness of our humanity involves the persuasion, that we cannot be owned as a tree or a brute. As men, we cannot justly be made slaves." All men possessed some rights by nature and "a being having rights cannot justly be made property; for this claim over him virtually annuls all his rights. . . . The right claimed by the master, to task, to force, to imprison, to whip, and to punish the slave, at discretion . . . is a virtual denial and subversion of all the rights of the victim of his power. The two cannot stand together. Can we doubt which of them ought to fall?"

Slavery had to fall also because it violated the principle of equality. Channing recognized the natural differences that divide men but contended that they were so ordained by God to secure the good of all by

---

[21] James Russell Lowell to C. E. Briggs, March 26, 1848, quoted in Nevins, *Ordeal of Union*, I, 447.

[22] Reproduced in *The Works of William E. Channing* (Boston: American Unitarian Association, 1878), II.

drawing on the different abilities and capacities of each, "to bind men together, and not to subdue one to the other." The advantages bestowed on some men, and the infirmities placed on others, were distributed without regard "to rank or condition in life. . . . Nature . . . pays no heed to birth or condition in bestowing her favors. The noblest spirits sometimes grow up in the obscurest spheres. Thus equal are men. . . ." In any case, men had many fewer differences than they had similarities. All shared an "essential equality . . . the same rational nature and the same power of conscience"; all were equally made for the "indefinite improvement of these divine faculties, and for the happiness to be found in their virtuous use." Disregard of this equality was plainly immoral.

Slavery, to Channing, was also contrary to God's law. God created men in His image and likeness; in the highest sense, therefore, men were God's children. From this, it followed that to seize a man and hold him in bondage would be "to offer an insult to his Maker, and to inflict aggravated social wrong." Did God make human beings to be owned as a tree or a brute? Channing asked. Indeed not. "Each human being was plainly made for an End in Himself. He is a Person, not a Thing . . . made to obey a Law within Himself," to develop his own potentialities, and to work for his own perfection. Because slavery made it impossible for men to do so, it was wrong.

Finally, Channing attacked slavery because of its influence on free institutions. The "idleness and impatience of restraint, into which the free of a slave holding community naturally fall," generated "an intenser party-spirit, fiercer political passions, and more desperate instruments of ambition" than ordinarily found in nonslaveholding communities. Abuse of the elective franchise and recourse to the sword, to violence, were more frequently encountered in slave than in free states. Even more fundamentally, slavery affronted the "great political virtues" of a free society: the love of liberty and the love of order. Liberty was not secure in the hands of those who had "the heart to wrest it from others." Law would not command respect from men in "the habit of command, not of obedience. The substitution of passion and self-will for law, is nowhere so common as in the slave-holding States. In these it is thought honorable to rely on one's own arm, rather than on the magistrate, for the defense of many rights." Slavery was a strange thing to mix with free institutions. It could not but endanger them. It was an open invitation to despotic power. "The liberties of a people ought to tremble until every man is free," and if slavery were a condition preceding republican government, "we are bound as a people to seek more just and generous institutions, under which the rights of all will be secure."

In a particularly cogent paragraph, Van Wyck Brooks summarized Channing's influence:

> Channing's little treatise on slavery . . . made a measure of opposition to it almost a condition of self-respect [in Boston]. This book was embarrassing to the prosperous classes, who for a generation had nursed the illusion that,

having won their independence, they had solved the problems of the world. The educated mind could not ignore a calm analytical essay that set the theme in a philosophical light. It showed, as no writer had . . . before, the disastrous effects of slavery, both on the slaves and on the masters, and thenceforth no one who professed to think defended the "peculiar institution" without reservations or misgivings. . . .[23]

Channing did more than this. In his *Tribute to the American Abolitionists for Their Vindication of Freedom of Speech* of 1836, Channing praised the abolitionists not only as "champions of the colored race," but also as "sufferers for the liberty of thought, speech and the press. . . ." Channing underscored America's incalculable debt to those who joined in this unending quest of freedom:

> To them [the abolitionists] has been committed the most important bulwark of liberty, and they have acquitted themselves of the trust like men and Christians. No violence has driven them from their post. Whilst, in obedience to conscience, they have refrained from opposing force to force, they have still persevered against menace and insult, in bearing their testimony against wrong, in giving utterance to their deep convictions. Of such men, I do not hesitate to say that they have rendered to freedom a more essential service than any body of men among us. *The defenders of freedom are not those who claim and exercise rights which no one assails, or who win shouts of applause by well-turned compliments to liberty in the days of her triumph. They are those who stand up for rights which mobs, conspiracies, or single tyrants put in jeopardy; who contend for liberty in that particular form which is threatened at the moment by the many or the few.*[24]

Abraham Lincoln: Free-Soiler

Garrison and Channing represented two of the three main schools of antislavery thought. Abraham Lincoln (1809–1865) spoke for a third. Garrison began from the radical premise of immediate emancipation, while Channing exposed the evils of slavery from a moral and philosophical point of view. Lincoln's approach was conditioned by the economics of Western agrarianism. Although Lincoln looked upon slavery with distaste and rising indignation, he never became an abolitionist and did not publicly condemn slavery until 1854. A realist, he recognized the validity of arguments based on natural rights, but built his case against slavery on the practical grounds he knew from experience. With each extension of slavery into the West, the free farmers for whom Lincoln spoke in politics saw their homesteads menaced by the prospect of slave labor. Cotton became a monster, consuming the land, degrading the labor market, and driving free white farmers out of existence. Although Western farmers had contempt for Negroes (Lincoln himself said his feelings would not

---

[23] Brooks, *Flowering of New England*, p. 390.
[24] *Tribute of William Ellery Channing to the American Abolitionists for Their Vindication of Freedom of Speech* (New York, 1861), pp. 3–24. Italics added.

admit of making Negroes "politically and socially our equals"), they began to agree with the abolitionists that slavery spelled pauperism for white and black alike. When Lincoln mounted the antislavery platform, he reflected this type of thinking. Rejecting Garrison's demands for abolition and Channing's denunciation of slavery as morally wrong, Lincoln embraced the Free-Soil argument. Slavery could, he thought, be confined to the states where it existed, be restricted from the western territory, and be neither totally abolished nor totally permitted. Even on the eve of the Civil War, he was not willing to take a more radical stand.

Lincoln's strategy, reflected in his speech at Peoria, Illinois, on October 16, 1854,[25] was to oppose any extension of slavery while indicating sympathetic understanding of the South's problems. He hated "the monstrous injustice of slavery," but he did not therefore hate slaveholders. "I think I have no prejudice against the Southern people," he declared.

Unlike Garrison and Channing, who regarded immediate abolition as a panacea, Lincoln recognized the complexity of "the existing institution." "If all earthly power were given me," he avowed, he would not know what to do about slavery in the South. Consequently, he would do nothing. But this furnished "no more excuse for permitting slavery to go into our own free territory than it would for reviving the African slave-trade by law. The law which forbids the bringing of slaves from Africa, and that which has so long forbidden the taking of them into Nebraska" were morally indistinguishable. Just as there were no advocates of repeal of the former (except, perhaps, a few "natural tyrants"), so there were no grounds on which to justify repeal of the latter. Instead, "for the sake of the Union," the Missouri Compromise ought to be restored. It had provided the Union with peace and quiet. It had constituted "a definite settlement of the slavery question, by which all parties were pledged to abide." It had embodied "the national faith," commanded the national confidence, created a "national feeling of brotherhood," and it represented "the spirit of concession and compromise . . . which has never failed us in past perils, and which may be safely trusted for all the future." The South ought to join with the North in its restoration. "It would be on their part a great act—great in its spirit, and great in its effect. It would be worth to the nation a hundred years' purchase of peace and prosperity."

Four years later, June 17, 1858, at Springfield, Illinois,[26] Lincoln sounded a somewhat stronger note. By then the decision in *Dred Scott* had been handed down, and the entrance of slavery into Kansas had caused the trouble Lincoln had feared. Thus he felt a more advanced position

---

[25] Reproduced in John G. Nicolay and John Hay, eds., *Abraham Lincoln, Complete Works* (New York: Appleton-Century-Crofts, 1894), II, 190–241. See also Richard N. Current, ed., *The Political Thought of Abraham Lincoln* (Indianapolis: Bobbs-Merrill, 1967).
[26] The Springfield speech is reproduced in Current, *Thought of Lincoln*, pp. 315–39.

justified. "A house divided against itself cannot stand. I believe this government cannot endure permanently half-slave and half-free." Man's natural love of justice demanded that it move in the direction of freedom. The lapse of four years had aroused Lincoln's concern, enabling him to object to Taney's underlying assumption in the *Dred Scott* opinion, that the lot of Negroes had improved since the Revolution. It had, in fact, deteriorated. "In those days," Lincoln recalled, "our Declaration of Independence was held sacred by all, and thought to include all; but now, to aid in making the bondage of the Negro universal and eternal, it is assailed and sneered at and construed, and hawked at and torn, till, if its framers could rise from their graves, they could not recognize it."

> The authors of that notable instrument intended to include *all* men, but they did not intend to declare all men equal *in all respects.* They did not mean to say all were equal in color, size, intellect, moral developments, or social capacity. They defined with tolerable distinctness in what respects they did consider all men created equal—equal with 'certain inalienable rights, among which are life, liberty, and the pursuit of happiness.' This they said, and this they meant. . . .

Brusquely dismissing the argument that its authors had only the white man in mind, Lincoln declared: "I had thought the Declaration contemplated the progressive improvement in the condition of all men everywhere." To read it merely as a statement equating white British colonials with their brothers at home enfeebled the Declaration and "left no more, at most, than an interesting memorial of the dead past . . . without the germ or even the suggestion of the individual rights of man in it."

Lincoln's concern was for the Negro's political and economic rights. He did not advocate social equality; indeed, he thought it "counterfeit logic" to argue that because Negroes were entitled to some rights, they should "vote, and eat, and sleep, and marry" with white people. "Because I do not want a black woman for a slave," did not mean "I necessarily want her for a wife. I need not have her for either. I can just leave her alone. In some respects she certainly is not my equal; but in her natural right to eat bread she earns with her own hands without asking leave of any one else, she is my equal, and the equal of all others."

Lincoln's concept was a simple one: "As I would not be a *slave,* so I would not be a *master*—This expresses my idea of democracy. Whatever differs from this, to the extent of the difference, is no democracy."

THE UNION TESTED AND PROVED

Before the slavery issue flared so tragically in 1860, any number of other subjects—the tariff, regulation of commerce, the exercise of the national taxing power—had threatened the existing nature of the Union. Indeed, the possibility of a confrontation had been raised by the Virginia and

Kentucky Resolutions, the Hartford Convention,[27] the extremity of John Taylor's views (especially in *New Views of the Constitution*), and the Webster-Hayne debates of 1830. Daniel Webster achieved enduring fame for his refutation of the states' rights thesis in those debates:

> When my eyes shall be turned to behold for the last time the sun in heaven, may I not see him shining on the broken and dishonored fragments of a once glorious Union, on States dissevered, discordant, belligerent; on a land rent with civil feuds, or drenched, it may be, in fraternal blood! Let their last feeble and lingering glance rather behold the gorgeous ensign of the republic, now known and honored throughout the earth . . . bearing for its motto not . . . those . . . words of delusion and folly, "Liberty first and Union afterwards"; but everywhere, spread all over in characters of living light . . . that other sentiment, dear to every true American heart,—Liberty *and* Union, now and for ever, one and inseparable!

Nullification was based on "total misapprehension." Indeed, the Constitution had been adopted to exclude such a possibility. The "very chief end, the main design, for which the whole Constitution was framed was to establish a government that should not be obliged to act through State agency, or depend on State opinion and State discretion." The right of a state to nullify an act of Congress could not be maintained, Webster declared, except upon the "ground of the inalienable right of man to resist oppression; that is to say, upon the ground of revolution." There was no other way by which a state government could, "as a member of the Union, interfere and stop the progress of the general government, by the force of her own laws. . . ."

Like Taylor, Webster held that the question dealt essentially with the nature of the Constitution and the Union. Whereas Taylor and Hayne traced the origin of the national government to the states, Webster found it in the people. "The people . . . Sir, erected this government. They gave it a Constitution . . . they . . . enumerated the powers which they bestow on it. . . . They . . . defined its authority. They . . . restrained it to the exercise of such powers as are granted. . . ." In short, it was their creature, their agent, "a people's government, made for the people, made by the people, and answerable to the people." Moreover, in its creation the people had deliberately "chosen to impose control on state sovereignties." They had deprived the states of the right to make war, to coin money, to make a treaty—all powers of a sovereign state. In the light of these and other restraints, arguments for state sovereignty were absurd.

The states need not fear, however, that the national government would violate their rights. Nor was nullification necessary as a safeguard. The

---

[27] See James M. Banner, Jr., *To The Hartford Convention: The Federalist and the Origins of Party Politics in Massachusetts* (New York: Knopf, 1970). This is a significant revisionist study of the 1815 crisis involving New England regionalism and national union.

people had provided in the Constitution itself "a proper, suitable mode and tribunal for settling questions of constitutional law"—in particular, those involving the several states: the judicial department of the national government, entrusted with the enforcement of the supremacy clause of the Constitution. These provisions were "the keystone of the arch. With these it is a government, without them it is a confederation." State legislatures had neither the power nor the need to interfere. Even if "intolerable oppression" should occur, there would be nothing state legislatures might do. "The people might protect themselves, without the aid of the State governments. Such a case warrants revolution. It must make, when it comes, a law for itself. A nullifying act of a State legislature cannot alter the case, nor make resistance any more lawful."

To Hayne's argument that the safety of the people required the "close guardianship of the State legislatures," Webster turned a deaf ear. The people had put their safety in other hands. They had chosen, first, to rely on the plain words of the Constitution and on their proper construction by Congress and the Executive. Second, they put their trust "in the efficacy of frequent elections, and in their own power to remove their own servants and agents whenever they see cause." They relied, finally, on an independent judiciary and on their own power to alter the Constitution "at their own sovereign pleasure." The people of the United States, Webster concluded, had "at no time, in no way, directly, or indirectly, authorized any State legislature to construe or interpret *their* high instrument of government; much less, to interfere, by their own power, to arrest its course and operation."

Webster saw, as most Southerners did not, the awful possibilities implicit in Taylor's and Hayne's divisive ideas. Beyond the Union Webster saw only a "dark recess," an abyss, hiding the breakup and destruction of the Union. Perhaps the most impelling reason for his lengthy refutation of Hayne was his desire to prevent that veil from being penetrated. Certainly during his lifetime he was successful. His reply to Hayne produced a great swell of Union feeling in the North and made no small contribution to the series of compromises that staved off the Civil War until 1861.

Jackson and the Union

Webster's defense, however, was powerless to prevent the precipitation of serious crises. In the sharp prewar differences over the nature of the Union Andrew Jackson played the starring role.

Although Jackson is remembered most for his contributions to the philosophy of economic democracy, his services in behalf of the Union should also be recalled. The Jefferson-Taylor-Hayne legacy affirmed that the Constitution was a compact of the states. It stressed state sovereignty and implied the right of secession. National supremacy, central to the thinking of Hamilton and Marshall, was rejected. Jackson was the logical

heir to their legacy, and on a number of occasions, including his first message to Congress, he seemed to accept this heritage.[28] At the end of his
first term, a practical situation arose out of enactment, in 1828, of the
so-called "Tariff of Abominations." Overnight Jackson renounced that
legacy and emerged a strong advocate of the Hamilton-Webster thesis
that the Constitution had founded "a government, not a league." The
national government was supreme and perpetual; the states had no right
to nullify national laws or to withdraw from the Union. South Carolina
objected strenuously to the higher duties imposed by the Tariff of Abominations, and in 1832 its legislature called a convention to protest it. That
body declared the tariff unconstitutional and hence null and void, further
resolving that, should federal officials attempt to enforce its terms inside
the state, South Carolina would withdraw from the Union and establish
an independent state. Subsequently, the South Carolina legislature passed
the sweeping Nullification Act of 1832. When Calhoun's rationale for
nullification provided a serious threat to the Union, immediate and forceful counteraction became inevitable. To a group returning to Charleston,
Jackson remarked: "Tell . . . [the Nullifiers] from me that they can talk
and write resolutions . . . to their hearts' content. But if one drop of
blood be shed there in defiance of the laws of the United States I will
hang the first man of them I can get my hands on to the first tree I can
find."[29]

When word came that South Carolina meant to push her claims to the
limits of nullification and perhaps secession, the President acted with purpose and dispatch. Secretary of State Edward Livingston was put to work
on the famous Proclamation of December 10, 1832; Unionist leaders in
South Carolina and other rebellious states were advised to stand fast; and
the garrisons in Charleston's forts were speedily replaced with troops the
President knew he could trust.

The proclamation itself is revealing, as was the even more famous toast
that Jackson directed pointedly at Vice-President Calhoun: "Our Union:
It must be preserved."[30] Characteristically, Calhoun replied: "The Union.
Next to our liberty, most dear." In typically untheoretical terms, the document spoke of nullification as "an impractical absurdity."[31] For a state to
assume the power to annul a national law was "incompatible with the
existence of the Union, contradicted expressly by the letter of the Constitution, unauthorized by its spirit . . . and destructive of the great
object for which it was formed."[32]

Jackson rejected the doctrine of nullification in toto. Using bold and
vivid language, he declared that the Constitution formed a government,

---

[28] In the strictest sense Jackson had no well-rounded "theory of the Union." Schlesinger, *Age of Jackson*, p. 15.
[29] James, *Jackson*, p. 306.
[30] James, *Jackson*, p. 235.
[31] James, *Jackson*, p. 313.
[32] Richardson, *Messages of Presidents*, II, 643.

not a league, and that secession could only be equated with revolution, and attempts at disunion with treason. Reminding South Carolina that the Constitution of the United States and the laws passed under it were supreme and that the Union formed by the Constitution was indissoluble, he warned that he intended to enforce federal laws with every power at his disposal and that he would hang anyone who caused blood to be shed in resistance.

Early in 1833 Congress passed the so-called Force Bill, which said in legislative terms almost precisely what Jackson had asserted in his proclamation. Simultaneously Congress consented to reexamine the tariff question, and under Henry Clay's leadership a compromise was reached that proved satisfactory to South Carolina. As a result the nullification ordinance was repealed and a showdown averted. Both sides claimed victory—South Carolina because she had secured a reduction of the hated tariff, friends of the Union because both the executive and legislative branches of the federal government had made it clear that national sovereignty would be defended by force if necessary. Jackson emerged from the nullification crisis a national hero. By "his masterly statesmanship . . . [in maintaining] the supremacy of the Union . . . he had committed himself to doctrines on the nature of the Union" in direct contradiction to states' rights.[33] In effect, he subscribed to the nationalistic view of the Constitution and of the Union and disassociated himself from the state sovereignty tenet, which soon became a divisive factor in American politics. Moreover, his "determined stand in 1833 provided the national government with a powerful precedent in 1861."[34] His was the most powerful voice raised in defense of the Union in the middle years of American history.

But even Jackson was unable to still the controversy; the argument continued between advocates of a Union grounded in the people and those of a Union created by the states. The resolution of a dispute dating from the Philadelphia Convention became inextricably linked with the controversy over slavery.

THE LINCOLN THESIS:
THE UNION—AN INDISSOLUBLE CHAIN

Amid a maze of conflicting theories, Abraham Lincoln charted the nationalist course. "My paramount object," he wrote Horace Greeley, "is to save the Union. . . . If I could save the Union without freeing any slave, I would do it; and if I could save it by freeing all the slaves, I would do it; and if I could do it by freeing some and leaving others alone, I would also do that. What I do about slavery and the colored race, I do because

---

[33] Schlesinger, *Age of Jackson*, p. 96.
[34] Alfred H. Kelly and W. A. Harbison, *The American Constitution. Its Origins and Development* (New York: Norton, 1948), p. 316.

I believe it helps to save the Union; and what I forbear, I forbear because I do not believe it would help to save the Union."[35]

A quasi-Jeffersonian and frontier Unionist, Lincoln had been a spokesman throughout his career for small farmers and midwestern entrepreneurs. As late as 1861, on the eve of the Civil War, he proclaimed his devotion to all the people, Northern and Southern. "Is there any better . . . hope in the world," he asked in his first inaugural address," . . . [than] in the ultimate justice of the people?"[36]

The first shots of the war having been fired and the Secession having been achieved, Lincoln searched for a theory of the Union that would probe more deeply than the constitutional debates. He determined that:

> in legal contemplation the Union is perpetual. . . . [It] is much older than the Constitution. It was formed, in fact, by the Articles of Association in 1774. It was matured and continued by the Declaration of Independence in 1776. It was further matured, and the faith of all the then thirteen States expressly plighted and engaged that it should be perpetual, by the Articles of Confederation in 1778. And finally, in 1787, one of the declared objects for ordaining and establishing the Constitution was "to form a more perfect Union."[37]

If the Union were perpetual, it could not be broken. No state could, "upon its own mere notion," lawfully get out of the Union, any state law or resolution to that effect notwithstanding. Even if the United States were "not a government proper," but merely an association of states, could the contract between them be broken lawfully except by *all* the parties to it? If only one or a few of the states could destroy the Union, it was less perfect after than before the Constitution. No, the Union remained unbroken and any attempt to break it was doomed to failure. For the United States was also a physical union. "We cannot remove our respective sections from each other, nor build an impassable wall between them." "They cannot but remain face to face, and intercourse, either amicable or hostile, must continue between them." Was it possible, he asked, "to make that intercourse more advantageous or more satisfactory after separation than before?" Even war, which someday must end, would not make continued division possible. It would result in "much loss on both sides, and no gain on either," and still the old question "as to terms of intercourse" would remain. Union, now and in the future, provided all the answers.

Lincoln concluded his inaugural address with a plea to his "countrymen" to think calmly. In their hands lay the issue of civil war; "though passion may have strained, it must not break, our bonds of affection." "The mystic chords of memory, stretching from every battle-field and patriot grave to every living heart and hearthstone all over this broad

---

[35] Letter of August 22, 1862, in answer to Horace Greeley's demand for emancipation. Nicolay and Hay, *Lincoln*, VIII, 15.
[36] Richardson, *Messages of Presidents*, VI, 12.
[37] Richardson, *Messages of Presidents*, p. 5.

land, will yet swell the chorus of the Union when again touched, as surely they will be, by the better angels of our nature."

Lincoln's Thesis Upheld: Texas v. White

Although victory at Appomattox was destined to confirm and enshrine his theory, Lincoln's words fell on deaf ears. His concept of the Union remained for some years only a paper pronouncement. Not until 1869 were Lincoln's ideas authoritatively confirmed. By then secession and its twin, nullification, had been disposed of forever. In that year the Supreme Court adopted Lincoln's reasoning—almost his very words.

The occasion for the Supreme Court's ruling came on an original bill testing the right of Texas as a Confederate state to redeem United States bonds under different conditions from those she had agreed to before seceding from the Union. The Court had to decide whether Texas had in fact seceded. Chief Justice Salmon P. Chase (1803–1873), delivering the opinion of the Court, recited the acts by which Texas proceeded "upon the theory that the rights of a State under the Constitution might be renounced, and her obligations thrown off at pleasure." Did Texas, in consequence, cease to be a member of the Union? The answer was an emphatic "No."

> The Union of the States was never a purely artificial and arbitrary relation. It began among the Colonies, and grew out of common origin, mutual sympathies, kindred principles, similar interests, and geographical relations. It was confirmed and strengthened by the necessities of war, and received definite form, and character, and sanction from the Articles of Confederation. By these the Union was solemnly declared to "be perpetual." And when these Articles were found to be inadequate to the exigencies of the country, the Constitution was ordained "to form a more perfect Union." It is difficult to convey the idea of indissoluble unity more clearly than by these words. What can be indissoluble if a perpetual Union, made more perfect, is not? . . . The Constitution, in all its provisions, looks to an indestructible Union, composed of indestructible States.[38]

Accordingly, when Texas entered the Union, she entered into an indissoluble relation. "The act which consummated her admission into the Union was something more than a compact; it was the incorporation of a new member into the political body. And it was final." Texas became united with the other states as completely and as indissolubly as the original union had united the original thirteen states. "There was no place for reconsideration, or revocation, except through revolution, or through consent of the States."

Finally, the Chief Justice disposed of secession and so indirectly of the claimed right of nullification. Texas' ordinance of secession and all the acts of her legislature since secession (considered in the light of the prin-

---

[38] *Texas* v. *White,* 7 Wallace 700 (1869), 725.

ciples he had just enunciated) were absolutely null, "utterly without operation in law." Texas' obligations as a member of the Union, and those of her citizens as citizens of the United States, remained "perfect and unimpaired." She did not cease to be a state, nor her citizens, citizens of the Union. Unilateral action did not and could not affect her status as a member of the Union. Her relations with the Union might have been altered, but her obligations and her status remained unchanged.

Although this final settlement seems as valid today as the day it was pronounced, the Court's decision was not uncontested. Justice Robert Grier (1794–1870), an associate Justice of the Supreme Court, dissented from the majority opinion "on all . . . points," arguing that the issue should have been decided "as a political fact, not as a legal fiction" "If I regard the truth of history for the last eight years," Justice Grier protested, "I cannot discover the State of Texas as one of these United States. . . ." Two other justices also dissented, but the objections were futile.

Texas v. *White* brought to a close the long controversy about the nature of the Union. From Marshall to Lincoln, the organic theory of the Union had steadily advanced. It had been repeatedly tested and sorely tried by the dialectics of Taylor and Calhoun. Finally, it was confirmed on the battlefield. The victory of the North carried with it triumph of the idea that the Union had been conceived by the people and fused, in Chase's words, "out of common origin, mutual sympathies, kindred principles, similar interests, and geographical relations." The counterproposition, that the Union was but a compact of sovereign states and dissoluble like a partnership, was left behind among the debris of battle.

Yet, as Chief Justice Chase himself pointed out, the concept of the Union as the creation of the people did not imply "the loss of distinct and individual existence, or of the right of self-government by the States." "Under the Articles of Confederation," the states retained their "sovereignty, freedoms, and independence, and every power, jurisdiction, and right not expressly delegated to the United States." Under the Constitution the states were still endowed with all the powers they needed for separate and independent existence. Their preservation and "the maintenance of their governments [came] as much within the design and care of the Constitution as the preservation of the Union and the maintenance of the National government." The only difference was their integration into the Union and its overriding supremacy. Within that essential unity, there was ample room and opportunity for diversity.

Justice Holmes, himself a soldier in Lincoln's army, gave the organic theory of the Union a classic formulation:

> When we are dealing with words that are also a constituent act, like the Constitution of the United States, we must realize that they [the framers] have called into life a being the development of which could not have been foreseen completely by the most gifted of its begetters. It was enough for them to realize, or to hope that they had created an organism; it has taken a century

and cost their successors much sweat and blood to prove they had created a nation.[39]

Yet within this strife-born nation fissures remain. Slavery itself was ended by the Emancipation Proclamation of 1863, by the advance of Union troops throughout the South, and by adoption of the Thirteenth Amendment in 1865. Freedom against state encroachments was spelled out in the sweeping provisions of the Fourteenth Amendment. The Fifteenth Amendment was employed to secure Negro suffrage against discriminatory state action. But the former slave states remained unwilling to grant Negroes the same measure of freedom as white citizens.[40] Although a century has elapsed and a racial revolution is under way, the extreme position of Calhoun, Harper, and Fitzhugh still has proponents.

Union, like the Constitution itself, has had to be "extorted from the grinding necessities of a reluctant nation."[41]

---

[39] *Missouri* v. *Holland*, 252 U.S. 416, 433 (1920).

[40] See Bruce Catton, "Unfinished Business of the Civil War, True Freedom for the Negro," *The New York Times Magazine*, April 4, 1965, pp. 28–29 ff.

[41] J. Q. Adams, *Jubilee of the Constitution*, p. 55. See Paul C. Nagel, *One Nation Indivisible. The Union in American Thought 1776–1861* (New York: Oxford University Press, 1964).

CHAPTER THIRTEEN

THE GOSPEL OF WEALTH

Liberal political thought between 1820 and 1860 had two main drives: to win universal manhood suffrage—thereby casting off the special constitutional safeguards for property written into the early state constitutions—and to abolish Negro slavery. The first goal was substantially achieved before the Civil War; the second, by 1865, when Appomattox spelled the end of slavery in the South and the Thirteenth Amendment in the nation. One might have anticipated that before long the last vestige of privilege in the United States would be abolished. Yet, after substantial progress had been made in attacking its bulwarks during the Age of Jackson and in the years immediately following, a new system of privilege began to emerge. Indeed, by 1870 plutocracy seemed more likely than economic and social democracy. Even in the heyday of Jacksonian Democracy, de Tocqueville foreshadowed a new tyranny: "I am of the opinion that the manufacturing aristocracy which is growing up under our eyes is one of the harshest which ever existed in the world."[1] The Civil War brought the industrial revolution in the United States into full flower, converting his prediction into fact.[2]

---

[1] de Tocqueville, *Democracy in America*, II, 197.

[2] Matthew Josephson, *The Robber Barons* (New York: Harcourt, Brace, 1934), p. viii.

THE GILDED AGE

In 1871 Charles Francis Adams of the eminent Adams family remarked on the "greatly enlarged grasp of enterprise and increased facility of combination" evident in America. "The great operations of war, the handling of large masses of men, the influence of discipline, the lavish expenditure of unprecedented sums of money, the immense financial operations, the possibilities of effective cooperation [had been] lessons not . . . lost on men quick to receive and to apply all new ideas."[3] Exploitation of America's vast resources had just begun, and the emotions of the people had "swung into a mundane fervor—for moneygetting and wealth enjoyment."[4] America had entered the Gilded Age. The five years after the war had

> witnessed some of the most remarkable examples of organized lawlessness, under the forms of law, which mankind has yet had an opportunity to study. If individuals have, as a rule, quietly pursued their peaceful occupations, the same cannot be said of certain . . . men at the head of vast combinations of private wealth. This has been particularly the case as regards those controlling the . . . railroad interests. These modern potentates have declared war, negotiated peace, reduced courts, legislatures, and sovereign States to an unqualified obedience to their will, disturbed trade, agitated the currency, imposed taxes, and, boldly setting both law and public opinion at defiance, have freely exercised many other attributes of sovereignty. . . . Single men have controlled hundreds of miles of railway, thousands of men, tens of millions of revenue, and hundreds of millions of capital. The strength implied in all this they wielded in practical independence of the control both of governments and of individuals; much as petty German despots might have governed their little principalities a century or two ago.[5]

Russell Conwell

These "modern potentates" found a host of apologists. Besides the new order's natural defenders—the industrialists—there were clergymen, novelists, lawyers, and educators. Perhaps no one was heard more often preaching the gospel of wealth than Russell H. Conwell.

Ten years before Adams noted the emergence of the "petty industrial despots," Conwell (1843–1925), later the founder and first president of Temple University, mounted the pulpit in a little church in Westfield, Massachusetts, and formulated the creed of post–Civil War America. His "Acres of Diamonds," delivered then for the first time, went on to set a lecture record seldom, if ever, equalled. During the next fifty years,

---

[3] Charles Francis Adams, Jr., "An Erie Raid," *North American Review*, CXII (April, 1871), 243.
[4] Nichols and Nichols, *Growth of Democracy*, p. 290.
[5] Adams, "An Erie Raid," p. 244.

Conwell delivered *Acres of Diamonds* more than six thousand times to audiences all over the United States. "Little did he foresee," wrote Conwell's official biographer, "how it would affect the lives of thousands of people; nor *the influence it would have upon the industries of this country.*"[6]

The lecture title was derived from an Eastern parable about the Persian Ali Hafed, who sold his land to search for the fabled Golconda diamond mines. In the end, he discovered the wealth he sought in his own backyard. The moral of the tale was "that the opportunity to get rich, to attain unto great wealth, is here in Jonesville now" (the location of the diamond mine shifted with every lecture). One had only to see and seize it. Within the compass of a few more such glittering phrases, Conwell effected the transition from the feudal emphasis on poverty to the modern preference for material prosperity—the path to godliness in the United States.

For Conwell no place on earth was more adapted to the acquisition of wealth than the United States; even a poor man without capital had the opportunity "to get rich quickly and honestly."[7] Indeed, he had more than an opportunity; he had an obligation to do so: "I say that you ought to get rich, and it is your duty to get rich." Moneymaking was a proper Christian objective, for money permitted men to do good, print Bibles, build churches, send missionaries abroad—and pay preachers! It was wrong to associate possession of money with dishonesty and immorality. Virtue and wealth were equated; "Ninety-eight out of one hundred of the rich men of America are honest. That is why they are rich." Covetousness was wrong, of course, but not the mere possession of money, even very large sums. "Money is power, and you ought to be reasonably ambitious to have it." "I say, then, you ought to have money. If you can honestly attain unto riches . . . it is your Christian and Godly duty to do so. It is an awful mistake . . . to think you must be awfully poor in order to be pious."

Conwell was often asked about his attitude toward the poor. We should sympathize with "God's poor—that is, those who cannot help themselves," the minister agreed. But to sympathize with or help a man "whom God has punished for his sins . . . is to do wrong, no doubt about it . . . let us remember there is not a poor person in the United States who was not made poor by his own shortcomings, or by the shortcomings of some one else. It is all wrong to be poor" when it is so easy to get rich. All one had to do was look around and find out what things people wanted, "set them down with your pencil, and figure up the profits you would make if you did supply them. . . ." Wealth was within easy reach. The chances were great that those who did not acquire money were unworthy or useless. "You can measure the good you have been to this city by what this city

---

[6] Agnes R. Burr, *Russell H. Conwell and His Work* (Philadelphia: Winston, 1926), p. 307.
[7] The quotations here from *Acres of Diamonds* (New York: Harper & Brothers, 1915), pp. 15–25, 48–49.

has paid you," Conwell told an audience in Philadelphia, "because a man can judge very well what he is worth by what he receives. . . ." To someone who complained that he had made no more than $1,000 in twenty years of storekeeping in Philadelphia, Conwell retorted: "It would have been better for Philadelphia if they had kicked you out of the city nineteen years and nine months ago. A man has no right to keep a store in Philadelphia twenty years and not make at least five hundred thousand dollars. . . ."

So preoccupied was Conwell with spreading the gospel of wealth that he professed no concern with politics. Indeed, he was cynical about free government and made derogatory remarks about the democratic process. "Young man," he warned an imaginary inquirer during his lecture, "won't you learn a lesson in the primer of politics that it is a *prima facie* evidence of littleness to hold office under our form of government? Great men get into office sometimes, but what this country needs is men that will do what we tell them to do." Nor was the so-called privilege of voting what it was considered to be. To women who looked forward to equal suffrage, Conwell declared, "You [won't] get anything that is worth while." One vote was nothing, nor were many, for "this country is not run by votes. . . . It is governed by influence. It is governed by the ambitions and the enterprises which control votes." Frederick Townsend Martin (1849–1914), author, traveler, and philanthropist, expressed the clergyman's philosophy even more brutally:

> It matters not one iota what political party is in power or what President holds the reins of office. We are not politicians or public thinkers; we are the rich; we own America; we got it, God knows how, but we intend to keep it if we can by throwing all the tremendous weight of our support, our influence, our money, our political connection, our purchased senators, our hungry congressmen, our public speaking demagogues, into the scale against any legislature, any political platform, any Presidential campaign that threatens the integrity of our estate.[8]

In those heady days of industrialization and emerging corporate power, the people were "in the mood for eager, unconservative exploitation of opportunity . . . business [sang] with swelling volume . . . 'prosperity and more prosperity.' " The worship of moneymaking and the moneymaker permeated all classes.[9] Conwell supplied a gospel to fit existing conditions.[10] His lecture was significant for the reinforcement it gave to the doctrine of *laissez faire*. Earlier *laissez faire* advocates had been insistent on the fewest possible relations between private economic activities and politics. Conwell, and the American people generally in the postwar

---

[8] Quoted in Thomas C. Cochran and William Miller, *The Age of Enterprise* (New York: Macmillan, 1942), p. 285.
[9] Nichols and Nichols, *Growth of Democracy*, p. 291.
[10] For a similar glorification of wealth, see William Lawrence, "The Relation of Wealth to Morals," *The World's Work*, (January, 1901), I, 286–92.

decades, accepted the former as the end-all of American life, condemning politics as little more than a farce. Political democracy seemed incompatible with economic oligarchy, the weight of "robber barons" being often decisive. Unwittingly, perhaps, Conwell demonstrated the validity of Webster's diagnosis of 1820: "A great equality of condition is the true basis, most certainly, of popular government."

Andrew Carnegie

A less flamboyant, but no less important, declaration of the same thesis came from the great steel magnate Andrew Carnegie (1835–1919), who heeded Conwell's cry as assiduously as if he had actually heard it. Beginning as a bobbin-boy, he became a superintendent for the Pennsylvania Railroad in 1859. During the Civil War he invested heavily in iron manufactures and in 1865 began to give them his full time. By 1873 he was the major steel producer in America, and by 1889, when he wrote his essay "Wealth," he was perhaps America's richest man.

When the *North American Review's* editor received Carnegie's manuscript, he was ecstatic, calling it "the finest article I have ever published."[11] Yet Carnegie had but "formulated a philosophy as universal in the United States as smoke in Pittsburgh."[12] Whereas Conwell put a supernatural base under his theory—making it virtually God's command to "get rich!" —Carnegie's approach was naturalistic[13] He regarded the new economic order as preordained. For "good or ill, it is upon us, beyond our power to alter, and therefore to be accepted and made the best of." "It is a waste of time to criticize the inevitable."[14] The new conditions must simply be accepted and accommodated. Carnegie conceded that in the transition from primitive equality to the civilized inequality of industrialism, human society had lost its homogeneity. "The ties of brotherhood" binding men together had been loosened, and the rich and poor were no longer "in harmonious relationship." But if the social cost, "the price we pay," was great, the process was nevertheless "highly beneficial." "It is well, nay, essential for the progress of the race, that the houses of some should be homes for all that is highest and best in literature and the arts, and for all the refinements of civilization, rather than that none should be so. Much better this great irregularity than universal squalor." "Today

---

[11] Quoted in B. J. Hendrick, *The Life of Andrew Carnegie* (Garden City, N.Y.: Doubleday, 1932), I, 330. See also Louis W. Hacker, *The World of Andrew Carnegie*: 1865–1901 (Philadelphia: Lippincott, 1968).

[12] Ralph H. Gabriel, *The Course of American Democratic Thought* (New York: Ronald Press, 1940), p. 146.

[13] Gabriel, *Democratic Thought*, p. 157.

[14] Andrew Carnegie, "Wealth," *North American Review*, CXLVIII (June, 1889), 651–64. See also Henry W. Lanier, "The Many-Sided Andrew Carnegie: A Citizen of the Republic," *The World's Work*, I (April, 1901), 618–30. For a painstaking and authoritative portrait, see Joseph Frazier Wall, *Andrew Carnegie* (New York: Oxford University Press, 1970).

the poor enjoy what the rich could not before afford." Paraphrasing the idea of natural selection basic to Charles Darwin's *Origin of Species*, published in 1859, Carnegie went on to say that "the law of competition, though sometimes hard for the individual, is best for the race, because it insures the survival of the fittest in every department." The operation of natural economic forces, which produced all these advantages, caused a few men with peculiar talents for organization and management to "be in receipt of more revenue than can be judiciously expended upon themselves." The result could be beneficial to the race, Carnegie explained, if these potentates followed an appropriate model for administering their tremendous fortunes. The only question the present generation had to answer was, "What is the proper mode of administering wealth after the laws upon which civilization is founded have thrown it into the hands of the few?"

There were only three answers: keep it in the family from one generation to another; bequeath it on death to public purposes; or administer it during the life of the possessor. The first way was neither compatible with republican institutions nor good for the welfare of the children. The second was satisfactory, "provided a man is content to wait until he is dead before [his wealth] becomes of much good in the world." Only the third way was practicable. It was "the true antidote for the temporary unequal distribution of wealth." It provided a means for "the reconciliation of the rich and the poor" and assured "a reign of harmony." "Under its sway, we shall have an ideal state." What a potent force for further advancement of the race it guaranteed!

> Even the poorest can be made to . . . agree that great sums gathered by some of their fellow citizens and spent for public purposes, from which the masses reap the principal benefit, are more valuable to them than if scattered among them through the course of many years in trifling amounts.

If the rich were to meet their obligations as stewards of society, they must live moderately and spend only to provide for their legitimate wants. The rest of their income must be considered trust funds, with themselves as trustees, to be administered in the manner "best calculated to produce the most beneficial results to the community." The "man of wealth thus become[s] the mere agent and trustee for his poorer brethren, bringing to their service his superior wisdom, experience, and ability to administer, doing for them better than they would or could do for themselves."

Like Conwell, Carnegie distinguished between the deserving and the undeserving poor. He cautioned against misdirected benefactions ("indiscriminate charity") and warned that it would be better in the long run if all the millions of the rich were thrown into the sea than "so spent as to encourage the slothful, the drunken, the unworthy." He would help only those who would help themselves. "Neither the individual nor the race is improved by alms-giving." Like Conwell's *Acres of Diamonds*, Carnegie's gospel of wealth tended to cramp government and limit its utility in solving social problems. Thus, the problem of rich versus poor, which Carnegie recognized as a major issue during his lifetime, would be solved by the rich themselves. "The laws of accumulation [and distribution] will be left free. . . . Individualism will continue, but the millionaire will be but a trustee for the poor; intrusted for a season with a great part of the increased wealth of the community, but administering it for the community far better than it could or would have done for itself."

Conwell and Carnegie sought to reestablish the equation of virtue and wisdom with wealth, so prominent in the early years of the Republic. Both emphasized "that the government of society in that most important of all areas, the economic, should be in the hands of a natural aristocracy,"[15] as in fact it seemed to be by 1871, when Adams made his comments. The composition of this aristocracy was dependent on the laws of competition. A corollary to the doctrine of natural leadership was a limited role for government. Conwell and Carnegie would have the state confined to police functions, specifically to the protection of property. They not only were fearful of the abuse of political power, and therefore wished to keep it minimal, but also were convinced that the usages and institutions of political democracy did not place men of ability into positions of power. While business produced a natural aristocracy of ability, politics "lifts mediocrity into the saddle."[16]

Carnegie practiced his stewardship theory. Benefactions during his lifetime amounted to $350 million. Although the bulk of Carnegie's own gifts went to foundations, which have since directed their interests primarily toward education, research, and peace, he donated a great deal also for the construction of libraries. In all, Carnegie, and later his major foundation, the Carnegie Corporation, "gave some $56 million to build 2,509 public libraries," 1,681 of them in the United States.[17]

Other millionaires were slower to respond, and a great many rejected Carnegie's ideas. John D. Rockefeller, Sr. (1839–1937), the American oil magnate, reinforced these ideas. "The growth of a large business is merely a survival of the fittest," Rockefeller declared. "The American beauty rose can be produced in the splendor and fragrance which bring cheer to its beholder only by sacrificing the early buds which grow up around it. This is not an evil tendency in business. It is merely the working out of a law of nature and a law of God." Wealth, however, implied responsibility. "The good Lord gave me my money," Rockefeller, a devout Baptist, told the first graduating class of the university he founded, "and how could I withhold it from the University of Chicago?"[18]

---

[15] Gabriel, *Democratic Thought*, p. 158. See also Professor Robert G. McCloskey, *American Conservatism in the Age of Enterprise* (Cambridge, Mass.: Harvard University Press, 1951).

[16] Gabriel, *Democratic Thought*, pp. 158–59.

[17] Florence Anderson, *Library Program, 1911–1961* (New York: Carnegie Corporation of New York, 1963), p. 4.

[18] Quoted in Mason, *Free Government*, p. 579.

To many Carnegie's interest in libraries and Rockefeller's benevolence to education have seemed the best way to meet their social responsibilities. Others, including Carnegie's contemporary Finley Peter Dunne (1867–1936), America's greatest satirist and an experienced journalist, were critical, even cynical. Dunne lampooned Carnegie's philanthropies. According to Mr. Dooley, the lovable creation of Dunne's imagination, Carnegie told an audience at the dedication of "th' libry at Pianola, Ioway":

> I don't want poverty an' crime to go on. I intind to stop it. But how? It's been holdin' its own f'r cinchries. Some iv th' gr-reatest iv former minds has undertook to prevint it an' has failed. They didn't know how . . . I do. Th' way to abolish poverty an' bust crime is to put up a brown-stone buildin' in ivry town in th' counthry with me name over it. That's th' way. . . . They'se nawthin' so good as a good book. It's betther thin food; it's betther thin money.[19]

Before Carnegie died (Mr. Dooley assured his sidekick, Mr. Hennessy) he hoped "to crowd a libry on ivry man, woman, an' child in th' counthry. He's given thim to cities, towns, villages, an' whistlin' stations. They're tearin' down gas-houses an' poor-houses to put up libries. . . . No beggar is iver turned impty-handed fr'm th' dure. Th' pan-handler knocks an' asts f'r a glass iv milk an' a roll. 'No, sir,' says Andhrew Carnaygie, 'I will not pauperize this onworthy man. Nawthin' is worse f'r a beggarman thin to make a pauper iv him. . . . Saunders, give him a libry. . . .' "

On the whole, however, Dunne's analysis of industrial oligarchy was restrained. Already the rationalization supporting it had become the folk philosophy of the nation. The fun he poked at Carnegie was not malicious, and though he was critical of prevailing customs and attitudes, even Dunne evidently had not remained immune to its appeal.[20]

Running through Mr. Dooley's conversations with Mr. Hennessy is the Conwell-Carnegie thesis that politics is a dirty business that honest men would do well to shun. "Look here," Mr. Dooley said, diving under the bar and producing a roll of paper, "Here's th' pitchers iv candydates I pulled down frim th' windy, an' jus' knowin' they're here makes me that nervous f'r th' contints iv th' cash dhrawer I'm afrid to tur-rn me back f'r a minyit."[21]

But by the time Dunne started Mr. Dooley's career, the folklore of capitalism had adopted the Conwell-Carnegie thesis. It was generally conceded that "government . . . could not be efficient because it did not operate for profit, . . . an essential element of efficiency." Nor could it

---

[19] Finley Peter Dunne, *Dissertations by Mr. Dooley* (New York: Harper & Brothers, 1906), pp. 177–82.

[20] Finley Peter Dunne, "The Pursuit of Riches," in *Mr. Dooley*, p. 36.

[21] Finley Peter Dunne, *Mr. Dooley: In Peace and In War* (Boston: Small, Maynard, 1899), p. 87.

administer charity, "because the Government would not know where to stop."[22]

THE TRIUMPH OF LAISSEZ FAIRE

The gospel of wealth, along with its corollary of laissez faire, was widely accepted in the United States. Together they demonstrated the "Triumphant Democracy."[23] The two great developers of laissez faire thought— Herbert Spencer and William Graham Sumner—elevated it to a science.

Herbert Spencer

Herbert Spencer (1820–1903) was an English philosopher, biosociologist, and agnostic. Oliver Wendell Holmes, Jr. did not exaggerate when he wrote in 1895: "H. Spencer you English never quite do justice to. . . . He writes an ugly, uncharming style, his ideals are those of a lower middle class British Philistine. And yet after all abatements I doubt if any writer of English except Darwin has done so much to affect our whole way of thinking about the universe."[24]

Spencer's creative endeavors spanned a half-century (1850–1900), a period in which political democracy forged strongly ahead in both England and the United States. The ever-increasing amount of social legislation achieved by newly enfranchised people in both countries disturbed him. How did it come to pass, he wanted to know, that the people, upon getting into power, began to dictate the actions of private citizens, thus in effect narrowing the range of their own freedom? By doing so, they were destroying the very liberalism in whose name they professed to act. Men could think of themselves as liberals only if they followed the historical pattern of throwing off government restrictions on individual liberty. Liberalism did not mean adding restrictions; it consisted of removing them, leaving men *free* and *independent*, not only of each other but also of the state. Liberalism thus meant a policy of laissez faire. The suggestion that the people imposed controls upon themselves through the agency of a government elected by and responsible to themselves Spencer thrust aside as irrelevant and immaterial. "The liberty which a citizen enjoys is to be measured, not by the nature of the governmental machinery he lives under, whether representative or other, but by the relative paucity of the restraints it imposes on him."[25] Liberalism and freedom from governmental restraint were one and the same thing.

[22] Thurman W. Arnold, *The Folklore of Capitalism* (New Haven, Conn.: Yale University Press, 1937), p. 204. This volume can be read with profit in connection with a study of the gospel of wealth.
[23] The title of a book by Andrew Carnegie (New York: Scribner's, 1886) .
[24] M. A. DeWolfe Howe, ed., *Holmes-Pollock Letters* (Cambridge, Mass.: Harvard University Press, 1941), I, 57.
[25] Herbert Spencer, *The Man Versus the State* (New York: Appleton-Century-Crofts, 1910), pp. 15–16.

Spencer's theory rested on precise views concerning man and his rights, society, and government. He was convinced that man was "shapen in iniquity and conceived in sin." Human frailties would be manifest and decisive regardless of the political system: there was no "political alchemy" by which leaden instincts could be changed into golden conduct. Such good as there is in man evolved from grim, even cruel, struggle. Just as universal warfare between lower animals ultimately produced types perfectly adapted to their environment, so the same beneficent, though severe, social struggle between humans brought forth men adapted to their environment and capable of the greatest happiness. The process was "rooted in the very nature of the organism [and] is constantly at work. . . ."[26] Through the years it tended to produce better men and, finally, human perfection.

> Progress . . . is not an accident, but a necessity. Instead of civilization being artificial, it is a part of nature; all of a piece with the development of the embryo or the unfolding of a flower.[27]

This natural process of selection, later described in Darwin's *Origin of Species*, worked not only toward evolution of the ideal man but also toward elimination of the unfit. The rigors of this divinely ordained struggle tested all men. If they were found "sufficiently complete to live," they emerged safe and victorious; if not, "they die, and it is best they should die."[28] Government had neither the capacity nor the authority to intervene in the struggle. "No power on earth, no cunningly devised laws of statesmanship, no world rectifying schemes of the humane, no communist panaceas, no reforms that men ever did broach or ever will broach" could affect it. The attendant suffering must be endured; government attempts to lessen it ultimately made it worse. Poverty Spencer ascribed to lack of ability, distresses to improvidence, starvation to idleness, and "shadows and misery" to weakness. The unfortunate deserved no sympathy; their status was the decree "of a large, far-seeing benevolence," "the nonadaptation of constitution to conditions." Spencer repudiated government aid to the poor and any other kind of state interference. Poor laws, state-supported education, sanitary supervision, regulation of housing conditions, tariffs, state banking, government-operated post offices, and even restrictions on medical quacks were all futile; all were destructive of true liberalism.[29]

Men's rights could be interfered with only at the cost of slavery to all. Government lacked the power to create human rights; these resulted from the operation of natural laws. Progress could be assured only if the functions of government were confined to enforcing contracts, repelling inva-

---

[26] Richard Hofstadter, *Social Darwinism in American Thought, 1860–1915* (Philadelphia: University of Pennsylvania Press, 1944), p. 26.

[27] This thesis is central to Spencer's *Social Statics* (New York: D. Appleton, 1866).

[28] Spencer, *Social Statics*, p. 415.

[29] Hofstadter, *Social Darwinism*, p. 27.

sions, suppressing insurrections, and protecting existing rights. A truly liberal government was therefore extremely limited.

In Spencer's thought old concepts appeared in new dress: *natural law* became the law of struggle, the necessary and beneficial competitive clash of men with men; *aristocracy*, those who emerged victorious from life's struggle; *natural and inalienable rights*, the right of those who survived and flourished in this divinely guided order. These concepts constituted the tenets of liberalism.

On first reading Herbert Spencer, Carnegie remembered

> . . . that light came in as a flood and all was clear. Not only had I got rid of theology and the supernatural, but I had found the truth of evolution. "All is well since all grows better," became my motto, my true source of comfort. Man . . . [has] risen to the higher forms. Nor is there any conceivable end to his march to perfection. His face is turned to the light; he stands in the sun and looks upward.[30]

Spencer's interpretation of laissez faire "won America as no philosophy ever won a nation before." "To an age singularly engrossed in the competitive pursuit of industrial wealth, [he] gave cosmic sanction to free competition. In an age of science, [he] 'scientifically' justified ceaseless exploitation. . . . [He defended the] cupidity [of American businessmen] as a part of the universal struggle for existence; their wealth, [he] hallowed as the sign of the 'fittest.' Business America . . . had supreme faith in itself; no wonder it embraced Spencer's philosophy, which sanctified business activities."[31]

Industrialists were not alone in accepting Spencer's creed. Charles W. Eliot and John Fiske sang his praises at Harvard, Nicholas Murray Butler at Columbia, Francis A. Walker at MIT. Theodore Dreiser, Jack London, Clarence Darrow, and Hamlin Garland were all influenced by him.[32] Lawyers and judges were his followers. All believed themselves to be liberal and argued that theirs was the only philosophy that, if followed, guaranteed industrial progress. On occasion his creed is proclaimed even today.[33]

William Graham Sumner

No one followed Spencer so devotedly and advanced his cause so diligently as William Graham Sumner (1840–1910). Sumner was tremendously impressed with Spencer's writings and was recognized as "the lead-

---

[30] *Autobiography of Andrew Carnegie* (Boston: Houghton Mifflin, 1920), p. 327.
[31] Cochran and Miller, *Age of Enterprise*, p. 119.
[32] Hofstadter, *Social Darwinism*, p. 21.
[33] One detects faint echoes of Spencer in Edward C. Banfield, *The Unheavenly City: The Nature and Future of Our Urban Crisis* (Boston: Little, Brown, 1970).

ing American exponent of Spencerian philosophy."[34] Sumner had been trained as a clergyman. Convinced that the church was destined to play a diminishing role in American life, he turned to education, accepting in 1872 a professorship of political economy at Yale. For more than a generation he exerted enormous influence. William Lyon Phelps, a student of Sumner's at Yale, recalled his teacher's devotion to Spencer:

> "Professor," a student inquired of Sumner, "don't you believe in any government aid to industry?"
> "No: it's root hog, or die."
> "Yes, but hasn't the hog got a right to root?"
> "There are no rights. The world owes nobody a living."
> "You believe, then, Professor, in only one system, the contract-competitive system?"
> "That's the only sound economic system. All others are fallacies."
> "Well, suppose some professor of political economy came along and took your job away. Wouldn't you be sore?"
> "Any other professor is welcome to try. If he gets my job, it's my fault. My business is to teach the subject so well that no one can take the job away from me."[35]

Sumner's defense of the *status quo* is presented in *What Social Classes Owe to Each Other*, published in 1883.[36] It rests on three premises: no class in society lay "under the duty and burden of fighting the battles of life for any other class, or of solving social problems for the satisfaction of any other class. . . ." No class had a right "to formulate demands on . . . other classes." Government and the State owed nothing to anybody save "peace, order, and the guarantee of rights." Life was hard. A certain number of ills were the natural lot of man; they must be accepted and lived with by everyone. "We cannot blame our fellow-men for our share of these." Nor ought we to call upon government to relieve us of them. Attempts "to apply legislative methods of reform to the ills which belong to the order of nature" were not only fruitless but also wrong, unwise, and self-defeating.

True liberals recognized that although attempts at reform were made in the name of the poor and the weak, these people were, in reality, only "the negligent, shiftless, inefficient, silly, and imprudent." In using the machinery of politics to fasten themselves "upon the industrious and prudent as a responsibility and a duty," they became "a dead-weight on the society in all its struggles to realize better things." Humanitarians, philanthropists, and reformers ignored the rights of the other classes. Glossing over the real cause of poverty and weakness, they "invent[ed] new

---

[34] J. Mark Jacobson, *The Development of American Political Thought* (New York: Appleton-Century-Crofts, 1932), p. 546.

[35] William Lyon Phelps, "When Yale was Given to Sumnerology," *Literary Digest International Book Review*, III (1925), 661.

[36] William Graham Sumner, *What Social Classes Owe to Each Other* (New York: Harper & Brothers, 1883). The citations quoted in this chapter are from pp. 12–168.

theories of property, distort[ed] rights and perpetrat[ed] injustice," prompting Sumner to observe: "[When I read some of these discussions,] I have thought it must be quite disreputable to be respectable, quite dishonest to own property, quite unjust to go one's own way and earn one's own living, and that the really admirable person was the good-for-nothing. The man who by his own effort raises himself above poverty appears . . . to be of no account." Yet, for Sumner, such a man was the rock upon which strong societies were built.

Sumner emphasized the contractual basis of the modern social structure. Realistic, "cold, and matter-of-fact" contracts were the roots of American progress. In a state "based on contract, sentiment is out of place in any public or common affairs." "A society based on contract is a society of free and independent men, who form ties without favor or obligation, and cooperate without cringing or intrigues. [Such a society] gives the utmost room and chance for individual development, and for all the self-reliance and dignity of a free man." Sumner's understanding of a truly liberal society—"a free democracy"—was "a society of free men, co-operating under [and united by] contract." Such a society would be strong and perfect if its full capabilities were ever attained.

Even in its imperfect state in America, it had become obvious that no one could claim help from or be required to help another. The rights of all to their freedom were guaranteed against "all arbitrary power, and all class and personal interest." Each man's life and career were objects of his personal destiny, not the responsibility of society. Freedom was not a right but *"a status created for the individual by laws and institutions, the effect of which is that each man is guaranteed the use of all his own powers exclusively for his own welfare."*

> It is not at all a matter of elections, or universal suffrage, or democracy. It is not to be admitted for a moment that liberty is a means to social ends, and that it may be impaired for major considerations. Any one who so argues has lost the bearings and relations of all the facts and factors in a free state.

Making men happy was not the function of government. "They must make themselves happy in their own way, and at their own risk." Free men were independent men, unrelated to their fellows save by the common bonds of "respect, courtesy, and good will." Each expected to take care of himself and his family, make no trouble for his neighbors or his community, honor his contracts, and contribute his share to a limited number of public interests and common necessities.

In an essay published in 1902,[37] Sumner declared his misgivings about democracy. "Every age is befooled by the notions which are in fashion in it," he wrote. "Our age is befooled by 'democracy.'" "If we could get rid

---

[37] "Consolidation of Wealth: Economic Aspects," *The Independent* LIV (May 1, 1902), 1036–40.

of some of our notions about liberty and equality," he snorted, "we might get some insight into societal organization; what it does for us and what it makes us do." It was nonsense to allow "analogies drawn from democracy to affect sentiment about industrial relations." The predominance of a few individuals and personal control were common characteristics of all joint-stock (corporate) enterprises. "Industry may be republican," Sumner declared, but "it never can be democratic, so long as men differ in productive power and in industrial virtue." Industrial oligarchies and monarchies were inevitable "because one or a few get greater efficiency of control and greater vigor of administration." Indeed, the "strongest and most effective organizations for industrial purposes were always formed by a few great capitalists." He believed that "these phenomena of growth" were ample "reason for public congratulation."

Sumner especially deplored the increasing tendency of the people "to turn to the politician to preserve [themselves] from the captains of industry." "When has anybody ever seen a politician who was a match for a captain of industry?" Neither the people who turned to legislatures nor the many legislators to whom they appealed understood the economic necessity for the concentration of wealth. Wealth "provided . . . things abundantly and cheaply"; it served to raise the general standard of living. "No man can acquire a million without helping a million men to increase their little fortune all the way down through all the social grades." What if there were "idle, or silly, or vulgar" millionaires? The bargain was still a good one for society.

In any case, Sumner asked, why complain of unequal fortunes? "What law of nature, religion, ethics, or the State is violated by inequalities of fortune?" Inequalities proved nothing. They had to be discussed in terms

of the institutions, laws, usages and customs which our ancestors have bequeathed to us and which we allow to stand. If it is proposed to change any of these parts of the societal order, that is a proper subject of discussion, but it is aside from the concentration of wealth. So long as tariffs, patents, etc., are part of the system in which we live, how can it be expected that people will not take advantage of them? What else are they for?

The only flaw in the existing economic order was the prevalence of "jobbery," "the voice of plutocracy,"—and this was the product of politics rather than of the industrial system. Jobbery is "any scheme which aims to gain, not by the legitimate fruits of industry and enterprise, but by extorting from somebody a part of his product under the guise of some pretended industrial undertaking."[38] Public buildings were "jobs"—few of them were needed and most were "costly beyond all necessity or even decent luxury." Internal improvements were "jobs," made more often to serve private ends than meet public needs. Pensions were "jobs," and so was every other device "for obtaining what has not been earned." The

---

[38] Sumner, *Social Classes*, p. 143.

only way to gain legitimately was to follow the socially ordained industrial pattern.

Sumner was especially concerned that the democratic form of government might not be able to prevent the possessors of large fortunes from becoming a ruling plutocracy and thereby eliminating "the possibility of free self-government." Democracy was "rooted in the physical, economic, and social circumstances of the United States" and consequently would be adhered to for an indefinite time. Yet its machinery constituted an open invitation to the plutocrats to take control. The lobby "is the army of the plutocracy." With good leadership, it could take any democratic redoubts. Vigilance and exertion must constantly be maintained to avoid the possibility of capture, for the plutocrats were always trying "to do what the generals, nobles, and priests have done in the past—get the power of the State into their hands, so as to bend the rights of others to their own advantage. . . ." In addition to vigilance and exertion, democratic society must develop social institutions that would work toward freedom. Specifically, Sumner suggested the development of voluntary combination of and cooperation among self-governing freemen "in furtherance or defense of their own interests."

Sumner did not share the mounting concern about concentrated wealth. "The millionaires are a product of natural selection, acting on the whole body of men, to pick out those who can meet the requirements of certain work to be done. In this respect they are just like . . . great statesmen, or scientific men, or military men. It is because they are thus selected that wealth aggregates under their hands. . . ."[39]

Great capitalists were entitled to great gains. "Wages of superintendence" were the just reward for "the time, the judgment, courage, and perseverance required to organize new enterprises and carry them to success. . . ." Many could do what they were told; but "men who can think and plan and tell the routine men what to do are very rare. They are paid in proportion to the supply and demand of them."

Sumner stated the essence of his philosophy in *What Social Classes Owe to Each Other*:

> Whatever we gain . . . will be by growth, never . . . by any reconstruction of society or the plan of some enthusiastic social architect. The latter . . . [only] postpon[es] all our chances of real improvement. Society needs first of all to be freed from these meddlers—that is, to be let alone. Here we are, then, . . . back at the old doctrine—*laissez-faire*. Let us translate it into blunt English, and it will read, Mind your own business. It is nothing but the doctrine of liberty. Let every man be happy in his own way. If his sphere of action and interest impinges on that of any other man, there will have to be a compromise and adjustment. Wait for the occasion. Do not attempt to generalize those interferences or to plan for them *a priori*. We have a body of laws and institutions which have grown up as occasion has occurred for adjusting rights. Let the same process go on. Practice the utmost reserve possible in your

---

[39] Sumner, "Consolidation," p. 1040.

interferences even of this kind, and by no means seize occasion for interfering with natural adjustments. Try first long and patiently whether the natural adjustment will not come about through the play of interests and the voluntary concessions of the parties.

To Sumner and to the industrialists of his own day—and indeed, to a considerable number even today—free government was weak government. Determined primarily to secure economic freedom for the entrepreneur, Sumner adapted Spencer's theories to the American situation and emerged as *primus inter pares* among the advocates of laissez faire. The fact that "let alone" in practice afforded no cure for all social ills did not concern him; he was willing to accept the troubles nature imposed. Laissez faire would at least guarantee that no ills caused by human meddling would increase the burdens of life. He recognized, too, that his credo was "a purely negative and unproductive injunction." It purposely excluded planning, for "true social advance" did not result from "arbitrary, sentimental, and artificial" schemes. It was "a product and a growth." Let alone, society would inevitably, if slowly, advance toward perfection. Social planning was based on the false premise that rights pertained to results. They did not, Sumner asserted. Rights pertained only to *chances*—"to the *conditions* of the struggle for existence . . . to the *pursuit* of happiness, not to the possession of happiness." How particular individuals fared in the struggle of life was determined strictly on their merit, and properly so. Social interference on behalf of certain persons only served to upset the operation of infallible natural laws, nourish "some of the meanest vices of human nature, waste capital," and in the end, "overthrow civilization." Social effort directed toward increasing and extending everyone's chances of success was, on the other hand, not only worthwhile but also desirable. This "is the work of civilization," the only proper concern of government in a free society.

CRITICISM MOUNTS

Some of Sumner's contemporaries were critical; a literature of opposition began to accumulate, and a reform movement of considerable strength sprang up. The critics had begun to realize that "if the accumulation of vast fortunes goes on for another generation with the same accelerated rapidity as during the present, the wealth of this country will soon be consolidated in the hands of a few corporations and individuals. . . ." How long could a few with vast estates live in "luxurious ease, while the great masses [were] doomed to incessant toil, penury and want?"[40]

In 1902 *The Independent* published a series of articles on the problem. One article was by John DeWitt Warner (1851–1925), a lawyer by profes-

---

[40] Lyman Trumbull, Speech to the Populist Convention, Chicago, Illinois, 1894, *Public Opinion*, XVII (October 18, 1894), 687.

sion, a trustee of Cornell University, and a member of Congress from 1891 to 1895, where he specialized in tariff and currency problems. Warner questioned the materialistic determinism implicit in both Carnegie's and Sumner's thinking and disputed Carnegie's smug dictum that "it is a waste of time to criticize the inevitable." Warner also queried the confident assumption that trusts were of little economic or political significance. Trusts had grown in power

> until they now control the leading necessaries of life and commerce; until today our Federal Government and many States are desperately seeking means to meet the appeal of a people deprived of meat, except at extortion rates. Concentration of wealth has so progressed that, through billion dollar trusts . . . American billionaire[s] . . . [are] wielding [their wealth] as a power in business and in politics—that is, in government.[41]

Warner foresaw revolution as the ultimate reaction to the abuses of concentrated wealth. In earlier times the masses had brought about reform. "Has Plutocracy," he asked, "more hold upon the regard, the affection or the prejudices of men than church, nobility, or [the] military? . . ." Were Americans less able or likely to assert themselves against plutocracy than were those "of other lands and other times"? The demands of the people had always proved irresistible; plutocracy would be no exception. The revolution, Warner thought, would produce socialism, for state socialism was the natural answer to private monopoly. The people would not hesitate to choose "Government administration for the public benefit by responsible officials" over "private extortion for private profit by irresponsible Trust magnates."

William J. Ghent

Whereas Warner criticized plutocracy because of the revolution it seemed certain to set in motion, William J. Ghent (1866–1942) deplored its social and economic effects. An editor of *The American Fabian* and a successful lawyer, Ghent had long been prominent in various social-reform movements. The burden of his argument in both *The Independent*[42] and in a book[43] was that the socioeconomic status of turn-of-the-century America contained "all the essentials of a renascent feudalism," characterized "by a class dependence rather than a personal dependence," as of old. Petty tradesmen and producers, laborers and mechanics, clerks and helpers, farmers—all had become economic dependents, dominated by "a few score magnates." Even the professions were affected. All found themselves "more and more confined to particular activities, to particular territories, and . . . to particular methods, all dictated and enforced by the pressure of the larger concerns." What Ghent identified in 1902 as a transforma-

---

[41] John D. Warner, "Consolidation of Wealth: Political Aspects," *The Independent*, LIV (May 1, 1902), 1045–49.
[42] W. J. Ghent, "Benevolent Feudalism," *The Independent*, LIV (April 3, 1902), 781–88.
[43] W. J. Ghent, *Our Benevolent Feudalism* (New York: Macmillan, 1902).

tion of the economy from individualism to a vast industrial feudalism was documented a generation later by Adolf A. Berle, Jr. and G. C. Means in their monumental *Modern Corporation and Private Property*.[44]

The new feudalism was, however, qualified and restricted by the operation of democratic processes. The possibility of exerting popular will still remained. Moreover, Carnegie's concept of trusteeship had been widely accepted; the "enormous benefactions for social purposes, which have been common of late years," Ghent observed, "could come only from men and women who have been taught to feel an ethical duty to society." To be sure, much of the giving was misdirected (Carnegie's libraries were perhaps a case in point), but the fact that the nabobs of the day recognized a duty to society was "of far-reaching importance." Indeed, America was well on its way toward becoming "a benevolent feudalism."

It was nonetheless a feudal system. Modern feudal barons were still seigneurs, and the masses were but serfs. "Popular discontent will naturally follow," but Ghent predicted it would be "barren of result." Governmental processes in America were perfectly suited to the exertion of power in subtle and extralegal ways. "From petty constable to Supreme Court Justice, the officials . . . understand, or [can] be made to understand, the golden mean of their duties; and except for an occasional rascally Jacobin, whom it may for a time be difficult to suppress, they will be faithful and obey." The barons would not even hesitate to use armed force "to overcome the discontented and to quiet unnecessary turbulence." Only one power on earth could prevent it: demonstration of "the collective popular will that it shall not be."

John B. Clark

John Bates Clark (1847–1938), professor of economics at Columbia University from 1895 to 1923 and a founder of the American Economic Association, refuted Ghent, arguing that "the people do not need to let it [monopoly] develop at all." He was not content to sigh resignedly, as Ghent seemed to be. In *The Independent*, the month after Ghent's article appeared, Clark centered on the loophole Ghent had discerned but rejected, and built a solid case around it.[45]

To Clark "the regime of monopoly" was a peril worse than "a feudal tyranny." No description could exaggerate the evil in store for a society "given hopelessly to a regime of private monopoly. . . . Monopoly checks progress in production and infuses into distribution an element of robbery. . . ."[46] At all costs it must be checked, and Clark set out to call "the righteous of his generation to go forth to war" against it.[47]

---

[44] Adolf A. Berle, Jr., and G. C. Means, *The Modern Corporation and Private Property* (New York: Macmillan, 1932).
[45] John Bates Clark, "Feudalism and Commonwealth," *The Independent*, LIV (May 29, 1902), 1275–79, *passim.*
[46] John Bates Clark, *Essentials of Economic Theory* (New York: Macmillan, 1907), p. 555.
[47] Gabriel, *Democratic Thought*, p. 302.

Laborers, farmers, and independent investors were in natural opposition to monopoly, and "great natural forces [were] working on their side." The state could be made "to discipline wrong-doers [and to] define and forbid the evil practices which [made] monopoly possible."

> Not this year nor the next will the satisfactory repressing of monopolies come; but to suppose that it will never come requires us to believe that a great majority of the people cannot ever get from their Government something that their interests demand.[48]

Clark thus turned his back on laissez faire while it was at the height of its popularity. In this he was joined by the other leading economists who subscribed, as he had, to the statement of principles of the American Economic Association: "We regard the state as an agency whose positive assistance is one of the indispensable conditions of human progress. . . . We believe in a progressive development of economic conditions, which must be met by a corresponding development of legislative policy."[49] In taking this stand, Clark and the other forward-looking academicians foreshadowed by almost a half-century the popular uprising implicit in the election of Franklin D. Roosevelt as president in 1932 and the extensive program of reform that followed.

Lester F. Ward

Warner, Ghent, and Clark criticized the effects of the new plutocracy; others attacked the validity of the dogma on which it was based. Darwinism did not necessarily imply laissez faire; on the contrary, it suggested the desirability and even the necessity of positive government action.

Among the first to reach this conclusion was Lester F. Ward (1841–1913), who has been described as "an American Aristotle." An educator, he was also a geologist, botanist, paleontologist, social statistician, systematic philosopher, linguistics expert, and a founder of the discipline of sociology.[50] In a series of writings beginning with *Dynamic Sociology*[51] in 1883 and concluding with his last book, *Applied Sociology*,[52] published in 1906, Ward attacked head-on the Darwin-Spencer-Sumner thesis. The laissez faire school, he concluded, had tried to use the jargon of science falsely. Adherents of laissez faire declared that neither social nor physical phenomena were capable of human control.

Moreover, they professed to want nothing to do with government. Yet, "Nothing is more obvious today," Ward declared, "than the signal inability of capital and private enterprise to take care of themselves, unaided

---

[48] Gabriel, *Democratic Thought*, p. 302.
[49] *American Economic Review*, Supplement, March, 1936, p. 144.
[50] Leonard W. Levy and Alfred Young, in the foreword to Henry S. Commager, ed., *Lester Ward and the Welfare State* (Indianapolis: Bobbs-Merrill, 1967), p. v.
[51] Lester F. Ward, *Dynamic Sociology* (New York: D. Appleton, 1883).
[52] Lester F. Ward, *Applied Sociology* (Boston: Ginn, 1906).

by the state."[53] Far from operating alone and unaided, private enterprisers and capitalists had from the beginning begged and obtained from legislatures subsidies and protective tariffs. While loudly decrying politics and deploring paternalism, the plutocrats made use of the former and enjoyed the benefits of the latter—a strangely inconsistent position. They thus acknowledged, in fact, if not in word, that progress depended on control, that human reason and knowledge, applied to specific phenomena, were the tools with which to build a better society. Man could "transform his natural and social environment and perpetuate a social tradition for his advantage." In "place of the prevailing individualistic competitive regime," Ward advocated the use of "scientific planning."[54] The science of sociology must be used to help man eliminate the barriers to progress.

More government, not less, was needed. Unfortunately, however, the government of the United States was not in a position to intervene. It, too, had become a tool of the favored classes. The whole "great system of jurisprudence, owing to entirely changed industrial conditions," now worked to throw "unlimited opportunities in the way of some" and to bar the rest from any opportunities whatsoever. If law had been devised originally to protect the lowly, it was now used to protect the strong.

Faults in the system needed immediate correction. "Modern society is suffering from . . . undergovernment, from the failure of government to keep pace with the changes which civilization has wrought. . . ." To stave off modern brigandage of the plutocracy and to save civilization, government must "not fetter . . . but . . . liberate the forces of society, not . . . diminish but . . . increase their effectiveness." Government must be recognized as "the most important among the instruments which man can use for the building of a better order."[55] "More than any other individual, Ward formulated the basic pattern of the American concept of the planned society." If he did not invent the welfare state, he was "its preeminent philosopher, protagonist, and architect."[56]

Walter Rauschenbusch

Ward's attack was directed against the "scientific" truth underlying plutocracy; other critics attacked it on religious grounds. Indeed,

"America's most unique contribution to the great ongoing stream of Christianity is the 'social gospel.' This indigenous and typically American movement, initiated in the 'gilded age,' was called into being by the impact of

---

[53] Lester F. Ward, "Plutocracy and Paternalism," *The Forum*, (November, 1895), XX, 300–310.
[54] Levy and Young, in Commager, *Lester Ward*, p. v.
[55] Gabriel, *Democratic Thought*, p. 376. For a modern restatement of virtually the same theme, see McGeorge Bundy, *The Strength of Government* (Cambridge, Mass.: Harvard University Press, 1968).
[56] Gabriel, *Democratic Thought*, p. 204, and Levy and Young, in Commager, *Lester Ward*, p. v.

modern industrial society and scientific thought upon the Protestanism of the United States during the half century following the Civil War . . . Defined by one of its leaders as 'the application of the teaching of Jesus and the total message of the Christian salvation to society, the economic life, and social institutions . . . as well as to individuals,' social Christianity involved a criticism of conventional Protestantism, a progressive theology and social philosophy, and an active program of propagandism and reform.[57]

Its proponents included Washington Gladden (1836–1918), George Davis Herron (1862–1925), and Shailer Mathews (1863–1941). Preeminent among them was Walter Rauschenbusch (1861–1918). Born of a line of ministers, Rauschenbusch held for eleven years, as a young Baptist preacher, a parish in a poor area of New York City. "The . . . years spent in ministering to this poverty-stricken congregation proved to be the great dynamic experience of Rauschenbusch's life."[58] Although he later became professor of church history at Rochester Theological Seminary, his life and philosophy were shaped by his conviction that the kingdom of God on earth could never be achieved without fundamental social and economic reform. *Christianity and the Social Crisis*[59] and *Christianizing the Social Order*[60] contain the core of his ideas. He saw capitalism, exemplified by postwar American business, bringing into play such base instincts as selfishness and covetousness rather than the mutual interest, good will, and (most importantly) solidarity of the good Christian. The great corporations were contradicting American ideals and profit was becoming increasingly associated with privilege and power, rather than with the idea of a just reward for work; indeed, it was becoming the supreme value of life, competing with man's worship of God. The answer to the evils of the time was a Christian economic order, emphasizing approximate equality and cooperation, social justice, collective property rights, and industrial democracy.

> The most striking of these was the demand for justice, which underlay all the others and which he regarded as 'the fundamental step toward Christianizing the social order.' Particularly in three areas ought injustice to be corrected: private property in land and resources, private control of transportation and communication, and private monopoly of inventions and industrial processes—all of which situations had been intensified by the rise of corporate combinations able to fix prices and dictate wages.[61]

In essence, Rauschenbusch called for recognition by American churches of the inevitability of change and for their enlistment in its service, in

---

[57] Charles Howard Hopkins, *The Rise of the Social Gospel in American Protestanism 1865–1915* (New Haven, Conn.: Yale University Press, 1940), p. 3.
[58] Hopkins, *Social Gospel*, p. 216.
[59] Walter Rauschenbusch, *Christianity and the Social Crisis* (New York: Macmillan, 1907).
[60] Walter Rauschenbusch, *Christianizing the Social Order* (New York: Macmillan, 1912).
[61] Hopkins, *Social Gospel*, p. 224.

place of their continued prostitution by American capitalism. His profound influence has continued to stimulate and inform Christian thought to the present day. Martin Luther King, Jr., one of his disciples, concluded that Rauschenbusch, more than any one else, "gave to American Protestantism a sense of social responsibility that it should never lose."[62]

Louis D. Brandeis

Still another attack on plutocracy was launched by Louis D. Brandeis (1856–1941). A distinguished Boston lawyer, social inventor, publicist, and later Associate Justice of the United States Supreme Court, Brandeis stressed the "contrast between our political liberty and our industrial absolutism." In the long run the two opposite forces could not exist in the same community. Employers had become "so potent, so well organized, with such concentrated forces and with such extraordinary powers of reserve and the ability to endure . . . strikes . . . that . . . even strong unions [were] unable to cope with the situation." How much worse for the many employees still unaffiliated with a union! Such great financial power created "a condition of inequality between the two contending forces," a condition against which

> no effort of the workingmen to secure democratization will be effective. The statement that size is not a crime is entirely correct when you speak of it from the point of motive. But size may become such a danger in its results to the community that the community may have to set limits. . . . Concentration of power has been shown to be dangerous in a democracy, even though that power may be used beneficently.[63]

Brandeis advocated the solution that William Graham Sumner had thrust aside—industrial democracy.

> We must bear in mind all the time that . . . the United States is a democracy, and that we must have, above all things, men. It is the development of manhood to which any industrial and social system should be directed. We Americans are committed not only to social justice in the sense of avoiding things which bring suffering and harm, like unjust distribution of wealth, but we are committed primarily to democracy. The social justice for which we are striving is an incident of democracy—not the main end. It is rather the result of democracy—perhaps its finest expression —but it rests upon democracy, which implies the rule by the people.

Whereas most of the prophets of the Gilded Age emphasized laissez faire to secure independence not only from government but also from their own employees, Brandeis wanted more than a fair division of the profits. In addition he wanted labor to share in the management of busi-

---

[62] Quoted in Robert T. Handy, ed., *The Social Gospel in America 1870–1920* (New York: Oxford University Press, 1966), p. 259.
[63] The quotations are from Brandeis' testimony before the U.S. Commission on Industrial Relations, Senate Document 415, 64th Cong., 1st sess., XXVI, 7659–68.

ness and to shoulder industrial responsibilities. Corporations must deal with employees on equal terms; "unless they treat on equal terms . . . there is no such thing as democratization." Industrial government meant "a relation between employer and employee where the problems as they arise from day to day . . . may come up for consideration and solution as they come up in our political government." Workers should have not only voices but also *votes*, not merely the right to be heard but also "a position through which [they] may participate in management." "This participation in and eventual control of industry," Brandeis contended, was "essential for obtaining justice in distributing the fruits of industry."[64]

Industrial democracy in such terms was and still is a revolutionary concept. Brandeis realized it could never be achieved without a struggle. "All of our human experience," he observed, "shows that no one with absolute power can be trusted to give it up even in part." He was not hopeful that the economic potentates would voluntarily adopt his suggestion or even admit the inconsistency of political democracy and industrial absolutism. If corporate power continued to oppose trade unionism, however, government should exert power in behalf of labor. "The state must in some way come to the aid of the workingman if democratization is to be secured."

REFORM ON THE WAY

The most important single development in American society in the years after Appomattox was the emergence of big business. With the momentum gained from a rapidly growing population and the organized exploitation of vast and varied resources, the nation became primarily industrial rather than agricultural. Although unplanned and often ruthless, these new industrial complexes provided the American people with services and products that were often superior to those to which they had been accustomed. Yet certain observers, like Brandeis, watched the advent of the corporate age with apprehension. In his address of 1873, the chief justice of Wisconsin, Edward G. Ryan, declared:

> There is looming up a new and dark power. I cannot dwell upon the signs and shocking omens of its advent. The accumulation of individual wealth seems to be greater than it ever has been since the downfall of the Roman Empire. The enterprises of the country are aggregating vast corporate combinations of unexampled capital, boldly marching, not for economic conquests only, but for political power. For the first time really in our politics, money is taking the field as an organized power. . . . The question will [soon] arise . . . "Which shall rule—wealth or man?" . . .[65]

---

[64] "The Social Thought of Mr. Justice Brandeis," in Felix Frankfurter, ed., *Mr. Justice Brandeis* (New Haven, Conn.: Yale University Press, 1932), p. 30. For a recent consideration of the same problem, see Robert A. Dahl, "Citizens of the Corporation," *New York Times*, March 17, 1971, p. 41.

[65] Quoted in James T. Adams, *Hamiltonian Principles* (Boston: Little, Brown, 1928), p. 297.

Despite the earnest defense of plutocracy by Conwell, Carnegie, and Sumner, there could be only one answer. Even the president of the United States lent his voice to the chorus. In his Fourth Annual Message to Congress, delivered in December 1888, Grover Cleveland declared:

> . . . We discover the existence of trusts, combinations, and monopolies, while the citizen is struggling far in the rear or is trampled to death beneath an iron heel. Corporations, which should be carefully restrained creatures of the law and the servants of the people, are fast becoming the people's masters.[66]

Cleveland urged businessmen to become trustees of the public. Before long more drastic remedies were being suggested; the days of the muckraker were at hand. Although the pendulum did not swing completely to industrial or social democracy, the spell of laissez faire on American political thinking had been broken. The door to government action in behalf of the people had not been opened wide, but at least it was ajar.

---

[66] Richardson, *Messages of Presidents*, p. 774.

CHAPTER FOURTEEN

THE GOSPEL
OF SOCIAL JUSTICE

By the beginning of the twentieth century, the tide of plutocracy had begun to ebb. "The ideal of an individualistic society had given way, at least in the minds of many intellectuals . . . to the concept of a society organized for collective action in the public interest."[1] Although critics of capitalism had built a theoretical case against it, they had not descended from their daises, rostrums, and pulpits to lead the people in a specific direction. Between 1890 and the end of World War I, reformers staged a drive for social justice. Marching under the liberal banner, a variety of individuals and groups joined the procession. Each group had its outstanding spokesmen; each had its adherents. Not without good reason have these years gone down in history as the Progressive Era—the Age of Reform.[2]

---

[1] Arthur S. Link, *Woodrow Wilson and the Progressive Era 1910–1917* (New York: Harper & Brothers, 1954), p. 1.
[2] See Richard Hofstadter, *The Age of Reform From Bryan to F.D.R.* (New York: Knopf, 1965); George E. Mowry, *The Era of Theodore Roosevelt, 1900–1912,* (New York: Harper, 1958); Link, *Woodrow Wilson,* and Louis Filler, *Crusaders for American Liberalism* (New York: Harcourt, Brace and World, 1939).
For a stimulating reappraisal of Progressive thinkers, see Christopher Lasch, *New Radicalism in America, 1889–1963: The Intellectual as a Social Type* (New York: Knopf,

Although wide disagreement among the "upward and onward" fellows, as Justice Holmes dubbed reformers, dissipated their effectiveness, all rooted their ideas in popular power; all believed in man's ability, through government or by other means, to master his own destiny.

Henry George

The most specific proposal came from Henry George (1839–1897), author of a perpetual best seller, *Progress and Poverty*, and independent candidate for mayor of New York in 1886 and 1897. Born in Philadelphia, George lived in California during the great land boom, acquiring there the obsession that remained with him. Land even in remote areas, George observed, began to increase tremendously in price; speculation in land "ran far in advance of its use." One day George asked a teamster how much land in a certain area was worth. The teamster replied that he did not know exactly, but referred George to a man who was offering land for a thousand dollars an acre. "Like a flash," George later recalled, "it came upon me that there was the reason of advancing poverty with advancing wealth. With the growth of population, land grows in value, and the men who work it must pay more for the privilege."[3] Land monopoly was thus the root source of poverty.

Largely self-educated, George was a man of tremendous emotional and intellectual power. His writings are infused "with a moral protest thoroughly familiar to readers of the social gospel literature."[4] As a result his ideas spread far and inspired many.

George believed that labor was the central economic force. His experience in California proved to him that private property in land was unjust. Property was fully the product of labor—"that which a man makes or produces is his own"—and it followed that "no one can be . . . entitled to the ownership of anything which is not the produce of his labor. . . ." If the "rightfulness" of the property derived from productive efforts be acknowledged, the "wrongfulness of individual property in land" must also be acknowledged. Recognition of the former "places all men upon equal terms, securing to each the due reward of his labor"; recognition of the latter denied "the equal rights of men, permitting those who do not labor to take [in the form of rent] the natural reward of those who do." The widespread desire for land he encountered throughout the West reaffirmed his conviction that economic rent—the unearned increment in land values landowners received for no services rendered—was counter to the traditions of democracy. His remedy was to tax all (or almost all) of

---

1965). Lasch has integrated the psychological roots of Progressive ideas and the goals they sought to achieve.

[3] Henry George, Jr., quoted in E. R. Lewis, *A History of American Political Thought from the Civil War to the World War* (New York: Macmillan, 1937), p. 273. See Steven B. Cord, *Henry George: Dreamer or Realist?* (Philadelphia: University of Pennsylvania Press, 1965) and Edward J. Rose, *Henry George* (New York: Twayne Publishers, 1968).

[4] Hofstadter, *Social Darwinism*, p. 88.

that rent and to channel the income into the alleviation of social distress. The land tax would yield enough to permit the abolition of all other taxes and would produce equality of condition among all economic classes.

> Poverty deepens as wealth increases, and wages are forced down while productive power grows, because land, which is the source of all wealth and the field of all labor, is monopolized. To extirpate poverty, to make wages what justice commands they should be, the full earnings of the laborer, we must . . . substitute for the individual ownership of land a common ownership. Nothing else will go to the cause of the evil—in nothing else is there the slightest hope. . . .
>
> We must make land common property.[5]

His solution, though radical, was not inspired by nihilism. An intensely religious man, George arrived at his conclusions confident in his belief in a benevolent God. "The laws of the universe," he wrote in *Progress and Poverty*, "do not deny the natural aspirations of the human heart. . . . [T]he progress of society . . . must be, toward equality, not toward inequality . . . economic harmonies prove the truth perceived by the Stoic Emperor, 'We are made for cooperation—like feet, like hands, like eyelids, like the rows of upper and lower teeth.' " Thus, while admitting that the law of justice could be satisfied, and all economic requirements met, by abolishing all private titles to land and declaring all land public property, George did not join Marx in advocating this revolutionary solution. "Such a plan, though perfectly feasible, does not seem to me the best." He proposed to accomplish the same end "in a simpler, easier, and quieter way," namely, by confiscating rent through taxation. Individuals under this scheme might retain title to their land; they would only be deprived of the profits from it. This simple but sovereign remedy would

> raise wages, increase the earnings of capital, extirpate pauperism, abolish poverty, give remunerative employment to whoever wishes it, afford free scope to human powers, lessen crime, elevate morals, and taste, and intelligence, purify government and carry civilization to yet nobler heights. . . .

All this would be accomplished through the operation of natural economic processes, with which the institution of rent and private property in land could only interfere, and not by the "needless extension of governmental machinery," which "is to be avoided."

The reform he proposed accorded with all that was "politically, socially, or morally desirable." It was "true reform" and within the spirit of the Declaration of Independence, for it promised to make political liberty of real value by providing economic liberty for all. Moreover, it would put a halt to "the popular unrest with which the civilized world is feverishly pulsing. . . . We cannot go on permiting men to vote and forcing them

---

[5] Henry George, *Progress and Poverty* (New York: D. Appleton, 1882), pp. 362–66.

to tramp. We cannot go on educating boys and girls in our public schools and then refusing them the right to earn an honest living. We cannot go on prating of the inalienable rights of man and then denying the inalienable right of the bounty of the Creator."

George was particularly influential upon the American labor movement and succeeded as did few others in awakening "journalists, intellectuals, small capitalists, and young lawyers to a comprehension of the grave economic and social problems of the rising urban world."[6] Although the Single Tax Movement initiated by George proved disappointing even to its promoters, there are still organizations in the United States advancing his ideas.

Edward Bellamy

A few years after the appearance of *Progress and Poverty*, a new liberal movement was born, exceeding George's in popular appeal. Edward Bellamy's *Looking Backward* became a runaway best seller.[7] Bellamy "centered his fire upon the fundamental principle of the competitive system and upon the institution of private property itself."[8] Born into a minister's family in Massachusetts and trained as a lawyer, Bellamy spent his life as a newspaperman and novelist. After a number of less-distinguished novels, he published *Looking Backward* in 1888. Within a year 210,000 copies had been sold.

A book of unpretentious style and vivid imagery, it tells the story of a young man, Julian West, who fell asleep in 1887 and awoke in the house of Dr. Leete in 2000, finding himself in a modern socialist utopia—a country without poverty, misery, or greed, wherein the determination of a man's needs turns not on the quantity of material goods he produces but on the simple fact that he is a man. When Mr. West asked Dr. Leete how each individual received his share of the national product—in short, how wages were determined—Dr. Leete replied, after meditative silence, "His title is his humanity."[9]

Whereas values in nineteenth-century society were based on competition, "the instinct of selfishness," values in Bellamy's utopia were built on "the secret of efficient production." All men enjoyed society's benefits; they were driven not by the prospect of material gain but by the spirit of cooperation and social recognition.

The new socialism Bellamy described had emerged naturally, without revolution or bloodshed. "The movement toward the conduct of business by larger and larger aggregations of capital, the tendency toward monopo-

---

[6] Chester M. Destler, *American Radicalism 1865–1901* (New London, Conn.: Connecticut College, 1946), p. 13.

[7] See Walter Teller, "Speaking of Books. Looking Back at 'Looking Backward,'" *The New York Times Book Review*, December 31, 1967, pp. 2 ff.

[8] Hofstadter, *Social Darwinism*, p. 93.

[9] Edward Bellamy, *Looking Backward* (Boston: Houghton Mifflin, 1889). The quotations in this chapter are from pp. 49–244.

lies, which had been so desperately and vainly resisted, was recognized at last," Dr. Leete explained to Mr. West, "in its true significance as a process which only needed to complete its logical evolution to open a golden future to humanity. . . . In a word, the people of the United States concluded to assume the conduct of their own business, just as one hundred-odd years before they had assumed the conduct of their own government, organizing now for industrial purposes on precisely the same grounds that they had then organized for political purposes." Socialism seemed only logical to a people accustomed to corporations and syndicates handling revenues larger than those of entire states and employing hundreds of thousands of men. It became an accepted axiom that the larger the operation the simpler the principles that could be applied to it. "Thus it came about that, thanks to the corporations themselves, when it was proposed that the nation should assume their functions, the suggestion implied nothing which seemed impracticable even to the timid."

To Conwell and Carnegie, as to Spencer and Sumner, government regulation or operation of any enterprise (to say nothing of socialism) seemed impractical, if not impossible. All distrusted politics and politicians. Bellamy's Mr. West revealed the same feeling. To him nothing could be worse than to entrust politicians "with control of the wealth-producing machinery of the country." In the ideal commonwealth there were no politics or politicians, and thus the problem of graft and corruption did not arise. Society was so constituted that no way remained by which an official could make any profit for himself or misuse his power. Nor would he desire to do so, for all men were equal; each received the same economic rewards, and the rate of living was "as luxurious as we could wish." The love of money, which supplied the motive power of the Gilded Age and inevitably corrupted men, no longer was an incentive to effort; "honor . . . the hope of men's gratitude, patriotism and the inspiration of duty" had replaced it. "Diligence in the national service [had become] the sole and certain way to public repute, social distinction and official power." The coarser motives no longer moved any man, and the politicians, who had responded to such motives, were no more. Nor was government itself important. The bulk of the laws had been concerned with private property, but with none remaining, it was only necessary to administer an essentially perfect system. "Law as a special science" was obsolete; social relations in the utopia were so much simpler that "only a few of the plainest and simplest legal maxims" were applicable. Except for direction of the national industrial army, which Bellamy did not conceive to be a very difficult task, government had little to do.

Believing in his utopia, Bellamy assumed editorship of the *New Nation*, the movement's monthly magazine, and lectured and wrote extensively. Nationalist clubs were formed throughout the nation; by 1890, there were 250 such organizations, all dedicated to putting into practice the ideas enunciated in *Looking Backward*. Although the clubs had no central organization, their influence was felt on the politics of the 1890s. Bellamy believed that the Populist platform of 1892 represented a triumph for his principles.[10] He might also have claimed some credit for formation of the Socialist Party later in the same decade.

Henry D. Lloyd

A few years after publication of *Looking Backward,* a third reform proposal was advanced by Henry Demarest Lloyd (1847–1903), a Chicago newspaperman and publicist. In an *Atlantic Monthly* article of 1881, Lloyd launched an attack on the Standard Oil monopoly, causing that number of the sedate Boston periodical to go through seven editions. *Wealth Against Commonwealth,* published in 1894, was "a venture in realism in a world of realities." The product of "six years of patient, exhaustive, and remarkably farflung investigation and research,"[11] it set a model for latter-day muckrakers. Quarried from official records, court decisions, reports of state legislatures and of Congress, and various other official inquiries, with full documentation throughout, Lloyd's book laid bare the practices of American industry and the evils of monopoly. The picture was "black and damning."[12]

The facts showed that the "Law of Competition" was ruthless. The head of one refinery testified before Congress that after he had refined the oil, it was "taken and sold by another organization. We agree to take the same prices that they take for their oil. It is kind of pooled—the sale of the oil." The purpose of this procedure, he said, was "simply to hold up the price of refined oil . . . to get all we can for it. . . ."[13] But suppose a potential competitor were unwilling to pool his oil? Other "market forces" were available to deal with him. One man, planning to build a refinery, was offered a salary for life if he would not build; when he refused, the oil trust put him out of business by rebate arrangements with the railroad. In at least one investigation, the independents showed that they could produce coal more economically than the trust that had combined with the railroads to eliminate them. From this Lloyd concluded: "the unfittest, economically, survives."

Obviously, change was required. Liberty would not long survive such tactics. Somehow "the vast multitudes" must organize to function as a people in business as they did in government. Somehow, Lloyd declared, the golden rule must be observed in business transactions; somehow "We must have honesty, love, justice in the heart of the business world." Lloyd

---

[10] Edward Bellamy, "Progress of Nationalism in the United States," *North American Review,* CLIV (June, 1892), 750. For an analysis of Bellamy's influence abroad, see Sylvia E. Bowman, *Edward Bellamy Abroad: An American Prophet's Influence* (New York: Twayne Publishers, 1962).

[11] Destler, *American Radicalism,* p. 143. See also Destler, *Henry Demarest Lloyd and the Empire of Reform* (Philadelphia: University of Pennsylvania Press, 1963).

[12] Lewis, *American Political Thought,* p. 315.

[13] H. D. Lloyd, *Wealth Against Commonwealth* (New York: Harper & Brothers, 1894), p. 420. The major part of Lloyd's book is concerned with the oil trust. The quotations in these paragraphs are from pp. 13–536.

visualized a new society in which both the economic and political scales would be redressed in labor's favor.[14] A well-ordered commonwealth of labor was his goal. Thousands of years of experience had taught "that government must begin where it ends—with the people. . . . Identical is the lesson we are learning with regard to industrial power and property." To call again on the owners of property, "as mankind called upon kings in their day, to be good and kind, wise and sweet," was to call in vain. Instead, as "liberty recast the old forms of government into the Republic, [it] must [also] remould our institutions of wealth into the Commonwealth." Mere regulation would not do; antimonopoly laws were futile. "The true law of business is that all must pursue the interest of all." Society must not only acknowledge that principle but also operate upon it, so that America would be a republic "in which all join their labor that the poorest may be fed, the weakest defended, and all educated and prospered. . . ." Such a republic would provide its citizens "a private life of . . . new beauty" and make them all "travellers to Altruria."

The influence of Lloyd's book was such that it "must be viewed as a catalytic and directive influence of first importance upon the confused, angry, intellectual currents" of the period. It affected the thinking of countless Americans—among whom were Ida Tarbell, Charles E. Russell, S. S. McClure, and the hardheaded reformers, such as Louis D. Brandeis and Robert M. LaFollette.[15]

Eugene Debs

Bellamy and Lloyd were led by reflection and study to democratic socialism as a solution for the nation's ills. Practical experience as a labor organizer in Terre Haute, Indiana, guided another dissenter to the same solution. Eugene V. Debs (1855–1926), a self-educated, sometime railroad fireman and member of the Indiana legislature, was one of America's outstanding early labor leaders. At thirty-five he became national secretary-treasurer of the Brotherhood of Locomotive Firemen, serving until 1892. In 1893 he organized and became president of a new industrial union of railroad workers, the American Railway Union. As a result of his leadership of union forces during the famous Pullman strike of 1894 (broken by federal troops sent by President Cleveland over the protest of Illinois governor John Altgeld), Debs was indicted and convicted of violating the blanket injunction against the trainmen and was sentenced to six months in prison. While in jail, he became convinced of the necessity of drastic reform.

> I wish to say in the broadest possible way that I am opposing the system under which we live today because I believe it is subversive of the best interests of the people. I am not satisfied with things as they are, and I know that no

---

[14] Jacobson, *American Political Thought*, p. 554.
[15] Nichols and Nichols, *Growth of Democracy*, p. 412.

matter what administration is in power, even were it a Socialist administration, there will be no material change in the condition of the people until we have a new social system based upon the mutual economic interests of the whole people; until you and I and all of us collectively own those things that we collectively need and use.[16]

Debs was convinced that social ills were due primarily to the economic framework of society. Poverty, crime, prostitution, prisons, the legal system, were inextricably linked to the division of society into a capitalist and a laboring class, with the capitalists using government to prevent labor from obtaining more than a subsistence wage. His experience as a labor organizer had shown him the strength and the single-mindedness of the capitalists, their determination to keep labor disorganized and subservient. Trade unionism was no match for concentrated economic power; Wall Street did not fear unions and so paid no attention to them.

Debs' goal was socialism.[17] Like Marx he believed that "the working class alone does the world's work," creating wealth only to be robbed by "the capitalist exploiters." Trade unionism marked the beginning of "a new era . . . for the human race," the first step in an impending social revolution. To achieve victory, the people must render harmless "the efforts . . . by the ruling class to restrain its march, impair its utility or stamp it out of existence."

Debs, like Marx, saw the inconsistency between economic democracy and political absolutism.

> They tell us that we live in a great free republic; that our institutions are democratic; that we are a free and self-governing people. This is too much, even for a joke. But it is not a subject for levity, it is an exceedingly serious matter. . . . Who appoints our federal judges? The people? In all the history of the country the working class have never named a federal judge. When they go to the bench they go, not to serve the people, but to serve the interests that place them there and keep them where they are.[18]

Particularly vicious and dangerous to trade unionism was the *injunction*. "All the judicial gunner has to do is to touch it off" at the command of the capitalists.

> Step by step the writ of injunction has invaded the domain of trade-unionism, limiting its jurisdiction, curtailing its powers, sapping its strength and undermining its foundations. . . . [T]he institutions [that the courts] were designed to safeguard . . . [they] have shamelessly betrayed at the behest of the barons of capitalism.

[16] Eugene V. Debs, *Writings and Speeches of Eugene V. Debs* (New York: Hermitage Press, 1948), p. 298.
[17] Eugene Debs, *His Writings and Speeches* (Chicago: Kerr, 1908), pp. 119–41.
[18] Debs, *Writings and Speeches*, pp. 422–23.

Eventually labor would be driven by the courts, if by nothing else, to the "inevitable conclusion that the labor question is also a political question and that the working class must organize their political power that they may wrest the government from capitalist control and put an end to class rule forever." The democratic system itself provided the instrument. "The ballot . . . is strong enough not only to disarm the enemy, but to drive that enemy entirely from the field." "There is nothing in our government the ballot cannot remove or amend. It can make and unmake presidents and congresses and courts. . . . It can sweep over trusts, syndicates, corporations, monopolies . . . [it] can do all this and more." *Violent* revolution was not a part of Debs' philosophy; he visualized the use of democratic methods to achieve his goal.[19]

Exertion of political power was not enough. In addition the economic emphasis of trade unionism must be joined by the political emphasis of industrial unionism. Trade unionism had been concerned primarily with wage increases and strikes. Although these were important, the labor movement meant "more, infinitely more." It had political purposes as well. "Its higher object is to overthrow the capitalist system of private ownership of the tools of labor, abolish wage-slavery and achieve the freedom of the whole working class and, in fact, of all mankind." Only *industrial* unionism, uniting all labor in a solid front, would effectively achieve this object. Debs planned for the United States what later came about in England—a Socialist party, identified with the labor movement and acting as the spokesman for labor in the political arena.

When socialism was finally established, the next phase of civilization would begin. Then the people would collectively own and operate "the sources and means of wealth production"; all would "have equal right to work . . . all [would] cooperate together in producing wealth and all [would] enjoy all the fruit of their collective labor." Private ownership and production for profit would be no more, and competition would be replaced by mutuality of interests. There would be work for all, and all would receive "their socially due share" of the national product. Civilization would receive "its crowning glory—the cooperative commonwealth."

Debs was five times the Socialist party candidate for president. Both on the campaign trail and in his columns of the Socialist weekly, *Appeal to Reason*, which he edited, he advocated his program. He succeeded in attracting a large audience. But the movement he headed won no political victories, and his pacifism during World War I put an end to his effectiveness. Even so, his conception of the democratic ideal contributed significantly to the development of liberal thought in America.

Samuel Gompers

For two decades or more Debs was American socialism's chief spokesman, bringing its gospel to the American workman. But labor as a whole was

---

[19] Debs, *Writings and Speeches*, p. 171.

much more attracted to Samuel Gompers (1850–1924) and his American Federation of Labor, which finally began to win for them the recognition Debs had long urged.

Gompers was born in England and came to this country with his parents in 1863. He immediately began to work as a cigar maker and in 1864 joined the local union. He rose quickly and in 1886 became the first president of the newly formed American Federation of Labor. Except for one year, 1895, when a Socialist uprising capitalizing upon widespread economic depression defeated him, he served in that capacity until his death.

The failure of those who put participation in the political process and in social goals above the pay envelope led Gompers to dissolve all connections with mere theory. He advocated practical solutions, step-by-step approaches to day-to-day problems—in short, ad hoc decisions, thoroughgoing pragmatism. Poverty, depressions, competition with immigrant labor, conflict with owners, and continuous war with left-wing elements within the ranks of labor—all went into the formulation of his ideas and program. Socialism, capitalism, and the miserable conditions of wage earners were at once the obstacles and foundations of his labor leadership.

"Unionism pure and simple" was his solution. Life in the shop had demonstrated that the immediate, pressing needs were higher wages, shorter hours, sanitary working conditions, and adequate housing. These gains for the wage earners could be won only through organization. Never should the union be subordinated "to any 'ism' or political 'reform.' We knew [Gompers wrote later] that the trade union was the fundamental agency through which we could achieve economic power, which would in turn give us social and political power."

> I strove to make the American movement practical, deep-rooted in sympathy and sentiment. I refused to concede one single inch of labor activity to any other movement."[20]

Gompers did not quarrel with the institutions of private property or capitalism. He simply wanted a larger share of the national income for labor. "More, more, more, now," was his goal. "The A.F. of L. stands squarely and unequivocally for the defense and maintenance of the existing order and for its development and improvement."[21]

> Economic betterment—today, tomorrow, in home and shop, was the foundation upon which trade unions have been built. Economic power is the basis upon which may be developed power in other fields. It is the foundation of organized society. Whoever or whatever controls economic power directs and shapes development of the group or the nation.[22]

---

[20] Samuel Gompers, *Seventy Years of Life and Labor* (New York: Dutton, 1943), pp. 209–10, 230.
[21] Louis S. Reed, *The Labor Philosophy of Samuel Gompers* (New York: Columbia University Press, 1930), pp. 12, 21.
[22] Gompers, *Life and Labor*, pp. 286–87.

Basically Gompers conceived of society in Spencerian terms. Labor and business should be left alone to fight it out between themselves. Governmental action, even on behalf of labor, weakened the moral fiber and virility of the community.

> Compulsory sickness insurance for workers is based upon the theory that they are unable to look after their own interest and the state must interpose its wisdom and assume the relation of parent or guardian. There is something in the very suggestion of this relationship and this policy that is repugnant to free born citizens.[23]

Labor must protect its own rights.

> I saw that leadership in labor could be safely entrusted only to those into whose hearts and minds had been woven the experiences of earning their bread by daily labor. I saw that betterment for workingmen must come primarily through workingmen.[24]

Like Spencer, Gompers was suspicious even of legislation covering working hours. "Political momentum" was as much of a bugaboo to one as to the other. If the workers

> surrender control over working relations to legislative and administrative agents, they put their industrial liberty at the disposal of state agents. They strip themselves bare of means of defense; they can no longer defend themselves by the strike. To insure liberty and personal welfare, personal relations must be controlled only by those concerned.[25]

And by that Gompers meant unions. Keeping his attention focused on the gradual improvement of the craft workers' status through unionization, Gompers provided the most immediately attainable results of any of the reformers of the period. The number of unions and union members climbed steadily, and under Gompers' leadership the American Federation of Labor became the dominant voice of the American workingman. Many of its demands—a six-hour day and a five-day week, unemployment insurance under government control, workmen's compensation, abolition of child labor, equal pay for men and women for equal work, compulsory education laws—later became law.

POLITICAL ACTION:
REFORM ACCOMPLISHED

Although each of the reformers advanced a specific remedy and worked hard to get it adopted, none were popular with the American people, for

---

[23] Reed, *Philosophy of Gompers*, p. 115.
[24] Gompers, *Life and Labor*, p. 115.
[25] Quoted in 1911 Annual Report, A.F. of L. Convention, quoted in Lewis, *American Political Thought*, p. 262.

they were ahead of their times. Parts of their philosophies were indeed adopted, but neither of the two dominant political parties embraced any of them until the 1930s.

Populism

Concrete action grew out of the discontent of farmers, whose plight had not been the central concern of the reformers. The Interstate Commerce Commission, established by Congress in 1887, was the direct result of the abuses farmers endured at the hands of railroads—discriminatory rates and rebates to favored customers. The ICC can also be regarded as a delayed triumph of the Granger movement and the Farmers' Alliance, the first organized agrarian protest movements in the United States. Both organizations, being essentially nonpartisan, could not move squarely into the arena of public-policy matters. As Ignatius Donnelly (1831–1901), agrarian reformer, editor, and a founder of the Populist party put it: "This creation of a nonpolitical organization was like making a gun that will do everything but shoot."[26] Needed was a reform-oriented political party—hence, the creation, in 1892, of the Populist, or People's, party.

The Populist platform contained a long list of agrarian grievances, along with specific reform suggestions. "It horrified the Eastern conservatives by proclaiming that 'tramps and millionaires' came from 'the same prolific womb of governmental injustice.' " "The time had come," the Populists declared, "when the railroad corporations will either own the people or the people must own the railroads. . . ."

> In deadly earnest, they were leading an impassioned campaign to relieve the misfortunes of the farmer. The smile faded from Republicans and Democrats alike as countless thousands of Populists sang, "Good-bye, My Party, Good-bye."[27]

In 1892 the Populist presidential candidate, James B. Weaver, received over one million popular votes and twenty-two electoral votes; ten Populist representatives, five Populist senators, three Populist governors, and fifteen hundred Populist members of state legislatures were elected. The concentration of Populist strength was in the semiarid agricultural regions of the West. In the elections of 1894, Populist strength increased. In 1896 the Populists supplied the Democratic party and its candidate, William Jennings Bryan, with the focal point of their campaign—free coinage of silver. The Populists were persuaded to support Bryan, though in a vain effort to retain their independence they nominated a different candidate for Vice President. With the election of the Republican standard bearer,

---

[26] Quoted in John Hicks, *The Populist Revolt* (Lincoln, Neb.: University of Nebraska Press, 1961), p. 206.
[27] Thomas A. Bailey, *The American Pageant. A History of the Republic* (Boston: Heath, 1966), pp. 585, 590.

William McKinley, and the increase in farm prices, the Populist party was undone—but not quite. For "to list their demands is to cite the chief political innovations made in the United States in recent times."[28] Moreover, Populism was the first large-scale movement to attack industrial dominance seriously. In unleashing a relentless flow of protest, it aroused Americans from their complacency and stirred in the masses a political awareness and a capacity for indignation.[29]

> The Populists' main service was to usher in a long-needed and long-delayed era of reform [in politics]. . . . [T]he Populists were the first important movement in this country to insist that laissez-faire economics was not the solution to industrial problems and that the federal government had some responsibility for social well-being.[30]

Theodore Roosevelt

Although the reform impulse seemed momentarily to subside, a crusade, supported by the Muckrakers, continued "in various levels and . . . in different directions. . . . The first reform wave came in the cities, with a great drive to overturn the politicians allied with corporations, railroads, and utilities. Considerable success in this endeavor led next to campaigns to capture the state governments. . . ."[31] With the Democrats in decline and confusion, reform, to be effective, had to permeate the Republican party and enlist its flamboyant leader, Theodore Roosevelt (1858–1919).

Roosevelt emerged from local and state politics in New York to a national prominence sufficient to win election as vice-president in 1900. With McKinley's assassination in 1901, he assumed both party and national leadership. During his administrations (he was elected in his own right in 1904) TR gave official recognition and leadership to reform in general and to individual projects. In his seven and a half years in office, Roosevelt tackled "trust-busting" with characteristic vigor, initiating forty-five actions against trusts.[32] He was also instrumental in securing passage of the first conservation legislation. He inspired the Elkins Act of 1903, which forbade railroad rebates on freight rates; the Hepburn Act of 1906, which gave the federal government greater power over railroads; and the first legislation protecting the consumer of meat, food, and drugs. In all his actions Roosevelt made it clear, however, that his concern was not to abolish big business but to regulate it. During his tenure in office,

---

[28] Hicks, *Populist Revolt*, p. 407.
[29] Hofstadter, *Age of Reform*, p. 60.
[30] John M. Blum, et al., *The National Experience* (New York: Harcourt, Brace and World, 1963), p. 484.
[31] Link, *Woodrow Wilson*, p. 2.
[32] The Sherman Anti-Trust Act was passed in 1890, as a necessary gesture on the part of Congress to increase public opposition to "combinations in restraint of trade." It was made virtually meaningless by the Supreme Court's decision in *U.S.* v. *E.C. Knight Company*, 156 U.S. 1, (1895).

the power of the national government—and of the presidency—was vastly
expanded.

Herbert Croly

Nevertheless, Roosevelt's presidency lacked an overall reform policy. If
during "the last few years of his presidency [he] . . . set forth his developing concept of the federal government as a dynamic force in the social
and economic affairs of men . . . he had not yet formulated a coherent
political philosophy. . . ."[33] Nor did he do so until after the publication
in 1909 of Herbert Croly's *Promise of American Life*.[34] Croly (1869–1930)
was the first editor of the *Architectural Record* and founder and editor of
the *New Republic*. *The Promise of American Life* was his first book,
marked, unfortunately, by a "heavy, Latinate and repetitious style."[35]
Even so, it was "easily the best political treatise to come out of the progressive ferment."[36] Croly's basic argument was that the original purpose
of the American people—to liberate and enlarge the individual—had
been lost, both in business and politics, in the pursuit of a false ideal—
laissez faire. He offered instead a "new nationalism," a redirecting of
America toward its avowed ends through the use of governmental power.
"What he demanded was nothing less than that . . . Hamiltonian means
[be adopted] to achieve Jeffersonian, or democratic, ends."[37] While retaining the stress on individual rights, he countenanced their restriction when
necessary for the greater good. The promise of American life, he wrote

> can never be redeemed by an indiscriminate individual scramble for wealth.
> The individual competition, even when it starts under fair conditions and
> rules, results, not only, as it should, in the triumph of the strongest, but in an
> attempt to perpetuate the victory; and it is this attempt which must be recog-
> nized and forestalled in the interest of the American national purpose. . . .
> No voluntary association of individuals, resourceful and disinterested though
> they be, is competent to assume the responsibility. The problem belongs to
> the American national democracy, and its solution must be attempted chiefly
> by means of official national action.[38]

Economic organization should be countered by political organization.
    Croly overlooked a number of areas—particularly agrarian issues—and
demonstrated, perhaps, an undue concern for efficiency. Yet he understood, perhaps better than anyone else, the pitfalls of yielding to the
"predominant yearning for individualism" in economic and political

---

[33] Link, *Woodrow Wilson*, p. 18.
[34] Herbert Croly, *Promise of American Life* (New York: Macmillan, 1909).
[35] Arthur M. Schlesinger, Jr., ed., Croly, *American Life*, John Howard Library ed.
(Cambridge, Mass.: Harvard University Press, 1965), p. xiv.
[36] Link, *Woodrow Wilson*, p. 18.
[37] Link, *Woodrow Wilson*, p. 19.
[38] Croly, *American Life*, p. 24.

affairs[39] and the necessity of giving the organization, administration, and management of national affairs a central focus. "To conceive [of] democracy as essentially a matter of popular political machinery" was to weaken it fatally. Equally necessary was a mechanism, a structure, "to give positive momentum and direction to popular rule."[40] Roosevelt responded to the challenge enthusiastically, making New Nationalism the leitmotiv of his unsuccessful 1912 campaign against Woodrow Wilson.

Roosevelt, retiring in 1908, virtually handpicked his successor, William Howard Taft, only to be grievously disappointed. Taft's basic conservatism also alienated the LaFollette[41] progressive wing of the Republican party. Thus, to preserve what he considered the essential liberal thrust of the GOP, Roosevelt reentered the political arena. The Republican-controlled convention of 1912 renominated Taft. Frustrated and angry, Roosevelt bolted the party and organized the Progressive—or "Bull Moose"—party, thereby virtually assuring the Democrats of victory.

Roosevelt had not intended that outcome. He entered the contest in all sincerity. His "Confession of Faith," delivered at the Progressive Convention in Chicago, was a thoughtful "statement of social and economic principles that was a classic synthesis of the most advanced thought of the time."[42] Like the Populist program of 1892, the Progressive platform of 1912 carried forward the liberal thrust of American thought. The things it called for were numerous: a minimum wage for women, prohibition of child labor, workmen's compensation, and social insurance; the adoption of the initiative, referendum and recall, and the recall for judicial officers; the institution of a nationwide presidential primary and full publicity to campaign contributions and expenditures; a federal trade commission with extensive power over business and industrial activity, and a tariff commission. The voters, however, rejected the Progressive party's candidate. Roosevelt won only 88 electoral votes to 435 for Wilson, but garnered 4,119,538 popular votes to Wilson's 6,293,454.

For Roosevelt the loss was crushing. But it was not so disastrous for exponents of social justice. The victorious candidate himself was a

---

[39] Hofstadter, *Age of Reform*, p. 6.

[40] Herbert Croly, *Progressive Democracy* (New York: Macmillan, 1914), pp. 213–14. Note should be made of the contribution to the Progressive campaign of 1912 by Walter E. Weyl (1873–1919), an associate editor of the *New Republic* and a close associate of Croly's. An economist, Weyl published in 1912 a penetrating survey of political and economic tendencies in the United States, entitled *The New Democracy* (New York: Macmillan, 1912). That book, like Croly's *Promise of American Life*, had a powerful influence on Roosevelt and, subsequently, on Wilson. Some of Weyl's specific suggestions were incorporated into the New Nationalism and the New Freedom.

[41] Robert M. LaFollette (1855–1925) of Wisconsin was an independent reformer with an exceptionally loyal following. The reforms he secured in Wisconsin in two terms as governor were firsts in the nation. He was elected to the U.S. Senate in 1906 as a Republican and became the foremost crusader for liberal reform. Later (in 1924) he broke with the Republican party and ran as candidate for president on his own Progressive party ticket.

[42] Link, *Woodrow Wilson*, p. 16.

reformer. In fact, modern historians tend to link Roosevelt's New Nationalism (the tag for his 1912 program, borrowed from Croly) and Wilson's New Freedom.

Woodrow Wilson

Between the Gilded Age and World War I, Woodrow Wilson (1856–1924) was America's most effective reformer. Virginia born and, in rapid succession, professor of jurisprudence at Princeton University, president of Princeton, Governor of New Jersey, and President of the United States, Wilson was a man of strong democratic sentiments. In quest of campus reform, he clashed with Princeton's conservative leadership. As Governor of New Jersey, he forced through the legislature an employers' liability act, a law providing for the direct primary and a forward-looking corrupt practices act. As President of the United States, he called for a "New Freedom." Whereas other reformers could command only limited audiences for their ideas, Wilson presented his platform to the entire nation. Had World War I not intervened and wrought even greater change, the national regulatory legislation he advocated might have altered the course of our history.

Wilson's contribution to American liberal thought lay not so much in the reforms he advocated—most of these had been suggested by others—as in the advanced theory of public power and leadership he developed. Throughout American history, he believed, popular power had been suspect—had been feared and denounced. At both the national and the state levels, various constitutional devices were fashioned to purify, frustrate, or even defeat it. Leadership rooted in public power and determined to use it in the service of mankind had often been accused of being inevitably demagogic. Americans had come to think of their constitution "as an admirable reservoir in which the mighty waters of democracy are held at rest," rather than as an active force for good.[43] They often overlooked the facts that progress is motion, government is action. Wilson's entire program was based on this last belief. "It is perfectly clear to every man who has any vision of the immediate future," he declared in 1913, "that we are just upon the threshold of a time when the systematic life of this country will be sustained, or at least supplemented, at every point by governmental activity."[44] It was vital that the waters of democracy "drive the wheels of policy and administration." Rather than permit them to remain useless in their reservoirs, leadership must canalize and direct them. The power that lies in the masses must be released. Leadership could liberate the "people's vital energies" and restore to them "in very truth the control of [their] government. . . ."[45]

[43] Woodrow Wilson, *An Old Master and Other Political Essays* (New York: Scribner's, 1893), p. 135.
[44] Woodrow Wilson, *The New Freedom* (New York: Doubleday, 1913), p. 205.
[45] Wilson, *New Freedom*, p. 277.

294 THE GOSPEL OF SOCIAL JUSTICE

Wilson often said he was not afraid of the American people doing something; he was more afraid that they would do nothing. Although a thoroughgoing conservative by temperament, he was frank to recognize what the Randolphs, the Kents, and the Upshurs had not dared to face: the inevitable shift of power from the few to the many. Indeed, he welcomed change. It was necessary for devising new political formulas to fit the new order to the convenience and prosperity of the average man. Wilson was convinced that the "treasure of America [lay in] the inventions of unknown men . . . the originations of unknown men . . . the ambitions of unknown men. Every country is renewed out of the ranks of the unknown. . . ." It was essential, therefore, that such men not be swallowed up in an industrial system made exclusively for the big fellows. Somehow the monopoly of industrial power must be broken. The government itself must be returned to the people and used as a positive force to create "the conditions which will make it tolerable for us to live." Wilson demanded that the Hamiltonian idea (long operative in the United States) that the masses need the guardianship of men of affairs be repudiated and the "original Americanism, . . . faith in the ability of a confident, resourceful, and independent people" be restored. Such a people could, through the use of their government, make and preserve the "perfect adjustments of human interests and human activities and human energies" that, taken together, constitute human freedom.

Woodrow Wilson's victory in 1912 seemed to herald the beginning of a new era. In much the same vein as Theodore Roosevelt a decade earlier, but even more forcefully, Wilson spoke in terms of the American ideal and expressed the widespread desire of "all the masses of humble and ordinary folk" for a fuller and richer life. During the first two years of his first administration, he demonstrated that his was not "the mere idealism of the impractical dreamer."[46] Under his leadership tariff rates were reduced to the lowest point in years, bringing goods of many kinds at less cost to American consumers. Sounder banking methods were assured. The Federal Trade Commission was established, and though the act creating it was vaguely worded, it left no doubt that Congress had "departed from the old faith that sharp competition [and laissez faire] would of itself bring prosperity, and indicated a trend toward a new faith—in government regulation of business enterprises for the public interest."[47] The Clayton Anti-Trust Act strengthened the possibility of government control of trusts and pointed in the direction of a return to freer enterprise. Use of the injunction in labor disputes was limited and an eight-hour day was provided for trainmen in interstate commerce. The Federal Land Banks were established to lend money to farmers at lower rates of interest than those offered in commercial banks, and the Smith-Lever Act of 1914 greatly expanded government aid to education in agriculture and home economics.

---

[46] Adams, *Epic of America*, pp. 363–64.
[47] Beard, *Basic History*, p. 392.

Drawing heavily on ideas developed earlier, Wilson believed his New Freedom would provide the American people with an opportunity to "square every process of our national life . . . with the standard we so proudly set up at the beginning and have always carried in our hearts. . . . We shall restore, not destroy. We shall deal with our economic system as it is and as it may be modified. . . . The Nation has been deeply stirred, stirred by a solemn passion . . . by the knowledge of wrong, of ideals lost, of government too often debauched and made an instrument of evil. . . ."

LIBERALISM TRIUMPHANT

Out of the struggle emerged a new and more liberal political philosophy, along with a new role for the national government. Social control seemed to be winning general acceptance, and the virtues of economic democracy were becoming generally recognized. The United States had, indeed, "reached a climax in democratic advance. . . ."[48]

By 1912 there was widespread concern for the greatest degree of freedom consistent with the conditions of modern life. Under the banner of Woodrow Wilson's New Freedom, widespread reform was achieved. The people had secured a more direct role at the local, state, and national level. Women had gained the right to vote. Railroads and trusts had been brought under regulation. Legislation had been enacted to control corrupt practices, and a great many social problems had received governmental attention. Laissez faire, "the old dog eat dog philosophy of free enterprise," had been considerably modified. In the ascendency was the view that the program of a government of freedom must in these days be positive," must, as Gompers put it, serve to channel human effort constantly "to the material, physical, social and moral betterment of the people."

---

[48] Nichols and Nichols, *Growth of Democracy*, p. 611.

CHAPTER FIFTEEN

RESISTANCE FROM
THE SUPREME COURT

By the turn of the century, reformist ideas had scored notable successes at the polls and in legislative halls, but a stable majority of converts to the broad new program of social action had not yet been won in the United States Supreme Court. Sharing the Court's views were leading lawyers and commentators. Arthur Twining Hadley (1856–1930), professor of political economy and first lay president of Yale, wrote in 1908:

> However much public feeling may at times move in the direction of social-istic measures, there is no nation which *by its constitution* is so far removed from socialism. . . . In America . . . the rights of private property are . . . formally established in the Constitution itself. . . .[1]

Pointing to the due process clauses of the Fifth and Fourteenth Amendments[2] and the clause that prohibits states from impairing the obligation of contracts, Hadley declared it "the positive authority of the judges" to safeguard property from the depredations of government.

---

[1] A. T. Hadley, "The Constitutional Position of Property in America," *The Independent*, LIV (April 9, 1908), 834–38.

[2] Hadley does not present the due process clauses as occurring in the amendments. The implication is that they were part of the original Constitution.

The general status of the property owner under the law cannot be changed by the action of the legislature or the executive, or the people of a State voting at the polls, or all three put together. It cannot be changed without either a consensus of opinion among the judges. . . .

When it is said, as it commonly is, that the fundamental division of powers in the modern State is into legislative, executive and judicial, the student of American institutions may fairly note an exception. The fundamental division of powers in the Constitution of the United States is between voters on the one hand and property owners on the other. The forces of democracy on one side, divided between the executive and the legislature, are set over against the forces of property on the other side, with the judiciary as arbiter between them; the Constitution itself not only forbidding the legislature and executive to trench upon the rights of property, but compelling the judiciary to define and uphold those rights in a manner provided by the Constitution itself.

This theory of American politics has not often been stated. But it has been universally acted upon. One reason why it has not been more frequently stated is that it has been acted upon so universally that no American of earlier generations ever thought it necessary to state it. It has had the most fundamental and far-reaching effects upon the policy of the country. To mention but one thing among many, it has allowed the experiment of universal suffrage to be tried under conditions essentially different from those which led to its ruin in Athens or in Rome. The voter was omnipotent—within a limited area. He could make what laws he pleased, as long as those laws did not trench upon property rights. He could elect what officers he pleased, as long as those officers did not try to do certain duties confided by the Constitution to the property holders. Democracy was complete as far as it went, but constitutionally it was bound to stop short of social democracy.

Hadley's widely approved thesis took the ground from under liberal pleas for political action. If it had been true, as he maintained, that his theory had been "universally acted upon," then any legislative action to secure social democracy would have been ruled out automatically. Woodrow Wilson, and others who advocated liberal ideas, would have been rated irresponsible demagogues. The fact is, however, that the theory Hadley described so graphically in 1908 was a recent development in America's constitutional jurisprudence. In a series of cases, including the landmark 1876 decision in *Munn* v. *Illinois*,[3] the Supreme Court had developed an attitude of toleration toward state regulatory legislation. It had held repeatedly that the Constitution imposed no impassable barriers against government regulation, including price fixing, in businesses "affected with a public interest." It was of the very essence of government, Chief Justice Waite remarked in the *Munn* case, that the manner in which property would be used might be regulated "when such regulation becomes necessary for the public good." The principle had been followed in England for over two hundred years and was not rejected in the Constitution. The Fourteenth Amendment did not alter its effectiveness. Waite reasoned that if facts could exist that might, in the legislature's

---

[3] 94 U.S. 111 (1876).

judgment, conceivably clothe a business with a public interest, and thus justify regulation, the Court would assume that they did exist. "We accept as true the statements of fact contained in the elaborate brief of one of the counsel of the plaintiffs in error."

In 1887 Justice John M. Harlan spoke for the Court in the same vein.[4] Because no contrary facts were presented of which the Court must take judicial cognizance, and because

> it does not appear upon the face of the statute [in question] . . . that it infringes rights secured by the fundamental law, the legislative determination of those questions is conclusive upon the courts. It is not a part of their functions to conduct investigations of facts . . . and to sustain or frustrate the legislative will, embodied in statutes, as they may happen to approve or disapprove its determination of such questions.

The Supreme Court also ruled that if a property owner felt aggrieved by a particular regulation, he should, under well-established principles of free government, resort to the polls and not to the courts. The primary control on government was political, as Madison had said in *Federalist* Number 51. Even in 1903 the Court, speaking again through Justice Harlan, reasoned that if the statute in the case before it were "mischievous in its tendencies," the responsibility for remedying its bad effects rested with "legislators, not upon the courts."[5]

Under this tolerant doctrine the Supreme Court upheld a substantial amount of social legislation in the years after the Civil War. Usury and granger laws, Sunday observance, lottery prohibition, and liquor regulation were all sustained as legitimate examples of the police power. Moreover, the Court recognized and approved legislative discretion in dealing with social and economic problems. It presumed such legislation constitutional "unless [it was] plainly and palpably, beyond all question, in violation of the fundamental law of the Constitution."[6] In the face of such pronouncements, Hadley's claim seems altogether unfounded.

THE COURT ENACTS LAISSEZ FAIRE

Thomas M. Cooley

By 1880, however, certain forces and factors were already at work moving the Court toward the position Hadley described so vividly. By the end of the first decade of the new century, the trend was unmistakable. In large part the Court was pushed into its new attitude by the nation's leading lawyers. The most notable onslaught came from the chief justice of Michigan, Thomas M. Cooley (1824–1898). Teacher, judge, publicist, and

---

[4] 127 U.S. 678 (1888), 685–86.
[5] *Atkin* v. *Kansas*, 191 U.S. 207 (1903), 224.
[6] *Atkin* v. *Kansas*.

for three generations a leading authority on American constitutional law, he published in 1868 his famous treatise on constitutional limitations.[7] That same year the Fourteenth Amendment, denying the states power to deprive any persons of "life, liberty or property" without "due process of law," was added to the Constitution. Laissez faire capitalism was thus supplied with both an authoritative constitutional ideology and a constitutional text to guard and promote its interests.

Benjamin R. Twiss described Cooley's work as "an expression in political and legal terms of American individualistic philosophy." As such it formed the groundwork for all laissez faire constitutional doctrine. "By identifying the constitutional clause, 'due process of law,' with the older doctrine of vested rights which had hitherto been used for the protection of property, [Cooley] performed his greatest service to lawyers and judges seeking to embody laissez faire in American constitutional law. . . ."[8] "By word or implication he made this small constitutional phrase comprehend most of the other implied limitations upon interference with property rights, including vested rights and even his concept of public purpose."[9]

In the *Slaughterhouse Cases* of 1873, the Supreme Court heard, for the first time, counsel argue the Cooley doctrine. The case involved the constitutionality of a Louisiana statute establishing a monopoly for the slaughter of livestock. Opposing the monopoly, former Supreme Court Justice John A. Campbell traced "the origins of several ideas and phrases through which the legalizing of laissez faire was accomplished."[10] Because it imposed an involuntary servitude on the consumers of Louisiana, Campbell argued, the state-created monopoly violated the Thirteenth Amendment. It also abridged the privileges and immunities of a thousand butchers, denied them the equal protection of the laws, and deprived them of liberty and property without due process of law.[11] The Fourteenth Amendment, Campbell declared, "was designed to secure individual liberty, individual property, and individual security and honor from arbitrary, partial, proscriptive and unjust legislation of state governments."[12]

Spurning Campbell's invitation to become (under the Fourteenth Amendment) a "perpetual censor" on all state legislation, the Court suggested that the aggrieved butchers seek remedy in the state courts. Undaunted, the campaigners for incorporating laissez faire into the Constitution continued. When the principles Cooley described were flouted by the Waite Court, he took up the cudgels in an article in *The Princeton*

---

[7] Thomas M. Cooley, *A Treatise on Constitutional Limitations* (Boston: Little, Brown, 1868).

[8] Benjamin R. Twiss, *Lawyers and the Constitution* (Princeton, N.J.: Princeton University Press, 1942), pp. 18, 25–26.

[9] Twiss, *Lawyers and the Constitution*, p. 26.

[10] Twiss, *Lawyers and the Constitution*, p. 43.

[11] Twiss, *Lawyers and the Constitution*, pp. 44–45.

[12] *Slaughterhouse Cases*, 16 Wallace 25 (1873), 36.

Review of 1878,[13] declaring that by far "the larger part of all doubtful legislation which the history of the country presents has taken place since . . . 1846, when radical ideas began to be characteristic of state constitutions, and the theory that officers of every department should be made as directly as possible responsible to the people after short terms of service, was accepted as a political maxim." Against this threat of popular power and "doubtful legislation," Cooley offered two safeguards: the Constitution itself and the operation of the inexorable law of supply and demand. Denouncing current legislative violations of property, he insisted that they violated both the "fixed and permanent" principles of the Constitution and the "laws . . . inherent in the nature and circumstances of civilized society," the operation of which were not "likely to be improved by legislative interference."

"It is not to be understood," Cooley asserted, "to be now pretended that any general right to fix the price of commodities or to limit charges for services can exist as a part of any system of free government." "Does . . . the mere fact," he inquired, "that one owns the whole supply of anything, whether it be of a certain kind of goods or of a certain kind of service, confer upon the state the authority to interfere and limit the price he may set upon his wares or his services? . . . Suppose in some state a single individual should own the only mine in the country of some metal important for use in mechanical arts; would it be competent for the state, on the ground that competition with him was impossible, to restrict at discretion the price he should be able to charge for it? . . . Whoever shall undertake to answer these questions in the affirmative should be expected to show how the power may be harmonized with the general principles of free government." Such a demonstration was precisely what Chief Justice Waite accomplished two years earlier in his opinion for the Court in *Munn* v. *Illinois*.

Pressure from the Bar

In the year Cooley's article appeared lawyers organized the American Bar Association and began a persistent propaganda campaign to have the Supreme Court's earlier attitude of toleration replaced by Cooley's doctrine that property was, in effect, a divine right. Slowly, members of the Supreme Court became converted. The arguments of such eminent lawyers as Joseph H. Choate and Roscoe Conkling of the New York bar were added to those of Judge Cooley and Justice Campbell. In his brief for the appellee in *Mugler* v. *Kansas*,[14] Choate stressed the fact that constitutional provisions for the security of person and property should be liberally construed and (like Hadley twenty years later) declared that it was "the duty of the courts to be watchful of constitutional rights" and of any encroach-

---

[13] T. M. Cooley, "Limits to State Control of Private Business," *Princeton Review*, March, 1878.
[14] 123 U.S. 623 (1887), 646.

ments thereon. Even earlier, Conkling, who as a United States Senator had been a member of the committee that drafted the Fourteenth Amendment, had told the Court that it was the intention of the framers to make it an additional device for the protection of property:

> At the time the Fourteenth Amendment was ratified, individuals and joint stock companies were appealing for congressional and administrative protection against invidious and discriminating state and local taxes. . . . Those who devised the Fourteenth Amendment . . . planted in the Constitution a monumental truth to stand foursquare to whatever wind might blow. That truth is but the Golden Rule, so entrenched as to curb the many who would do to the few as they would not have the few do to them.[15]

A majority of the Court justices continued for a while, nevertheless, to restrain themselves and to uphold state regulatory action; on one occasion the Court even noted that the contrary views current among corporation lawyers afforded "abundant evidence" that they had "some strange misconception" of a broad power vested in the judiciary to "frustrate the legislative will."[16] However, the dissenters—notably Justices Stephen J. Field, Rufus W. Peckham, and William Strong—not only took exception to the majority's construction of the Constitution but also claimed to find additional protection for property against legislative interference in the spirit of the age and the character of American institutions.

Yet the most detailed search, conducted in 1890 by Charles C. Marshall (1860–1938), a distinguished lawyer, uncovered no support for any such doctrinal dragnet. Marshall concluded that a number of Supreme Court cases, of which *Munn* v. *Illinois* was only one, demonstrated the existence of an inherent power in state legislatures on which state constitutions imposed no check: "What the citizen owns is not absolute property but a *qualified* and *contingent* interest in property. Control by the legislature is its necessary incident, and such control, when exercised through a statute, is in its very self 'due process of law.' " Only by a constitutional amendment could a change be introduced. There was no possibility of reversing judicial precedent, except by repudiating the idea: "The possibility of retracing steps, of reversing or distinguishing, or of otherwise [acting] through the courts is . . . quite beyond possibility."[17]

The Court Capitulates

But Marshall had taken into account neither the impact of the American Bar Association's campaign nor the probable effect of a change of judicial

---

[15] Quoted in B. B. Hendrick, *The Journal of the Joint Committee of Fifteen on Reconstruction,* 39th Cong., 1865–1867 (1914), pp. 32, 34. Writing in 1938, Howard Jay Graham showed that Conkling was guilty of a fraud, or at least of a trick unworthy of a great lawyer. See "The 'Conspiracy Theory' of the Fourteenth Amendment," *Yale Law Journal,* XLVII (January, 1938), 371.

[16] *Davidson* v. *New Orleans,* 96 U.S. (1878), 97, 103–4.

[17] Charles C. Marshall, "A New Constitutional Amendment," *American Law Review,* XXIV (November–December, 1890), 908–31.

personnel. Nor did he understand (as Webster did in 1820) the property owners' peculiar genius for finding new ways of limiting and controlling popular power. Suddenly, in 1890, the Supreme Court accomplished by judicial decision what Marshall had said was possible only by constitutional amendment: the Court shifted its position regarding legislative power over property and virtually overruled *Munn* v. *Illinois*. In *Chicago, Milwaukee and St. Paul Railroad Company* v. *Minnesota*,[18] the Court declared that the Minnesota legislature's rate-making power, even in businesses affected with a public interest, was limited; that rates set by statute must yield a fair return on a fair valuation of the property in question; and that the Supreme Court, not the state legislature, was the final arbiter of fairness. In effect, the Court virtually established itself as a third legislature.

For this achievement no small amount of credit must go to the counsel for the railroad, John W. Cary, whose brief Justice Samuel Blatchford (1820–1893) followed in his opinion for the Court.

> The question of the reasonableness of a rate of charge for transportation by a railroad company, involving as it does the element of reasonableness both as regards the company and as regards the public, is eminently a question for judicial investigation, requiring due process of law for its determination. If the company is deprived of the power of charging reasonable rates for the use of its property, and such deprivation takes place in the absence of an investigation by judicial machinery, it is deprived of the lawful use of its property, and thus, in substance and effect, of the property itself . . . in violation of the Constitution of the United States.[19]

Three justices dissented. Justice Joseph P. Bradley, speaking for himself and for Justices Horace Gray and L. C. Q. Lamar, denounced the Court's decision as "an assumption of authority on the part of the judiciary which . . . it has no right to make. . . . It may be that our legislatures are invested with too much power, open, as they are, to influences so dangerous to the interests of individuals, corporations, and society. But such is the Constitution of our republican form of government; and we are bound to abide by it until it can be corrected in a legitimate way."[20]

Such misgivings were of no avail. A majority of the justices were persuaded. In *Allgeyer* v. *Louisiana* of 1897,[21] Justice Rufus Peckham (1837–1909) reached out toward issues that need not have been raised, and chose —with the consent of his brethren—to view the Louisiana Act regulating insurance companies as a "real" interference with "the liberty of the defendants to place insurance on property of their own" as they pleased. It is idle to argue that he went out of his way to do it; for, to the individualistic mind of Mr. Justice Peckham, his was the only way. It was

---

[18] 134 U.S. 418 (1890).
[19] 134 U.S. 418 (1890), 458.
[20] 134 U.S. 418 (1890), 462, 466.
[21] 165 U.S. 578 (1897).

a superb opportunity to bring the orthodoxy of classical economics into the higher law, and he was not going to allow it to pass. In the name of due process of law, freedom of contract was thrown up as a fence about the domain of business enterprise against the incursions of the state. And no one on the high bench ventured a contrary opinion.[22]

The new principle was reaffirmed the next year in *Smyth* v. *Ames*:

> The idea that any legislature, state or federal, can conclusively determine for the people and for the courts that what it enacts in the form of laws, or what it authorizes its agents to do, is consistent with the fundamental law, is in opposition to the theory of our institutions. The duty rests upon all courts, federal and state, when their jurisdiction is properly invoked, to see to it that no right secured by the supreme law of the land is impaired or destroyed by legislation.[23]

In *Lochner* v. *New York* of 1905,[24] Justice Peckham, speaking in the same vein on behalf of the Court, tested and found wanting a New York law restricting work in bakeries to ten hours a day:

> The question whether this act is valid as a labor law . . . may be dismissed in a few words. There is no reasonable ground for interfering with the liberty of person or the right of free contract, by determining the hours of labor, in the occupation of a baker. . . . The mere assertion that the subject relates though but in a remote degree to the public health does not necessarily render the enactment valid. The act must have a more direct relation.

In making such a judgment the Court was not substituting its judgment for that of state legislatures. If the act were within the power of the state to enact, then certainly it was valid, "although the judgment of the Court might be totally opposed to the enactment of such a law. But the question would still remain: Is [the particular act] within the . . . power of the state? and that question must be answered by the Court."[25]

In case after case, the Court answered, "No." So directly related did it require an act to be to its avowed social objective that virtually no state legislation emerged unscathed. To all intents and purposes, laissez faire was enforced as the Constitution. The Court had appointed itself final judge of state and federal policy; it conceived of itself as standing between property and social democracy. The judiciary had become preeminent and was to remain so until 1937.

Nor was it only in its opinions that the Court preached the laissez faire gospel. David J. Brewer (1837–1910), Associate Justice of the United States Supreme Court from 1889 to 1910, defended the faith before the

---

[22] Walton H. Hamilton, "The Path of Due Process of Law," quoted in Francis H. Heller, *Introduction to American Constitutional Law* (New York: Harper & Brothers, 1952), pp. 310–11.
[23] *Smyth* v. *Ames*, 169 U.S. (1898), 466, 725.
[24] 198 U.S. 45 (1905).
[25] 198 U.S. 45 (1905).

New York State Bar Association in 1893. Brewer admitted that judicial intervention in the political arena might raise questions about the fate of "the essential idea of government of and by the people," but he reminded his audience of the judicial responsibility for interpreting the written Constitution, itself a limitation on the power of the majority to affect the rights of minorities. It was thus a guarantee against despotism, defined as the "control of the many over the few." Nothing in the power of the judiciary detracted in the least from the idea of popular government. "The courts hold neither purse nor sword; they cannot corrupt nor arbitrarily control. They make no laws, they establish no policy, they never enter into the domain of popular action. They do not govern." Amid "wide unrest" and impending "vast social changes," when property was endangered from every side, "what factor in our national life," Brewer asked, "speaks most emphatically for stability and justice? . . . I am fairly persuaded that the salvation of the nation, the permanence of government of and by the people, rests upon the independence and vigor of the judiciary."[26]

OBJECTION FROM WITHIN

James Bradley Thayer

Brewer believed that the Supreme Court was property's only protection against the haste and the passions of the people and the pressures of democracy. But several eminent lawyers, including James Bradley Thayer (1854–1902), warned against judicial intervention. Taking a restrictive view of judicial power, they argued that progress along economic lines might cease if the courts had the power to rely on vague clauses in the Constitution to fasten the economic views of the past onto the present as matters of constitutional law. They argued that it was self-defeating to forget that legislatures, within the limits of their power, were final arbiters of what is right and wrong in matters of public policy. If they were not allowed to be such, the legislatures would cease to be sovereign, and their power would be transferred to the courts.

Thayer, professor at the Harvard Law School, noted that whereas what the courts were doing seemed to be a "mere judicial function, it involves, owing to the subject-matter with which it deals, taking a part . . . in the political conduct of government." That being the case, there could only be a "*modus vivendi* between the different departments" if the courts confine their actions "to [a] reasonable and fairly permissible view of [their] constitutional power. The ultimate arbiter of what is rational and permissible is indeed always the courts, so far as litigated cases bring the question before them. This leaves to our courts a great and stately juris-

---

[26] David J. Brewer, "The Movement of Coercion," *Proceedings of the Sixteenth Annual Meeting of the New York State Bar Association*, XVI (1893), 37–47.

diction. It will only imperil the whole of it if it is sought to give them more. They must not step into the shoes of the law-maker. . . . Under no system can the power of courts go far to save a people from ruin; our chief protection lies elsewhere. . . ."[27]

Roscoe Pound

Thayer's sober counsel was to no immediate avail. Soon he was joined, however, by other eminent legal voices in protesting judicial intervention.

Roscoe Pound (1870–1964), professor and later dean of the Harvard Law School, "one of the distinguished social scientists of the Progressive era," with "intimate experience with and resentment of plutocracy,"[28] told his students that "judicial decisions are not babies brought by constitutional storks but are born out of the travail of economic circumstances.":

> Formerly it was argued that common law was superior to legislation because it was customary and rested upon the consent of the governed. Today we recognize that the so-called custom is a custom of judicial decision, not a custom of popular action. We recognize that legislation is the more truly democratic form of law-making. We see in legislation the more direct and accurate expression of the general will. We are told that law-making of the future will consist in putting the sanction of society on what has been worked out in the sociological laboratory. That courts cannot conduct such laboratories is self-evident. Courts are fond of saying that they apply old principles to new situations. But at times they must apply new principles to situations both old and new. The new principles are in legislation. The old principles are in common law. The former are as much to be respected and made effective as the latter —probably more so as our legislation improves. The public cannot be relied upon permanently to tolerate judicial obstruction or nullification of the social policies to which more and more it is compelled to be committed.[29]

Louis D. Brandeis

While Pound was resisting judicial activism in defense of property, Louis D. Brandeis introduced his epoch-making factual brief to the Supreme Court. As counsel for Oregon in *Muller* v. *Oregon*,[30] involving an eight-hour law for women, Brandeis accepted traditional legal principles but combined them with economic and social data showing the evil of long

---

[27] James Bradley Thayer, "The Origin and Scope of the American Doctrine of Constitutional Law," *Harvard Law Review*, VII (October, 1893), 129–36.

For a penetrating discussion of the contemporary battle between advocates of judicial activism and judicial self-restraint, see Arnold Paul, *Conservative Crisis and Rule of Law: Attitudes of Bar and Bench, 1887–1895* (New York: Harper & Row, 1969).

See also A. T. Mason, "Judicial Activism: Old and New," *Virginia Law Review*, LV (April, 1969), 385–426.

[28] Hofstadter, *Age of Reform*, p. 154.

[29] Quoted in Twiss, *Lawyers and the Constitution*, p. 259. See also Roscoe Pound, "Common Law and Legislation," *Harvard Law Review*, XXI (1908), 383–407.

[30] 208 U.S. 412 (1908).

hours and the possible benefits to be derived from legislative limitation. Many pages of his brief were devoted to evidence culled from a variety of foreign and domestic official reports, all proving that long hours were in fact injurious to health and morals and that short hours resulted in economic and social benefits. The Court upheld the Oregon law, going out of its way to compliment Brandeis on his technique. In 1909 Brandeis successfully applied the same technique before the Illinois Supreme Court and, in 1915, in a case in New York State. A dent was thus made in the judicial armor, but even Brandeis realized that the struggle to put more life in the law was not yet won.

When facts were confronted by "stubborn theory," the latter prevailed. "Facts are more pliable than stubborn theories. Facts can be ignored, explained away, or denied. But theories are mental habits which cannot be changed at will."[31]

Brandeis was not discouraged. Before his own ascension to the Supreme Court in 1916, he made notable contributions to both theory and action. A highly successful corporation lawyer, he achieved an extraordinary grasp of complex social-economic relations. Recognizing the explosive nature of popular power and the danger lurking therein for men of wealth, he addressed himself to the specific question of how "recent dissatisfaction with [the] law as administered" by the courts could effectively be overcome. As early as 1905 he anticipated that "immense wealth would in time develop a hostility from which much trouble will come to us unless the excesses of capital are curbed. . . ."[32] He was acutely conscious of the Socialist peril. Whereas conventional corporation lawyers traced this danger to agitators, muckrakers, corrupt politicians, and labor leaders, Brandeis pointed to the great captains of industry as the chief makers of socialism. Power was moving from the few to the many. Informed lawyers and judges would not try to maintain the status quo by freezing privilege and indiscriminately thwarting social change. Rather, they would seize a signal opportunity to enter the rich field reserved for "those who wish to serve the people." It lay within their power to chart the course of political and social action, "to determine whether it is to be expressed in lines of evolution or in lines of revolution." Too long had the leading lawyers of the United States confined themselves to "supporting the claims of the corporations," expending their ability "almost wholly in opposition to the contentions of the people." If the problems of the time were to be settled right, Brandeis declared, "this condition cannot continue. Our country is, after all, not a country of dollars, but of ballots. . . . There will come a revolt of the people against the capitalists, unless the aspirations of the people are given some adequate legal expression. . . ."

---

[31] Morris R. Cohen, "The Process of Judicial Legislation," *American Law Review*, XLVIII (1914), 164.

[32] Louis D. Brandeis, "The Opportunity in the Law," an address delivered May 4, 1905, before the Harvard Ethical Society, reprinted in *Business—A Profession* (Boston: Small Maynard, 1914), 333–47.

Members of the bar must take a leading part themselves and urge their corporate clients to join them in "constructive legislation designed to solve in the public interest our great social, economic and industrial problems." If they would not, the initiative would be taken by others. Social revolution was a real possibility. If the nation were to be preserved and the commonweal promoted, the people must be led in thought and action along wise and temperate lines. "Here, consequently, [was] the great opportunity in the law."

Brandeis never concurred in President Hadley's caveat that democracy was constitutionally "bound to stop short of social democracy." In the years since the adoption of the Constitution, the longing for social justice had steadily increased. The American ideal was now democracy and social justice. To achieve it, the states need not amend the Constitution. "It has not lost its capacity for expansion to meet new conditions unless interpreted by rigid minds which have no such capacity. Instead of amending the Constitution, I would amend men's economic and social ideas."[33] Specifically, Brandeis would seek to change the nation's legal and judicial mind, making it "conform to contemporary conceptions of social justice."

"What we need is not to displace the courts, but to make them efficient instruments of justice; not to displace the lawyer, but to fit him for his official or judicial task." When, in earlier days, lawyers were general practitioners, they handled all types of cases and came in contact with all aspects of contemporary life. Thus, they gained considerable "breadth of view." Industrialization, however, had tended to make lawyers specialists; the growing intensity of professional responsibility in the corporate age had acted to discourage participation in public affairs. The broadening influences were removed from the average lawyer's experience, and gradually the legal profession became characterized by "vast areas of ignorance and grave danger of resultant distortion of judgment." This trend must be halted; indeed, reversed. Lawyers must once again develop an "intimate relation to contemporary life," and judges must be equipped "with the necessary knowledge of economic and social science." Broader education was the remedy: "study undertaken preparatory to practice—and continued by lawyers and judges throughout life; study of economics and sociology and politics which embody the facts and present the problems of today." " 'Every beneficent change in legislation,' " Brandeis quoted Professor Henderson as saying, " 'comes from a fresh study of social conditions and social ends, and from such rejection of obsolete laws to make room for a rule which fits the new facts. One can hardly escape from the conclusion that a lawyer who has not studied economics and sociology is very apt to become a public enemy.' "[34]

At a time when the leaders of the American bar were "mostly self-

---

[33] Louis D. Brandeis, "The Living Law," an address delivered before the Chicago Bar Association, January 3, 1915, *Illinois Law Review*, X (1916), 461–70.
[34] Quoting Charles R. Henderson, professor of practical psychology, University of Chicago.

satisfied economic Pharisees who did nothing but make a good living out of things as they were and who were distinctly opposed to any form of social change," wrote a prominent New York lawyer years later, "Brandeis was the only major exception."[35] "He was the first great lawyer I ever knew who had a social conscience and a genuine desire to make a better world." He did not share the "smugness and self-satisfaction in existing conditions" that characterized the majority of the members of the legal profession. He had doubts about the sanctity of some of the economic institutions that had been developed in industrial America and was not afraid to say so.

Brandeis was not the first to stress the need for judicial education. The antimonopoly economist Richard T. Ely (1854–1943) expressed the same view in 1891. Noting that our government exerted "a force on the whole adverse to the interests of labor," Ely declared that the "only practicable remedy . . . seems to be broader, more liberal, and more thorough education of the lawyers who are our ruling class. At the present time, the training which our American lawyers receive is, as a rule, woefully deficient, and cannot entitle them, as a whole, to the rank of a liberal profession. The condition of legal education in this country becomes apparent when it is stated that the political and economic science implied and expressed in Blackstone's *Commentaries on the Laws of England* is still regarded as sound doctrine by at least nine American lawyers out of ten." Ely's remarks were made in 1891; Brandeis made the same observation twenty-five years later. During those years, the situation had worsened.

Oliver Wendell Holmes, Jr.

A few voices on the Court itself were raised against judicial intervention. In his scathing dissent in *Lochner* v. *New York* of 1905, Associate Justice Oliver Wendell Holmes, Jr. (1841–1935), son of the famous poet and more famous in his own right as a lawyer, jurist, and essayist, reminded his colleagues that

> the Fourteenth Amendment does not enact Mr. Herbert Spencer's *Social Statics* . . . a Constitution is not intended to embody a particular economic theory, whether of paternalism and organic relation of the citizen to the State or of laissez-faire. It is made for people of fundamentally differing views, and the accident of our finding certain opinions natural and familiar or novel and even shocking ought not to conclude our judgment upon the question whether statutes embodying them conflict with the Constitution of the United States.

"This case," Holmes commented, "is decided upon an economic theory which a large part of the country does not entertain."

Although the Court upheld legislative power to take steps that con-

---

[35] George W. Alger, quoted in A. T. Mason, *Brandeis: A Free Man's Life* (New York: Viking Press, 1946), pp. 105–6.

siderably affected the public welfare, it justified the decision with "apologetic phrases like the police power, or the statement that the business concerned has been dedicated to a public use." Holmes did not believe in such apologies. The Court should recognize "that a state legislature can do whatever it sees fit to do unless it is restrained by some express prohibition in the Constitution of the United States or of the State. . . ." Thus, unless constitutionally forbidden, a legislature "may forbid or restrict any business when it has a sufficient force of public opinion behind it." Courts "should be careful," he cautioned, "not to extend [the express] prohibitions [found in the Constitution] beyond their obvious meaning by reading into them conceptions of public policy that the particular Court may happen to entertain." It was not the Court's affair to decide whether a law before it was wise and rational; it was enough for the judges that "the people . . . speaking by their authorized voice say that they want it. . . ."[36] "Of course I enforce whatever constitutional laws Congress or anybody else sees fit to pass, and do it in good faith to the best of my ability, but I don't disguise my belief that the Sherman Act is a humbug based on economic ignorance and incompetence."[37]

Holmes distrusted the tendency to rely on formulas, knowing that this practice, if "prolonged, means death." On the other hand, he had seen enough of reformers to distrust them as "come-outers" and to chastise them as "the greatest bores in the world," "cocksure of a thousand nostrums." His liberalism was the byproduct of an ingrained naturalism that led him to reject all absolutes, whether in economics, ethics, or politics. He defined truth "as the system of my limitations" and left "absolute truth for those who are better equipped."[38]

Holmes shared Spencer's doubts about the beneficial effects of social legislation. The words he used in addressing the graduating class at Harvard in 1895 might have been drawn from Spencer himself:

> We have learned the doctrine that evil means pain and the revolt against pain in all its forms has grown more and more marked. From societies for the prevention of cruelty to animals up to socialism, we express in numberless ways, the notion that suffering is a wrong which can be and ought to be prevented, and a whole literature of sympathy has sprung into being which points out in story and verse how hard it is to be wounded in the battle of life, how terrible, how unjust it is that anyone should fail.

Social legislation did little more than "shift disagreeable burdens from the shoulders of the stronger to those of the weaker." "Wholesale social regeneration" could only be effected appreciably by individuals taking life in hand "and trying to build a race."

---

[36] *Tyson* v. *Banting*, 273 U.S. 418 (1927), 446–47.
[37] Quoted by Francis Biddle, in A. Dunham and P. Kurland, eds., *Mr. Justice* (Chicago: University of Chicago Press, 1956), p. 8.
[38] The quotations are from Oliver Wendell Holmes, *Collected Legal Papers* (New York: Harcourt Brace, 1921), pp. 303–7.

Law, Holmes recognized, is constantly growing and usually behind the times.[39] Even when it seemed at last to have caught up with social change, room for growth remained. That is why it is so dangerous to be dogmatic in dealing with social problems. The "law embodies beliefs that have triumphed in the battle of ideas and then have translated themselves into action. . . ." While doubt persists, while opposite points of view still fight each other for dominance, "the time for law has not come; the notion destined to prevail is not yet entitled to the field." Judges often spoke too soon, having allowed fear to convert their "conscious or unconscius sympathy with one side or the other" into law, and forgetting that what they had just declared to be first principles was still believed "by half [their] fellow men to be wrong." The Court's fear of socialism had resulted in the enunciation of doctrines that had no proper place in either the Constitution or the common law.

"Certainty generally is illusion," Holmes wrote in an essay of 1897,[40] "and repose is not the destiny of man. . . . No concrete proposition is self evident, no matter how ready we may be to accept it, not even Mr. Herbert Spencer's 'Every man has a right to do what he wills, provided he interferes not with a like right on the part of his neighbors.'" Judges and lawyers were particularly prone to accept absolutes. "The logical method and form flatter that longing for certainty and for repose which is in every human mind." Any conclusion could be given a logical form, and Holmes charged that the courts and the bar, in wholeheartedly accepting the doctrine of laissez faire, had allowed logic to lead them astray. Judges had "failed adequately to recognize their duty of weighing considerations of social advantage." As with many others, fear of the unknown, and of the specter of socialism in particular, had led them to rely on rigid theory and dogma and to overlook the fact that a large part "of our law is open to reconsideration upon a slight change in the habit of the public mind." If lawyers would undertake to justify the rules they laid down on the basis of social advantage, "they sometimes would hesitate where now they are confident, and see that really they were taking sides upon debatable and often burning questions."

Even the natural law, on which Spencer and his followers relied as a bulwark for their arguments, evoked Holmes' skepticism. "The jurists who believe in natural law" seemed to him "to be in that naive state of mind that accepts what has been familiar and accepted by them and their neighbors as something that must be accepted by all men everywhere." Those who professed belief in the operation of natural law were in reality merely seeking to enforce their particular creed upon others. If they were in the majority, then "natural law" was operative. Those who wished to live in the society had to do so on those terms. That, to Holmes, was the

---

[39] Holmes dealt with this point particularly in his speech on "Law and the Court," delivered February 15, 1913, and reproduced as Senate Document 1106, 62nd Cong. 3rd sess. It also appears in Holmes, *Legal Papers*, pp. 291–97.

[40] Holmes, "The Path of the Law," *Legal Papers*, pp. 167–85.

whole of the matter: natural law was simply a statement of what men must do if they wished to remain in a particular society. "If I do live with others, they tell me that I must do and abstain from doing various things or they will put the screws on to me."

Holmes' liberalism meant rare open-mindedness in an age in which most lawyers and judges were singularly obtuse. He pleaded for tolerance, not only of the views we dislike but also for those we detest. John Dewey, singling out Holmes' great capacity for tolerance, cited a passage from the Justice's *Abrams* opinion as "the only enduring type of liberal faith."[41]

> When men have realized that time has upset many fighting beliefs, they may come to believe even more than they believe the very foundations of their own conduct that the ultimate good desired is better reached by free trade in ideas—that the best test of truth is the power of the thought to get itself accepted in the competition of the market, and that truth is the only ground upon which their wishes safely can be carried out. That, at any rate is the theory of our Constitution. It is an experiment, as all life is an experiment.[42]

On a less formal occasion, Holmes put the same thought in cosmic terms: "Life is painting a picture; not doing a sum."

VEBLEN AND THE ECONOMIC RATIONALE

By 1900 both aspects of Daniel Webster's prophecy of 1820 had come true. Popular power, in the form of legislation enacted by duly elected representatives of the people, had broken in on the rights of property, and the "influence of property" had found new ways "to limit and control the exercise of popular power." The most remarkable accomplishments were the translation of laissez faire into the idiom of constitutional law and the elevation of the Supreme Court to its position as guardian of economic privilege. Central to this achievement was the American Bar Association.

> As a group they [lawyers] sought to insulate the judges from any theories or facts but those consistent with their own outlook. As increasing industrialism widened the distance between the few and the many, adherence to this legalistic creed disguised its transition from the faith of a people to the dogmatic propaganda of a dominant minority. In sum, the achievement of the lawyers and judges was to bring together the American political philosophy of government limited by absolute fundamental rights, the theory of non-interference with self-regulating economic laws, and the legal and constitutional devices of property, contract, states rights, and judicial review to

---

[41] John Dewey, "Justice Holmes and the Liberal Mind," quoted in Frankfurter, *Mr. Justice Holmes*, p. 42.

[42] *Abrams* v. *U.S.*, 250 U.S. 616 (1919), 624.

form the American constitutional doctrine of freedom of private economic enterprise.[43]

How could leading American jurists confuse personal preference and political dogma with the Constitution of 1787? What made possible the sudden elevation of the Supreme Court to a position of preeminence in American politics? The understanding necessary for answering these questions was supplied by the satirical iconoclast Thorstein Veblen (1857–1929) in 1904 in his *Theory of Business Enterprise*. Born of Norwegian ancestry on a farm in Wisconsin, Veblen graduated from Carleton College in Minnesota and was a graduate student of William Graham Sumner at Yale. Throughout his hectic teaching career, he was delving into the psychological bases of industrialism and its dominant rationale and laying the foundations for a school of institutional economics. What Spencer and his American disciples saw as the inevitable working of natural forces, Veblen explained as the pecuniary drive for profit. "Profit is a business proposition, livelihood is not. Industrial man is chained in an economic prison where law and politics bear the pecuniary imprint, to the exclusion of all else."[44]

All modern institutions rested for the most part on business principles; those principles controlled not only "the terms of livelihood from day to day," but also "the larger affairs of life"—"both for the individual in his civil relations and for the community at large in its political concerns." So deeply entrenched was the habit of seeing all things in terms of profit and loss that public affairs fell by common consent into the hands of businessmen and were guided by business considerations. "Hence modern politics is business politics." Every function and activity of government was concerned primarily with pecuniary interests and had "little more than an incidental bearing on other human interests."

Modern America's preoccupation with business and with efforts to maintain the greatest liberty with which to pursue it was, in Veblen's opinion, a natural result of earlier emphasis on natural rights. "The movement of opinion on natural-rights grounds converged to an insistence on the system of natural liberty." As industrialism developed, natural rights became identified with the rights of ownership and natural liberty with the "system of free pecuniary contract." The great freedom became "freedom to buy and sell," and the only limit on freedom was "the equal freedom of others to buy and sell; with the obvious corollary that there must be no interference with others' buying and selling, except by means of buying and selling." Pecuniary obligations replaced other natural rights as the most sacred objects in the community. Prestige and esteem

---

[43] Twiss, *Lawyers and the Constitution*, pp. 3–4.
[44] Thorstein Veblen, *The Theory of Business Enterprise* (New York: Scribner's, 1904, 1932). The quotations here are from pp. 268–92. For a biography of Veblen, see Douglas F. Dowd, *Thorstein Veblen* (New York: Washington Square Press, 1966).

began to flow in some rough proportion to what men were paid for their work. If the pioneers "brought with them a somewhat high-wrought variant of the English preconception in favor of individual discretion," that preconception developed into an obsession. Even civil rights were molded to accommodate the development of individualism and private initiative. America became the habitat of the self-made man, "and the self-made man is a pecuniary organism."

Naturally, Veblen concluded, "the metaphysics of natural liberty" would be embodied in the Constitution in the guise of freedom of contract. Thus, although under the Constitution "one individual or group of individuals [might] not legally bring any other than pecuniary pressure to bear upon another individual or group," pecuniary pressure itself could not be barred. The constitutional proclamation of freedom of contract, however, came too late to fit the actual economic situation of the United States. Conceptions of natural rights were suited to the eighteenth century, when men were "situated on a plane of at least constructive equality" with each other. But by the time freedom of contract was declared the fundamental tenet of the American legal creed, "a new standardizing force, that of the machine process," had invaded the field and had rendered that tenet practically if not legally obsolete. When the relations between men contracting with each other were altered by the impersonal economic pressure of specialization and the concatenation of industrial processes, a legal principle based on equality of parties no longer applied. The result was a discrepancy between law and fact that consistently benefited employers and owners and deprived workmen of all hope of remedying their unfavorable position.

The so-called common man was not only made subservient to property by judicial invocation of the principle of free contract, but also was hindered by the operation of the principles of sentiment on which popular approval of a "government for business ends" rested. Just as the former was obsolete, so the latter was a descendent of a past whose institutional facts "differed substantially from the present situation." Both principles were advanced as "a matter of course, as self-legitimating grounds of action which . . . admit[ted] of no question as to their ulterior consequences or their value for the life-purposes of the community." One principle was patriotism, the other property. The former had been a habit of society since barbaric days and through the years had been regarded as essential to institutional survival. By force of "this happy knack of clannish fancy, the common man is enabled to feel that he has some sort of metaphysical share in the gains which accrue to the business men . . . of the same 'commonwealth,' so that whatever policy furthers the commercial gains of . . . business men . . . is felt to be beneficial to all the rest of the population." The second principle in support of business politics —property—had also been handed down from the past, and like patriotism, "though perhaps in a less degree, [it was] out of touch with the discipline of the more recent cultural situation." That principle held that the ownership of property is the material foundation of human well-being, and that this natural right of ownership is sacred . . . the acquisition of property by any person is held to be, not only expedient for the owner, but meritorious as an action serving the common good.

By such institutional devices the common man was tied ever more tightly to a system that worked toward his ultimate disadvantage.

In 1921 Veblen developed the social and political implications of the modern industrial system. In his book *The Engineers and the Price System*,[45] he noted that under eighteenth-century liberal principles, income was "a sure sign of productive work done." Businessmen were thus accorded full credit for having created this productive capacity, ignoring such contributory factors as continued advances in technology, further development of available natural resources, and ever-increasing population. Observers of the progress of capitalism also overlooked the way in which industrial management held "productive industry in check." "It is today an open question," he observed, "whether the businesslike management of the captains [of industry] is not more occupied with checking industry than with increasing its productive capacity"—that is, more interested in making money than in making goods and supplying services.

What Veblen lost sight of, or at least did not take fully into account, was the counterforce in the American system—popular power and the dynamic strength that Woodrow Wilson saw latent in freedom under leadership. He did not recognize, as did V. L. Parrington, that "broadly two great movements were going forward side by side in the unconscious drift of political tendency—the democratic and the plutocratic."[46] Indeed, Veblen's thinking was hardly less narrowly deterministic than Spencer's. But whereas Spencer saw man driven by the natural urge to survive, Veblen saw him in the grip of an implacable pecuniary motive. Incisive and original though Veblen was, he "never crossed the periphery of American life"[47] and was recognized only after his death. Yet it is clear today that the insights Veblen provided go a long way toward explaining the psychological bases of the distinct preference for property that for so many years permeated the United States in general and the Supreme Court in particular.

BROOKS ADAMS
AND THE FACTS OF HISTORY

While Veblen probed the psychological foundations of industrialism to explain the judicial preference for property, Brooks Adams (1848–1927) showed how Veblen's thesis was grounded in history. A member of the

---

[45] See Veblen, *The Theory of the Leisure Class*, first published in 1912 (New York: Modern Library, 1934).
[46] Quoted in Mason, *Free Government*, p. 642.
[47] Charles A. Madison, *Critics and Crusaders* (New York: Henry Holt, 1947), p. 308.

famous Massachusetts family, he was an acute social critic and historian. Boston's financial center, State Street, was to him the "symbol of all that was crass. . . . The more he detested this crassness . . . the more his mind became preoccupied with it, and he struggled with it during the remainder of his life even as the orthodox Puritan contended with sin."[48] His study of history enabled Adams to see, as Veblen never did, that the dominant capitalists' preoccupation with profits and property was precipitating the very development they desired most to allay: the rise of popular power and, ultimately, of revolution. Civilizations usually broke down because of "administrative difficulties"; men in positions of leadership failed to adapt themselves to change, and sooner or later a corrective process of deterioration set in. In the modern world the cycle was accelerated, and social revolutions were quite common occurrences.

> Under the stimulant of modern science, the old types [of mind] fail to sustain themselves, new types have to be equally rapidly evolved, and the rise of a new governing class is always synonymous with a social revolution and a redistribution of property.[49]

Unless the modern capitalist hierarchy adapted itself to the social changes the Industrial Revolution had wrought and reevaluated its position toward the sanctity of property, a new governing class, or a succession of them, would rise, only to be followed by a redistribution of wealth.

For historical evidence Adams pointed to the dominant commercial aristocracy of 1776, who "misjudged the environment, adhered to Great Britain, were exiled, lost their property, and perished"; to the cotton-planter aristocracy of the Old South, who, similarly failing "to comprehend their situation . . . were conquered, suffered confiscation of their property, and perished." The new dominant class had come to power because of its mastery of steam power, and for about two generations had ruled the land. "If this class, like its predecessors," Adams warned, "has in its turn mistaken its environment, a redistribution of property must occur. . . . The last two redistributions have been painful, and, if we examine passing phenomena from this standpoint, they hardly appear to promise much that is reassuring for the future."

Adams had little faith that the revolution he foresaw would or could be avoided, because capitalists and their lawyers alike "think with specialized minds." They could not "comprehend a social relation . . . beyond the narrow circle of [their] private interests." They tended to put their faith in one weapon, money, never realizing that thereby they were precipitating a conflict "instead of establishing an adjustment." Without being aware of it, they were, in essence, revolutionists.

Capitalists lacked the essential power of effective administration—

---

[48] Madison, *Critics and Crusaders*, pp. 286–87.
[49] Brooks Adams, *The Theory of Social Revolution* (New York: Macmillan, 1913), pp. 203–29.

namely, "the power of recognizing [and coordinating] a series of relations between numerous special social interests" "into a single organism, so adroitly that they shall operate as a unity." The capitalist mind had developed in an environment that demanded "excessive specialization in the direction of . . . money-making. . . . To this money-making attribute all else has been sacrificed." "The modern capitalist not only thinks in terms of money," Adams observed, corroborating Veblen, "but he thinks in terms of money more exclusively than the French aristocrat or lawyer ever thought in terms of caste."[50] His concentration on pecuniary matters led him to neglect all other interests, to abjure any social responsibility, and to resist any restraint by legislation.

It was not that capitalists and lawyers were venal; they were, on the whole, conscientious men. They were merely inflexible. They did not understand the changes going on around them. Their singlemindedness was inadequate to meet the need of modern civilization for "the administrative or generalizing mind." Even the universities, which "capital has long owned . . . by right of purchase," were not capable of producing such minds, for education had been commercialized and quality sacrificed for quantity. "The more the mind dwells upon the peculiarities of the modern capitalistic class, the more doubts obtrude themselves touching their ability to make the effort to carry [society] safely from an unstable to a stable equilibrium."

These considerations led Adams to the pessimistic conclusion that America could move no other way than downhill. The modern world being too much for the capitalistic mind, drastic social change could not be prevented; "signs of disintegration" were all about him: the universal contempt for law, the continual war between labor and capital, the slough of urban politics, and the dissolution of the family. All these things presaged the end of capitalism.

> Unless capital can, in the immediate future, generate an intellectual energy beyond the sphere of its specialized calling . . . and unless it can besides rise to an appreciation of diverse social conditions, as well as to a level of political sagacity, far higher than it has attained within recent years, its relative power in the community must decline.

Social disintegration, Adams predicted, would intensify, capital weaken still further, and finally the contest become so costly that it would be abandoned. "Then nothing remains but flight." The forces of revolution would triumph and a new governing class emerge.

Given this psychological orientation, the Supreme Court would naturally adopt a class bias in its interpretation of the Constitution. "This propensity in the court system irritated [Adams] as much as any other deficiency in our national life. He argued that 'a court should be rigid and emotionless' and that any attempt on the part of judges to use the courts to control legislation must result in disaster." Having been trained

---

[50] Quoted in Mason, *Free Government*, p. 643.

in the law and his family having been long attached to the profession, Adams was enraged that the legal fraternity itself had turned "the Constitution into a fetish" in an attempt to halt "the efforts of social reformers to adapt the . . . economy to changing conditions for the benefit of the people as a whole."[51]

Like Thayer twenty years earlier, Adams predicted that the judicial blockade erected against "social democracy" would prove to be a Maginot Line:

> The American lawyer has come to believe that a sheet of paper soiled with printer's ink and interpreted by a half-a-dozen elderly gentlemen snugly dozing in arm chairs has some inherent and marvelous virtue. . . . Capital finds the judicial veto useful as a means of at least temporarily evading the law, while the bar believes that the universe will obey a judicial decree. No delusion could be profounder and none, perhaps, more dangerous.

A Jeremian critic of capitalism, Adams did not permit any positive program of action to lighten his pessimism. Although the essence of his thought is socialistic, he did not join in Socialist activities, remaining primarily an individualist. Like Veblen's, Adams' impact on his contemporaries was slight. Time, however, has added to his stature, giving him a place alongside the more famous members of the Adams family.

THE COURT STANDS FIRM

Repulsing all attacks, the majority of the Supreme Court retained the point of view Justice Brewer expressed seventeen years before his death in 1910:

> The great body of judges are as well versed in the affairs of life as any, and they who unravel all the mysteries of accounting between partners, settle the business of the largest corporations and extract all the truth from the mass of sciolistic verbiage that falls from the lips of expert witnesses in patent cases, will have no difficulty in determining what is right and wrong between employer and employees, and whether proposed rates of freight and fare are reasonable as between the public and the owners. . . .[52]

Combining certitude ("never the test of certainty," according to Justice Holmes) with the strongly held belief that judicial intervention was entirely proper—indeed, necessary to block the assaults of communism, socialism, and populism—the Supreme Court had a rationale enabling it to frustrate government; it was not until 1937 that the Supreme Court took account of the fact that liberty can be, and often is, interfered with by industrial corporations and other private power groups, as well as by government.

---

[51] Madison, *Critics and Crusaders*, pp. 303–4.
[52] Brewer, "Movement of Coercion."

CHAPTER SIXTEEN

THE AGE OF CYNICISM

During its first few years the Wilson administration rode the crest of a reform wave. That wave ebbed quickly after 1916. What the courts did not frustrate, the war did. The presidential election that year turned on the two-year-old war in Europe. Reelected by a narrow margin, President Wilson had been watching developments abroad apprehensively. Finally on April 2, 1917, he asked Congress to declare war on Germany. Before long America was fighting, along with her allies, against the Central Powers. The focus of Wilson's—and the nation's—attention shifted from social advance to preparedness, and then to all-out war effort.

Although historians generally hold that "the American people [were] finally dragged into the conflagration against their will,"[1] once involved, they were carried along by President Wilson's idealism. It was a "war to end war," a crusade "to make the world safe for democracy." Walter Lippmann (1889–   ), then an editorial associate of the *New Republic*, voiced the prevailing feeling: "For ourselves, we . . . stand committed as never before to the realization of democracy in America." After the war

---

[1] Bailey, *American Pageant*, p. 725. See also Christian Gauss, *Why We Went to War* (New York: Scribner's, 1919).

[we] shall turn with fresh interests to our own tyrannies—to our Colorado mines, our autocratic steel industries, our sweatshops and our slums. We shall call that man unAmerican and no patriot who prates of liberty in Europe and resists it at home. A force is loose in America as well. Our own reactionaries will not assuage . . . or control [it]. . . .[2]

The war was not all inspiration. Much of it was unpleasant, for those at home, as well as for the "Doughboys" overseas. World War I necessitated the first regimentation of the American people, the first heavy taxation, and the first detailed regulation of industry and private life— government control of railroads, control of production, and food rationing. On the battlefield the four million members of the armed forces overseas developed an aversion to "barbed wire, mechanical monsters called tanks, lethal poison gas, dirt, and lice ('cooties')."[3] As time went on and emotion mounted, whipped up by George Creel's Committee on Public Information, strong anti-German sentiment developed. Congress reacted with two repressive measures—the Espionage Act of 1917 and the Sedition Act of 1918. Eugene Debs was one of almost two thousand persons prosecuted under those acts. The climate of American life became one of suspicion and intolerance, doing violence to our tradition of freedom. The Prohibition Amendment, ratified in 1919, was the most conspicuous example of war-inspired self-righteousness.

Suddenly the war ended; the pressure was off. From this experience "the world," Mark Sullivan observed, "was . . . half-blind, half-deaf, and chronically dazed" and "shell-shocked besides."[4] Almost immediately, reaction set in. Disillusionment was widespread. The American people had come to believe that the lofty purposes of the war, enunciated by Wilson and Lippmann and embellished by Creel and others, could in fact be achieved. This miracle did not happen. "The greatest disillusionment may have been provided by President Wilson [himself], who on Armistice Day [had] said: 'Everything for which America fought has been accomplished.' " His optimism was reflected in the *New Republic*: "At this instant of history, Democracy is supreme." But Wilson could not prevail in the peace negotiations, at which his Fourteen Points were defeated. Disillusionment was a byproduct of the drastic changes wrought by the war itself. "The prewar world had been a comprehensible place, with Americans completely satisfied [with their role in it]. Now they were inhabitants of a major power, perhaps the strongest nation on earth. From an affirmative people, aware of their place in the sun, Americans . . . turned into a bewildered group, off-balance and uncertain. It was as if

---

[2] Walter Lippmann, "The World Conflict in its Relation to American Democracy," *Annals of the American Academy of Political and Social Science*, LXXII (July, 1917), 10.

[3] Bailey, *American Pageant*, p. 746.

[4] Mark Sullivan, *Our Times. The United States 1900 to 1929* (New York: Scribner's 1935), VI ("The Twenties"), 2.

the nation, looking into a mirror, neither recognized nor liked what it saw."[5]

The war accelerated, if it did not cause, urbanization. The day of the village and small town was ending. The automobile provided greater mobility; movies and other forms of mass entertainment homogenized national attitudes and tastes. With a sense of relief America turned to gaiety as a way of life. "Roaring Twenties," "Incredible Era," "Prosperity Decade," were not merely figures of speech; these tags reflected the pattern of life. In 1928 Herbert Hoover envisaged the day when poverty "will be banished from this nation." Happy days were the norm of American life. In politics the period was marked by complacency and conservatism.

Joseph Wood Krutch (1893–1970), author, early contributor to *The Nation*, editor, and professor of English at Columbia University, remembered that the "most threatening enemies were . . . not Capitalism, Race Prejudice, or the Neglect of the Undeveloped Countries, but Puritanism, Provincialism, and the Genteel Tradition." "Significantly," Krutch observed, "*The Nation*'s most publicized series of articles during the Twenties . . . was devoted, not to any economic or political questions, but to 'Our Changing Morals.' " Americans seemed content to get "drunk on bathtub gin" and were "criminally unaware of the various Waves of the Future (good or bad) which were soon to overwhelm them."[6]

Intellectual activity, not wholly abandoned, queried "the American form of society; particularly the political and governmental aspects."[7] Questioning soon became cynicism—the hallmark of the age. America the Beautiful had become "The Waste Land."

> The most moving and pathetic fact in the . . . life of America today [1921] is emotional and aesthetic starvation, of which the mania for petty regulation, the driving regimentation, and drilling, the secret society and its grotesque regalia,[8] the firm grasp on the unessentials of material organization of our pleasures and gaieties are all eloquent stigmata. We have no heritages or traditions to which to cling except those that have already withered in our hands and turned to dust. One can feel the whole industrial and economic situation as so maladjusted to the primary and simple needs of men and women that the futility of a rationalistic attack on these infantilisms . . .

---

[5] Allen Churchill, *Over Here! An Informal Re-creation of the Home Front in World War I* (New York: Dodd, Mead, 1968), pp. 22, 225.
[6] Joseph Wood Krutch, *More Lives Than One* (New York: William Sloane, 1962), pp. 173, 178.
[7] Mark Sullivan, *Our Times*, p. 13. See the volume edited by Harold E. Stearns, *Civilization in the United States. An Inquiry by Thirty Americans* (New York: Harcourt, Brace, 1922) for a survey of contemporary conditions in various fields. In almost every essay criticism and dissatisfaction are the keynotes.
[8] A reference to the new Ku Klux Klan, which mushroomed in the early 1920s. For a short while it conducted a "reign of hooded terror." "It was anti-foreign, anti-Catholic, anti-Negro, anti-Jewish, anti-pacifist, anti-Communist, anti-internationalist, anti-evolutionist, anti-bootlegger, and anti-birth control. It was also pro-Anglo-Saxon, pro-native American, and pro-Protestant." Bailey, *American Pageant*, p. 782.

becomes obvious. There must be an entirely new deal of the cards in one sense; we must change our hearts.[9]

The need for thinkers to show how so fundamental a change might be brought about was not met. During the twenties the courts continued to block reform, and even the intellectuals were largely negative, pessimistic, and despondent.[10] Some sought refuge abroad. Others saw the necessity of revolting against the machine civilization, against materialism—against destroying humanistic values in the name of progress. But they offered no constructive suggestions suited to accomplish regeneration.

RANDOLPH BOURNE: CRITIC OF WAR

Had he lived a little longer, Randolph Bourne (1886–1918) might well have been the spokesman for the 1920s. A native of Bloomfield, New Jersey, a hunchback whose life was cut short at thirty-two by the influenza epidemic of 1918, Bourne was a precocious student at Columbia University and later became a free-lance writer and critic whose interests ranged widely—literature, politics, society, and travel. His articles and essays appeared in the *Atlantic Monthly*, the *New Republic*, and in other magazines of wide circulation. Others were published in book form. His *Unfinished Fragment on the State* has been described as "one of the most notable American attempts at a theory of the state."[11] In Bourne's pages hatred of war became a monotonous refrain. War, he contended, was perpetrated by the state because it served to aggrandize its own power and glory. It was, indeed, welcomed by the "significant classes," who in the name of patriotism silenced minorities, enforced conformity, and destroyed those differences and disagreements that in peacetime threatened their rule. "Only when the State is at war does the modern society function with that unity of sentiment, simple and uncritical patriotic devotion, cooperation of services, which have been the ideal of the State lover."[12] In wartime privileged Americans enjoyed the "peacefulness of being at war." Their gregarious nature made them "feel powerful by conforming." At the same time war destroyed the cultural balance and variety that made life worthwhile. In the vanguard promoting war one found the intellectuals, one's teachers and friends, identifying themselves with "the least democratic forces in American life," giving their "reactionary opponents a rationalization for the war." Bourne directed his thoughts toward these traitors, especially those holding an "honorable place in a University—the republic of learning."

---

[9] Bailey, *American Pageant*, p. vii.
[10] See Henry May, *The Discontent of the Intellectuals. A Problem of the Twenties* (Chicago: Rand McNally, 1963).
[11] Quoted in Mason, *Free Government*, p. 724.
[12] Bourne's *Unfinished Fragment on the State* is included in James Oppenheim, ed., *Untimely Papers* (New York: Viking, 1947), pp. 140–230.

To those of us who still retain an irreconcilable animus against war, it has been a bitter experience to see the unanimity with which the American intellectuals have thrown their support to the use of war-technique in the crisis in which America found herself. Socialists, college professors, publicists, new-republicans, practitioners of literature, have vied with each other in conforming with their intellectual faith the collapse of neutrality and the riveting of the war-mind on a hundred million more of the world's people.[13]

Although he detested war as an evil in itself, Bourne was primarily concerned with its destructive effect on spiritual and cultural life, whose diversity demanded an open society conducive to the free interchange of unorthodox ideas and opinions. Sapping the vitality and creativity of a nation, "war is a vast complex of life-destroying and life-crippling forces."[14]

Bourne's productive period was only seven years, from 1911 to his death in 1918; yet he left an enduring imprint. He was a bannerman of values during the general collapse that followed. What he wrote found compelling proof not only in the fantastic regimes that arose after him, but also in what one reads in today's newspaper.

> If any man has a ghost
> Bourne has a ghost,
> a tiny twisted unscared ghost in a black cloak
> hopping along the grimy old brick and brownstone
> streets still left in downtown New York,
> crying out in a shrill soundless giggle:
> War is the health of the State.[15]

DEMOCRACY DEBUNKED

Sinclair Lewis

Perhaps no one caught the spirit of America's "golden age of mediocrity" better than Sinclair Lewis (1885–1951). "The critics may debate the niceties of his style; the literary historian may place him in an orderly niche. The fact remains that Lewis' books roused the world to a better understanding of America and affected the course of our national thinking about America and Americans."[16] His "Unpublished Introduction" to *Babbitt* provides a graphic description of the twenties. To tell the story of America was to portray the business man, "the man with toothbrush mustache and harsh voice who talks about motors and prohibition in the

---

[13] Quoted by James Oppenheim, "The Story of the Seven Arts," *American Mercury*, XX (June, 1930), 163.
[14] Quoted in Madison, *Critics and Crusaders*, p. 442.
[15] John Dos Passos, *1919* (New York: Harcourt Brace, 1932), pp. 105–6.
[16] Harry E. Maule and Melville H. Cane, eds., *The Man From Main Street. A Sinclair Lewis Reader* (New York: Random House, 1953), pp. xxiv. The Lewis quotations are from pp. 21, 25, 28, 29.

smoking compartment of the Pullman car, the man who plays third-rate golf and first-rate poker at a second-rate country club near an energetic American city." Lewis mercilessly lampooned parochialism and synthetic culture.

"Mr. Jones himself—ah, that rare and daring and shining-new creator of industrial poetry, votes the Republican ticket straight, he hates all labor unionism, he belongs to the Masons and the Presbyterian Church, his favorite author is Zane Grey, and in other particulars . . . his private life seems scarce to mark him as the rough, ready, aspiring, iconoclastic, creative, courageous innovator his admirers paint him. He is a bagman. He is a pedlar. He is a shopkeeper. He is a camp-follower. He is a bag of aggressive wind." This was "our conqueror, dictator over our commerce, education, labor, art, politics, morals, and lack of conversation."

All across the land there was no variation from this model, nor from his physical environment. "So powerful is our faith in standardization," wrote Lewis, that when "a new hotel, factory, house, garage, motion-picture theater, row of shops, church, or synagogue is erected in gray Charleston, rambling New Orleans, or San Francisco of the '49ers, that structure is precisely, to the last column of reinforced concrete and the last decorative tile, the same as a parallel structure in the new cities of Portland or Kansas City. And the souls of these structures . . . are increasingly as standardized as the shells."

Vernon L. Parrington (1871–1929), himself a critic of the times, summarized Lewis's lesson:

> What is the tremendous discovery that Sinclair Lewis makes? . . . It is no other than this: that the goodly United States of America are peopled by a mighty herd, . . . stuffed with conceit of their own excellence, esteeming themselves the great end for which creation has been in travail, the finest handiwork of the Most High . . . with a vast respect for totems and fetishes; purveyors and victims of the mysterious thing called Bunk, who valiantly horn to death any audacious heretic who may suggest that rumbling about the plains, filling their bellies, bellowing sacred slogans, and cornering the lushest grass, are scarcely adequate objectives for such immense power: a vast middleman herd, that dominates the continent, but cannot reduce it to order or decency.[17]

Lewis's *Main Street, Arrowsmith, Elmer Gantry,* and *Babbitt* were directed as much toward politicians as toward the prototype businessman. In a self-composed obituary, he spoke of "his jeering yet essentially kindly shafts at the pomposity and inefficiency of contemporary politicians and industrialists." Patriotism was only "brazen mawkishness."[18] Lewis hated "equally, politicians who lie and bully and steal under cover of windy and banal eloquence, . . . manufacturers who pose as philanthropists

---

[17] Vernon L. Parrington, *Sinclair Lewis. Our Own Diogenes* (Seattle: University of Washington Book Store, 1927), pp. 11–12.
[18] Maule and Cane, *Man from Main Street,* pp. 104–5.

while underpaying their workmen [and] professors who in wartime try to prove that the enemy are all fiends. . . ."[19] The antics of all three bored the people and turned them away. "Why, nobody is interested, not one doggone bit," a Lewis character responded to a question about politics in "Main Street's Been Paved."[20]

Many of Lewis's subjective judgments were borne out by Robert S. (1892–1970) and Helen M. Lynd[21] (1896–   ) in their monumental *Middletown*, the first objective sample ("after the manner of social anthropology") of a typical American public—the town of Muncie, Indiana. The Lynds found that "the activity of getting a living [had] come to dominate the time, the energy, and the habitual attitudes of the . . . population to a degree undreamed of in the quiet days" before the war. By and large, "unless his particular interests [were] interfered with, a Middletown citizen [did] not concern himself greatly" with politics. If he voted at all, he voted "the good-fellow straight ticket." Most Middletonians paid little attention to elections and automatically identified politics with fraud. They learned "new ways of behaving towards material things more rapidly than new habits addressed to persons and non-material institutions." The times were bewildering, and in self-defense the average citizen clung to old habits and old ways, defending them heatedly against innovation.

Henry L. Mencken

Lewis and the Lynds described the desert America had become. The Baltimore journalist and critic Henry L. Mencken (1880–1956) subjected it to analysis. In his pessimistic, cynical *Notes on Democracy*,[22] published in 1926, the editor of the *American Mercury* looked about him and found a great deal of wickedness and far too much foolishness. Why should this be so? It was all due, he replied, to natural causes—to stupid, boobish, wicked men, and to that worst of human contrivances, democracy. In witty and sophisticated prose Mencken burlesqued his own times. An admirer of Nietzche, and like him a believer in the superiority of certain individuals, he wrote about popular government—a racy, acidulous rehash of what aristocrats and authoritarians at home and abroad had been gossiping about for centuries.

Democracy, Mencken suggested, was first offered to the world as a "cure-all." It was supported on the basic premise that "any boil upon the body politic, however vast and raging, may be relieved by taking a vote; any flux of blood may be stopped by passing a law." What was all this but

---

[19] Maule and Cane, *Man from Main Street*, p. 48.
[20] Reprinted in Maule and Cane, *Man from Main Street*, p. 323.
[21] Robert S. Lynd and Helen Merrill Lynd, *Middletown. A Study in Contemporary American Culture* (New York: Harcourt, Brace, 1929). The quotations are from pp. vi, 416, 420–22, 427, 434, 499, 500. See Alden Whitman, " 'Middletown' Revisited: Still in Transition," *New York Times*, December 3, 1970, pp. 45 ff.
[22] H. L. Mencken, *Notes on Democracy* (New York: Knopf, 1926), *passim*.

"hocus-pocus," an attempt to rationalize democracy by using "concepts borrowed from theology." Democracy was a "substitute for the old religion"; it was "shot through with . . . banal mysticism . . . [and] preposterous postulates." Yet to expose it as such was impossible. The people had and would continue to have absolute faith in its healing power. It simply was not "vulnerable to logical attack." All this was not to say, Mencken protested, that he was ready to abandon the democratic ship. Democracy at least "surpasses and shames the polity of the Andaman Islanders or the Great Khan. . . ." He simply denied that *"vox populi* is actually *vox Dei."*

It was a matter of little moment anyhow, for democracy was "a self-limiting disease" and would in the end devour itself. There were "obvious paradoxes in its philosophy, and some of them have a suicidal smack." Thus to offer one man equality with a second was counter to the first's natural tendency as an inferior man" to acknowledge the second's superiority upsets the foundations on which a stable society was built. "The democrat, leaping into the air to flap his wings and praise God, is for ever coming down with a thump. The seeds of his disaster . . . lie in his own stupidity: he can never get rid of the naive delusion—so beautifully Christian!—that happiness is something to be got by taking it away from the other fellow."

Most discouraging of all, Mencken observed, was democracy's "ineradicable tendency to abandon its whole philosophy at the first sign of strain." Whenever the national safety was threatened, despotism was adopted with "an almost fabulous ferocity." Echoing Bourne, he noted that war was waged upon "mere academic advocacy" of democratic doctrines.

> I offer the spectacle of Americans jailed for reading the Bill of Rights as perhaps the most gaudily humorous ever witnessed in the modern world. Try to imagine monarchy jailing subjects for maintaining the divine right of Kings! Or Christianity damning a believer for arguing that Jesus Christ was the Son of God! This last, perhaps, has been done; anything is possible in that direction. But under democracy the remotest and most fantastic possibility is a commonplace of every day.

Notwithstanding its defects, Mencken found democracy delightful. "It is incomparably idiotic, and hence incomparably amusing. Does it exalt dunderheads, cowards, trimmers, frauds, cads?" If so, the pain of seeing them exalted was balanced by the joy of seeing them brought down. Was it wasteful, extravagant, dishonest? Well, so was every other form of government. Did it enshrine "rascality"? "Well, we have borne that rascality since 1776, and continue to survive. In the long run, it may turn out that rascality is necessary to human government, and even to civilization itself —that civilization, at bottom, is nothing but a colossal swindle. I do not know: I report only that when the suckers are running well the spectacle is infinitely exhilarating."

Walter Lippmann

Walter Lippmann, student of politics, political columnist, and editor of *The New York World*, expressed his distrust of democracy in less vituperative terms. In several books written between 1913 and 1922, Lippmann concluded that traditional democratic theory, as developed in the United States, was a failure. It was based on the idea of self-government, on the conviction that government should be directly responsive to the expressed will of an informed people, whereas in fact the modern world had incapacitated people for self-government by making it impossible for them to be informed on public issues. Instead of by knowledge, the people were guided by fear and prejudice.

> No financial power is one-tenth so corrupting, so insidious, so hostile to originality and frank statement as the fear of the public which reads the magazine. For one item suppressed out of respect for a railroad or a bank, nine are rejected because of the prejudices of the public. This will anger the farmers, that will arouse the Catholics, another will shock the summer girl. Anybody can take a fling at poor old Mr. Rockefeller, but the great mass of average citizens . . . must be left in undisturbed possession of its prejudices. In that subservience, and not in the meddling of Mr. Morgan, is the reason why American journalism is so flaccid, so repetitious and so dull.[23]

By 1920, when he wrote *Liberty and the News*, he had concluded that the great obstacle confronting democratic government was not so much the prejudices of the people as their ignorance. What assurance was there that, even with facts to guide them, people would use them rationally to formulate policies in the best interests of the nation? Very little, he answered in his classic *Public Opinion*, published in 1922.

Lippmann began with the premise that "in any society that is not completely self-contained in its interests . . . ideas deal with events that are out of sight and hard to grasp."[24] In order to establish contact with those events, men form their own pictures—"maps of the world"[25]—in their heads. These pictures are their public opinions and constitute their peculiar "social set." It subsequently provides a filter of acceptability for facts and helps to determine how they are evaluated. But the "social set" is only one perceptual distortion among many imposed by the observer between himself and his observations.[26]

In short, "Men react to their ideas and images, to their pictures and

---

[23] Quoted in Arthur M. Schlesinger, Jr., "Walter Lippmann: The Intellectual *vs.* Politics," *The Politics of Hope* (Boston: Houghton Mifflin, 1962), p. 130. See the collection of short pieces Lippmann wrote for the *New Republic* between 1914 and 1920, annotated by Arthur M. Schlesinger, Jr. G. A. Harrison, ed., Lippmann, *Early Writings* (New York: Liveright, 1970).

[24] Walter Lippmann, *Public Opinion* (New York: Macmillan, 1956), p. 12.

[25] Lippmann, *Public Opinion*, p. 15.

[26] Lippmann, *Public Opinion*, p. 76.

notions of the world, treating these pictures as if they were the reality."[27]
Men live by stereotypes, a particular type of mental picture conforming to
their habits, tastes, capacities, and hopes. They do not constitute a mirror
image of the world but rather of the world as we have adapted it and in
which we have come to feel at home. Eventually, our sense of personal
worth, our social position, and our privileges in society derive from our
stereotypes.

These stereotypes are converted into a common will by means of sym-
bolism; the symbol is the "common bond of common feelings, even though
these feelings were originally attached to disparate ideals." "A leader or
an interest that can make itself master of current symbols is master of
the current situation."[28]

> Since in order to have spontaneous self-government, you had to have a simple
> self-contained community . . . [it was taken] for granted that one man was
> as competent as the next to manage these simple and self-contained affairs.
> . . . There was no serious trouble with the doctrine of the omnicompetent
> citizen until the democratic stereotype was universally applied, so that men
> looked at a complicated civilization and saw an enclosed village. . . .
>
> This meant that men formed their picture of the world outside from the
> unchallenged pictures in their heads.[29]

The Scopes trial, involving a Tennessee statute proscribing the teaching of evolution in its public schools, provided Lippmann with a perfect
illustration. The people of Tennessee believed the first chapter of Genesis
to be historically more reliable than the biology of Charles Darwin; they
so declared through a majority of their representatives. To Lippmann this
suggested the belief that any opinion or action was inherently as good as
any other. The conviction of the speaker was the test of the statement's
truth.

> Since no value can be placed upon an opinion, there is no way . . . of
> deciding between opinions except to count them. [Without a way through
> which] the worth of a soul can be measured, . . . the mere counting of souls
> [becomes] the final arbiter of all worth. It is a curious misunderstanding Mr.
> Bryan brought into high relief during the Tennessee case. The spiritual
> doctrine that all men will stand at last equal before the throne of God meant
> to him that all men are equally good biologists before the ballot box of
> Tennessee.[30]

What all this meant, Lippmann concluded, was that while the rule of 51
percent was a convenience, it might easily become an absurd tyranny if

---

[27] Walter Lippmann, *Essays in the Public Philosophy* (Boston: Little, Brown, 1955),
p. 73.
[28] Lippmann, *Public Opinion*, pp. 206–7.
[29] Lippmann, *Public Opinion*, pp. 272–73.
[30] Clinton Rossiter and James Lare eds., *The Essential Lippmann: A Political Philosophy for Liberal Democracy* (New York: Random House, 1963), pp. 10–11.

regarded worshipfully, as though it were more than a political device.[31]

People generally failed "to transcend their casual experience and their prejudice" and arrive at logical conclusions about anything; thus, there seemed to be little prospect, "in any time which we can conceive," that the people would be able to arrive at "sound public opinions on the . . . business of government." Even if there were such a prospect, Lippmann thought it extremely doubtful that many people would want to be bothered. The most he hoped for was that somehow "standards of living and methods of audit by which the acts of public officials and industrial directors are measured"[32] might be devised. These revisions would at least enable the people to have some means of social control that would make the specialized governing class ultimately responsible to them.[33]

Frank R. Kent

Frank R. Kent (1877–1957), another eminent Baltimore journalist, substantiated Mencken's and Lippmann's conclusions concerning the low status of democratic government in postwar America. In the foreword to his *Political Behavior*,[34] he entertained "a low view of the popular intelligence" and saw no evidence of the American voters' "inherent distaste . . . for corruption." Rather, the American voter preferred "the stupid and insincere" and lacked the ability "to discriminate between good and bad." Such conclusions were "merely . . . inescapable deductions from . . . evidence . . . given . . . in all parts of the country and in great abundance." It would be good if the people did have the capacity to get at the truth and could be depended on to act wisely and righteously, and it was perhaps wise to retain the pretense that they did so. "But . . . the evidence," Kent found, "is overwhelmingly against it. . . ."

"Give them a good show," he urged politicians seeking election. "At bottom, what [the people] want is to be amused, not instructed. The thing they abhor is to be bored. Actually, except in times of industrial depression and unemployment or when some national crisis impends, it is a difficult thing to get the voters really aroused over any issue. Constructive proposals as a rule leave them cold." Therefore, Kent advised office seekers to give "them hokum . . . bunk . . . bull . . . banana oil. . . ." The voters loved it and had a limitless capacity to absorb it.

Yet Kent, like Mencken, protested that he did not write "with any desire to reflect upon the democratic scheme of government, which with all its faults is probably the best yet devised—for us anyway—and for which there seems to be no practical or acceptable substitute."[35]

[31] Rossiter and Lare, *Essential Lippmann*, p. 13.

[32] Lippmann, *Public Opinion*, p. 236.

[33] For a study of Lippmann's influence, see Edward L. and Frederick H. Schapsmeier, *Walter Lippmann, Philosopher-Journalist* (Washington, D.C.: Public Affairs Press, 1969).

[34] Frank R. Kent, *Political Behavior* (New York: Morrow, 1928).

[35] Kent, *Political Behavior*, pp. vii, xiv, 97, 146.

HERBERT HOOVER
AND RUGGED INDIVIDUALISM

What Bourne and the debunkers said was largely ignored by the American people, or if noticed, resented.[36] If their attitude made it hard for iconoclasts, it also made it difficult for the new political philosophies developing elsewhere in the world. They were largely unaffected even by the "hysterical fear of Red Russia," which colored official American thought for several years after the Communist coup of 1917, and which led Attorney General A. Mitchell Palmer to go on an anti-Communist witch hunt.[37] By and large the people were content to enjoy life. "The Twenties were probably regarded by most Americans as a fairly satisfactory period of peace and prosperity."[38]

Favored by the unhappy exhaustion of her principal foreign business competitors and organized by and for the leadership of high finance, postwar America was able to sell a flood of mass-produced goods in the most profitable world markets, to draw the gold of the world into her coffers in payment, and to return to American stockholders and employees enormous sums in bonuses, profits, and wages. These in turn further expanded demand, production, and investment and caused the cycle to be repeated. The incredible boom, and the glow of optimism that accompanied it, created a golden age for crafty industrialists and financiers—an age made all the more glorious by the acquiescent administrations of Warren G. Harding, Calvin Coolidge, and Herbert Hoover. All seemed wholeheartedly satisfied with the condition of affairs as they found them; none suggested resumption of the liberal political programs of the prewar years. Their acquiescence reflected the mood of the nation—supreme confidence that prosperity was unending. It was hardly a time for radical political change.

To ward off possible setbacks in prosperity's onward march, businessmen should exercise political leadership and control and perhaps make the two synonymous. President Coolidge summed up the thought in the terse, oft-quoted admonition: "Take politics out of business and put business in politics." The argument ran then, as it did thirty years later, that "what was good for General Motors was good for the country."

> The welfare of business, especially of big business, the product of intense individualism, necessarily means the *public* welfare. The two are inseparable! . . . No citizens . . . were so well qualified to steer legislation and government as its top-notch business and professional men; none had such great interests at stake; none could judge of effective organization and transaction of public business so well as they. None could so well forecast the immediate and remote economic consequences of any given legislation.

---

[36] May, *Discontent of Intellectuals*, p.1.
[37] Bailey, *American Pageant*, pp.773–74.
[38] May, *Discontent of Intellectuals*, p.2.

> For Government is nothing but big business—the biggest kind of business. There is no better training for success in government than success in business. There is no better material for making legislators and administrators than is found among our captains of industry and their professional advisers. . . . With [business's] powerful associations it can and ought to . . . re-establish the moral basis of capitalism and effectively put Business in Politics.[39]

Herbert Clark Hoover (1874–1964), thirty-first president of the United States, did not specifically adopt such a platform, but when he ran on the Republican ticket in 1928, he articulated a philosophy of rugged individualism based on the same reasoning. Hoover, a mining engineer and promoter, a wartime administrator and cabinet member under Harding and Coolidge before being elected President of the United States, believed in efficiency, enterprise, equality of opportunity, individualism, substantial laissez faire, personal success, material welfare. These were the components of true liberalism.

As Secretary of Commerce, Hoover gained a reputation as the advance agent of American business abroad. The record of American investments in foreign countries during his secretaryship indicates how richly he deserved it. In his speech after receiving the 1928 presidential nomination, he voiced his faith in our "whole business system" and praised its "high sense of moral responsibility." "The whole practice and ethics of business has made great strides of improvement in the last quarter of a century, largely due to the effort of business and the professions themselves." To "far-sighted leadership in industry" he gave much of the credit for the advances America had made during the 1920s. Having himself worked his way up the economic ladder and benefited from the profit system, he was stubborn in its defense. Even when the national economic picture was radically altered by war and depression, he insisted that this system should remain comparatively unregulated. "When industry cures its own abuses, it is true self-government."[40] To enjoy that kind of self-government, politicians must severely limit their actions. It was enough that "through free and universal education," government provide "the training of the runners" for the economic race and as umpire, guarantee the fairness of the race. "The winner is he who shows the most conscientious training, the greatest ability and the greatest character." Government action would only create handicaps for the runners and destroy the drive that stimulated men and women "to endeavor and to achievement."

When Senator G. W. Norris of Nebraska passed through Congress his bill providing authority for the government-owned hydroelectric plant on the Tennessee River at Muscle Shoals, Alabama, to sell electric power and nitrates, Hoover vetoed it, saying:

---

[39] Charles N. Fay, *Business in Politics* (Cambridge, Mass.: Cosmos Press, 1926), pp. ix–x. For a brilliant analysis of the businessman's philosophy during the 1920s, see J. W. Prothro, *The Dollar Decade* (Baton Rouge: Louisiana State University Press, 1955).
[40] *New York Herald Tribune*, August 12, 1928, p. 14.

I am firmly opposed to the Government entering into any business the major purpose of which is competition with our citizens . . . I hesitate to contemplate the future of our institutions, of our Government, and of our country if the preoccupation of its officials is no longer the promotion of justice and equal opportunity but is to be devoted to barter in the markets. That is not liberalism, it is degeneration.[41]

The fact that the high prices charged by the monopoly for electric power in the Tennessee Valley had motivated Norris to propose public owner-ship and development as a remedy was of no consequence. If industry abused its power, a little regulation would remedy it; if the people wanted Muscle Shoals to manufacture and sell power and fertilizers, it could be done effectively only by private industry in the area. "Muscle Shoals," Hoover declared, "can only be administered by the people upon the ground, responsible to their own communities and not for purposes of pursuit of social theories or national politics."

For Hoover the picture was black and white: on the one hand, the choice of freedom and individualism, on the other, the hard alternative of tyranny. The moment a step was taken away from a policy of minimal government activity, the brakes would be released and maximal govern-ment would inevitably follow. Hoover published his political testament in 1922 under the title *American Individualism*.[42] The title sounded his unvarying themes: the "good life" in America and American prosperity were the result of "individualism." Individualism, left free from govern-ment regulation and control, had industrialized the nation and given it the highest standard of living in the world. Competition assured the pub-lic that it would receive the best leadership and the best products at the lowest prices. Economic power was limited by the fact that "production is for the mass of society and dependent therefore on the public good will." No group "can dominate the nation and a few successes in imposing the will of any group is its sure death warrant." The role of government was that of "umpire." It might regulate but never regiment. At all costs government must be kept out of the production and distribution of goods and services. The test of proper governmental action was, "Does it safe-guard an equality of opportunity? Does it maintain the initiative of our people?"

In Hoover's analysis democracy was the handmaiden of individualism.

Democracy is merely the mechanism which individualism invented as a device that would carry on the necessary political work of its social organiza-tion. Democracy arises out of individualism and prospers through it alone.

Economic and social injustices, though not unheard of, were so local-ized and infrequent as to be practically nonexistent. The great danger, indeed the only one, was that home-grown American individualism might

---

[41] Quoted in Hofstadter, *American Political Tradition*, p. 293.
[42] Herbert Hoover, *American Individualism* (Garden City, N.Y.: Doubleday, 1934).

become infected with alien "isms." Socialism was the major threat. Its evils must be avoided by repulsing any tendency toward reliance on government for social and economic benefits.

The sum of Hoover's faith was

> that while we build our society upon the attainment of the individual, we . . . safeguard to every individual an equality of opportunity to take that position in the community to which his intelligence, character, ability, and ambition entitle him; that we keep the social solution free from frozen strata of classes; that we . . . stimulate effort of each individual to achievement; that . . . we . . . assist him to this attainment; while he in turn must stand up to the emery wheel of competition.

Put into practice, that philosophy meant "a smack and a dab of government regulation here and there to prevent 'abuses.' "[43] Human progress was largely a voluntary, individual matter. Government action beyond the safe limits he described merely hindered progress and retarded individual development.

Responsibility for health, welfare, housing, and full employment should rest wholly upon private enterprise. Entrance of the federal government into these areas would lead to mastery. "It is significant," Karl Schriftgiesser pointed out, "that Herbert Hoover thought of federal aid as *mastery*, rather than as part of the democratic function of a government of the people, by the people, and for the people."[44] A strong and active government was too easily identified in his mind with socialism.

Even in the depths of the depression, it was

> a question as to whether the American people on the one hand will maintain the spirit of charity and mutual self-help through voluntary giving and the responsibility of local government as distinguished on the other hand from the appropriations out of the Federal Treasury for such purposes. My own conviction is strongly that if we break down this sense of responsibility of individual generosity to individual and mutual self-help in the country in times of national difficulty and if we start appropriations of this character we have not only impaired something infinitely valuable in the life of the American people but have struck at the roots of self-government.[45]

To the end of his life, Hoover retained his assumptions: that wealth is tangible goods in the hands of owners who actually control and direct its use, that the profit motive keeps industry going, and that the property owner's enterprise, daring, and initiative supply the dynamics of American business. Hoover took no account of the silent revolution which, in the last half-century, had transformed our basic economic institutions so as to center control in the managers of a scant two hundred large corpora-

---

[43] Hofstadter, *American Political Tradition*, p. 290.
[44] Karl Schriftgiesser, *This Was Normalcy* (Boston: Little, Brown, 1948), p. 264.
[45] Quoted in Schriftgiesser, *Normalcy*, p. 277.

tions, who frequently owned little stock in the complex economic empires they governed.

THE CORPORATE REVOLUTION

In a book published in 1932, Adolf A. Berle, Jr. (1895–1971), a lawyer and financial expert, presented, with economist Gardiner C. Means (1896–), irrefutable evidence that such a revolution had indeed taken place. Considered by critics one of the most important works bearing on American statecraft since the publication of *The Federalist, The Modern Corporation and Private Property*[46] made it amply clear that individualism and private enterprise were no longer realistic concepts in the United States. The "corporate system," like the feudal system centuries before, had "attracted to itself a combination of attributes and powers, and . . . attained a degree of prominence entitling it to be dealt with as a major social institution." Moreover, by 1932 the corporate system, under unified direction, had become "the principal factor in economic organization through its mobilization of property interests."

"Characteristic of the new system were the surrender of control by investors over their own wealth and the concentration of the wealth of a great many individuals "into huge aggregates." No longer was the typical business unit owned and managed by one or a few men and limited in size by the economic resources of their owners, as in the days of Hoover's youth. Such units had been replaced by tremendous enterprises "in which tens and even hundreds of thousands of workers and property worth hundreds of millions of dollars, belong to tens or even hundreds of thousands of individuals, are combined through the corporate mechanism into a single producing organization under unified control and management." The American Telephone and Telegraph Company, then with $5 billion in assets, 454,000 employees, and 567,694 stockholders, was the prime example of the new order. To all intents and purposes, some two hundred concerns formed economic empires, empires "bounded by no geographical limits, but held together by centralized control." Separation of ownership and control became almost complete. In the American Telephone and Telegraph Company, for example, there was not even a substantial minority interest—the largest holder owned less than 1 percent of the company's stock.

Such corporations had lost the right to be called private. They were quasipublic, depending on "the investing public" for their capital and responsible only to the public for their actions. Although American law made no distinction between the private corporation and the quasipublic, the economics of the two were vastly different. Size alone gave

---

[46] Adolf A. Berle, Jr., *The Modern Corporation and Private Property* (New York: Macmillan, 1932). The quotations in this chapter are from pp. 1–9, 345–57.

them "a social significance not attached to the smaller units of private enterprise" and imposed on them new responsibilities "towards the owners, the workers, the consumers, and the State. . . ." Separation of ownership from control produced in them "a condition where the interests of owner and of ultimate manager may, and often do, diverge, and where many of the checks which formerly operated to limit the use of power disappear, thus requiring a certain degree of governmental protection for the owners. By their reliance on the open market for securities, they assumed legal obligations to the investing public.

"In creating these new relationships, the quasi-public corporation may fairly be said to [have] work[ed] a revolution." The very foundations on which the old economic order had rested had been destroyed and entirely new ones built in their stead. No longer could anyone assert, as Hoover did, "that the quest for profits will spur the owner of industrial property to its [most] effective use" or, for that matter, that individual initiative was a fundamental economic principle in America. The whole question "of the motive force back of industry, and the ends for which the modern corporation can be or will be run" was opened for reexamination. The self-interest of the property owner no longer bore any necessary relation to the disposition of the property.

The corporate system, Berle and Means predicted, "bids fair to be as all-embracing as was the feudal system in its time." Indeed, the corporate system had already achieved a concentration of power in the economic field comparable to the religious power in the medieval church or political power in the national state. Just as feudalism eventually developed its peculiar rationale, so the corporate system devised terms and concepts suited to itself. The future might well "see the economic organism, now typified by the corporation, not only on an equal plane with the State, but possibly even superseding it as the dominant form of social organization." So pervasive had the corporation become that the "long-fought issue of power and its regulation," presumed settled in the United States, was raised anew and with a far greater sense of urgency.

Berle and Means's statement is coldly factual. Although the implications of their data—that big government must meet and conquer big business on behalf of the people if democracy and the corporate system are to live together in harmony—were clear, the authors were content to let these conclusions suggest themselves. Published in 1932, Berle and Means crystallized the issues and furnished realistic foundations for the New Deal.[47]

---

[47] See the authors' later books, which extend their reasoning into more recent times. Adolf A. Berle, *Power Without Property. A New Development in American Political Economy* (New York: Harcourt, Brace, 1959) and Gardiner C. Means, *The Corporate Revolution in America; Economic Reality vs. Economic Theory* (New York: Crowell-Collier, 1962).

AN AGE OF CYNICISM AT BAY

When the stock market—America's symbol of prosperity—crashed in October 1929, the nation literally went to pieces. By the end of 1930, between six and seven million workers were unemployed; by 1932 that number had doubled. Banks collapsed, mortgage payments were halted, bread lines formed, some thirty thousand citizens rushed police at Madison Square Garden, demanding relief, and in Chicago a mob shouting, "We Want Bread" cheered the Communist flag. "Brother, Can you Spare a Dime?" became the national refrain. Crisis fed upon crisis until the situation became desperate. The very foundations of the Old Order were shaken, the premises of the old faith queried. The economic crisis penetrated every corner of the land, creating unrest and dissatisfaction. For the first time in American history men began to doubt the survival of capitalism—indeed, of free government. As the months and years dragged on, people craved a positive program. Above all, they wanted action. In search of a new leader, a new philosophy, and a new policy, they turned to politics, so maligned and neglected in more prosperous days.

The Democratic candidate for president in 1932, Franklin D. Roosevelt, offered voters all three. In accepting the nomination, he promised America "a new deal." Once again, American political thought was forced into new and exciting channels. The prevailing cynicism of the twenties proved to be only skin deep.

CHAPTER SEVENTEEN

FREEDOM REVITALIZED: ROOSEVELT AND THE NEW DEAL

Even in 1932, after the country reached the depth of depression, President Hoover continued to affirm his belief in individualism and to predict dire results if it were abandoned. "Such down-at-the-mouthism contrasted sharply with Roosevelt's tooth-flashing optimism."[1] "Let me assert my firm belief that the only thing we have to fear is fear itself," Franklin D. Roosevelt (1882–1945) proclaimed. "I pledge you, I pledge myself, to a new deal for the American people. Let us all . . . constitute ourselves prophets of a new order of competence and of courage. This is more than a political campaign; it is a call to arms." When the people heeded his call in unprecedented numbers, Roosevelt disdainfully dismissed the past:

> They tried, but their efforts were cast in a pattern of an outworn tradition. Faced by the failure of credit, they proposed only an extension of credit. Stripped of the lure of profit, they resorted only to exhortations and confidence. They knew only the rules of a generation of self seekers. They have no vision, and where there is no vision, the people perish.

Roosevelt was not quite fair. President Hoover—much against his own convictions—had belatedly asked Congress for public relief funds (federal

---

[1] Bailey, *American Pageant*, p. 833.

aid through a Reconstruction Finance Corporation) to resuscitate business. His requests were granted. In the end, Hoover was unwilling to see the people perish, moving significantly away from his own principles to bring them aid. But he acted without conviction; his steps were hesitant—too little and too late.[2] It remained for the new president to act boldly.

The New Deal, at first, embodied no well-rounded ideology. "At the President's request," Miss Perkins recalled, "we steered clear of people who were too theoretical." "What is your philosophy," a young reporter once asked, "Communist, . . . Capitalist, . . . or Socialist?" "Philosophy?" the president asked blandly: "Philosophy! I am a Christian and a Democrat—that's all."[3]

Conceding that his approach was pragmatic and experimental, FDR remarked: "There are counselors these days who say: 'Do nothing'; other counselors say: 'Do everything.' Common sense dictates an avoidance of both extremes. I say to you: 'Do something'; and when you have done that something, if it works, do it some more; and if it does not work, then do something else." Like children in a progressive school, New Dealers learned by doing—by trial and error. What doctrine the New Deal had was largely a doctrine of action, a policy of bold experimentation, aimed at recovery from the rigors of depression. Far from being a deliberate plan (or plot, as its enemies inferred) its ultimate objective was not "clear or specific in Roosevelt's mind, in the mind of the Democratic Party or in the mind of anyone else taking part in the 1932 campaign."[4] "At the heart of the New Deal," Richard Hofstadter has concluded, "there was not a philosophy but a temperament."[5] With the banks closed or closing, with farm and home owners faced with mortgage foreclosures, and with the vast numbers of unemployed mounting daily, the new administration could ill afford the luxury—usual among earlier saviors of society—of debating various approaches and philosophies. Forced by circumstances to act at once, the New Deal's basic concepts emerged as the program developed. Crisis, not preconceived ideology, produced whatever theory the New Deal finally came to embody. No blueprint for a new social order, it was in the beginning hardly more than a shining slogan happily hit upon to win votes and to advance and solidify the Roosevelt administration politically. Even as finally developed, it rested to a large extent

---

[2] See David A. Shannon, *Between the Wars: America 1919–1941* (Boston: Houghton Mifflin, 1965) and Albert V. Romasco, *The Poverty of Abundance: Hoover, the Nation, the Depression* (New York: Oxford University Press, 1965). See also Clarke A. Chambers, *Seedtime of Reform: 1918–1933* (Minneapolis: University of Minnesota Press, 1963); Stanley Coben, *American Economic History: Essays on Interpretation* (Philadelphia: Lippincott, 1966); and Allan F. Davis, *Spearheads for Reform* (New York: Oxford University Press, 1967). All have argued that the picture Roosevelt painted and most Americans have accepted of the twenties as a "prelude to disaster" is not wholly in accord with the facts. The twenties were "years of quiet preparation" for the reform of the thirties.

[3] Frances Perkins, *The Roosevelt I Knew* (New York: Viking, 1946), p. 330.

[4] Perkins, *Roosevelt*, p. 167.

[5] Hofstadter, *American Political Tradition*, p. 311.

on tradition, and it expressed ideas or interests that could be traced far back in American history. For Harold Laski what was remarkable in the New Deal

> is the degree in which it is, in fact, simply the completion of a continuous development of discontent with traditional individualism which goes back, in a sense, to Shays' Rebellion, and, in another, at least to Populism in the period after the Civil War. In these aspects the struggle waged by Jefferson and Jackson against the financial interests embodied first in the Federalist movement, and then in the Bank of the United States, must be regarded in direct line of ancestry. So, too, if from a somewhat different approach, was the tradition of the Republican Progressive movement which Theodore Roosevelt offered to take to Armageddon.[6]

The New Deal, of course, cannot be separated from its leader, Franklin Roosevelt. Some commentators have contended that Roosevelt had developed his own political philosophy long before the Depression struck, and it is now certain that he did more hard thinking and planning before and during his campaign for the presidency than was earlier supposed. Robert E. Sherwood referred to Roosevelt's early orientation toward Jeffersonian principles and underscored Theodore Roosevelt's influence on his cousin, Franklin. The first Roosevelt's 1910 speech at Osawatomie, Kansas, in which TR proclaimed his New Nationalism, urging the national government to exert the power needed to remedy social and political deficiencies, was of "great importance in shaping the structure of the New Deal. . . ."[7]

THE CORE OF ROOSEVELT'S IDEAS

The other tenets of Roosevelt's political creed were similarly familiar. He believed that government not only could but should subordinate private interests to collective interests and substitute cooperation for selfish individualism. "He had a profound feeling for the underdog, a real sense of the critical unbalance of economic life, a very keen awareness that political democracy could not exist side by side with economic plutocracy.[8]

These ideas, though not original, had been slowly developing in Roosevelt's own mind. As early as 1912 he expressed his dissatisfaction with laissez faire individualism.

> Conditions of civilization that come with individual freedom are inevitably bound to bring many questions that mere individual liberty cannot

---

[6] Harold Laski, *The American Democracy* (New York: Viking, 1948), p. 69. See also David Mitrany, "The New Deal: An Interpretation of its Origin and Nature," *American Interpretations* (London: Contact Publications, 1946).

[7] Robert E. Sherwood, *Roosevelt and Hopkins* (New York: Harper & Brothers, 1948), p. 41. See also Rexford Guy Tugwell, *The Democratic Roosevelt* (Garden City, N.Y.: Doubleday, 1957).

[8] Raymond Moley, *After Seven Years* (Harper & Brothers, 1939), pp. 23–24.

solve. This is to my mind exactly what has happened in the past century. We have acquired new sets of conditions of life that require new theories for their solution. . . . I have called this new theory the struggle for the liberty of the community rather than liberty of the individual. . . . Every new star that people have hitched their wagon to for the past half century, whether it be anti-rebating, or anti-trusts, or new-fashioned education, or conservation of our natural resources, or state regulation of common carriers, or commission government, or any of the thousand and one other things that we have run after of late, almost without any exception come under the same heading. They are all steps in the evolution of the new theory of the liberty of the community.

The right of any one individual to work or not as he sees fit, to live to a great extent where and how he sees fit is not sufficient. . . . To put it another way, competition has been shown to be useful up to a point and no further. Cooperation must begin where competition leaves off and cooperation is as good a word for the new theory as any other.[9]

By the 1920s government experience had deepened his understanding:

We are approaching a period similar to that from 1790–1800 when Alexander Hamilton ran the Federal government for the primary good of the chamber of commerce, the speculators and the inside ring of the national government. He was a fundamental believer in an aristocracy of wealth and power—Jefferson brought the government back to the hands of the average voter, through insistence on fundamental principles, and the education of the average voter. We need a similar campaign of education today, and perhaps we shall find another Jefferson.[10]

As Governor of New York, Roosevelt foreshadowed what was to come. "Those who in retrospect look for Franklin's theory of government," Rexford Guy Tugwell observed, "for his conception of the State, will find it [in his speeches as Governor]." "What is the state?" Roosevelt asked in 1930:

It is the duly constituted representative of an organized society of human beings, created for them for their mutual protection and well-being. . . . Our government is not the master but the creature of the people. The duty of the state toward the citizens is the duty of the servant to its master. The people have created it; the people, by common consent, permit its continued existence.

One of the duties of the State is that of caring for its citizens who find themselves the victims of such adverse circumstances as to make them unable to obtain even the necessities for mere existence without the aid of others. . . .

While it is true that we have hitherto principally considered those who through accident or old age were permanently incapacitated, the same responsibility of the State undoubtedly applies when widespread economic conditions render large numbers of men and women incapable of supporting either them-

---

[9] Quoted in Daniel R. Fusfeld, *The Economic Thought of Franklin D. Roosevelt and the Origins of the New Deal* (New York: Columbia University Press, 1956), p. 49.
[10] Fusfeld, *Economic Thought of Roosevelt*, p. 86.

selves or their families because of circumstances beyond their control which make it impossible to find remunerative labor. To these unfortunate citizens aid must be extended by Government, not as a matter of charity, but as a matter of social duty.[11]

At Oglethorpe University on May 22, 1932, Roosevelt developed his concept of an enlarged role for government:

> We cannot review carefully the history of our industrial advance without being struck with its haphazardness, the gigantic waste with which it has been accomplished. . . . Much of this waste is the inevitable by-product of progress in a society which values individual endeavor and which is susceptible to the changing tastes and customs of the people of which it is composed. But much of it, I believe, could have been prevented by greater foresight and by a larger measure of social planning. Such controlling and directive forces as have been developed in recent years reside to a dangerous degree in groups having special interests in our economic order, interests which do not coincide with the interests of the Nation as a whole. . . .

Old-fashioned liberals and conservatives alike accepted this statement as a commitment to collectivism. It was not, however, until late in the campaign, on September 23 at San Francisco's famous Commonwealth Club, that the Brain Trust[12] succeeded in putting Roosevelt's approach in the idiom of political theory. Roosevelt originally planned to deliver a brief, inconsequential greeting to members of the distinguished San Francisco club. But he was persuaded to make a major address, summing up his political philosophy.

The Commonwealth Club speech[13] begins with a summary of the American political tradition, pointing out that the American colonies were an outgrowth of the struggle in Europe against all-powerful central governments. They were founded by people seeking "a balancing—a limiting force." The people were anxious to make their rulers bear "responsibility for the welfare of [their] subjects." Through the American Revolution they accomplished the first steps in securing these objectives, but even after the Revolution the struggle continued. It was especially evident in the first decade under the new Constitution, when Hamilton's belief in powerful government by an elite clashed with Jefferson's faith in individualism and government as servant, not master. Jefferson's view triumphed "in the great election of 1800"; the Hamiltonian effort to establish "a dominant centralized power" was slowed. Jefferson saw government as a means to an end, not as an end in itself. It existed primarily to preserve the rights of the people against harm. In Jefferson's view its business was "not to destroy individualism, but to protect it."

---

[11] Quoted in Tugwell, *Democratic Roosevelt*, p. 204.
[12] Raymond Moley (1886–   ), A. A. Berle, Jr., and Rexford Guy Tugwell (1891–   ) were Roosevelt's chief aides in the 1932 campaign and during the early days of the New Deal. They were dubbed the "Brain Trust."
[13] The Commonwealth Club speech is included in *The Public Papers and Addresses of Franklin D. Roosevelt* (New York: Random House, 1938), I, 742–56.

For a long time economic facts in the United States were such that they fitted Jeffersonian political theory to a "T." Land in the West was substantially free, and opportunities to make a living were numerous enough to permit everyone "who did not shirk the task of earning a living" to do so. Our national resources were sufficient not only for the American people but also for vast numbers of immigrants. The changes produced by the Industrial Revolution promised even greater prosperity and happiness. An unfortunate incidental result of that Revolution, however, was that almost immediately a group of "financial Titans" began to dominate American economic life.

Under the still prevalent Jeffersonian theory of uninhibited individualism, the government was restrained from interfering with their methods, despite the fact that ruthless, wasteful, and corrupt means were frequently employed. As long as the economic plant so much desired was being produced, the ambitious men directing its production were given "free play and unlimited reward," and the government was powerless to interfere. Gradually the public became aroused. Clearsighted men began to see the dangers of corporate power, of having "great uncontrolled and irresponsible units of power within the State" and began to demand government action to alleviate them. At last, under Theodore Roosevelt and Woodrow Wilson, action was taken to assure more effective competition. If World War I had not come along, Roosevelt concluded, a great deal more might have been accomplished. Wilson understood the problem: the American political system, keyed to Jeffersonian concepts, had been built to prevent "the encroachment of political power on the lives of individuals"; now the power that threatened their lives was commercial and financial. Government must take cognizance of this new condition. The problem Wilson "saw so clearly is left with us as a legacy."

Up to this point Roosevelt spoke in the tradition of reformist liberalism. There was nothing in his approach, nothing in his analysis, to set him apart from other liberal spokesmen in the three or four previous decades. It was not until the second half of the Commonwealth Club speech that the theoretical motif peculiarly identified with the New Deal emerged. In 1928 Herbert Hoover spoke of "equality of opportunity" as if it were a reality. Four years later, Roosevelt flatly stated that "equality of opportunity as we have known it no longer exists." The American economy had been so altered by monopolization and depression that a more positive role was required of government.

"As I see it," Roosevelt observed, "the task of Government in its relation to business is to assist the development of an economic declaration of rights, an economic constitutional order." The proper policy of government was to create conditions in which "prosperity is uniform [and] purchasing power is well distributed throughout every group in the Nation," "a form of organization which will bring the scheme of things into balance, even though it may in some measure qualify the freedom of action of individual units within the business" world. Roosevelt did not, however, believe these ideas were contrary to the "American way":

The Declaration of Independence discusses the problem of Government in terms of a contract. Government is a relation of give and take, a contract, perforce, if we would follow the thinking out of which it grew. Under such a contract rulers were accorded power, and the people consented to that power on consideration that they be accorded certain rights. The task of statesmanship has always been the re-definition of these rights in terms of a changing and growing social order. New conditions impose new requirements upon government and those who conduct Government.

Hoover "totally failed to plan ahead in a comprehensive way."[14] Like all adherents of the old order, he never understood that "new conditions impose new requirements," never recognized the necessity for a redefinition of individual rights. To defenders of the status quo, the facts Berle and Means uncovered in 1932 did not alter one iota the responsibilities and functions of government; the American system had been cut from the Jeffersonian pattern and could not be changed. To Roosevelt, however, the picture Berle and Means painted called "for a re-appraisal of values." He was not only willing and anxious to make such a reappraisal but also convinced that the contract on which the American government rested demanded it. Nowhere did Roosevelt support the abandonment of the Jeffersonian ideal and its replacement with one of his own fashioning. Instead, he called (as in the Commonwealth Club speech) for another look at that ideal in the light of new circumstances, with a view toward action.

Jefferson declared that all men possessed "certain inalienable rights," but he mentioned only life, liberty, and the pursuit of happiness. Roosevelt wholeheartedly accepted both the general statement and the specific rights listed, but he was convinced that additions were in order. "Every man has a right to life," of course; but "this means that he has also a right to make a comfortable living." Moreover, it was the government's duty actively to enforce that right. "Our Government," Roosevelt declared, "formal and informal, political and economic, owes to everyone an avenue to possess himself of a portion of [our] plenty sufficient for his needs, through his own work." Roosevelt agreed with Jefferson that every man has a right to his own property. But he interpreted that right in practical terms: the paramount value was the "right to be assured, to the fullest extent attainable, in the safety of his savings"; "all other property rights must yield to it." If, in accord with this principle, governmental restrictions were placed on "the operations of the speculator, the manipulator, even the financier," the restrictions must be accepted as needful— imposed "not to hamper individualism but to protect it." Roosevelt thus thought of himself not as a blurry-eyed radical, but as a "true conservative" who sought

to protect the system of private property and free enterprise by correcting such injustices and inequalities as arise from it. The most serious threat to

---

[14] Rexford Guy Tugwell, "The Progressive Orthodoxy of Franklin D. Roosevelt," *Ethics*, LXIV (October, 1953), 11.

our institutions comes from those who refuse to face the need for change. Liberalism becomes the protection of the farsighted conservative.

Wise and prudent men—intelligent conservatives—have long known that in a changing world worthy institutions can be conserved only by adjusting them to the changing time.[15]

Despite Roosevelt's willingness to use the power of government to achieve greater equality of opportunity, he believed that the possibilities of voluntary action should be exhausted first; government should assume "the function of economic regulation only as a last resort, to be tried only when private initiative, inspired by high responsibility, with such assistance and balance as Government can give, has finally failed."

Looking about him in the years of the Depression, Roosevelt recognized that the time for government action had come. It was necessary then, as never before, not only to prevent a "rising tide of misery" from engulfing the nation, but also to fulfill the terms of the American contract and achieve the utopia "which Jefferson imagined for us in 1776, and which Jefferson, [Theodore] Roosevelt and Wilson sought to bring to realization." Indeed, a larger role for government was implicit in the times themselves.

The day of the great promoter or the financial Titan, to whom we granted anything if only he would build, or develop, is over. Our task now is not the discovery or exploitation of natural resources, or necessarily producing more goods. It is the soberer, less dramatic business of administering resources and plans already in hand, of seeking to reestablish foreign markets for our surplus production, of meeting the problem of underconsumption, of adjusting production to consumption, of distributing wealth and products more equitably, of adapting existing economic organizations to the service of the people. The day of enlightened administration has come.

The New Deal apparently broke with precedent only in its assumption of a mature and finished economy, in which the people could be secure in their economic rights only with the aid of a strong central government. Its primary concern was with the "economic man" and his welfare. Roosevelt saw that

democracy in government could not exist unless, at the same time, there was democracy in opportunity. . . .

In our national life, public and private, the very nature of free government demands that there must be a line of defense held by the yeomanry of business and industry and agriculture—those who have an ownership in their business and a responsibility which give them stability. Any elemental policy, economic or political, which tends to eliminate these dependable defenders of democratic institutions, and to concentrate control in the hands of a few small, powerful groups, is directly opposed to the stability of government and to democratic government itself.

---

[15] Roosevelt, *Papers and Addresses*, V, 389.

> Mechanization of industry and mass production have put unparalleled power in the hands of the few. No small part of our problem today is to bring the fruits of this mechanization and mass production to the people as a whole.[16]

Only government could ultimately provide that kind of service for the people. On their behalf the New Deal was inaugurated.

For a considerable time after taking the oath of office on March 4, 1933, Roosevelt concerned himself with meeting the current crises. He evidently had little opportunity to amplify his ideas or crystallize his thinking. In retrospect the Commonwealth Club speech seemed to provide a theoretical framework, but, as Miss Perkins said, the New Deal "grew out of . . . emerging and necessary rescue actions. . . . The action was not projected from a central pattern. . . ."[17]

But action there was. To some the feverish, almost harum-scarum activity during the famous first 100 days, described in Hugh S. Johnson's *The Blue Eagle, From Egg to Earth*,[18] seemed almost activity for activity's sake, "amorous of devices, contemptuous of ideas."[19] From March 9 to June 16, 1933, a great many pieces of "must legislation" were enacted to assist recovery from the Depression, provide relief to the hard-pressed, and accomplish reform in national institutions. Between 1933 and 1939 additional measures were enacted, directed toward the same purposes. For the most part these measures were lineal descendants of earlier proposals in the Populist, Progressive, and New Freedom programs. Some had already been put into effect in some states or tried overseas and could be patterned partly on actual experience. Together they provided the basis for a revived nation. The necessity of government action had been conclusively proved. Having been so close to the brink of disaster, the country would never return to its previous habits.

But as far reaching as so much government intervention seems in retrospect, the measures establishing it were never integrated into an overall plan. Some were improvisations and had to be altered or abandoned; others were frankly experimental or temporary. Roosevelt did not commit himself indefinitely to any particular New Deal program. Nor did he state his policies in terms of theory. He left it to others to synthesize and rationalize action and events.

HENRY WALLACE: PHILOSOPHER OF THE NEW DEAL

The most systematic thinker of the New Deal's early years was Henry Agard Wallace (1888–1965), an erstwhile Theodore Roosevelt Progressive,

---

[16] Perkins, *Roosevelt*, p. 173.

[17] Roosevelt, *Papers and Addresses*, V, 211, 299.

[18] Hugh S. Johnson, *The Blue Eagle, From Egg to Earth* (Garden City, N.Y.: Doubleday, 1935).

[19] G. Lowes Dickinson, *Appearances* (Garden City, N.Y.: Doubleday, 1914), p. 153.

and Franklin Roosevelt's secretary of agriculture. Wallace's effectiveness in supplying a conceptual framework lay partly in his solid grounding in economics but even more, perhaps, in his ability to give the New Deal program a highly moral, even a religious, cast. Elaborating candidate Roosevelt's theme of 1932[20] and restating the New Deal's basic premise, Wallace said that physical frontiers in the United States were gone, and with their passing, economic affairs had grown in both number and complexity until they dominated American life. To deal with new issues, we must equal our forefathers in courage and persistence and conquer the new frontiers of the mind and heart. We must do more than merely "patch [the] outworn economic structure" our ancestors had erected; we must devote ourselves to the urgent task of "trying to build seaworthy vessels in which to reach a new world. . . ." The New Deal was designed to achieve, through cooperation and willingness to experiment, "a plan of national coordination, realistic, yet idealistic," by which a more equitable distribution of the national income and a better balance between our major producing groups might be secured. In contradistinction to those who argued that the economy was at the mercy of the dictates of supply and demand, its direction determined by natural laws, Wallace stressed the necessity of economic planning under the auspices of politically responsible government:

> Our land of tomorrow must be surveyed and trails hacked out. To go in and take possession means mental and spiritual toil, comparable with the physical toil of those who built the New England stone fences, cleared the Ohio woods, drained Northern Iowa and built the great highways of the past and present . . . [all this was done by] men with a rare capacity for planning. They had no romantic illusions; they knew the cost and decided to pay it. Hearts, minds, and wills were set to the accomplishments of definite physical tasks, and the jobs were done with a rather remarkable continuous joy in their accomplishment.

That same enthusiasm must be re-created and brought to bear by the present generation in the invention, building, and effective operation of "new social machinery," and used to "carry out the Sermon on the Mount" instead of "the law of the jungle." It was the great opportunity of the New Deal, Wallace declared, to symbolize this "new state of heart and mind" and lead the nation to "new standards of accomplishment."

The program Wallace conceived had two parts: "planning in the physical sense of the term," on the one hand, and change in "the rules of the game," on the other. Both were necessary, but in the 1930s the second part was the most important. As Roosevelt pointed out in the Commonwealth Club speech, the bad effects of individualism must be curbed. "If the

---

[20] Wallace's chief work in this period was *New Frontiers* (New York: Harcourt, Brace, 1934). The quotations here are from pp. 3–29, 272–76. Louis D. Brandeis, no visionary, read Wallace's book carefully. *New Frontiers* was among the most extensively "marked up" books in his library.

majority of us are to have automobiles," Wallace commented, "we must obey the traffic lights and observe certain rules of common decency in order to get speedily and safely from one place to another." Once these "habits of mutual consideration" were well established, everyone on the highways found the advantages of regulation to outweigh the handicaps. The same was true of the economy: economic traffic rules must be enacted and limits placed on competition and individualism as they were placed on highway driving. Wallace declared that it was "absolutely necessary for the state to assume its true functions" of "directing, watching, stimulating and restraining" the process of production and distribution as circumstances suggested or necessity demanded. The goal of government should be to establish a reasonable relationship between the prices the several economic groups in society received for their goods and services and to assure an economic commonwealth in America in which all men were "members of a common body, lending each other mutual help and services." When this goal was reached, America would be a democracy "worthy of the name . . . guided by concern for social justice and social charity—in other words, the greatest good for the greatest number." If agriculture, labor, and industry could achieve this balanced relationship of national income through their own efforts, so much the better; the degree to which they actually did accomplish it would determine the extent to which government power must be exerted.

Wallace felt a peculiar urgency about effecting change. The "New Deal spirit ebbs and flows," he warned; "progressive liberals get a real opportunity to change the rules only about once in a generation." Complacency was more common in politics than the spirit of reform. The opportunity to act must be seized as soon as it presented itself, and the New Deal offered such an opportunity. Experience demonstrated that there might be only eight to sixteen years in which to rebuild America; so Wallace called for immediate action, especially by the young people. If the necessary changes were made in time by "an aroused, educated Democracy," socialism, communism, and fascism could and would be avoided. Even though these ideologies seemed to offer a shorter, straighter road to tomorrow, the very fact that the new rules were evolved from "the clash of free opinion" would make them better rules. Under them America would go further than under "the precise, decisive dogma of Communism or Fascism."

Wallace noted the limits he envisaged for the New Deal program. There was no likelihood of its leading to a dictatorship, and he saw no reason "why we in the United States should go into precise detailed planning. . . ." In fact, the United States had a good chance to escape the regimentation that had long been common in Europe. "It is necessary in a democracy," he declared, "to furnish the red and green lights to guide the traffic, but not to supply drivers for every car on the road."

In essence, Wallace demanded a new unity and a new hope. We have come to a new frontier, he declared; to cross it, we must rely upon cooperation and "social invention." Conquering the old frontier demanded individualistic competition and mechanical invention; conquering the new frontier would demand new forces. "Power and wealth were worshipped in the old days. Beauty and justice and joy of spirit must be worshipped in the new." Devices must be developed to permit that worship. Only if the men tackling the new frontier were subject to "social discipline" and were moved by the spirit of "cooperative achievement" toward "social justice and social charity" could success be assured. With that success

> men [might] rightfully feel that they are serving a function as high as that of any minister of the Gospel. They will not be Socialists, Communists or Fascists, but plain men trying to gain by democratic methods the professed objectives of the Communists, Socialists and Fascists: security, peace, and the good life for all.

By 1936, as the effect of the New Deal measures were being felt in the nation, Roosevelt turned his attention, as Wallace had urged, to a frontal attack on economic privilege. FDR struck this new note in his annual message to Congress on January 3, 1936. The New Deal would now endeavor "to restore power to those to whom it rightfully belonged." Under its aegis the federal government had become what it should be in a democratic society, "the representative and the trustee of the public interest," whose constant and rightful concern was "the adjustment of burdens, the help of the needy, the protection of the weak, the liberation of the exploited and the genuine protection of the people's property." Roosevelt resumed the battle waged by Jefferson, Jackson, Theodore Roosevelt, and Wilson against a power-seeking minority. This time, however, the battle was being won. For the first time "an economic constitutional order" was being created in America. Now the government, with "new instruments of economic power," stood between the people and the selfish financial and industrial groups that had long dominated American economic life, preventing them from pursuing their age-old policies of "Autocracy toward labor, toward stockholders, toward consumers, toward public sentiment."

The New Deal, Roosevelt declared, demonstrated the constitutional flexibility of the American political system, its ability to act energetically when the occasion demanded. At the same time it indicated the limits of that system, for although the New Deal introduced variations and relied on experiment, it clung to proven theoretical concepts. It was truly conservative. It was, clearly, "not a work of revolution, but of restoration. Its historic function was not to inaugurate but to save. . . ." "A new chapter in the history of popular government" had been written.[21] "We have," the president proudly proclaimed, "returned the control of the Federal Government to the City of Washington."

---

[21] D. W. Brogan, *The Era of Franklin D. Roosevelt* (New Haven, Conn.: Yale University Press, 1950), p. 361.

JOHN DEWEY
CRITICIZES THE NEW DEAL

Others were not so sure the millennium was at hand. No one argued the need for further reconstruction more convincingly than America's distinguished philosopher and outstanding liberal, Professor John Dewey (1859–1952) of Columbia University. In his book *Liberalism and Social Action*[22] Dewey noted that modern men had found a method better than violence for accomplishing change—"that of cooperative and experimental science," of social planning. The discovery of that method—and its utilization by the New Deal—precluded any future assumption "that democratic political institutions are incapable either of further development or of constructive social application." Utilizing organized intelligence as its method, society had "through an authorized majority entered upon the path of social experimentation leading to great social change" and had done it peacefully, despite the opposition of a decidedly "recalcitrant minority." Social legislation—"measures which add performance of social services to the older functions of government"—had become part of the political edifice without the predicted toppling of the structure. "The value of this addition," Dewey concluded, "is not to be despised. It marks a decided move away from laissez-faire liberalism, and has considerable importance in educating the public mind to a realization of the possibilities of organized social control."

To realize these possibilities necessitated far more than a New Deal. If "the cause of liberalism" were not to be lost, "the liberty of individuals [would] eventually [have to] be supported by the very structure of economic organization." The New Deal had only begun to accomplish all that the application of "socially organized intelligence" might be expected to produce. In other words, Dewey confirmed the basic conservatism of the New Deal and called upon it to raise the flag of "renascent liberalism." Now that it was mechanically possible for the material needs of all to be met, the truly liberal program must insist that men be liberated from the bonds of economic necessity and enabled to realize their individual creative and spiritual capacities. "We should either surrender our professed belief in the supremacy of ideal and spiritual values and accommodate our belief to the predominant material orientation, or we should through organized endeavor institute the socialized economy of material security and plenty that will release human energy for pursuit of higher values."

> The ultimate place of economic organization in human life is to assure the secure basis for an ordered expression of individual capacity and for the satisfaction of the needs of man in non-economic directions. . . . [Such a basis now] can be brought about by organized social reconstruction that puts

---

[22] John Dewey, *Liberalism and Social Action* (New York: Putnam's, 1935), pp. 33, 41, 54, 79–93.

the results of the mechanism of abundance at the free disposal of individuals.

Liberalism has to gather itself together to formulate the ends to which it is devoted in terms of means that are relevant to the contemporary situation. The only form of enduring social organization that is now possible is one in which the new forces of productivity are cooperatively controlled and used in the interests of the effective liberty and the cultural development of the individuals that constitute society. Such a social order cannot be established by an unplanned and external convergence of the actions of separate individuals, each of whom is bent on personal private advantage. . . . Organized social planning, put into effect for the creation of an order in which industry and finance are socially directed in behalf of institutions that provide the material basis for the cultural liberation and growth of individuals, is now the sole method of social action by which liberalism can realize its professed aims.

Because the New Deal had not adopted the social regimentation necessary for fully achieving the objective of a truly liberal creed, Dewey believed, it had failed the cause of liberalism.

STILL LOOKING FORWARD

When Roosevelt restated his beliefs in the famous Four Freedoms speech to Congress on January 6, 1941,[23] he did not adopt Dewey's suggestions. His faith in positive government, both for the United States and for the world, remained undaunted. Instead of disregarding individual rights, as opponents charged, the New Deal had preserved and enlarged them. One of its greatest accomplishments was to make the "people conscious of their individual stake in the preservation of democratic life in America," giving them the stamina and courage to defend it. The rights men would fight and die for were

Equality of opportunity for youth and for others;
Jobs for those who can work;
Security for those who need it;
The ending of special privilege for the few;
The preservation of civil liberties for all;
The enjoyment of the fruits of scientific progress in a wider and constantly rising standard of living.

Nor was this the time to sidetrack a program to achieve those rights. Social and economic problems were the "root cause of the social revolution which is today a supreme factor in the world." Only by continuing to work toward a solution could the United States become strong enough internally to stave off aggression and assure "the happiness of future gen-

---

[23] The words as well as the ideas of his Four Freedoms speech must be credited, Robert Sherwood has told us, to the President himself. Sherwood, *Roosevelt and Hopkins*, p. 231. The speech is reproduced in Roosevelt, *Papers and Addresses*, V, 663–72.

erations of Americans." "Men do not live by bread alone; they do not fight by armaments alone." The source of their strength and of their willingness to fight ultimately lay in their "unshakeable belief" in the worth of their own way of life.

Social betterment must now be made a world goal. The "four essential human freedoms" that had meaning and inspired devotion were the—

freedom of speech and expression—everywhere in the world;

freedom of every person to worship God in his own way—everywhere in the world;

freedom from want—which, translated into world terms, means economic understandings which will secure to every nation a healthy peacetime life for its inhabitants—everywhere in the world;

freedom from fear—which, translated into world terms, means a world-wide reduction of armaments to such a point and in such a thorough fashion that no nation will be in a position to commit an act of physical aggression against any neighbor—anywhere in the world.

The achievement of such a world was "no vision of a distant millennium." It could be won "in our own time and generation." It required that other countries adopt the same methods that were then being utilized in America—quiet and steady adjustment to change without reliance on "the concentration camp or the quick-lime in the ditch." America had begun what Roosevelt hoped would become "a perpetual peaceful revolution," and he urged the rest of the world to follow suit. The New Deal had demonstrated that the nation could "quietly adjust itself to changing conditions" and emerge stronger than before. Therein lay a constructive lesson for the world.

Although the war practically brought the New Deal to a halt, forcing America's energies to be focused on defense for the remainder of Roosevelt's life, he continued to look ahead. No one was more conscious than he that the New Deal had not solved all the nation's social and economic problems. The country had resolutely taken a new direction, and it showed no signs of wishing to retrace its steps or flee with Herbert Hoover back to the nineteenth-century paradise of individualism. The people's command was still, *Forward.*

SECURING ECONOMIC RIGHTS

In his 1944 State of the Union address to Congress, Roosevelt summed up the "one supreme objective for the future" in the word "security"—"not only physical security . . . [but] also economic security, social security, moral security—in a family of nations." "It is our duty now to begin to lay the plans and determine the strategy for . . . the establishment of an American standard of living higher than ever before known. We cannot be content, no matter how high that general standard of living may be, if some fraction of our people—whether it be one-third or one-fifth or one-tenth—is ill-fed, ill-clothed, ill-housed, and insecure." America had learned that political rights alone were not enough "to assure . . . equality in the pursuit of happiness." We had come to a clear realization that true individual freedom could not exist without economic security and independence. " 'Necessitous men are not free men.' People who are hungry and out of a job are the stuff of which dictatorships are made." If we would avoid dictatorship in the United States, we must make economic rights and freedom as secure as political rights and freedom.

A second bill of rights must be implemented "under which a new basis of security and prosperity can be established for all—regardless of station, race, or creed." Such a bill of rights should be the nation's primary goal "after this war is won." It should include—

The right to a useful and remunerative job in the industries, or shops or farms or mines of the Nation;

The right to earn enough to provide adequate food and clothing and recreation;

The right of every farmer to raise and sell his products at a return which will give him and his family a decent living;

The right of every businessman, large and small, to trade in an atmosphere of freedom from unfair competition and domination by monopolies at home or abroad;

The right of every family to a decent house;

The right to adequate medical care and the opportunity to achieve and enjoy good health;

The right to adequate protection from the economic fears of old age, sickness, accident, and unemployment;

The right to a good education.

Convinced that "unless there is security here at home there cannot be lasting peace in the world," the president urged Congress, even in wartime, to explore ways of developing an economic constitution. "Our fighting men abroad—and their families at home—expect" a progressive program to be enacted "and have the right to insist upon it. It is to their demands that this Government should pay heed rather than to the whining demands of selfish pressure groups. . . ." But, the president warned, Congress must at once apply itself to this task for another and much more important reason. Unless a program of positive action were set in motion, a rightist reaction in the United States would remain a real danger. If such a reaction should develop, "if history were to repeat itself and we were to return to the so-called normalcy of the 1920s—then it is certain that, even though we shall have conquered our enemies on the battlefields abroad, we shall have yielded to the spirit of fascism here at home." This disaster must be avoided at all cost, and the best way to do it was to begin a broad program of counteraction at once. It "is definitely the responsibility of the Congress so to do"; to shirk their duty would be to shirk their "solemn obligation under God to serve this Nation in its most critical hour—to keep this Nation great—to make this Nation greater in a better world."

CHAPTER EIGHTEEN

CONFLICT
AND ACCEPTANCE

The New Deal's philosophy and program, following a stubbornly conservative decade, aroused anger and reaction.[1] The most vehement opposition came from businessmen, who predicted collapse even as the New
Deal was attempting to answer their anguished pleas for help.

THE AMERICAN LIBERTY LEAGUE

In August 1934 a bitter, outspoken, well-financed opposition organized
the American Liberty League. Its purposes were "to defend and uphold
the Constitution of the United States," "to teach the necessity of respect
for rights of persons and property," "to encourage and protect individual
and group initiative and enterprise, to foster the right to work, earn, save
and acquire property, and to preserve the ownership and lawful use of
property when acquired." Under its appealing battle cry, "The Constitution, Its Restoration and Preservation," the league declared:

---

[1] See Joseph Boskin, *Opposition Politics: The Anti-New Deal Tradition* (Beverly Hills,
Calif.: Glencoe Press, 1968), pp. 33–57.

The Constitution is perfect; we do not seek to change it, or to add to or subtract from it; we seek to rescue it from those who misunderstand it, misuse and mistreat it. To correct these evils amendments may be required later, but we hope not.[2]

"The Constitution," wrote the league's vice-president, Raoul E. Desvernine, is "our king." Property is "the arch upon which civilized government rests," "the very foundation of American tradition." Ignoring these maxims, New Dealers misconceived the basic tenets of American politics:

We find latent in their conception of law that law emanates solely from the will of the majority of the people, and can, therefore, be modified at any time to meet majority wishes. This doctrine is absolutely totalitarian. . . . Our political system is predicated on the doctrine that there are some immutable laws of nature and certain other divinely sanctioned rights, which the Constitution and our tradition recognized as being above and beyond the power of the majority, or of any other group of individuals or officials of the Government. . . .[3]

Americans must soon decide which road they wished to take. The signposts, as Desvernine identified them, were Washington, Hamilton, Madison, and other Founding Fathers; the guidebooks were the Declaration of Independence and the Constitution. On the other road were mountebanks, whose professed objectives bore little resemblance to the traditional democratic dogma and whose moves must be carefully watched. The New Dealers were deceitfully attempting to manipulate the "democratic processes, to maneuver democratic forces, and finally . . . to convert, improperly, Constitutional machinery to the furtherance of their designs." These attempts were clearly visible to Desvernine in Roosevelt's 1936 State of the Union address: "We have undertaken a new order of things, . . . *a permanent readjustment of many of our ways of thinking and therefore of many of our social and economic arrangements.*" In Wallace's *New Frontiers*, Desvernine found additional evidence that the New Deal would provide the means for "plain men . . . *to gain by democratic methods the professed objectives of the Communists, Socialists, and Fascists.*"

"Has any economic, social, or human activity been left out of their 'spheres' of governmental authority and control?" asked Desvernine. "Surely, no comparable control over our economic and social life was ever contended for by any other group or individual. Other economic autocrats, if there be any, were mere little fish alongside of this Leviathan." So stark was Desvernine's image of the emerging autocrat, and so firm his

[2] Records of the American Liberty League, Firestone Library, Princeton University. See also Frederick Rudolph, "The Liberty League, 1934–1940," *American Historical Review*, LVI (October, 1950), 19–33.
[3] Raoul E. Desvernine, *Democratic Despotism* (New York: Dodd, Mead, 1936). The quotations here are from pp. 6, 22, 27–28, 175–77. Italics added.

faith in the ruling plutocracy, that he indicted the whole New Deal program.

The voters did not heed Desvernine and other prophets of doom within the American Liberty League, and by 1939 the league virtually gave up. A last-gasp attempt was made that year, when Albert J. Nock brought out a new edition of Herbert Spencer's *Man Versus the State*. It would provide, the publisher's blurb suggested, "the present lover of freedom with a dialectic basis that will serve him as fundamentally as Marx's *Das Kapital* serves the Communist." Only by adherence to Spencer's principles could America be saved from the goblins of statism.

> All that the State can do for the best interests of society—all it can do to promote a permanent and stable well-being of society—is by way of these purely negative interventions. Let it go beyond them and attempt the promotion of society's well-being by positive coercive interventions upon the citizen, and whatever apparent and temporary social good may be effected will be greatly at the cost of real and permanent good.[4]

Depression-ridden Americans had already seriously prejudiced their future; if they would yet save themselves, if they would check "the riotous progress of Statism," they must return to the philosophy of Spencer.

Hoover as Critic

In vehemence and unyielding persistence none of the New Deal's critics matched Herbert Hoover. His books and speeches presented a rapid-fire attack. The very length of his battle and the eminence of his position, quite apart from the merits of his case, focused attention on his pronouncements. Like Desvernine, Hoover threw the New Deal and all its works into the totalitarian cesspool, which contained fascism, nazism, and communism. "The New Deal forgets it is solely by production of more goods and more varieties of goods and services that we advance the standard of living and security of men," the former President remarked in 1936. "If we constantly decrease costs and prices and keep up earnings, the production of plenty will be more and more widely distributed." "These laws may be restitched in new phrases," he admitted, "but they are the very shoes of human progress."

Hoover labeled Roosevelt's resort to government to stimulate economic recovery "Mother Hubbard economics." Refusing to admit that the nation had benefited from such efforts, he claimed to see in them only "an attack on the foundations of freedom," the enslavement of the people by the imposition of new taxes, the surrender of Congress to personal leadership, and the "violation of the rights of men and of self-government." For Hoover the choice was easy: there were certain economic laws "which neither tricks of organization nor the rigors of depression, nor the march

---

[4] Albert J. Nock, Introduction to Herbert Spencer's *The Man Versus the State* (Caldwell, Idaho: Caxton Printers, 1940), pp. vii–viii.

of time, nor New Dealers, nor Socialists, nor Fascists can change. There are some principles which came into the universe along with the shooting stars of which worlds are made, and they have always been and ever will be true." Under their beneficent reign, America had "so triumphed in this long climb of mankind toward plenty that we had reached Mount Pisgah, where we looked over the promised land of abolished poverty." The fruits of that triumph could be saved only if "the little prophets of the New Deal" would return to the time-tested economic principles, only if they would forego "unstable currencies, unbalanced budgets, debts and taxes."[5]

Hoover's objections were shared by more temperate critics, including Senator Robert A. Taft (1889–1953), son of William Howard Taft, who likewise condemned the New Deal as "inspired by a hostility to the entire pre-existing economic system." "The New Deal has failed," Senator Taft wrote in 1939.

> The rights asserted by the Declaration of Independence and conferred by the Constitution are individual rights. They are conferred on each individual, not on any class of people or on society in general. The whole history of America reveals a system based on individual opportunity, individual initiative, individual freedom to earn one's own living in one's own way, and to conduct manufacture, commerce, agriculture, or other business; on rugged individualism, if you please, which it has become so fashionable to deride. . . .
>
> Opportunity, and not security, is still the goal of young America, and even of middle-aged and old America. The burden of security for those who cannot work must not be so heavy as to destroy or seriously reduce opportunity for those who can work.[6]

CONFLICT WITH THE COURT

After Roosevelt's landslide reelection in 1936, criticisms of the New Deal program from politicians, some of them self-serving, could be tolerated. Opposition from the Supreme Court was an entirely different matter. A majority, still fervently devoted to laissez faire, had invalidated not only the National Industrial Recovery Act, which the President had described as "the most important and far-reaching [act] ever enacted by the American Congress," but also the first Agricultural Adjustment Act and several other measures the Roosevelt administration considered important to the success of the New Deal. It began to appear that the entire New Deal legislative package was in danger of being lost "in a maze of constitu-

---

[5] The quotations are from Herbert Hoover, *Crisis to Free Men*, reprinted in his *American Ideals versus the New Deal* (New York: Scribner's, 1936), *passim*.

[6] *A Republican Program*, Speeches and Broadcasts of Robert A. Taft (Washington, D.C.: Ransdell Incorporated, 1939), pp. 45, 47. The same ideas appear in Thomas E. Dewey, *The Case Against the New Deal* (New York: Harper & Brothers, 1940).

tional metaphors."[7] "A dead hand was being laid to stay it all. It was the hand of the Supreme Court of the United States."[8] Like the Federalists, in 1801, the Old Guard had taken refuge in the judiciary. "They steal," President Roosevelt declared, "the livery of great national constitutional ideals to serve discredited special interests."[9]

During the 1936 presidential campaign, Roosevelt muted his attitude toward the Court. The Democratic platform merely declared:

> If these [social and economic] problems cannot be effectively solved by legislation within the Constitution, we shall seek such clarifying amendment as . . . [we] shall find necessary, in order adequately to regulate commerce, protect public health and safety and safeguard economic security. Thus we propose to maintain the letter and spirit of the Constitution.[10]

But after his triumph at the polls, Roosevelt submitted to Congress a plan to reorganize the federal judiciary. He proposed giving a Supreme Court justice past the age of seventy six months in which to retire. If he failed to do so, he could continue in office, but the Chief Executive would appoint an additional justice—presumably younger and better able to carry the heavy load. Because six justices were in this category, the president would have at once six appointments to make. His proposal would, he said, "bring to the decision of social and economic problems younger men who have had personal experience and contact with modern facts." "I will appoint Justices who will act as Justices and not as legislators,"[11] the president explained.

> Unless the complexion of the Supreme Court be changed, two or three elderly judges living in cloistered seclusion and thinking in terms of a bygone day can block nearly all the efforts of a popularly elected President and a popularly elected Congress to correct these ills. . . . Those who oppose this plan are not afraid *for* democracy. They are afraid *of* democracy.[12]

In the president's original proposal there was no hint of a desire to change the decisions of the Court or to subordinate the views of the justices to those of the executive and Congress. Roosevelt indicated that he wished only to clear a crowded docket. In his message of March 4, 1937, however, he moved closer to the real issue, likening the judiciary to an unruly horse on the government gang plough, unwilling to pull with its teammates, the executive and Congress.[13] The crucial question was not whether the

---

[7] Assistant Attorney General Robert H. Jackson, *Reorganization of the Federal Judiciary*, Hearing before the Committee on the Judiciary, U.S. Senate, 75th Cong., 1st sess., Pt. 1, 1937, p. 44.

[8] Roosevelt, *Papers and Addresses*, VI, 1.

[9] Roosevelt, *Papers and Addresses*, V, 14.

[10] "Democratic Platform of 1936," *New York Times*, June 26, 1936, p. 13.

[11] Roosevelt's Fireside Chat of March 9, 1937, quoted in Brogan, *Era of Roosevelt*, p. 231.

[12] Sherwood, *Roosevelt and Hopkins*, p. 108.

[13] Roosevelt, *Papers and Addresses*, VI, 116.

Court had kept up with the calendar, but whether it had kept up with the country. In a nationwide Fireside Chat on March 9, the president explained:

> When the Congress has sought to stabilize national agriculture, to improve the conditions of labor, to safeguard business against unfair competition, to protect our national resources, and in many other ways, to serve our clearly national needs, the majority of the Court has been assuming the power to pass on the wisdom of these acts of the Congress—and to approve or disapprove the public policy written into these laws. . . . We have, therefore, reached the point as a nation where we must take action to save the Constitution from the Court and the Court from itself. We must find a way to take an appeal from the Supreme Court to the Constitution itself. We want a Supreme Court which will do justice under the Constitution—not over it. In our courts we want a government of laws and not of men.[14]

To support the charge that "the Court has been acting not as a judicial body, but as a policy-making body," the president drew his most devastating ammunition from the dissenting justices themselves. Of the majority opinion, holding the Agricultural Adjustment Act invalid, the dissenters said that it was a "tortured construction of the Constitution"; in another case they charged the majority with reading their "personal economic predilections" into the Constitution. "In the face of these . . . opinions," the president said, "there is no basis for the claim made by some members of the Court that something in the Constitution had compelled them regretfully to thwart the will of the people."[15]

From the start the president's proposal, dubbed "Court Packing," ran into noisy opposition. Supreme Court justices were once again pictured as demigods far above the sweaty crowd, weighing public policy in the delicate scale of immutable law. "Constitutionality" was intoned as if it were an esoteric treasure, as undeviating and precise as the orbits of the spheres. "The Constitution," organic and deific—not the currently dominant judicial view of right and wrong—was the barrier to action. In its adverse report the Senate Judiciary Committee said, in words Alexander Hamilton might have written:

> If the Court of last resort is to be made to respond to a prevalent sentiment of a current hour, politically imposed, that Court must ultimately become subservient to the pressure of public opinion of the hour, which might at the moment embrace mob passion abhorrent to a more calm, lasting consideration.
> True it is that courts, like Congresses, should take account of the advancing strides of civilization. True it is that law, being a progressive science, must be pronounced progressively and liberally; but the milestones of liberal progress are made to be noted and counted with caution rather than merely

---

[14] Roosevelt, *Papers and Addresses*, VI, 125–26.
[15] Roosevelt, *Papers and Addresses*, VI, 125–26.

to be encountered and passed. Progress is not a mad mob march; rather, it is a steady, invincible stride.

With us, the committee concluded, democracy could not be equated with majority rule. Reliance on political responsibility declared and enforced at the ballot box and in legislative halls—the very essence of democracy in most free societies—was not enough for us.

> Our law reports are filled with decisions scattered throughout those long years reassuring the citizen of his constitutional rights, restraining States, restraining the Congress, restraining the Executive, restraining majorities, and preserving the noblest in rights of individuals.[16]

For the committee this was the design and purpose of a "written Constitution and uncontrolled judiciary."

The controversy over the president's plan raged for over five months. He had few supporters, and in the end Congress refused to enact the legislation. "The public may have been irritated by the obstructionism of the Supreme Court, but it did not wish that revered institution to be tampered with."[17] As it turned out the Court settled the issue itself.[18] While the president was bearing down on the justices and the Congress was debating his proposal, one of the most important New Deal enactments—the National Labor Relations Act—was before the Court for decision. Several cases had been argued. On April 12, 1937, Chief Justice Hughes put forward a broad and encompassing definition of commerce, conceding to Congress the power to protect the lifelines of national economy from private industrial warfare. Arguments that had proved effective in previous cases now availed nothing. "These cases," Hughes commented summarily, "are not controlling here."[19]

The chief justice's colleagues, and others, naturally supposed that the man who now took a position apparently at odds with his earlier pronouncements must have seen a new light. "Every consideration brought forward to uphold the Act before us was applicable to support the Acts held unconstitutional in cases decided within two years,"[20] Justice

---

[16] Senate Report No. 711, 75th Cong., 1st sess., 1937, pp. 19–23.

[17] Morison, *History of American People*, p. 970.

[18] At the end of the struggle, FDR reflected: "I feel convinced . . . that the change would never have come, unless this frontal attack had been made on the philosophy of the majority of the Court. That is why I regard it as a turning point in our modern history." Roosevelt, *Papers and Addresses*, Introduction, 1937 vol., p. lxvii.

Professor Schmidhauser, endorsing the president's observation, writes: "With a few important exceptions, the decisions of the pre-1937 Hughes Court were simply continuations of the judicial policies of the Fuller, White, and Taft Courts. After 1937, however, came a tremendously important period of reevaluation and sometimes of reversal of earlier doctrinal trends." John R. Schmidhauser, *The Supreme Court as Final Arbiter in Federal-State Relations 1789–1957* (Chapel Hill, N.C.: University of North Carolina Press, 1958), p. 162.

[19] *National Labor Relations Board* v. *Jones-Laughlin Steel Corporation*, 301 U.S. 1 (1937), 41.

[20] *Board* v. *Jones-Laughlin*, p. 77.

McReynolds growled in dissent. Although Hughes denied to his dying day that he had changed his position, President Roosevelt firmly believed that this "clear-cut victory [for his program] on the bench . . . did more than anything else to bring about the defeat of the plan in the halls of Congress." Before a single judge resigned, before any appointments were made, "the Court began to interpret the Constitution instead of torturing it."[21]

The historic Court-packing episode underscored the most characteristic aspects of our tradition—its ambiguity, its richness, its complexity. It highlighted what might be our major contribution to the theory and practice of government—rejection of all absolutes, whether under the auspices of majorities or minorities, of interests or of numbers. In this bitter controversy the arguments on both sides were framed in terms of our tradition. In this struggle both sides won, both lost. The inconclusiveness of the outcome was itself significant.

POTSHOTS FROM THE FRINGES

Opposition to Roosevelt and the New Deal was not limited to the conservative viewpoint, expressed by businessmen and Supreme Court justices. They were also criticized—and just as vehemently—from the extremes of the Left and the Right. Among early critics of the New Deal was Earl Browder (1891–   ), general secretary of the Communist party in America from 1930 to 1945. While he attacked the Old Deal for its resistance to change and emphasis on the interests of big business, he condemned the New Deal as merely "a new form [of]) the fundamental Old Deal policies." The New Deal sought to put government "*at the head* of big business, with the proclamation that thereby business had been 'subordinated to the general good.' " Only the Communist party adhered to the principles of the Declaration of Independence. Indeed, in 1934 those principles required "the dictatorship of the proletariat . . . [in] the form of . . . workers' and farmers' councils—the Soviet power," not simply a new variety of the Old Deal.[22]

Socialists also objected to the New Deal. The perennial candidate for president on the Socialist ticket, Norman Thomas (1884–1968),[23] chided Roosevelt for failing to move far enough to overcome poverty and insecurity. Public housing, Thomas alleged, was mere "boondoggling" and "made work"; one-third of the people were still "housed in shacks and slums fit only for destruction,"; the so-called "social security legislation" omitted "altogether the vital matter of health insurance or any equivalent for it"; unemployment compensation was totally inadequate.

---

[21] Roosevelt, *Papers and Addresses*, VI, lxvi.
[22] The quotations here are taken from Browder's Manifesto of the eighth Convention of the Communist Party of the United States of America, April, 1934, published as an appendix to Earl Browder, *What is Communism?* (New York: Vanguard, 1936).
[23] Norman Thomas, *After the New Deal, What?* (New York: Macmillan, 1936), pp. 16–21.

The most that one can say is that . . . Roosevelt had to act in a crisis. The principles to guide any effective action were not be found in his own platform, and certainly not in the musty Republican document. Like many a politician before him, he had to turn to ideas advanced by Socialists. The trouble is not that he took some of them, but that he took so few and carried them out so unsatisfactorily.

From the far right home-grown demagogues condemned the New Deal. Charles E. Coughlin (1891–   ), a Roman Catholic priest, used the radio to broadcast, along with his anti-Semitic propaganda, denunciations of capitalism itself and of Roosevelt and the New Deal for attempting to save it.

By 1935 Coughlin's case against the administration achieved some coherence. As long as the bankers remained untouched, he said, the Old Deal of economics reigned supreme. The administration had sought to nationalize industry while leaving banking in private hands, whereas it should have nationalized banks and left industry in private hands. "We demand ownership of the banks . . . [but] I protest most vehemently against any government going into business." In this way Coughlin was seeking to unite agrarian radicals and the small businessmen of the cities against the president.[24]

Dr. Francis E. Townsend (1867–1960) attacked the New Deal for its failure to provide adequate relief for the elderly. The simplicity of the plan he offered—a pension of $200 a month, financed by a federal sales tax, for every person sixty years of age or older, the total to be spent within a month of receipt—and Townsend's own messianic zeal in its behalf won converts by the thousands. Townsend's efforts doubtless hastened passage of the Social Security Act in 1935, but his ideas thereafter lost much of their popular appeal.

Of all the demagogues on the right, Senator Huey P. Long of Louisiana (1893–1935) was the sharpest thorn in Roosevelt's side. Roosevelt considered Long one of the most dangerous men in America. Capitalizing on popular discontent, Long openly sought to become "Kingfish" not only in Louisiana but also in the United States. He utilized his shrewd mind and rabble-rousing talents to push a pie-in-the-sky "Share-the-Wealth" program, under which every family would receive $5000 at the expense of the more prosperous citizens, whose incomes above a certain level would be taxed for the purpose. Long's criticism was chiefly a personal feud with Roosevelt—his rival for the people's attention—not a rational commentary on the New Deal's shortcomings.[25] His assassination in 1935 brought an end to the movement, although it was carried on for a while by another demagogue, the Reverend Gerald L. K. Smith (1898?–   ) of Michigan, who, along with Lawrence Dennis (1893–   ), was a leader of

---

[24] Arthur M. Schlesinger, Jr., *The Politics of Upheaval* (Boston: Houghton Mifflin, 1960), p. 28. See also Charles Tull, *Father Coughlin and the New Deal* (Syracuse: Syracuse University Press, 1965).
[25] See T. Harry Williams, *Huey Long* (New York: Knopf, 1970), p. 699 ff.

a native fascist movement. Smith moved from one cause to another, but always in opposition to Roosevelt and always toward four goals: the preservation of private property, the sanctity of the Constitution, the glory of the American flag, and the expulsion of Communists from the United States.[26] Dennis was an ex-soldier, diplomat, and banker who had become disenchanted with capitalist foreign policy and business and frankly advocated fascism. In *Is Capitalism Doomed?*[27] and *The Coming American Fascism*,[28] he argued for "a middle-class revolution." Big business itself had made fascism logical for the United States. Dennis also advocated abolition of states' rights, elimination of unemployment by government spending, and nationalization of banks.

Too much attention to the opposition is misleading. The New Deal was overwhelmingly popular from the outset, and though the election of 1938 dented the Democratic majority, it did not endanger it. World War II altered the climate of American politics, but Roosevelt's success in bucking the two-term tradition in 1940 and again in 1944 proved his popular appeal. Despite a plethora of voices raised in opposition, continuing even during the war years, none drowned out Roosevelt's clarion calls for change. Indeed, the voters hardly acknowledged the presence of opposition.[29] So fervently did they embrace the New Deal that no significant departures from it have yet been made. Indeed, President Nixon, going beyond it, envisaged in his 1970 State of the Union address a political millenium unprecedented in scope. Designed to give the nation the "lift of a driving dream," it makes the New Deal program pale by comparison.

THE IMPACT OF THE AGE OF ROOSEVELT

So massive was the impact of the New Deal on American political thought and action that the time of its origin and development has aptly been called the Age of Roosevelt.[30] The legacies of that age continue to be determinative in American politics and government.

Redirection of Government's Role

For Old Dealers the objectives of government had been relatively narrow. Liberty meant primarily the right of those who own property to control it; social power was annexed to private right. The scope of politically responsible governmental authority was narrowly circumscribed. New

[26] See *Current Biography, 1943* (New York: Wilson, 1943), pp. 708–9.
[27] Lawrence Dennis, *Is Capitalism Doomed?* (New York: Harper & Brothers, 1932).
[28] Lawrence Dennis, *The Coming American Fascism* (New York: Harper & Brothers, 1936).
[29] See Boskin, *Opposition Politics*, p. 36.
[30] See the two-volume study by Arthur M. Schlesinger, Jr., *The Age of Roosevelt* (Boston: Houghton Mifflin, 1958).

Dealers, denying that freedom is possible under conditions of economic dependence on a ruling industrial oligarchy, invoked government power on behalf of the underprivileged and the economically weaker groups in society. After 1932 the orientation of American political thought became basically collectivist. Thereafter, government enacted programs designed to promote the general welfare directly. It was recognized that no individual, no group, could profit or suffer without affecting the interests of all. Economic rights must be added to the roster of our freedoms, and government, rather than industrial ownership or management, be made the dominant power. In his message to Congress on January 4, 1935, President Roosevelt said:

> We have . . . a clear mandate from the people, that Americans must forswear that conception of the acquisition of wealth which, through excessive profits, creates undue private powers over public affairs and, to our misfortune, over public affairs as well. In building toward this end we do not destroy ambition, nor do we seek to divide our wealth into equal shares on stated occasions. We continue to recognize the greater ability of some to earn more than others. But we do assert that the ambition of the individual to obtain for him and his a proper security, a reasonable leisure, and a decent living throughout life, is an ambition to be preferred to the appetite for great wealth and great power.

The policy he formulated and translated into action was not designed merely to meet the current emergency. "The plans we make for this emergency . . . may show the way to a more permanent safeguarding of our social and economic life to the end that we may . . . avoid the terrible cycle of prosperity crumbling into depression. In this sense I favor economic planning, not for this period alone but for our needs for a long time to come."[31]

The New Deal brought about a shift from implicit faith in the operation of so-called natural forces to the belief that social processes can and must be controlled by government in the interest of the many, no less than in the interest of the few. It was now clear that a politically responsible government must insist on monopolizing coercive power as against any and all private aspirants for such power. It must do so not because there was any special virtue in established authority, or because government was or could be omniscient, but because this was the only way to prevent individuals and groups from taking law into their own hands. It was also clear to New Dealers that the welfare of the people must be, in a broad sense, a basic concern of government. In 1934 Justice Roberts observed: "This Court from the early days [has] affirmed that the power to promote the general welfare is inherent in government."[32] No longer could the government stand aside when groups or individuals need assistance or relief.

---

[31] Quoted in Tugwell, "Orthodoxy of Roosevelt," p. 11.
[32] *Nebbia* v. *New York*, 291 U.S. 502.

Redistribution of Power

"Roosevelt and the New Dealers," William Leuchtenburg observed, "almost revolutionized the agenda of American politics." They focused on the national government as the center of problem-solving and decision-making. Its concerns became for the first time the concerns of the American people themselves. In the process the balance of federalism was shifted from state capitals to Washington. The presidency was virtually re-created. "Under Roosevelt, the White House became the focus of all government—the fountainhead of ideas, the initiator of action, the representative of the national interest."[33] At the same time the separation of powers was being altered, and much greater reliance was being placed on the executive than ever before. By 1940 government lay increasingly in the hands of administrative authority. Changes imposed on society by statute had perforce to be administered and amplified by a bureau or commission. These official agencies were not easily subject to the "auxiliary devices" on which the Founding Fathers had relied for compelling the government "to control itself." Both private individuals and large corporations were often unable to determine, by reference to fixed rules, their rights, duties, and responsibilities. A multitude of government agencies now dealt with technical matters and made decisions on a case-to-case basis. Drastic changes in policy became fixed in precedent without public approval. Sometimes even the opportunity for public comment was denied by civilian and military officials, who, by invoking such familiar tags as "confidential" or "top secret," classified information and screened operations from public scrutiny. Moreover, the ease with which powerful private interests might influence complex administrative processes was quickly demonstrated, enabling private enterprise—losers of the battle for laissez faire—to win its way by dominating the very machinery created for its control.[34]

Finally, the judiciary, after impeding the development of active government for more than a generation, retired from the battle. The Court now found little reason to put obstacles in the way of governmental power.

Responsibility Endangered

The outbreak of war compounded the problem. Congress had had little experience in handling such complex matters as those involved in fight-

---

[33] William E. Leuchtenburg, *Franklin D. Roosevelt and the New Deal* (New York: Harper & Row, 1963), pp. 326–33.

[34] Walton H. Hamilton, "The Smouldering Constitutional Crisis," *New Republic*, January 19, 1943, p. 74. See also J. W. Fulbright, "The Decline—and Possible Fall—of Constitutional Democracy in America," An Address to the Yale Law Journal's annual banquet, April 3, 1971, reproduced in *Congressional Record*, CXVII (April 14, 1971), S 4784–86.

ing World War II and almost gratefully relinquished power and responsibility to the executive branch. Government became almost exclusively an executive show, with a cast of thousands, reading different scripts. With so many agencies and so much to oversee and understand, the president alone could not supply effective coordination and control, and there was no one else to do so. As a result an increasing number of agencies began to wander off in directions of their own choosing. The element of responsibility, imposed by checks and balances, was gone. The "operating government" was in effect separated from popular sources of power, and the way to bring the two together again had not been found.

The will of the people moved in one domain—their influence was exerted chiefly upon Congress—and the operations of government in quite another. Between them a chasm developed. Left on their own, these agencies often failed to accomplish their ends and began unwittingly to work at cross purposes. Although the New Deal's jerry-built machine made progress and the war effort was extraordinarily successful, the question whether the nation had lost its ability to keep its own creatures in line became urgent:

> The government moves into a new orbit. . . . There is no easy way of getting real questions of policy—enlarging personal opportunity, ensuring the economy against breakdown, advancing the standard of life, laying the foundations of a durable peace—raised. And adequate answers can emerge only from an almost miraculous conjunction of unlike wills. In our order of society, agencies of control must be expert, flexible, able to act with speed. But they must be informed, considerate of interests involved, responsive to the public will. As the state changes in character, it occupies an area where the older safeguards do not operate. Our friends to the right, sensitive to the trend, have not been idle. They have attempted to move "independent agencies" under judicial, and away from popular, authority. And, as judicial review runs into difficulties, they have set out to capture—or to sabotage—the new controls. The counter task, at which . . . liberals have made far less headway, is to contrive ways and means for subduing these agencies to the democratic process . . . A breach . . . threatens . . . between a popular executive and an operative government which the voters cannot reach. Unless "We, the people" can make the industrial system the instrument of the general welfare, the dominant interests will take over the government. For the separation of state and economy is gone.

In pursuit of a broader freedom through government action, the New Deal might have given birth to a monster that could destroy that freedom. "The real concern is that the whole establishment is drifting away from responsible government."[35]

Franklin Roosevelt's successor, President Harry S. Truman, took account of the drift almost as soon as he took office, asking Congress to appropriate funds for a study. Congress responded by creating the Com-

---

[35] Hamilton, "Smouldering Crisis," p. 74. See also Walton H. Hamilton, *The Politics of Industry* (New York: Knopf, 1957), pp. 152–60.

mission on Organization of the Executive Branch of the Government, with a former president, Herbert Hoover, as its chairman. In accepting the appointment, Hoover agreed to refrain from comment on the substance of government action and confine the commission to matters of organization and control. The commission demonstrated that big government can be made to operate within the confines of the democratic process; that it can, in short, be made responsible and accountable to Congress and to the people. In general the commission recommended that more power be given to the president. "Somebody had to be responsible, and that responsibility had to be with the only person whom all the people selected as top man. If any effective expression of majority rule was to be obtained, he had to be the man to unite the other two million government employees to get it. Power had to go with responsibility. The administrative house [had to be] redesigned around this simple but important idea."[36] Hundreds of specific recommendations in line with this general principle were made and since 1949 Congress has enacted a good many of them. But if Congress has thus helped reduce them, the dangers have since increased alarmingly.

FREE GOVERNMENT STRENGTHENED

"The domestic principles and policies which were laid down and put into practice by President Roosevelt," Harry S. Truman wrote in 1946, "have come almost to be accepted as commonplace today. Yet they constitute a program of social reform and progress unequalled in the history of the United States. In a very practical sense, this program was a social revolution which swept out obsolete notions cluttering our economy and substituted a bold program of decisive action designed to improve the standard of living and the level of security of the common man."[37]

During much of our history, liberty had been narrowly conceived, requiring the protection of private rights, especially those of property and contract, against invasion by government. In actual practice there had been only one exception to this narrow view in our history—the emancipation of the slaves. Roosevelt, realizing the tremendous potentialities for social betterment latent in positive government action, forged the New Deal as a weapon to convert them into actualities. Equality was also a basic New Deal tenet, as in the Declaration of Independence, and in the Fourteenth Amendment. Traditionally confined in its meaning to equality of opportunity, it had been adhered to primarily as an ideal,

---

[36] *The Hoover Report, Half a Loaf*, Occasional Papers Series, No. 3. The Public Affairs Institute, 1949, p. 7. See also "Big Government. Can it be Managed Efficiently?" Supplement to *Fortune*, May, 1949. See also Paul H. Appleby, "The Significance of the Hoover Commission Report," *Yale Review*, n.s. XXXIX (September, 1949), 20.

[37] President Harry S. Truman to Bruce Bliven, March 19, 1946, reproduced in *The New Republic*, April 15, 1946, 523.

which Americans might strive toward but perhaps never fully reach. During the Age of Jackson that ideal had considerable substance in fact, despite the absence of political equality. The latter was finally achieved, but the rise of industrialization created in its wake vast economic inequalities; thus, it was gradually recognized that political equality alone was not enough in a society characterized by dependence and interdependence. We had passed to a subtler civilization. Barriers, for privilege and against progress, unknown in the simpler days of Jacksonian agrarianism, were raised. To repel these new inroads on both economic and political equality, government must act positively.

The conviction that governments derive their just powers from the consent of the governed likewise continued as an article of our political faith under the New Deal. During much of our history, however, that concept had been narrowly defined. Consent of all the people or even of a political majority had never been unqualifiedly accepted. It had been held to mean only such consent as could run the gamut of our delaying checks and balances system, and, more particularly, such government action as the Supreme Court might approve. Under the New Deal the notion of popular consent was considerably broadened. With the erosion of many of the institutional checks on power, it connoted greater responsiveness to majority will reflected at the ballot box, in Congress, and by the president; and greater reliance than in the past upon political rather than structural, legal, and judicial control of government policy and action.

It is tempting to draw parallels between Jacksonian Democracy and the New Deal. There are points of comparison: both were manifestations of popular revolt against entrenched economic power; in both, the revolt was headed by a powerful political leader. However, these and other similarities must not blur important differences. The Jacksonian revolution took place at a time when the dominant groups in American society were small property owners—independent farmers, petty traders, and merchant-manufacturers; the Roosevelt revolution emerged against a totally different background. A propertyless "forgotten third" was the focal point of its endeavors. "The Jacksonian movement grew out of expanding opportunities and a common desire to enlarge those opportunities . . . by removing restrictions and privileges that had their origin in acts of government . . . it was essentially a movement of laissez-faire, an attempt to divorce government and business . . . it was . . . a phase in the expansion of liberated capitalism." The New Deal, on the other hand, was "frankly based upon the premise that economic expansion had come to an end and economic opportunities were disappearing; it attempted to cope with the situation by establishing governmental ascendancy over the affairs of business."[38] Thus, the New Deal operated on the assumption that government power was a positive instrument to be used in the service of the general welfare.

"Government is action," Woodrow Wilson wrote in an essay of 1893,

---

[38] Hofstadter, *American Political Tradition*, p. 55.

"and democratic government more than any other needs organization to escape disintegration."[39] What is more, democratic government demands leadership in thought and action. President Roosevelt came close to fulfilling these Wilsonian specifications. Since Roosevelt's day we are no longer content with a government that does not govern.

---

[39] Quoted in Mason, *Free Government*, p. 798.

CHAPTER NINETEEN

FOCUS ON
CIVIL LIBERTIES

Roosevelt's New Deal, like Woodrow Wilson's New Freedom, was cut short by the intervention of war. In 1939 Adolf Hitler unleashed his Nazi forces, and within two years Europe was aflame. Gripped by fear, men have ever been ready, as de Tocqueville reminded us, "to throw away their freedom at the first disturbance before they discover how freedom itself serves to promote it."[1]

Whatever measures the government takes to advance our security seem inevitably to cut into our most precious freedoms. For the exalted purpose of security, the channels of information between government and people are blocked, so that the main arteries of free government—discussion, dissent, opposition, nonconformity—are in constant danger of strangulation. As Alexander Hamilton foresaw in 1787, "safety from external danger" can become "the most powerful director of national conduct." Liberty can give way to the dictates of national security. "To be more safe a nation can become willing to run the risk of being less free."[2]

Hamilton's dictum was given its first severe test during World War I.

---

[1] Quoted by Henry Steele Commager, "Democracy in America: One Hundred Years After," *New York Times Magazine*, December 15, 1935, p. 15.
[2] Alexander Hamilton, *Federalist* Number 8.

Even before America's involvement President Wilson had prophesied (almost in Randolph Bourne's words) that if war should come, "conformity will be the only virtue. And every man who refuses to conform will have to pay the penalty."[3] Almost as soon as war was declared, Congress, taking the President at his word, passed the Espionage and Sedition Acts, severely curtailing the traditional constitutional guarantees of free speech, free press, and free assembly. At the same time the Post Office Department undertook to exclude "subversive literature" from the mails. The states, following the national government's lead, passed innumerable laws restricting or denying basic civil rights. To bolster governmental attempts to assure conformity and quell dissent, the Ku Klux Klan, the American Legion, and other private groups joined in the coercive drive for "national unity."

The Armistice did not halt these activities; indeed, the Russian Revolution of 1917 so frightened America that antiradical movements of heroic proportions were organized. Hallowed freedoms were impaired, religious prejudices fanned into hate, textbook investigations undertaken, loyalty oaths imposed on teachers, censorship of books introduced, and nativism revived. "Altogether," Arthur S. Link wrote, "it is . . . astounding . . . the way in which fear of a largely mythical Bolshevik danger stimulated wholesale federal, state, and private assaults against civil liberty and free thought and expression."[4]

During the postwar wave of prosperity, these excesses were largely forgotten, and the Great Depression dimmed their memory still further. By the late 1930s, however, war clouds again hung threateningly over the United States, and once more the question of national security began to loom large in public and private discussions. This time President Roosevelt continued to stress fundamental human rights. Unlike Woodrow Wilson, FDR did not recommend restrictive legislation as a security measure. Nor is there evidence that any large segment of the people disagreed with him. The nation was therefore shocked when, on April 21, 1940, Justice Felix Frankfurter (1882–1965) read the majority opinion for the Supreme Court in the case of *Minersville School District* v. *Gobitis*.[5] This case involved the first in a series of attempts by Jehovah's Witnesses to defend their unorthodox beliefs before the Supreme Court. Interpreting the Bible literally, they refused to permit their children to salute the flag and take the pledge of allegiance, arguing that this ceremonial requirement was incompatible with the command of the Scriptures. Thus, when the Minersville, Pennsylvania, school board required the flag salute of teachers and pupils, Lillian and William Gobitis did not participate.

[3] Quoted in Harold U. Faulkner, *From Versailles to the New Deal* (New Haven, Conn.: Yale University Press, 1950), p. 141.
[4] Arthur S. Link, reviewing Robert K. Murray, *Red Scare: A Study in National Hysteria* (Minneapolis: University of Minnesota Press, 1955), in *Annals of the American Academy of Political and Social Science*, CCC (July, 1955), 142. That whole volume of the *Annals* is devoted to "Internal Security and Civil Rights."
[5] 310 U.S. 586 (1940).

They were expelled from school. To relieve himself of the financial burden of putting his children in private schools, their father brought suit to enjoin the board from requiring participation in the flag ceremony as a condition of school attendance.

In his opinion for eight justices upholding the school board's regulation, Justice Frankfurter, ignoring the Court's role as guardian of "preferred freedoms,"[6] declared that the "precise issue" was "whether the legislatures of the various states and the authorities in a thousand counties and school districts of this country [were by judicial action to be] barred from determining the appropriateness of various means to evoke that unifying sentiment without which there can ultimately be no liberties, civil or religious." Apparently convinced, as Wilson had been, that conformity was essential in wartime, Frankfurter held that the states could not be so barred, despite the specific words of the First Amendment enjoining legislation abridging freedom of speech, press, and religion. A free society, he thought, rested on the binding tie of cohesive sentiment; national unity was the basis of national security and such unity might, if necessary, be achieved by legislative coercion, even to the extent of forcing school children to salute the flag in violation of their family's religious belief. The Court could not intervene, Frankfurter declared, without pronouncing "pedagogical and psychological dogma" in a field wherein it had "no marked and certainly no controlling competence." To legislatures, and through them to school boards, no less than to courts, "is committed the guardianship of deeply cherished liberties."

> For ourselves, we might be tempted to say that the deepest patriotism is best engendered by giving unfettered scope to the most crochety beliefs. . . . [But it] is not our province to choose among competing considerations in the subtle process of securing effective loyalty to the traditional ideas of democracy, while respecting at the same time individual idiosyncrasies among a people so diversified in racial origins and religious allegiances. So to hold would in effect make us the school board for the country. That authority has not been given to this Court, nor should we assume it.

Justice Harlan F. Stone (1872–1946), later chief justice, alone dissented. To his mind the Minersville school board had not merely chosen an ineffective means of evoking unity and inspiring patriotism; it had struck at the very heart of a basic constitutional guarantee—the Gobitis children's religious freedom. No cautious hesitation to use judicial power should keep the Court from defending that freedom. Stone recognized the necessity of "tempering together" liberty and restraint. But he saw the courts as peculiarly responsible for determining "whether such accommodation is really possible." If it were not, the justices had no alternative but to rule in favor of freedom. "The Constitution," Stone reminded his

---

[6] See *Whitney* v. *California*, 274 U.S. 357 (1927); *Stromberg* v. *California*, 283 U.S. 359 (1931); and *Near* v. *Minnesota*, 283 U.S. 697 (1931).

brethren, "expresses more than the conviction of the people that democratic processes must be preserved at all costs. It is also an expression of faith and a command that freedom of mind and spirit must be preserved, which government must obey, if it is to adhere to that justice and moderation without which no free government can exist." Freedom of mind stood highest in the hierarchy of constitutional values and was thus beyond legislative reach. The duty of the Court was to keep it beyond reach. Moreover, such freedom—not coerced national unity—was the basis of national security.

For the time being, Stone's conception was ignored. The ruthlessness of the European dictators impressed the Court as it impressed the people. Looking ahead to the imminent probability of war, and remembering the social confusion following World War I, the majority felt that considerations of national unity and security must have precedence. "Certainly it is relevant," Frankfurter argued, "to make the adjustment that we have to make within the framework of present circumstances and those that are clearly ahead of us." Confronted with an authoritarian threat, Frankfurter suggested the necessity of meeting it with authoritarian measures. Stone, the lone dissenter, upheld the long-established tradition of freedom.

COERCION REJECTED

Before long, however, his position was adopted by a new majority. Three justices—Black, Douglas, and Murphy—dissenting in *Jones* v. *Opelika*[7] in 1942, took the unusual step of announcing that they now believed that the *Gobitis* case had been wrongly decided. With Justice Stone this meant that the Court's decision stood by the narrow margin of five to four. The scales were finally tipped against Frankfurter when two newly appointed justices, Robert H. Jackson and Wiley Rutledge, joined the four in the leading case of *West Virginia State Board of Education* v. *Barnette*,[8] decided in 1943. It, too, involved the flag salute issue. Justice Jackson, speaking for the Court, adopted Stone's position:

> If there is any fixed star in our constitutional constellation, it is that no official, high or petty, can prescribe what shall be orthodox in politics, nationalism, religion, or other matters. . . . The very purpose of a Bill of Rights was to withdraw certain subjects from the vicissitudes of political controversy, to place them beyond the reach of majorities and officials and to establish them as legal principles to be applied by the courts. One's right to life, liberty, and property, to free speech, a free press, freedom of worship and assembly, and other fundamental rights may not be submitted to vote; they depend on the outcome of no elections.

---

[7] 316 U.S. 584 (1942).
[8] 319 U.S. 624 (1943).

Unity was not secured by coercion; security did not depend upon smothering dissent. "Those who begin coercive elimination of dissent," Justice Jackson warned, "soon find themselves exterminating dissenters. Compulsory unification of opinion achieves only the unanimity of the graveyard." Like Stone, Jackson believed that the First Amendment meant what it said, that it had been designed to support a government by consent of the governed, denying "those in power any legal opportunity to coerce that consent. Authority here is to be controlled by public opinion, not public opinion by authority."

> To believe that patriotism will not flourish if patriotic ceremonies are voluntary and spontaneous instead of a compulsory routine is to make an unflattering estimate of the appeal of our institutions to free minds. We can have intellectual individualism and the rich cultural diversities that we owe to exceptional minds only at the price of occasional eccentricity and abnormal attitudes. Freedom to differ is not limited to things that do not matter much. That would be a mere shadow of freedom. The test of its substance is the right to differ as to things that touch the heart of the existing order.

Indeed, Jackson argued that such freedom increased our national strength:

> Government of limited power need not be anemic government. Assurance that rights are secure tends to diminish fear and jealousy of strong government, and by making us feel safe to live under it makes for its better support. Without promise of a limiting Bill of Rights it is doubtful if our Constitution could have mustered enough strength to enable ratification. To enforce those rights today is not to choose weak government over strong government. It is only to adhere as a means of strength to individual freedom of mind in preference to officially disciplined uniformity for which history indicates a disappointing and disastrous end.

Jackson's position was not accepted by three[9] of his brethren. So diverse were the individual opinions of the six majority members that three[10] of them wrote separate concurring opinions. Justice Frankfurter, now a dissenter, argued that the Constitution gave the Bill of Rights no special priority, despite the "preferred freedoms" doctrine. Nor were courts the primary protectors of liberty. The "very essence of our constitutional system and the democratic conception of our society" was a primary reliance on legislatures and on the democratic process. "Judges should be very diffident in setting their judgment against that of a state [legislature] in determining what is and what is not a major concern, what means are appropriate to proper ends, and what is the total cost in striking the balance of imponderables."

Nothing in our tradition, Frankfurter argued, gave dissidents an

---

[9] Justices Owen J. Roberts, Stanley Reed, and Felix Frankfurter.
[10] Justices Hugo Black, William O. Douglas, and Frank Murphy.

"exceptional immunity from civic measures of general applicability, measures not in fact disguised assaults upon such dissident views."

> The State is not shut out from a domain because the individual conscience may deny the state's claim. The individual conscience may profess what faith it chooses. It may affirm and promote that faith—in the language of the Constitution, it may 'exercise' it freely—but it cannot thereby restrict community action through political organs in matters of community concern, so long as the action is not asserted in a discriminating way either openly or by stealth.

Frankfurter still insisted that community action might require, in the interest of national security, formal obedience to laws that ran counter to an individual's beliefs, particularly in time of emergency.

> Where all the effective means of inducing political changes are left free from interference, education in the abandonment of foolish legislation is itself a training in liberty. To fight out the wise use of legislative authority in the forum of public opinion and before legislative assemblies rather than to transfer such a contest to the judicial arena, serves to vindicate the self-confidence of a free people.[11]

Underlying the cleavage between Stone and Jackson, on the one hand, and Frankfurter, on the other, are basic differences about the meaning and requirements of free government and of the Court's role in securing those requirements. The divergent points of view expressed in the Flag Salute Cases have not yet been reconciled. Indeed, recent events have exacerbated the split. In reaction to Communist aggression abroad and suspected infiltration at home, the drive toward conformity for security's sake has mounted in intensity, catapulting this issue to top position among the political enigmas of our time.

WHO IS LOYAL?

The issue of conformity arose also in answering the question of what constitutes loyalty, asked increasingly in the days after World War II. In the Eightieth Congress (1946–1948) the Committee on Un-American Activities of the House of Representatives encouraged a "witch-hunting spirit both in government and in private life," while failing to "demonstrate the existence of a . . . serious threat of internal subversion. . . ."[12] Taking account of these irregularities, Chief Justice Earl Warren (1891–), speaking for the Court in the landmark case of *Watkins* v. *United States*,[13] limited the power of congressional committees in making investigations, and read the Un-American Activities Committee a stern lecture

---

[11] Justice Frankfurter in *Minersville School District* v. *Gobitis*.
[12] Robert K. Carr, *The House Committee on Un-American Activities, 1945–50* (Ithaca, N.Y.: Cornell University Press, 1952), pp. 452, 455.
[13] 354 U.S. 178 (1957).

on the laxity of their procedures. Said the chief justice: "Abuses of the investigative process may imperceptibly lead to abridgment of protected freedoms. . . . There is no congressional power to expose for the sake of exposure." The trend toward coerced conformity was also manifest in the loyalty program instituted for federal employees, all of whom became, for a while in the 1950s, subject to government security clearance, the burden falling on the individual employee to prove his loyalty.

But what were the standards by which loyalty could be judged? Was an American disloyal because he advocated the right of revolution? because he criticized big business? because he joined the Socialist party? Where could the substance of loyalty be found? We must remember, an eminent historian reminds us, "that the only criterion for disloyalty is superior loyalty to another country, and that reservations about the capitalist system or skepticism concerning the wisdom of the business community are by themselves no evidence at all of external loyalties."[14] Yet the government program was operated on the assumption that loyalty could be measured precisely. Although the program, on the whole, was administered fairly, it nevertheless produced marked injustices and further weakened the meaning of civil rights. Francis Biddle (1886–1968), Attorney General of the United States from 1940 to 1945 and an outstanding student of civil liberties, summarized the operation of the loyalty program from 1947 to 1953:

> Under the order [establishing the program] and regulations, charges were only as specific "as security considerations" would permit; the employee could only introduce such evidence as the [Loyalty Review] Board deemed proper; could cross-examine witnesses—but not informants; had no right to subpoena witnesses; and appeared before a board in his own department which in fact was acting also as a prosecutor. . . . [Cases were decided] on the "unsworn" reports in . . . secret files . . . purporting to connect [employees] . . . with Communism; not on knowledge, but on belief.[15]

In none of these procedures were the rights of the accused protected.

Something of the same trend was developing elsewhere. Under the Taft-Hartley Act of 1947, passed only after heated debate in Congress and over President Truman's excoriating veto, labor union officials are required to sign non-Communist affidavits before their unions can be certified as bargaining agents or be eligible for the services of the National Labor Relations Board, thus putting unions under a restraint not imposed on other segments of society. State educational institutions and city school boards began to require loyalty oaths of teachers. In 1954 California enacted a law requiring representatives of churches that desired exemption from state taxation to sign a loyalty oath. Some of the laws proved

---

[14] Arthur M. Schlesinger, Jr., "What is Loyalty? A Difficult Question," *New York Times Magazine*, November 2, 1947, p. 51.
[15] Francis J. Biddle, "Subversives in Government," *Annals of the American Academy of Political and Social Science*, CCC (July, 1955), 56.

unworkable and have been declared unconstitutional. All such measures constituted a threat to free government.

> If the loyalty oath has certain practical advantages, the fact that its spirit is repugnant to our free institutions should be recognized. The loyalty oath is negative rather than positive; it is actually what someone has called a non-disloyalty oath, and it is particularly offensive if one special group [government employees] . . . is singled out to take it. The emergency of the moment may demand a limited employment of the loyalty oath. But . . . its use involves potential dangers only less great than the external peril we face.[16]

Textbooks also came in for their share of attack as subversive. In 1951 the New York State Board of Regents appointed the Commission on Subversive Textbooks, authorized to examine, upon complaint, all texts alleged to contain subversive matter. Texas prohibited the purchase of any text "unless and until the author takes the [non-Communist] oath. . . ." If the author "is dead or cannot be located, the publisher may take the oath instead." Alabama passed a bill requiring that every one of the millions of books used in Alabama's schools—and the official reports of the State Superintendent of Education as well—be labeled to show whether the author and all those in the bibliographies were Communists, followers of the Communist line, or Socialists.[17] The protest these measures evoked underscored the stern requirements of free government:

> To tell an American child—the inheritor of Thomas Paine, Thomas Jefferson, Walt Whitman, and Abraham Lincoln—*what he must think* is to deny him his inheritance. Certainly any indigenous American education cannot, above all, do that. Would not such a perversion . . . show lack of faith that in the free market place of ideas "our way" will be able to hold its own? Are not our children discerning enough to see the discrepancies between history that glorifies our dissenters—the Pilgrim Fathers, Roger Williams, William Penn, the signers of the Declaration of Independence—and immediate attempts at censorship and stifling of inquiry?[18]

In June 1950 the cold war became hot in Korea. A state of near hysteria soon enveloped the country, causing Justice William O. Douglas (1898–   ) to fear that "we will so limit or narrow the range of permissible discussion and permissible thought that we will become victims of the orthodox school."[19] The Internal Security (McCarran) Act of 1950,

---

[16] "Loyalty by Oath," *Commonweal*, January 2, 1953, p. 319. See also Howard Mumford Jones, "Do You Know the Nature of an Oath?" *American Scholar*, XX (Autumn, 1951), 457–67.

[17] For a brilliant treatment of the textbook problem, interlarded with telling illustrations, see Walter Gellhorn, *Individual Freedom and Governmental Restraint* (Baton Rouge: Louisiana State University Press, 1956).

[18] Virgil M. Rogers, "Textbooks under Fire," *Atlantic*, February, 1955, pp. 42, 48.

[19] William O. Douglas, "The Black Silence of Fear," *New York Times Magazine*, January 13, 1952, p. 38.

reflecting this fear, was framed in such vague and general language that President Truman suspected that it could be used to curb critics of the capitalist system, thus striking at American liberties instead of at communism. Truman's classic veto message[20] propounded the basic American doctrine of security through freedom. In response to it Congress promptly passed the measure over the president's veto. In August 1954 Congress passed the Communist Control Act, a measure apparently designed to outlaw the Communist party as a political organization.

Before the issue was decided irrevocably in favor of government-imposed conformity, the pendulum began to swing back toward the side of civil rights. President Truman gave it a significant push in that direction in 1946, when he appointed the Committee on Civil Rights to review the state of civil rights in the nation and to recommend remedial action where necessary for achieving "more adequate and effective means and procedures for [their] protection. . . ." The president believed that "the preservation of civil rights . . . is essential to . . . national security . . . and the continued existence of our free institutions."[21] He left no doubt that freedom from fear, fully protected and implemented, was vital to a free society. The committee, in its report in 1947, agreed. What was needed was not only protection of the people's rights *against* the government, but also protection of their rights *by* the government.[22] Civil rights, indeed, "should assume more of the aspect of mutual obligations and should be a positive, vital, active concern of men in government and of the whole body of our citizens.[23] The President's Committee expressed the faith that people in a free society could make sound, rational judgments and reasonably satisfactory adjustments. As Robert K. Carr put it: "The reconciliation of authority and liberty may be a never-ending process, but it is always possible."[24]

What was the proper role of government in the sphere of civil rights, measured by the liberal tradition of American politics? In the interests of security, must government dominate men's ideas? Or laissez faire still possible in the realm of the mind and spirit? Could a strong nation depend in the long run on orthodoxy and conformity? Or would diversity and conflict actually strengthen government? To none of these questions have clear-cut answers been found. In trying to persuade Justice Stone not to dissent in the *Gobitis* case, Justice Frankfurter wrote: "When it comes to these ultimate civil liberties, . . . we are not in the domain of absolutes. Here . . . we have an illustration of what the Greeks thousands of years ago recognized as a tragic issue, namely, the clash of rights,

---

[20] House Document No. 708, 81st Cong., 2nd sess., September 22, 1950, pp. 1–10.
[21] Executive Order 9808, December 5, 1946.
[22] *To Secure These Rights. The Report of the President's Committee on Civil Rights* (Washington, D.C.: Government Printing Office, 1947), pp. 4–10, 139–49.
[23] "Address by the Honorable George M. Leader," April 2, 1955, reproduced in *Annals of the American Academy of Political and Social Science*, CCC (July, 1955), 1.
[24] Carr, *Committee on Un-American Activities*, p. x.

not the clash of wrongs. For resolving such clash, we have no calculus."[25] There remained, however, the Supreme Court.

Having adopted self-restraint toward economic legislation, the justices refused to apply that limiting concept of judicial power in passing on issues involving civil rights. In the famous *Carolene Products* footnote of 1938,[26] Justice Stone suggested there would be narrower scope for operation of the presumption of constitutionality when legislation infringed upon specific prohibitions in the Bill of Rights. Any legislation restricting political processes that could ordinarily be expected to bring about repeal of undesirable legislation, any statutes directed against particular religious, national, or racial minorities, called for *"more exacting judicial scrutiny."*

ATTACK ON SEGREGATION

In no area of public policy did legislative and executive action, especially in the South, offer more opportunity for judicial correction under the *Carolene Products* test than in that of racial segregation. Indeed, the application of that test furnished the theoretical foundations of much of the Warren Court's constitutional jurisprudence. Some progress had been made in providing meaningful equality for people of minority races, but until 1964 the legislative arms of national and state government had virtually avoided the challenge. In contrast the Supreme Court under Chief Justice Warren asserted its responsibility on May 17, 1954—that historic day on which the Justices handed down their unanimous judgment in the school segregation cases.[27] The anxiously awaited opinion was short and incisive. Warren found neither history nor precedent an adequate guide to action. Special studies of the intention of the framers of the Fourteenth Amendment were inconclusive.

"In approaching this problem," the chief justice remarked, "we cannot turn the clock back to 1868, when the Amendment was adopted, or even to 1896 when *Plessy* v. *Ferguson*[28] was written. We must consider public education in the light of its full development and its present place in American life throughout the Nation." In support of the proposition that segregation may affect hearts and minds in a way unlikely ever to be undone, the Court cited six sociological and psychological texts, concluding that

> in the field of public education the doctrine of "separate but equal" has no place. Separate educational facilities are inherently unequal. Therefore, we

---

[25] Felix Frankfurter to Harlan F. Stone, May 27, 1940. Frankfurter's entire letter, reproduced in A. T. Mason, *Security Through Freedom* (Ithaca, N.Y.: Cornell University Press, 1955), pp. 217–20 is worth careful study.
[26] *United States* v. *Carolene Products*, 304 U.S. 144 (1938), 152–54.
[27] *Brown* v. *Board of Education of Topeka*, 347 U.S. 483 (1954), 492–94, *passim*.
[28] 163 U.S. 537 (1896).

hold that the plaintiffs and others similarly situated for whom the actions have been brought are, by reason of the segregation complained of, deprived of the equal protection of the laws guaranteed by the Fourteenth Amendment.

In so-called *Brown II*,[29] the chief justice reiterated "the fundamental principle that racial discrimination in public education is unconstitutional," and went on to say that "all provisions of federal, state, or local law requiring or permitting such discrimination must yield to this principle." Realizing that adjustment to the requirements of the 1954 ruling would not be easy, and that a period of transition must be allowed, the chief justice concluded that the defendant school boards must make a "prompt and reasonable start" toward full compliance "with all deliberate speed."

Public reaction to the Court's rulings was electric and vehement. While many observers applauded them as overdue adjustments to principle, others blasted the decisions, especially their requirements of remedial action. In most jurisdictions the orders were complied with without great difficulty or opposition. "Ten states," however, "adopted patterns of avoidance, evasion, and delay under color of law, seeking judicial acceptance of pupil assignment laws, private schools supported with public monies, and other . . . stratagems designed to avoid integration."[30] When the Little Rock, Arkansas, school board petitioned the Supreme Court for additional time to put its program into effect in the wake of considerable violence, the request was unanimously denied. The Court held that the state must exercise

the responsibility for public education . . . consistently with federal constitutional requirements as they apply to state action. . . . [T]he constitutional rights of children not to be discriminated against in school admission on grounds of race or color . . . can neither be nullified openly and directly by the state legislators or state executive or judicial officers, nor nullified indirectly by them through evasive schemes for segregation whether attempted "ingeniously or ingenuously."[31]

Notwithstanding so positive a declaration that natural rights must be upheld, the judicial mandate against school segregation was, for ten years after *Brown* v. *Board of Education*, only a paper right. The Segregation-Desegregation Status Table prepared by the Southern Education Reporting Service for the school year 1964–1965 revealed that the South had successfully resisted the Supreme Court's decision. Only 2.14 percent of the nearly 3 million Negroes in Southern schools were receiving anything approaching a nonsegregated education.[32] Voicing its dissatisfaction in

---

[29] *Brown* v. *Board of Education,* 349 U.S. 294 (1955).
[30] Albert P. Blaustein and Robert L. Zangrando, eds., *Civil Rights and the American Negro. A Documentary History* (New York: Trident Press, 1968), p. 453.
[31] *Cooper* v. *Aaron,* 358 U.S. 1 (1958).
[32] Blaustein and Zangrando, *Civil Rights and the Negro,* p. 415.

Griffin v. *Prince Edward School Board*,[33] the Court declared that there had been "entirely too much deliberation and not enough speed." Subsequently, still other ways were found to drag feet. Full compliance has yet to be secured.

The desegregation decisions demonstrated conclusively that the only agency of government that could protect minorities when a majority, albeit a local one, errs is the courts.

> The limitations which the Constitution, and in particular the Bill of Rights, impose, were and are an exercise of self-restraint by a national majority, intended to be permanent until changed by a subsequent national (not local) majority. So long as they remain unchanged, they may fairly be taken to reflect the continuing and present popular will of the nation, much more accurately than a school board's regulation, a town's ordinance, or even a State's statute. The essential principle of the Bill of Rights is certainly that the protection of the fundamental rights of minorities is a matter of national concern. . . . In other words, the majority which makes and continues the constitutional compact . . . is not identical with the local majority which . . . has indicated its will by local legislation. In a clamor of conflicting commands, ought not the Court, when it is ultimately required to act in a litigated matter, to make some inquiry as to which is the authentic voice of the people?[34]

The Warren Court had no doubt that the constitutional voice would be listened to; nor has the Court under the leadership of Chief Justice Burger yet reversed this course. Perhaps that is why the intellectual descendants of the Jeffersonian tradition of states' rights have been so vehement in opposition. "The Tenth Amendment is not a mere truism," Senator Strom Thurmond of South Carolina declared. "It was not incorporated in the Bill of Rights just to bring the number of amendments to a round ten."[35] If we must "surrender our precious states rights in order to establish a program of civil rights," Representative Noah Mason of Illinois asked, "isn't the cure much worse than the disease?"[36]

Similar opposition was expressed to judicial action in other than racial matters. In August 1958 the chief justices of thirty-six states issued a

---

[33] 377 U.S. 218 (1964).

[34] J. R. Green, review of Henry Steele Commager, *Majority Rule and Minority Rights*, in *California Law Review*, XXXII (1944), 117. See also Henry J. Abraham, *Freedom and the Court. Civil Rights and Liberties in the United States* (New York: Oxford University Press, 1972).

[35] Strom Thurmond, "Constitutional Government," an address delivered December 6, 1957, in *Vital Speeches*, January 15, 1958, pp. 209–13. In July 1970, when the Justice Department announced it would send lawyers and other officials to the South "for the purpose of assuring forced integration of the public schools," the South Carolina senator exploded, condemning this step "wrong as social policy . . . wrong as law." He warned the Nixon administration that "such unreasonable policies" might lead to President Nixon's defeat in 1972. *New York Times*, July 18, 1970, p. 1.

[36] Noah Mason, "Preservation of Our Constitution," an address delivered February 6, 1957, in *Vital Speeches*, March 1, 1957, pp. 305–6.

report declaring that there was "at least considerable doubt" whether the United States had a government of laws and not of men. The chief justices' resolution expressed the hope "that the Supreme Court of the United States, in exercising the great powers confided to it for the determination of questions as to the allocation and extent of national and state powers, respectively, and as to the validity under the federal Constitution of the exercise of powers reserved to the states, [would] exercise one of the greatest of all judicial powers—the power of judicial self-restraint. . . ."[37]

Like earlier conflicts involving the nature of the Union, the present controversy arose in part out of an ambiguity contained in the Constitution itself. Those adhering to strict construction of Article I, section 8 could find nothing in the United States Constitution about integrated schools. On the other hand, those who believed that in cases affecting human rights, political arrangements in a federal union are but means to an end considered the matter one for national action. The Warren Court, adopting the latter view, accomplished what Congress was "powerless" to achieve.

"What has occurred," Robert J. Harris explained, "has been the atrophy of the fifth section of the fourteenth amendment [authorizing Congress to enforce provisions of the amendment by appropriate legislation] as a result both of judicial decisions and of the continuing influence of John C. Calhoun, whose mischievous device of the concurrent veto finds current expression in the Senate filibuster and seniority rule in the organization of congressional committees, either of which is a sufficient barrier to legislative implementation of the Fourteenth Amendment. If the Fourteenth Amendment is to have meaning, the Court must provide it, and, in doing so, it must have regard to all relevant factors."[38]

Nor is racial segregation the only field in which the Warren Court responded to a larger responsibility. At a single sitting, June 17, 1957, the Court shouldered other tasks in the civil rights orbit. In the *Yates* case[39] it upheld the right of anyone to advocate overthrow of the government, as long as the preaching does not openly advocate specific action. In the *Watkins* case,[40] it qualified the power of congressional committees to make investigations and require witnesses to testify. In *Sweezy* v. *New Hampshire*,[41] it limited the state's power to require witnesses to testify in investigations authorized by state law. In the *Jencks* case,[42] earlier in the term, the justices held that the FBI and other government agency reports must be made available to defendants in criminal trials if the persons who made the report are called as witnesses.

---

[37] Report of Committee on Federal-State Relationships as Affected by Judicial Decisions, Conference of Chief Justices, Chicago, 1958.

[38] R. J. Harris, "The Constitution, Education, and Segregation," *Temple Law Quarterly*, XXIX (Summer, 1956), 431.

[39] *Yates* v. *United States*, 354 U.S. 298 (1957).

[40] *Watkins* v. *United States*, 354 U.S. 178 (1957).

[41] 354 U.S. 234 (1957).

[42] *Jencks* v. *United States*, 353 U.S. 657 (1957).

"We cannot simply assume," Chief Justice Warren commented in the *Watkins* case, "that every congressional investigation is justified by a public need that overbalances any private rights affected." To do so "would be to abdicate the responsibility placed by the Constitution upon the judiciary to insure that the Congress does not unjustifiably encroach upon an individual's right of privacy nor abridge his liberty of speech, press, religion, or assembly." Even Justice Frankfurter, the most persistent exponent of judicial laissez faire on the Court, recognized that the Court must balance the contending claims of a citizen to political privacy and the right of the state to self-protection. "This is the inescapable judicial task," Frankfurter wrote, concurring in the *Sweezy* decision, "and it is a task ultimately committed to this Court."

RATIONALE FOR JUDICIAL ACTION

As it undertook action in behalf of civil liberties, the Warren Court was not unmindful of the bounds set by the principle of judicial self-restraint. Here the contrast with the Court of 1935–1936 is sharp. That Court vitalized old constitutional barriers and refashioned new ones against the power to govern. Even the well-worn principle of presumption of constitutionality was sometimes ignored. This flouting of judicial self-restraint, this destruction of a national legislative program having strong popular support, meant the raising of bars that could be removed only by constitutional amendment or by reversal of judicial decisions. The Warren Court, on the other hand, achieved libertarian objectives largely by statutory interpretation. Thus any ill-effects of momentous decisions like *Yates*, *Watkins*, and *Jencks* could be removed by an ordinary act of Congress.

The Hughes Court precipitated a crisis by blocking legislation that the Constitution itself did not enjoin. The Warren Court became the focus of controversy by responding to popular aspirations, perhaps in moving ahead of them. It had the courage to face the challenge of the separate but equal doctrine and bring the law of the American Constitution into line with the social conscience of the world. The Court also evoked criticism from less localized quarters. By curbing legislative effort to achieve national security in a time of unprecedented peril, it found itself in the awkward position of frustrating the government's attempt to stave off the onslaught of Nazism, the diabolical connivings of an incredibly monstrous tyrant. Little wonder the Court came under fire. Like that headed by John Marshall, the Warren Court attempted to dam a powerful current in our politics. Just as Marshall's fervent nationalism stirred violent criticism among Democratic-Republicans, so the Warren Court's defense of our basic freedoms roused bitter denunciation from those inclined to equate security with repression.

The Warren Court, like those who won our independence and framed the Constitution, believed that the only security worth having is built on freedom. By 1790 American society had already reached a degree of stability sufficient to prompt the First Congress to write into the Constitution provisions protecting the right of political disagreement. In piloting the Bill of Rights through the First Congress, Madison observed:

> The prescriptions in favor of liberty ought to be levelled against that quarter where the greatest danger lies, namely, that which possesses the highest prerogative of power. But this is not found in either the Executive or Legislative departments of Government, but in the body of the people, operating by the majority against the minority. . . . If they [the Bill of Rights] are incorporated into the Constitution, independent tribunals of justice will consider themselves in a peculiar manner the guardians of those rights; they will be an impenetrable bulwark against every assumption of power in the Legislative or Executive; they will be naturally led to resist every incroachment upon rights, expressly stipulated for in the Constitution by the declaration of rights.[43]

"There is nothing covert or conflicting," Justice Robert Jackson commented 150 years later, when he was appointed to the bench, "in the recent judgments of the Court on social legislation and on legislative repressions of civil rights. The presumption of validity which attaches in general to legislative acts is frankly reversed in the case of interferences with free speech and free assembly, and for a perfectly cogent reason. Ordinarily, legislation whose basis in economic wisdom is uncertain can be redressed by the processes of the ballot box or the pressures of opinion. But when the channels of opinion or of peaceful persuasion are corrupted or clogged, these political correctives can no longer be relied on, and the democratic system is threatened at its most vital point. In that event the Court, by intervening, restores the processes of democratic government; it does not disrupt them."[44]

An appointive body such as the Supreme Court, exercising political control in a system of government whose powers are supposed to derive from the people, has sometimes been considered an alien offshoot from an otherwise democratic polity. The dilemma was once resolved by invoking the fiction that the Court had no power—that it merely applied the Constitution, which somehow was always presumed the highest expression of the people's will. Although this ancient theory still shows signs of vitality, it is not altogether satisfying. The real problem is to protect individuals and minorities without thereby destroying capacity in the majority to govern. Majorities—and this is the key point of democratic theory—are always in flux. Tomorrow's majority may have a different composition as well as different goals. Defense of the political rights of minorities thus becomes not the antithesis of majority rule, but its very foundation. The Supreme Court can contribute toward realization of free government by guaranteeing all minority groups free access to the political process and

---

[43] *Annals of Congress*, 1st Cong., 1st sess., June 8, 1789, I, 454–55, 457.
[44] Jackson, *Struggle for Judicial Supremacy*, pp. 284–85.

the instruments of political change, while allowing the majority government—as long as the political process is open and untrammeled—to rule.

In a free society no organ of government can be defended solely in terms of its symbolic value. The Supreme Court is a forum. Its contribution consists in what it does, in the deliberative process that precedes judgment. In a society that values the power of reason, an act of judgment can have a moral force far exceeding that of the purse or sword. Thus, the Court's worth consists not only in its restraining power, but also in the part it plays in making audible the ideals and values that may otherwise be silenced. The Court explores and passes judgment on living issues. As Chief Justice Warren put it: "Our system faces no theoretical dilemma but a single continuous problem: how to apply to ever changing conditions the never changing principles of freedom."[45] By precept and example the Court demonstrates what free government means.

---

[45] Earl Warren, "The Law and the Future," *Fortune*, November, 1955, p. 107.

CHAPTER TWENTY

THE
CONTINUING PREDICAMENT

As the nation enters the last three decades of the twentieth century, conflict, deepened and intensified, continues on many fronts. The several years anticipating the 1970s constitute a microcosm of the entire development of American political thought—a heightening and continuation of old dilemmas. Once again the Supreme Court is bound to be at the "storm center."

POLITICAL EQUALITY

Nearly a century after the Civil War, a drive has been mounted in behalf of equality for the black minority at the polls. The Fourteenth and Fifteenth amendments[1] and the Reconstruction Congress attempted to secure the right to vote unaffected by race, color, or previous condition of servitude,[2] but the Supreme Court, in a series of decisions from 1873 to 1883, virtually negated their efforts.[3] Southern states enacted a variety of

---

[1] William Gillette, *The Right to Vote: Politics and Passage of the Fifteenth Amendment* (Baltimore: Johns Hopkins, 1969).
[2] 16 Stat. 140 (1870); 17 Stat. 13 (1871).
[3] See especially *The Slaughterhouse Cases*, 16 Wall. 36 (1873).

restrictions, effectively disfranchising Negro voters. Among the devices employed were the poll tax, the grandfather clause, harshly enforced (for blacks at least) residence requirements, literacy tests, and the so-called white primary. Despite challenges,[4] it was not until 1915 that the Supreme Court held Oklahoma's grandfather clause unconstitutional.[5] In 1939 the Justices killed Oklahoma's attempt to continue the practice in a different guise,[6] evoking Justice Frankfurter's famous remark that the Fifteenth Amendment "nullifies sophisticated as well as simple-minded modes of discrimination."

In 1944, before white primaries were declared unconstitutional, the Court held that the franchise included the citizen's right to vote in a congressional primary and to have his vote properly counted:

> It may now be taken as a postulate that the right to vote in . . . a primary for the nomination of candidates without discrimination by the State, like the right to vote in a general election, is a right secured by the Constitution.[7]

Poll taxes and literacy tests, however, continued in full operation.[8] Congressional opposition was finally mustered against the poll tax, leading in 1962 to the Twenty-fourth Amendment, prohibiting any tax as a requirement for voting in federal elections. The amendment was ratified in 1964. Poll taxes for state elections were not ended until 1966, when the Court concluded

> that a State violates the equal protection clause of the Fourteenth Amendment whenever it makes the affluence of the voter or payment of any fee an electoral standard. Voter qualifications have no relation to wealth nor to paying or not paying this or any other tax.[9]

Literacy tests have presented a more difficult problem, as have residence requirements. Justice Douglas, again speaking for the Court, said in 1959: "The ability to read and write . . . has some relation to standards designed to promote intelligent use of the ballot." The states are empowered to set the standards required of voters, and a state may "conclude that only those who are literate should exercise the franchise."[10] If a literacy test is used to determine voting qualifications, however, it

---

[4] *Grovey* v. *Townsend*, 295 U.S. 45 (1935). The Court had earlier disallowed two Texas arrangements to keep Negroes from voting. *Nixon* v. *Herndon*, 273 U.S. 536 (1927) and *Nixon* v. *Condon*, 286 U.S. 73 (1932), but Texas was able to circumvent the effect of the rulings.
[5] *Quinn* v. *United States*, 238 U.S. 347 (1915).
[6] *Lane* v. *Wilson*, 307 U.S. 268 (1939).
[7] *United States* v. *Classic*, 313 U.S. 299 (1941); *Smith* v. *Allwright*, 321 U.S. 649 (1944).
[8] *Breedlove* v. *Suttles*, 302 U.S. 277 (1937) and *Lassiter* v. *Northhampton Election Board*, 360 U.S. 45 (1959).
[9] *Harper* v. *Virginia State Board of Elections*, 383 U.S. 663 (1966).
[10] *Lassiter* v. *Northhampton Election Board*.

must be both "fair on its face" and fairly administered. Literacy tests may not be used as traps

> to stop even the most brilliant man on his way to the voting booth. The cherished right of people in a country like ours to vote cannot be obliterated by the use of laws . . . which leave the voting fate of a citizen to the passing whim or impulse of an individual registrar. . . .[11]

Although the Supreme Court resolved the conflict between state power and individual rights in a number of landmark cases, it could not, on a case-by-case basis, commit the federal government to securing for every citizen the full enjoyment of his political rights. In sections of the Federal Criminal Code, Congress provided remedies for discrimination, and laid the basis for civil action against the improper denial of the right to vote. But as the Civil Rights Commission noted:

> These provisions . . . were weak . . . the Federal Government was empowered only to bring criminal cases, and the criminal statutes were unwieldy and difficult to apply. Civil cases, with their flexible remedies and relative ease of proof, could be brought only by private persons, who are not always able to bear the expense and difficulty involved in long and complicated litigation.[12]

To make the Fifteenth Amendment truly meaningful, Congress enacted the Civil Rights Act of 1957, the first civil rights legislation since Reconstruction. The Supreme Court's decision outlawing racial segregation in public schools may have been an essential prelude. Among other things the statute prohibits action preventing persons from voting in federal elections and authorizes private parties and the Attorney General to bring suit when a person is deprived of his voting rights. Title II of the act provides for the substitution of federal voting referees for local registration officials when discriminatory practices are found to exist.

All this notwithstanding, the right to vote was still being abridged in certain states. A provision in the Civil Rights Act of 1964 prohibits differential standards of qualification for applicants for registration and denial of the right to vote in federal elections because of trivial errors or omissions on the applicant's part; required literacy tests must be wholly in writing. In the face of determined opposition, however, even these proved inadequate. Finally, Congress, under pressure from President Lyndon B. Johnson, enacted the Voting Rights Act of 1965. Section 2 states that "no voting qualification or prerequisite to voting, or standard, practice, or procedure shall be imposed or applied by any State or political subdivision to deny or abridge the right of any citizen of the United States to vote on account of race or color." In Alabama, Alaska, Georgia, Louisiana,

---

[11] *Louisiana* v. *United States*, 380 U.S. 145 (1965).
[12] U.S. Civil Rights Commission, *Voting* (Washington, D.C.: Government Printing Office, 1961), p. 75.

Mississippi, South Carolina, Virginia, and in twenty-six counties of North Carolina, literacy tests and other discriminatory devices were suspended. Immediately challenged, the act was upheld by the Court in 1966.[13]

"Hopefully," Chief Justice Warren commented, "millions of non-white Americans will now be able to participate for the first time on an equal basis in the government under which they live. We may finally look forward to the day when truly 'the right of citizens of the United States to vote shall not be denied or abridged by the United States or by any State on account of race, color, or previous condition of servitude.' "

The chief justice's use of "hopefully" was not amiss. He knew that in the act itself lay opportunity to delay full possession of the right to vote. In his commencement address at Harvard University, June 4, 1965, President Johnson said: "The voting rights bill [is] the latest, and among the most important, in a long series of victories [for Negroes]." This victory, the President concluded, paraphrasing Winston Churchill, "is not the end. It is not even the beginning of the end. But it is, perhaps, the end of the beginning."[14]

The determined and persistent campaign for voting equality on behalf of racial minorities also inspired a drive on behalf of urban majorities. State legislatures, more representative, as they had been from the first days of the Republic, of rural than of urban citizens, were unwilling to reform themselves. Because the same malapportioned bodies devised congressional districts, Congress reflected rural dominance long after the country had become predominantly urban. Attacks on malapportionment were based on the claim that it violated the constitutional guarantee to each state of "a republican form of government" and that it contravened the Fourteenth Amendment's equal protection clause. In an inconclusive ruling of 1946,[15] a sharply divided Court found the apportionment issue nonjusticiable. "Nothing is clearer than that this controversy concerns matters that bring courts into immediate and active relations with party contests. From the determination of such issues this Court has traditionally held aloof. It is hostile to a democratic system to involve the judiciary in the politics of the people."

But in 1962, under different leadership, the Court reversed itself. A landmark case—*Baker* v. *Carr*[16]—found apportionment justiciable and malapportionment a denial of equal protection of the laws. The Justices followed *Baker* v. *Carr* with a series of other decisions. *Gray* v. *Sanders*, the next year, invalidated the notorious county-unit system of Georgia, which gave disproportionate weight to smaller counties in state primary elections. Justice Douglas, speaking for the majority, observed:

---

[13] *South Carolina* v. *Katzenbach*, 383 U.S. 301 (1966).

[14] The text of President Johnson's address is quoted in Blaustein and Zangrando, *Civil Rights and the Negro*, pp. 559–66. See also Allen Weinstein and Frank O. Gatell, eds., *The Segregation Era, 1863–1954* (New York: Oxford University Press, 1970).

[15] *Colegrove* v. *Green*, 328 U.S. 549 (1946), sustained in *South* v. *Peters*, 339 U.S. 276 (1950).

[16] 369 U.S. 186 (1962).

Once the geographical unit for which a representative is to be chosen is designated, all who participate in the election are to have an equal vote—whatever their race, . . . sex, . . . occupation, . . . income, and wherever their home may be in the geographical unit. This is required by the Equal Protection clause of the Fourteenth Amendment. . . . The conception of political equality . . . can mean only one thing—one person, one vote. . . .[17]

In *Wesberry* v. *Sanders*, decided in 1964, the Court applied the "one man, one vote" concept to congressional districts. "We hold," Justice Black wrote, "that the command of Article I, Section 2" of the Constitution—Members of the U.S. House of Representatives shall be chosen " 'by the People of the several States' "—means "as nearly as practicable one man's vote in a Congressional election is to be worth as much as another's."[18] In *Reynolds* v. *Sims* the same year, the Court held that both houses of bicameral state legislatures were required by the Fourteenth Amendment's Equal Protection Clause to be apportioned wholly on the basis of population. In *Reynolds* v. *Sims*, Chief Justice Warren made his famous observation:

Legislators represent people, not trees or acres. Legislators are elected by voters, not farms or cities or economic interests. As long as ours is a representative form of government, and our legislatures are those instruments of government elected directly by and directly representative of the people, the right to elect legislators in a free and unimpaired fashion is a bedrock of our political system.[19]

The reapportionment decisions led to the deepest probe into representation theory since the state constitutional conventions in the 1820s.[20] As a result of that examination and of the court rulings it produced, state legislatures began the arduous task of reapportionment. Whether it is possible to achieve the perfect one-man one-vote ratio the Court requires remains to be seen. But the ultimate goal is nearer than it has been at any other time in American history. It is little wonder that Chief Justice Warren rated the reapportionment decisions his Court's major contribution to American life. Under his leadership the Supreme Court, in structure and organization the most oligarchical organ of our government, was in the vanguard, bringing us closer to the democratic ideals professed in the Declaration of Independence.

---

[17] 372 U.S. 368 (1963).
[18] 376 U.S. 1 (1964).
[19] 377 U.S. 533 (1964).
[20] M. Glenn Abernethy, *Civil Liberties Under the Constitution* (New York: Dodd, Mead, and Company, 1968), p. 249. See also Robert G. Dixon, *Democratic Representation: Reapportionment in Law and Politics* (New York: Oxford University Press, 1968), Gordon E. Baker, *The Reapportionment Revolution: Representation, Political Power, and the Supreme Court* (New York: Random House, 1966).

THE DRIVE FOR SOCIAL JUSTICE

With the crusade for political equality largely won, an effort to achieve the broader goal of economic equality was made. Unlike the crusade for political equality, which utilized legal and judicial processes and was largely nonviolent, the latter heralded a new development in American political thought—the substitution of action for rhetoric.

Although the concept of social justice had become deeply imbedded in American theory, it had yet to be applied in specific cases. A significant beginning coincided with the outbreak of World War II, when President Roosevelt established a Fair Employment Practices Committee in the Office of Production Management and endowed it with investigatory and recommendatory power to bring an end to discrimination in hiring in defense industries and related government agencies. A permanent Equal Employment Opportunity Commission was subsequently established. Their programs had considerable success, but in the face of congressional opposition, they were not continued after the war.[21] In the Civil Rights Act of 1964, however, Congress, sensing the more liberal temper of the times, prohibited discrimination by both employers and unions.

President Truman added other elements—his order integrating the armed forces[22] and his trailblazing message to Congress on civil rights (February 2, 1948), the first special presidential message in history devoted specifically to that problem. Among "the basic civil rights which [were] the source and support of our democracy," the president declared—rights that the federal government had a clear duty to safeguard anywhere in the Union—were the rights to "equal opportunities for jobs, for homes, for good health and for education." Those rights, as well as "the right to equal justice under law," the traditional freedoms of thought, expression, and religion, and the right to have a voice in government, were "essential human rights" to be enjoyed equally by all.[23] To secure these rights, President Truman made ten specific recommendations, but Congress refused to act. Many of the recommendations, however, were acted on in the 1957 Civil Rights Act.

The Supreme Court addressed itself to housing discrimination in 1948,[24] barring private arrangements—restrictive covenants—designed to maintain segregated housing. "It cannot be doubted that among the civil rights intended to be protected from discriminatory state action," Chief Justice Fred Vinson (1890–1953) wrote for the Court, "are the rights to secure, enjoy, own and dispose of property." It matters not that there may be no positive state legislative action denying equality in the enjoyment of property. The requirements of the Fourteenth Amendment are

---

[21] Executive Order 8802, June 25, 1941, 6 Fed. Reg. 3109 (1941).
[22] Executive Order 9981, July 26, 1948, 13 Fed. Reg. 4313 (1948).
[23] House Document No. 516, 80th Congress, 2nd Session.
[24] *Shelley* v. *Kraemer*, 334 U.S. 1 (1948).

met fully only if state courts do not support private arrangements to promote segregation. "The Constitution confers upon no individual the right to demand action by the state which results in the denial of equal protection of the laws to other individuals." The "coercive power of government" may not be used to deny any right "on the grounds of race or color."

The Civil Rights Acts of 1964 and 1968 carry these gains further. The former prohibits discrimination in public accommodations; the latter bars discrimination in the sale or rental of about 80 percent of all housing in the United States. Litigants in Georgia immediately sought to test the validity of the prohibitions, and the Supreme Court responded with a strong affirmation of the right of Congress to legislate under the commerce clause of the Constitution.[25]

The social equality of Negroes and whites had thus been largely achieved by 1968, at least as far as Congress and the courts could bring it about. But such progress has not overcome the handicaps that the Negro's background imposes upon him. As the Negro population has grown, as prosperity has increased, the ghettos have become more unbearable and inexcusable. Summarizing the problem, the *New York Times* commented that it is now time to face up "to the larger social problems of race. They are problems of poverty, of education, of delinquency. . . . As long as Negro unemployment runs twice the rate of white, as long as central cities continue to become Negro ghettos surrounded by white suburbs, as long as the slum child enters school with his capacity for learning already severely damaged, so long as these facts are unaltered, the law will not solve America's race problem." One wonders, the *Times* concluded, "whether the country's political and social institutions [will] deal as effectively with the new aspects of the racial problem in the next decade as the Supreme Court [has] dealt with the legal aspects in the last."[26]

Black Power

In recent years, inspired by the writings and actions of Malcolm X (1925–1965), Stokely Carmichael (1941–   ), and Eldridge Cleaver (1935–   ),[27] the civil rights movement has moved away from the slow course of legal endeavors. The thrust of the current phase is "Black Power," a militant drive toward the immediate achievement of economic and political power for black citizens of the United States. Black Power advocates recognize that black people, particularly those in the ghettoes of American cities, have "already witnessed and suffered too much and [have] seen too much economic impoverishment to endure the standard

---

[25] *Heart of Atlanta Motel* v. *United States*, 379 U.S. 241 (1964).

[26] *New York Times*, December 20, 1968, p. E3.

[27] See John H. Clarke, ed., *Malcolm X—The Man and His Times* (New York: Macmillan, 1969); Malcolm Little, *The Autobiography of Malcolm X* (New York: Grove Press, 1965); Stokely Carmichael and Charles V. Hamilton, *Black Power: The Politics of Liberation in America* (New York: Vintage Books, 1967); and Eldridge Cleaver, *Soul on Ice* (New York: McGraw-Hill, 1968).

procedures readily accepted by most liberal Americans as evidences of reform. They [feel they] must develop a base of political and economic power from which to identify and define their own needs in their terms."[28] Renouncing integration, Black Power advocates demand "self-determination," i.e., black control of economic and political institutions affecting black people. They challenge the American political system head-on: they reject the Supreme Court and the judicial process as too slow and cumbersome; they do not accept the two-party system, preferring "participatory democracy" and direct confrontation. Militancy and collective action are their chief methods of operation.[29]

"Black people do not want to 'take over' this country," Stokely Carmichael has observed. "They don't want to 'get whitey'; they just want to get him off their backs. . . . The white man is irrelevant to blacks, except as an oppressive force. . . . We won't fight to save the present society, in Vietnam or anywhere else. We are just going to work, in the way *we* see fit, and on goals *we* define, not for civil rights but for all our human rights."[30]

Not surprisingly, considering the current tinderbox of racial relations, the reaction of the white majority has been antagonistic. Thus, "whether American society as a whole is capable of understanding [what the blacks want] and responding sensibly without panic, fear, and repression is an open, but devastatingly crucial question."[31]

MILITARISM

Fear has also been evoked by the growing military preeminence in the United States.[32] Congress is continually subjected to pressure by the military services and by lobbies for the weapons industry. Nor is pressure on Congress (and the resultant increase in military-minded Congressmen) the only tactic used to enhance the military. In 1970 Eliot Janeway reported

---

[28] Blaustein and Zangrando, *Civil Rights and the Negro*, p. 598.
[29] Charles V. Hamilton, "Black Militancy," *New York Times Encyclopedic Almanac 1970* (New York: New York Times, 1970), p. 308 and August Meier and Francis L. Broderick, *Negro Protest Thought in the Twentieth Century* (Indianapolis: Bobbs-Merrill, 1968). See also William H. Grier and Price M. Cobbs, *The Politics of Protest*. A Task Force Report submitted to the National Commission on the Causes and Prevention of Violence (New York: Simon & Schuster, 1968).
[30] Stokely Carmichael, "What We Want," a statement of the Student Nonviolent Coordinating Committee (1966), reprinted in Blaustein and Zangrando, *Civil Rights and the Negro*, p. 605.
[31] Hamilton, "Black Militancy." See also Staughton Lynd, *Class Conflict, Slavery, and the United States Constitution* (Indianapolis: Bobbs-Merrill, 1969).
[32] See Tristram Coffin, *The Passion of the Hawks; Militarism in Modern America* (New York: Macmillan, 1964) and John M. Swomley, Jr., *The Military Establishment* (Boston: Beacon Press, 1964). See also Jack Raymond, *Power at the Pentagon* (New York: Harper & Row, 1964); William Proxmire, *Report from Wasteland: America's Military-Industrial Complex* (New York: Praeger, 1970); and Seymour Melman, *Pentagon Capitalism: The Political Economy of War* (New York: McGraw-Hill, 1970).

that by the mid-1960s, "the Pentagon operated a government within a government, its power base enjoying insulation from not only the grumblings but also the findings of critics."[33] Pressure to solve the great problems facing the nation increasingly involve action by the military. Army teams have discussed riot-control plans with local officials; "order at the point of the bayonet" has been imposed,[34] perhaps nowhere with such chilling effect as in Washington in May 1971 against the "Mayday Tribe." Many and larger segments of the population—lawyers, students, publishers, university administrators—have been aroused by our continued military involvement in Southeast Asia.

Even before the situation became extremely critical, President Eisenhower warned gravely against the military-industrial complex. "In the councils of government," President Eisenhower said, "we must guard against the acquisition of unwarranted influence, whether sought or unsought, by the military-industrial complex. The potential for the disastrous rise of misplaced power exists and will persist." The possibility of abuse of power arose chiefly from the tremendous stake American industry has in defense supply, an interest that industry may use with the acquiescence of the American people to force a buildup of military power or to perpetuate or accelerate a war when the need to do so does not in fact exist. By such techniques, Eisenhower feared, the military aspects of the federal programs might sidetrack compelling economic and social needs and lead to a garrison state. President Kennedy reiterated Eisenhower's concern in his first defense budget message to Congress, and since then the warning has been frequently repeated by many, inside and outside government.[35] The dire situation President Eisenhower foresaw in 1961 has worsened. The Pentagon is now successfully competing with other centers of power, old and new.[36]

THE POLITICS OF DISSENT

All these issues—civil rights, black power, antimilitarism—have won significant support from the nation's young people. Opposing the "Establishment," they have raised their voices in dissent and joined in confrontation politics. A study reporting in early 1970 found that in 1968–1969 a majority of the nation's 2,300 college campuses had experienced incidents in connection with one or all of those causes—22 percent of them violent

---

[33] Eliot Janeway, "Defense Business is Bad Business," *Saturday Review*, April 25, 1970, p. 29.

[34] See Donald McDonald, "Militarism in America," *Center Magazine*, January, 1970, reprinted in *Congressional Record*, CXVI (March 10, 1970), 53334–42.

[35] See C. Wright Mills, *The Power Elite* (New York: Oxford University Press, 1965); Fred J. Cook, *The Warfare State* (New York: Macmillan, 1962); and William Proxmire, *Report from Wasteland*. See also Tom Wicker's New York Times News Service syndicated column of May 17, 1971, "John Mitchell's Dragnet."

[36] Hans J. Morgenthau, "Who's Running the Country?" *Saturday Review*, April 25, 1964, p. 31.

or disruptive. Although perhaps no more than 15 percent of college students were actively engaged, the study found that "there is widespread sympathy among students for the aims of protestors."[37]

Nowhere was the right to dissent more dramatically challenged than in the Chicago trial of eight youthful antiwar demonstrators, arrested during the 1968 Democratic National Convention and charged with violating the antiriot section of the Civil Rights Act of 1968. The trial itself provoked so many challenges to traditional procedures that it was difficult to keep the central point in focus. The first test of a law making it illegal to cross a state line with "intent" to incite riots, the Chicago trial is expected "to go far toward determining how much dissent is permitted in America under the Constitution."[38]

The brutal episode at Chicago was only one in a series of actions taken against political dissenters, prompting the *New York Times* to remark editorially: "Under the guise of essential attacks on crime, police and investigatory power are being sharpened for potential use against political offenders." The nation needed to be reminded, the *Times* thought, that its "greatness springs from its dream of greater freedoms for all, not from a nightmare of restricted liberties for some."[39]

Whether from the Left or Right, the most extreme thoughts and the most offensive rhetoric are entitled to protection under the Bill of Rights. But when thought is translated into unlawful or violent action, it is equally imperative that the community be protected, not only from coercion but also from its consequent aftereffects. The social compact has room for tolerance, patience, and restraint, Justice Douglas has argued, but not for sabotage and violence.[40] This applies with particular force to the academic community, in which protection of freedom is most precious and its security most fragile. Neither the government nor a dissident group can indulge in violence or the abridgment of rights without being guilty of the ultimate and intolerable subversion of the American ideal and the democratic reality.[41]

---

[37] The study was conducted by a committee named by the American Council on Education and was chaired by Sol M. Linowitz. See also Seymour M. Lipset and P. G. Altbach, eds., *Students in Revolt* (Boston: Houghton Mifflin, 1970) and Garry R. Weaver and James H. Weaver, eds., *The University and Revolution* (Englewood Cliffs, N.J.: Prentice-Hall, 1970).

[38] *New York Times Encyclopedic Almanac 1970*, p. 36.

[39] *New York Times*, April 27, 1970, p. 32, and April 29, 1970, p. 40.

[40] William O. Douglas, *Points of Rebellion* (New York: Vintage Books, 1970), pp. 3–33, *passim*.

[41] *New York Times*, April 29, 1970, p. 40. Probing beneath surface manifestations of disorder and unrest on our campuses, Alexander Bickel points persuasively to a deeper crisis—the breakdown of rationality, civility, ethical standards, measure, and balance. Instead of commiserating with each other, Bickel urges, heads of leading universities should "announce their intention to institute a reform which is the pre-condition of all other reforms: the use of disciplinary power to keep discourse and action within the bounds of order. No more vandalism; no more assaultive, vicious speech; no more bullying, simulated or actual." Alexander M. Bickel, "We've Been Shouted Down," *Washington Post*, June 14, 1970. Reprinted from the *New Republic*.

The Quality of American Life

The greatest challenge in the politics of confrontation is the call for basic change in the quality of American life. Some argue that change has long since taken place—for the worse—and that this is what the protest is about. Although directed toward specific issues—the spread of war in Southeast Asia, the privileged position of ROTC units on college campuses, alleged discrimination against minorities—each protest, runs the argument, is part of a general campaign against what America has become: "one great wasteland, a big, monstrous, mechanized desert, a place without roots or feelings."[42] Jerry Rubin has observed:

> The biggest social problem in the country today is loneliness. . . . Loneliness is not an individual problem—it's the collective problem of millions of Amerikans [sic], growing out of the alienating environment we live in. We work in one part of town with people who are not our friends, and we sleep in another part of town and don't know our neighbors. We waste much of our life dying in mobile concentration camps called freeways or commuter trains. . . . The car, a box, transports lonely people from the box where they sleep to the box where they work, and then back to the box where they sleep. Amerikans [sic] relate to each other as drivers of other cars; the only good driver is the one who takes another road.[43]

Less strident voices are being raised against the vacuous quality of American life. "Will [the American] people long be content with the rather mundane goal of ever-increasing affluence which the system espouses as the highest aim of man?" John Kenneth Galbraith has asked. "Might there not one day be discontent with a society in which there is single-minded concentration on the goal of economic success? Might there not one day be suspicion of leadership and prestige that is so universally associated with economic achievement? Might not one wish for such a revolt?"[44]

Galbraith stopped short of calling for drastic change; Mayor John V. Lindsay of New York did not. In an address at the University of California at Berkeley, in April 1970, he told the students that they stand "as an alternative—as a check on how we work—as a warning system to men and to organizations which are not helping to make this country what it can be." Lindsay interpreted student activism as a "plea for help in the urgent task of turning this nation on a different course," as a warning against the "real danger that, out of the tumult and turmoil of recent years will come a set of simplistic, illusory solutions that will destroy what chance we have to build something better. . . ."[45]

---

[42] A student comment in *The Chronicle*, Duke University, March 17, 1971, p. 6.
[43] Jerry Rubin, *DO IT!* (New York: Simon & Schuster, 1970), p. 231. See also Peter Schrag, "Out of Place in America," *Saturday Review*, May 9, 1970.
[44] John K. Galbraith, "The Affluent Society after Ten Years," *Atlantic*, May, 1969, p. 44.
[45] Reported in the *New York Times*, April 3, 1970, p. 21.

PHILOSOPHICAL ALTERNATIVES

A debate reminiscent of earlier times has developed, as proponents of the "counterculture" offer solutions ranging across the spectrum of political thought. For convenience, they can be divided into the New Right, traditional conservatism, responsible business leadership, socialism, philosophical radicalism, civil disobedience, and the New Left.

The New Right

New Right solutions are in reaction to two fears: of excessive centralization of power in the national government and of the loss of individual identity. The New Right sees in the increasing activity of the national government more "than the mere proliferation of federal programs of grants-in-aid; more . . . than the tens of thousands of rules and regulations that turn up in the *Federal Reporter*." Deplored is the abandonment of the "two principal safeguards devised by the founding fathers against the abuses of excessive power"—namely, federalism and separation of power.[46] In the 1960s the John Birch Society, leading proponent of the New Right, feared the capitulation of the United States to communism and expressed concern lest this country fall under domination of the United Nations, "designed by its founders for the . . . purpose of increasing the rigidity of government controls over the lives and affairs of individual citizens."[47] Convinced that in modern America, where there is nothing but "contempt for the individual," "the human spirit withers," the New Right demands *self*-government by responsible individuals. What little governmental aid is needed should come primarily from state and local governments and be given to "executive agencies . . . kept strictly within the surveillance of the legislative branch."[48] Only so will free men survive.

Traditional Conservatism

The conservative does not go so far as his brethren further to the Right; he recognizes the validity of government action, operating within the traditions of the American people. Aristotle's "polity" is his model, a governmental arrangement balancing and checking the interests of the several classes. Civil freedom comes from just and prudent government, supporting what past experience has shown to be important, but not depriving individuals of the opportunity to make the most of their talents

[46] James J. Kilpatrick, "The New Right: What Does It Seek?" *Saturday Review*, October 8, 1966, pp. 29–30. See also Seymour Martin Lipset, "New Perspectives on the Counter-Culture," *Saturday Review*, March 20, 1971, pp. 25–28.
[47] *Beliefs and Principles of the John Birch Society, 1962*, reprinted in Mason, *Free Government*, p. 853.
[48] Kilpatrick, "The New Right," pp. 124–25.

in the achievement of prosperity and happiness. Conservatives do not choose between conforming and nonconforming but between conforming to the shifting, stereotyped values of the moment and conforming to the lasting, archetypal values shared by all mankind.[49] The conservative sees the danger of blind obedience to the transient majority and the value and necessity of protecting the minority for the benefit of the majority itself. Thus, he is unhappy with modern America, convinced that in slavishly embracing such current fads as the New Deal, the Fair Deal, the New Frontier, and the Great Society, we have turned our backs on our heritage. Exemplified by President Richard M. Nixon, the conservative calls on the nation to return to a better balance: "We live in a deeply troubled and profoundly unsettled time . . . on every hand we find old standards violated, old values discarded, old precepts ignored . . . [in jeopardy is] the process by which a civilization maintains its continuity: the passing on of values from one generation to the next."[50] Needed is recognition of the merit of that process and determination to guard and preserve it.

Responsible Business Leadership

Despite passage of the Full Employment Act of 1946, declaring it the federal government's responsibility to "create and maintain" conditions of full employment and maximum production, the principles of private ownership and free enterprise have not been abandoned. Far from it. Even with increasing governmental involvement in the economy, the United States is still committed to private enterprise. But whereas big business formerly stressed natural rights and the sanctity of property, it is now more inclined to place considerations of general economic interest more nearly on a par with its own interests and to espouse a philosophy of business responsibility and leadership. The antagonism between economic oligarchy and political democracy, so troublesome to Louis D. Brandeis at the turn of the century, has been mitigated in recognition of the concept of cooperation for the general welfare. For the first time in history, "the really great corporation managements have reached a position," Adolf Berle observed, "in which they . . . consider the kind of a community . . . they intend to help construct and maintain. . . . The present current of thinking . . . clearly [leads] the largest corporations toward a greater . . . acceptance of the responsibility that goes with power."[51]

As a result "the present-day corporation stands not on the periphery

---

[49] See Peter Viereck, *Conservatism Revisited and the New Conservatism* (New York: Macmillan, 1965).

[50] Remarks at General Beadle State College, Madison, South Dakota, June 3, 1969, White House press release, p. 3.

[51] Adolf A. Berle, Jr., "The Emerging Common Law of Free Enterprise," an address before the Brandeis Lawyers Society, December 13, 1949, p. 7. See also Berle, *Twentieth Century Capitalist Revolution* (New York: Harcourt, Brace, 1954).

of the democratic process, as it did in the last half of the 19th century, but in its dead center."[52] Business does not seek to take over government but, in recognition of the increasingly blurred line between what is "public" and what is "private" in the United States, to cooperate with government in achieving social objectives, to join with it in attacking and solving social problems for the ultimate benefit not only of itself but also of all American citizens.[53]

Acceptance by business of responsibility for the general welfare has not invalidated the truth so much stressed by the Founding Fathers that "power has laws of its own."[54] Testifying in 1915 before the United States Commission on Industrial Relations, Louis D. Brandeis observed: "The result in the case of these large corporations may be to develop a benevolent absolutism, but it is absolutism all the same; and it is this which makes the great corporations so dangerous. There develops within the State a state so powerful that the ordinary social and industrial forces existing are insufficient to cope with it."

Despite the political dominance achieved by the New Deal, and the "social conscience" of corporations so reassuring to Berle, Brandeis's observations may still be true. Ralph Nader's objective, reminiscent of the thought and methods of Brandeis, is to bring the power of corporations under public control. Nader's words echo Berle's in *The Modern Corporation and Private Property*: "In Russia the enemy would be the Government. In this country, it is the big corporations which have become private governments." So while others dream of revolution and strike out in all directions, Nader works within the "system," quarries in the hard rock of reality, exposing the facts concerning engineering of automobiles, meat-inspection standards, and the laxity of the Federal Trade Commission. Nader is doing on a small scale what he would like to see in operation on a large scale—ten thousand professionals in Washington lobbying in the public interest as vigorously as an estimated fifteen thousand lobbyists working for corporations and trade associations.[55]

In a perceptive review of Adolf Berle's *Twentieth Century Capitalist Revolution*, Walton Hamilton wrote:

> The pages of the book ring with the reiterated demand that conscience, not the acquisitive urge, be the corporate guide. But even in a simple and unvexed society, conscience has never been able to stand alone, for conscience has always been a flexible thing, easily receptive to values of personal interest. . . . In headlong times like ours, when the small voice within cannot

---

[52] William T. Gossett, vice-president and general counsel, Ford Motor Company, quoted in *Congressional Record*, CXII (July 17, 1966), 11730.

[53] Gaylord A. Freeman, Jr., "For Business, a Call to Commitment," *Wall Street Journal*, January 22, 1970, p. 10.

[54] Berle, *Capitalist Revolution*, p. 172.

[55] William V. Shannon, "The Man Who Beat the System," *New York Times*, August 23, 1970, Sec. 4, p. 12.

keep up with the course of events, conscience needs help over the hard places.[56]

Conscience needs, in short, the help of government. For of one thing we can be certain: government alone can create and re-create the broad firmament of order under which individuals and groups, including so-called free enterprise, can function for the good of all. "Neither the claims of ownership nor those of control can stand against the paramount interest of the community."[57] Whenever "any organization or combination of individuals, whether in a corporation, a labor union or other body, obtains such economic or legal advantage that it can control or, in effect, govern the lives of other people, it is subject to the control of the Government. Liberty requires that coercion be applied to the individual, not by other individuals, but by the Government after full inquiry into the justification."[58]

Socialism

It is precisely to the possibilities of self-interest, still not ruled out, that objections are raised by critics of capitalism. Michael Harrington finds it difficult to discern conscience in the heart of the capitalist process[59] and joins with others in calling for a Socialist corrective. A Socialist state would take over the private sectors of the economy (to a greater or lesser degree depending on where the particular Socialist or Communist stands) and run them collectively in behalf of the people. No longer would power be solely in the hands of those with money—the capitalists. Henceforth it would be possessed by the people themselves. The great division in Socialist thought is not over ends—a collectivist society—but over means. Generally, the split is between those who are willing to accomplish the objective through existing forms and procedures (Democratic Socialism) and those who accept Marx's dictum that it can be accomplished only by revolution.

The latter group has found a spokesman in Tom Hayden (1940?–   ), leader of the Students for a Democratic Society (SDS). Hayden declares that the welfare state, inaugurated by the New Deal, is a "myth." "The entire reformist trend has weakened the poor under the pretense of helping them and strengthened elite rule under the slogan of curbing private enterprise."[60] The only way to remedy the situation is to organize "a community" composed of its poor, blacks and "middle-class insurgents," who

---

[56] Walton Hamilton, "Human Reports in a Corporate Society," *Nation*, December 18, 1954, p. 534.

[57] Berle and Means, *The Modern Corporation*, p. 356.

[58] Robert H. Jackson, *The Supreme Court in the American System of Government* (Cambridge, Mass.: Harvard University Press, 1955), p. 69.

[59] Michael Harrington, *The Accidental Century* (New York: Macmillan, 1969).

[60] Irving Howe, ed., *The Radical Papers* (Garden City, N.Y.: Doubleday, 1966). pp. 353–55. See Thomas Hayden, *Trial* (New York: Holt, Rinehart, & Winston, 1970).

will destroy that state and put in its place a new type of entity based on participatory democracy and featuring some sort of "parallel structures" instead of government.[61] After a period of emphasizing the negative, destructive part of its program, giving little thought to the new society it hopes to bring about, the SDS has quieted down. It has yet to come up with a viable Socialist alternative.

Philosophic Radicalism

Still another revolutionary alternative has been suggested by the philosopher Herbert Marcuse (1898–   ).[62] Marcuse elevates Freud's theory of instincts to the operating principle of a new society. He proposes the establishment of a "nonrepressive" society in which man's erotic instincts, or the Pleasure Principle, will reign. Capitalism has too long been allowed to produce a self-serving, stifling morality; "freedom" has been a hollow thing—"unfreedom" in reality—for society has been structured to delay individual gratification for the benefit of the system. A biological-psychological transformation is necessary if the fundamental experience of human instincts is to be permitted and the proper goals of life established. A new social structure based on Eros must be created.

> We should keep our seriousness for serious things and not waste it on trifles . . . while God is the real goal of all beneficent serious endeavor, man . . . has been constructed as a toy for God and this is, in fact, the finest thing about him. All of us, then, men and women alike, must fall in with our role and spend life in making our play as perfect as possible—to the complete inversion of current theory.[63]

Only so will man realize "the full potentials of his humanity—to live a life as free as possible from toil, dependency, and cruelty under conditions which fully liberate imagination, intellect, and the capacity for sensuous pleasure."[64] Revolution will be necessary to bring this drastic change about. "When the rights of the existing society contradict the right of men to greater freedom, 'the two rights must come into violent conflict. . . . The opposition cannot change [the] state of affairs by the very means which protect and sustain the state of affairs.' "[65]

---

[61] Tom Hayden, quoted in Norm Fruchter, "The New Radicalism: Round IV," *Partisan Review*, Winter, 1966, p. 54. Some of these same ideas were expressed at the Revolutionary People's Constitutional Convention, Philadelphia, September, 1970, sponsored by the Black Panther party. See the Associated Press dispatches for September 7, 1970 and *Washington Post*, September 9, 1970, p. A14.

[62] Marcuse's ideas appear in three major recent works, *Negations; Essays in Critical Theory* (Boston: Beacon Press, 1968); *An Essay on Liberation* (Boston: Beacon Press, 1969); and *Five Lectures (Psychoanalysis, Politics, and Utopia)* (Boston: Beacon Press, 1970).

[63] Marcuse, *Five Lectures*, p. 43.

[64] Richard Goodwin, "The Social Theory of Herbert Marcuse," *Atlantic*, June, 1971, p. 69. This is perhaps the best short analysis of Marcuse's theory in print.

[65] Goodwin, "Social Theory of Marcuse," p. 75.

Civil Disobedience[66]

Marcuse rejects the lesson Thoreau taught, as did most Americans until recently. Martin Luther King, Jr. (1929–1968), a disciple of Ghandi, made nonviolent resistance the key to his successful efforts to mobilize support for full civil rights for Negroes. For Dr. King, civil disobedience was an alternative course for today's disaffected. Civil disobedience as a tactic of protest requires action in response to the dictates of higher law, interpreted by conscience in behalf of what one believes to be moral, just, or right, regardless of the consequences. Philip Berrigan, convicted of burning draft files in the exercise of civil disobedience in 1968, declares:

> I am an American and a Christian insofar as I face my country and humanity under the Declaration of Independence and the Gospel. As a democratic man I must cling to a tradition of protest going back to our birth as a nation— traditions which brightened our finest hours as people. Jefferson, Washington, Madison, Thoreau, Emerson, Whitman, and Twain; they also stand in the dock today; they judge you as you judge me. They judge our uses of political power, our racism, our neglect of the poor, our courts serving the interests of war. I do not hesitate to assert that were these men alive today, they would disobey as I have disobeyed and be convicted as I am convicted.[67]

Berrigan, along with his brother Daniel and a good many others, has moved beyond passive civil disobedience to the incitement of riot and violence, raising questions about the continued viability of the concept.

The New Left

Some remain unsatisfied with any solution that does not promise immediate change in "the system." For the most part they have become part of the radical protest movement labeled the New Left.

Of all the philosophies competing for attention in modern America, the New Left is the most difficult to explain within a brief compass. Its proponents—largely young people—have widely divergent goals and differing views of how they should be achieved. On certain subjects there is agreement: America's participation in the Indochina conflict must be ended; civil rights must be expanded;[68] the fight against poverty must be waged with dedication. But beyond that there is little coherence.

"The 'New Left' does not fit within the political spectrum," Edward M. Keating of *Ramparts*, a New Left publication, explains. "If anything, it belongs to the social spectrum. The end sought is not a new system,

---

[66] See Carl Cohen, *Civil Disobedience: Conscience, Tactics and the Law* (New York: Columbia University Press, 1971). See also the works cited in footnote 8, Chap. 1.
[67] Philip Berrigan, *Prison Journal of a Priest Revolutionary*, (New York: Holt, Rinehart, & Winston, 1970), p. 12.
[68] See Nat Hentoff, "Why Students Want Their Constitutional Rights," *Saturday Review*, May 22, 1971, pp. 60–63, 73–74.

since systems . . . are irrelevant. What *is* relevant is justice. Whereas the 'Old Left' sought economic justice, the 'New Left' has a far broader concern that encompasses social, economic, and political justice. Its ultimate goal is peace—domestic and international—and peace is impossible without justice."[69]

> The enemy is not Communism; it is disease, poverty, ignorance and oppression. . . . We should replace our power to destroy with our power to create. We should care about the suffering of human beings—and we should do something about it.
>
> What impels us is an unshakable conviction that the old ways won't work anymore—if they ever worked at all, which we doubt. To achieve peace—through justice—will prove a wrenching task. We will have to let go of traditional rhetoric, stereotyped thought, preconceptions, and everything else that inhibits man from fulfilling himself. We wish to cooperate, not compete, so that the family of Man might become one. We see what can be. And we seek the ineffable. We will never grasp it in this life, but we can reach out—and live.[70]

In a perceptive essay Irving Howe concludes:

> The New Left has had a notable effect on campus life; it has exerted an oblique but measurable influence on the more extreme black militants; and it has contributed to the growth of a distinctive "Youth Culture." . . . So far the New Left has made few serious contributions to political thought or cultural experience. Whatever interest the New Left shows in political theory is usually directed toward the work of older writers whose work it appropriates and sometimes twists to its own ends.[71]

Seymour Martin Lipset reminds us that countercultural behavior is not new in the United States: earlier rebels have challenged the Establishment; indeed, conflict with authority goes back to ancient times.[72] It is endemic in a free society. As Robert Dahl suggests, democracy seems to "encourage demands for new systems of authority."

> Democracy has never been fully achieved. . . . [E]very system purporting to be democratic is vulnerable to the charge that it is not democratic enough, or not "really" fully democratic. The charge is bound to be correct, since no polity has ever been completely democratized.[73]

---

[69] Edward Keating, "The New Left: What Does It Mean?" *Saturday Review*, September 24, 1966, p. 25. For another perceptive analysis and interpretation see Irving Howe, "New Course for the New Left," *Saturday Review*, May 30, 1970, pp. 8–11.

[70] Keating, "The New Left," pp. 27, 64.

[71] Irving Howe, "New Course for the New Left," pp. 8–11.

[72] Lipsit, "New Perspectives," pp. 25–26.

[73] Quoted in Lipset, "New Perspectives," p. 27. See Robert A. Dahl, *After the Revolution? Authority in a Good Society* (New Haven, Conn.: Yale University Press, 1971).

The Quest Continues

In part, the problem of modern America may be, as Herbert Marcuse insists,[74] that the principles and practices of free government, though vital in the earlier stages of industrial development, are outmoded with the maturity of society. They were devised to meet an entirely different set of needs, Marcuse argues. Until means are again related to needs, the United States will be "out of phase" with its own best interests.

The real thrust today, C. P. Dippel writes, is that "of technological domination."

> A new faith, the belief in science and technology, is driving out the old faith. It is thought that science has at last found the key to all reality and truth. . . . We fear the domination of technology. A religion that takes fright at the absolute realization of its faith and hope is a very dubious affair. Yet it is this religion that prepares the way for an ever encroaching technology. . . . If man is to retain his freedom in the face of this technology, he must reverse the order he presently supports, an order that gives priority first to things and then to "anonymous man." If we do not do so, we choose against ourselves.[75]

Probing more deeply, René Dubos writes:

> The present century is called the technological age not because there is a great abundance of machines and man is dependent on them, but because we accept the fact that our lives are the manifestations of consequences rather than expressions of purposes. . . .
>
> Despite our scientific and technological triumphs, we suffer from a loss of nerve and have become a conservative society satisfied with continuing our present course. We are no longer willing to construct models of possible futures that we really desire. . . .[76]

Accepting Dubos's analysis and interpretation, Harrison Brown holds that society suffers from a malady of which technology is only a manifestation:

> We must learn how to stabilize populations, and how to provide all persons with adequate nutrition. We must learn how to utilize our vast reserves of low-grade resources. We must learn how to recycle our wastes in such a way that we do not pollute our environment. We must learn how to create beauty to replace the ugliness we have created.[77]

---

[74] See Herbert Marcuse, *One Dimensional Man* (Boston: Beacon Press, 1964).
[75] C. J. Dippel, "What Price Freedom: Discontent in a Technological Society," *Delta*, Spring, 1970, pp. 67, 75–76.
[76] René Dubos, *Reason Awake: Science for Man* (New York: Columbia University Press, 1970). Quoted by Harrison Brown in *Saturday Review*, June 6, 1970, p. 68.
[77] René Dubos, *Reason Awake.*

Zbigniew Brzezinski, professor of government at Columbia University, thinks American society may be at a parting of the ways—at "the transition state between two ages." Just as the agrarian age gave way to the age of industrialism, so the age of industrialism is now yielding to a new age—the "technetronic era."[78] In *Between Two Ages*, Brzezinski, taking into account the various and often antagonistic forces at work in our society, tries to understand their social, philosophical, and political implications. His approach is optimistic: "Until now, man has lived in combat with nature. Man has won that war, and pollution is part of the carnage of his victory. We are now, more or less, standing on the battlefield, having won that battle." Thanks to technetronics, man will be free of the drudgery imposed by "the plow and the sweatshop."[79]

Such divergent opinions as these will occur again as America turns to attacking new problems. Involved will be not only controversy and fresh challenges but enduring basic principles in American political thought. Vietnam has been diversionary, explaining—even justifying—postponement of an all-out effort to deal with domestic issues. When, and if, values and priorities are reassessed and serious effort is made to achieve peace with nature, one may confidently predict divisions and fissures in American society reminiscent of earlier times. Conflicts between those who share a vision of what America may become and those determined to keep things as they are may, indeed, become so disruptive as to make disagreements over Vietnam pale. It is conceivable, moreover, that with change in Supreme Court justices, the banner of judicial self-restraint, raised in 1937 to legitimatize New Deal reform legislation, may once again be lowered, reviving the earlier judicial negativism that had prevented government from regulating the economy. If that should be the case, it would be difficult, indeed, to supply a satisfactory answer to the "supreme question" posed by Walter Lippmann on the occasion of his eightieth birthday: "How will men be able to make themselves willing and able to save themselves?"[80]

---

[78] Zbigniew Brzezinski, *Between Two Ages* (New York: Viking, 1970).

[79] "For the first time, we are able to inquire, 'To what end? What purpose should society serve—what am I, who am I, what am I for?' Without science, modern philosophy cannot possibly supply answers to such concrete problems as ecology, survival, pollution, even peace. Without philosophy, science would be directionless, possibly destructive." From an interview with McCandlish Phillips, *New York Times*, August 12, 1970, p. 18.

[80] *New York Times Magazine*, September 14, 1969, p. 140.

ENDURING PRINCIPLES
OF FREE GOVERNMENT

Americanism is multiform; and it is also, at its very roots, nonconformist. No one can fully shape it the way he wants it to go—no President and no millionaire, no labour leader and no intellectual; and it is not even shaped by all the objective consequences of its mass production system. Something is always escaping to be itself; something is always emerging to protest that things must be done another way; there is always an ardent clash between traditionalist and reformer which makes the consequential Americanism different from what either of them dared both to hope and to fear.[1]

Multiform American political society leads to a decided preference for a political blend—a mixture of diverse and often antagonistic elements. Conflict and change have been the normal pattern in achieving this fusion. The result of this continuous process has often been disorder, sometimes verging on chaos, so much so that each generation, including our own, thinks itself obligated to save free government for the next. Far from deploring unrest, Adlai Stevenson called it "the kind of noise that, to the inner ear, is the sweet music of free institutions." Solutions achieved have not been permanent. In his "Song of the Open Road" Walt

---

[1] Harold Laski, *The American Democracy* (New York: Viking, 1948), p. 719.

Whitman in 1856 divined the unending quest: "It is provided in the very essence of things that from any fruition of success, no matter what, shall come forth something to make a greater struggle necessary." Free government is, indeed, a *"method"* of "finding *proximate* solutions for *insoluble* problems."[2]

The Founding Fathers inherited the axiom that property was the basis of politics, the true measure of power. Alexander Hamilton and James Madison agreed that liberty leads inevitably to inequality.[3] Their guiding principles rested on this assumption. For them, the primary function of government was to safeguard the fruits of this inequality, i.e., property, against the ever-present threat of "mere numbers." Latter-day Americans burnished this doctrine even brighter and promoted it as the most distinctive facet of our culture.

From the outset, however, exponents of the property-power nexus have been confronted by those upholding the sovereign authority of government, by those stressing the role of public power rooted in persons and numbers, by those who would make politics dominant over, not subordinate to, economics. The Declaration of Independence dedicated the American people to the doctrine that just governments rest on the consent of the governed. We are committed, in some measure, to majority rule, and to the idea that government is a positive, creative force in society. The preamble of our Constitution proclaims that government is instituted to promote the general welfare. In 1826 Edward Livingston declared: "Political society owes perfect protection to all its members in their persons, reputations and property; and it also owes necessary subsistence to those who cannot procure it for themselves. . . . The preservation of life is the first object, property is only a secondary one." "Can it be supposed," Livingston inquired, "that any just contract could stipulate that one of the contracting parties should die of hunger, in order that the others might enjoy, without deduction, the whole of their property?"[4]

---

[2] Reinhold Niebuhr, quoted in Mason, *Free Government*, p. 906.

[3] "It was certainly true," Hamilton remarked on the floor of the Philadelphia Convention, June 26, 1787, "that nothing like an equality of property existed; that an inequality would exist as long as liberty existed, and that it would unavoidably result from that very liberty itself. This inequality of property constituted the great and fundamental distinction in Society." *The Records of the Federal Convention of 1787*, 1, 424. In *Federalist* Number 10 Madison said: "The diversity in the faculties of men, from which the rights of property originate, is not less an insuperable obstacle to an uniformity of interests. The protection of these faculties in the first object of government."

"It is a great and dangerous error," Calhoun once wrote, "to suppose that all people are equally entitled to liberty. It is a reward to be earned, not a blessing to be gratuitously lavished on all alike. . . . Inequality of condition, while it is a necessary consequence of liberty, is, at the same time, indispensable to progress." (R. K. Cralle, *Works of Calhoun*), I, 55–56.

[4] Edward Livingston, Introductory Report to the Code of Reform of Prison Discipline, 1826, in *Criminal Jurisprudence* (New York: National Prison Association of the United States of America, 1873), I, 528–29, 533.

At every turning point in our history, conflicting claims concerning property and persons have been made. Spokesmen for property have met rebuttal from those who valued the human personality. The dominant trend has been democratic. "We march and rest and march again."[5] Democracy, "like death, gives back nothing."[6] De Tocqueville reminded us that the passion for equality is even more relentless than the quest for freedom. This radical strain in our tradition has not been, however, an unmixed blessing. If reformers have been necessary to counterbalance fossilism, then adherents of the status quo have been indispensable as a safeguard against reformers. It was a reformer who said that "the greatest dangers to liberty lurk in insidious encroachment by men of zeal, well-meaning but without understanding."[7]

These divergent, interwoven strands constitute the essence of American politics. Whether one reads Madison's notes of the debates in the Philadelphia Convention of 1787, the discussions held in the 1820s in Massachusetts, New York, and Virginia, then engaged in broadening the constitutional base of power, the long and bitter wranglings that preceded Lincoln's Emancipation Proclamation, the nationwide controversy engendered by FDR's Court-packing proposal, or the literature of student protest, one notes a baffling and continuing paradox. Pitted against each other are the moral ideals of freedom and the stubborn defense of inequality. As John Quincy Adams said: "The government of our country, instead of a Democracy the most simple, is the most complicated government on the face of the globe."[8]

The American political tradition is self-renewing; it rests on certain principles on the basis of which regeneration can be accomplished. First, we acknowledge that man is born for freedom, not for slavery. "Legislators represent people, not trees or acres." "God gave man the same amazing diversity that He gave the flowers in the mountain meadows."[9] Differences of opinion are inevitable and natural. Men as widely separated in times as Thomas Jefferson and William O. Douglas have believed that

> our real power is our spiritual strength, and that spiritual strength stems from our civil liberties. If we are true to our traditions, if we are tolerant of a whole market place of ideas, we will always be strong. Our weakness grows when we become intolerant of opposing ideas, depart from our standards of civil liberties, and borrow the policeman's philosophy from the enemy we detest.[10]

---

[5] Lloyd, *Wealth Aganist Commonwealth*, p. 533.
[6] Quoted in Ghent, *Our Benevolent Feudalism*, p. 783.
[7] Justice Brandeis, dissenting in *Olmstead* v. *U.S.*, 277 U.S. 438 (1928), 479.
[8] Adams, *Jubilee of the Constitution*, p. 115.
[9] William O. Douglas, address delivered in Denver, Colorado, May 20, 1948, reproduced in Mason, *Free Government*, p. 842.
[10] William O. Douglas, "Black Silence of Fear."

Second, our political heritage takes cognizance of man's natural propensity for freedom, his "providential" drive for equality. It keeps open the channels for the expression of ideas, good, bad, and indifferent. It guarantees the people the right to "assemble freely and speak their minds freely and criticize their government, . . . not for the pleasure of the citizens but for the health of the state."[11]

Third, these basic freedoms are sanctified in formal declarations and in the Constitution itself. "The very purpose of the First Amendment is to foreclose public authority from assuming a guardianship of the public mind through regulating the press, speech, and religion. In this field every person must be his own watchman for truth, because the forefathers did not trust any government to separate the true from the false for us."[12]

Fourth, in addition to our constitutional safeguards and our recognition that "man's capacity for justice makes democracy possible; but man's inclination to injustice makes democracy necessary,"[13] we have further fortified our freedoms by shying away from absolutes. What distinguishes our political system from that of totalitarians, Right and Left, is the methods and means followed, not the ends professed. "The history of man's struggle to be free is in large degree a struggle to be free of oppressive procedures," William O. Douglas has declared.[14] Although rarely in accord with Douglas in civil liberties cases, Justice Frankfurter agreed that "the history of human freedom is, in no small measure, the history of procedure."[15] The most distinctive aspect of our society lies in the methods free government must follow. No opposition means no democracy, no freedom. Out of difference, diversity, and conflict, emerges a quickened sense of the common interest. "If there were no different interests the common interest would barely be felt, as it would encounter no obstacles. All would go of its own accord, and politics would cease to be an art."[16]

Fifth, despite the freedom of the majority to choose a particular means, we preserve the right of the minority to suggest others and to try to persuade the majority to adopt them. "As a free society," Adlai Stevenson once said, "we must rely primarily on persuasion. We can use coercion only rarely, and usually only as a defensive measure."[17]

Sixth, we recognize that liberty has meaning only within "an organized society, in which law and order are maintained and the security of the

---

[11] Archibald MacLeish, "Freedom to End Freedom," *Survey Graphic*, XXVIII (February, 1938), 118.

[12] *Thomas* v. *Collins*, 323 U.S. 516 (1945), 545.

[13] Reinhold Niebuhr, quoted in Mason, *Free Government*, p. 899.

[14] William O. Douglas, *An Almanac of Liberty* (Garden City, N.Y.: Doubleday, 1954), p. viii.

[15] *Malinski* v. *New York*, 324 U.S. 401 (1945) 419.

[16] J. J. Rousseau, *The Social Contract and Discourses*, (Everyman Library ed., Book 2, Chap. iii,) p. 25.

[17] Adlai E. Stevenson, *Call to Greatness* (New York: Harper, 1954), pp. 103–4.

group is safeguarded."[18] In the interest of order and national security, we admit that some restrictions on liberty may from time to time be necessary. "Liberty . . . must be limited to be possessed," Edmund Burke remarked. "The degree of restraint it is impossible in any case to settle precisely. But it ought to be the constant aim of every wise public counsel to find out by cautious experiments, and rational, cool endeavours, with how little, not how much, of this restraint the community can subsist."

Seventh, although there is no doubt about the reality of latter-day menaces to our peace and security, it is usually conceded that these threats can be taken care of within our existing legal framework. "The present police power . . . should enable a people devoted to democracy to protect their democracy; and the present control of radio, movies and the press should enable the defenders of the existing order to talk at least as loud as those who would replace the existing order with something else."[19] Mere advocacy of any nonconformist philosophy can safely be left to the tests of the marketplace.

Finally, because we live in an age of propaganda, subtle infiltration, and mass hypnosis, an age in which it is not difficult to become expert at bewitching and confusing, we must guard against the use of free institutions by those determined to subvert them. We must devise ways of restricting their use by such people and still leave them free for the rest of society. As Max Eastman has written: "Those who . . . love freedom not as an abstract idea, but as a concrete fact . . . ought to be ready to suspend its purity in order to defend its existence." Quoting Edouard Heimann, Eastman concludes, " 'Democratic liberty can never include the liberty to destroy democracy by organized slander or armed force.' "[20]

These are the fundamentals of our tradition. Whatever compromise is reached on the civil rights issue must take cognizance of them to be in keeping with our heritage.

Principles are arid things; they become meaningful only when given life. "The truth is," Leslie Lipson notes, "that institutions are strong to the extent that a large enough section of the public feels keenly enough to have them so. Exactly the same applies to civil liberties. If enough people are sufficiently determined to preserve and exercise their rights, those rights will be exercised and preserved, and the institutions will then be found to do the job. . . . The ultimate sanction, therefore, of all civil liberties resides in the same source that creates the constitution initially and renders it effective—the political will of the people. Freedom in any society is what the people earn and guard for themselves."[21]

Do we "not rest our hopes too much upon constitutions, upon laws,

[18] Carr, *Committee on Un-American Activities*, p. x.
[19] MacLeish, "Freedom to End Freedom," p. 119.
[20] Max Eastman, "The Dilemma of Free Speech," *Modern Quarterly*, XI, No. 7, as revised and reproduced in Hillman M. Bishop and Samuel Hendel, eds., *Basic Issues of American Democracy* (New York: Appleton-Century-Crofts, 1948), p. 91.
[21] Leslie Lipson, *The Great Issues of Politics* (Englewood Cliffs, N.J.: Prentice-Hall, 1954), p. 267.

and upon courts," Judge Learned Hand wondered. "These are false hopes. Liberty lies in the hearts of men and women; when it dies there, no court, no laws, no constitution can save it."[22]

But the structure of our political system can assist. The Founding Fathers, Justice John M. Harlan declared, "staked their faith that liberty would prosper in the new nation not primarily upon declarations of individual rights but upon the kind of government the Union was to have."[23] Our political system reflects distrust; the Founding Fathers feared above all unchecked power. The written Constitution, the detailed Bill of Rights, separation of powers, federalism, judicial review—all are evidence that we have institutionalized the feeling Jefferson expressed: "Free government is founded in jealousy."[24]

A careless or indifferent or frightened people can undermine—even destroy—the effective operation of free government. Even while working within the principles suggested above, we can suffer self-destruction; it is hard to suppress by degrees. The tendency is to carry restrictions beyond those necessary to protect society. A free people must therefore be continually on guard, lest in its anxiety to choke the poison ivy, it also destroy essential vegetation, leaving only barren soil. George Kennan's warning with respect to our opposition to communism has general application:

> If our handling of the problem of Communist influence in our midst is not carefully moderated—if we permit it, that is, to become an emotional preoccupation and blind us to the more important positive tasks before us— we can do a damage to our national purpose beyond comparison greater than anything that threatens us. . . . The subjective emotional stresses and temptations to which we are exposed in our attempt to deal with this domestic problem are not an external danger; they represent a danger within ourselves —a danger that something may occur in our minds and souls that will make us no longer like the persons by whose efforts this republic was founded and held together, but rather like the representatives of that very power we are trying to combat: intolerant, secretive, suspicious, cruel, and terrified of internal dissensions because we have lost our own belief in ourselves and in the power of ideals.[25]

Not until our own time have we fully appreciated the apparent rashness of the venture of 1776. It was, indeed, a "bold and doubtful election" we then made for our country. Whether a government based on reason and consent is a match for totalitarian force, whether in the coura-

---

[22] Quoted in *Congressional Record*, CXVII (May 3, 1971), H 3377.
[23] Address of John M. Harlan at the Dedication of the Bill of Rights Room, New York City, August 9, 1964, quoted in *Congressional Record*, CXVII (March 23, 1971), S 3940.
[24] See the testimony of Alpheus Thomas Mason before the Committee on Foreign Relations, U.S. Senate, March 25, 1971. *Hearings*, 92nd Cong., 1st sess., pp. 251–59, 317–29. Reprinted in *Congressional Record*, CXVII (March 23, 1971), S 3938–40.
[25] George F. Kennan, "Where Do You Stand?" *New York Times Magazine*, May 27, 1951, p. 53.

geous spirit of our heritage we can conquer a whole range of domestic troubles—poverty, pollution, racial inequities—is still uncertain. Free government's inexorable demands are measured by periodic departures from it, by the temptation, not always resisted, to adopt at both the domestic and international levels the adversary's way as our own. In an essay rich in specific illustrations pointing to a new period of repression, Henry Steele Commager paints a gloomy picture:

> Not since the days when . . . Joseph McCarthy bestrode the political stage, fomenting suspicion and hatred, betraying the Bill of Rights, bringing Congress and the State Department into disrepute, have we experienced anything like the current offensive against the exercise of freedom in America. If repression is not yet as blatant or as flamboyant as it was during the McCarthy years, it is in many respects more pervasive and more formidable. For it comes to us now with official sanction and is imposed upon us by officials sworn to uphold the law. . . .[26]

There is a brighter side. During World War I Randolph Bourne wrote satirically of war as "the health of the State," and of the "peacefulness of being at war," setting in motion "throughout society those irresistible forces for uniformity, for passionate cooperation in coercing into obedience the minority groups and individuals who lack the larger herd sense." Contrast with the 1960s and 1970s is sharp. Peacefulness is not the mood of the country. The lifeblood of free government—protest, dissent, opposition—is mounting. Some of it is foolish and self-defeating. But better this than nothing, as Albert Speer's memoirs poignantly demonstrate.[27]

Is modern America willing to gamble on our commitment to free government? Can we entertain the possibility that dissenters may exceed the bounds of reason or use speech that may result in violence and destruction of property? Are we willing to tolerate the prospect of radical change in the organization and structure of government itself? Can we, in short, accept the risk entailed by enforcement of the Bill of Rights?

"Safety from external danger is the most powerful director of national conduct," Hamilton remarked in *Federalist* Number 8. "To be more safe nations at length become willing to run the risk of being less free." The danger is lest we throw away freedom on the altar of security, of law and order—increasingly a euphemism for unlawful use of force—only to discover how freedom serves to promote both. Repression of the values we profess seems the more ironical, for the real threat is within our own borders—indeed, within ourselves—not ten thousand miles away in Indochina.

The problem now, as always, is to combine individual freedom with social justice, to fuse that degree of initiative necessary for progress with

---

[26] Henry Steele Commager, "Is Freedom Dying in America?" *Look*, July 14, 1970, pp. 16–17.

[27] *Inside the Third Reich. Memoirs by Albert Speer*, trans. Richard and Clare Winston (New York: Macmillan, 1970).

the social cohesion needed for survival. No adjustment will ever be perfectly and finally achieved. It is the tediousness of its method and the stress on human values, rather than efficiency, that seemingly place free government at a disadvantage. So many minds have to be consulted, informed, and brought into agreement. Herein lies free government's strength, the only assurance that whatever course it may have to take, freedom will survive.

Nearly 200 years ago, Julian Boyd reminds us, the nation made a difficult choice. Then it "hammered out its fundamental institutions not in tranquility but in agony." It may be necessary to do so again. The outcome can be faced with confidence "if we understand better the complications of our kind of society. . . ."

> This is a not inconsiderable if. John Adams once remarked that he had been obliged to study government so that his descendants might be free to devote themselves to arts and letters. . . . But John Adams would have made government his first and indispensable preoccupation in whatever age he lived. . . . Adams and his generation understood that government . . . is the first and most difficult of the arts and the one on which the well-being of all others depends. . . . It would be a counsel of prudence for all of us, at this critical juncture, to do our best to emulate their as yet unparalleled example of creative achievement in the art of government.[28]

---

[28] Boyd, "A People Divided," pp. 174–75.

INDEX

All references are to the text; references are made to footnotes only when a substantive matter is discussed therein.

Progressive (Bull Moose) Party, 292, 338, 344

property, 5–6, 7, 8–9, 12, 14, 15–17, 41, 52, 53–54, 58–59, 64, 66, 73, 78–79, 80, 91–92, 93, 107, 109, 114, 118, 137, 165–66, 171–88, 195–97, 202–4, 211–12, 228, 236, 241, 254, 260, 266, 274, 279, 281–83, 284, 286–88, 296–97, 299, 300, 301–4, 311, 312–14, 315, 332–34, 342, 352–53, 361, 365, 389, 396, 405–6

Puritans, influence of, 22–35, 38

Putney, debates at, 4–7, 8, 14, 36, 91–92

Randolph, Edmund, 62, 72, 75–76, 86, 126, 135

Randolph, John, of Roanoke, 178–81, 186, 187, 294

Rauschenbusch, Walter, 273–75

reason, in politics, 9–13, 16, 32, 154, 167, 383, 409

Reconstruction Finance Corporation, 337

Reed, Stanley, 372

religion, freedom of, 4, 17, 29, 147, 153, 166, 346, 369–71

representation. *See also* representative government; 2, 6, 67, 82–83, 84–86, 102, 110, 170–88, 191–92; in Parliament, 38–40, 42, 46, 48

representative government, 26–27, 29, 31, 43, 82–83, 91–93

republican government, 63–64, 67, 70, 73, 80–81, 84, 87, 91, 94–95, 107, 109–11, 149, 154, 156–58, 163, 166, 177, 186, 242, 302

Republican Party, 289, 290, 292, 330, 360

Resolutions, Kentucky, 83, 151, 233, 246; Virginia, 83, 150, 164

revolution, 270, 280, 285, 286, 306–7, 350, 398–99; right of, 12, 14, 33–35, 36, 41, 53, 56, 156, 221–22, 246, 247

Revolution, American, 14, 17, 19, 33, 35, 37–54, 55–70, 73, 144, 149, 179, 238, 245, 315–16, 340, 409

Rexroth, Kenneth, 228, 229n

Reynolds v. *Sims*, 388

Rhode Island, 26, 28–29, 53, 58, 72, 97, 171

rights (civil, natural, private). *See also* limited government; 4, 14, 22, 29, 33, 35, 42 45–48, 52–54, 56, 65, 73, 101, 107, 120, 146–48, 153–56, 158–69, 171, 174, 177, 178, 179, 205, 230, 234, 237, 240, 241, 243, 245, 263–64, 265–66, 269, 281, 291, 312, 314, 342, 349–51, 352–53, 355, 362, 368–83, 389–90, 396, 407, 408

Roberts, Owen J., 362, 372

Rockefeller, John D., Sr., 260–61

romantic individualism, 207–30

Roosevelt, Franklin D., 272, 335, 336–51, 352–67, 368, 369, 389, 406

Roosevelt, Theodore, 290–91, 294, 338, 341, 343, 347

Rubin, Jerry, 394

Rush, Benjamin, 65

Rutledge, John, 87, 90

Ryan, Edward G., 276

Santayana, George, 54

Schlesinger, Arthur, Jr., 191

Schmidhauser, John R., 358 fn 18

Schriftgeisser, Karl, 332

Seabury, Samuel, 48, 56

secession, 83, 164, 166–67, 168, 233–34, 247–49, 250, 251

sectionalism, 92, 93, 102, 160, 166, 179, 190–91, 198–99, 233–35, 239, 243–45, 250

Sedition Act of 1918, 319, 369

segregation, 377–81

separation of powers, 12, 16–17, 18–20, 43, 62, 65, 76, 79, 87, 88, 92, 120, 171, 194, 233, 362–63, 395, 409

Shays's Rebellion, 67–68, 137, 338

Shelley v. *Kraemer*, 389

Sherman, Roger, 51, 84, 86

Sherman Anti-Trust Act, 290, 309

Sherwood, Robert E., 338, 349

Sidney, Algernon, 14

Slaughterhouse Cases, 299

slavery, 54, 102, 163, 166, 179, 206, 207, 208, 213, 214, 220, 221, 222, 231–45, 249, 253, 254

Slocum, Holder, 183

Smith, Adam, 125

Smith, Gerald L. K., 360–61

Smith-Lever Act (1914), 294

Smyth v. *Ames*, 303

socialism, 270, 281–83, 285–86, 287, 296, 306, 309, 310, 317, 332, 346–47, 353, 359–60, 375, 395, 398–99

Social Security Act, 360

South Carolina, 58, 96, 172, 248–49, 387

speech, freedom of, 147, 153, 160, 243, 346, 369, 370

Spencer, Herbert, 262–64, 269, 272, 282, 288, 308, 309, 310, 312, 314, 354

Stamp Act, 38, 39, 41, 45

Stamp Act Congress, 41

state sovereignty, 55–62, 71–83, 100, 101, 104, 105, 106, 115–16, 141, 150–51, 167–68, 193, 194, 246, 247, 249, 252

states, under the Articles of Confederation, 56–62, 68–69, 73; in Constitutional Convention, 76–83, 86; in American government, 126–28, 133, 141–44, 150–51, 152–53, 158–59, 166, 193, 198–99, 212, 226, 246–47, 252, 297–98, 299, 300, 301–4, 307, 309, 369–73, 375, 377–80, 385–90

states' rights, 147, 166–68, 196, 198–99, 200, 246, 249, 311, 361, 379

Stevenson, Adlai, 404, 407

Stone, Harlan F., 370–71, 372, 376, 377
Story, Joseph, 174, 176, 185, 186
Stowe, Harriet Beecher, 239
Students for a Democratic Society (SDS), 398
suffrage. *See also* elections; 6–7, 33, 54, 73, 78, 91–92, 170, 171, 172–88, 206, 225, 254, 257, 266, 295, 297, 385–88
Sullivan, Mark, 319
Sumner, William Graham, 264–69, 270, 275, 277, 282, 312
Supreme Court, 89, 90, 111, 136–45, 157–58, 166–67, 191, 193–94, 199–202, 251–52, 296–317, 355–59, 363, 366, 369–74, 376–83, 384–90, 391, 403, 406
Sweezy v. *New Hampshire*, 380, 381

Taft, Robert A., 355
Taft, William Howard, 292, 355
Taft-Hartley Act of 1947, 374
Taney, Roger B., 190n, 194, 196, 197, 199–202
Tariff of Abominations, 232, 248
taxation, Parliament and, 37, 38–39, 42, 43–44, 46; Hamilton and, 133–34; Marshall and, 143–44
Taylor, John, 164–68, 246, 247, 252
Tennessee, 173, 327, 330–31
Texas, 214, 239, 251–52
Texas v. *White*, 251–52
Thayer, James Bradley, 304–5
theocracy, 22–24, 31
Thirteenth Amendment, 253, 254, 299
Thomas, Norman, 359
Thoreau, Henry, 208, 214, 216–23, 224, 225, 228, 229, 230, 231, 400
"Three-Fifths" Compromise, 93
Thurmond, Strom, 379
Tocqueville, Alexis de, 191, 206, 254, 406
Townsend, Francis E., 360
Townshend Acts, 43
transcendentalism, 213, 224–25, 229–30
Truman, Harry S., 364, 365, 374, 376, 389
trusts. *See* monopoly
Tugwell, Rexford G., 340
Turner, Frederick Jackson, 170
Twiss, Benjamin R., 299

Union, nature of. *See* federalism
United States Bank. *See* Bank of the United States
U.S. v. *Corolene Products*, 377
Upshur, Abel P., 178–79, 186, 195, 294
utopia, 15, 214–15, 228, 281–83

Van Buren, Martin, 190, 197, 202–4
Veblen, Thorstein, 312–14, 316, 317

veto, power of, 31, 49, 58, 65, 88, 110, 111, 158, 191
Vietnam, 391, 392, 394, 400, 403, 410
Vinson, Fred, 389–90
Virginia, 17, 21, 55, 58, 62–63, 71, 73, 82, 96, 97, 99, 103, 133, 150, 160, 164, 171, 174, 178–81, 183–85, 186, 187, 231, 238, 245, 387, 406
Virginia Constitutional Convention, 1829–1830, 115n
Virginia Plan, 75–76, 77, 79, 80–93
Virginia, University of, 155, 160, 164
voluntarism, 230, 268, 291, 332, 343
Voting Rights Act of 1965, 386, 387

Waite, Morrison R., 297–98, 300
Wallace, Henry, 344–47, 353
Ward, Lester F., 272–73
Ward, Nathaniel, 24
Warner, John De Witt, 269–70, 272
War of 1812, 170, 172
Warren, Earl (The Warren Court), 200, 373–74, 377–83, 387, 388
Washington, George, 17, 55, 58, 61–62, 68, 72, 73, 74, 93–94, 97, 119–20, 122–23, 124, 126, 133, 135, 141, 147, 148, 150, 168, 198, 238, 353
Watkins v. *United States*, 373, 380, 381
Webster, Daniel, 140, 145, 174, 177–78, 185, 188, 197, 210, 228, 246, 248, 258, 302, 311
Wesberry v. *Sanders*, 388
West Virginia Board of Education v. *Barnett*, 371
Weyl, Walter E., 292n
Whig Party, 212
Whiskey Rebellion, 133–35
Whitman, Walt, 208, 223–29, 375, 405
Williams, Roger, 27, 28–29, 30, 31, 32, 33, 53, 375
Williamson, Hugh, 86
Wilson, James, 45–46, 56, 74, 81, 83, 84, 86, 87, 90, 91, 105
Wilson, Woodrow, 164, 292, 293–95, 297, 314, 318, 319, 341, 343, 347, 366–67, 368, 369, 370
Wiltse, Charles M., 190
Winthrop, John, 23, 25
Wise, John, 27, 31–33
World War I, 286, 293, 318–22, 341, 368–69, 371, 410
World War II, 361, 368, 369, 373, 389
Writs of Assistance Case (1761), 42
Wythe, George, 74

X, Malcolm, 390

Yates, Robert, 99–100, 138
Yates v. *United States*, 380, 381